Methodologies of Pattern Recognition

THE PROCEEDINGS OF THE INTERNATIONAL CONFERENCE ON METHODOLOGIES OF PATTERN RECOGNITION

Co-sponsored by the University of Hawaii
and the Air Force Office of Scientific
Research with Program Participation by
the Systems Science and Cybernetics
Group of I.E.E.E.
Held at Honolulu, Hawaii
January 24-26, 1968

Organizing Committee:

Satosi Watanabe *Chairman*

Norman Abramson
Harold Brown
Rowena Swanson
Hans Oestreicher
Timothy Ewald
Janet Yamamoto

Methodologies of Pattern Recognition

Edited by

Satosi Watanabe

University of Hawaii
Honolulu, Hawaii

Academic Press • New York • London • 1969

ACADEMIC PRESS, INC.
111 Fifth Avenue, New York, New York 10003

United Kingdom Edition published by
ACADEMIC PRESS, INC. (LONDON) LTD.
Berkeley Square House, London W.1

LIBRARY OF CONGRESS CATALOG CARD NUMBER: 69-13489
AMS 1968 Subject Classifications 6230, 6241, 68XX, 9310, 9401

PRINTED IN THE UNITED STATES OF AMERICA

CONTRIBUTORS

M. A. Aiserman (U. S. S. R.)

E. Andreewsky (France)

G. H. Ball (United States)

J. P. Benzecri (France)

D. B. Brick (United States)

P. W. Cooper (United States)

T. M. Cover (United States)

M. J. B. Duff (England)

T. G. Evans (United States)

K. S. Fu (United States)

E. E. Gose (United States)

A. Grasselli (Italy)

J. K. Hawkins (United States)

J. H. Holland (United States)

B. Julesz (United States)

L. Kanal (United States)

T. Kasvand (Canada)

V. A. Kovalevsky (U.S.S.R.)

P. F. Lambert (United States)

H. M. Lipp (Germany)

D. M. MacKay (England)

J. H. Munson (United States)

S. Noguchi (Japan)

T. Sakai (Japan)

S. D. Shapiro (United States)

J. T. Tou (United States)

I. Vajda (Czechoslovakia)

S. Watanabe (United States)

E. Wong (United States)

PREFACE

To the layman's ear, the term pattern recognition sounds like a very narrow esoteric field of electronic computer applications. But, actually, it is a vast and explicit endeavor at mechanization of the most fundamental human function of perception and concept formation. It represents, indeed, one of the most ambitious scientific ventures of this century, requiring collaboration of electronic engineers, physicists, physiologists, psychologists, logicians, mathematicians, and philosophers.

In recent years, pattern recognition has definitely emerged from the status of a programming stunt to become a respectable branch of scientific art. This implies that from now on the progress in the field will no longer be as dazzling as in the past, but that it has to become more solid and systematic. We can no longer congratulate ourselves because "it works,"but we should ask why it works and explore the limits beyond which it will not work. Today, therefore, is a good time for researchers in this field to sit back awhile to evaluate the significance of their past achievements and to dream, prospect, and plan their future paths. This will require above all a soul-searching methodological examination of the entire enterprise of pattern recognition. Such was the motivation behind compilation of the volume you are holding in your hand at this moment.

I am very happy to have been instrumental in making this unique collection of papers on pattern recognition available to those who are interested in this fascinating new field of science. The articles in this volume were written by 29 outstanding authorities of 10 different national origins presently active in the field, who have critically reviewed their own methods and projected their present activities into the future. Each author was requested to place emphasis on the "philosophy" of his approach rather than on mathematical derivations and experimental data, and to provide the reader with a self-contained survey of lasting value.

These papers were presented, or were intended to be presented, at the International Conference on Methodologies of Pattern Recognition which was held on January 24-26, 1968 at the University of Hawaii, Honolulu, under the co-sponsorship of the University of Hawaii and the Air Force Office of Scientific Research with program participation by the Systems Science and Cybernetics Group of I.E.E.E. From the inception of the idea of the conference to the final redaction of these proceedings, Mrs. Rowena Swanson of the A.F.O.S.R. has tirelessly helped this project with wise advice and "motherly" care. Dr. Hans Oestreicher, representing I.E.E.E., participated actively in preparing the program. Dr. Norman Abramson and Col. Harold P. Brown of the University of Hawaii were always at hand, ready to help us in organizing the conference. The Organizing Committee of the Conference consisted of the four names mentioned above, myself (who served as the chairman), and Mr. Timothy Ewald. If there was a single person who contributed most to the successful completion of this project, it was the secretary of the Committee, Miss Janet H. Yamamoto. She not only typed up everything from the original letters of invitation to all the articles which are photocopied and reproduced in this volume, but also actively participated in planning, organizing, and carrying out the project. The expert collaboration by the University of Hawaii Conference Center considerably alleviated the burden of our work in organizing the Conference.

I appreciate particulary the friendly act of Dr. M. Aiserman and Dr. V.A. Kovalevsky of U.S.S.R. who kindly contributed their papers to this book although the insufficiency of time between the invitation and the conference did not permit them to be personally present at the meeting. Heavy daily schedules prevented Dr. C. Masson (France), Dr. G. Sebestyen (United States), and Dr. L. Zadeh (United States) from preparing their written manuscripts. This is so much more regretted as their presentations aroused considerable interest and discussion at the Conference. I may also add that I deeply regret the absence of many other valuable papers which could have been contributed by equally outstanding scholars had the scale of the Conference only been large enough to allow us to invite them all. To everybody who in one way or another has helped us in organizing the conference and preparing its proceedings, I repeat

Mahalo and Aloha

Satosi Watanabe

Honolulu, Hawaii
April 1969

CONTENTS

CONTENTS

REMARKS ON TWO PROBLEMS CONNECTED WITH PATTERN RECOGNITION

M.A. Aiserman

INSTITUTE OF AUTOMATICS AND TELEMECHANICS
ACADEMY OF SCIENCES OF THE U.S.S.R.
MOSCOW, U.S.S.R.

To my regret, I was not able to take advantage of Professor Watanabe's kind invitation to participate in the "round table" discussion on questions of pattern recognition organized by him at the University of Hawaii. So it is with the greatest satisfaction that I take advantage of his kind proposal that I send a written copy of my presentation so that it can be published with the rest of the papers presented at this discussion. I decided to use this occasion to answer the following two questions, which in recent years have been asked of me by audiences at universities in the U.S.A. (in 1964), Canada (1967), Italy (1967) and other countries.

First Question: How do you evaluate the two different approaches which are developing in the area of pattern recognition—the geometrical approach, associated with the automatic construction of a partitioning surface, and the structural approach, associated with the automatic construction of a pattern description?

Second Question: What is the connection between the Robbins-Monro procedures of the method of stochastic approximation and the method of potential functions, developed collectively by you?

Since these questions probably interest not only the small circles of engineers and mathematicians who happened to be present at my lectures, I will try to answer them briefly.

I. Geometric and Structural Approaches to Problems of Machine Instruction in Pattern Recognition

The geometric approach to problems of pattern recognition in Western countries developed gradually along with an understanding of the principle of operation of Rosenblatt's perceptron. In the U.S.S.R. this approach was investigated and reported by E.M. Braverman, resulting in a great number of scientific publications. The essence of this approach can be described thus: We consider a space X of objects lying within a partition, such that every object is a point (vector) of this space; and the collection of objects is related to some pattern-region in it. The partition of patterns is interpreted as the construction of a characteristic function assigned on X, that takes on numerical values of different signs on points of X belonging to different patterns. The problem lies in the construction of a characteristic function, when its signs are known only at a comparatively small number of points randomly chosen from the regions subjected to the partition.

Such an interpretation of the pattern recognition problem allowed us to relate it to a distinct extrapolation problem. The usual methods of extrapolation function theory turned out to be of little use in its solution mainly because of the high dimensionality of the space X and because of the random method used for the selection of points, for which information about the extrapolating function is known. However, a strict statement of the problem allowed us to introduce implicit bounds, with which it became possible to not only propose extrapolating algorithms, but also to prove their convergence to the extrapolating characteristic function; and sometimes to even estimate the speed of convergence.

Such a geometric approach was successfully used in a number of countries to solve important applied problems. However, it appeared weak in solving some quite elementary examples. So, for example, V.M. Glushkov studied the extremely difficult uses of the geometrical approach in cases where objects of one class are different collections of horizontal straight lines, and objects of another class are different collections of vertical straight lines. Another example of this type is the separation of the handwritten Latin letters "capital O" and "capital Q", or the Russian letters ш and щ.

The reason for these difficulties is understandable. In the first case (horizontal and vertical lines), the boundaries of the region with which the space X must be divided are extremely complex and devious, and therefore the form of the characteristic function is highly complex (for example, in its series representation by any "usual" system of functions, a great many harmonics must be present). In the second case (the letters O and Q or ш and щ) it is difficult to divide the regions due to another reason: they are too closely adjoined to one another and can only be well partitioned on subspaces of small dimensionality. Nevertheless, man easily discerns the differences between these forms; moreover, many animals (for example, rats) can be easily taught to perceive this difference, for example, by means of evoking their various reflexes.

Dissatisfaction with this situation led to the appearance of another important approach – the structural approach. In the West it was successfully investigated by R. Narasimhan, M. Eden and R. Kirsch and many others. In the U.S.S.R. this approach is associated with the name of M.M. Bongard.

The basic ideas of the structural approach are these: initially, one considers a given set of simpler fragments of objects of the partitioned collections (for example, for representation, the simpler details are intersections, curves, angles, line ends, etc.). This initial set is used as letters of the language; and the grammar of the language is given (the rules of construction of letters give words, rules of words give sentences, and so on). The problem then lies in the composition of a description for previously shown objects of the given space in this language. During the observation of a new object the program checks the conformity of its construction with its description. It is easy to see that in the above examples (horizontal and vertical straight lines and letters O and Q) the application of the structural approach does not cause any difficulties.

Actually, in the first example, everything is straightforward, since horizontal and vertical lines can be simply the first letters of a language. The second example, is not much more complicated; thus, to describe the patterns of letters O and Q, it is sufficient to have such simple concepts as the oval, "intersection", "left" and "right", "up" and "down".

As far as I know, the structural approach has not yet been used in practice to solve any complex problems.* But, as the International Symposium at Sukhanovo (USSR), showed, the number of its adherents is growing rapidly.

In my opinion, any of these methods is of itself of little use in solving complex problems and the future will demand their combination.

Having understood this idea, it is not difficult to construct any number of examples that are not realizable in practice by the geometrical method and almost trivial for the structural method and vice versa. However, such examples are of no interest to us. We will try to give a structural description of a topographical or meteorological map, geological section or such a pattern as a "man's portrait" – this is enough to show how extremely difficult it is to describe an intricate pattern as in these cases. This intricacy is usually associated neither with the presence of an excessively large number of initial letters in the language alphabet nor with the excessive number of words that can be formed. The intricacy of the description arises on higher "grammatical levels" and is closely associated with the initial complexity of the pattern.

In order to understand the nature of this difficulty we will now proceed to consider the space Y of descriptions constructed in the chosen language. Every description of the pattern is a point (vector) of this space. Thus the whole process of composing the description is only a process of constructing a transformation which carries a region of space X into a point of space Y. It is clear that a transformation of this type can be simple in particular cases, but in general it is complex and cumbersome.

Naturally the thought arises – is it necessary to transform a region into a point. Would it not be better to consider an "intermediate space" Z, for example, the space of phrases or other fragments of the language not complete enough to fully describe it, and to choose this space so that in the considered problem, the regions of X that are difficult to divide would transform themselves into well-partitioned (e.g. distantly spaced from one another) regions of Z. Assignment of traits and partitioning, not in the initial space X, but in the space of traits is an example of this type. By such an approach the use of structural linguistical ideas does not lead to absurdity, and the language emerges as a means of transforming space or forming a space adequate for the problem. In this case both approaches, the geometrical and the structural do not compete, but are used to their full extent, with a common purpose and means to reach their goals.

* Perhaps the symposium at Honolulu will show the opposite. The participants should then forgive and correct me.

In the structural approach there is yet one more difficulty. To overcome it the geometrical method can be used. The question lies in forming the initial language alphabet, that is, those initial concepts to which grammatical rules apply from the first, for the construction of words and sentences. In all the programs known to me, this alphabet is introduced "from without" by the programmer. Now there are two alternatives. First the programmer can every time "creatively" find a specific alphabet, adapted to a given particular problem, and introduce it into the program. Thus, for example, he can notice that four or five concepts are sufficient (oval, stroke, right-left, up-down), to give a description of the pattern of the letters O and Q. But if the person deals with the situation thus, the problem for the machine vanishes. A person with such success could introduce into the program the completed description of the pattern also. As the second alternative, some "standard" alphabet could be proposed, sufficient for a wide class of problems (e.g. for all line drawings). But programs using such an alphabet, as is known, excessively overload the machine memory, complicate all steps in the construction of the description and always leave a feeling of uncertainty: will symbols for the understood description of the pattern be included in the alphabet for every new, arbitrary, complex problem? The issue is as follows: the program itself in every problem, considering the underlying distribution of the objects, should build an alphabet, convenient for their description.

In our laboratory a program of this type was realized.* The idea of this program consists of looking over the representation to assign "information fragments" (this concept can be formalized) and then using the geometrical approach to automatically divide these fragments into several groups according to their similarity. Typical patterns of each group of fragments thus assigned are taken as letters of the alphabet for describing the representation.

Thus the controversy between geometric and structural approaches for problems of pattern recognition seems to me historically inevitable, but temporary. There are problems to which the geometric approach is ideally suited. Also there are some well known problems which, though solvable by the geometric method, are more easily solvable by the structural approach. But any difficult problems require a combination of these approaches, and methods are gradually crystallizing to combine them; the structural approach is the means of construction of a convenient space; the geometric is the partitioning in it.

II. The Method of Potential Functions and the Robbins-Monro Procedure

We will now consider one part of the question associated with the geometric method in pattern recognition.

The question which is often asked of me is usually stated as follows: what is there in common between the method of potential functions and

* See article by I.B. Muchnik: "Algorithms for forming local traits for visual patterns" in "Automatics and Remote Control", No. 10, 1966.

their application to the same problems treated by the Robbins-Monro procedure of the method of stochastic approximation? Is there a difference between them, and of what does it consist?

To a great extent this question is terminological: it contains two indistinct concepts (the "method of potential functions" and the "method of stochastic approximation") and the answer to this depends only on how these concepts are defined.

Attempting to clarify what my questioners in fact had in mind when talking about the different methods, I was almost always convinced that they understood, strictly speaking, not a comparison of methods, but a comparison of procedures: the recursive procedures of the method of potential functions and the Robbins-Monro procedures.

In connection with this, we will note, first of all, that the idea of "method" is a significantly wider concept than that of "utilized procedure", so that a method, besides containing a procedure, contains facts and considerations, allowing one in every concrete problem to first choose a procedure in a reasonable fashion (such as, parameters entering into it; the form of the functions contained in it; its sequence, etc.) and then to establish that it converges to the solution of the considered problem. Usually, these initial and final steps of the application of the method are considerably shorter but more complex than the corresponding steps of an actual realization of the procedure.

The term "method of potential functions" was introduced through me, and it is easier for me to start with it. We call any recursive procedure of solving approximation problems a method of potential functions when it satisfies the following two conditions:

1) It can be represented in the form:

$$f^{n+1}(x) = q^n f^n(x) + r^n K(x, x^{n+1}) . \qquad (i)$$

or, if it is possible to assume that $f^n(x)$ can be represented in a series $f^n(x) = \sum_{i=1}^{\infty} c_i^n \phi_i(x)$ by a certain system of functions $\phi(x)$, then the procedure takes the form:

$$\tilde{c}_i^{n+1} = q^n \tilde{c}_i^n + r^n \psi_i(x^{n+1}) \qquad i = 1, 2, \ldots \qquad (ii)$$

In formulas *(i)* and *(ii)* we designate: x as a finite dimensional or infinite dimensional vector; x^{n+1} as the vector "indexed" on the (n+1)-st step of the procedure; $f^n(x)$ as the n-th degree estimate of the approximating function $f^*(x)$; q^n and r^n as numerical series, which differ with the choice of the method of potential function; and the potential function

$K(x, x^{n+1}) = \sum_{i=1}^{\infty} \lambda_i^2 \phi_i(x) \phi_i(x^{n+1})$ and designate $\tilde{c}_i = \dfrac{c_i}{\lambda_i}$; $\psi_i(x) = \lambda_i \phi_i(x)$.

2) This procedure with any choice of $f^0(x)$ (or correspondingly c_i^0, $i = 1, 2, \ldots$) with $n \to \infty$ in this or another sense converges to the approximating function $f^*(x)$.

In the method of potential functions, the very establishment of the procedure *(i)* or *(ii)* in itself already suggests that in every concrete problem preliminary work is done for the selection of a potential function $K(x, x^{n+1})$ or of a system $\phi_i(x)$, without yet considering a choice of a series q^n and r^n. For this reason the method includes not only exact facts but many other intuitive considerations which as a group are an important component part of the method.† Another component part of the method is the group of concepts and theorems serving to establish the convergence of the procedure.

We will now consider the method of stochastic approximation. This method is used in mathematical statistics to solve the so-called regression equations.

We consider N functions $\Phi_i(c,x)$, $i = 1, \ldots, N$, where x is a random quantity and $c = \{c_1, \ldots, c_N\}$ is some vector. The system of regression equations is

$$M_x \{\Phi_i(c,x)\} = 0 ; \quad i = 1, \ldots, N \tag{1}$$

in which the unknowns are the components c_i of vector c, and $M_x\{\cdot\}$ is the mathematical expectation.

It is assumed that the probability distribution of the random variable x is unknown beforehand, and consequently the left hand sides of equation (1) evidently cannot be calculated. Let us suppose, however, that at consecutive moments of time $(1, 2, \ldots, n)$ there appear points $x^1, x^2, \ldots, x^n$ with probability distribution P; then with any c the quantities $\Phi_i(x^n, c)$ can be calculated. For this case Robbins and Monro proposed the following recurrent procedure.*

$$c_i^{n+1} = c_i + \gamma_n \Phi_i(c^n, x^{n+1}) \quad i = 1, \ldots, N \tag{2}$$

† See for example, M. A. Aiserman, E. M. Braverman, and L. I. Rozonoer, "On the Selection of Potential Functions in Symmetrical Spaces". "Automatics and Remote Control", No. 10, 1967.

* In the work of Robbins and Monro, procedures (2) and (3) were proposed for the scalar case; where c is a scalar. In the case where c is an n-dimensional vector it was extended by Bloom. I think that my audience under the term "Robbins-Monro procedures" understood procedures (2) and (3) in the case where c is a vector. Recently several works have appeared in which the terms "Robbins-Monro procedures" are understood in a broader sense. Undoubtedly my audience did not have in mind this widened terminology, simply because the work containing it appeared after the basic results of the method of potential functions had been published.

where γ_n is a series of non-negative numbers satisfying the condition

$$\sum_1^{\infty} \gamma_n = \infty ; \quad \sum_1^{\infty} \gamma_n^{\ 2} < \infty \tag{3}$$

It was shown that within certain limits on the form of function Φ_i, the procedures (2) and (3) converge in probability to the root of the system of equations (1). The method of stochastic approximation, aside from procedure (2), includes also theorems on convergence which define the bounds on the choice of functions Φ_i.

If the Robbins-Monro procedure (2) is compared with the general procedure *(i)* and *(ii)* of the method of potential functions, then these procedures turn out to be essentially different, even if only because expression *(i)* and *(ii)* admit, generally speaking, any dependence q^n and r^n on the number n, which evidently enters into consideration from the time that (2) and (3) depended on n and (in this special case) only on the "convergence factor" γ_n. Besides this, the procedures of the method of potential functions can be applied both in cases where vector c is finite dimensional and where vector c is infinite dimensional (in this case the procedure *(i)* is used). The Robbins-Monro procedures (2) and (3) are introduced for finite vectors c.* Therefore, only one special form of procedures *(i)* and *(ii)*, and not the general procedures, can be compared to the Robbins-Monro procedure.**

$$c_i^{\,n+1} = c_i + \gamma_n [r (\sum_{i=1}^{N} c_i\phi_i(x^{n+1}), x^{n+1}) + \xi^{n+1}] \ \phi_i^{\,n+1}(x) \tag{\textit{iii}}$$

where c is a finite dimensional vector and ξ^n is a disturbance with zero mathematical expectation.

Procedure *(iii)* can be considered*** as a Robbins-Monro procedure (2), adapted to the solution of the following system of regression equations:

$$M_{x,\xi} \ \{ [r \sum_{i}^{N} c_i\phi_i(x), x) + \xi] \ \phi_i(x) \} = 0 \tag{4}$$

If we consider as a given condition that the mathematical expectation of disturbance ξ is zero, then for every fixed x, the system (4) assumes the form:

---

* In recent works (see the note on page 11) the term "Robbins-Monro procedure" was used in the case where c was an infinite vector. It is not immediately clear, however, how one can realize in this case procedures (2) and (3) in practice, without restricting oneself to the specific case of procedures (2) and (3) which lead to procedure *(i)* of the method of potential functions (see further).

** Many algorithms, considered in our publications had the form *(iii)*, but it is understood, that this is only a special case of the general procedure *(i)*.

*** If we do not consider the here non-essential circumstances that in *(iii)* it is not assumed (in contrast to (2)), that γ_n satisfies condition (3).

$$M_x \{ r(\sum_i^N c_i\phi_i(x), x) \phi_i(x) \} = 0 \tag{5}$$

We will now consider that the sought after parameters c_i enter in the regression equation (4) and (5) in quite a special form. In the same way, procedure *(iii)* of the method of potential functions defines a specific subclass of regression equations (4) and (5) and a corresponding specific subclass of Robbins-Monro procedures. Such procedures have a series of special properties, because of which they can be studied in more detail than Robbins-Monro procedures of the general form. We will next consider some of these properties.

1. The possibility of machine realization of the procedure: Procedure *(iii)* is obtained from the assumption that the building functions $f^n(x)$ can be represented by a series of the system $\phi(x)$. It is understood, that an inverse transformation from the correspondence *(iii)* to procedure *(i)* of the special form is always possible. Indeed, this circumstance allows one to realize the procedure *(iii)* with the help of calculating machines, and in those cases where vector c is infinite dimensional--that is, where functions $f^n(x)$ can be represented only by an infinite series. It is not immediately clear how for an infinite dimensional case, the general Robbins-Monro procedure can be brought to form *(i)* and thus realized in practice.

2. Existence of an extremizing functional: For procedures of the form *(iii)* a functional can be written extremizing this procedure. On the assumption that vector c^n is finite dimensional, procedure *(iii)* can be represented in the form of a stochastic gradient procedure and the regression equation (5) assumes the form:

$$M_x \{ \frac{dG(c,x)}{dc_i} \} = \frac{dJ(c)}{dc_i} = 0 \quad i = 1, \ldots, N \tag{6}$$

where the function G and the functional J are defined by the formulas:

$$G(c,x) = Q[f(x), x] = \int_0^{f(x)} r[u,x]\, du \tag{7}$$

$$J(c) = M_x \{G(c,x)\} \tag{8}$$

It is understood that in the general case the regression equation (1) does not have a gradient form (6). The existence of an extremizing functional for procedure *(iii)* allows one to give a specific meaning to the extrapolating problem that is being solved*. For such a particular form of the Robbins-

* The first to consider such a possibility was Ya.Z. Tzypkin. He found an extremizing functional for the series of procedures of the method of potential functions of the form *(iii)* establishing by this that these procedures can be interpreted as Robbins-Monro

Monro procedure all the preliminary work can be transferred from the choice of a procedure to the choice of a functional (which we discussed earlier, when we explained why the concept of "method" is broader than the concept of "procedure"). Of course, all difficulties with which this preliminary work is attended still remain. Thus, in establishing a gradient procedure, it is necessary to give an expression of an approximating function through the parameters c_i^n and consequently to choose a system of functions $\phi_i(x)$.* The method of stochastic approximation does not contain (and does not have to contain, because the problem for which it is used does not require it) facts and recommendations which would allow one to intelligently perform this initial step in solving the problem. Of itself it is understood that the problem of studying convergences remains in this case too, and does not become simpler.**

3. The possibility of using a functional for defining the idea of procedure convergence. If, proceeding from the regression equation, the Robbins-Monro procedure is constructed, this of itself does not give a solution of

---

(continue from previous page)

procedures. Developing these procedures, B.M. Litvakov showed that for the procedure of the method of potential functions of the form *(iii)* the extremizing functional always exists, and he gave a method for its calculation. He also gave the conditions under which procedure *(iii)* converges to the minimum of the functional. Because of this work it was established for the first time that the procedures of the method of potential functions and Robbins-Monro procedures overlap and that lying in this overlap, procedure *(iii)* corresponds to the subclass of the gradient procedures of Robbins-Monro procedures.

* Here it is assumed that the function $f(x)$ is represented in the form of a series so that the coefficients c_i enter linearly into the expression of this function. Of course, one could say that $f(x)$ depends on the parameters c_i in some different way—in this case the Robbins-Monro gradient procedure can be written simply as the functional is known. With this arises the problem of how specifically must the function $f(x)$ depend on the parameters c_i—in any case a problem that is not simpler than the choice of a system of functions $\phi_i(x)$.

** If the initial step of the method is the choice of a functional, it is necessary to consider, besides this, the following additional circumstances. The initial functional cannot be assigned arbitrarily. The explanation is that the procedure for construction of approximating functions must contain only values which can in fact be measured, that is, such quantities whose values at every step of the procedure can be calculated according to the information in the step (for example, to communicate with the "teacher"). In these cases, when the initial step of the method is the establishment of the procedure itself, this circumstance is directly taken into consideration. If it proceeds from the assignment of a functional, then its choice is essentially bounded by this circumstance. Often to simple, intuitively understood procedures there correspond complex and at first glance difficult to interpret functionals. On the other hand, an attempt to proceed from simple, well-interpreted functionals, can lead to useless procedures if they contain quantities that cannot be measured.

the problem, but only a "candidate" to such a solution. The problem is solved only if it is shown that the procedure so constructed "converges as a whole", with the solution of the regression equation*; that is, with any choice of initial vector c° (or at least with some specific c°). The criteria of convergence used in the method of stochastic approximation (for example the criteria of Bloom, Gladishev and others), proceed from the assumption that the considered regression equations have a solution, and that this solution is unique. It is understood that this assumption is often far from true.**)

The presence of an extremizing procedure *(iii)* of the functional allows one to define for it the concept of convergence even in those cases when the regression equations (6) do not have solutions in general, for example, when at the point of minimum of the functional, the derivative dJ/dc does not exist, or when $J(c)$ has a strict lower bound, but does not have a minimum point. In cases of a similar nature it is senseless to talk about the convergence of the Robbins-Monro process to the solution of the regression equations. Together with this, for procedures of type *(iii)*, the very concept of convergence can be defined as the approach of the value of the functional to its strict lower bound when $n \to \infty$. Conditions under which convergence in this sense has a place are a constituent part of the method of potential functions.

We can now formulate an answer to the question about the relation of the two considered methods:

First: As methods (and not only procedures) they are basically different; they are aimed at the solution of different problems and contain therefore theorems, criteria, recommendations and other material touching different sets of questions.

Second: The procedures of the method of potential functions and the procedures of the method of stochastic approximation generally "overlap each other" but do not coincide nor do they encompass each other.

Third: The region of "overlap" of the procedures of the two different methods defines a subclass of procedures of the Robbins-Monro method, which have a series of important and useful properties (not extending to Robbins-Monro procedures of a general form). Therefore, the definition of this subclass and its detailed study becomes an interesting and useful problem in all its aspects.

---

* "Convergence in the small" in a given case is insufficient, since the solution itself is unknown beforehand.

** Thus, for example, almost all published algorithms of the method of potential functions have the form *(iii)* and consequently can be obtained from the corresponding regression equations of form (6). Among these algorithms, only for those establishing the functions can one assume that the regression equations (6) have a unique solution. In all remaining cases (deterministic and probabilistic problems of pattern recognition, and the problem of learning without a teacher) such an assumption cannot be made, and therefore the method of stochastic approximation appearing in works on the method of potential functions, was not useful for the solution of such problems.

RESEARCH ON PATTERN RECOGNITION IN FRANCE

Evelyne Andreewsky

I. N. S. E. R. M.
PARIS, FRANCE

A double rhythm of progression is necessary to science: it must develop simultaneously on both mathematical and experimental grounds, the theoretical analysis allowing the mind to view the relations between facts and events brought up by the experimental analysis. We will try to give some views on Research on Pattern Recognition in France on both theoretical and experimental level. The "keywords" of those researches are "Theoretical studies on learning process, classification, adaptative networks and perceptrons; applications such as character and speech recognition, optical information processing . . . "

Theoretical Research

All the numerous mathematical researches for pattern classification in the field of pattern recognition seem suitable to many other fields, such as, for example, human science, where in the same way as for pattern recognition, the immediate data are multiform and the appearance extremely diversified. Examples can be found in the works of investigators such as Levi-Strauss[6]. He tried to find in the framework of structuralism, by means of mathematical formalization (in the particular case of primitive people), different features built up in structure. But it is also possible, on the other hand, that the research in the field of pattern recognition finds its inspiration in the works of human sciences. We present such a way in the first theoretical work described as "establishment of a code."

Let us show how psychological experiments, statistical analysis, and analysis of simulation with a view to examine a certain type of learning process were treated simultaneously at the *Institut de Statistiques of the University of Paris* under Professor Benzecri.

Learning is considered here not as a behavior imposed a priori but as the collective synthesis of the solution of a problem. The experiment which was chosen–*setting up of a code*, enabling two persons to designate to each other, on a given field B, the objects situated in space A–resulted in:(a) an experimentation on human subjects, (b) a mathematical model, (c) simulation of this model on a computer.

One imagines that if space B of the signals is smaller than space A of the objects to be designated, the code which established a correspondence between these two spaces enables one to effect:(a) a reduction of the number of dimensions, giving rise to a certain structure of the objects in space A, (b) facilitation of the classification of the objects of space A, especially if a geometrical representation of space B is easy.

1. PSYCHOLOGICAL EXPERIMENTATION

The psychological experiment is a game which is played as follows:

Space A of the objects to be designated is the map of Europe.

Space B of the signals at our disposal for so doing is a segment of a straight line.

To communicate to each other the names of the countries, the players h and h′ have only one possibility, that of placing marks on segment B. The game leader has to estimate each exchange of information according to a given scale:

Player h, intending for example to ask for "Spain," places a mark on segment B:

Player h′, seeing the mark, replies for instance "Italy." The game leader declares the results: the number of points which players h and h′ have won or lost depends upon the proximity of the countries requested and replied. Thus we have a classical sequence–classical in psychology–"stimulus, reply, conclusion." The game goes on, players h and h′ making in turn requests and replies. Generally, we see that, after some thirty or forty moves, a satisfactory "comprehension" between the players is established.

A statistical examination of this type of experiment was made and led to a model of simulation on a computer:

STUDY OF THE LAWS OF BEHAVIOR LEADING TO SIMULATION:

Two stimuli s_1 and s_2 are considered as close if $\forall a$: $k(s_1,a)/k(s_1)$ differs only slightly from $k(s_2,a)/k(s_2)$; $k(s_1,a)$ being in the experiment the number of times when stimulus s_1 gives rise to a reply a; k(s) being the number of presentations of s in the same experiment.

If we write

$$\begin{cases} C^D(i) \\ C^R(i) \end{cases}$$

the mean abscissa of the points of the segment used to code the country i (or of the points which were given i as a reply), we can say that the mean code is defined by a function on the set I, which must be defined.

2. MATHEMATICAL MODEL-SIMULATION ON A COMPUTER

Subjects h and h′ of a set H make use of the signals of a space B in order to designate and to ask each other the objects of a space A, open to all. We suppose that A and B are metrical spaces. We can define the distances $|a\ a'|$ and $|b\ b'|$. The behavior of the subjects of H will be described by the probabilities that they make such and such requests or give such and such replies. The variables of behavior will therefore be measures of probabilities and probabilities of transition.

If h requests a by means of signal b, and receives reply a′ from h′ :

If $|a\ a'|$ is weak, that is to say $|a\ a'| < dA$, highest limit of the short intervals, the communication is satisfactory, which causes for h and h′ an increase of the probability of bringing the objects of A close to a and a′ in correspondence with zone b.

The density of probability that subject $h \in H$ may have in view the object $a \in A$ is $\overset{*}{h}_A(a)$. $\overset{*}{h}_A(a)da$ is the measure of probability on A, with $\int_A \overset{*}{h}_A(a)da = 1$. The density of conditional probability that h, speaking of a, utilizes to designate signal b is $h_B^A(a,b)$; it is the *code* of h. In the same way, $h_A^B(a,b)$ is the density of conditional probability that h, having received from h′ message b, may reply with object a. $h_A^B(a,b)$ is the uncoding by h of the messages received. We suppose that h_B^A and h_A^B do not depend upon the subject h′ to whom h is speaking.

Adaptation

The h_B^A evolve in order to make the communication effectual.

Let an initial communication between subjects h and h′ be noted: (a_o, b_o, a'_o).

For a given a, we have: $h_B^A(a,b)db$, the measure of probability on B which must be modified in terms of the conclusion (value of the interval $|a_o\ a'_o|$ of the initial communication):

$$\Delta\ h_B^A(a,b) = \Delta\ a_o, b_o, a'_o\ h_B^A$$

where $\Delta\ a_o, b_o, a'_o$ is a linear operator depending upon the value of

$$|a_0\ a'_0|,\ |a\ a_0|,\ |a\ a'_0|,\ \text{etc.}$$

The Monte Carlo method was used for the simulation on a computer. In this simulation, space A was also the map of Europe; and in the structure of the codes which appeared, it was found the main elements noted in the game played by human subjects: division of the space of the objects into zones, each one coded on an interval of S and, inside each zone, a way of continuous representation.

The programs of simulation offer interesting outlets as regards to the possibility of competitive classification from the point of view of speed and a certain capacity for the representation of a system of points of R^n within a space R^p, where $p < n$. One sees the possible applications to the problems of preselection in pattern recognition.

******

We shall mention other groups which pursue theoretical studies related to the different problems of pattern recognition. In these studies the nature of learning process is no more investigated. It is in terms of applications and performances that more or less "classical" learning algorithms are built up.

At the *University of Toulouse*, MM. Castan and Perennou studied various algorithms relative to learning processes. The studies were carried out by means of simulation on IBM 7044. The research of this group is based upon the speed of the algorithms of discriminators working by linear separation and the optimization of the general performances of these discriminators. The papers published[5] deal with algorithms of minimization of the moment of inertia of the misclassified patterns, in the case when the data are not linearly separable, or with methods relative to the surfaces of separation (such as the hyperquadric or hypercubic) minimizing the quadratic terms in order to avoid prohibitive calculations.

A system of the perceptron type simulated on a computer leads to applications in the fields of recognition of optical patterns (printed and handwritten characters, aerial photographs, etc.) and the recognition of speech (with a vocoder, manufactured by CNET, which must be on line with IBM 7044 to allow recognition in real time).

At the CERA (Centre National d'Etudes et de Recherche en Automatisme) in Paris, a study was made on a system of "diachronic" recognition. The group of CERA, directed by M.J.C. Levy, studied by simulation on a computer, the behavior of a system which was made up of elements E_i, and the connections of which are built up by learning[7].

The application of a diachronic pattern, that is to say of a sequence of signs called alphabets, will correspond for the system to the setting up of alot of connections oriented between elements E_i (each element E_i of the system corresponds to one of the signs of the alphabet). The connections A_{ij} between the elements E_i and E_j are stored.

1. A_{ij} will be modified during the period of learning with the eventual external application of a new pattern and with the time (progressive decrease: forgetfulness).

2. The set of the A_{ij} will be used after the period of learning to recognize the sequences stored previously if sequences more or less similar are applied to the system and to insure recognition, even if the rhythm of input differs from the stored rhythm, which gives the possibility, among other applications, of recognition of speech, where the phonems occur with any kind of rhythm.

At the *Faculty of Sciences in Paris*, Department of Theoretical Calculus under the supervision of Professor Fortet, Mme. M. Parvu and B. Bru, they have undertaken a research on the generative and linguistic theory of patterns. For the first time in France, this department will give a set of lectures on "pattern recognition" for the postgraduate students.

Research in Pattern Recognition in the Field of Applications

1. SYSTEM OF OPTICAL READING OF TYPEWRITTEN CHARACTERS

This system is studied at CNET (Centre National d'Etudes des Télécommunications) by M. Bordes with the proposed application to sorting of the mail[4]. The object of the system is the recognition of words belonging to a limited list, i.e., the names of the French districts and the codes of the departments. The redundancy produced by comparison with this list makes it possible to reach the percentage demanded by the P. & T. (maximum of errors $2^0/_{00}$. This comparison is carried out on a computer; it is the second part of the system. We shall now describe its first part, realized in hardware, and which aims at the recognition of typewritten capital letters.

A first experiment was made only on a set of four alphabets. It showed that it was necessary to make a preprocessing of the data before classification, for a machine for the reading of *all* the capital letters of typewriters utilized in France.

Description of the three levels of the present machine:

[See Figure 1]

I. Input of the Line of Text. The envelopes are in continuous running. The reading head is made up of a system for the research of the lower line of the text on the envelope (by means of a servo-mirror) and of a set: optical devices, vibrating mirror, photo-diodes mosaic. The vibrating mirror, which oscillates at 12 khz, is destined to recapture the residual, vertical aframes: (± 1,5 mm). The envelopes are running at the speed of 2,5m/sec. One is sure to obtain, among others, a framed projection of the character to be identified on the photo-diodes mosaic. To each of the photo-diodes is attached an amplifier giving out electrical, analogical signals V_j. Thus (see Figure 1)

$$x_j = \frac{V_j}{V_{max}}$$

$0 \leqslant x_j \leqslant 1$; V_{max} depends upon the contrast between ink and paper.

II. Preprocessing. The level of preprocessing has an analogical and parallel structure. It is made up of p threshold logic units, associating to each vector X delivered by the input, a vector Y of p components defined as follows:

$$Y_k(X) = \begin{cases} 1 & \text{if} \quad A_k X > 0 \\ 0 & \text{if} \quad A_k X \leqslant 0 \end{cases}$$

Each threshold logic unit corresponds to a vector A_k, the components of which are fixed. The selection corresponding to the choice of p vectors A_k has been made by means of different methods: intuitive remarks, learning algorithms, algorithms (described by Ho and Kashyap) minimizing the moment of inertia of the misclassified characters. These algorithms were adapted in terms of the problems of tolerance of the threshold logic unit. The adjustment of the A_k entailed a complete sampling of all the typewritten capital letters.

Prior to making use of the algorithms, a certain number of definitions, essentially intuitive, of the significance points of the letters have been made (points of the periphery of the line, the slope of which has a given value, intersection with the axes of symmetry, etc.). With these definitions, vectors A_k can be built up, for vectors X duly framed on the photo-diodes mosaic; and the problem of recognition can be eliminated from that caused by the continuous running of the characters.

The system of preprocessing, with its set of threshold logic units (each element of which detects in the character to be recognized, the eventual presence of an outline centered on a significant point), sets off the structure of the character and leaves for the next level of identification a relatively simplified work.

III. Identification. The third level of the machine is as far as now simulated on a digital computer. The object of this simulation is to compute the analogical circuits of the machine (plain hardware, analogical circuits).

The principle of identification is based upon a process of linear separation. Vector Y obtained at the output of the second level must be placed in the most probable class to which it belongs, that is to say, P_{r_i} being the probability that Y belong to class i ($1 \leqslant i \leqslant 36$):

$$P_{r_i}(Y) = P_r(C^i) \prod_{k=1}^{p} P_r[Y_k | C^i] \ ,$$

with $P_r(C^i)$ being the probability of presence of a character of the class C^i and $P_r(Y_k | C^i)$ being the probability that component Y_k be present if C^i is the class of the character to be recognized. Class m which will be chosen for Y will correspond to P_r maximum. It is obvious that a correct determination of Y_k by the second level is essential to reach a satisfactory classification (85% recognition).

Let us recall that the process of identification is not ended at the output of the third level. The character is sent to a computer to make up a word, to be recognized in order to sort the envelopes (the words are the names of the French districts and the departmental codes).

Let us hope in the near future that this kind of research will relieve the tedious task of sorting the mail that thousands of employed persons are doing daily.

2. SYSTEM OF OPTICAL READING OF ANY PRINTED CHARACTERS

The object of the research undertaken at *C.N.R.S.* (Centre National de la Recherche Scientifique) under the supervision of Professor de Possel is the automatic reading of all and any printed texts, unconditioned: current printed texts, texts in different alphabets (latin, cyrillic, hebrew, chinese...).

At present, the level of data input, a flying-spot sensing unit, has been built in hardware. This level is for the data input on a computer where the levels of preprocessing and identification are simulated with the aim of testing the algorithms in terms of statistics on the percentage of recognition, determining the optimum hardware feature necessary to design each level, and showing that the number of storages necessary for the classification of characters belonging to numerous alphabets (all the learning experiments being stored) does not increase in proportion with the number of alphabets "learned" but tends towards a reasonable limit, which permits to foresee for the design of hardware,a permanent storage.

I. Level of Data Input. A flying-spot sensing unit proceeds to the input of the data on a magnetic tape. With the help of various devices (different automatic controls, "box for books" for the reading of a book without tearing out the pages, "automatic page-turner," etc.) it will be used as direct input in fast core storage for the hardware device.

The technical characteristics of the sensing unit are the flying-spot sensing unit, which analyzes the image, column after column, and sends it, bit after bit, on a magnetic tape. There are 96 points per column. The speed of the sensing unit is limited by the magnetic tape. It can go as high as 250,000 bits/sec.

The different parameters are suitable for their satisfactory tolerance limits (height of the letters, contrast between ink and paper, etc.).

Let us mention that this sensing unit was used, with different aims, for input on magnetic tape of:(a) bee-wings (the study of connected components of the veins enabling one to discern the races of bees), (b) star configurations (for studies relative to the automatic determination of position), and (c) cartoons (to study the animation on a display, output of a computer). . .

II. Preprocessing. The method consists in independent tests, after cleaning and separation[(1)] of the characters. These tests can give a limited number of possible results.

Example: The character is divided into vertical sections and we can get properties from them. These elementary tests are, in most cases, sufficient for a correct classification.

A set of tests, so-called "of the second order", are added to those of the first order when there are not enough of them.

Example: The beginning and the ending of white and black intervals, so-called "events", are examined. These different tests have been built up after numerous experiments with intuitive methods.[11]

III. Identification Level. There are m tests of the first and second order. Let n_i be the number of different possible results of test i. Identification of the character will be made with a Boolean matrix with N lines: classes $C_1, C_2, \ldots, C_N$ of the characters; $n_1 + n_2 + \ldots + n_m$ columns. Learning (or storage of a new alphabet) consists in putting in core storage for each letter the results of the different tests. Identification is made by different successive tests on the character, which permits the elimination of a certain number of classes C^i. The tests cease when only one class not eliminated (or eliminated only a few times as compared with the eliminations incurred by the other classes) is left.

IV. Simulation and Study of Hardware. The works of simulation of the preprocessing and identification levels show very clearly different possibilities of perfecting the algorithms and their speed. In particular, the matrix representing exploration of the letter may be transposed several times

(1) Separation may require a set of operations corresponding to a search for connected components of a set for characters of this kind: 

during the process of recognition. It has seemed necessary to study a cross access memory to avoid these transpositions.

V. Experiments. A large number of experiments have been made for the design of the hardware of the reading machine. At present, effective recognition is delivered with some ten alphabets in core storage *(unconditioned* alphabets).

3. PATTERN RECOGNITION IN COHERENT LIGHT

The method employed in the *Laboratoire d'Electro-Optique* at C.S.F. in Paris directed by M.S. Lowenthal is based on spatial filtering in coherent light and is applied to the recognition of printed characters, fingerprints and map matching.

As it is known[9] in a coherent optical system, a function (object) in the form of a transparency, for example, is introduced in the input (object) plane of the system. By diffraction, the two dimensional Fourier transforms of the input are delivered in a plane called "Fourier plane." A second diffraction performs and gives in a third plane (image plane) an image of the input. By suitable filtering in the Fourier plane, the input function can then be processed in different manners.

The method employed to recognize an element in an object, for example a letter in a text, consists to cross-correlate the two dimensional derivatives of the text with the two dimensional derivatives of the letter by acting only on the Fourier spectrum. For this purpose, two filters are used simultaneously: (1) a matched filter which is realized by holography (van der Lugt) whose transparency is proportioned to the complex conjugate of the Fourier transform of the researched letter; and (2) a filter (parabolic transmission) which performs the above double differentiation (Lowenthal).

The auto-correlation of the derivatives of the researched function is then characterized in the image plane by a sharp maximum. With this method the ambiguities often encountered in ordinary correlation are greatly reduced. An example will show that if the capital letter I is researched in a text by ordinary cross-correlation, the capital letters, such as E, F, H, etc. containing the I, will equally give a response. By differentiation, the letters are transformed in their contours or outlines and it is evident that the contour of the I is no more contained in the contour of the E, F, H, . . . In this way, only the researched letter will give a sharp maximum. Satisfactory results are obtained.

BIBLIOGRAPHY

[1] M. Benzecri–"Lecons sur l'Analyse Factorielle et la Reconnaissance des Formes"; Third cycle course, taught at the Institut de Statistiques de l'Université de Paris (1967).
9, Quai St. Bernard, Paris 5°

[2] M. Benzecri–"Sur l'instauration d'un code", Publication of the Institut de Statistiques de l'Université de Paris.

[3] D. Bertaux–"Methodes mathématiques de la Reconnaissance des Formes", Internal technical report (October 1966), C.E.R.A., Vélizy-Villacoublay.

[4] M. Bordes–"Etude expérimentale d'un système d'identification automatique des caractères dactylographiés", Symposium on médical data processing, Toulouse (1967).

[5] S. Castan, G. Perennou–"Etudes sur les discriminateurs", Symposium on médical data processing, Toulouse (1967).

[6] C. Levi-Strauss–"La Structure et la Forme" in "Cahiers de l'I.S. E.A., 35, Bd. des Capucines, Paris (2°), No. 99, March 1960.

[7] J.C.Levy–"Système autoadaptatif de reconnaissance des configurations dynamiques", Symposium on médical data processing, Toulouse (1967).

[8] S. Lowenthal, Y. Belvaux–Optical Acta, 14, 245, 1967.

[9] A. Marechal, P. Croce–"Comptre-rendus Académie des Sciences", 237, 1953.

[10] M. Nadler "Empyrean", An alternative paradigm for pattern recognition, International Symposium on Information Theory, San Remo (1967).

[11] R. de Possel–"La lecture automatique: un essai de réalisation", Automatisme, X, October 1965.

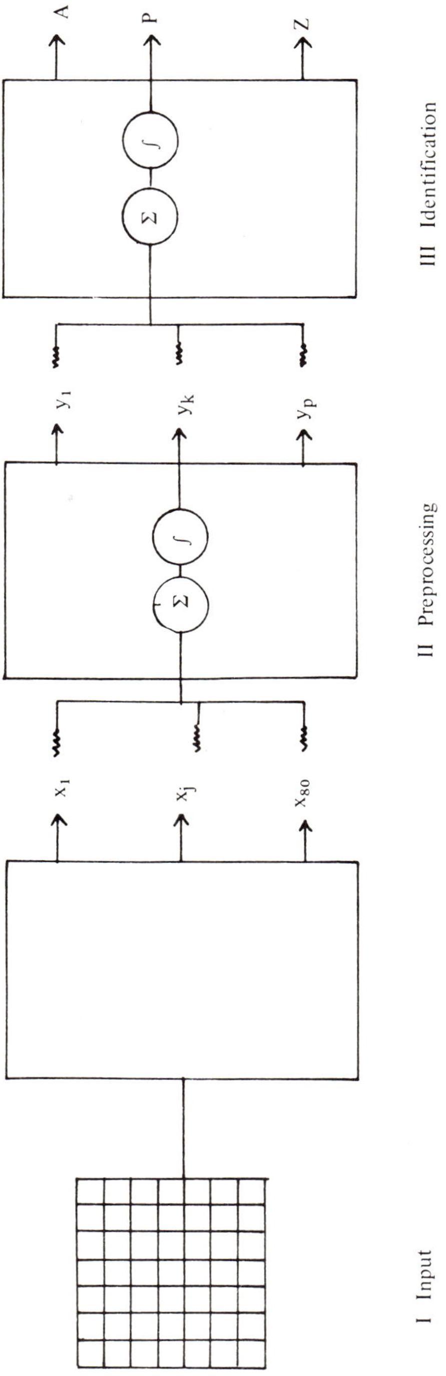

Figure 1: Mosaic of 80 Photodiodes

(8) How is the classification to be used in a given application?

(9) What interaction exists between various parts of the system? How should the data be organized? What overall configuration should the system have?*

More questions could be asked. Our purpose, however, is to show that interactive computer graphics can play an important role in pattern recognition. PROMENADE, ENVIRON, the Signature Analysis Research Facility (SARF) (Stanley, Lendaris, and Nienow, 1967) and the facility at Rome Air Development Center developed under Dr. John Sammon all use interactive graphic computers for pattern recognition. We now describe these systems and relate their capabilities to the questions asked above.

3. PROMENADE

Since PROMENADE is described by Hall (1967), only a short description will be given here. PROMENADE results from a two-year research effort** to explore, implement, and evaluate the feasibility and usefulness of an interactive graphic computer system for pattern recognition. This system is an attempt to integrate graphic plots with numeric analysis and data manipulation to provide for the pattern recognizer a tool to explore and analyze his data. The system is programmed in FORTRAN for a CDC 3100 computer with "Digigraphics" display and an IBM 1311 disk pack.

The various parts of the system complement each other. For example, the link node plot shown in Figure 2 complements the ISODATA cluster-seeking program. This plot indicates the distances between cluster centers. In Figure 3 we have listed programs now available in PROMENADE. The 3–D, 4–D plots are shown in Figure 4.

PROMENADE requires vector-valued numerical data as input. The plots available are most suitable for real-valued data, less useful for ordinal data and nominal data. Therefore, PROMENADE seems most useful in the preprocessor-to-classifier stages (points 5 through 7 in Figure 1). For example, this system allows examination of the details of the data. Individual data points can be selected in 3–D, 4–D plot and their numerical values printed out. The ability to select individual data points can be used to make explicit the regions of overlap between classes, the modes within classes, and wild shots.

---

* We assume that good engineering practice will be used to design specific hardware. Our emphasis is on the development of the concepts needed to guide the engineering design.

** Supported by Rome Air Development Center, Rome, N.Y., under Contract F30602-67-C-0351.Dr. John Sammon of RADC is developing an interactive graphic-data-analysis system using a CDC 1604. This facility will not be described separately since it examplifies many of the same characteristics as PROMENADE.

Eventually, it will be possible to partition non-homogeneous data sets into homogeneous sub-sets, to specify sub-sets of variables as being useful for specific sub-sets, to evaluate error performance over a local region, and to use non-numerical data associated with each data point (such as laboratory notebook comments) to suggest new measurements that could be made or to point to specific equipment or operator deficiencies.

PROMENADE is interactive. The graphics programs allow detailed operations on data sets. The numeric packages,* at this time, are half-way between batch-processing programs and fully interactive routines. The user can modify program control parameters but has little control over the details of the program.

In the future we will modify these programs in two ways. First, we will allow the user more control over details of the program, while at the same time using graphic presentations to convey rapidly the "state" of the program. Second, we will develop a system of program segments that can be flexibly linked together. The second way will reduce our dependence on particular arrangements of program blocks captured in a given algorithm and allow the user to create his own algorithms.** Careful design of data structures will be crucial in chaining program blocks since the output of one program will be the input of another.

4. SARF

SARF (Signature Analysis Research Facility—Stanley *et al.*, 1967) is programmed for an IBM 360/50 Computer with 2250 display unit. SARF includes a diffraction-pattern-sampling system that can be controlled from the interactive console. This allows the user to modify the characteristics of the transducer, thus controlling and modifying Stages 3 and 4 of the pattern-recognition system. The user can then see the effects of this modification of the transducer in all parts of the system.

The ring data structure and the bookkeeping method that describes to the user the processing of any data sub-sets are also significant parts of SARF.

5. ENVIRON***

ENVIRON is a computer system for the interactive graphic display facilities at Stanford Research Institute that provides the user the capability of

---

* The Health Sciences Computing Facility at University of California, Los Angeles under Prof. Wilfred Dixon has programmed several statistical packages to work on an IBM 2250 display (see Dixon, 1967).

** See Beaton (1964) for a particularly effective set of blocks. Beaton was able to define five matrix operators that are sufficient to perform most multivariate statistical routines.

*** Supported by the Office of Naval Research under Contract N0014-68-C-0454.

mixing English text with a linear graph representation of the "structural" relationships between the paragraphs of English text. The program was designed by David A. Evans, a graduate student in Civil Engineering at Stanford University. His goal in designing the program was to provide the planner with a tool capable of manipulating complex concepts such as might arise in planning in an urban context.

ENVIRON provides a non-hierarchical structure within which a person can express the complex relationships he subjectively feels are important.* The nodes of the linear graph are associated with concepts as expressed in the English text paragraphs that lie behind the nodes. The links established between the nodes of the graph are created when the user feels that relationships exist between the concepts. By using the combination of English text and the linear graph the user is able to see the structure of his ideas as well as the ideas themselves. In Figures 5(a) and 5(b) we show the presentations provided to the user when he is using the graphic and the textual presentation of his ideas. The graphic and textual representations are directly connected, since each node and link of the graph is associated with a paragraph of text. The system allows the user to conveniently indicate, using the graph, those paragraphs he wishes to juxtapose.

We feel that the structure is important by itself and that by looking at the linear graph the user arrives at a different understanding of his problem than he would if he merely looked at the English text. The structure is also important because it allows us a second representation to examine by computer. The computer can be programmed to search the linear graph for certain graphical structures. These graphical structures may suggest interrelationships between concepts that might not have been apparent as the ideas were being developed.

In addition to searching the graph it will also be possible eventually to search the text to pull together ideas that from their textual description appear to be related.

When we do such searching it is clear that we need to be able to conveniently modify the concepts that we have generated. For example, three concepts that seem quite distinct when first conceived may, after the subject is better understood, be seen as two distinct concepts. The ENVIRON program makes it possible for the user to replace the three concepts with the two concepts, with the computer keeping a history of these modifications.

We see ENVIRON's use in pattern recognition as providing a tool that will allow the pattern recognizer to organize the complex constraints that exist in most pattern-recognition problems (Stages 1, 8 and 9). We further see ENVIRON as being used to provide an "explicit group memory" for a

* Hierarchy (for example, see Engelbart *et al.,* 1967) forces in a useful way the organization of ideas but it also can prevent presentation of more richly connected conceptual structures. The less constraining structure of the linear graph seems particularly appropriate for the process of forming concepts about a particular subject.

team working on a pattern-recognition problem. The hunches and feelings of all the members of the team can be reflected in the ENVIRON representation of the problem. Because it is explicit, everyone can see and comment upon it.

Two important aspects of ENVIRON need to be reemphasized. It allows the person to work with quantitative and subjective feelings about his problem and it uses the computer's power to allow him to manipulate his concepts to arrive at the conceptualization most appropriate to his problem.

6. Implications

Using PROMENADE, SARF, and ENVIRON as examples we have indicated some of the implications of convenient, flexible interactive computer graphics for pattern-recognition methodology. In this section we summarize these and other implications we consider significant.

The implications can be separated under three headings:

(1) Recognition algorithm design

(2) Analysis of data

(3) Intra-team communication

We consider each of these in turn.

a. RECOGNITION ALGORITHM DESIGN

The interactive graphic computer allows us to create algorithms by concatenating operators (program blocks). This means that development emphasis will shift to defining blocks of various complexities and to putting the blocks together in useful ways. This will tend to shift discussion to the *various* ways that a problem can be approached (and, hopefully reduce the number of discussions as to which technique is "best"). The best way will depend on the data. File and data structures will assume increasing importance, since the output of any block has the possibility of serving as input to any other block.

An interactive system is to us more than a collection of batch programs that can be conveniently called from the display console. Interaction implies control* and selection over the way blocks are fitted together. This will allow appropriate tailoring of the processing to the individual situations. Changes in performance can then be related immediately to the kind of classifier used.

* Truly interactive control will require the presentation of the "state" of the machine to the user.

b. ANALYSIS OF DATA

We need to analyze our data to determine its structure and to suggest to ourselves new measurements that could be made to improve the performance of the system. Most of all we need to be able to move easily from overall summarizations to the individual data point and back. We portray by

overview ⟵ zoom ⟶ details

this necessary characteristic.

Details of interest include wild shots–i.e., isolated points in the data space–and non-numerical information, such as text from an observation notebook, that might indicate useful new measurements to be taken. To observe details requires a high-capacity channel. The graphic console meets this need. Computer assistance in doing the bookkeeping is essential to keep the user sane as he looks through these details.

At some middle level of detail the data analysis can indicate multimodal data and regions of overlap, and can examine measurements or patterns in sub-regions. This analysis can be used to guide classifier* and preprocessor selection and design, and to provide indications of performance locally so that proprocessors and transducers can be evaluated.**

c. INTRA-TEAM COMMUNICATION

The graphic display provides a medium that several people can observe at one time. Fortunately the interactive control should also allow a greater variety of analyses to be performed. Coupled together, these suggest that communication within a team of people can be enhanced. It seems to us that this has particularly interesting implications for interdisciplinary efforts.***

* Possibly different kinds of classifiers should be used in different sub-regions of the data space.

** See also the discussion in Tukey and Wilk (1966) for the relationships of data analysis to statistics.

*** There are also interesting implications when similar research is carried on by several individual researchers who are not geographically close. If these researchers had available the same analysis system, then it would be possible for one researcher to analyze his data and at the same time write a magnetic tape giving the operations he performed on the data. Then he could provide his data and his tape to the other person who could then use the magnetic tape to control his analysis system and (perhaps via an audio recording) key the first researcher's comments to this sequence of analysis steps. He would see the data in the same detail as the original person saw it and could make detailed comments on the other person's interpretations.

7. Major Remaining Problems

There are many additional subtle and difficult problems. We need a much better understanding of the "active graphic" representations that will be used in interactive graphic computers. This understanding needs to be tied to a firmer understanding of the nature of man's physiology. It appears to us that active graphics will provide a major new representation for work on complex topics. It will allow a person to develop his own special symbol set and his own set of structural relationships and operations in order to describe a particular discipline. Much work remains to be done before this will come to pass, however.

We need more convenient and flexible compiler and data structures. Particularly important is work toward meta-compilers. These allow a person to define convenient operators within the language in which he wishes to work, and provide the possibility of machine-independence. Thus the code required to run one machine can be converted to code that runs another machine.

For a long time data analysis was viewed, at least academically, as applying this or that *most appropriate* technique to a particular set of data. With the advent of more powerful multivariate data analysis systems new strategies for performing data analysis will be required. As we learn more, it will probably be appropriate to incorporate checklists within these computer systems that use the characteristics of the data to suggest that such and such techniques be tried.

The work of Beaton in multivariate statistics and of others in the areas of pattern recognition and cluster-seeking need to be extended so that we develop blocks appropriate to the kinds of pattern-recognition work we wish to do. As we develop new operators, it may be appropriate to develop hardware to implement some of these operators. For example, computers for numerical data analysis may have hardware for a variety of matrix operations and not just hardware for multiplying pairs of floating-point numbers.

8. Conclusions

Let us conclude with what are essentially a series of slogans for the new era of interactive graphic computer systems. We feel that these systems will change the rules to the extent that in addition to doing the old things better, we will actually be able to do new things. We will be able to examine the details of the data and then zoom to a summarized overview of the data in a way that will give us the feeling that we are flying in hyperspace. In short, we feel that the interactive graphic computer system will give us a powerful new tool for organizing complexity.

REFERENCES

A.C. Beaton, "The Use of Special Matrix Operations in Statistical Calculus," Ed.D. Thesis. Grad. School of Education, Harvard University, 1964.

W.J. Dixon, "Use of Displays with Packaged Statistical Programs," *Proc. AFIPS Fall Joint Computer Conf., 31,* Thompson Books, Washington, D.C., pp. 481–484, 1967.

D.C. Engelbart, W.K. English, "A Research Center For Augmenting Human Intellect," *Proc. AFIPS Fall Joint Computer Conf., 33,* Thompson Books, Washington, D.C., pp. 395–410, 1968.

D.J. Hall, "PROMENADE–An On-Line Pattern Recognition System," Final Report, Contract AF 30(602)–4196, 1967. (DDC number AD822174).

G.L. Stanley, G.G. Lendaris, W.C. Nienow, "Pattern Recognition Program," Technical Report 567–16, AC Electronics–Defense Research Laboratories, Santa Barbara, Calif., November 1967.

J.W. Tukey, M.B. Wilk, "Data Analysis and Statistics: An Expositary Overview," *Proc. AFIPS Fall Joint Computer Conf., 29,* 1966, 695–709.

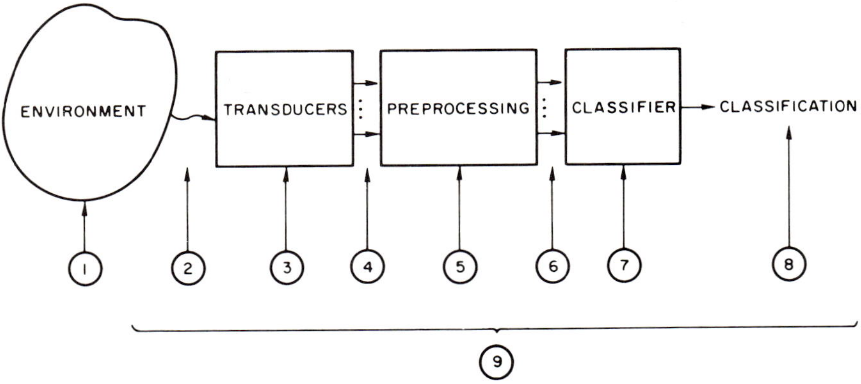

Figure 1: A Pattern-Recognition System with Stages Indicated

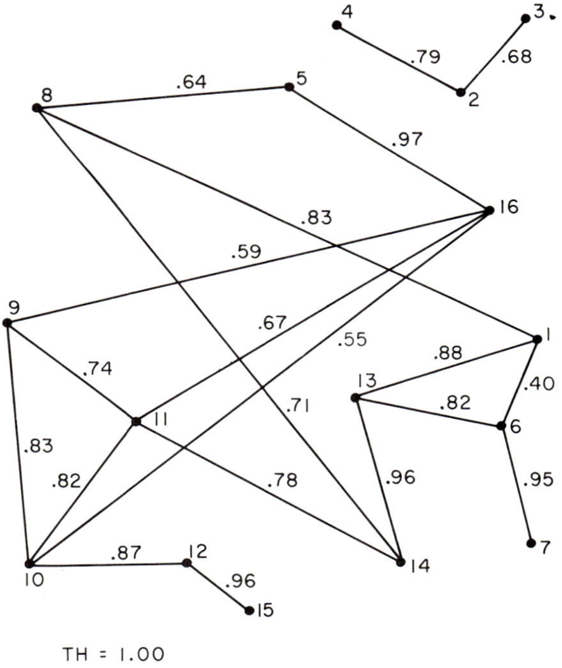

Figure 2: Link-Node Plot
(Numbers on links indicate between cluster distances)

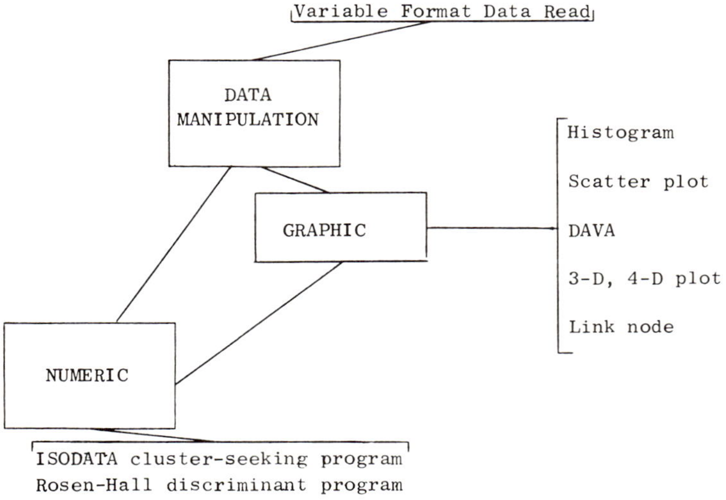

Figure 3: Programs Now Available within PROMENADE

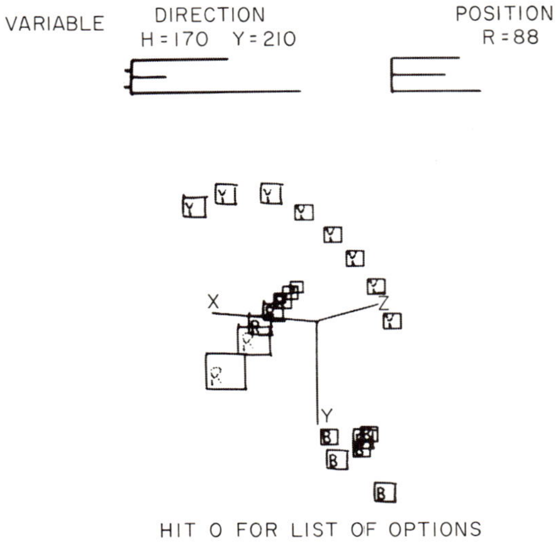

Figure 4(a): Three-dimensional Plot Taken from CRT Display

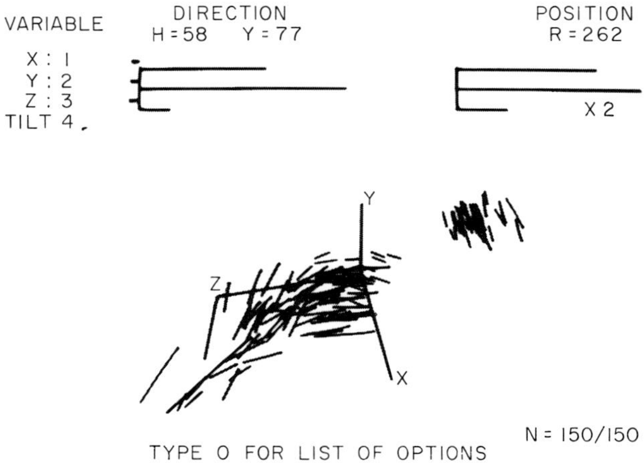

Figure 4(b): Four-dimensional Plot Taken from CRT Display

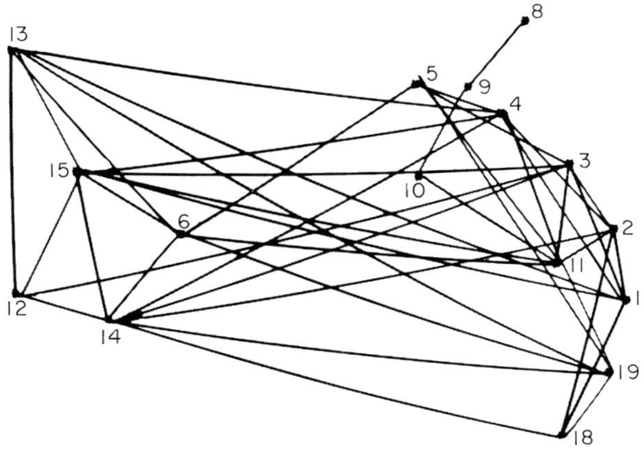

Figure 5(a): Linear Graph Representation of Conceptual Structure

12 DEVELOPMENT OF VILLAGE INDUSTRY

15 NO OVERCROWDING ...

13 EASY ACCESS TO DRINKING WATER ....

Figure 5(b): English Text Representation of Three Maximally Associated Concepts

STATISTICAL ANALYSIS AS A TOOL TO MAKE PATTERNS EMERGE FROM DATA

Jean-Paul Benzecri

UNIVERSITY OF PARIS
PARIS, FRANCE

Forward

Before we say anything about recognition, it should be fair to speak of patterns. The most common idea we have of a pattern is that given by a word of some natural language. Although dictionaries have been available for centuries, none has succeeded to give a clearcut algorithm by which it is to be decided when and to which objects any word can be applied. Some logicians claim that semantical definitions do exist, yet unstated, which provide lists of features determining the class of things corresponding to each meaningful sound. However, it is wise to notice that such a simple noun as, e.g., a neighbor, can be understood only in a complex situation where one can ask such questions, as: to whom is he a neighbor?, or: is it enough to be at walking distance from each other to be called neighbors? After all your neighbor is just someone who seems presently closer to you than a number of others.

The same difficulty is met when we are to distinguish a letter d from a letter a in a manuscript: is a **d** which it makes sense to call a d, and besides is taller than a class of resembling letters which we have advantage to read as **a**. Indeed a very efficient reading machine, and possibly a not too complicated one, should be built on this program; segment what is handed to you into resembling units which you label from 1 to at most 100; and just let another program guess, possibly from frequency tables, possibly by use of a dictionary or even a grammar, that item No. 13 is capital D, and item No. 29 is small z.

This is enough I think to suggest that what has been contributed those last five years in France and mainly in my laboratory in the field of automatic classification and multivariate analysis is of interest to the science of shapes, and that the page you have just read is a promising introduction to my coming lecture!

1. Data Analysis Versus Models and Discriminant Analysis

When faced with intricated sets of data, human scientist or biologist calls for help from the statistician, the former generally has some hypothesis, or even an accepted theory, while the latter has none. Besides, only in the last decade has statistical science received from electronic devices due to help to cope with the huge mass of digits that has to be handled in order to submit the flesh of data to the soul of formulae. It is therefore quite natural that the opinions, which the sociologist or psychologist brought with him, were made the main ingredients of the mathematical answer he received. In some cases, common-sense-concepts were built into a model with just enough parameters in it to outnumber the data. In others, an a priori classification was recovered up to but not always much less than 50% error-rate, using an ad hoc discriminant function; or else which in a sense is the worst of all, an evidently true statement was rejected on the basis of a parametric test which involved many more hypotheses and by far less natural ones than did the statement itself. But since those good old days when it was thought that it was enough to have two to make out an average, the statistician has acquired certain rights not seldom stronger than those of evidence.

That such a practice takes us back to fictions which we thought had been ruled out of science by Newton's "Hypotheses non fingo" (which could be properly paraphrased: "I don't use hypotheses as an ingredient in their own proof") should be clear to any scientist. However, there is a growing evidence, too, that Baconian methodology does not suffice to make out a knowledge in a context of numerous fluctuating variables. If one is willing to study sociology by letting all parameters constant but one, it is to fear that nobody will have neither power nor time to produce and observe all of the various situations relevant to the field. The notion of a shape or a pattern should emerge from a sea of data, not through a priori nominalistic postulates or axioms or by unduly fragmentary measurement of isolated facts which in themselves are meaningless since they depend on the environment and quickly change their mode but through the simultaneous synthesis, in the ethymological sense of putting together a number of elementary facts which help us ascend a step in the hierarchy of causes. But multidimensional synthesis cannot be achieved inside a human brain is without many arbitrary choices which often make the result devoid of significance. Therefore, the help of a computer is needed to apply to the data previously collected a set of quasi-universal computations or rather transformations which give them such a shape that the man of the field may unarbitrarily read on the output what was undecipherable in the input.

This certainly raises a question: To what extent are we able to fulfill this magnificient program? If factor analyses strongly rely upon arbitrary rotations to extract anything significant, how can it be claimed that the statistician should do nothing more to the data than the multidimensional analogue (or even the non-euclidean generalization) of computing an average or adjusting a straight line? that determinate purely mathematical handling of data tables is enough to make emerge such significant results that the man of the field may read them and accept them with as little doubt as he welcomes a nose in the middle of a face?

Let us not boast of too great a success. Alternating the study of the numerical data and of the concepts of the field is sound and besides unavoidable. Already several times the results of our computational analysis did suggest extending the measurements or rebuilding the experimental framework. But too intricate a mixture between what we observe and measure and what we think to be the underlying structure of it is an obvious danger against which we claim our new statistical methods – a few years old as they are, they provide a significant weapon. And without indulging in more philosophizing, we will try to put before you a few mathematical principles illustrated by examples. Colleagues interested in more details, including listings of programs, are welcome to write to Paris Statistical Institute and will receive our articles and reports.

2. Automatic Classification and Similarity Indexes

Although we don't believe that a splendid future is promised to taxonomic hierarchies, it seems unavoidable to start our review with automatic classification techniques.

Usually a classification algorithm consists of two fairly independent parts: (1) the computation of a similarity index, (2) the formation of clusters. Let us study these two points successively and state recent French contributions to the art.

In their now classical treatise devoted to the "Principles of Numerical Taxonomy," Sokal and Sneath offer a great number of similarity indexes, most of which are computed from data of the following (or a resembling) format: an I x C table (I = {i}, set of items; C = {c}, set of characters) is filled with ones and zeros. There is a one at the intersection of column **C** with line **i**, if item **C** possesses character **c**, and there is a zero when the contrary happens to be true. Actually, set C may very well be a set of vegetal or animal species, and set I a set of patches of land with character **c** possessed by item **i** if animal **c** is found in land **i** . . . but these semantic peculiarities are not relevant to the mathematical treatment which is concerned only with format.

Given two items **i** and **i′**, four numbers may be defined

$$Y\ Y(i,i'); \ Y\ N(i,i'); \ N\ Y(i,i'); \ N\ N(i,i')$$

of which the first is the number of **c**'s possessed jointly by **i** and **i′**, etc. It is clear at first that Y Y and N N correspond to match while Y N and N Y number differs. It is not clear, however, whether a N O N O match is just as meaningful as a Yes Yes match. Indeed whales and slugs both lack feathers and shell which do not make them look much the same. While the fact of having non-dark hair being just equivalent to that of having light hair, it is a negation which amounts to the same as an assertion. This is only one among the problem involved in coding characters and computing similarities.

Inspired by a paper of R.N. Shepard, about which we will speak fully later on (Cf. No. 7), we thought that the notion of similarity-index (or pseudo-distance) should be replaced by that of "ordonnance" or set of inequalities between the distances and consider themselves irrelevant. This implies, of course as will be seen immediately, that the clustering algorithms should be devised to rely only on the inequalities and *not* on the distances. But it has various advantages empirically tested by S. Regner and M. Roux:

(1) The host indexes enumerated by S. and S. is essentially reduced to two, which differ mainly (and do definitely differ!) according to the part played by N N matches.

(2) Cluster techniques become much less sensitive to arbitrary choices since a monotonic transformation on the index now becomes totally irrelevant.

Let us come now to clustering. Although ascending techniques, i.e., grouping elements into islets and these islets into islands or various clumpings have been suggested, we think that, as M.S. Watanabe made it already clear years ago, the partitioning of a set I into p distinct non-overlapping classes should, and to a certain extent can, rely on the following criterion: To each partition is associated a test quantity T and that partition is chosen which gives T the highest value. Unless we run into combinatorial infinity, not all partitions can be considered, but the following algorithm, pointed out to us by S. Regner (then at Maison des Sciences de l'homme, Paris), is convenient. Starting from one partition (coded as a function on set I with values ranging from 1 to p), we consider only those which can be obtained from it by changing the class of only one item **i** in I (that is, by changing only one value at a time of the function). The algorithm stops when no improvement of T can be obtained by such a restricted change in the partition. As for computing test quantity T, there is an ingenuous principle for which we are again indebted to S. Regner. Consider the data (a similarity matrix, or an ordonnance) as an element of a set S of mathematical structures to which the unknown (a partition) also belongs and then compute T as the inverse of a distance (of some kind or another) in set S. Indeed a partition may readily be interpreted as a (partial) ordonnance. It suffices to consider distances between elements inside one class as smaller than distances between elements belonging to different classes. There is still some choice left for the T-test distance used on set S of all (partial or total) ordonnances and only after some mathematical trials and practical experiments was de la Vega (again an investigator from M.S.H.) able to define a T better than the one we first suggested. This led to a program by M. Renaud which has been satisfactorily used to process archaelogical, psychiatrical, ecological data.

Whatever may have been this success, of which it is difficult to give here proper account in a few words without an explanation of the intricate data involved, we do think that the part played by automatic classification in data analysis should be modest. Let us state our opinion in few points.

(1) Some automatic ascending clustering seems necessary when too large sets of items are considered, in order to come down, let us say, from 5,000 elements to 500 islets.

(2) When processing a moderately large table, the very partitioning technique should use as an input not distances or ordonnance but the very table I x C itself. If both I and C are simultaneously partitioned, the former in a set Q of classes, the latter in a set K, there comes out a Q x K table:

cell (q,k) contains the total sum n_{qk} of the number of qualities in class k, each item i in class q possesses. For such a table a χ^2 may be computed:

$$\Sigma_{q,k}\ (n_{qk})^2/n_q\ n_k$$

The bigger this quantity, the more correlation there is between classes in I and C. It can therefore properly be chosen as T with this definite advantage that the data have been submitted to as little arbitrary treatment as possible. Since this χ^2 program has not been tested yet, we cannot however assert anything in its favor.

(3) After previous classifications have reduced the initial set from a few thousands to a few hundreds and then from a few hundreds to a dozen, it is probably a nuisance to partition further, since for the tables of which the least dimension is a few dozens, we have a very satisfactory and cheap factoring technique, about which we will speak in the next paragraph. Indeed, classification always involves much arbitrariness, much more than does a continuous geometrical representation of the data using, as coordinates in the map the factors extracted by some suitable analysis (or should we rather say, see above, synthesis). The only reason why classification has played such a prominent part in the history of science is that it is quite convenient for human memorizing and processing. But now we have machines, the storage as well as computation facilities of which allow us to give some rest to our brains!

3. The Analysis of Correspondences (Principles)

Let us start this paragraph with a typical example borrowed from linguistics. Let set I be the set of all characters appearing in a play and set J the set of the 40 (e.g.) words most frequently used in that play. We can fill an I x J table with integers by letting n(i,j) be the number of times character **i** has used word **j** in the whole course of the play. From such a table we wish to derive some compact information about both characters and words by which we mean the following. We think that words **j** and **j′** are close to each other, irrespective of their absolute frequencies, if they are predominantly used by the same characters, that is, of columns **j** and **j′** in our table are close to being proportional to each other. The same can be said of two characters, **i** and **i′**, although one may speak much more than the other. If both have the same sociocultural status or personal taste, they will prefer or avoid the same words. Therefore, lines **i** and **i′** in our table will be similar in profile, whatever different their total weights may be. Again it is natural to say that word **j** and character **i** are close to each other, if the relative frequency with which **i** uses **j** is above the average. All these notions are precisely what we intend to extract from our table and to display in a compact diagram. We want both sets I and J to be inserted in the same map (be it linear, plane or spacial) so that all their mutual proximities be immediately visible. Before we go into more details, let us give the result of our analysis as applied to Racine's Phèdre (Figure 1). Here, the main contrast is between Phèdre, the passionate queen, and Théramène, a respectful servant: between characters who say tu and assez (enough!) and those who address the latter by Vous, Madame and Seigneur.

How can such an analysis be achieved and in what does it differ at first sight from many variants of factor analysis you may have heard of? Let us indulge here in a few mathematical formulae:

$$n(i) = \Sigma_j\ n(i,j);\ n(j) = \Sigma_i\ n(i,j);\ n = \Sigma_{i,j}\ n(i,j);$$

$$f(i/j) = n(i,j)/n(j);\ f(j/i) = n(i,j)/n(i)$$

$$f(i) = n(i)/n;\ f(j) = n(j)/n;\ f(i,j) = n(i,j)/n$$

As is well known to all of you, the f(i) f(j) and f(i,j) are called frequencies and the f(i/j) f(j/i) conditional frequencies (of i when j and of j when i respectively). If we had the exact identity:

$$\forall\ i,j:\ \ f(i,j) = f(i) \times f(j)$$

that is, if we had statistical independence between i and j (all subjects use all words with the same conditional frequencies), nothing could be said, according to our viewpoint, about the data-table submitted to our analysis. In statistical terms, one can say that we have selected independence as a null hypothesis, H_0. But the use we make of a null hypothesis is quite different from what is common place in applied statistics. We are not interested in the question of accepting or rejecting a null hypothesis (indeed if H_0 has to be accepted, it means that our data are devoid of significance which we don't want! But that H_0 has to be rejected is only an indication that something may be done. It is not an interesting output in itself.) We want to see displayed as clearly as possible *how* our data differ from H_0, in what direction they deviate from independence. Again our null hypothesis differs from those commonly accepted in factor analysis where one would rather seek to what extent and along which directions do the lines and columns deviate from mere equality, while we are only interested in differences between *profiles*. By doing so we eliminate from the scope of our study the differences in weight (the n(i), n(j) or f(i), f(j)), which generally bring in an amount of noise of the same order of magnitude as the signal we are interested in and therefore prevent the factors extracted from being readily interpretable, even if the situation is obviously undimensional! Let us indicate here before we are misunderstood that we don't restrict our method to cases where f(i) is indeed just noise. It may very well happen that raw marginal frequencies are in themselves a useful information, which will be wise to compare with the factors; but even then it is a great advantage to compute the factors as independently as possible from the marginal frequencies.

And now what do we have to compute? How expensive is it to perform our analysis; what is the rationale for those computations? The computation cost first is as low as possible; it amounts to looking for the eigenvectors (as many eigenvectors as we extract factors) of some symmetrical square matrix, the dimension of which is equal to the number of elements in the smallest of sets I and J. Actually, if I is the smallest set, the matrix is the table of the s(i,i′) given by the following formula:

$$s(ii') = \Sigma_j(n(i,j).n(i'j)/n(j).(n(i).n(i'))^{1/2})\ .$$

As for the rational, the situation is more complicated; and it is quite fortunately so, since our formulae happen to be a crossroad to which one is led from several different approaches. Let us explain it as briefly as possible.

Our first principle was that of distributional equivalence. Actually we were mainly concerned with linguistic applications and included our statistical studies in a course on mathematical linguistics. The very word distribution was borrowed from Z.S. Harris, a famous linguist who in many a stimulating but indeed not universally approved paper, has been claiming that statistical analysis of the distributional facts (namely, environments, co-occurrences of words, etc.) could suffice to give all, or almost all of the structure of a language without any consideration of meaning being involved. An extreme corollary, as you may see, to the statement that to build science is to decode the universe . . . a bold project in pattern recognition. I am afraid it would not be easy to find a sponsor for! Anyway, even without a sponsor, a mathematician can define a formula for a so-called distributional distance, and so we did, letting the square of the distance between i and i′ be:

$$d^2(i,i') = \Sigma_j(f(j/i) - f(j/i'))^2/f(j) \;;$$

a formula in which a statistician recognizes immediately the χ^2 distance between two laws of frequencies, and to which we were led not so much by analogy than by the requirements that the distance be quadratic and that melting into one two individuals with the same conditional frequencies (two elements **i** and **i′** distributionally equivalent or synonymous in the sense that

$$\forall j\colon\ f(j/i) = f(j/i')$$

would not change anything to the whole pattern. After a distance had been defined, it was only natural to do multidimensional scaling (that is briefly stated to make out an euclidean map, extracted axis by axis that would gradually adjust as closely as possible to the computed distances), and so we did. Besides, we also devised some conjectural principle in order to put together both sets I and J on the same map, and with no more theorems behind us, we started writing programs and testing them on data.

The situation gradually grew better; we first recognized that the program was efficient, and then the programmer (B. Cordier) noticed a number of peculiarities she could prove to be theorems and afterwards the mathematician was somewhat ashamed he did not notice at first sight.

Here are those theorems. If the various factors F_1, F_2, etc., relative to the eigenvalues λ_1^2, λ_2^2 (all of which between 0 and 1) are considered simultaneously as functions on both sets I and J, one has the following expansion formula:

$$f(i,j) = f(i)\, f(j)(1+\lambda_1\ F_1(i)\ F_1(j)+\lambda_2\ F_2(i)\ F_2(j) + \ldots \qquad (1)$$

and factors on sets I and J are related to each other by a center of mass principle:

$$F(i) = \lambda^{-1} \Sigma_j F(j)\ f(j/i). \qquad (2)$$

Formula (1) means that marginal frequencies f(i), f(j) plus factors F_1, F_2 . . . is indeed equivalent to the sum of the information contained in the data table. Besides from some statistical considerations (χ^2 test!), it may be roughly stated how many factors are needed to represent the significant part of this information. Formula (2) quite satisfactorily asserts that up to a λ factor an individual **i** will appear on the map (our output) with coordinate F(i) at the center of masses of the **j**, themselves given as masses the conditional frequencies f(j/i).

Besides, now this formula had been proven, it was possible to compare our method with Eckart and Young Factor analysis (this comparison was suggested to us in 1965 by Douglas Carrol, then at Bell Laboratories), and with Guttman views on principal components in scalogram analysis. The latter comparison was especially fruitful since it revealed that, starting from Formula (2) as a rationale, Guttman had first contemplated doing the same analysis we did (and of which scalogram analysis is a particular case) but never went to computations, probably simply because in 1941 there were no computers available! From contacts with scalogram analysis, we benefited the following:

(1) Our attention was focused on the fact that a factor may be an algebraic function of another: e.g., F_2 may be a parabolic function of F_1. This actually happened several times and once to an amazing degree of accuracy (see below).

In the work of Guttman, successive factors depending algebraically on each other were given names such as intensity closure; such rigid interpretations do not always agree with facts, but they may be helpful if carefully handled.

(2) When a parallelogrammatic situation underlies the data table (i.e., when through due permutation of the lines and columns, the proeminent coefficients in the table could be clustered roughly into parallelogrammatic neighborhood of the diagonal), it sometimes happens that unlike what could be predicted through the theory of perfect scalograms, the second factor F_2 is *not* a quadratic function of the first one. This second factor may be used to extract a perfectly parallelogrammatic submatrix and eventually gives a second interpretable dimension.

(3) When the data matrix is filled not with various integers but only with one's and zeroes (Yes and No; Cf. Paragraph 2 above), it is convenient to give two columns to each character (as Guttman did) – a yes column and a no column – so that the underlying factor can be recovered most clearly.

Before we illustrate what has been said by a set of examples, let us speak briefly of the relationship between correspondence analysis on one side and some models on the other.

Let us first suppose that there exists two partitions, $\{I_1, \ldots, I_q, \ldots, I_p\}$ and $\{J_1, \ldots, J_q, \ldots, J_p\}$ of sets I and J respectively into p disjoint sets such that n(i,j) is non zero only if **i** and **j** belong to classes numbered by the same integer [i.e., if n(i,j) $\neq$ 0 and i ϵ I_q, then j ϵ J_q]. This may be paraphrased by saying that the data matrix may be (through suitable permutations) rewritten as a sequence of rectangular blocks along the diagonal. Then these partitions are discovered using the first factors extracted. Classes I_1, I_2, . . . and J_1, J_2, . . . are concentrated into points on the output map, with classes I_q and J_q exactly at the same point. Such a situation, which was actually discovered from an example before it was proved, is especially important since when the hypothesis is only approximately fulfilled, the program is still able to recover an interesting structure.

Let us now suppose that there exists a normally distributed random vector with two components (x,y) (actually the situation readily generalizes to any number of components) underlying our data matrix in the following sense: to the i's (resp. j's) are associated successive intervals on the X (resp. Y) axis; and n(i,j) is proportional to the probability that the random vector is in the i x j rectangle. Then the first factor extracted F_1 will approximate x on set I (F_1(i) will be the abscissa of a middle point in interval i) and y on set J. And the following factors (assuming that there is no noise, or rather no other interesting structure involved) approximate the successive Hermite polynomials.

4. Analysis of Correspondence (Examples)

In the preceding paragraph we took as a standard example of a correspondence the case where the n(i,j) were integers, representing roughly speaking, how many times individual i from set I had been found to match individual j from set J in same process, be it textual or psychological. However, we also suggested that our technique could also be used when the n(i,j) were but zeroes and one's corresponding to No and Yes answers. And actually we did consider successfully as correspondence matrices the tables of lines of which corresponded to individuals in some set I and the columns to continuous non-negative variables [n(i,j) being, e.g. the length of some part j of a plant i].

Our first three examples will be concerned with confusion matrices; in which case set I and J happens to coincide: n(i,j) being the number of times item i (stimulus) has been mistaken for item j (response). Example 2 is actually concerned with pair-wise comparison: how many times is i (first presented) judged similar to j (second). Then there will come two cases of logical (Yes–No) description matrices and finally continuous variables.

We can only mention here that in ecology our analysis of correspondence has proven to compete successfully with classification algorithms.

Example 1: A classical experiment in learning (Data by le Ny) – six sounds of increasing frequencies have to be associated with letters. On the output (a tridimensional map) each sound appears twice, once as a stimulus and once as a response. It should be noticed that the answers are systematically lower than the stimuli; besides, all points appear on a parabola; the second factor is a quadratic function of the first (Guttman, effect, see above). [See Figure 2]

Example 2: Comparing morse code signal pairs (Data by Rothkopf) – A 36 x 36 matrix is analyzed; signals as i and j almost perfectly coincide (because the comparison matrix is close to being symmetrical). The first factor correlates to .95 with the total duration of the signal (measured in Bodes); the second factor is a perfect parabolic function of the first (Guttman effect); the third factor is interpretable as the opposition of dots versus dashes.

The total duration and dot-dashes being relevant have already been found by Shepard (No. 7), but his technique gave a two dimensional chart without separating factors, and nothing like a .95 correlation with a physical quantity (the duration) *not* involved in the data (integers: how many times has i been judged equal to j) could have emerged. [See Figure 3]

Example 3: Inventing a code (experiment by J.F. Richard and J.P. Benzecri) – It is impossible to explain in a few words the experiment. Let us say that subjects were set by pairs and had to communicate to each other the names of European countries using only as signals a point marked on a 12 centimeters long straight-line; the psychologist said them if the communication had been successful. From this experiment we got:

(1) a confusion matrix–How many times had this country been answered for that;

(2) an average code–By which point on the line did the subjects code Spain, Italy, etc. (in most cases the subjects simply enumerated the countries from left to right, i.e., from Portugal to Russia; but very few errors affected Russia).

The output was brilliant. The first factor (labeled f_1 with index R for responses and D for questions) separated Russia from all other countries (since few confusions have arisen, this suggested proving the partition theorem as stated above) The second factor (f_2 on the diagram) had .94 correlation to the average code (labeled 1) (of all countries excluding Russia). Again a physically measurable quantity not included in the data matrix was recovered, and this times as a second factor (of course, with *no* rotation!). [See Figure 4,5,6]

Example 4: A descriptive matrix (Chinese pottery data by Eliseev)– This author suspected the existence of a parallelogrammatic structure; he applied with some success to Guttman's technique. Factor analysis revealed that the second factorwas not a quadratic function of the first: Characters (having an ear with flowers like that and so on) with non-zero second factor were excluded; a perfect scalogram appeared with no pottery rejected.

Example 5: Are you afraid of . . . (see below) – Thirty-four questions were asked to 150 children. By duplicating each question into two columns (Yes and No) a 68 x 150 matrix resulted. The first two factors extracted are readily interpretable. The psychologist, who thought only galvanic responses were meaningful and verbal (Yes–No) behaviour was just noise, was much astonished at what we recovered. The first factor accounts for the no-yes opposition: No, I don't fear any damage; Yes, I do fear. It is very remarkable that both yes and no answers were coded exactly the same. The analysis could distinguish them through their mutual correlations. The second factor concerns the agent: a natural little known and actually not much damageable agent as a mouse, or even thunder versus family problems (Data from Zlotowicz). [See Figure 7]

QUESTIONS

1. Are you afraid your father will fall sick?
2. Are you worried when your father is late to come back home?
3. Are you worried when your mother is late to come back home?
4. Are you afraid your mother will fall sick?
5. Are you afraid of what father will tell you?
6. Are you afraid of what your mother will tell you?
7. Are you frightened of rats?
8. Are you afraid of spiders?
9. Are you frightened of mice?
10. Are you afraid of snakes?
11. Are you frightened to be bitten by a dog?
12. Are you afraid of the wolf?
13. Are you afraid of thieves?
14. Are you frightened when you have to come into a dark room?
15. Are you worried when you have to go to sleep by night?
16. Are you worried when you are alone at home and somebody is knocking?
17. Are you afraid when you are alone in a room and you are hearing some noise?
18. Are you afraid when you are alone at home at night?
19. Are you afraid of coming home alone by night?
20. Are you afraid of what may happen?
21. Are you worried in situation which do not matter?
22. Are you worried about what people think of you?
23. Are you frightened of storm?
24. Are you afraid of falling sick?

1. Est- ce que tu as peur que ton pere tombe malade?
2. Est-ce que tu es inquiet quand ton pere est en retard pour rentrer a la maison?
3. Est-ce que tu es inquiet quand ta mere est en retard pour rentrer a la maison?
4. Est-ce que tu as peur que ta mere tombe malade?
5. Est-ce que tu as peur de ce que ton pere te dira?
6. Est-ce que tu as peur de ce que ta mere te dira?
7. Est-ce que tu as peur des rats?
8. Est-ce que tu as peur des araignees?
9. Est-ce que tu as peur des souris?
10. Est-ce que tu as peur des serpents?
11. Est-ce que tu as peur d'etre mordu par un chien?
12. Est-ce que tu as peur du loup?
13. Est-ce que tu as peur des voleurs?
14. Est-ce que tu es effraye quand tu dois entrer dans une piece ou il fait noir?
15. Est-ce que tu es inquiet quand tu dois aller te coucher le soir?
16. Quand tu es tout seul a la maison et qu'on frappe à la porte, est-ce que tu es inquiet?
17. Quand tu es tout seul dans une piece et que tu entends du bruit est-ce que ca te fait peur?
18. Est-ce que tu as peur quand tu es tout seul à la maison la nuit?
19. Est-ce que tu as peur de rentrer tout seul chez toi la nuit?
20. Est-ce que tu as peur de ce qui va arriver?
21. Est-ce que tu t'inquiètes pour des choses qui n'en valent pas la peine?
22. Est-ce que tu es inquiet de ce que les gens pensent de toi?
23. Est-ce que tu as peur de l'orage?
24. Est-ce que tu as peur de tomber malade?

25. Are you frightened of seeing a dead animal?	25. Est-ce que ca t'effraye de voir un animal mort?
26. Do you feel bad when you touch a sharp edge?	26. Est-ce que ça te fait un drôle d'effet de toucher quelque chose de très coupant?
27. Are you worried about your work at school?	27. Est-ce que tu t'inquiètes pour ton travail a l'école?
28. Are you frightened when you are at a high place and you are looking down?	28. Est-ce que tu es effrayé quand tu es dans un endroit élevé et que tu regardes par terre?
29. If you have to climb a ladder, will you feel afraid of falling?	29. Si tu devais grimper a une échelle est-ce que tu aurais peur d'en tomber?
30. Don't you like to fight because you are afraid of being hurt?	30. Est-ce que tu n'aimes pas te battre parce que tu as peur d'être blesse?
31. Are you afraid of being hurt in an accident?	31. Est-ce que tu as peur d'être blessé dans un accident?
32. Do you have sweaty hands?	32. Est-ce que tes mains transpirent?
33. Have you often a lump in your throat?	33. Est-ce que tu as souvent la gorge serrée?
34. Are you often feeling your heart beating like mad?	34. Est-ce que tu sens souvent ton coeur battre très fort?

Example 6: Testing 4,186 children (finishing what roughly correspond in France to High School and averaging 16 years old). (Data from Benedetto and Reuchlin; analysis by Lacourly)

Let C be a set of 6 knowledges:

C_1 = grammatical analysis
C_2 = Syntax I (phrases to be completed)
C_3 = Syntax II (time concordances)
C_4 = French literature
C_5 = Arithmetic and Algebra
C_6 = Geometry

A 6 x 6 correspondence matrix k(C,C′) was built, the analysis of which provides the same factors as that of the full 6 x 4186 matrix, namely:

$$k(C,C') = \Sigma_e \; [C(e)\, C'(e) \;/\; \Sigma_{e''}\, C''(e)]$$

where C(e) is the note obtained by the pupil $e \in E$ (E is a set of 4186 children) to the knowledge C. The analysis of this matrix showed that the two first factorial axes gave 82% of the total inertia; a quite agreeable and interpretable organization of the whole set of test was obtained. [See Figure 8]

Example 7: Factor analysis of medical data (Data from Hotel-Dieu Rennes; Prof. Bourel, Prof. Lenoir; analysis by M. Kerbaol) – The rates of six substances have been measured in the blood of 613 patients. In order to give to all substances approximately the same importance, each column was divided by its average and its deviation. The data matrix was then analyzed according to our standard program. Two significant factors were obtained and on the map (Cf. Figure 7) hemochromatosis of first and second kind appeared to be well-grouped which encouraged us to resume an analysis with only 180 patients including all concerned with hepatic pathology (namely, ethilism, cirrhosis, hemochromatosis, 1° and 2°). Up to slight changes the same factors were extracted, a stability which increased the doctor's confidence in the method. The separation between various classes were satisfactory (Cf. Figure 8) and some anomalous positionings could be explained either by errors in punching data (!) or by the curation of the patient, who traveled across the diagram (isolated black squares on the left). An interesting feature is that when a new set of data comes in, it can be inserted readily in the map by computing its factors through linear combination of the various rates; in various terms, the doctors took advantage of this facility.

Data for new investigations are now being collected and coded at Hotel-Dieu de Rennes. [See Figures 9 and 10]

5. Factor Analysis of a Random Process

Classical statistics have been concerned with such questions: Is the process Markovian; and if not, to what depth should we go back to get all information relevant to the prediction of the future? Or, can the hypothesis be accepted that the process is Markovian and belongs to a certain parametric class; and if this is true, how to estimate properly the parameters, etc.?

Much has been done to define the spectrum of a fluctuating random variable, such as a pressure or a magnetic field. Our problem here is quite different: Given a finite a priori structureless set I and a long string of items i(1), i(2), . . . , i(n), all belonging to set I, define a structure on set I from the statistical analysis of string {i(n)}. To achieve this, we use, of course, the frequencies of the various pairs of elements in I; that is, we compute how many times element i has been found coming put after element i′; it is possible to use also the number of times element i is found coming after element i′ with just one element in the between. Very beautiful things can be dreamt of, I am sure, if one consents to use triplets; but since a set with a decent number of elements as 50 may generate an undecently memory consuming three dimensional table, it is wise to be careful about triplets – my fellow mathematicians asking for n-uplets anyway.

So we have one program (a variant of the correspondence analysis program) working – honestly working I mean, with no rule of thumb such as rotation whatsoever, and we had up to now the opportunity to have it run on three sets of data.

(a) A monkey on the typewriter: As a typewriter, we actually used the keyboard of an IBM 026, which was equipped with an aluminum screen which let visible only one line of ten characters. As a "monkey" we took one of our youngest programmers; we instructed him to type at random with only one finger. The result was a hundred of cards representing a sequence of about 10 thousand elements which we call digits. The sequence was analyzed by using the standard program; and the first factor extracted gave, up to two inversions, the correct order of the digits on the keyboard.

This can actually be explained by the fact that when a boy is instructed to type at random, he will alternately stay around the same spot on the keyboard or jump from one end to the other. In both cases, the probability of the pairs of digits following each other will depend continuously on the position of the keys. [See Figure 11]

(b) A phonemically coded Spanish text: Since the pronunciation of the Spanish language is rigorously determined from the spelling and the set of phonemes is among the shortest found among natural languages, it is possible to write a simple program to transform a Spanish-written text into a sequence of phonemes. Such a sequence was analyzed from a corpus of 4,200 letters using the standard program, and the first factor was found to separate quite clearly the vowels (one side of the null point) from the consonants (clustered on the other side, with the semi-vowel jod identified to i). With the second factor, it was possible to get a moderately distorted vowel-triangle; but this point deserves further study. It is presumable that much better results will be achieved, taking advantage of the already obtained vowel-consonant opposition. The main interest of such an elaborate study would be to get evidence from the frequential data of the evolution of a sound system and also to compare different languages. Analogous results have been obtained for Italian [See Figures 12 and 13].

(c) A phonemically coded Portuguese text: One may wonder why Portuguese was chosen as a second language to study, since its sound system is almost as intricate as that of French or English, but as we started from Spanish . . .

The separation between vowels and consonants was again successfully achieved (with a corpus of 8,000 letters). But nothing has emerged up to now about the vowel triangle which obviously requires more elaborate tools, especially in Portuguese where nasal vowels should have to be recognized.

Let us notice that since a vowel is more frequently followed by a consonant than by another vowel, sequential frequencies should suffice to distinguish between vowels and consonants; and an ad hoc classification program divised by SUKHOTIN (in *Problemy Strukturnoi Linguistiky,* Moskva 1962) could actually achieve this distinction. But here a standard program was used which gives besides a continuous coordinate.

6. Analysis of Preference Ranking

From psychological, sociological, and other investigations, there frequently emerge such data as the following: all subjects from a set S rank from first to last (or possibly they rank only a few first) the items of a set I. Such preferences rankings may be coded into points representing each subject choice as exemplified on Figure 6a in the two dimensional case. Now the set of subjects and also the items become a cloud of points in a euclidean space; and therefore, it is only natural to achieve a multidimensional scaling. What comes out of such a scaling is first a center of masses = the average preference ranking, which very often is not significantly different

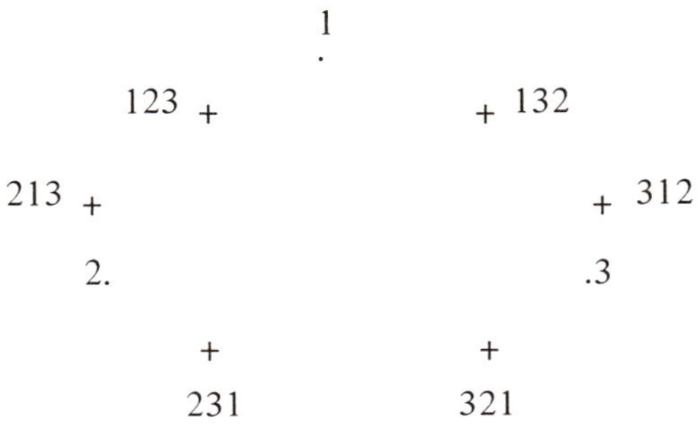

Figure 6a: Geometrical coding of preference rankings; dots represent items and plus signs represent possible rankings (and therefore subjects).

from indifference, or is absurd (whatever may be your feelings in favour of collegial decisions, from a mixture of divergently motivated choices quite absurd an average is liable to emerge); but sometimes it indicates the general acceptation or rejection of this or that item. And second, which in all cases we had the opportunity to study turned out to be genuinely significant, dispersion factors expressed under what respect the various choices were opposed to each other. Here are a few examples:

(a) Ranking six pictures: Two hundred and nine subjects were asked to rank six paintings reproduced as postcards and all concerned with flowers. The pictures were respectively:

(1) A common place "Chromo" picture printed in Italy;
(2) by a Japanese artist;
(3) Sun flowers by Van Gogh;
(4) by Dufy;
(5) by Douanier Rousseau (a famous "naive");
(6) by Paul Klee (a thoroughly abstract piece where it was impossible to diagnose flowers, except from the title).

The only information given by the center of masses was that almost all subjects rejected (6).

Four factors were extracted of which the first two accounted for more than 75% of the total inertia and could *without* rotation be readily interpreted as follows:

–The first factor accounts for the sensibility of subjects to the figurative qualities of the pictures.

–The second factor accounts for the opposition between Rousseau at one end, and Dufy, Van Gogh at the other (Klee is out of the question because almost everybody refuses it; and 1, 2 are not concerned with this factor). Actually although naive painting is considered by critics as distinct from figurative and close to abstract, it may be accepted by people naive enough themselves to welcome the naive style as a variant of the figurative one. As a matter of fact, Rousseau considered himself a figurative painter!

–Factor 3 is concerned with the splitting of Western from Eastern figurative art.

–Factor 4 is with the opposition between Dufy and Van Gogh. It is indeed remarkable that those two pairs (1,2) and (3,4) of pictures were most generally kept close by generating an axis, just as the latent conflict of the naive (5) and the abstract (3,4).

The correlation of factor one with the sociocultural background was as could be expected. The sociologist who had previously used with little success the methods available previously to ours (e.g., Coombs unfolding techniques) was very satisfied with our treatment. But she saw with disappointment that Rousseau so strongly interfered with the abstract–realistic opposition which she intended to study. [See Figure 14]

(b) Multiple-choice Tests: A few years ago, multiple choice test was introduced in France as a standard procedure to grade students in medical schools and Faculties of Medecine. Although most teachers were reluctant, the system was widely accepted to cope with the increasing number of students. As you may know, various types of questions may be used and the teachers were asked to state their preference order among eight possible types.

A – Compléments simples,
B – Compléments groupés,
C – Variation relative,
D – Association simple,
E – Association composee,
F – Relation de cause a effet,
G – Comparaison quantitative,
H – Schéma, planche,

I state those types in French, since the English precise equivalents, which are unknown to me, may certainly be guessed better from the original than from a poor translation!

As far as the average order is concerned, all that can be said is that A is universally accepted while G, H are universally rejected. The remainder is, statistically speaking, non-significant and happens to be poorly interpretable.

Factor one *(extracted without rotation)* accounts satisfactorily for the opposition between questions relying on memory, and question relying on judgment. Factor two (again *without* rotation) accounts for the opposition between simple and compound (or group).

Information brought by factor three and four was found to be non-negligible but it will not be explained here.

The analysis was also resumed, including only the teachers of morphological disciplines anatomy, etc., and those of physiology, chemistry and physics. It turned out that (.86 x second factor + .14 x first factor) .79 correlation with the partition function = 1 to morphologists (who use preferably type B), -1 to physicists, etc. (who use preferably type F). This discrimination or recognition was achieved by processing only the behavioral information (the rankings) and not the fields of the subjects (teachers), which were only introduced afterwards on the map generated by the first two factors (of which the second could almost have been used as an optimal discriminent function). [See Figures 15 and 16].

(c) Why do you practice sport? The subjects (about 1,500 sportsmen) had to state and rank the first six of a list of 24 motivations. The analysis, again completed using the standard program for the analysis of preferences, gave as first two factors (non-rotated) two dimensions considered classically as most relevant = . . . ; . . .

(1) Nature and beauty versus *Combativity*
(2) Friendship and play versus *Self-affirmation*

[See List of Motivations]

LIST OF MOTIVATIONS

1.	Attraction for a natural element	Attrait pour un élement de la nature
2.	Instinct of competition	Instinct combatif
3.	Self-affirmation	Affirmation de soi
4.	Cultivate one's cleverness	Cultiver son habileté
5.	Taste for beauty	Goût du beau
6.	Social accomplishment	Réussite sociale
7.	Attraction for danger	Attract du danger
8.	Fame	Briller–gloire
9.	Live for game	Amour du jeu
10.	Compensation	Compensation
11.	To build up one's character	Se forger le caractère
12.	To bustle about	Se remuer
13.	To fill up one's spare time	Remplir les loisirs
14.	Money	Gain lucratif
15.	To make friends	Avoir des camarades
16.	To spare no troubles	Se dépenser à fond
17.	To cultivate one's strength	Cultiver sa robustesse
18.	Evasion	Evasion
19.	Health	Hygiène–Santé
20.	Spirit of competition	Esprit de compétition
21.	Relax	Détente–Distraction
22.	Sense of corporeal dignity	Sentiment de dignité corporelle
23.	To be gifted	Possession de dons
24.	Adventure	Aventure

7. On the Factor Analysis of Proximities

R. N. Shepard (1,2) has published, in a few recent papers, an interesting discovery about the following geometrical problems.

Given a set I of elements (of any nature) for which not distances but only inequalities between distances are known (i.e., for any four i_1, i_2, i_3, i_4 in I, we know whether i_1 is closer to i_2 than i_3 to i_4 , or the contrary). We construct a model J for I in an Euclidean space having as little dimensions as possible, and such that the given inequalities be realized (i.e., if i_1 is said to be closer to i_2 than i_3 to i_4, then $|j_1j_2| < |j_3j_4|$).

It turns out, Shepard noticed, that approximately the solution to this problem is unique; especially if one started from the inequalities between the interpoint-distances of a set I in the plane or the ordinary space, this set can be recovered (and first its dimension discovered) with good approximation. Shepard writes: " . . . an underlying Euclidean configuration . . . can be metrically recovered by an analysis based essentially upon the rank order . . . This conversion from a non-metric to a metric representation seems to be tantamount to getting something from nothing."

Shepard's construction involves rather complicated iterative computations since it requires, he says, a few minutes on a 7090 computer. Relying on a mathematical theory devised for the purpose (3), we are now able to go much faster and even by hand (in 15 minutes!) especially in the cases solved by Shepard in his paper.

It turns out that the squared interpoint-distances between the points of a finite subset taken at random in R^p are a fairly good sample of a p-degrees of freedom χ square distribution. Therefore, it is easy to recover approximate distances (up to a constant multiplier) by just using the proximity–inequalities and a χ-square table.

Given the number of points (e.g. 9), we have the number of interpoint distances (36). We assign to each a *precise* value d_r (taking into account only its rank r) by reading the squared distance on the χ^2–axis against the coordinate r/36 on the cumulative probabilities axis.

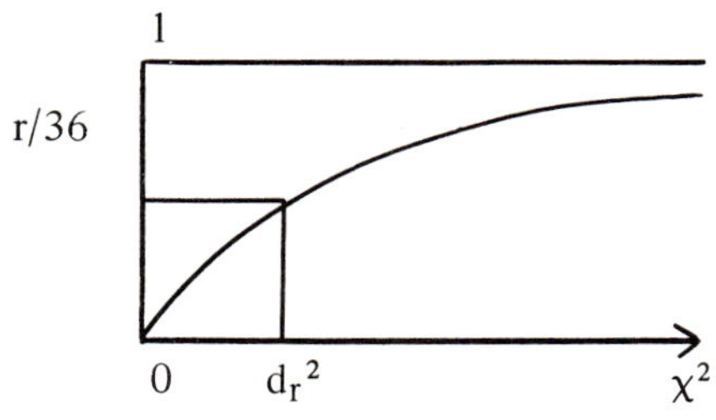

It is very easy, in case p = 2, to put the points in a diagram just using those approximate distance d_r and working from point to point with a compass. We solved this problem without having to resort to any iterative technique.

However, a program for multidimensional scaling can be used to extract a p-dimensional picture from the approximate distances computed according to the χ^2 rule. And this is actually the only possible solution when p is greater than (or even equal to) three.

Here is an example taken from Shepard. On a table there are found the original distances between 9 points in the plane. Then the same is multiplied by a constant so that they have an average of 100. Then the d_r is computed from χ^2 table and then the same is averaged to 100. At last, the distances on the diagram are reconstructed with a compass.

Actually, just try to do it yourself: put 9 points "at random" on the plane; call them 1 . . . 9; measure the interpoint distances 1–2, 1–3, . . . , 8–9; rank them first 3–6, second 7–9, third 8–2, etc.; take 3–6 = 146, 7–9 = 125, 8–2 = 115, etc. (middle column on the table); and then work a diagram out of those distances using a compass. There is a high probability that you nearly come back to the same shape you started from (But be aware of one thing–there is one chance out of two, just as if you had had the precise distances, that the reconstructed diagram is a mirror-image of the original one.).

However, although, from the viewpoint of the geometer, to recover distances from mere inequalities is an achievement, the factor analysis of proximities as an applied technique is not so useful as could have been expected. The reasons for this are the following:

(1) The statistician is not a man trapped by a Sphynx who asks him geometrical puzzles, but he is a man faced with natural phenomena whose structure he has to decode;

(2) From what is known of natural phenomena, inequalities between proximities cannot be straightforwardly computed. Various formulae are available, as stated above, may sometimes lead to opposite results. There is no sphynx on the way to provide him at least with the appropriate inequalities;

(3) In non-artificial cases where factor analysis of proximities has been successfully used (e.g., Rothkoff's morse-code confusion matrix, analyzed by R.N. Shepard; or a set of similarities between wave lengths given in Coombs' book and successfully analyzed by our all-hand technique), the data as seen above have a beautiful correspondence matrix structure which it is wiser to keep than to convert into proximities.

8. Conclusion

I understand I should now bring my report to an end. Certainly I have omitted many important mathematical arguments or positive examples that could have helped you to appreciate the real scope of our work. On the contrary, I have more than once indulged in mixing dreams with facts because with the little time allowed it is so much easier to suggest a pleasant potentiality than to describe what precisely has been achieved. But we all suspect that if our congresses have been called symposia (after a Greek word which means a banquet) since the days of Platon, it is because scientists reporting on their own work or that of their teachers, fellows or pupils are indeed to be somewhat intoxicated, in order that they may speak more freely.

On this confession I will stop, since my conclusion could but repeat what my introduction said, and you certainly all still have in mind.

9. Acknowledgement

The work of our Laboratory at the Institut de Statistique de l'Universite de Paris has been made possible by support received from the French University and by contract grants D.R.M.E. No. 66–34–557 and D.G.R.S.T. No. 66 FR 001.

BIBLIOGRAPHY

Section 2

J.P. Benzecri–Problemes et methodes de la taxinomie (1965).

J.P. Benzecri–Sur les algorithmes de classification (1965) (Both papers included in "Lecons sur l'analyse factorielle et la reconnaissance des formes; 1965–66, I.S.U.P., Paris).

S. Regner, M. Renaud, W.F. de la Vega–technical reports some of which include programs issued by Laboratorie de Calcul de la Maison des Sciences de l'Homme. (M.S.H. Paris,, rue Puiseux); work now continued by I.C. Lerman.

M. Roux–Sur l'application de quelques methodes de classification en phytosociologie, in Revue de statistique appliquee, 1967.

Section 3

J.P. Benzecri–Cours de linguistique mathematique; 3eme et 4eme lecon; Rennes 1963–64. Mimeographed notes available from I.S.U.P. Paris.

B. Cordier–L'analyse des correspondances; These Rennes 1965. This work includes program-listings and the proofs of various theorems; it is available from I.S.U.P. with successive paper by the same author.

Ch. Rousse–Lagordaire & W. Moussatat–(unpublished) proof of the theorem stated above regarding the normal case.

Section 5

B. Cordier (Mme Escofier)–Sur l'analyse des correspondances, These, Faculte des Sciences de Rennes (1965).

Programs and analysis by B. Cordier and Ph. Marano.

Section 6

On the method:

(1) J.P. Benzecri–Analyse des preferences (I.S.U.P. 1965).

(2) J.P. Fenelon–id–in Sciences (Hermann edit.), Paris, 1967.

On the data:

(3) Y. Bernard–C.N.R.S. (1966), Esthetique experimentale.

(4) M. Bouet–Thesis to appear, On the sociology of sport.

(5) J.J. Guilbert & Ch. Rousse Lacordaire–Opinions des enseignants sur les examens en faculte de Medecine (avec un appendice de J.P. Fénelon). Paris–Ministère de l'Education Nationale et Imprimerie Nationale (1967).

Programs by J.P. Fénelon; Analysis by J.P. Fénelon, Ch. Rousse Lacordaire & M.O. Lebeaux.

Section 7

(1) Shepard, Roger N. – *The Analysis of Proximities,* Scaling with an Unknown Distance Function I, published in Psychometrika, June, 1962, Vol. 27, No. 2.

(2) Shepard, Roger N. – *The Analysis of Proximities,* Scaling with an Unknown Distance Function II, published in Psychometrika, September, 1962, Vol. 27, No. 3.

(3) Benzecri, J.P.–*Analyse Factorielle des Proximités*, Publication de l'Institut de Statistique de l'Universite de Paris, 1964–65.

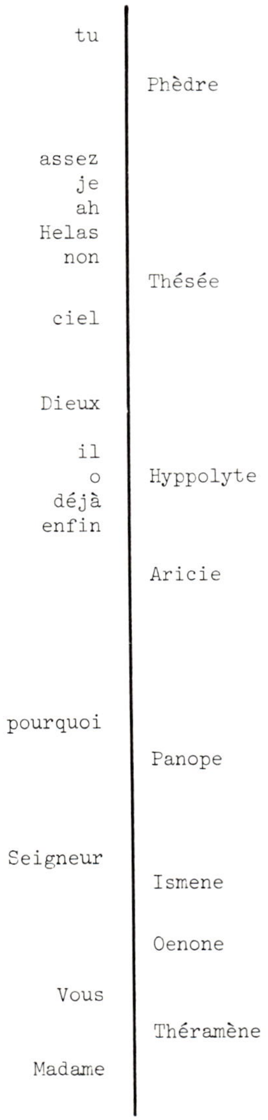
tu
Phèdre
assez
je
ah
Helas
non
Thésée
ciel
Dieux
il
o
Hyppolyte
déjà
enfin
Aricie
pourquoi
Panope
Seigneur
Ismene
Oenone
Vous
Théramène
Madame

Figure 1

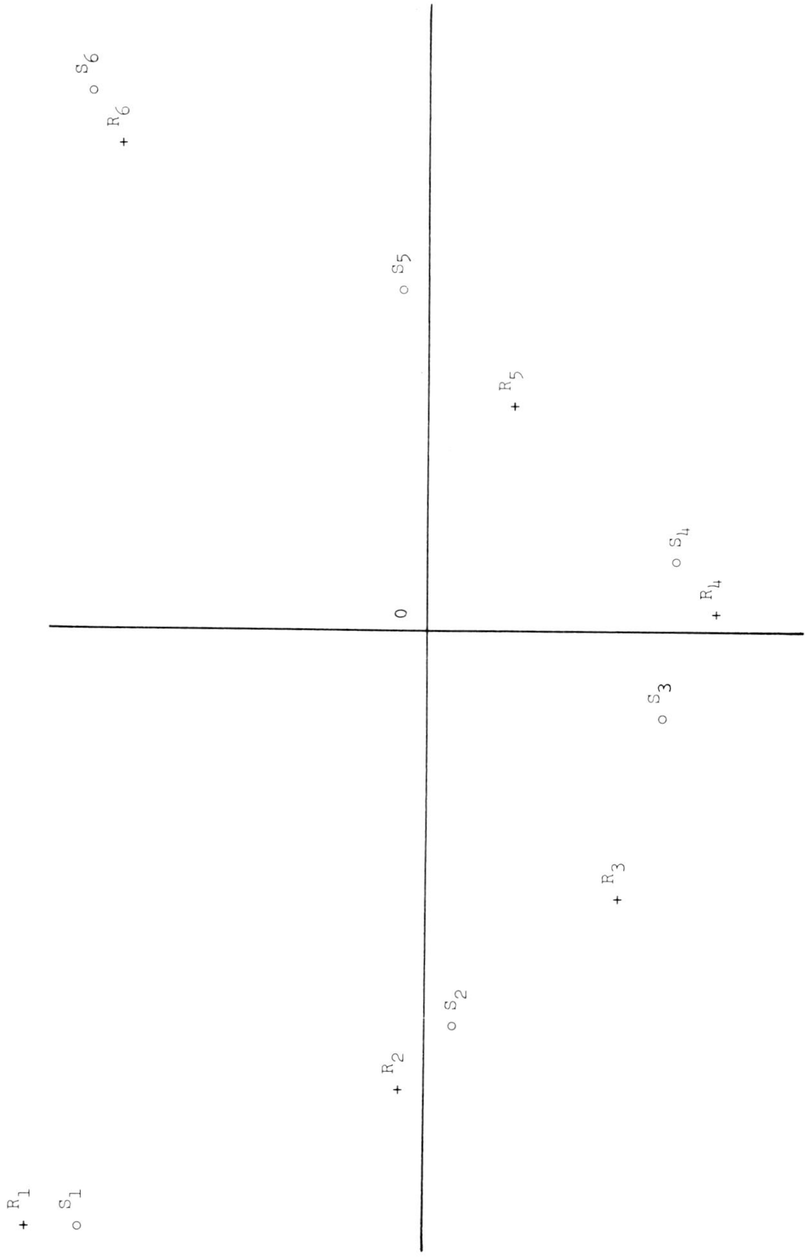

Figure 2: Experience d'apprentissage d'association de lettres de sons

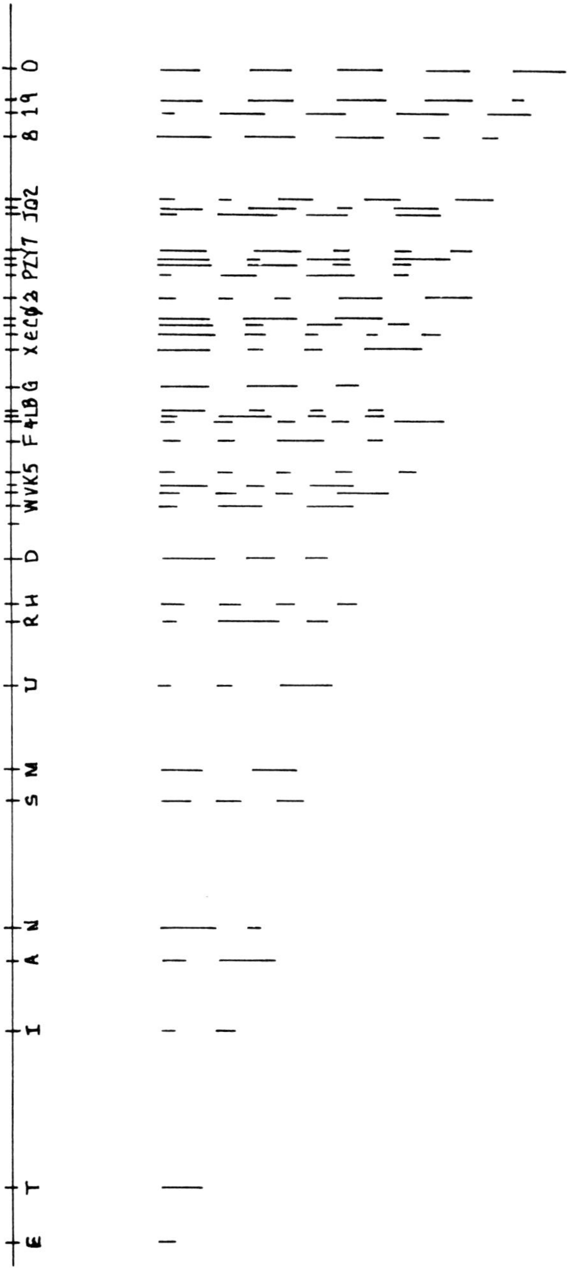

Figure 3

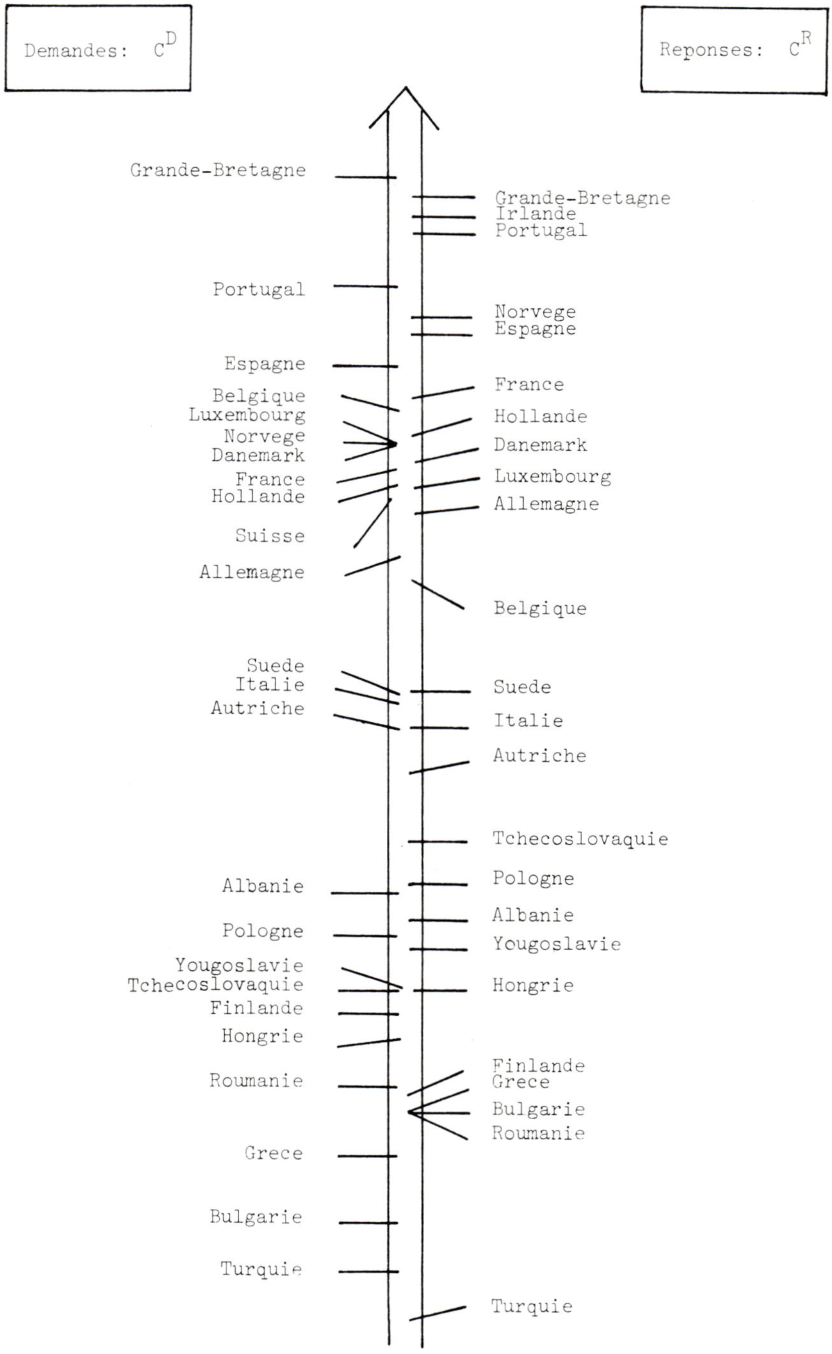

Figure 4: Le code moyen

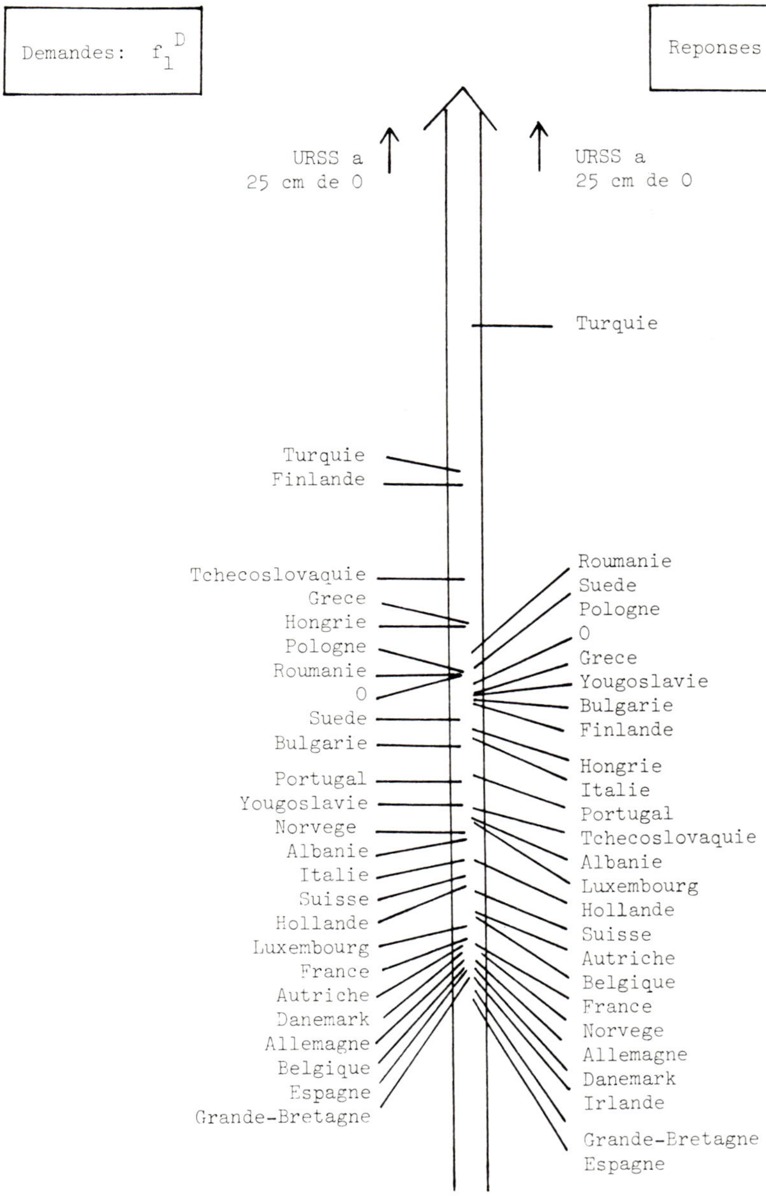
Demandes: f_1^D
Reponses: f_1^R
URSS a 25 cm de 0
URSS a 25 cm de 0
Turquie
Turquie
Finlande
Tchecoslovaquie
Grece
Hongrie
Pologne
Roumanie
0
Suede
Bulgarie
Portugal
Yougoslavie
Norvege
Albanie
Italie
Suisse
Hollande
Luxembourg
France
Autriche
Danemark
Allemagne
Belgique
Espagne
Grande-Bretagne
Roumanie
Suede
Pologne
0
Grece
Yougoslavie
Bulgarie
Finlande
Hongrie
Italie
Portugal
Tchecoslovaquie
Albanie
Luxembourg
Hollande
Suisse
Autriche
Belgique
France
Norvege
Allemagne
Danemark
Irlande
Grande-Bretagne
Espagne

Figure 5

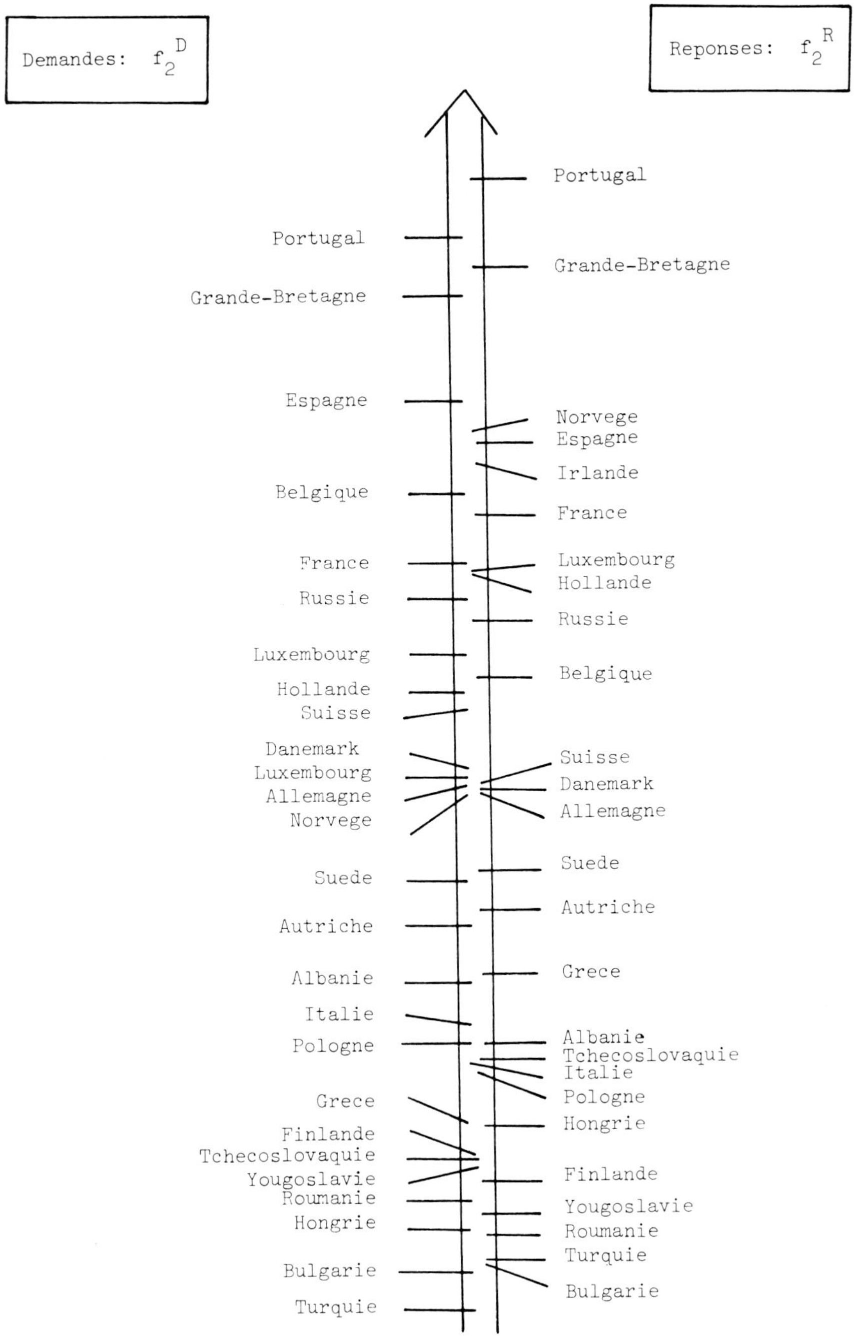
Demandes: f_2^D
Reponses: f_2^R
Portugal
Grande-Bretagne
Espagne
Belgique
France
Russie
Luxembourg
Hollande
Suisse
Danemark
Luxembourg
Allemagne
Norvege
Suede
Autriche
Albanie
Italie
Pologne
Grece
Finlande
Tchecoslovaquie
Yougoslavie
Roumanie
Hongrie
Bulgarie
Turquie
Portugal
Grande-Bretagne
Norvege
Espagne
Irlande
France
Luxembourg
Hollande
Russie
Belgique
Suisse
Danemark
Allemagne
Suede
Autriche
Grece
Albanie
Tchecoslovaquie
Italie
Pologne
Hongrie
Finlande
Yougoslavie
Roumanie
Turquie
Bulgarie

Figure 6

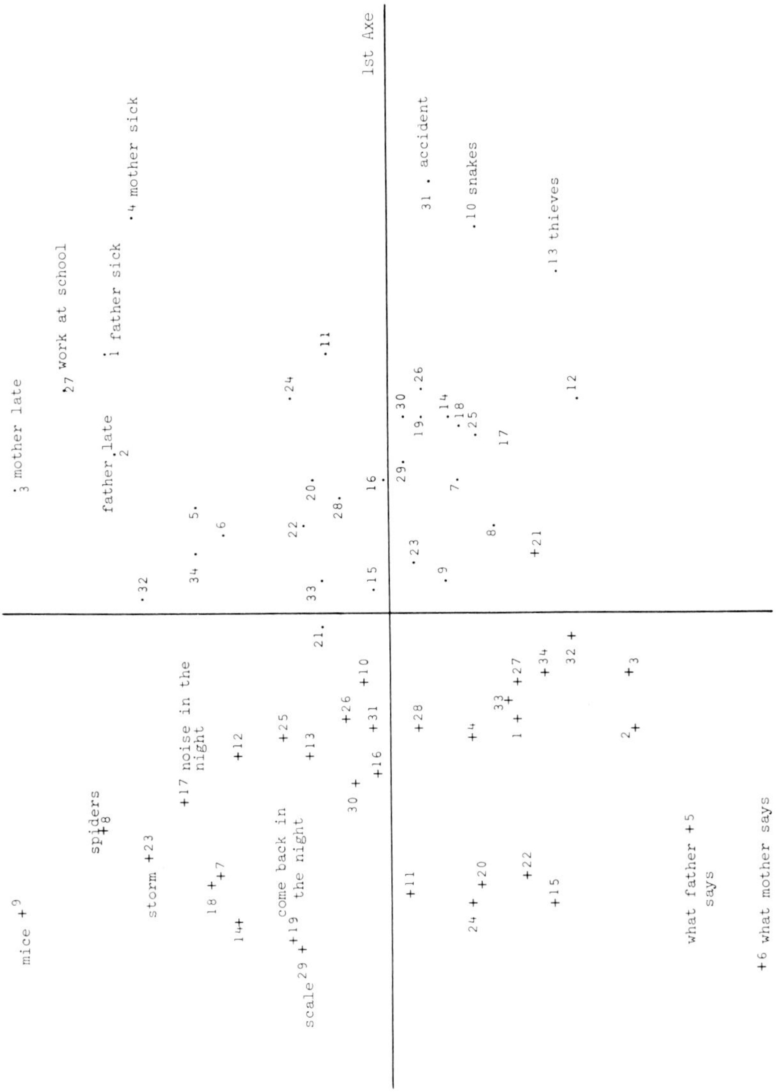
1st Axe
3 mother late
27 work at school
1 father sick
4 mother sick
father late 2
31 accident
10 snakes
13 thieves
mice +9
spiders +8
storm +23
+17 noise in the night
come back in the night
scale 29 + +19
what father +5 says
+6 what mother says

Figure 7

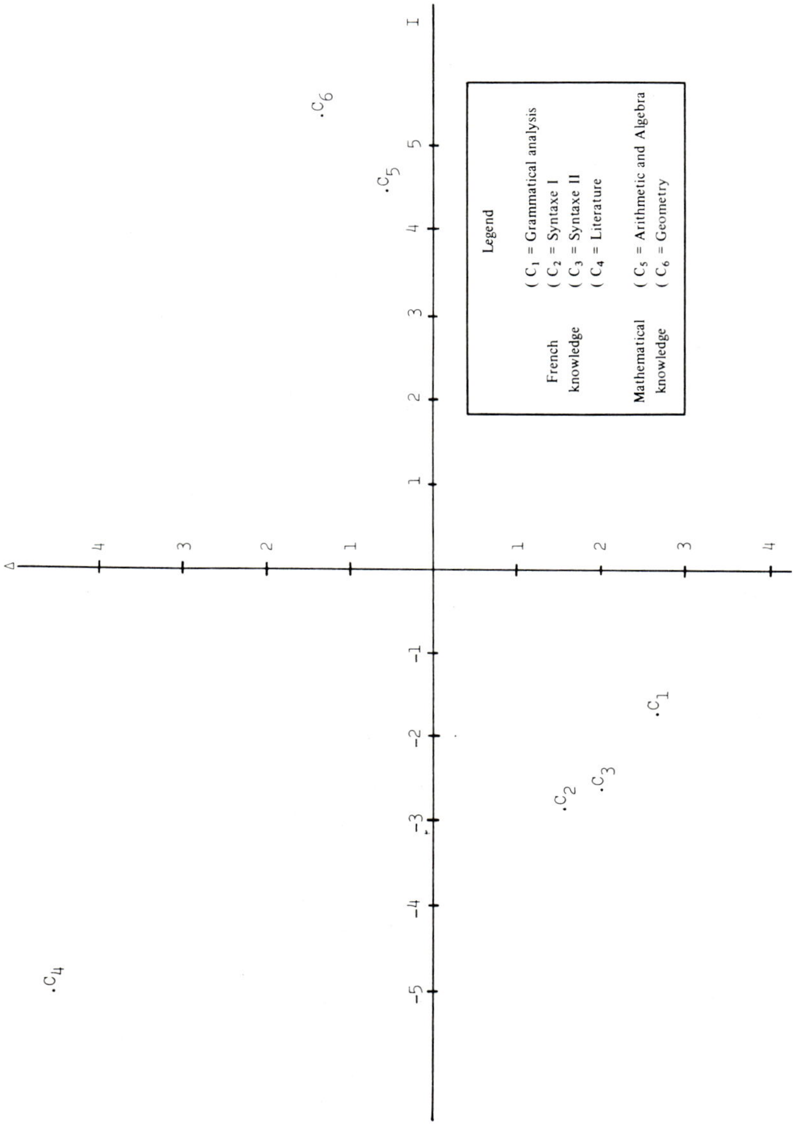
Legend
French knowledge
(C_1 = Grammatical analysis
(C_2 = Syntaxe I
(C_3 = Syntaxe II
(C_4 = Literature
Mathematical knowledge
(C_5 = Arithmetic and Algebra
(C_6 = Geometry
C_1
C_2
C_3
C_4
C_5
C_6
I

Figure 8

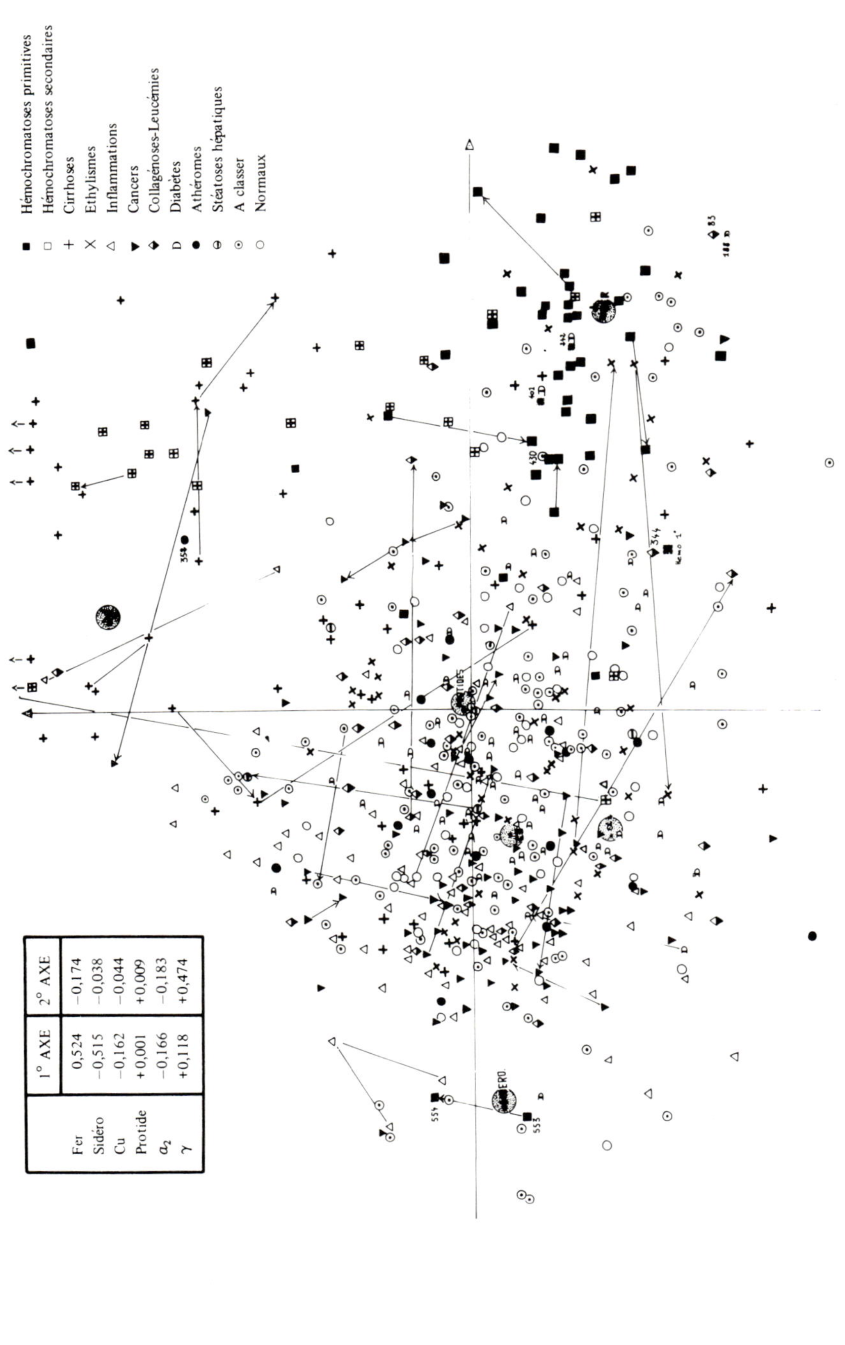

	1° AXE	2° AXE
Fer	0,524	−0,174
Sidéro	−0,515	−0,038
Cu	−0,162	−0,044
Protide	+0,001	+0,009
α_2	−0,166	−0,183
γ	+0,118	+0,474

Figure 9: Analyse Factorielle Globale (613 cas)

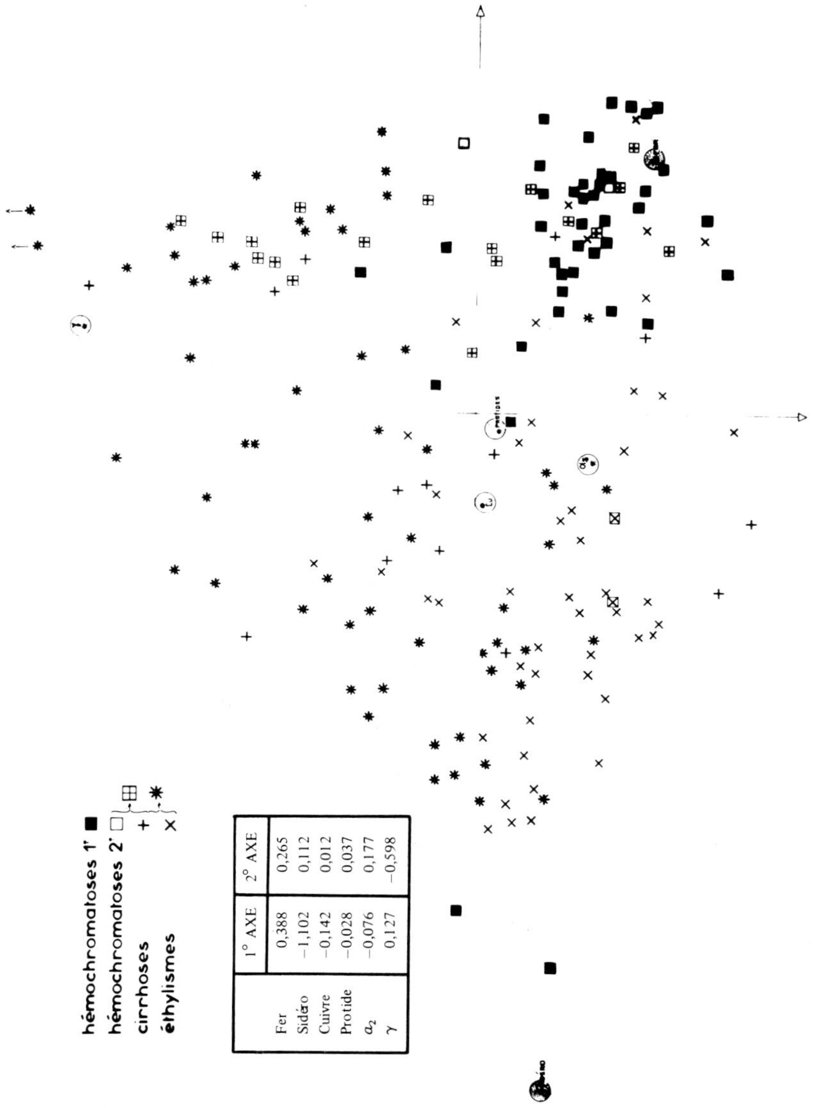

	1° AXE	2° AXE
Fer	0,388	0,265
Sidéro	−1,102	0,112
Cuivre	−0,142	0,012
Protide	−0,028	0,037
α_2	−0,076	0,177
γ	0,127	−0,598

Figure 10: ANAEMO (180 cas)

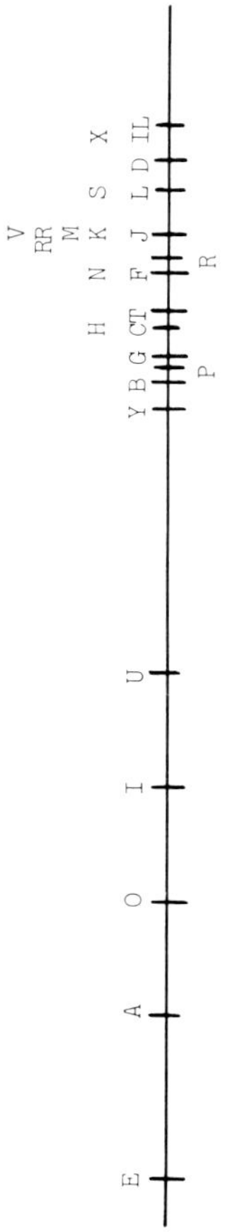

Figure 11

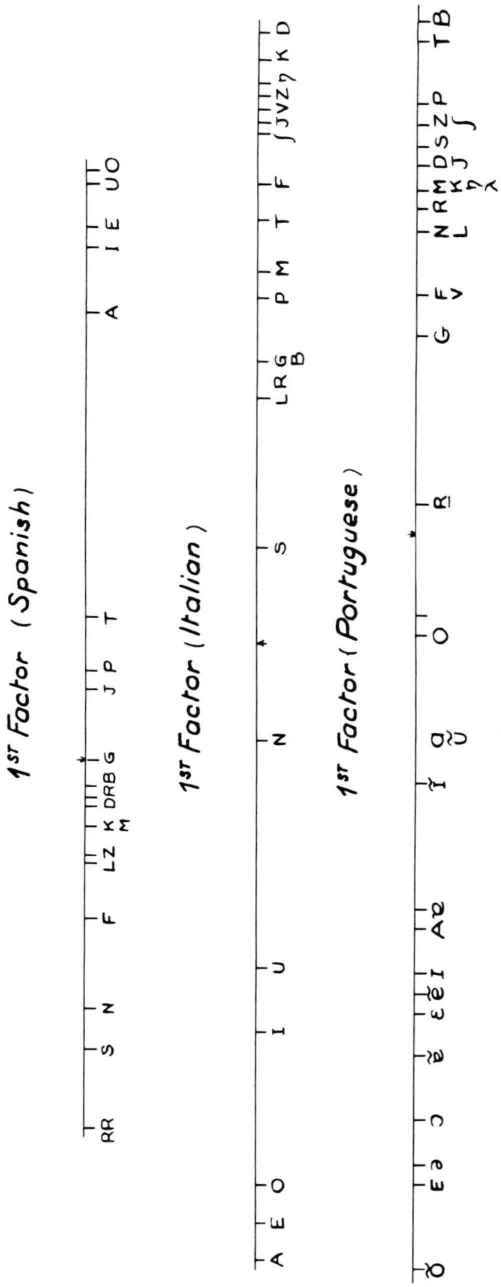

Figure 12: Séparating Vowels from Consonants

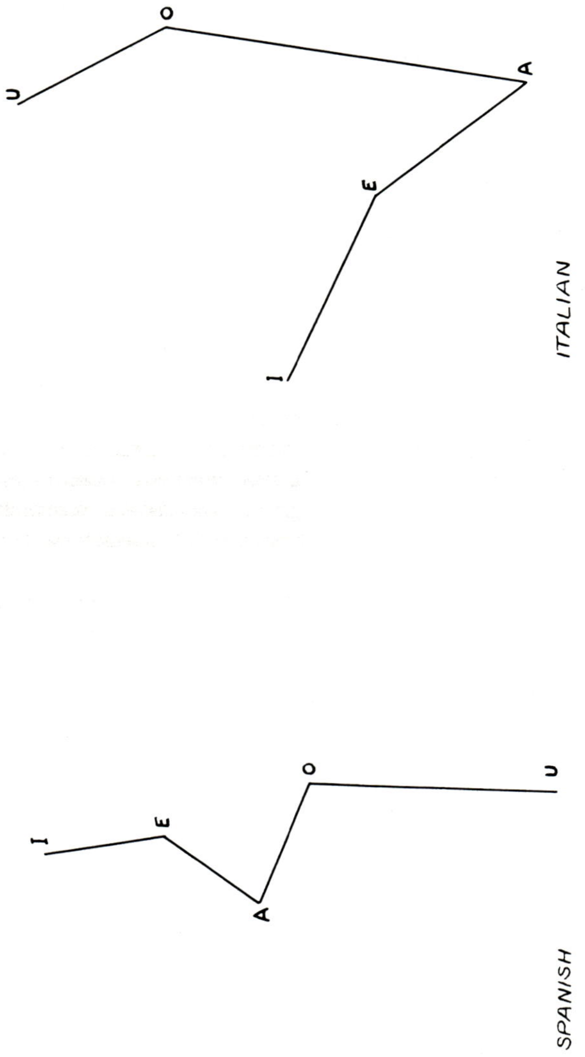

Figure 13: Recovering an Approximate Vowel Triangle

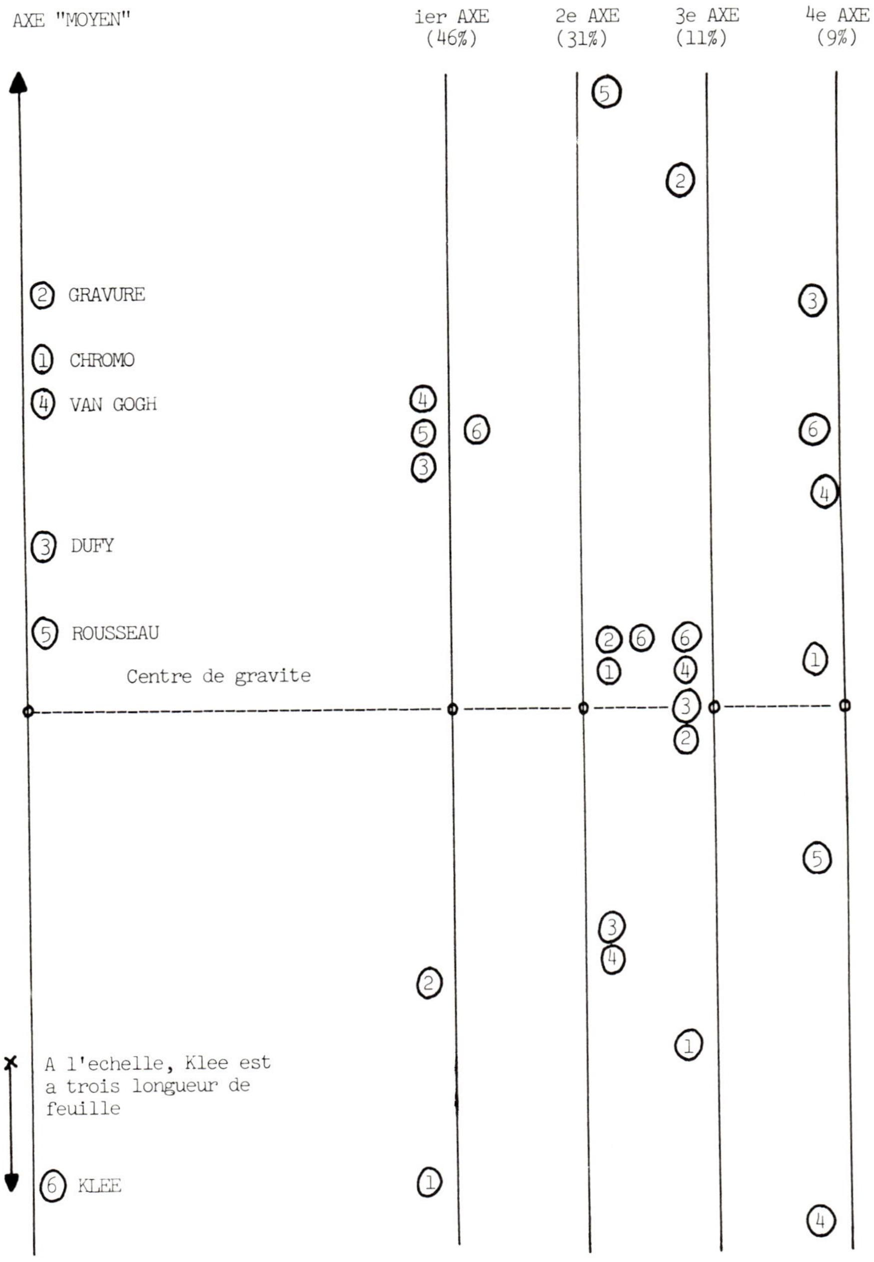

Figure 14: Les Axes

2 axe
1 axe
A
complement simple
C
variation relative
F
relation de cause
a effet
G
comparaison
quantitative
association simple
D
complements
groupes
B
H
schemas planches
E
association composee

Figure 15

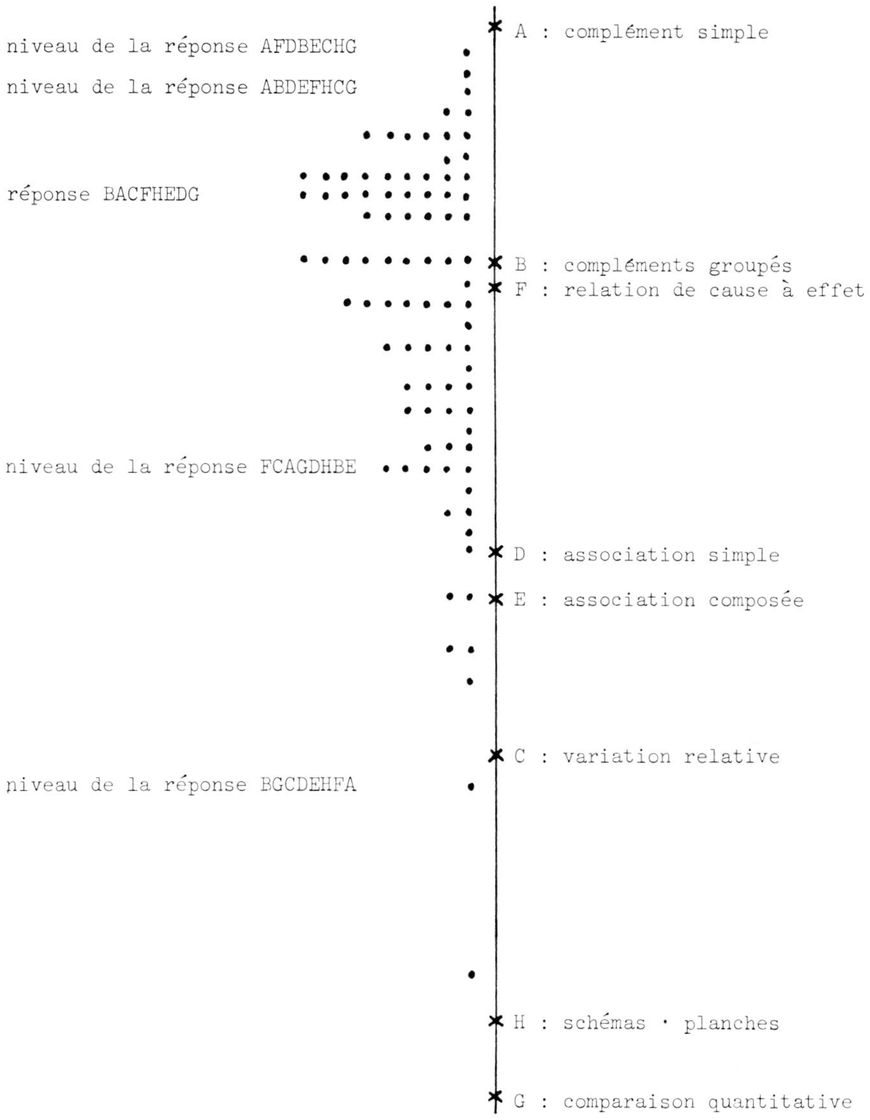
A : complément simple
niveau de la réponse AFDBECHG
niveau de la réponse ABDEFHCG
réponse BACFHEDG
B : compléments groupés
F : relation de cause à effet
niveau de la réponse FCAGDHBE
D : association simple
E : association composée
C : variation relative
niveau de la réponse BGCDEHFA
H : schémas · planches
G : comparaison quantitative

Figure 16

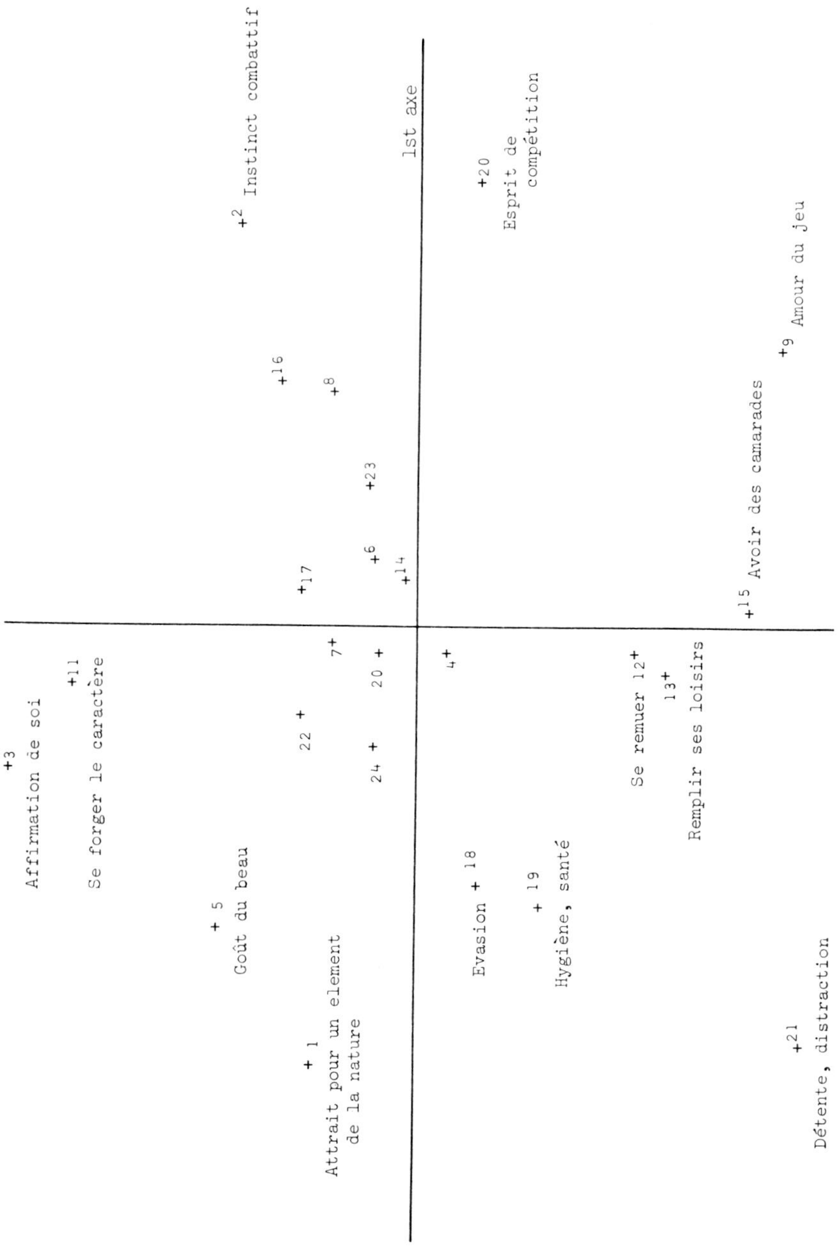

1st axe
+2 Instinct combattif
+20 Esprit de compétition
+9 Amour du jeu
+16
+8
+23
+6
+14
+17
+15 Avoir des camarades
+3 Affirmation de soi
+11 Se forger le caractère
+5 Goût du beau
+1 Attrait pour un element de la nature
22 +
24 +
20 +
7+
4+
Se remuer 12+
13+ Remplir ses loisirs
Evasion + 18
+ 19 Hygiène, santé
+21 Détente, distraction

Figure 17

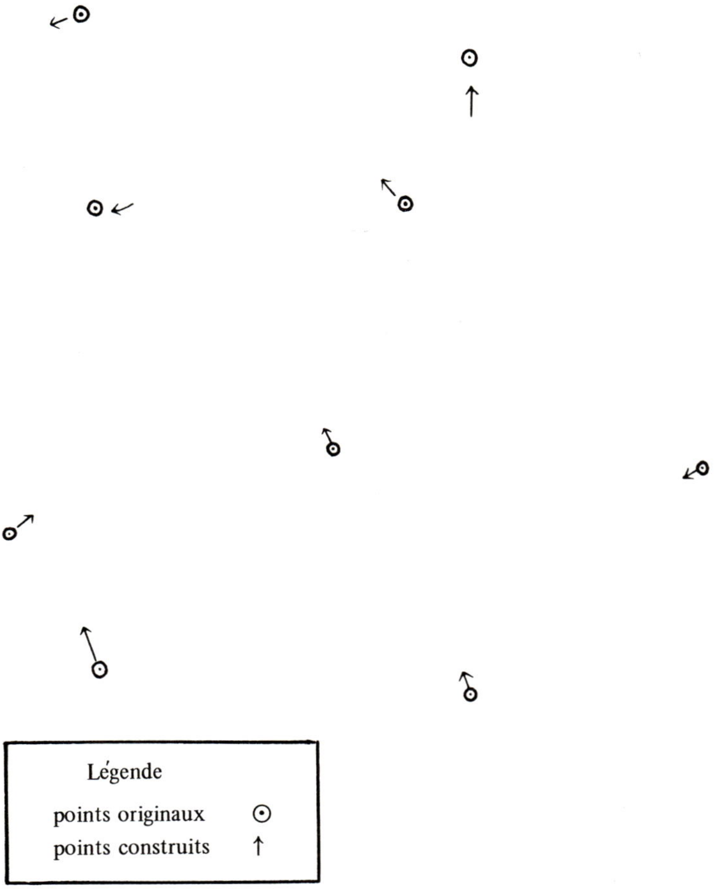

Figure 18

TABLE 1

An example from R.N. Shepard, solved by our method.

No	Nom	d mesuree	d norma- lisee dx 100	χ mesure	χ norma- lise χ=100	d experi- mentale
1	6-9	67	182	146	235	175
2	1-9	66	180	125	201	172
3	3-9	64	174	115	185	165
4	1-8	57	155	109	175	158
5	1-6	56	153	102	164	158
6	2-9	53,5	146	98	158	136
7	4-6	52	142	93	148	136
8	2-6	48,5	132	89	143	130
9	1-7	48	131	85	137	121
10	6-7	47,5	130	81	130	124
11	5-9	46	125	77	124	123
12	2-8	45	123	74	119	121
13	8-9	44	120	71	114	117
14	3-7	42,5	116	68	109	105
15	1-4	38,5	105	66	106	102
16	3-4	38,5	105	64	103	102
17	1-5	37	101	62	100	100
18	3-8	37	101	60	97	99
19	4-8	36	98	57	92	97
20	2-7	34	93	55	89	82
21	3-6	29,5	81	53	85	81
22	4-9	29	79	51	82	70
23	7-8	27,5	75	48	77	78
24	1-3	27	74	46	74	78
25	5-6	27	74	44	71	72
26	2-5	25	68	41	66	66
27	4-5	25,0	68	39	63	66
28	2-4	24,5	67	37	60	66
29	6-8	24,5	67	34	55	61
30	5-7	24	65	31	50	60
31	2-3	23	63	29	47	60
32	7-9	22,5	61	25	40	60
33	5-8	20,5	56	22	35	57
34	3-5	19	52	18	29	50
35	1-2	14	38	14	23	39
36	4-7	12	33	8	13	23

PATTERN RECOGNITION, THE CHALLENGE, ARE WE MEETING IT?

Donald B. Brick

INFORMATION RESEARCH ASSOCIATES, INC.
WALTHAM, MASSACHUSETTS

Introduction

Although a number of *real* applications in the field of pattern recognition can be identified, the number is not large compared to the total effort and in many cases the techniques utilized have been primitive and not at all indicative of the advanced state of sophistication of much of the research. (However, often the simple techniques have been sufficient.) The earliest investigations were goal-directed or had as their motivating force particular applications or well-defined objectives. Motivation was provided by, for example, attempts to (a) understand and/or model neural systems, their structure, their functional behavior, or their cognitive or 'intelligent' properties; (b) obtain a better understanding of the fundamentals of the 'pattern-recognition problem'; (c) develop intuitive or ad hoc algorithms, heuristics, or system concepts to provide *immediate* solutions to pressing problems; or (d) design and evaluate new data processing concepts (or structures) using a pattern-recognition problem as a test or design input. As the field grew, much of the subsequent work tended towards specialized or isolated aspects, details, or the solutions of very limited problems, often in apparent disregard of ultimate overall objectives and applications and directions of the field. Many of the applications made to-date have resulted from a need to justify one's method or technique by finding or inventing a particular problem that it solves, rather than the other way around. This often results in applications that are not of great utility, or in solving problems that are either unrealistic or poor approximations to real problems.

This is not an uncommon tendency during the early research phase of a particular field. However, we are ultimately faced with the challenge of reversing this trend. The elements which are to play significant roles will have to fit into the overall scheme. In pattern recognition, the overall scheme must, by the very nature of the subject, be motivated by real, clearly-defined, and, in many cases, pragmatic objectives (or problem solutions) and goals. If we are to justify our efforts to date (as well as future efforts) and provide the basis for future direction, it is encumbent upon us to define, continually redefine, and guide our efforts by the particular needs and objectives that must of necessity motivate the field.

For the purposes of this paper, let us direct our attention to the problem of the potential user (who is not a 'pattern-recognition expert'†) who has, or thinks he has, a pattern recognition problem. His problem may or may not fit into one of the categories investigated earlier. If it does, and if he happens to realize it, a satisfactory solution may exist. However, the available solution(s) might not be satisfactory for his particular problem for a variety of reasons, such as cost, complexity, hardware problems, error or response rates, efficiency, reliability, etc. Conversely, his class of problem might not fall into one of the already-treated categories. His only alternative to abandoning the problem might be to use an approximate or best-available solution, a new technique, or a synthesis of existing techniques. However, in order to arrive at this point, the user should be able to satisfy himself concerning these factors. In most cases, this requires expertise above and beyond that of the vast majority of potential users.

It is our thesis that the field has progressed to the point where we in the field should begin to concern ourselves with the needs of such potential users (or general practitioners as opposed to specialists). The challenge, in this author's opinion, is to provide a library of useful techniques and guidelines for the non-researcher and to continually update and modernize them. Techniques and methodologies are required for analyzing a particular problem, for deciding upon the preferred approach(es), and for analytically determining and specifying the merits of each. Measures, means, methods, and facilities for evaluating and testing the effectiveness of competing techniques are required so that the relative advantages of each can be quantitatively assessed (or alternatively rank-ordered) in the context of a particular problem. Furthermore, it is becoming obvious that, from a functional point of view, there is no best solution to a particular pattern-recognition problem. There are a host of competing techniques, one or some combination of which may be chosen, but not strictly on the basis of a clear operating superiority over its competitors. User preferences and engineering considerations will dictate the final choice. Redundancy, reliability, and uncertainty considerations may make it advantageous to avoid a clear-cut decision, therefore indicating a modus operandi whereby several solutions are encompassed as lower-level processes within a higher-level framework. The ultimate resolution might therefore reside in a meta-structure designed to take advantage of the inherent redundancies. Such a structure would suffer graceful rather than catastrophic degrada-

† The question as to what constitutes a pattern-recognition expert is a moot one. Most people so-identified are experienced, conversant, and/or capable of applying and evaluating work in only particular sub areas or techniques in pattern recognition. This is so because the activities lumped under the category 'pattern recognition' are so diverse.

tion in the event of failure of the individual lower processes.

Thus, the challenge posed here for the pattern recognition community is to provide the necessary information, tools, and facilities to assist and guide the user so that he can make intelligent and sound decisions (from an engineering and economic point of view) in his choice, design, and use of pattern recognition systems. It is believed that at this juncture the best way to accomplish this would be to initiate an examination of the field from a systems point of view. The conclusions and recommendations from such an effort could serve (a) as a guide to the user and (b) as a guiding, unifying, motivating, and stimulating force for the pattern recognition community. The responsibility for this effort should reside with the experts in the field. It is hoped that they would be convinced of the importance and impact of their efforts, the overall objectives, the effect on the total picture, and, therefore, would be motivated to participate. The task should be initiated with the concept of a continuing effort since the picture is not a static one and the effort will not, in the foreseeable future, result in 'final' conclusions, only interim ones. The output data and recommendations should be presented clearly and concisely in a form that makes them readily-available and identifiable to both the researcher in pattern recognition and the non-specialist who wishes to utilize pattern-recognition techniques. Consideration should be given to providing results and conclusions (tentative or final) in handbook form, to be updated and modified as required, with conditions and assumptions clearly spelled out.* It would also be well to consider either a specific design, test, and evaluation facility or the use of one or more available interactive pattern-recognition design facilities in conjunction with or as recommended facilities for this effort and the user.

The User's Problem

With these objectives in mind, let us examine the problems faced by a potential user. He must ask himself the following questions:

(1) Is my application one of pattern recognition?

(2) Is there an obvious approach? Has the problem, its analogue, or its homologue been solved previously?

(3) Are the pattern classes defined, undefined, to be derived teleologically, etc.?

---

* The nomenclature "handbook" is used to indicate a form of presentation (aimed at the user) rather than a final end item.

(4) Is the classification problem one of taxonomy or can it contain synonymies? †

(5) Do the pattern classes overlap or is an error-free (non-overlapping) classification possible?

(6) Should several approaches be tried or is there one best approach?

(7) Should a multi- or general-purpose solution be attempted as opposed to one limited to the particular application at hand?

(8) What intraclass (similarity) and/or interclass (discriminating) features, if any, should be extracted and emphasized or suppressed. Should preprocessing be performed and is there a preferred type? Should this be done automatically, manually, interactively, etc.?

(9) What are the merits of an adaptive or learning capability for this particular type of problem, i.e., should the processing be rigidly structured or of a heuristic nature?

(10) What capabilities should be provided on-line versus off-line (i.e., in the laboratory or on the prototype)?

(11) What, if any, capacity for intelligent behavior should the processor possess? Should a capability to generalize be attempted?

(12) What factors govern the decision and recognition process, e.g., should it be statistically motivated, deterministic, algorithmic, heuristic, etc? In each case, what a priori assumptions about the behavior of the pattern classes can and should be made?

(13) Finally, the method of implementing the design has to be considered in terms of the data medium (i.e., the form of input), the hardware techniques and equipment available, their costs, and environmental and other constraints imposed.

The user, faced with this myriad of choices, is usually forced to resort to a course of action based upon intuition, personal feelings, and preferences, unless he also happens to be very knowledgeable in the field. If, as stated earlier, research in pattern recognition is to justify its existence, the researcher must guide himself according to meaningful end objectives. One of these is to provide the non-specialist with useful and readily-available tools.

† Is the correct classification for a particular pattern unique or can it belong to more than one class like synonyms in a thesaurus?

Proposed Direction

It is suggested that a continuing effort in the future be concerned with overall or global aspects with the aim of providing to the potential user a set of guidelines, programs, or facilities to assist him in his utilization of the accomplishments in the field. Perhaps, the objective of the systems study can best be represented by a flow chart as shown in Figure 1. The output of the proposed effort should result in algorithms to fill in each of the blocks in this flow chart. For example:

In box A, the question is asked if the problem is one of pattern recognition. In the obvious cases, this is a ridiculous question. In less-obvious cases, however, the data and the objectives or goals of the questionner must be critically examined to determine the answer.

The answer to the question asked in box B cannot be answered without reference to the flow chart as a whole. In fact, the answers to the questions asked in boxes B, C, D, and E are intertwined and require us to examine some of the following questions and derive indicators or algorithms for them in a form that can be understood and utilized by the non-specialist.

Are the patterns discrete or are they members of classes?

(a) If classes, do the classes overlap? If yes, is the problem amenable to and readily describable in statistical terms? In terms of fuzzy sets? etc.

(b) If discrete, will a simple template or other ad hoc scheme such as a matched or inverse filter or a background (interference or noise) eliminator work? Can they be realized or approximated by simple algorithms? Are the patterns prototype-derived? (These questions can also be asked if the classes overlap, if one admits a finite error probability.)

Can we break the problem down into sub-problems and is the sum greater than or less than the whole (i.e., is it synergistic or not)?

Are there features that can aid in (1) reducing the complexity (dimensionality) of the class description, i.e., constitute sufficient descriptors, (2) clustering the class members (intraclass features), (3) separating different classes (interclass discriminators), (4) eliminating unwanted classes, (5) maximizing the information (a) about the class or (b) between classes for discrimination (e.g., Kullback's divergence),[1] (6) improving the geometry of the problem, (7) minimizing or maximizing the sensitivity to pattern variations; (8) are there extraneous, redundant or useless measurements or features or are there redundancies between features (efficiency and sufficiency)?

For box F one might ask:

Are statistical tools appropriate?

Are the statistical behaviors known? If not, are they readily and accurately approximated?

Are parametric, non-parametric, or quasi-parametric techniques appropriate?

With regard to the boxes following F, we might ask:

Should adaptive techniques be included?

Should a learning capability be considered? (Heuristics as opposed to algorithms? Heuristics composed of algorithms?)

Should interactive techniques be included?

In the light of the last two questions should sequential or deferred techniques be incorporated in the decision rule? Should these be used for updating the algorithms or decision rules?

Specifically with regard to the boxes following J we find the following to be important:

Is there a useful measure of the objective function of the pattern recognizer? (What do we wish it to do?)

What is the measure of effectiveness, reliability?

Fundamental to the overall process are the following questions:

How do we tell when a new pattern class or even an old pattern class occurred, i.e., is there a pattern present? Learning, if included--should it be supervised or unsupervised?

The problem of whether the phenomena are time varying or stochastic and if so, whether they are ergodic or not is extremely important to the procedure since a different class of techniques is available for time-varying processes.

Earlier mention was made of the question of whether a special purpose or general (or multi–) purpose procedure should be sought. Intertwined with this is the question of intelligence in the processor, in particular, inductive powers of reasoning over and above the normal cognitive powers.

In the practical realization we must come to grips with two questions which intimately affect in at least a qualitative way the evaluation and decision, i.e., the operational question of what features should be implemented on-line versus off-line (i.e., in the laboratory) and how should the technique be realized in hardware.

Although the natural order of things would normally be to learn, to extract features, and then, to establish rules for classification, this orderly procedure is often not the best one to follow. Frequently we find it more to our advantage to permute and juxtapose these procedures during our learning phase, and sometimes even subsequent to the formal supervised learning phase.

Incidentally, the corresponding flow chart for the designed pattern recognizer (corresponding to Figure 1) is shown in Figure 2.

Modus Operandi of Systems Study

The modus operandi of the suggested effort should be such as to be knowledgeable of, take into account, and provide comparative evaluations of *all* potentially valuable processing alternatives, techniques, and modi operandi vis a vis the various classes of pattern and data sets. In the following sections a preview of this approach is given (at this point no presumption of completeness is made):

(a) How are the data obtained?
Table I lists several ways in which data in the various forms and media can be measured and entered into the pattern recognizer.

(b) If these data are to be transformed prior to processing proper, on what basis will these transformations be made? This is treated in Table II. Feature extraction can be considered to be essentially a manipulation of the measurement space for the purpose of simplifying the final decision procedure.

(c) Many of the techniques listed in Table II cannot be separated from those used in developing the classification or recognition rules. In particular the clustering, clumping, eigenfunction, mode-seeking, perceptron-like, hill-climbing, and some of the stochastic process techniques can be used not only to develop the features but also to determine the existence and extent of pattern classes, the partitioning rules and functions, and metric reference points. This is so because frequently the transformation and recognition procedures are intimately related. In most cases the decision portion of the recognizer can be considered to be the result of either a partitioning operation or a metric-type or similarity-type relationship.† These may or may not be time-varying, or sequentially or adaptively variable.

Often, the metric (similarity) or partitioning function depends upon, or includes, the probability distribution of the pattern behavior explicitly if a probabilistic model is applicable. If the probabilistic behavior is unknown, as is often the case, either an approximation to it or an assumption concerning the distributional form is made either explicitly or implicitly in the partitioning or metric relationships; for example, assuming that the actual distribution is well-approximated by one or a combination of several known distributional forms. Such a procedure, whose degree of applicability to inexact situations is termed robustness, is to be compared in each case with competing ones which do not require such assumptions or approximations (so-called nonparametric techniques). In both cases something is lost as compared with complete knowledge.

---

† In a partitioning operation, the unknown pattern is to be identified with a region in either measurement or feature space, each point in space being uniquely identified with a pattern class. In a metric relationship, the distance of the pattern with respect to (or similarity to) characteristic points or sets in measurement or feature space is used to classify the pattern.

One of the major problems faced by nonparametric techniques† is that they have been hampered by the problem of extension to more than one dimension. (Only in the time-varying or stochastic problem has any degree of success been achieved.) One is forced then to resort to the use of a feature or a functional to extend the methods derived to the many-dimensional problem. In so doing the vector space is usually mapped onto a real line. In our work[14,15] for example, we have used a general functional for a metric rather than the commonly used projection or dot-product procedure (in which one finds the projection of vectors on a line), see Table IV.

In those approaches based upon a probabilistic formulation, one form of learning is encompassed in the actual operation of estimating the probabilities. Ideally these should be of such a nature as to be robust, i.e., they are subject to a minimum of dependence on the shape or the functional characteristics of the actual distribution functions.

Table III contains a comprehensive listing of classification and recognition (decision) techniques used in pattern recognition.

The decision rule, if the Bayes' (minimum risk) philosophy is to be adhered to, is a member of one of several well-known standard forms, i.e., it can vary fundamentally only as to whether, for example, a sequential, non-sequential, or composite decision criterion, etc. is to be utilized and what loss criteria are imposed. These, in turn, are defined by the overall considerations of the problem.

(d) Of pertinent interest to the previous two categories are the relevant metric or similarity relationships and the techniques used to approximate probability distributions. These are listed in Tables IV †† and V respectively.

(e) Finally, the various methods for implementing or realizing the pattern-recognition processors are pertinent in any systems application. Some of these are listed in Table VI.

The question of learning or adaptation and whether it should be carried out on-line or off-line transcends the breakdown in Tables II – V. The considerations leading to the choice of a method of implementation, Table VI, will also govern the choice of a rigid versus an adaptive structure.

It is recommended that each technique be critically evaluated and its capabilities documented relative to the user's needs, and made available to

† Those which are independent of the form of the probability distribution.

†† Ball's work was used freely in deriving Table IV.[2]

workers in the field as a guiding force. As suggested earlier, we should consider an evaluation facility or capability in order to realize, test, and implement a procedure such as that suggested in Figure 1 in an interactive manner.

Conclusions

Upon examining the present stage of achievement and applications in the field of pattern recognition and projecting ahead, it has been concluded that the future of the field both in direction and existence is critically dependent upon the types and degree of use to which the results of research are applied. It is therefore recommended to the pattern recognition community that in order to (a) facilitate the useful applications of pattern recognition techniques, (b) unify the field, and (c) aid the pattern-recognition researcher in orientation and direction, a system effort of a continuing nature be initiated. The diversity of techniques, results, applications, and factors motivating workers in the field; the scarcity of and means for carrying out comparative evaluations of different approaches; and the comparatively small number of *real* applications seem to indicate a need for such an effort. The suggested effort should be the responsibility of the community as a whole and, in particular, its leaders and authorities.

Appendix

With regard to the non-parametric procedures applicable to time varying or stochastic processes, one approach has been to apply Wiener's Canonical procedure to the recognition, decision, and estimation operations.[29]

The procedure leads to a linear filter bank (Wiener chose Laguerre filters, but any filter set which forms a complete orthonormal set or which completely spans the space of functional processes can be used) followed by a non-linear (no-memory) set of operations on the filter outputs (Wiener chose Hermite polynomials to match the marginal probability distributions of the normal white-noise process which he used as an input to his black boxes, but any set of functions which is complete and orthonormal over the space of amplitudes of the process is satisfactory. To wit, Bose chose non-overlapping amplitude gates or window functions). For digital waveforms, the structure is composed of a shift register, followed by a weighting structure, followed in turn by a layer of majority or threshold logic functions. The outputs of the layer are again weighted by variable weight or gain functions and summed. Although the structure is similar in form to others, the convergence and adaptive considerations are different.

The advantages of the procedure † are (a) it leads to realizable networks or computer programs, (b) it is canonical; that is, the structure is the same for

† Before applying the procedure one must be sure that the incoming process is an allowable one.

all acceptable processes of a particular class (e.g., the class of stochastic processes or the class of digital random series); the only difference between processes of the same class being in the gain functions, and (c) because these coefficients are attainable as averages of the responses of the non-linear (Hermite-Laguerre or majority logic) terms themselves, it is possible to determine the coefficients or gain functions as either ensemble averages (expectations of samples of the input processes), or, if the input processes are ergodic (locally-ergodic is sufficient), they can be determined from time-averaging the respective outputs. This leads to interesting learning and adaptive possibilities.

Another promising approach has utilized sequential rank-order statistics.[30] However, to date, the technique has been limited to independent observations and the case where the alternative to the desired pattern class is a Lehmann alternative, i.e., its cumulative distribution function is equal to that of the pattern class raised to a positive power. It does have the advantage of providing a sequential or deferred decision rule.

REPRESENTATIVE REFERENCES

1. Kullback, S., *Information Theory and Statistics,* John Wiley, N. Y., 1959.
2. Ball, G. H., "Data Analysis in the Social Sciences: What About the Details?" *Proceedings-Fall Joint Computer Conference,* 1965, Spartan Press.
3. Sebestyen, G. S., *Decision Making Processes in Pattern Recognition,* Macmillan, N. Y. and London, 1962.
4. Watanabe, S., P. F. Lambert, C. A. Kulikowski, J. L. Buxton, and R. Walker, "Evaluation and Selection of Variables in Pattern Recognition," *Computer and Information Sciences II,* edited by J. T. Tou, Academic Press, N. Y., London, 1967, pp. 91–122.
5. Tou, J. T. and R. P. Heydorn, "Some Approaches to Optimum Feature Extraction," *ibid.,* pp. 57–89.
6. Ball, G. H. and D. J. Hall, "ISODATA, A Novel Method of Data Analysis and Pattern Classification," *Stanford Research Institute Report,* April 1965.
7. Cover, T. M. and P. E. Hart, "Nearest Neighbor Pattern Classification," *IEEE Transactions on Information Theory,* Vol. IT–13, No. 1, January 1967, pp. 21–27.
8. Bledsoe, W. W. and J. Browning, "Further Results on the N-tuple Character Recognition Method," *IRE Trans. on E. C.,* Vol. EC–10, No. 1, March 1961, pp. 96 ff; "Pattern Recognition and Reading by Machine," *Proc. of the Eastern Joint Computer Conference,* 1959, pp. 225–232.
9. Uhr, L. and C. Vossler, "A Pattern Recognition Program that Generates, Evaluates, and Adjusts Its Own Operators," *Proc. Western Joint Computer Conference,* Nos. 9–11, 1961.
10. Highleyman, W. H., "Linear Decision Functions with Application to Pattern Recognition," *Proc. IRE,* Vol. 50, No. 6, June 1962, pp. 150 ff.
11. Cooper, P. W., "The Hyperplane in Pattern Recognition," *Cybernetica,* Vol. V, No. 4, 1962.
12. Nilsson, N. J., *Learning Machines, Foundations of Trainable Pattern Classifying Systems,* McGraw-Hill, N. Y., 1965.
13. Cooper, P. W., "Hyperplanes, Hyperspheres, and Hyperquadrics as Decision Boundaries," *Computer and Information Sciences,* edited by Tou and Wilcox, Spartan, Washington, D.C., 1964.
14. Brick, D. B. and Owen, J., "A Mathematical Approach to Pattern Recognition and Self-Organization," *Computer and Information Sciences,* edited by Tou and Wilcox, Spartan, Washington, D.C., 1964.
15. Owen, J., "Non-Parametric Pattern Recognition Part I: The Locally Disjoint Case," *Information Research Associates, Inc., Technical Report No. 1,* July, 1965. Owen, J., "Non-Parametric Pattern Recognition Part II: The Non-Disjoint Case," *Information Research Associates, Inc., Technical Report No. 2,* October, 1965.
16. Rao, P.S.R.S., "On Selecting Variables for Pattern Classification," *Information Research Associates, Inc., Technical Report No. 11,* 1967 (Presented at the IEEE International Symposium on Information Theory, 1967).
17. Baran, P. and G. Estrin, "An Adaptive Character Reader," *Rand Report,* August 10, 1960.
18. Rosenblatt, F., *Principles of Neurodynamics: Perceptrons and the Theory of Brain Mechanisms,* Spartan, Baltimore, 1962.

19. Block, H. D., "Analysis of Perceptrons," *Proc. WJCC,* May 1961, pp. 281–289.
20. Marill, T. and D. M. Green, "Statistical Recognition Functions and the Design of Pattern Recognizers," *IRE Trans. Electron. Computers,* Vol. EC–9, No. 4, December 1960, pp. 472–477.
21. Marill, T., *et al,* "Cyclops 1: A Second-Generation Recognition Systems," *Proc. AFIPS Fall Joint Computer Conference,* 1963, Spartan, pp. 27–33.
22. Highleyman, W. H., "Character Recognition System," U. S. Patent 2,978,675, issued April 4, 1961.
23. Anderson, T. W., *An Introduction to Multivariate Statistical Analysis,* John Wiley & Sons, Inc., N. Y., 1958.
24. Kailath, T., "Optimum Receivers for Randomly Varying Channels," *Information Theory,* edited by C. Cherry, Butterworth's, Washington, D. C., 1961.
25. Jakowitz, C. V., R. L. Shuey, and G. M. White, "Adaptive Waveform Recognition," *Information Theory, op. cit.*
26. Watanabe, S., "Information Theoretical Analysis of Multivariate Correlation," *IBM Journal of Research & Development,* Vol. 4, No. 1, January 1960, pp. 66–82.
27. Marill, T. and D. M. Green, "On the Effectiveness of Receptors in Recognition Systems," *IEEE Trans. on IT,* Vol. IT–9, No. 1, January 1963, pp. 11–17.
28. Lewis, P. M., II, "Approximating Probability Distributions to Reduce Storage Requirements," *IEEE Trans. on Information and Control,* Vol. 2, No. 3, September 1959, pp. 214–225.
29. Brick, D. B., "On the Applicability of Wiener's Canonical Expansions," *IEEE Trans. SS&C,* January 1968.
30. Fu, K.S. and Y. T. Chien, "On the Finite Stopping Rules and Nonparametric Techniques in a Feature-Ordered Sequential Recognition System," *Purdue Univ.,* TR–EE66–16, October 1966.
31. Minsky, M., "Steps Toward Artificial Intelligence," *Proc. IRE,* Vol. 9, No. 1, January 1961, pp. 8–30.
32. Minsky, M., and O. G. Selfridge, "Learning in Random Nets," *Information Theory, op. cit.*
33. Alt, F. I., "Digital Pattern Recognition by Moments," *Journal of the ACM,* Vol. 9, No. 2, April 1962.
34. Meyer, R. F., V. E. Giuliano, P. E. Jones, "An Analytic Approximation and Translation Invariance in Character Recognition," *Optical Character Recognition,* edited by Fischer, Pollock, Radack, and Stevens, Spartan, Washington, D.C., 1962, pp. 181 ff.
35. Braverman, D. J., Although the theory presented is general, illustrative examples in the following are restricted to the normal case.
    a.———, *Machine Learning and Automatic Pattern Recognition,* Stanford Electronics Laboratory, Tech. Rpt. No. 2003–1, February 17, 1961.
    b.———, "A Decision Theoretic Approach to Machine Learning and Pattern Recognition," Report 3813, WESCON 1961.
    c.———, "Learning Filters for Optimum Pattern Recognition," submitted to *IRE Trans. Information Theory.*
36. Chow, C. K., "An Optimum Character Recognition System Using Decision Functions" *IRE Trans. Electron. Computers,* Vol. EC–6, No. 4, December 1957, pp. 247–254.

37. Bahadur, R. R., "Probability and Statistics in Item Analysis and Classification Problems," Air University, School of Aviation Medicine, USAF, Randolph AFB, Texas, January 1959, also published in *Studies in Item Analysis and Prediction,* edited by H. Solomon, Stanford University Press, 1961.
38. Chow, C. K., "A Class of Nonlinear Recognition Procedures," to be published.
39. Sebestyen, G. and J. Edie, "An Algorithm for Non-Parametric Pattern Recognition," *IEEE Trans. on Electronic Computers,* Vol. EC–15, No. 6, December 1966, pp. 909–915.
40. Abend, K., T. J. Harley, and L. N. Kanal, "Classification of Binary Random Patterns," *IEEE Transactions on Information Theory,* Vol. IT–11, No. 4, October 1965, pp. 538–544.
41. Kanal, L., "Evaluation of a Class of Pattern Recognition Networks," *Biological Prototypes and Synthetic Systems,* Vol. 1, edited by Bernard, E. E. and M. R. Kare, Plenum Press, N. Y., 1962.
42. Specht, D. F., "Generation of Polynomial Discriminant Functions for Pattern Recognition," Presented at IEEE Pattern Recognition Workshop, October 24–26, 1966; also *Technical Report No. 6764-5, Stanford Electronics Laboratories, Stanford University,* May 1966.
43. Sammon, J. W., "An Adaptive Method for Decomposition of Mixed Distribution," presented at *IEEE Pattern Recognition Workshop,* October 24-26, 1966.
44. Stanat, D. F., "Nonsupervised Pattern Recognition Through the Decomposition of Probability Functions," presented to *IEEE Pattern Recognition Workshop,* October 24–26, 1966; also *Tech. Report, the University of Michigan,* April 1966.
45. Furey, William N., Jr., and Arthur R. Williams, "Least Squares Fit to Optimum (Bayes) Decision Surface (Revised)," *Information Research Associates, Inc., Technical Note No. 21,* August 1967.
46a. Wald, A., *Sequential Analysis,* Wiley, New York, 1947.
b. Wald, A., *Statistical Decision Functions,* Wiley, New York, 1950.
47. Sebestyen, George S., "On Pattern Recognition with Application to Silhouettes," unpublished thesis, Massachusetts Institute of Technology, September 1959.
48. Minsky, M. L., "Some Methods of Heuristic Programming and Artificial Intelligence," *Proceedings of Symposium on Mechanisation of Thought Processes,* published by Her Majesty's Stationery Office, London, 1959.
49. Ablow, C. M. and D. J. Kaylor, "A Committee Solution of the Pattern Recognition Problem," *IEEE Trans. IT,* Vol. IT–4, No. 3, July 1965 (Correspondence), pp. 453–455.
50. Aizerman, M. A., E. M. Braverman, and L. I. Rozonoer, "Theoretical Principles of Potential Function Method in the Problem of Teaching Automata to Recognize Classes," *Automation and Remote Control, 25,* No. 6, (1964), pp. 821–837.
51. Spragins, John, "Use of the Principle of Maximum Entropy in Pattern Recognition," published in the *1965 Boulder Conference on Information Theory.*
52. Spragins, John, "Learning Without a Teacher," *IEEE Trans. IT,* Vol. IT–12, No. 2, April 1966, pp. 223–230.
53. Zadeh, L. A., "Fuzzy Sets," *Information and Control,* Vol. 8, No. 3, June 1965, pp. 338–353.
54. Fu, K.S., and W. G. Wee, "On Generalizations of Adaptive Algorithms and Application of the Fuzzy Sets Concept to Pattern Classification," Purdue University, School of Electrical Engineering, Lafayette, Indiana, June 1967.

55. Cooper, D.E. and P.W. Cooper, "Adaptive Pattern Recognition and Signal Detection Without Supervision," *IEEE International Convention Record, Part I,* 1964, pp. 246–256.

TABLE I. MEDIA AND MEASUREMENTS

Optical

Flying-Spot Scanners, Image Disectors
Retinal Scanners
Sub-Retinal Scanners (Lines, Sub-Arrays, etc.)
Special Feature-Scanners
Vidicons, Image Orthicons
Holographic and Fourier Transform Systems

Acoustic, Electromagnetic, Heat, Seismic Sensors

Other Radiation Detectors

Measurement of Spatial Variations

Multi Sensor and/or Directional Sensors

Measurement of Time Variations

Continuous and/or Sampled

Measurement of Frequency Variations

Frequency Scanning, Sampling, and/or Parallel Filtering
Transform Techniques

Physical Measurements

Length, Height, Width, Depth, etc.
Mass, Volume

Static, Dynamic, Kinematic Measurements

Other Graded Data

Etc.

TABLE II. TRANSFORMATIONS, FEATURE EXTRACTORS, ETC.

Clustering[2,3,4,5,6]

(For compacting classes or for maximally separating patterns)

Clumping[2,7]

(For developing class centers)

Intuitive Transformations or Features[8,9]

Functionals and Operators

(Such as linear discriminants,[10,11] piecewise linear discriminants,[12] or quadratic functionals,[13] etc.[14,15])

Dimensional Reduction

(Via, e.g., coordinate transformations followed by rejection of least important dimensions[3,4,5] or straightforward rejection[16])

Templates[17]

(Prototypes or the most characteristic shapes)

Perceptron-like or Neural (Brain-like) Techniques[18,19]

Eigenfunction Generators[2,3,5]

Decision Theory Techniques[14,20]

Mode Seeking[2]

Interactive Techniques (e.g., using displays)[21]

Correlation Type Techniques[22]

Factor Analysis[23]

Matched or Inverse Filtering[24,25]

Entropy Techniques[1,26,27,28]

Stochastic Process Techniques[29,30]

(Table II. cont.)

Hill-Climbing Algorithms[31, 32]

Other Techniques for Picking the Most Important Features (with relevance to the objective function of the recognition problem)

Moments, etc.[33, 34]

TABLE III. CLASSIFICATION AND RECOGNITION (DECISION) TECHNIQUES IN PATTERN RECOGNITION

Probabilistic Techniques—Partitioning

- **Bayes Rule Techniques**[46]
  - Probability Distribution Known
- **Approximate Bayes Rule Techniques**
  - Partitioning Surface Approximated by Simple Surface (e.g., Linear,[10, 11] Piecewise Linear,[12] Quadratic,[13,36] etc.)
  - Probability Distribution Estimated[28, 35-44]
  - Functional of Exact or Estimated Probability Distribution Used[14, 15, 16]
  - Estimation of Decision Rule[36, 37, 38]
  - Combinations of Above[42, 45]
- **Deferred or Sequential Bayes Techniques**[29, 30, 46]
- **Techniques Using Metric or Similarity Relationships** (Table IV)
  - Know and Use Probability Distribution
  - Need Not Use Probability Distribution
  - Must Estimate Probability Distribution
- **Stochastic Techniques**[29, 30] (See Appendix)

Non-Probabilistic Techniques

- **Use Metrics or Similarity Relationships Directly 47** (Table IV)
- **Partition Based on Metric or Similarity Relationship**[47]
- **Partition Intuitively**
- **Partition by Interactive Means**[20]
- **Partition by Frequency of Co-occurrences**
- **Neural or Perceptron-like Partitioning**[18, 19]
- **List Processing Techniques**[31, 48]
- **Committee Solutions**[49]

TABLE IV. METRIC OR SIMILARITY RELATIONSHIPS[2]

[Used either for intraset similarities or interset discrimination. Applied to the unknown and either the class or a point characterizing the class as a similarity measure or between classes as a dissimilarity measure.]

DOT PRODUCT
NORMALIZED DOT PRODUCT (Similarity Ratio)
EUCLIDEAN DISTANCE, EITHER WEIGHTED OR UNWEIGHTED
MEAN SQUARE FITS
CORRELATION FUNCTIONS OR FUNCTIONS OF CORRELATION FUNCTION
NORMALIZED CORRELATION
BOOLEAN 'AND' AND BOOLEAN CORRELATION
ENTROPY TYPE MEASURES INCLUDING KULLBACK'S DIVERGENCE FUNCTION AND EQUIVOCATION[1,26,27,28]
PROBABILITY OF ERROR
WEIGHTED PROBABILITY OF ERROR OR RISK
FREQUENCY OF CO–OCCURRENCES (e.g., Perceptron-like Systems)
INTUITIVE AND OBSERVED SIMILARITIES

TABLE V. TECHNIQUES USED TO APPROXIMATE PROBABILITY DISTRIBUTION

HISTOGRAM TECHNIQUES[16,39]
EMPIRICAL CUMULATIVE DISTRIBUTION[14,15]
EMPIRICAL CUMULATIVE ESTIMATE OF DECISION RULE[14,15]
ORDER STATISTICS[15,30]
SEQUENTIAL RANK–ORDER STATISTICS[30]
PARZEN APPROXIMATION–TYPE TECHNIQUES[39,42–45]
POTENTIAL FUNCTION TECHNIQUES[50]
ENTROPY TECHNIQUES[28,51]
ASSOCIATION (CLUSTER-LIKE) TECHNIQUES[7,47]
RECURSION TECHNIQUES[35,52]
STOCHASTIC OR TIME FUNCTION TECHNIQUES (SIGNAL DETECTION)[29,30] (See Appendix)
ADAPTIVE AND NEURAL TECHNIQUES[18,19]
FUZZY SETS TECHNIQUES (?)[53,54]
QUASI–PARAMETRIC TECHNIQUES[13]
UNSUPERVISED ESTIMATION TECHNIQUES[29–31,52,55]

TABLE VI. IMPLEMENTATION OF PATTERN RECOGNITION PROCESSES

(Following Measurements)

GENERAL PURPOSE COMPUTERS
PARALLEL–ORGANIZED COMPUTERS
SPECIAL–PURPOSE COMPUTERS
ASSOCIATIVE PROCESSORS
ANALOG SYSTEMS
OPTICAL TECHNIQUES (CORRELATORS)
HOLOGRAPHIC SYSTEMS
INTERACTIVE (e.g., DISPLAY) SYSTEMS
NEURAL OR PERCEPTRON-LIKE SYSTEMS
(ELECTRONIC, BIOLOGICAL, CHEMICAL, ETC.)
ETC.

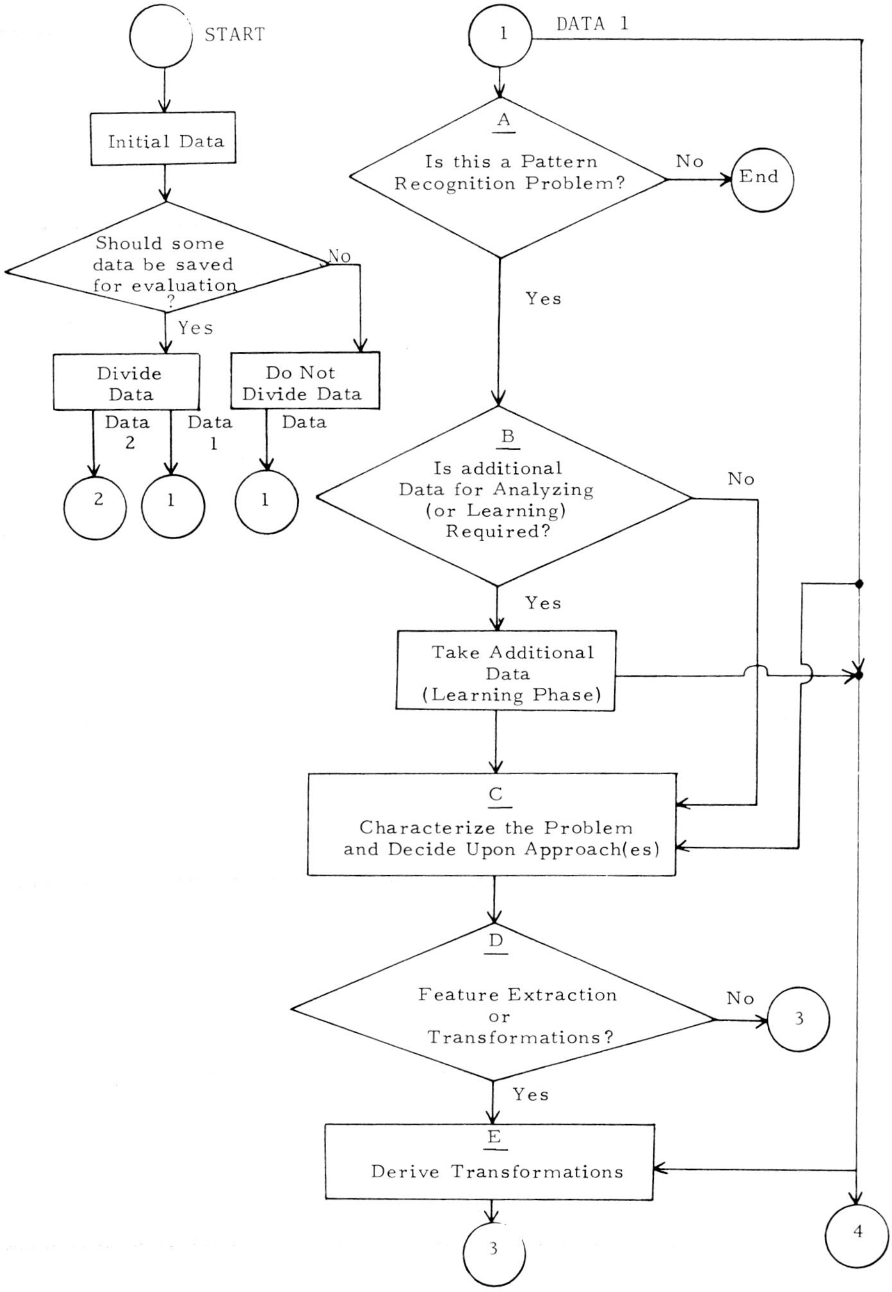

Figure 1a: Flow Chart for Derivation of Pattern Recognition Procedure

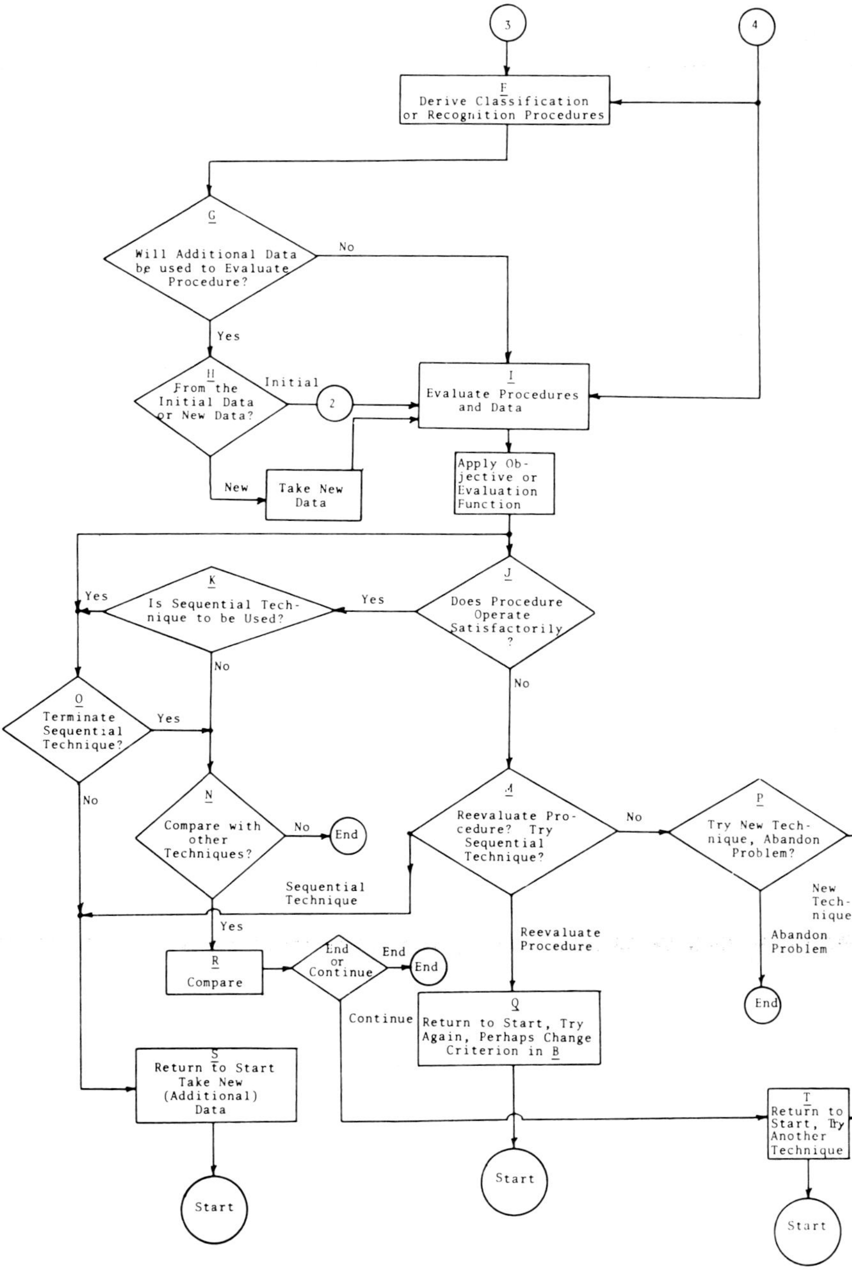

Figure 1b: Flow Chart for Derivation of Pattern Recognition Procedure (continued)

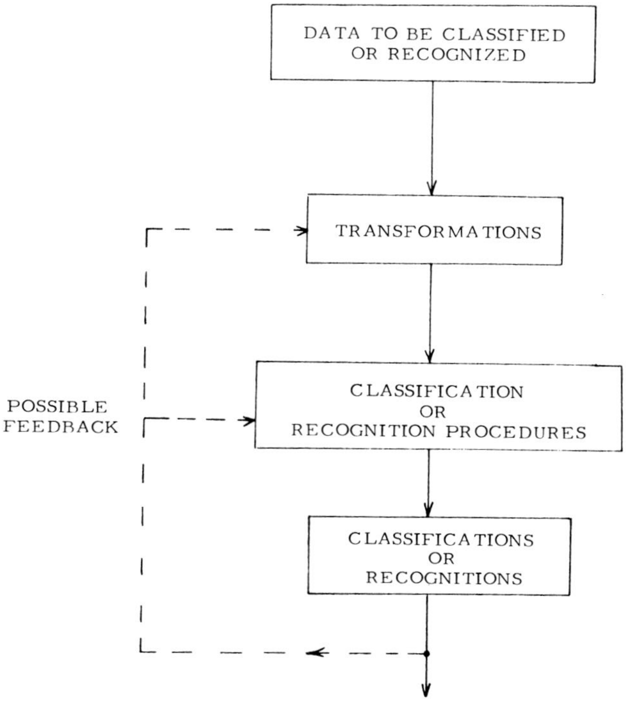

Figure 2: Pattern Recognition Procedures

NONSUPERVISED LEARNING IN STATISTICAL PATTERN RECOGNITION

Paul W. Cooper

CONSULTANT
2 FOREST STREET
CAMBRIDGE, MASSACHUSETTS

Abstract

Pattern recognition and learning can be treated as problems in statistical decision theory and estimation. Nonsupervised *learning arises when the decision parameters must be gleaned from a sequence of samples of unknown category association known* only *to have been drawn from the aggregate categories. This paper discusses some of the underlying philosophy of* nonsupervised *learning which has led to solutions and considers aspects of the problems arising therein.*

I. Introductory Remarks

Statistical decision theory provides one of the mathematically powerful approaches to pattern recognition. Members of the categories are represented each by a set of n numerically describable attributes, and the categories are represented with probability distributions. One can proceed to obtain (and to understand the capabilities of and limitations of) a classification procedure optimally satisfying a (subjectively chosen) classification criterion, as, e.g., minimum probability of misclassification. To the extent that the characteristics of the probabilistic model adequately represent the real problem (as deduced from statistical measurements or from analysis of the physical model), the mathematical-statistical[1] approach can be excellent.

Data samples are represented as vectors in n-space, and the categories each have associated with them a probability distribution describing the distribution in n-space of the members of the category. In real classification problems important questions arise first in deciding upon the number of and types of attributes to form this space, but this paper proceeds for the model wherein one is constrained to a specific n-space in which to perform.

Among the several broad aspects of statistical pattern recognition are the problem of the classification procedure itself, the question of choosing (where desired) the best subspace of a particular dimensionality, and the problems of learning (supervised and *nonsupervised*). For some of these aspects theoretical limitations are not posed, but difficulties can arise in obtaining analytic expressions for practical solutions. The aspect of *nonsupervised* learning, however, can not only offer formidable practical obstacles but often encounters fundamental theoretical barriers.

After touching briefly on these various aspects, the paper focusses on the philosophy underlying *nonsupervised* learning, as presented originally in *Ref.* 2. In the spirit of this conference, this paper reviews philosophy and examines the nature of some of the problems thereby arising. Any specific treatment of mathematical techniques here is for illustrative purposes, and simple examples are used as a vehicle for this.

The starting point is the *criterion problem*, as the subjective selection of a classification criterion sets the goal, regardless of the framework of approach. Within the framework of statistical decision theory[3,4,5] classic decision criteria allow for minimizing probability of misclassification, minimizing expected cost (loss) arising from misclassifications, and combinations of these depending upon what is known concerning prior probabilities and the loss matrix.

Given the probability distributions, the decision procedure optimally satisfying the chosen decision criterion is precisely defined. For the minimum-probability-of-misclassification criterion, for example, the decision procedure assigns the unknown vector $\mathbf{x}$ to that one of the K categories for which $q_k p_k(\mathbf{x})$ is largest, where $p_k(\mathbf{x})$ is the probability density function associated with the kth category, q_k is the *a priori* probability of the kth category, and $k = 1, 2, \ldots, K$. The inherent probability of misclassification associated with the known distributions is the *irreducible error*, and it is the goal of any system involving learning procedures.

As an illustration, for multivariate normal distributions

$$p_k(\mathbf{x}) = (2\pi)^{-n/2}\ |\Sigma_k|^{-n/2}\ \exp[-\tfrac{1}{2}(\mathbf{x}-\mathbf{u}_k)'\Sigma_k^{-1}(\mathbf{x}-\mathbf{u}_k)]$$

$k = 1, 2, \ldots, K$, having covariance matrix Σ_k and mean $\mathbf{u}_k$, and denoting transpose with accent $'$, the decision procedure is to assign $\mathbf{x}$ to that category having the smallest decision function

$$(\mathbf{x}-\mathbf{u}_k)'\ \Sigma_k^{-1}(\mathbf{x}-\mathbf{u}_k) + \log_e|\Sigma_k| - 2\log_e q_k$$

Viewed geometrically, such a decision procedure corresponds to partitioning the n-dimensional hyperspace into category regions with segmented hyperquadric boundaries. In a 2-category problem, the partition would be made by a single hyperquadric, and, depending upon the relationship among the two distribution means and covariance matrices, could be any of the possible forms of the hyperquadric.

Given the probability distributions, the classification problem is straightforward, basically. In attempting to make wider use of the more simply-implementable decision procedures, attention has been focussed on exploring some of the general properties of the simple decision boundaries, as, e.g., the aforementioned hyperquadrics. Among results obtained have been the following: capacity theorems[6] for the number of possible partitions for a finite data set; demonstration[7] that the hyperquadrics are the optimal partition not only for normal but for other interesting probability distributions as well, as, e.g., multivariate Pearson Types II and VII.

The aspect of reducing the dimensionality of the sample space arises in the desire to reduce the numerical complexity of decision-making by discarding the least important attributes. Within a statistical framework this is a problem in finding in n-space the most *significant directions*[7] of the decision boundaries, and is equivalent to finding that c-subspace which allows for the closest fulfillment of the chosen decision criterion. In principle this could involve determining for each possible c-subspace the optimal decision procedure and its degree of fulfillment of the criterion, e.g., evaluation of probability integrals to decide which c-subspace affords the lowest probability of misclassification. But, except for special cases, in practice such an evaluation procedure can be overwhelming. So, a variety of approaches[8,9] have been explored and developed for choosing features on the basis of various other more-easily-satisfied criteria, some of which are of interest in their own right and some of which hopefully might approximate under certain circumstances the requirements set by the chosen decision criterion. (These latter works[8,9] have also been concerned with the important problems of pre-selection of features).

II. Learning

Learning is needed when the category distributions are inadequately known or not known at all. From a sequence of samples drawn from these categories, the unknown category distributions are estimated. (In some interesting cases it is only necessary to estimate certain parameters, not the complete distributions, as, e.g., ellipsoidal monotone distributions with equal covariance matrices wherein, for certain criteria, just the means and matrices need be determined).

Supervised learning[10,5](learning with a teacher) is applicable for known samples, whereby there is given a set of "learning" samples for each category. *Supervised* learning can always be done, no matter how complicated the problem may be. In the parametric problem, where the distributions' functional forms but not their parameters are known, the parameters are estimated and these estimates are inserted into the decision functions and used as though they were the true values. Many forms of estimators for the unknown parameters converge to true values whereby the decision procedure also converges to its irreducible optimum. It is a matter of using estimators that display a balance between rapidity of convergence and computational simplicity. When the functional forms of the distributions are unknown, nonparametric estimation can be used to obtain the empirical distributions, which are in turn used in the decision functions as though they were the true distributions.

When the associations of the "learning" samples with their respective categories are unknown *a priori* learning is *nonsupervised.*

A transitional case[11,12,13] arises when the "learning" samples are not identified in advance but where all but one of the category distributions are completely known *a priori*. This transitional case is always possible.

III. Nonsupervised Learning

Nonsupervised learning (self-learning, learning without a teacher), wherein the "learning" samples are of *a priori* unknown category association, at the outset invites question as to its possibility at all. That is, given a sequence of samples known *only* to have been drawn from the aggregate categories, is it possible from examination *only* of these samples to estimate the unknown distributions defining the desired decision functions?

Until several years ago it had been widely felt that this was not possible. And, in fact, it is not possible in general. There are, for example, many possible organizations of the data. A machine could disclose its own behavioral patterns, and an observer could learn about the machine or person rather than obtain the desired organization of the data.

But *nonsupervised* learning *is* possible in many important cases of interest. That this is so was shown originally in our *Ref.* 2. That work showed that *nonsupervised* learning is possible for a wide range of situations, presented a philosophy for viewing the problem, developed considerations of structural requirements among the distributions, and explored methods of effective estimation. *Ref.* 14 delves into and presents the fundamental structural requirements in greater depth. As it develops, some related questions had been under examination[15,16,17] in the statistical literature. The material in this paper draws primarily upon *Ref.* 2, and in part upon 14.

It should be noted that the amount of *a priori* knowledge concerning the distributions determines the complexity of and in fact the possibility of effecting such learning, but it is that the "learning" samples are associated with the categories in a way unknown *a priori* that makes it a *nonsupervised* learning problem.

Nonsupervised learning assumes importance because of the fact that in some problems of interest *supervised* learning may be impossible, inconvenient, or too expensive.

The viewpoint we took is one in which the samples are considered having been drawn from an over-all distribution p(x) which is itself a mixture of the component category distributions, i.e.,

$$p(\mathbf{x}) = \sum_{k=1}^{K} q_k p_k(\mathbf{x}) .$$

Given the sequence of samples $\{\mathbf{z}_m\}$, m = 1, 2, . . . , M , one would like to estimate these component distributions (or at least the decision-determing parameters). Viewed in this way *nonsupervised* learning is an estimation problem involving a single (possibly very complex) distribution, even though the underlying category distributions themselves may be of simple form. (Although it is also possible to have a relatively simple over-all distribution comprised of complex component distributions). The questions which arise are:

1. If it is possible at all, under what conditions is this so?

2. What are good estimators to use?

The over-all distribution can always be estimated – if necessary by nonparametric means wherein the empirical distribution is obtained. Therefore, the first question is rephrased – given the true over-all distribution, can it be broken down into the component distributions, at least in theory? That is, is there a unique decomposition?

The answer in general is *no*. With adequate probability structure, *yes*. (The reason why the transitional case, mentioned earlier, can always be done is that an estimate of the one unknown distribution can be obtained as the difference between the estimated over-all distribution and the remaining known component distributions).

IV. Probability Structure[2,14]

Any over-all distribution can be comprised of an infinity of combinations of component distributions. But when there is adequate *probability structure* to the problem the combination of component distributions giving rise to the over-all distribution can be unique. Equivalently, with adequate *probability structure* (known), the component distributions, given the over-all distribution, are uniquely defined (in principle), i.e., the distributions are identifiable.

In any specific problem it is first necessary to determine whether there is in fact adequate structure relating the category distributions for a unique decomposition. Among interesting cases where there is adequate *probability structure* are the following:

1. Many problems involving finitely parameterized category distributions, e.g., multivariate normal distributions. That is, if the class is specified, e.g., that they are normal distributions.
2. Certain nonparametric situations involving completely unknown category distributions of any (unknown) functional form. A very interesting situation for which this is true is the one involving two equally-likely distributions differing only in translation, i.e., $p(x) = (1/2)[g(x-a) + g(x+a)]$. If a is known, this is true for any functional form. If a is unknown, this is true for essentially all a and $g(x)$ of possible interest (there are certain restrictions). (With unknown translation parameter this could correspond to detection of two unknown signals in unknown additive noise of any distribution form).

The concept of *structure* is actually more general than just described. There are classes of problems for which there is not adequate structure for obtaining the component distributions, yet for which there is adequate structure for obtaining the decision parameters (complete distributional knowledge not being necessary).

We term this more general (and less stringent) situation one involving *decision structure* (corresponding to a decision identifiability), whereas the previously described situation is labeled *distribution structure* (corresponding to a distribution identifiability).

V. Statistical Estimators[2,18]

Even though there may be adequate structure, *statistical estimators* for the component distributions or the decision parameters can be complicated, and this can be especially so for nonparametric *nonsupervised* learning. Interest, then, focuses on developing manageable convergent estimation procedures. For parametric problems, among the estimators of the desired parameters are sample moments, maximum-likelihood, Bayesian, and rank order.

The *Maximum-likelihood* estimator (MLE), that gem of statistical estimators, can become computationally complex even for the simplest situations here. This is illustrated for the simple minimum-probability-of-misclassification 2-category problem where the two equi-probable distributions are each univariate normal differing only by translation $2a$, having standard deviation σ, and over-all mean μ. The only parameter needed is μ, which is the threshold in the decision process. The MLE for μ is obtained from simultaneous solution of three algebraic equations involving the three unknown parameters μ, a, and σ. Even if we were to already know a and σ, the MLE for μ involves solution of an algebraic equation in which the estimator $\hat{\mu}$ appears both within and without the arguments of hyperbolic functions, the number of these functions equal to the number M of "learning" samples, as here shown:

$$\hat{\mu} = \frac{1}{M} \sum_{m=1}^{M} z_m - \frac{a}{M} \sum_{m=1}^{M} \tanh[(a/\sigma^2)(z_m - \hat{\mu})] .$$

The MLE of course displays various optimal statistical properties. Its desirable convergence properties are apparent whether the distributions over-lap significantly or are somewhat spaced. And with the availability of the large computer, the difficult numerical problems appear less imposing. Furthermore, the MLE, even as a sidelight, gives insight into approximative procedures.

Moment estimators, despite their antiquity, have a great deal of merit. In certain cases they are neat and fairly simple. Moments of the over-all distribution can be expressed in terms of the parameters of the component distributions. Simultaneous solution of these relations gives expressions for the desired parameters in terms of the over-all moments. The over-all moments are easily estimated directly with *sample moments.*

Many problems (particularly 2-category cases) are amenable to easy solution in relatively simple analytic form for the desired parameters in terms of the over-all moments. Aesthetically and computationally this is appealing. For so many problems of interest sample moments converge, although not as rapidly as MLE. Memory requirements for sample moments are small, as the estimate can be updated with a new sample without having had to store all previous samples. For example, the sample mean adjusting to the $(m+1)^{st}$ sample is

$$\hat{\mu}_{m+1} = \frac{m\hat{\mu}_m + z_{m+1}}{m+1}$$

Moment solutions do not always fall easily into place, however, and this becomes readily apparent in multiple-category problems.

To illustrate some simple moment solutions, consider two normal distributions of equal prior probability. For a minimum-probability-of-error criterion, for the case of univariate normal distributions of equal variance the sample mean $\hat{\mu}$ provides the complete estimate. For two spherically-symmetric multivariate normal distributions of equal variance the optimal hyperplane partition is defined by the over-all mean and the principle eigen-vector of the over-all covariance matrix. From the over-all sample covariance matrix, the principle eigenvector can be determined directly from the elements of the matrix or by any of a number of iterative procedures.

Consider two general multivariate normal distributions having covariance matrices Σ and Ω (equivalent, respectively, to notation Σ_2 and Σ_1) and mean separation $2a = \mathbf{u}_2 - \mathbf{u}_1$. Since the over-all covariance matrix and other moments can be estimated directly, from these we would like to obtain Σ, Ω, a, and μ, the latter determined directly from $\hat{\mu}$. There is much value in having a little prior knowledge. With everything unknown it is not so easy. If any single parameter is known, *a priori*, the problem is much simplified. With everything unknown, there are easy solutions when some restrictions are put on the matrices, e.g., being diagonal. For arbitrarily general matrices, means and matrices unknown, the parameters can be obtained, but there is an association problem. For example, the unsigned values of the components are obtained, but to associate these with their appropriate signs involves a partial trial procedure – i.e., the various possibilities are tried pair-wise and a statistical measure indicates which is appropriate.

However, there are neat complete solutions for the slightly restricted matrices. To illustrate, we make use of the over-all covariance matrix **B** and the third central cross-moment matrix Φ, having elements ϕ_{ij}, where

$$\mathbf{B} = a\,a' + \tfrac{1}{2}(\Sigma + \Omega)$$

$$\phi_{ij} = \overline{(x_i - \mu_i)^2 (x_j - \mu_j)} \ .$$

For the case of diagonal matrices, all parameters unknown: $b_{ij} = a_i a_j$, $a_i^2 = b_{21} b_{31} / b_{32}$, $a_i = b_{i1}/a_1$. Taking a_1 positive and associating Σ with $+\,a$, one obtains

$$\sigma_{ii} = b_{ii} - a_i^2 + (1/3)\frac{\phi_{ii}}{a_i}$$

and ω_{ii} by replacing the + with a – in the above expression. For the case of arbitrarily general matrices, one mean known *a priori*: $\mathbf{u}_1$ known, a is obtained from $a = \mu - \mathbf{u}_1$, σ_{ii} and ω_{ii} are obtained as before, and from $b_{ij} = a_i a_j + (1/2)(\sigma_{ij} + \omega_{ij})$ one obtains

$$\sigma_{ij} = (b_{ij} - a_i a_j) + \frac{\phi_{ij} - \frac{1}{2} a_j(\sigma_{ii} - \omega_{ii})}{2a_i}$$

and ω_{ij} by replacing the + with a − in the above expression.

Different prior probabilities for each category are easily incorporated into any of the equations, slightly modifying them when known and requiring an extra moment equation when unknown.

The multiple-category case gets more complicated. Not only are there brought in higher-order equations for the additional distribution parameters, but cross-term association problems become more difficult. (However, the modern large computer can help out here). Various related questions can be readily answered. For example, for K spherically symmetric category distributions differing only in location (could correspond to K signals in additive white gaussian noise), the number of categories (i.e., K), unknown *a priori*, can be determined from the over-all covariance matrix

$$\mathbf{B} = \mathbf{I}\sigma^2 + \frac{1}{K} \sum_{k=1}^{K} \underset{\sim}{a}_k \underset{\sim}{a}_k' \; .$$

The smallest eigenvalue λ_K is of multiplicity (n−K+1), where $\underset{\sim}{a}_k = \mathbf{u}_k - \mu$

Bayesian estimators[10,11,19] are of theoretical interest, but they involve arbitrary assumptions of distributions of the parameters themselves, and from practical considerations are very cumbersome computationally. Rank order statistics require storage of all samples, but can be of interest in certain situations.

VI. Some Sub-Optimum Estimation Procedures

Sub-optimum techniques can be brought to bear, sometimes to achieve by successive approximations a solution not readily available directly, or sometimes to achieve a more easily implementable solution. For minimum-error-probability criterion, we illustrate with two procedures.

HILL–CLIMBING[2]

This type of procedure is sometimes suitable, and is especially so in the case of two equi-probable normal distributions with equal (arbitrarily general) covariance matrices, for which case direct statistical solutions still partly involve a trial procedure. The hyperplane representing the optimum decision rule is defined by perpendicular vector $\Sigma^{-1} a$. In this direction the marginal kurtosis (kurtosis defined as ratio of fourth central moment to the square of the second central moment) is minimal over all possible directions. Therefore, start with any possible hyperplane passing through the over-all mean, estimate the marginal kurtosis (e.g., with sample moments) perpendicular to this plane, and progressively shift the orientation of the plane in direction of decreasing kurtosis until a minimum is reached. This minimum (valley) corresponding to the desired solution is unique. There are no other valleys enroute, and the hill-climbing (or, in this case, descending) could be achieved monotonically. This procedure is not confined to normal distributions, and would apply also to any ellipsoidal monotone distributions.

NONLINEAR ESTIMATION PROCEDURES[20]

Nonlinear systems (decision-directed), applicable to n-space discrete models, can be very simple. They are sub-optimum in convergence properties, and some do not even converge to the irreducible optimum. But certain situations lend themselves to partially decision-directed systems which do converge to the irreducible optimum.

We illustrate with an interesting system couched in terms of a communications problem. Consider two equi-probable spherically symmetric normal distributions differing only in location, corresponding to two signals in white gaussian noise. The optimal partition is the hyperplane perpendicularly bisecting the line of means, and what is desired then is the over-all mean μ and the principal over-all eigenvector ν. Although there are various simple statistical solutions, we describe now a nonlinear system, shown in Fig. 1, called a synchronous NASD (Nonsupervised Adaptive Signal Detector) for two signals in band-limited white noise, all initially unknown at the receiver. Although not optimum, the system does converge to the irreducible optimum.

Instead of vectors and spaces, we speak here of waveforms. A synchronous train of Mark and Space waveforms in noise is received, and, knowing nothing initially of the signal characteristics or noise or of which signal is received at any time, the system processes the received data and adapts to the configuration of the optimum detector. The Mark and Space waveforms and the delay lines all have duration T. The parameter W lies between 0 and 1, preferably close to 0. Assuming first that the system is in synchronism, i.e., that the decision is made at the end of a baud (where bauds are transmitted contiguously), the system operates as follows. The loop at the left averages what comes in, and therefore derives an estimate of the over-all mean. This mean is subtracted out, and what remains are two anti-correlated signals in noise. The multiplier, integrator, and decision box together comprise the correlation detector. The remaining system (except for the sync box) estimates the waveform $\nu(t)$, corresponding to the principal eigenvector, i.e., the vector perpendicular to the partitioning hyperplane. The gate operates on the basis of whether the decision was Mark or Space. Waveform $\nu(t)$ represents, therefore, a scaled estimate of the difference between the Mark and Space waveforms, Mark and Space losing their absolute significance.

The system can perform synchronization. If the instants of transition between bauds are not known, the sync circuit would measure the average energy in the delay line and slowly and progressively shift the sampling time of the decision circuit until the measured energy is maximum. At this time the system is in synchronism, i.e., the decision is made at the end of each baud. If T is not known, it can be determined most easily with an autocorrelator on the input.

The weighting W controls the rate of convergence. For fixed W, the averaging is based upon progressive decrease in weighting for earlier samples. The weighting factor W is chosen small enough to achieve adequate convergence and large enough to allow for tracking for slowly nonstationary signals. If W were connected to a counter so that it was set equal to N^{-1}, where N is the number of received bauds, all samples would be averaged equally, e.g., the averager on the input would give the sample mean.

The synchronous NASD, given a train of noisy general Mark-Space waveforms, can start in initial ignorance, knowing nothing of the noise variance, of the Mark and Space waveforms, of the identification of the waveforms appearing, of the baud transition times, and of the baud duration T, and adapt and converge to the system corresponding to that which would be optimum if all this were known.

VII. Concluding Remarks

To summarize and comment, there are problems remaining in all of statistical pattern recognition, particularly so in feature selection and also, to some extent, in *nonsupervised* learning. Given the distributions, the classification procedures are defined, and remaining questions largely concern simplifying implementation through approximations. Feature selection as a problem in reducing a given n-space to a good c-dimensional subspace can be described theoretically, but for some cases of interest still awaits the development of effective procedures. The problem of choosing the features in the first place is of fundamental importance, and ultimately must relate to the decision criterion and decision procedure thereby dictated, and this too requires further work. Supervised learning is clear-cut. Of all the aspects of the learning-recognition problem, *nonsupervised* learning is the one that can face rigid theoretical limitations. *Nonsupervised* learning cannot always be done, and this fact sets a limit on the types of problems which can be solved. Furthermore, even where theoretically solvable, the actual techniques derived can be complex, and with any new problem there is the challenge to getting a good estimation procedure.

Nonsupervised learning is a concept of fundamental importance and rich in potential, and there will continue to appear problems where there is no choice but to do *nonsupervised* learning, or not do learning at all. (And there can be problems where no learning can be done). What is important in viewing *nonsupervised* learning is the underlying philosophy. That is the key, as are the basic questions of structure and of estimators. The underlying philosophy is clear. The samples are treated as having been drawn from an over-all distribution, and estimation procedures are directed toward determining the needed decision parameters (or the component distributions themselves). *Nonsupervised* learning can be done when there is adequate known probability structure allowing for obtaining the desired decision parameters from the over-all distribution. Estimators are developed to exhibit an acceptable balance among analytic simplicity, computational tractability, and rapidity of convergence.

The discussion on *nonsupervised* learning in this paper draws upon our earlier work, where all of this is treated in far greater detail and scope. In particular, early treatment of all topics appears in *Ref.* 2. More detailed treatment of structure, of associated existence theorems, and of conditions for nonparametric statistical decomposition of mixtures appears in *Ref.* 14.

Specific treatments of estimators in this paper are for illustrative purposes. (Normal distributions are a convenient vehicle for illustrating what is involved, as well as being of interest in their own right). In any problem one can proceed to solve for all sorts of similar procedures as needed, as the basic considerations in determining these for different distributions with or without known prior probabilities are essentially the same.

In a real problem one would first decide whether the distributions were of a known parameterized class. If so, one would develop the estimators (e.g., moments) for that situation.

Or, if not known whether parameterization is applicable, one would attempt to determine whether there is a suitable structural relation among the distributions, as, e.g., translates. If so, the solutions can be brought to bear.

If neither of these are apparent, one is left somewhat in the dark. Merely getting the over-all distribution is useless. Physical knowledge of the problem or generating process can guide one in deciding something of the nature of the distributions or of the probability structure.

All of this treatment of *nonsupervised* learning has focused on a precise probabilistic-statistical model wherein any degree of over-lap is allowed among the category distributions and where solutions converge to the irreducible optimum. The questions of structure and of deriving convergent estimators are directed primarily toward those (more difficult) situations of large measure of over-lap. In a problem, however, where the distributions are far apart and essentially disjoint, the exact nature of the distributions or of the structure is not important, and there will be essentially disjoint clusters corresponding to the different categories. One can then proceed to get the over-all distribution and thereby the component clusters. Such fortunate situations cannot be counted upon, however. But, in practice, some pattern recognition problems do allow for almost perfect classification, and for these problems the distributions are essentially disjoint. (Perhaps, in a way, it might be said that their disjointedness is their structure. Although, in some cases the category distributions can be mutually disjoint yet close and in fact have interleaved modes, in which cases structural information continues to be important.) For such problems, effort to achieve *nonsupervised* learning can be directed simply to developing the most effective algorithms.

REFERENCES

1. Wilks, S.S., "Mathematical Statistics". Wiley, New York, 1962.
2. Cooper, D.B., and Cooper, P.W., Nonsupervised adaptive signal detection and pattern recognition. *Information and Control, 7*, 416–444 (1964).
3. Wald, A., "Statistical Decision Functions". Wiley, New York, 1950.
4. Van Meter, D., and Middleton, D., Detection and extraction of signals in noise from the point of view of statistical decision theory. *Jnl. Soc. of Industrial and Applied Math.*, part I, *3*, 192–253 (1955) and part II, *4*, 86–119 (1956).
5. Anderson, T.W., "An Introduction to Multivariate Statistical Analysis". Wiley, New York, 1958.
6. Cover, T., Geometrical and statistical properties of systems of linear inequalities and applications in pattern recognition. *IEEE Trans. on Electronic Computers, EC–14*, 326–334 (1965).
7. Cooper, P.W., Hyperplanes, hyperspheres, and hyperquadrics as decision boundaries. *In* "Computer and Information Sciences" (J.T. Tou and R. H. Wilcox, eds.), 111–138. Spartan Books, Washington, D.C., 1964.
8. Watanabe, S., *etal.*, Evaluation and selection of variables in pattern recognition. *In* "Computer and Information Sciences–II" (J.T. Tou, ed.), 91–122. Academic Press, New York, 1967.
9. Tou, J.T., and Heydorn, R.P., Some approaches to optimum feature extraction. *In* "Computer and Information Sciences–II" (J.T. Tou, ed.), 57–89. Academic Press, New York, 1967.
10. Abramson, N., and Braverman, D., Learning to recognize patterns in a random environment. *IRE Trans. on Information Theory, IT–8*, 558–563 (1962).
11. Daly, R.F., The adaptive binary detection problem on the real line. *Stanford University Tech. Report* 2003–3 (1962).
12. Jakowatz, C.V., Shuey, R.L., and White, G.M., Adaptive waveform recognition. *In* "Information Theory" (C. Cherry, ed.), Butterworths, Washington, 1961.
13. Hinich, M.J., A model for a self-adapting filter. *Information and Control, 5*, 185–203 (1962).
14. Cooper, D.B., On the existence of nonsupervised adaptive signal detectors; and detector estimation using stochastic approximation methods. *Ph.D. doctoral dissertation*, Columbia University, New York, April 1966.
15. Medgyessy, P., "Decomposition of Superpositions of Distribution Functions". Hungarian Academy of Sciences, Budapest, 1961.
16. Teicher, H., Identifiability of finite mixtures. *Annals of Math. Stat., 34*, 1265–1269, (1963).
17. Robbins, H., The empirical Bayes approach to statistical decision problems. *Annals of Math. Stat., 35*, 1–20 (1964).
18. Cooper, P.W., Some topics on nonsupervised adaptive detection for multivariate normal distributions. *In* "Computer and Information Sciences–II" (J.T. Tou, ed.), 123–146. Academic Press, New York, 1967.
19. Fralick, S.C., Learning to recognize patterns without a teacher. *IEEE Trans. on Information Theory, IT–13*, 57–64, (1967).
20. Cooper, D.B., and Cooper, P.W., Adaptive pattern recognition and signal detection without supervision. *IEEE Intern. Conv. Record, Part I*, 246–256 (March 1964).

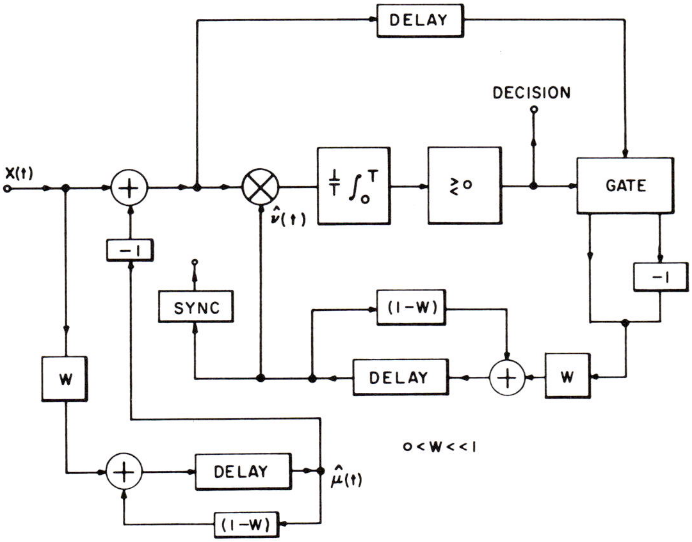

Figure 1: A Synchronous NASD

LEARNING IN PATTERN RECOGNITION

Thomas M. Cover †

STANFORD UNIVERSITY
STANFORD, CALIFORNIA

Abstract

This paper is specifically concerned with the problem of inferring from a finite set of patterns the classification of an unknown pattern. A discussion of the general problems inherent in the concept of "learning" and "data reduction" are discussed from a standpoint of measurement selection for the general pattern recognition problem. A brief history of the existent work in empirical Bayes and compound sequential Bayes procedures will be presented. It is felt that these procedures are basically non-Bayesian, despite their names, and are therefore especially suited to problems arising in pattern recognition. Finally, a discussion is made of some nonparametric approaches to the problem of the classification of an unknown pattern when the only information on the underlying distributions associated with the various categories is that which can be obtained from a finite number of samples.

I. Patterns and Measurements

I.1 THE PATTERN SPACE

This paper is concerned with the general problem of inferring from a set of patterns the correct classification of a new pattern. No attempt will be made to provide an overall point of view or to provide a complete history of the approaches tangent to those considered herein. I wish simply to present several trains of thought on the subject.

Let P be an indexed family of patterns $\{P_\alpha\}$. The indexing of the patterns in P by the parameter α does not imply that P is countably infinite, nor does it imply that the parameterization is "nice" in the sense that

† This work was supported in part by Joint Services Contract NONR–225(83), NR 373 360 and Air Force Contract AFOSR AF49(638)1517.

a being close to a' implies P_a is in some sense close to $P_{a'}$. We mention in passing that the usual distinction between the parametric and nonparametric approaches to statistics (and pattern recognition) lies not in the fact that the set of distributions (or patterns) may be parameterized—since this may always be done—but in the fact that there exists a "nice" parameterization in the parametric case but not in the nonparametric. Thus, in the true parametric case, the parameters should enter significantly into the simplification of the statement of solution of the problem. In the nonparametric case, no parameterization is useful.

The following are examples of possible pattern sets P : the set of all subsets of the plane; the set of all points in Euclidean n-space; the set of all smells, paintings, thoughts, or sensory experiences.

One is tempted immediately to begin to solve the problem, before it is well defined. For example, one might attempt to establish an interesting parameterization on P. Also, it might be interesting to define a "degree of association" of the elements in P or to define a metric on P. There is certain empirical evidence, especially in the field of art, music, and literature, that humans try blindly to compare and order in an attempt to establish a linear ordering on P. (For what it is worth, those who believe in linearly ordering the arts are termed "absolutists" as opposed to "relativists" in the amusing book "Precious Rubbish".)

We shall be concerned throughout this paper with the following fundamental statement of the pattern recognition problem: Let P_1 and P_2 be two indexed families of patterns, and let P be a new pattern. It is desired to associate P with one of the two classes P_1, P_2. On what basis should this assignment be made?

I.2 AN ALGEBRA OF THE SPACES OF MAN'S SENSES

While on the subject of pattern specification, it is appropriate to mention the interesting problem of pattern rerepresentation. I have in mind a systematic description of the algebras of the spaces of man's senses, with special attention to be paid to the formal relationships existing between them. If the rules of combination are well understood in the areas of sight, hearing, smell, taste, and touch, it should be possible to rerepresent the perceptions of one sense in an appropriate form for the perception by another sense. Thus auditory rerepresentations of the visual field for the blind, and visual rerepresentations of sounds for the deaf could be found. It is important, however, that any such rerepresentation be a homomorphism in the sense that the rerepresentation of the superposition of several perceptual experiences in one domain should yield the superposition of the rerepresentations in the other domain. If one object obscures another in the visual field we might like the corresponding sound to "obscure" the other sound in the auditory field. Similarly, complementary images should yield complementary sounds.

Consider for a moment the pattern spaces of sight and sound. Both the ear and the eye are affected pleasurably by pure tones and pure light frequencies respectively. However, the ear has the capability of distinguishing the basic frequency components present in the superposition of a small number of pure audio frequencies. The eye, on the other hand, receives the subjective impression of another pure frequency when presented with the superposition of two pure frequencies. To confuse the picture even further, we note the lack of a corresponding concept in audition to the concept of the color wheel in vision–there are no "primary" audio tones from which the others may be generated.

From these well-known examples and others it may be seen that any attempt to rerepresent one space in terms of another must face the fact that most simple 1-to-1 correspondences will fail to have consistent rules of combination and therefore will not be an adequate sensory rerepresentation.

I.3 SUFFICIENCY IN MEASUREMENTS

In statistics the concept of a sufficient statistic is instrumental in reducing the order of complexity of calculations and the conceptualization involved in hypothesis-testing and estimation problems. For example, $\overline{x}_n = (1/n)\,\Sigma x_i$ is a sufficient statistic for the estimation of the mean of n independent identically distributed random variables $x_1, x_2, \ldots, x_n$ drawn according to a normal distribution with unknown mean and known variance.

Similar considerations may be fruitful in the general area of data reduction, measurement selection, and preprocessing for pattern recognition. Let us introduce the following ideas. Let M be a measurement function, defined on $\mathcal{P}$, taking values in an arbitrary space.

i) Sufficiency with respect to $\mathcal{P}$: M is said to be *sufficient with respect to* $\mathcal{P}$ if M is 1:1. Of course this definition is trivial in the sense that no data reduction is accomplished. M merely rerepresents the patterns. However, several interesting examples of measurements are in this category.

Example. Let M assign to every function P(t), $-\infty \leqslant t \leqslant \infty$, defined on the real line the values that P(t) takes at the points $t = 0, \pm 1/2W, \pm 2/2W, \ldots$ By the Nyquist sampling theorem, if $\mathcal{P}$ is restricted to the set of all band-limited functions with bandwidth W, then M is 1:1.

Example. Let M assign to every subset P of 3-space the set of all its shadow appropriately indexed by the planes upon which the shadows are cast. Then if $\mathcal{P}$ is the set of all convex sets, M is 1-to-1.

Example. Let M assign to every object in 3-space the set of all X-ray photographs of the object appropriately indexed by the directions in which the photographs were taken. Let $\mathcal{P}$ be the set of all everywhere-nonzero X-ray transmissivity functions defined on E^3. Then M is 1:1. It is an interesting exercise to derive an explicit reconstruction scheme for P from its X-rays.

Example. Let M map the horizontal-vertical axes of the visual field into a frequency-time audio signal. (Imagine a black and white scene being played by a player piano or harmonica.) Thus the visual field is rerepresented as a tapestry of sound for the ear. A device implementing this mapping was invented in 1914 under the name "Optophone". Unfortunately, as indicated in the previous section, although the mapping is 1-to-1, the ear does not resolve sounds in the same way the eye resolves visual fields.

ii) Sufficiency with respect to Classification: M is said to be *sufficient with respect to the classification* problem with classes $\mathcal{P}_1$, $\mathcal{P}_2$ if $M(P_1) \neq M(P_2)$, for all $P_1 \in \mathcal{P}_1$, $P_2 \in \mathcal{P}_2$.

Example. Size and shape may be ignored in distinguishing blue objects from red.

Example. Translation, rotation, and scale may be ignored in distinguishing circles from squares.

iii) Sufficiency with respect to an intermediate operation: Let ϕ map $\mathcal{P}$ into another pattern set $\mathcal{P}'$. Then M is sufficient with respect to $(\phi, \mathcal{P})$ if M is sufficient with respect to $\mathcal{P}'$.

Again, this is a trivial definition in the sense that it is merely definition *(i)* with respect to the new set $\mathcal{P}'$. We had the following example in mind:

Example. Let $\mathcal{P}$ be the set of all waveforms. Let $\phi_1(\mathcal{P}) = \mathcal{P}'$ be the set of all waveforms distinguishable in a certain sound conducting medium. Let $\phi_2(\mathcal{P}') = \mathcal{P}''$ be the set of all sound waveforms distinguishable by the human ear. Let M assign every waveform P a canonical waveform with arbitrary preassigned phase relationships among the component frequencies. Then certain physiological evidence indicates that M is sufficient with respect to $(\phi_2 \circ \phi_1, \mathcal{P})$.

iv) Sufficiency with respect to a family of decision procedures: Let $G = \{g_\beta\}$ be a family of decision mappings g_β: $\mathcal{P} \rightarrow \{1,2\}$. *Then* M *is sufficient with respect to* G *and* $\mathcal{P}$ if, for every α, $M(P_\alpha) = M(P_\alpha') \Rightarrow g(P_\alpha) = g(P_\alpha')$ for all $g \in G$.

Example. Let $\mathcal{P}_1$ and $\mathcal{P}_2$ be two indexed sets of points in E^n. If G is the set of all decision procedures of the hyperplane type (in which a hyperplane is passed through E^n in such a manner as to minimize the number of errors of misclassification of $\mathcal{P}_1$ and $\mathcal{P}_2$), then the indices of the patterns in $\mathcal{P}_1$ and $\mathcal{P}_2$ may be forgotten—because a hyperplane rule is "symmetric in the data".

v) Statistical Sufficiency: Let $\mathcal{P}_1$ and $\mathcal{P}_2$ be two pattern sets. Let the random pattern $\tilde{P}$ be drawn according to a probability distribution f_1 if the underlying pattern $P \in \mathcal{P}_1$ and according to f_2 if $P \in \mathcal{P}_2$, where f_1 and f_2 are defined on a pattern space $\widetilde{\mathcal{P}}$. Then M *is sufficient with respect to* (f_1, f_2) if there exists a factorization $f_i(\widetilde{P}) = g_i(M(\widetilde{P}))h(\widetilde{P})$, $i = 1, 2$, where the first factor may depend on i but depends on $\widetilde{P}$ only through $M(\widetilde{P})$ while the second factor is independent of i. This is the well-known factorization criterion [see, for example, Lehman, E.L., "Testing of Statistical Hypotheses", Wiley, 1959, pp. 17–21.]

Example. Let $\mathcal{P}_1$ and $\mathcal{P}_2$ be the single point sets $\{+1\}$ and $\{-1\}$ respectively, and let $P = (\widetilde{P}_1, \widetilde{P}_2, \ldots, \widetilde{P}_n)$ be a vector of n independent identically distributed observations on the underlying pattern P, where $\widetilde{P}_i$ is drawn according to a normal distribution $N(\mu, \sigma^2)$ with known variance σ^2 and mean $\mu = +1$, if $P \in \mathcal{P}_1$, and mean $\mu = -1$, if $P \in \mathcal{P}_2$. The factorization theorem may be used to show that the sample mean

$$M(P) = \frac{1}{n} \sum_{i=1}^{n} P_i$$

is sufficient with respect to f_1, f_2.

II. Data Reduction and Finite Memory

II.1 INTRODUCTORY REMARKS

A great amount of attention seems to have been paid to the general problem of data reduction from the standpoint of reducing the demands on the memory required for a particular data processing scheme. Those data reduction schemes which focus on the existence of many-to-one information-lossless maps and sufficient statistics have only a superficial application to memory reduction, as we shall indicate in the next section. In this chapter we shall mention a new approach, which attacks the memory reduction problem directly. The proofs of Theorems 1 and 2 will appear in [1, 2]. A time-varying solution to the famous two-armed bandit problem with finite memory [3,4] will appear in [5].

II.2 SUFFICIENT STATISTICS AND FINITE MEMORY

Let $X_1, X_2, \ldots$ be a sequence of independent identically distributed random variables (i.i.d. r.v.'s) drawn according to some unknown probability density f(x) defined on the real line. Throughout this section we shall be interested in the hypothesis test $H_0 : f = f_0$ vs. $H_1 : f = f_1$. For a given decision procedure, which assigns each possible observations $(x_1, x_2, \ldots, x_n)$, $n = 0, 1, 2, \ldots$, to H_0 or H_1, we may define $\alpha_n = \Pr\{\text{Decide } H_1 | H_0\}$ and $\beta_n = \Pr\{\text{Decide } H_0 | H_1\}$. Thus α_n and β_n are the probabilities of error of each kind, based on the first n observations, for the given decision procedure.

It is well known that the standard likelihood-ratio decision procedure results in $\alpha_n \to 0$ and $\beta_n \to 0$ exponentially in n, with rates which depend on an information distance between f_0 and f_1. To apply this procedure at time n requires a memory capacity sufficient to store the observations x_1, $x_2, \ldots, x_n$. Thus, even in the simplest case, the memory must grow indefinitely with time. Any truncation of memory to the last k observations, for example—as in the most familiar definition of finite memory [see 3,4]—will preclude the convergence of α_n and β_n to 0, except in the singular case.

It has been frequently observed that the data may be reduced by a sufficient statistic without loss of information. For example,

$$\bar{x}_n = (1/n) \sum_{i=1}^{n} x_i$$

is a sufficient statistic for testing the mean of a normal distribution. However, while it is true the mapping corresponding to a sufficient statistic is many-to-one, and is in this sense data reducing, it is generally not true that the cardinality of the required memory is reduced. For example, in the case of the univariate normal, the mapping from $(x_1, x_2, \ldots, x_n) \in R^n$ to $\bar{x}_n \in R$ leaves the memory requirement uncountably infinite. A possible alternative information-lossless mapping from R^n to R is given by the simple trick of interleaving the digits in the decimal expansions of $x_1, x_2, \ldots, x_n$ to form a single real number. (The possible objection that this mapping lacks the continuity possessed by $\bar{x}_n$ will be obviated shortly.) Clearly, then, if one can store one real number, one may store any finite number of real numbers. We conclude that the statistic $\bar{x}_n$ has not decreased the memory requirement at all.

Particular attention in the work of Dynkin, Spragins, and Abramson [6,7,8] has been paid to the existence of finite-dimensional sufficient statistics (such as $\bar{x}_n$ for the normal). Here, by implication, it would seem that the memory is bounded in some sense by the dimension of the minimal sufficient statistic. Again, from the standpoint of memory capacity, there is no resultant saving in memory. The previously mentioned interleaving decimal expansion yields a mapping of an arbitrary number of univariate observations into a 1-dimensional sufficient statistic, thus accomplishing the same task as the perhaps nonexistent finite-dimensional sufficient statistic.

Even the nice continuity properties of the usual minimal sufficient statistic are not difficult to duplicate. The work of Denny [9,10] establishes the existence of a 1-1 uniformly continuous map of R^n into R, excluding a set of Lebesgue measure zero. If used as a statistic, small errors in memory would be reflected in uniformly small errors in the reconstruction of the data, and conversely. Thus there always exists a continuous 1-dimensional sufficient statistic with respect to $\{f_\theta\}$.

A first step toward defining a statistic with a realistic memory constraint might be to consider rounding off the statistic at each stage. Hopefully, the infinite-accuracy theory would apply directly, and α_n, β_n would still tend to 0, although at slower rates. Even this is not the case, as the following simple example will show: Let $X_1, X_2, \ldots$ be i.i.d. r.v.'s drawn according to a normal $N(\mu,\sigma^2)$ distribution with unknown mean μ and known variance σ^2. We wish to test $\mu = 1$ vs. $\mu = -1$. Observe that the new statistic $\bar{x}_{n+1}$ may be expressed in terms of the old statistic $\bar{x}_n$ and the current observation x_{n+1} in the form

$$\bar{x}_{n+1} = \frac{n}{n+1} \bar{x}_n + \frac{1}{n+1} x_{n+1}$$

Suppose now that $\bar{x}_n$ may be recalled only to some arbitrary decimal place accuracy. Let $[\bar{x}_n]$ denote the rounded-off version of $\bar{x}_n$. Rounding off at each stage results in the algorithm

$$[\bar{x}_{n+1}] = [\frac{n}{n+1} [\bar{x}_n] + \frac{1}{n+1} x_{n+1}] .$$

To what random variable does $[\bar{x}_n]$ converge? The best hope is that $[\bar{x}_n] \rightarrow [\mu]$ wpl. Thus the decision procedure that decides $\mu = \pm 1$ accordingly as $[\bar{x}_n] \gtrless 0$ would result in $\alpha_n, \beta_n \rightarrow 0$. Instead, the worst possible situation occurs. As we have shown in [1], $[\bar{x}_n]$ converges wpl to a random variable which has strictly positive probability mass on each of the countably infinite number of lattice roundoff values. In particular, there is positive mass on both sides of the origin. Consequently, α_n, β_n converge to nonzero limits. So the first realistic approximation to the data reduction problem will not resolve the hypotheses. This is true despite the fact that we have used an eminently reasonable procedure and a countably infinite memory. Apparently the memory-constrained hypothesis testing problem must be approached from first principles.

To our surprise, we find that this same problem may be solved with a memory of only 2 states (1 bit). Consider the sequence of statistics $\{T_n\}_1^\infty$, $T_n \in \{-1,1\}$, defined recursively by

$$T_n = \begin{cases} 1, & x_n > \sqrt{2 \log n} \\ -1, & x_n < -\sqrt{2 \log n} \\ T_{n-1}, & \text{otherwise} \end{cases}$$

$$T_0 \text{ arbitrary} \in \{-1,1\}.$$

We make use of the fact that, for $X_1, X_2, \ldots$ i.i.d. $\sim N(\mu,\sigma^2)$, $\max\{X_1, X_2, \ldots, X_n\} - \sqrt{2\sigma^2 \log n} \rightarrow \mu$, in probability. As a consequence of this and the Borel zero-one law, for $\mu > 0$, the event $X_n > \sqrt{2\sigma^2 \log n}$ occurs infinitely often, while the event $X_n < -\sqrt{2\sigma^2 \log n}$

occurs only finitely often, wp1. A corresponding statement holds for $\mu < 0$. Therefore $T_n \to 1$ or -1 accordingly as $\mu > 0$ or $\mu < 0$. We have thus furnished an example of a 2-state memory which resolves the composite hypothesis testing problem $\mu > 0$ vs. $\mu < 0$ with probabilities of error α_n, $\beta_n \to 0$. We generalize this example to arbitrary distributions in the next section.

To summarize our point of view, we admit the utility of sufficient statistics, finite-dimensional or otherwise, in computation, but doubt their utility in the problem of data reduction. First, for multivariate data, there exist trivial data preserving mappings into the unit interval. Denny's work provides uniformly continuous such mappings. Second, the straightforward sequential rounding off of sufficient statistics generally fails to yield α_n, $\beta_n \to 0$. Thus a memory constraint requires a more careful approach than the simple rounding off of the infinite-memory procedures. Third, we might add that the existence of a finite dimensional sufficient statistic is destroyed by a slight distortion of the distribution (without greatly affecting the resolving power of the old statistic). In this sense, the existence of a finite-dimensional sufficient statistic is a "measure-zero" phenomenon, not to be taken too seriously.

In the next sections we shall provide the beginnings of a theory of hypothesis testing with finite statistics in which the hypotheses are learned despite nontrivial data reduction at each stage. Specifically we shall demonstrate the existence of a four-valued (and in some cases two-valued) sequentially updated statistic achieving $\alpha_n \to 0$ and $\beta_n \to 0$. Sole concern will be with the algorithm

$$T_{n+1} = f_n(T_n, x_{n+1}) ,$$

where the memory (or statistic) T_n takes values in the set $\{1, 2, \ldots, m\}$. Thus the new value of T depends explicitly only on the old value of T and the current observation.

II.3 LEARNING WITH FINITE MEMORY

Let $X_1, X_2, \ldots$ be a sequence of independent identically distributed random variables drawn according to a probability density function f(x). Consider the hypothesis test $H_0 : f = f_0$ vs. $H_1 : f = f_1$. Define the likelihood ratio $\ell(x) = f_1(x)/f_0(x)$. Let us consider f_1 and f_0 such that ℓ is unbounded above and unbounded away from zero, with probability one, under each hypothesis. We shall refer to this as the unbounded likelihood ratio case. The proof of the following theorem is given in Cover [1].

Theorem I: In the unbounded likelihood ratio case, there exist sequences of thresholds $\{\overline{\ell}_n\}$, $\{\underline{\ell}_n\}$ such that the algorithm

$$T_{n+1} = \begin{cases} 1, & \ell(x_n) > \overline{\ell}_n \\ -1, & \ell(x_n) < \underline{\ell}_n \\ T_n, & \text{Otherwise} \end{cases}$$

results in $T_n \to 1$ wpl under H_1 and $T_n \to -1$ under H_0. Thus $\alpha_n \to 0$ and $\beta_n \to 0$ with a 2-state memory, under either hypothesis. With probability one, only a finite number of mistakes will be made by $\{T_n\}$.

There are certain heuristic considerations which make it appear unlikely that learning is possible in the bounded likelihood ratio case. In the Bayesian formulation, for example, where prior probabilities are associated with the two hypotheses, the rule which stores the Bayes decision at each stage will not learn. Eventually the posterior probabilites will be such that no single observation will yield a change in decision.

Fortunately, experiments of arbitrarily large information may be compounded from experiments of bounded information by the artifice of looking for sequences of events before changing the state of the memory. (This point of view yields some interesting comments [5] on the 2-armed bandit problem with finite memory [3].)

Consider the basic problem of testing the compound hypothesis that a coin with bias p has bias $p \geqslant p_o$ vs. the compound hypothesis that $p < p_o$. Note that the general two-hypothesis testing problem with $\{\widetilde{X}_1\}$ i.i.d. may be put in this framework under the correspondence

$$X_i = \begin{cases} 1, & \ell(\widetilde{X}_i) \geqslant 1 \\ 0, & \ell(\widetilde{X}_i) < 1 \end{cases}$$

and

$$P_o = \frac{1}{2}(\Pr\{X_i = 1 | H_1\} + \Pr\{X_i = 1 | H_0\}) .$$

Theorem 2: Let $X_1, X_2, \ldots$ be a sequence of i.i.d. Bernoulli r.v.'s with $\Pr\{X_i = 1\} = p$. There exists an algorithm with a 4-state memory for which the hypothesis $p \geqslant p_o$ vs. $p < p_o$ is resolved with limiting probability of error zero under either hypothesis. (Proof given in [1].)

Example 1: Let $X_1, X_2, \ldots$ be i.i.d. real valued normal random variables with mean zero and unknown variance σ^2. Let

$$Y_i = \begin{cases} 1, & X_i^2 > c^2 \\ 0, & X_i^2 \leqslant c^2 \end{cases} .$$

Note that $\Pr\{Y_i = 1 | \sigma^2\} = 2\Phi(c/\sigma)$. Let $p_o = 2\Phi(c/\sigma)$. Then the 4-state test described in this section will test $\sigma^2 \geqslant c^2$ versus $\sigma^2 < c^2$, with limiting probability of error zero. In the final analysis, we are testing the hypothesis $\Pr\{X \in X_1\} \geqslant p_o$ vs. $\Pr\{X \in X_1\} < p_o$.

Example 2: In the univariate case, let

$$Y_i = \begin{cases} 1, & X_i \geqslant c \\ 0, & X_i < c\,. \end{cases}$$

The test in this section resolves $F(c) \gtrless p_o$, where F is the unknown cdf of x. If $p_o = 1/2$, we have a nonparametric finite-memory test of whether or not the median is greater than c.

II.4 COMMENTS ON THE ALGORITHM

In an attempt to solve the hypothesis-testing problem under realistic memory constraints, we have investigated the straightforward quantization of infinite-memory schemes based on sufficient statistics. Somewhat to our surprise we found that in general such schemes will not learn (i.e. α_n and β_n are bounded away from 0.) However, a different approach establishes that a four-state memory is sufficient for learning under any two hypotheses.

We should remark that the hypothesis-testing problem is essentially infinite in the sense that no finite number of samples yields $\alpha_n = 0$, $\beta_n = 0$, except in the singular case. Thus some capability must be retained for accepting this infinity. The variation of f with n is a natural way to meet this requirement. Thus the algorithm has been factored into two parts. That dealing with the data is finite, while the part concerned with the data processing is unbounded. The important point is that the data processing algorithm $f_n(\cdot)$ is specified independently of the data. We do not cheat by storing data in the description of f_n (See further discussion in Reference 5.)

There is a nice complementary between the theory of Turing machines and that of hypothesis testing with finite statistics. Turing machines have essentially infinite memory (an infinite tape) with finite computation (i.e., an f_n which is independent of n), while the finite-memory algorithm has finite memory and unbounded complexity of computation f_n. Each problem seems to be stated in its most natural form. Bounding the length of the tape for a Turing machine results in a hopelessly combinatorial theory. Similarly, for finite-memory hypothesis testing algorithms, allowing the memory to be infinite yields the theoretical trivial classical hypothesis-testing problem, while restricting f_n to be independent of n yields a hopelessly combinatorial theory which, in any case, precludes the convergence of α_n and β_n to 0.

III. Nonparametric Pattern Recognition

III.1 CHOOSING THE BEST NONPARAMETRIC CLASSIFICATION RULES

Suppose that n labeled observations (x_1,θ_1), (x_2,θ_2), . . . , (x_n,θ_n) are presented and a new pattern (or observation) x_{n+1} is to be classified. Here we assume that the x_i's take values in some observation space and that each θ_i equals 0 or 1. Let $g(x_{n+1}; (x_1,\theta_1), \ldots, (x_n,\theta_n))$ be an arbitrary estimator defined on $X \times (X \times \Theta)^n$ which assigns to every x_{n+1} an estimate $g = 0$ or 1 based on the n training samples. Thus g induces a partition of X into 2 sets, this partition partaking of the randomness of the training set $\{(x_i,\theta_i); i = 1, 2, \ldots, n\}$. Let $G = \{g_\alpha\}$ be a set of such decision rules. For example, G might be the set of all k-nearest-neighbor procedures, for all k, together with all procedures of the separating hyperplane type [11, 12,13]. How is one to select the "best" procedure for the assignment of x_{n+1}?

Either of the following basic assumptions about the homogeneity of $\{(x_1,\theta_1), \ldots, (x_n,\theta_n), (x_n,\theta_{n+1})\}$ will suffice for our further remarks:

i) $(x_1,\theta_1), \ldots, (x_{n+1},\theta_{n+1})$ is a collection of n+1 independent identically distributed random variables. Dependence between x and θ is allowed.

ii) $\tilde{x}_1, \tilde{x}_2, \ldots, \tilde{x}_n, \tilde{x}_{n+1} \in X$ and $\tilde{\theta}_1, \tilde{\theta}_2, \ldots, \tilde{\theta}_n, \tilde{\theta}_{n+1} \in \Theta$ are arbitrary sequences. A permutation π of $\{1, 2, \ldots, n+1\}$ is chosen at random according to a uniform distribution on the set of (n+1)! permutations. Then the assignment $x_i = \tilde{x}_{\pi(i)}$; $\theta_i = \tilde{\theta}_{\pi(i)}$; $i = 1, 2, \ldots, n+1$, is made.

Let $S(\hat{g})$ be the proportion of incorrect assignments obtained by $\hat{g}$ when $\hat{g}$ is used to assign each of the x_i's, $i = 1, 2, \ldots, n$ in terms of the remaining x_i's. To be precise, let σ be a permutation of $\{1, 2, \ldots, n\}$. Let $\delta(\theta,\hat{\theta}) = 1$ or 0 accordingly as $\hat{\theta} \neq \theta$ or $\hat{\theta} = \theta$. Then $S(\hat{g}) = 1/n! \sum_{\sigma} \delta[\theta_{\sigma(i)} ; \hat{g}(x_{\sigma(i)} ; (x_{\sigma(j)}, \theta_{\sigma(j)}), j = 1, 2, \ldots, n, j \neq i)]$. Observe that $0 \leqslant S(\hat{g}) \leqslant 1$. Now, for a given $\hat{g}$, $S(\hat{g})$ will be a random variable, the distribution of which is governed by the distribution of the (x_i,θ_i)'s.

It is understood that $\hat{g}$ will be used to classify x_{n+1} in the following randomized way. First a permutation σ of $\{1, 2, \ldots, n\}$ will be chosen according to an equiprobable distribution on the n! permutations, and then x_{n+1} will be given the classification $\hat{\theta}_{n+1} = \hat{g}(x_{n+1} ; (x_{\sigma(1)}, \theta_{\sigma(1)}), \ldots, (x_{\sigma(n-1)}, \theta_{\sigma(n-1)}))$. The permutation σ plays the role of symmetrizing the data so that the order in which the observations occur is irrelevant. Clearly this precaution is unnecessary under assumption *(i)*. Note also that the $(x_{\sigma(n)}, \theta_{\sigma(n)})$ sample is deleted so that $\hat{g}$ is defined on the same number of variables for which it was evaluated. We define the risk, or probability of error, of this procedure to be $R(\hat{g})$ where

$$R(\hat{g}) = \Pr\{\hat{\theta}_{n+1} \neq \theta_{n+1}\},$$

where the probability is taken with respect to the distribution of the (x_i,θ_i)'s (under either assumption *i)* or *ii)*) as well as the distribution on σ.

Now we note the interesting fact that $S(\hat{g})$ is an unbiased estimate of the probability of error in using $\hat{g}$ on x_{n+1} in the sense that $E\{S(\hat{g}) | R(\hat{g})\} = R(\hat{g})$ where again the expectation is taken over the distribution on $(x_1, \theta_1), \ldots, (x_n, \theta_n)$ and σ. We shall not give the simple proof here.

The optimal classifier in $G = \{g_a\}$ is the one which minimizes $R(g_a)$. Since, in the nonparametric case, $R(g_a)$ is unknown, we propose to choose the classifier which minimizes $S(g_a)$. The hazards are obvious—comparing means on the basis of the comparison of random variables having the corresponding means may yield arbitrarily poor results, depending on the distributions. In spite of this, I feel that this procedure will result in good decision rules in practice. The next section illustrates some of the families of decision rules which we have in mind for G.

It may be worth noting that with high probability the best procedure in G may be chosen if one is willing to discard a large portion of the samples. Let the n samples in the training set be divided into k disjoint subsets each containing r samples. Let g be defined on $X \times (X \times \Theta)^r$. Then g will achieve scores $S_1(g), S_2(g), \ldots, S_k(g)$ on the corresponding blocks of data. Under assumption *(i)* the blocks are independent. Thus $S_i(g)$, $i = 1, 2, \ldots, k$, is a set of independent identically distributed random variables with common mean $R(g)$. Hence

$$S = \sum_{i=1}^{k} S_i(g)/k$$

is an unbiased estimate of $R(g)$ for which the variance tends to zero at the rate $0(1/k)$.

Notice that G dichotomizes the family of all distributions $\{f_a(x,\theta)\}$ into sets for which G does and does not perform well. This point of view complements the usual point of view in which a nonparametric family of probability distributions $\{f_a(x,\theta)\}$ is presented and one is asked to find a set G of reasonable decision procedures with respect to it. Here, we specify G first and then ask for the natural family (or families) of distributions for which G is best suited.

III.2 NEAREST NEIGHBOR ESTIMATE OF THE BAYES RISK

Let $(x_1, \theta_1), (x_2, \theta_2), \ldots, (x_n, \theta_n)$ be a set of n independent identically distributed random variables drawn according to a joint probability density $f(x,\theta)$. Let $\Theta = \{1,2\}$. If f is known, the minimum risk incurred in estimating the unknown parameter θ associated with a random variable observation x is defined to be the Bayes risk R^* (see Section IV.2). Now suppose that we are in the nonparametric case in which the only knowledge of f is that which may be inferred from the n samples. In the previous section we have asked how to classify a new sample. The question we ask here is "What is R^*?".

We wish to propose a "deleted nearest-neighbor" rule as a measure of the *intrinsic complexity* or *interleavedness* of the data in the classification problem. As a biproduct, an estimate of the Bayes risk will be obtained.

To be specific, let R_{n-1} denote the probability that the nearest neighbor to the ith observation x_i has a different classification from x_i, where the probability is defined with respect to the overall distribution of $\{(x_i,\theta_i)\}_1^n$. (Since the (x_i,θ_i)'s are independent identically distributed, R_n is independent of i.) Let S_{n-1} = [number of indices i = 1, 2, . . . , n for which the classification of the nearest neighbor to x_i disagrees with θ_i]/n. Since S_{n-1} may be considered the sum of identically distributed 0-1 random variables each with mean R_{n-1}, we see that

$$E\{S_{n-1}\}=R_{n-1} .$$

Now, R_{n-1} is seen to be, by definition, the (n−1)-sample nearest-neighbor risk investigated in Cover and Hart [11]. In that investigation it was proved that $R_n \to R_\infty$, almost without restriction on f, where $R^* \leqslant R_\infty \leqslant 2R^*(1-R^*)$. It is further shown in Cover [14] that, under slight further assumptions on the allowable family of f's, $R_n \leqslant R_\infty + c/n^2$, where c is some constant depending on f. Thus we see that the score S_{n-1} of the NN rule is a random variable having the property that

$$E\{S_{n-1}\}= R_{n-1}$$

and

$$R^* \leqslant E\{S_{n-1}\}\leqslant 2R^*(1-R^*) + c/n^2 \leqslant 2R^* + c/n^2.$$

Inverting the two most extreme inequalities we have

$$\frac{1}{2}(E\{S_{n-1}\} - c/n^2) \leqslant R^* \leqslant E\{S_{n-1}\}.$$

Thus R^* is bounded in terms of $E\{S_{n-1}\}$. If it is also true that $S_{n-1} \to E\{S_{n-1}\}$ in probability, as $n \to \infty$, which seems reasonable, then S_{n-1} is more firmly established as a bound on R^* in the sense that

$$\Pr\{S_n/2 \leqslant R^* \leqslant S_n\}\to 1$$

as $n \to \infty$. Thus we claim that the interval $[S_n/2, S_n]$ is a good estimate of R^*.

For ease of explication, the upper bound $2R^*(1-R^*)$ was replaced by the weaker bound $2R^*$ in the inversion of inequalities. So all the preceding remarks hold for the tighter interval bound $[(1-\sqrt{1-2S_n})/2, S_n]$.

The idea that the NN risk may be used to bound the Bayes risk seems to have been arrived at independently by Cover, Hart, and Whitney[15].

Whether or not it is felt that n is sufficiently large for S_{n-1} to be interesting bound on R^*, the score S_{n-1} yields a great amount of information about the interleavedness or intrinsic complexity of the data. In fact, a large difference between S_{n-1} and its limit R_∞ reflects a small sample size with respect to $f(x,\theta)$. Although S_{n-1} is, in this case, a poor estimate of R_∞, it is probably a very good estimate of the best that any nonparametric decision rule may do in terms of the small sample $\{(x_i,\theta_i)\}_1^n$. In other words, we feel that the failure of the NN rule score to be near its limit is a good indication that every other decision rule based on the n samples will also be doomed to poor behavior. A small sample with respect to the NN rule is probably a smaller sample with respect to more complicated data processing rules.

IV. Asymptotically Bayes Non-Bayesian Procedures

IV.1 PRELIMINARY REMARKS

It is clear in many pattern recognition problems that elaborate statistical assumptions are not justified. Certainly this is the case in character recognition problems. But it is equally clear that many procedures from the realm of classical statistical hypothesis testing are eminently reasonable. The procedures arising in Bayes decision theory, in particular, fall in this class. The reasonableness of these procedures suggests that they may be applicable in a wide variety of problems in which the standard statistical assumptions do not hold or do not make sense.

The purpose of the next few sections is to study statistical decision procedures which are variously known, in the engineering literature, as learning without a teacher, and nonsupervised identification, and, in the statistics literature, as compound and sequential compound Bayes decision procedures. It will be shown that, with a little bit of care (sometimes involving the use of randomized decision procedures), Bayes-like decision rules are asymptotically Bayes even in problems in which the concept of an underlying prior distribution makes no sense. However, we wish to first to review the existent Bayes formulation of the sequential decision problem.

IV.2 THE BAYESIAN FORMULATION

Let $\Theta = \{1,2\}$ be a parameter space with two elements. Let $\mathcal{X}$ be an observation space or pattern space. Consider the pattern recognition problem in which the random variable θ is drawn according to the distribution

$$\theta = \begin{cases} 1, \text{ with probability } \eta \\ 2, \text{ with probability } 1-\eta \,. \end{cases}$$

Suppose that a random observation X is drawn according to the probability density function $f_1(x)$, if $\theta = 1$, and $f_2(x)$, if $\theta = 2$, where f_1 and f_2 are defined on $\mathcal{X}$. Let $\delta(x)$ be a decision function defined on $\mathcal{X}$ taking values in $\{1,2\}$. Then, the probability of error R of the decision rule δ is simply given by

$$R = \eta \int (1-\delta(x)) f_1(x) dx + (1-\eta) \int \delta(x) f_2(x) dx.$$

The minimum value R^* of R, over all decision rules δ, is achieved by the decision rule

$$\delta^*(x) = \begin{cases} 1, & \Pr\{\theta=1 \mid X=x\} \geqslant \Pr\{\theta=2 \mid X=x\} \\ 2, & \Pr\{\theta=1 \mid X=x\} > \Pr\{\theta=2 \mid X=x\} \end{cases}$$

where $\Pr\{\theta=1 \mid X=x\} = \eta f_1(x)/(\eta f_1(x) + (1-\eta) f_2(x))$ (by application of Bayes rule). The resulting risk R^* is then $R^* = R^*(\eta, f_1, f_2) = \int \min\{\eta f_1(x), (1-\eta) f_2(x)\} dx$. R^* and δ^* are termed the Bayes risk and Bayes decision rule respectively. We shall frequently draw attention to the dependence of R^* on η, f_1, and f_2 by explicitly writing $R^* = R^*(\eta, f_1, f_2)$ as we have in the last equation.

IV.3 SEQUENTIAL BAYES LEARNING

We shall attempt to review some of the work on the general problem of learning in the classification problem. Let $\underline{\theta}_n = (\theta_1, \theta_2, \ldots, \theta_n)$ be an arbitrary sequence of integers $\theta_i \in \{1, 2, \ldots, k\}$, where θ_i denotes the category of the ith sample. Let $\underline{x}_n = (x_1, x_2, \ldots, x_n)$ be the resulting sequence of random observations, where x_i is drawn according to probability density function $f_{\theta_i}(x)$. It is assumed that the x_i's are conditionally independently distributed (conditioned on the θ_i's). Let $\underline{f} = (f_1, f_2, \ldots, f_k)$ denote the set of k probability density functions on $\mathcal{X}$. We shall be concerned with classifying the x's given various states of knowledge about $\underline{x}$, $\underline{\theta}$, and $\underline{f}$.

Frequently we shall not know the f_i's precisely but only that they belong to some set $\mathcal{F}$. When there exists no "interesting" parameterization of $\mathcal{F}$ the problem lies in the domain of nonparametric statistics. Let us define

$$\overline{L}_n = (1/n) \sum_{i=1}^{n} L_i$$

to be the random variable losses incurred by a given decision rule $\delta(x)$. A 0-1 loss function (i.e., a probability of error loss function) will be assumed. Let R_n be the expected value of $\overline{L}_n$, where the expectation is taken with respect to the distribution on $\underline{\theta}$, $\underline{x}$, $\underline{f}$, and δ.

The earliest, and one of the most ambitious, treatments in the engineering literature of the unsupervised learning problem is given in Cooper and Cooper [16]. They consider the problem in which the θ_i's are independent identically distributed Bernoulli random variables with $\Pr\{\theta_i = 1\} = \Pr\{\theta_i = 2\} = 1/2$. It is assumed that the functional forms of the f_i's are known up to some unknown parameters. The authors show that the classification problem has a solution if the two equiprobable distributions differ only in location parameters. They exhibit a classification procedure based solely on $\underline{x}_n$ and the knowledge of the family $\mathcal{F}$ of all translates of a given prototype density f, which yields an expected proportion of errors R_n such that

$$R_n - R^*(\tfrac{1}{2}, f_1, f_2) \to 0 ,$$

for any $f_1, f_2 \in \mathcal{F}$. Thus the underlying densities f_1 and f_2 are effectively learned from $\underline{x}$.

Fralick [17] considers a learning system in which the prior probability η is unknown and the f's $\in \mathcal{F}$ are known only up to some unknown parameters. The unknown parameters are treated as random variables; that is, it is assumed that the unknown parameters are distributed according to a certain joint prior distribution. The posterior distribution function is updated after each observation x_i by use of Bayes' rule. The formulation is entirely Bayesian. Procedures are exhibited, based on knowledge of $\underline{x}_n$, achieving $R_n - R^*(\eta, f_1, f_2) \to 0$. The novelty in Fralick's approach consists of his formulation of a sequential decision procedure which requires minimal memory of past observations at each stage. The work in Section II was motivated by similar memory-reducing considerations. A summary of Bayesian learning may be found in Spragins [8].

Hancock and Patrick [18] consider an unsupervised identification problem in which little or nothing is known about the family of probability density functions $\mathcal{F}$. It is assumed that $\underline{x}_n$ but not $\underline{\theta}_n$ is known. The sample space $\mathcal{X}$ is divided into a finite number of bins and the resulting empirical multinomial distribution is calculated. From this, estimates $\hat{\eta}_1, \hat{\eta}_2, \ldots, \hat{\eta}_k, \hat{f}_1, \hat{f}_2, \ldots, \hat{f}_k$ are formed of the mixing priors and densities. A Bayes classification rule is used with respect to these estimates.

There are two weaknesses in this procedure. First, no allowance is made for the number of bins to grow with the number of samples. Consequently R_n does not in general converge to the Bayes risk $R^*(\underline{\eta}, \underline{f})$. Second, multinomial distributions are inherently unidentifiable (even when $\mathcal{F}$ is identifiable), and it is necessary for the authors to demand that $2k-1$ samples be drawn at a time from the same unknown distribution. These objections may be overcome by further development of this approach in terms of the work of Parzen [19] and Cacoullos [20], with regard to the question of bin growth; and Yakowitz and Spragins [21] and Cooper [22], with regard to the identifiability problems for $\mathcal{F}$.

IV.4 COMPOUND SEQUENTIAL BAYES LEARNING

The learning without a teacher problem may be compared with parallel studies in statistics by Robbins [23], Samuel [24,25], Van Ryzin [26], Swain [27], and Johns [28]. In most of this work it is *not* assumed that $\theta_1, \theta_2, \ldots, \theta_n$ are independent identically distributed random variables. In fact, there is no probability distribution assumed on the θ_i sequence, in any sense. Nevertheless, sequential procedures will be described which asymptotically achieve the Bayes risk defined on the *empirical* distribution of the actual θ_i sequence encountered. These procedures are commonly referred to as compound sequential Bayes rules following the initial work of Robbins and Hannan [29]. However, since the traditional Bayes structure is lacking, namely with regard to the assumption of a prior distribution on the θ_i's, the problem is essentially non-Bayesian, or, at best, empirical Bayesian. (We remark that the designation "empirical Bayes" refers to a slightly different problem, also introduced and studied by Robbins [Refs. 30–44].)

Samuel [24] considers the compound sequential decision problem in which, at the time of the kth decision, the statistician has knowledge only of $\underline{x}_k = (x_1, x_2, \ldots, x_k)$ and $\underline{f} = (f_1, f_2)$. No distribution is assumed on the θ_i sequence. She exhibits a sequential decision rule $\delta_k(\underline{x}_k, \underline{f})$ which achieves a probability of error $R_n = E\{(1/n) \Sigma_1^n L_i\}$ such that $R_n - R^*(\overline{\theta}_n, f_1, f_2) \to 0$ as $n \to \infty$, uniformly in all θ sequences in $\{0,1\}^\infty$, where $\overline{\theta}_n$ equals the proportion of 1's in $\underline{\theta}_n$. The decision rule used is essentially the Bayes decision rule with respect to a consistent estimate of the empirical prior probability $\overline{\theta}_n$ given by Hannan and Robbins [29]. When $R^*(\eta, f_1, f_2)$ is not a differentiable function of η, the decision rule involves some artificial randomization. When R^* is differentiable, the observations x_i effectively provide the needed randomization, and a deterministic decision rule may be used.

Obviously, in the Bayesian formulation with θ_i's i.i.d., $\Pr\{\theta_i = 1\} = \eta$, it follows that $\overline{\theta}_n \to \eta$ with probability one. Consequently $R^*(\overline{\theta}_n, f_1, f_2) \to R^*(\eta, f_1, f_2)$ with probability one, and R_n approaches the true Bayes risk $R^*(\eta, f_1, f_2)$. Thus Samuels' work demonstrates that, with a small amount of care, possibly involving some artificial randomization, a Bayes-like decision rule will perform optimally in a much wider class of problems than had been previously thought possible [38]. This is characteristic of the compound Bayes approach. In a subsequent paper [25] Samuel obtains stronger results and demonstrates convergence with probability one of $(1/n) \Sigma_1^n L_i - R(\overline{\theta}_n, \underline{f})$ to zero. Robbins [23] extends the results of Samuel to a finite number of states of nature (range of θ) in a general discussion of the empirical Bayes approach to statistics. Tainiter [45] shows that, for an appropriate family of decision rules, $R_n - R^*(\hat{p}_n(\theta_j | \theta_{j-1}, \theta_{j-2}, \ldots, \theta_{j-k}), f_1, f_2)$ converges to zero, for any k, where $\hat{p}_n$ is the *empirical* k^{th} order

Markov dependence exhibited by the sequence $\underline{\theta}_{n-1}$. Swain [27] investigates an estimation problem of similar structure. Thus Markov dependence, real or imagined, may be learned.

Van Ryzin [26] considers the compound and sequential compound decision problem with a finite number of states of nature and actions. Van Ryzin makes precise the artificial randomization and differentiability requirements in Samuel [24] and shows that the rate of convergence of R_n is $0(n^{-1/2})$.

Van Ryzin [46, 47, 48] is able to dispense with knowledge of the underlying densities $\underline{f}$ at the cost of introducing knowledge of $\underline{\theta}_n$. This is the so-called learning with a teacher problem in which the underlying distributions are unknown. Using Parzen [19] probability density function estimators, Van Ryzin finds decision rules $\delta_k(\underline{x}_k, \underline{\theta}_{k-1})$ for which $R_n - R^*(\bar{\theta}_n, \underline{f}) \to 0$, for all θ sequences in $\{0,1\}^\infty$. Johns [28] considers the two-action compound decision problem extended to an infinite number of states of nature and establishes rates of convergence of R_n to the Bayes risk defined on the mth order empirical joint distribution on the states of nature.

The nonparametric unsupervised learning problem in the compound Bayes framework is considered by Alens and Cover [49,50]. Let $\mathcal{F}$ be a family of probability densities, perhaps infinite in number. Nature is allowed to choose an arbitrary set of k probability density functions $\underline{f} = (f_1, f_2, \ldots, f_k)$ where $f_i \in \mathcal{F}$. These are then fixed for all time. She may then choose an arbitrary sequence of categories $\underline{\theta}_n$. The statistician has knowledge only of $\underline{x}_n$ at the time of his decision. After n observations, it is desired to partition $\{x_1, x_2, \ldots, x_n\}$ into k sets (or categories) with minimum probability of misclassification with respect to the true partition induced by $\{\theta_1, \theta_2, \ldots, \theta_n\}$.

For the sake of comparison, consider the statistician who has complete knowledge, not only of $\underline{x}_n$, but of $\underline{f}$ and $\bar{\underline{\theta}}_n$, where $\bar{\underline{\theta}}_n$ denotes the empirical frequencies of occurrence of the categories in $\underline{\theta}_n$. His minimum expected proportion of misclassifications, over all partitioning procedures on $\underline{x}_n$, will be denoted by $R^*(\bar{\underline{\theta}}_n, \underline{f})$. This is the Bayes probability of error, in the one-shot case, with respect to densities $\underline{f}$ and prior $\bar{\underline{\theta}}_n$.

Under certain identifiability and completeness conditions [22] on $\mathcal{F}$ a decision rule is exhibited by Alens and Cover based only on $\underline{x}_n$, which incurs a risk R_n for which $R_n - R^*(\bar{\underline{\theta}}_n, \underline{f}) \to 0$, for every $\underline{f} \in \underline{\mathcal{F}}$ and every infinite sequence $\theta_1, \theta_2, \ldots$. In other words, the penalty the statistician pays for having no knowledge of the classifications or of the underlying statistics is asymptotically negligible, even in the worst possible cases. This represents a generalization of the work of Fralick, Hancock and Patrick, and Cooper and Cooper in that no probability distribution is assumed on the category sequence $\underline{\theta}_n$. Thus this rule is asymptotically Bayes even in non-Bayesian problems. The compound Bayes work of Van Ryzin is also generalized, from cases in which $\underline{x}_n$ is known and either $\underline{f}$ or $\bar{\underline{\theta}}_n$ is known, to the case in which neither $\underline{f}$ nor $\bar{\underline{\theta}}_n$ is known.

Shubert [51], [52] has examined a problem of the compound Bayes type and obtained very exciting results. Consider a decision-maker who knows only the space D of his possible decisions and an observation space $\mathcal{X}$. In particular, he does not know $\mathcal{F}$ nor does he know the range of θ (which may be infinite). Upon the observation of the ith sample x_i, a decision $d \epsilon D$ is made and a loss $L(\theta_i, d_i)$ is incurred. The loss function itself may, moreover, be random with an unknown distribution depending, of course, on θ and d. No statistics whatsoever are assumed on the sequence of θ_i's. After each decision d_i is made, the decision-maker is told the value of the random loss incurred by him.

Under mild assumptions Shubert [52] is able to demonstrate a sequential decision procedure based on $\underline{x}_n$ and $\underline{L}_n$ which has an average risk which approaches the Bayes risk R* of the underlying problem evaluated at the hypothetical prior distribution on θ equal to the empirical distribution of the sequence of parameters $\underline{\theta}_n$. Thus, the decision-maker is performing as well asymptotically as if he knew *i)* the distributions $f_\theta(x)$; *ii)* the random loss structure $L(\theta,d)$; and the (possibly time-varying) empirical "statistics" of the parameter sequence $\theta_1, \theta_2, \ldots$.

V. Concluding Remarks

The mathematical theory of pattern recognition, I feel, is differentiated from the classical theory of statistics in that pattern recognition problems do not generally lend themselves to precise statistical formulations. In this sense the field of nonparametric statistics lies closest in spirit to practical problems in pattern recognition. One role that statistics rightfully plays in pattern recognition is that of testing various ad hoc procedures under carefully specified conditions, thus answering the question, "When is this procedure good?" or "What is the natural class of problems for which this procedure is useful?"

For this reason, we have emphasized throughout this paper various "nonstatistical" procedures. By this we mean procedures which are insensitive to the underlying statistical structure, if any, and are robust in the sense that moderate deviations from the underlying assumptions do not invalidate the qualitative goodness of the procedure. Thus the nearest-neighbor classification ideas mentioned in section III are nonstatistical in the sense that the description of the procedure is solely in terms of the data and depends in no way on the underlying distributions. Nevertheless, when there is an underlying statistical structure, it has been demonstrated that procedures of the nearest-neighbor type are good. Since this goodness is insensitive to the underlying statistics, the nearest-neighbor procedure may also be considered robust in the sense just mentioned.

Similarly, the compound Bayes procedures discussed in Chapter IV are nonstatistical, to a lesser extent, in the sense that the crucial assumption of an underlying distribution on the sequence of nature's choices of classifications is shown to be unnecessary for the compound Bayes procedure to have good behavior with respect to a similar procedure in a closely related problem in which that assumption is made and is utilized.

Finally, we have made some remarks in Chapter III about the problem of letting the data choose the best procedure for use on future data.

Although our remarks on this problem have been quite elementary, we hope that there will be much more of a theoretical nature which can be said. In any case, we hope that experimentalists in pattern recognition will take a careful analytical point of view about their reasons for recommending one pattern recognition scheme over another.

REFERENCES

[1] Cover, Thomas M., "Hypothesis Testing with Finite Statistics", to appear, *Ann. Math. Stat.,* June, 1969. Based on paper "Learning with Finite Memory" delivered at IEEE International Conference on Information Theory, San Remo, Italy, September 1967.

[2] Cover, Thomas M., and Martin E. Hellman, "A Solution of the Two-Armed Bandit with Finite Memory," to be submitted to *IEEE Transactions on Inf. Theory, 1968.*

[3] Robbins, H., "A Sequential Decision Problem with Finite Memory", *Proc. Nat. Acad. Sci., 42,* 920–923, 1956.

[4] Smith, C. V. and Pyke, R., "The Robbins-Isbell Two-Armed Bandit Problem with Finite Memory", *Annals of Mathematical Statistics, 36,* 1375–1386, 1965.

[5] Cover, Thomas M., "A Note on the Two-Armed Bandit Problem with Finite Memory", IBM Yorktown Heights Technical Report RC-1913, October 1967, *Information and Control,* May-June, 1968.

[6] Dynkin, E.B., "Necessary and Sufficient Conditions for a Family of Probability Distributions", in *Selected Translations in Mathematical Statistics and Probability, 1,* 17–40, 1961.

[7] Abramson, N. and Braverman, D., "Learning to Recognize Patterns in a Random Environment", *IEEE Transactions on Information Theory, IT–8,* 58–63, 1962.

[8] Spragins, J., "Learning Without a Teacher", *IEEE Transactions on Information Theory, IT–12,* 223–230, 1966.

[9] Denny, J.L., "On Continuous Sufficient Statistics", *Annals of Mathematical Statistics.*

[10] Denny, J.L., "A Continuous Real-Valued Function on E^n Almost Everywhere 1-1", *Fund. Math.*

[11] Cover, Thomas M., and Hart, Peter, "Nearest Neighbor Pattern Classification", *IEEE Trans. on Information Theory, IT–13,* 21–27, 1967.

[12] Cover, Thomas M., "Estimation by the Nearest Neighbor Rule", *IEEE Trans. on Information Theory,* January 1968.

[13] Cover, Thomas M., "Geometrical and Statistical Properties of Systems of Linear Inequalities with Applications to Pattern Recognition", *IEEE Trans. on Electron. Computers, EC–14,* June 1965.

[14] Cover, Thomas M., "Rates of Convergence of Nearest Neighbor Decision Procedures" paper delivered at First Annual Hawaii International Conference on Systems Theory, January 1968.

[15] Whitney, A.W., Ph.D. Dissertation, University of Missouri, Columbia, Missouri, January 1967.
[16] Cooper, D. B. and Cooper, P.W., "Nonsupervised Adaptive Signal Detection and Pattern Recognition", *Inform. Control, 7,* September 1964.
[17] Fralick, S.C., "Learning to Recognize Patterns Without a Teacher", Rept. SEL-65-011 (TR No. 6103-10), Stanford Electronics Laboratories, Stanford, California, March 1965.
[18] Hancock, J.C. and Patrick, E.A., "Learning Probability Spaces for Classification and Recognition of Patterns With or Without Supervision", TR No. EE 65-21, School of Electrical Engineering, Purdue University, Lafayette, Indiana, September 1965.
[19] Parzen, E., "On Estimation of a Probability Density Function and Mode", *Ann. Math. Stat., 33,* September 1962.
[20] Cacoullos, T., "Estimation of a Multivariate Density", TR No. 40, Department of Statistics, University of Minnesota.
[21] Yakowitz, S. and Spragins, J., "On the Identifiability of Finite Mixtures", *Ann. Math. Stat., 39,* February 1968.
[22] Cooper, D.B., "On the Existence of Nonsupervised Adaptive Signal Detectors; and Detector Estimation Using Stochastic Approximation Methods", Ph.D. Thesis, Columbia University, New York, April 1966.
[23] Robbins, H., "The Empirical Bayes Approach to Statistical Decision Problems", *Ann. Math. Stat., 35,* February 1964.
[24] Samuel, E., "Asymptotic Solutions of the Sequential Compound Decision Problem" *Ann. Math. Stat., 34,* September 1963.
[25] Samuel, E., "Convergence of the Losses of Certain Decision Rules for the Sequential Compound Decision Problem", *Ann. Math. Stat., 35,* December 1966.
[26] Van Ryzin, J.R., "The Compound Decision Problem with m x n Finite Loss Matrix", *Ann. Math. Stat.,* 37, April 1966.
[27] Swain, D.D., "Bounds and Rates of Convergence for the Extended Compound Estimation Problem in the Sequence Case", TR No. 81, Department of Statistics, Stanford University, Stanford, California, June 1965.
[28] Johns, M.V. Jr., "Two-Action Compound Decision Problems", TR No. 87, Department of Statistics, Stanford University, Stanford, California, March 1966.
[29] Hannan, J.F. and Robbins, H., "Asymptotic Solutions of the Compound Decision Problem for Two Completely Specified Distributions", *Ann. Math. Stat., 26,* January 1955.
[30] Choi, K., "A Note on the Empirical Bayes Approach to Statistical Decision Problems", Mathematical Sciences Technical Report No. 19, University of Missouri, 1966.
[31] Choi, K., "Composite vs. Composite Hypothesis Testing (Empirical Bayes Approach)", Mathematical Sciences Technical Report No. 20, University of Missouri, 1967.
[32] Deely, J.J., "Multiple Decision Procedures from an Empirical Bayes Approach", Mimeograph Series No. 45, Purdue University, Department of Statistics, 1965.
[33] Johns, M.V. Jr., "Contributions to the Theory of Non-Parametric Empirical Bayes Procedures in Statistics", Ph.D. Dissertation, Columbia University, 1956.
[34] Johns, M.V. Jr., "Non-Parametric Empirical Bayes Procedures", *Ann. Math. Statistics, 28,* 649–669, 1957.
[35] Johns, M.V. Jr., "An Empirical Bayes Approach to Non-Parametric Two-Way Classification", *Studies in Item Analysis and Prediction,* Stanford University, Stanford, California, 1961.
[36] Kagan, A.M., "An Empirical Bayes Approach to the Estimation Problem" *Doklady of the Academy of Sciences of the USSR, 147,* 1020–1021, 1962.

[37] Miyasawa, K., "An Empirical Bayes Estimator of the Mean of a Normal Population", *Bull. International Statist. Inst. 38,* 181–188, 1961.
[38] Neyman, J., "Two Breakthroughs in the Theory of Statistical Decision Making", *Review International Statist. Inst. 30,* 11–27, 1962.
[39] Robbins, H., "An Empirical Bayes Approach to Statistics", *Proceedings of Third Berkeley Symposium on Statistics and Probability,* 157–164, 1955.
[40] Robbins, H., "The Empirical Bayes Approach to Testing Statistical Hypotheses", *Review of International Statist. Inst., 31,* 195–208, 1963.
[41] Rutherford, J.R., "The Empirical Bayes Approach: Estimation of Posterior Quantiles", Unpublished Paper. Royal Military College, Kingston, Ontario, Canada, 1966.
[42] Rutherford, J.R. and Krutchkoff, R.G., ' The Empirical Bayes Approach: Estimating the Prior Distribution", Unpublished Paper. V.P.I., 1966.
[43] Samuel, E., "An Empirical Bayes Approach to the Testing of Certain Parametric Hypotheses", *Ann. Math. Stat., 34,* 1370–1385, 1963.
[44] Sastry, R.M.V., "Empirical Bayes Estimation in Regression Analysis", Calif. State College at Fullerton, Unpublished Paper, 1966.
[45] Tainiter, M., "Sequential Hypothesis Tests for the R-dependent Marginally Stationary Processes", *Ann. Math. Stat., 37,* February 1966.
[46] Van Ryzin, J.R., "Non-Parametric Bayesian Decision Procedures for (Pattern) Classification with Stochastic Learning", *Transactions of the Fourth Prague Conf. on Information Theory, Statistical Decision Functions, Random Processes,* Prague, Czechoslovakia, 1965.
[47] Van Ryzin, J.R., "Repetitive Play in Finite Statistical Games with Unknown Distribution", *Ann. Math. Statist., 37,* 976–994, 1966.
[48] Van Ryzin, J.R., "Bayes Risk Consistency of Classification Procedures Using Density Estimation", *Sankhyā, Series A, 28,* 1966.
[49] Alens, N., "Compound Bayes Learning Without a Teacher", Rept. SU-SEL-67-019 (TR No. 6151-2), Stanford Electronics Laboratories, Stanford, California, August 1967.
[50] Alens, N. and Cover, Thomas M., "Compound Bayes Learning Without a Teacher" (Abstract) Proceedings of the First Annual Princeton Conference on Systems Theory, April 1967.
[51] Shubert, B.O., "Repetitive Play of an Unknown Game Against Nature", SEL Tech. Rept. No. 6151-3, Stanford University, Stanford, California, December 1967.
[52] Shubert, B.O., "Learning With a Lack of Prior Data", SEL Tech. Rept. No. 6151-4, Stanford University, Stanford, California, December 1967, submitted to *Ann. Math. Stat.*

PARALLEL COMPUTATION IN PATTERN RECOGNITION

Michael J. B. Duff

UNIVERSITY COLLEGE LONDON
LONDON, ENGLAND

1. Introduction

One of the rather curious factors hindering any coordinated attack on the problems of pattern recognition is the difficulty experienced in reaching agreement as to what is meant by a 'pattern'. Because the word has a common everyday usage, its significance is only loosely defined and tends to be appreciated more intuitively than analytically.

The need to give some precision to the definition of the word is felt as soon as one attempts to devise a pattern recognition system. Sooner or later, the question is invariably asked: 'Does the system have any generality or will it only recognise patterns in a narrowly defined field?'

It is convenient, if not essential, to regard any pattern recognition system as including in its early stages some form of input device which will represent the input as an ordered set of numbers. The input may be a train of sound waves, a projected optical image of a page of writing, or a view out of a satellite window; it can be assumed that the essential quality of 'pattern' in the input can be translated into the ordered number set by means of microphones or photocells, together with amplifiers, digitizing electronics, or whatever apparatus may prove necessary. The actual method used, although it may require the application of very sophisticated techniques and a depth of understanding of the properties of the input which may not be readily available, is irrelevant to the present argument. The important assumption is that the input device will not destroy any of that part of the input information which is necessary for the pattern to be recognised by analysis of the ordered number set. Accepting the validity of this assumption, we may now refer to the ordered number set itself as 'the pattern', allowing us to ignore physical peculiarities of the original input. In order to fix our ideas, let us assume that the numbers are arranged in a square array with twenty rows and twenty columns. Initially, and for the sake of simplicity, we may further assume that the numbers can take only the values one or zero.

There would seem to be two opposing definitions of what is meant by a pattern, using the model we have discussed as a basis for the argument:

1. A pattern is *any* arbitrary ordered set of numbers, each representing particular values of a finite number of variables (in our example: 400). Each arbitrary set is given a label which thereby defines its class, with the result that two such sets might be associated within a particular class, although there may be no obvious similarity between the two sets.

2. A pattern is an ordered set of numbers, each representing particular values of a finite number of variables, in which there are certain *definable relationships* between the numbers in the set, involving both the values of the numbers and their positions in the set. Two such sets would only be given the same classifying label if they are observed to conform to the same definable relationships.

Formally, there would appear to be no essential difference between these two definitions, since it is possible to find common relationships in any number of arbitrarily selected number sets, although one should not expect such relationships to be either simple or obvious. For example, the four patterns (e) to (h) in Figure 1 are results of applying the same random spatial transformation to the figures (a) to (d). The four transformed figures, whilst appearing to have nothing in common, need only the inverse transformation to reveal their intrinsic similarity, although to an observer without a knowledge of their origin, they would appear to be four unrelated random patterns.

Thus the difference between the two definitions lies in the *simplicity* of the definable relationships within the sets. Patterns best described by the first definition include arrays of parameters whose values indicate the state of a control system. Recognition of the pattern implies recognition of the current state of the control system and hence, the appropriate control action to be taken. Aleksander[1] has devised methods to deal with this class of pattern.

The second definition seems closer to the popular idea of what a pattern should be. Number sets showing simple internal relationships are likely to look like patterns when displayed graphically. It can be surmised intuitively that numbers which are near together in the ordering of the set, or which can be brought close together by a simple transformation, will be strongly coupled. Two numbers are said to be coupled if knowledge of the value of one of them leads to a knowledge of the value of the other with a certainty greater than that of a statistical guess. The stronger the coupling, the higher will be the certainty.

It will be noted that this concept has much in common with the idea of *clustering* of points in n-dimensional space. Transforms which lead to clustering are a necessary prerequisite to the construction of hyperplanes for the separation of points in n-dimensional space into class clusters (see, for example, Sebestyen[2] for a discussion of this process). Restatement of the idea in its present form, however, leads more naturally to the local operator concept.

2. Pattern Types

It is pertinent to ask what types of pattern would be included in the second definition. The five principal types of pattern are, retaining the number set representation:

(a) *Random Patterns,* being patterns of the type described in the first definition.
(b) *Point Patterns,* in which the essential quality of the pattern could be represented by a set of points distributed with a particular relative orientation in the input field.
(c) *Texture Patterns,* in which there is a repetition of well defined groups across the input field (although the group itself may be a random pattern; it is the presence of repetition which is significant here).
(d) *Line Patterns,* figures in which the essential quality of the pattern could be represented by a system of zero width lines (connected points).
(e) *Area Patterns,* figures in which the essential quality of the pattern could be represented by a system of areas. (For example, note that a circle is obviously a line pattern, as is, perhaps, an annulus of finite width, but a disc must be regarded as an area pattern if confusion with a circle is to be avoided).

Composite patterns, involving all or some of these five main properties, can often be treated as being essentially in one of the five classes. It is considered that patterns of types (b) to (e) are all included in the second definition of the word 'pattern'.

As an example of the coupling process within patterns, consider the texture pattern shown in Figure 2. The repeated group is the four by four set comprising three ones and thirteen zeros. Suppose it is known that a sample pattern is of the class shown in Figure 2 and further suppose that one particular element of the array is known to have the value one. Then it can be said with certainty that the immediate ring of eight neighbours surrounding the given number will contain exactly two ones and six zeros. If, on the other hand, the given element is a zero, then the chances of the neighbouring ring containing 0, 1, 2 or 3 ones are approximately 7½%,

54%, 31% and 7½% respectively, giving the average chance of any particular neighbour being a one to be 17.3%. This compares with 12½% for a random pattern of the same density. Prediction based on the calculated figure for the pattern will therefore be more reliable than prediction based on the pattern density. However, note that if two adjacent ones are located and given, then it becomes immediately possible to fill in the details of the entire input pattern. If slight irregularities in the pattern are allowed, then the estimate of the pattern details should at least give a good approximation to the input.

3. Local Operators

This philosophy leads to the local operator concept. A local operator acts on groups of close neighbours in the number set and can be devised so as to be sensitive to particular relationships between the members of the neighbour groups. For example, the pattern shown in Figure 2 could be detected by a local operator which responded to rings comprising two ones and six zeros, surrounding each one. But the same operator would respond equally well to the same pattern after translation or rotation. If this is not acceptable, then an operator with orientational properties must be used in preference to the simple counting operator.

It is common practice to use certain local operators to preprocess patterns prior to their recognition. The best known of these is the smoothing operator. A neighbour set of numbers is summed and the sum compared with a predetermined level, called a threshold. If the sum is equal to or exceeds the threshold, a one is passed on to the next stage of processing. If the sum is less than the threshold, a zero is passed on to the next stage. The process is repeated over the entire field of the pattern. This type of operator can be used to fill gaps in line patterns, to thicken lines, or to remove small irregularities. It is usual to take a symmetrical group, such as a square array, for this operator, with the result that the operator is almost non-directional in its action. Such directional properties that it has stem from the intrinsic 'squareness' of the summation group and the finite number of elements in the group. A square array has only two axes of symmetry, vertical and horizontal. Three axes of symmetry are exhibited by a hexagonal array, resulting therefore in some reduction in the directional action of the smoothing operator.

Other non-directional operators include those designed to eliminate either ones completely surrounded by zeros or zeros completely surrounded by ones (these are noise removal operators), edge or contrast detectors, line end and line junction detectors, and other operators with properties which are less easily described.

It is interesting to note at this point that Lewis and Coates[3] in their book 'Threshold Logic' expound the view that all logical functions can be represented by a particular combination of threshold gates, the general form of which is illustrated in Figure 3. Two forms of the gate are necessary in order to cope with the requirement for inversion. The gate is a summation unit, the sum being compared with the threshold t in the usual way. To take two simple examples: a three input AND gate would require $t = 2\frac{1}{2}$ whereas a three input OR gate would require $t = \frac{1}{2}$. The local operators which have been discussed so far can obviously be achieved by means of the threshold gate. Lewis and Coates discuss the relevance of this method to pattern recognition in Chapter 10 of their book.

Not all local operators are designed to be direction independent. Following investigations which have been made on the visual systems of various animal species, interest has been aroused in the potential use of operators with distinct directional properties. In this connection, a study of the visual system of the frog by Lettvin *et al*[4] has resulted in a device constructed by Herscher and Kelley[5] which simulates the known properties of the system. The work of Hubel and Wiesel[6] on the visual cortex of the cat has, for example, provided clear evidence of local operators designed to detect line elements at particular orientations in the retinal field. Attempts are being made by Evans and his collaborators[7] to relate measurements of the type made by Hubel and Wiesel to the human visual system, using stabilised retinal images as the experimental stimulus, and verbal reporting as the experimental probe.

It is encouraging that the intuitively satisfying definition of a pattern, the second previously stated, leads to the local operator concept, which might well be the basis of the human pattern recognition system. Human observers are not equipped to recognise random arrays of dots spread over a large field and would seem to be unable to co-classify such patterns unless some simple internal relationships are present.

4. Parallel Operation

If a local operation is to be carried out at every point of an input field, then there is a choice between carrying out these operations either serially or in parallel. When the process is to be performed within a conventional digital computer, then the choice does not exist; its operation is bound to be serial. But if special hardware is to be constructed, then the choice must be made. Furthermore, a fully parallel system would have a parallel input, parallel processing and a parallel output. It might be thought advisable to construct a system in which only one or more of these is parallel, the others being serial. There would appear to be three major considerations:

(a) Which system is likely to be most economic in hardware?
(b) Which system should give the highest throughput of data?
(c) Which system allows the use of the most effective logic, within limitations imposed by (a) and (b)?

Economy in hardware can be a rather misleading factor since costs of microminiature circuit blocks are falling rapidly at the present time. Also, the ubiquity of serial circuitry in digital computers has led to very low prices for certain circuit elements. Another factor is that, at the present state of development of parallel circuitry, it is far less easy to construct multipurpose parallel hardware than multipurpose serial hardware, so that adaptability tends to be cited as an economic advantage of serial systems. Nevertheless, it can be shown that parallel systems can compare favourably with serial systems when a well defined function is intended.

On the question of throughput there can be no doubt. Unless the multiplication of circuitry in the parallel system makes it impracticable to use fast components, then one might expect speeds which are of the order as many times faster than the serial system as there are channels through the parallel system. In practice this would appear to be a gross underestimate especially when input and output times are included in the comparison.

The final point, which is in many respects the most important point, concerns the effectiveness of the logic. Can it be said that every physical system can be simulated in a serial digital computer? Clearly, this will depend on how well the system is understood before simulation is attempted, and on how many parameters are required to describe the various interactions between the elements of the system to be represented. One of the most successful ways of solving complex problems has been to set up an analogue model and to allow the model to provide a solution in real time. It should be noted, however, that the process is, in essence, parallel. The serial nature of the solution method is merely a representation of a sequence of events in the history of the process being simulated, not a serial representation of events which actually take place simultaneously in different regions of the system.

It is a matter for discussion as to whether the character of a pattern recognition process is such that a parallel representation is likely to be the most fruitful. It has been opinioned that too much notice has been taken of physiological neural parallel circuitry, which might well be designed so as to allow circuit redundancy and regeneration rather than as a maximally efficient logical circuit. Notwithstanding this objection, it would surely be foolish to ignore this evidence from what is indisputably a highly effective working system.

5. UCPR1

UCPR1 is a system for the automatic location of vertices in bubble chamber track photographs.[8] It was originally conceived as a preliminary stage of processing to precede a polar scanner device for the measurement of tracks radiating from vertices[9, 10]. The work now being carried out should be regarded as the first stages in an extensive study of automatic pattern recognition. In fact, wherever possible, attempts are being made to generalise the problem and to eliminate those parts which are peculiar to a particular class of input data.

Three guiding principles have been adopted in the research programme:

(a) Only parallel input, parallel processing systems are being considered.
(b) Components and methods which are fundamentally incapable of being microminiaturised will not be used.
(c) Wherever possible, physiological systems will be examined with a view to incorporating useful techniques in the designs.

UCPR1 was first designed and simulated on an Atlas Computer. The simulation did not take into account the precise electrical characteristics of the circuits to be used, but was an accurate representation of the logic employed.

The complete logic diagram is shown in Figure 4. The input system comprises a 20 by 20 square array of Mullard ORP60 photodetectors mounted in a reflecting grid. Each detector is followed by a two transistor amplifier which saturates when the photodetector is at least 40% obscured. The amplifier outputs are then grouped in sets of 3 by 3 and summed, the summation being compared with a threshold of 2 units. Each output will take part in nine such summations.

This smoothing operator is followed by a second summation; this time, the summation group is the sixteen points which surround the original 3 by 3 array. The threshold can be varied from 16 units down to zero and is used to search for the highest sum in the summation field. A vertex is characterised by a sum, somewhere in its locality, which exceeds 11 units, this being the maximum count which can be obtained from a straight line of unit width at the input.

A display bank of pilot bulbs is used to indicate those points which have summations exceeding the current value of the threshold. A control circuit is incorporated to allow the threshold to be swept from high to low values, halting the sweep as soon as a vertex is found anywhere in the field. Alternatively, the threshold can be preset at a fixed level. The full circuit diagram of the logical system is shown in Figure 5. Constructional details of the apparatus, which is illustrated in Figure 6, are given in a published paper.[8]

A vertex in a bubble chamber track is a special case of a junction or sharp direction change in a line pattern. UCPR1 can therefore be regarded as a system for locating such features in line patterns. Further design studies have been carried out, and construction work commenced, to extend the range of the system to include the detection of line ends and also to enable ends and vertices to be separately detected in up to nine regions in the output field. With the existing system, it is possible to detect vertices in four fixed regions; this facility permits the identification of a stylised font of ten numerics. It is expected that the new arrangement will considerably extend the range of the method. UCPR1 should provide a useful test-bed for the practical evaluation of local operators, particularly those in which component characteristic spreads are likely to modify the properties of the operators.

6. Acknowledgements

The author is grateful to Dr. B. M. Jones and Mr. L. J. Townsend, both of whom have contributed to this paper in many useful discussions, and to the Science Research Council for their support of some of the work discussed.

REFERENCES

1. Aleksander, I., Proc. of Spring Joint Computer Conf., pp. 707–712 (1967).
2. Sebestyen, G. S., Decision-Making Processes in Pattern Recognition, p. 11 (1962), (Macmillan).
3. Lewis, P. M. & Coates, C. L., Threshold Logic, Chapters 1 & 10 (1967), (Wiley).
4. Lettvin, J. Y., Maturana, H. R., McCulloch, W. S. and Pitts, W. H., What the Frog's Eye Tells the Frog's Brain, Proc. IRE *47*, pp. 1940–1951 (1959).
5. Herscher, M. B. & Kelley, T. P., Functional Electronic Model of the Frog Retina Trans. IEEE MIL–7, (April-July 1963), pp. 98–103.
6. Hubel, D. H. and Wiesel, T. N., Receptive Fields, Binocular Interaction & Functional Architecture in the Cat's Visual Cortex., J. Physiol. *160*, pp. 106–154 (1962).
7. Evans, C. R., Some Studies of Pattern Recognition Using a Stabilized Retinal Image, Brit. J. Psychol. *56*, pp. 121–133 (1965).
8. Duff, M. J. B., Jones, B. M. & Townsend, L. J., Parallel Processing Pattern Recognition System UCPR1, Nuc. Inst. & Meths. *52*, pp. 284–288 (1967).
9. Robinson, C. J. and Duff, M. J. B., A Polar flying spot scanner for the measurement of bubble chamber photographs, Nuc. Inst. & Meths. *35*, pp. 1–12 (1965).
10. Robinson, C. J. and Duff, M. J. B., The polar scanner, Nuc. Inst. & Meths. *35*, pp. 334–336 (1965).

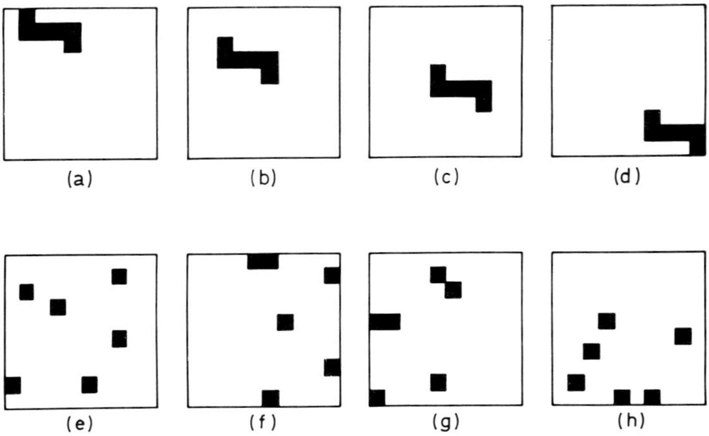

Figure 1

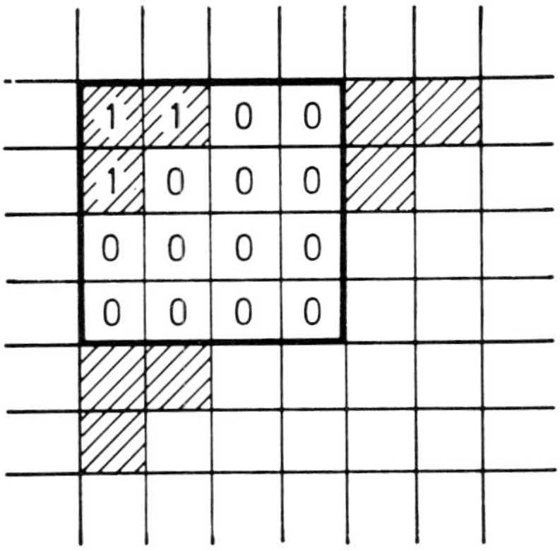

Figure 2

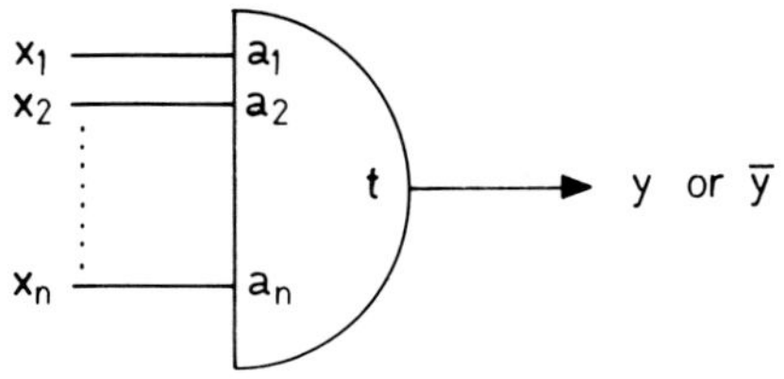

$$y = 1 \quad \text{if} \quad \sum_{j=1}^{n} a_j x_j \geq t$$

$$y = 0 \quad \text{if} \quad \sum_{j=1}^{n} a_j x_j < t$$

Figure 3

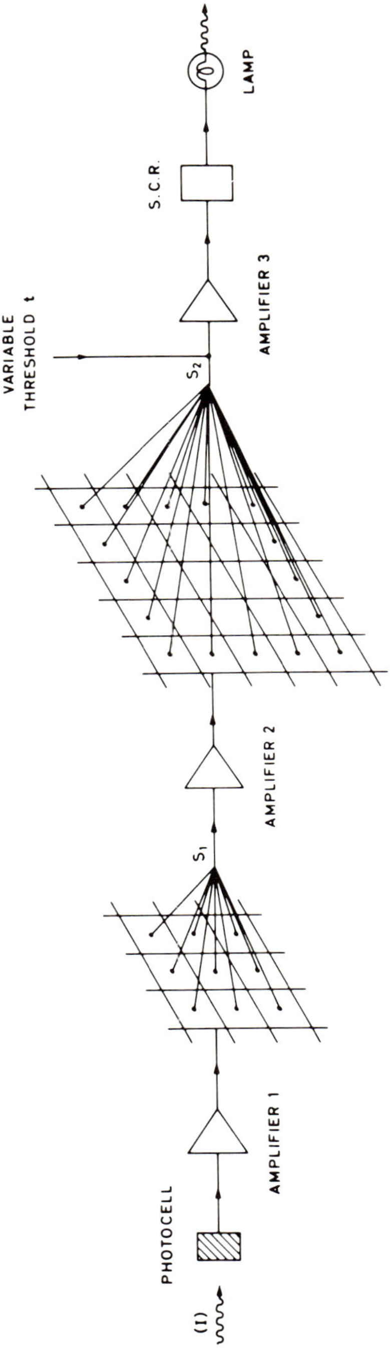

(I)
PHOTOCELL
AMPLIFIER 1
S_1
AMPLIFIER 2
S_2
VARIABLE
THRESHOLD t
AMPLIFIER 3
S.C.R.
LAMP

Figure 4

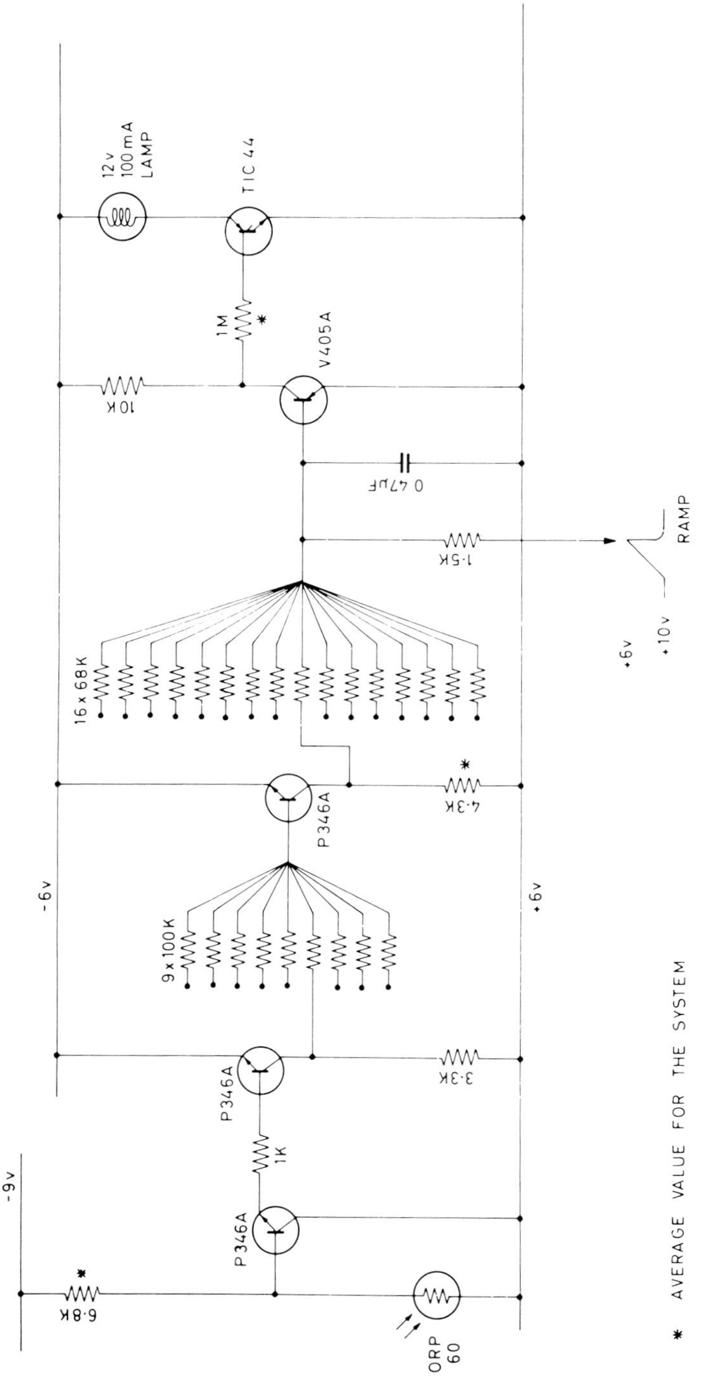
12v
100 mA
LAMP
TIC 44
1M
*
V405A
10K
0 47μF
1·5K
RAMP
+6v
+10v
16 x 68K
*
4·3K
P346A
-6v
+6v
9 x 100K
P346A
3·3K
1K
-9v
P346A
*
6·8K
ORP
60
* AVERAGE VALUE FOR THE SYSTEM

Figure 5

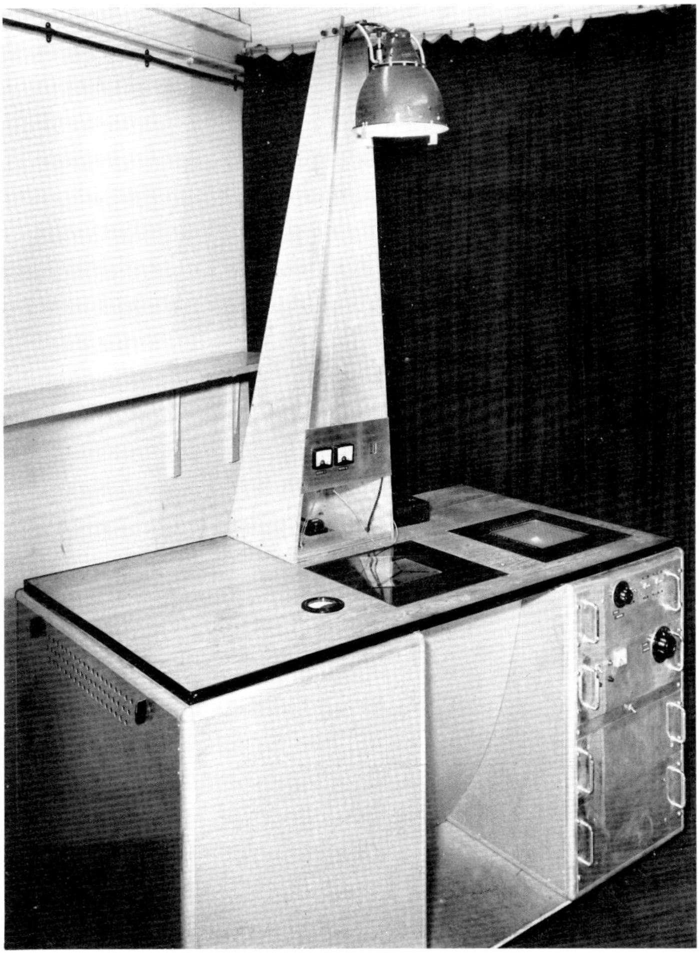

Figure 6

DESCRIPTIVE PATTERN-ANALYSIS TECHNIQUES: POTENTIALITIES AND PROBLEMS

Thomas G. Evans
AIR FORCE CAMBRIDGE RESEARCH LABORATORIES
BEDFORD, MASSACHUSETTS

In examining the application to date of the available pattern-classification techniques, it is difficult to avoid the conclusion that, despite substantial successes in sufficiently limited problem domains (of the order of complexity of, say, isolated hand-printed letters), rather little has been achieved by way of comparable success when the patterns of interest are appreciably more complex. If this evaluation is substantially correct, it is our responsibility to seek the reasons and consider alternative approaches, if necessary. To fix ideas, consider the following paradigmatic sketch of the organization of a "classical" pattern recognizer: the input pattern, perhaps after the intervention of some preprocessing, is examined by a number of "feature extractors" (property filters, attribute detectors) each of which computes a result (typically a single number). These results are passed to a "decision maker," which uses them (and only them) to compute a number which specifies into which one of a number of pre-established categories the input pattern is to be placed. In this purposely rather vague description, we have not, for example, said whether part or all of the device is implemented as special-purpose hardware vs. as program in a general-purpose computer or whether the feature extractors operate in parallel (either physical or logical) vs. in a sequential decision arrangement in which the use of some feature extractors is contingent on the results produced by others. All these details are irrelevant for our purposes here. This loose description has been made precise in many different ways in the literature and much interesting work has been done in exploring, both theoretically and experimentally, the behaviour of a number of such devices, but the details which distinguish one from another will not concern us here, since we wish to consider the problems of applying any representative from the broad class of devices we have described to some class of patterns, to see where the difficulties arise.

The place where the guidance provided by the pattern recognition literature stops is in the design of a suitable set of feature extractors (with the exception of some work on procedures for automatically generating better feature extractors by modifying existing ones and considerable work in choosing a "best" subset of features from a set of available ones subject to various criteria for performance and cost). Thus, one might argue that lack of success in applying the results of work on the above-described pattern recognition model to any particular class of patterns represents simply a failure to develop a suitable set of features for that application. It is no doubt true that, with more sophisticated features, the model can be applied successfully to pattern classes that have not yet been conquered. However, the point of view to be expressed below is that the model itself is inadequate for the treatment of many pattern recognition problems, though the results developed so far in studying this model will in time find a useful place within the study of models of greater scope.

The limitations inherent in the ability of the "classical" model to treat complex patterns are based on its inability to cope with what we think of intuitively as the structure of a pattern and to concentrate its attention as necessary on the subpatterns whose relationships form this structure. That is, the model is a "global" one, capable only of computing a set of properties defined on the whole input pattern, then making a choice based on them. That the model lends itself well to mathematical treatment is inadequate recompense for its failure in this respect. Logically, of course, one can remain within the model and perform any analysis one wishes on an input pattern by burying the complexity of the analysis within the feature extractors. Furthermore, one can then pass on any arbitrary amount of information so obtained as the output by encoding it as a choice of one of a sufficiently large number of pattern categories. As to the latter point, it is worth noting that the practical application of much of the body of knowledge that has been obtained on, for example, convergence of training procedures depends on the number of pattern categories remaining reasonably small. As to the former, if it is necessary to get the desired flexibility by concealing extremely sophisticated processing within the feature-extraction "black boxes," a reasonable inference would seem to be that an excessive proportion of the research effort in pattern recognition has been concentrated on an inadequate model and that the time has come to direct more of this attention to models reflecting more of the desired features.

If we try to formulate a model of a process that may be more appropriate to the treatment of complex, highly-structured patterns, the central notion which arises is that of a description. We are led to talk of what we can call pattern analysis, a procedure which, given a "raw" pattern as input, produces as output a description of it, that is, some structured object (perhaps an expression in a formal language, perhaps something else) that *(i)* is in a form convenient for whatever further processing may be required (this usually means, among other things, that it will be much more compact than the "raw" pattern itself) and *(ii)* reflects the "essential features" of the pattern relative to the purpose for which the pattern processing is being done.

It is perhaps worth remarking that the classical pattern-classification model is a special (two-stage) case of pattern analysis, so defined, where the output of each "feature extractor", usually a single number, is a very simple form of description of the input pattern and the decision-making stage consolidates these descriptions into one description of the input pattern, a single number of specifying one of n categories. Thus the entire effect is a mapping of a class of patterns into one of n possible descriptions. Stretching our notion of description in this way to cover classification would appear to be an empty exercise. However, there seems to be some tendency to think of classification as an end in itself, while talk of description-making more strongly suggests some subsequent use of the description; viewing classification as a special case of description may be useful as a reminder that it is the use made of classification or description which is the reason we are concerned with processing the patterns in question at all. A tendency to think of the problem of classifying hand-printed characters, rather than say, the interpretation of an aerial photograph, as the paradigmatic problem is perhaps responsible for this habit of mind, since in the former case, the classification of the input blob as an "A" is a satisfying terminal point and completely answers the most natural question which comes to mind about the pattern, while, in the latter, a large number of reasonable questions could plausibly be asked.

We have noted that a classification is a kind of description; however, we have in mind a notion of description that contains much more or there would be no reason for the stress we are placing on this idea. To avoid drawing an arbitrary and unedifying line, let us make a very general definition of description; the result of *any* processing of a pattern is a description of that pattern. In a subsequent section we shall consider pattern analyzers for each of which the class of available descriptions is quite precisely defined and is capable of expressing quite rich pattern structures. However, those classes of descriptions, too, will certainly prove inadequate or inconvenient for some processing on some classes of patterns. Thus, in advocating description-based pattern processing, we wish to avoid any commitment to some such particular class of descriptions. However, we are always thinking of descriptive formalisms that at least permit one to talk about subpatterns of any specified types and of relations of any specified types among them and to express a pattern as hierarchially composed of as many levels of such structure as desired.

The notion that description-based techniques for treating patterns have considerable merit is by no means new. In Minsky[1] (1961), for example, the advantages of what are there called "articular" descriptions are quite clearly expressed. Still earlier, Grimsdale *et al* (1959)[2] described a program for the recognition of hand-printed letters that operates by calculating a kind of a description of the input in terms of strokes and matching this description in a fairly complex fashion against stored descriptions of labeled patterns.

In[3] (1963) techniques based on the making and using of descriptions are applied to the solution of a class of figure-analogy intelligence-test questions. Descriptions at several levels of abstraction of the simple line drawings occurring in the test questions are used. The interest of this problem in the present context is that it provides a simple, stylized example of a problem with a strong pattern recognition flavor in which classification techniques are inadequate. Since solution of the test questions typically involves viewing the question figures as composed of parts and detecting changes in the relationships of these parts in passing from one question figure to another, a natural way to proceed is to find, for each problem figure, one or more "reasonable" decompositions into parts, and generate for each an expression stating how its parts are related, that is, build a description, then find possible rules taking one figure into another by processing these expressions. Finally it is necessary to choose a "best" rule from the possibilities discovered and select the corresponding answer figure.

Another example of a program with a considerable element of description-processing is CYCLOPS[4] (1963), which had some ability to separate and recognize overlapping characters by finding in the input the appropriately-related strokes specified by each of the programs (written in a special-purpose language) defining the characters in question. An ambitious effort in analyzing complex visual scenes forms a major part of the work on the so-called "robot project" at MIT under the direction of M. Minsky and S. Papert. Extensive use is made of various kinds of descriptions in the course of the very complex processing required to convert a variety of pieces of partial information into a coherent model inside the computer of what it "sees."

The pattern description mechanisms employed in [2,3] and [4] and the MIT robot project work all have a certain kinship, since the subject matter of each is pictorial (and primarily concerned with contours). However, in each case descriptions were devised on an *ad hoc* basis to meet the particular needs of the task at hand. The "classical" classification model effects a convenient partition between the subject-matter-dependent aspects of a particular problem (represented by the contents of the feature-extractor "black boxes") and the subject-matter-independent classification mechanism. Thus it is possible to study the latter in considerable generality and apply the results so obtained to a wide variety of subject matter. We have advocated consideration of pattern analysis models of wider scope; does this mean that we cannot have such a division; that the creation and manipulation of descriptions must always be entirely on the *ad hoc* basis mentioned above? It appears that this is not the case—a small but growing body of work in pattern recognition reflects a concern with pattern analysis mechanisms in which a sharp separation into problem-dependent and problem-independent portions occurs, along with a stress on user convenience in specifying the problem-dependent part. The influence which initially stimulated this line of development was the prior work in the syntactic analysis of natural and formal languages. There, given a string and a grammar, one performs a syntactic analysis to determine if the string is one of the class defined by the grammar and, if so, to produce the so-called structural description (or descriptions) assigned to the string by that grammar (where such a structural description typically consists of a tree structure expressing relationships between the grammatical constituents into which the string has been analyzed). It is natural to consider the analogy in which a pattern of some sort replaces the string and the linguist's grammar becomes a set of rules in some formalism specifying how sub-patterns may be combined to form larger patterns. The reason for making the grammar explicit and disjoint from the analysis procedure, apart from conceptual clarity, is the same one which has made the notion of a syntax-directed compiler so attractive to many investigators in the programming language field; that is, the same underlying analysis procedure can be applied to a variety of tasks simply by changing the grammar.

A device of the type we have indicated, given any grammar of the form acceptable to it, can produce descriptions, just as a classical pattern recognizer, equipped with an appropriate set of feature extractors, can turn out classifications. Given the motivations we have sketched for working with descriptions as, in many cases, a suitable vehicle when complex processing of complex patterns is required and given the attraction of the generality inherent in the idea of "syntax-directedness," it is not surprising that attempts have been made to design and implement systems exploiting these ideas. In the remainder of this paper we shall give a broad outline of some of the developments to date along these lines and consider some of the problems facing research of this nature and affecting its future prospects.

First it may be useful to try to say something about the degree of generality we shall find. Typically the investigator has chosen some relatively broad class of patterns, perhaps as inclusive as the class of all line drawings. He then chooses a set of primitive objects (i.e., patterns) and one of primitive relations, from which everything else will be built up. For example, the primitive objects might be a set of strokes of various sizes, orientations, and curvatures, with which an arbitrary line drawing could be conveniently approximated. The primitive relations might then specify various ways in which these strokes could be concatenated to form larger objects. Then a formalism is specified in which a set of definitions of new objects can be made in terms of these primitives; that is, one can write a grammar. Two things are still required:

(i) a preprocessor, which given a "raw" pattern, finds the primitive objects and passes them to

(ii) a parser, which, given the preprocessed pattern and any acceptable grammar, produces a description of the pattern in terms of its composition

out of related subpatterns, to any depth required. Thus, for line drawings, if one had built a system rich enough in primitives, one could write one grammar for the English alphabet and another for the Russian alphabet, then do parsing according to either with the same underlying mechanism. Thus, to the extent that a desired change in pattern processing can be reflected simply through changes in the grammar, the partitioning of the processor into a fixed part and an easily modifiable subject-matter-dependent part has been achieved.

Now we can proceed to sketch some of the progress to date. (It should be noted that much of the work referenced below consists of reports on research in progress, rather than published results of finished work.) Narasimhan was one of the first investigators to propose and study syntax-directed pattern analysis methods. He has published two papers[5,6] and produced a number of reports describing this work. In [6] we find one of the few published examples of a picture grammar. Contrived for illustrative purposes only, it defines the printed English alphabet in terms of a few primitive strokes and a simple scheme for concatenating them.

Kirsch[7] in 1964 discussed the analogies between linguistic and pictorial syntax and examined some of the problems involved in trying to exploit this analogy. More recently A. Shaw[8,9] at Stanford and Guzman[10] at MIT have explored grammatical formalisms for describing pictures. Guzman has investigated one scheme in which the primitives are line elements and another in which they are regions. Shaw has introduced an interesting set of primitives in terms of a definition of "head" and "tail" for each primitive and derived object, (with incidentally, physics photographs, as in Narasimhan's case, the principal intended subject matter). Clowes[11,12], Sauvain[13], and Knoke and Wiley[14] have also considered grammatical representations of the structure of line drawings. Kovalevsky[15] has proposed a pattern analysis formalism based on, in effect, a finite-state grammar. Watt[16,17] has considered the problem of constructing a grammar for the Nevada cattle brands, together with the problem of automatically generating the name (blazon) of the brand from its pictorial structure. Ledley[18] has applied conventional string grammar techniques to the analysis of certain classes of pictures, where the boundary of an object such as a chromosome is decomposed into strokes and the linearly ordered list of types so obtained is parsed as a string to identify the object. Rankin[19] *et al* have studied grammars for Chinese ideographs, and Eden and Halle[20] have devised a formalism of strokes and their concatenations as a description of handwriting. Finally, Grasselli[21] has applied syntactic techniques to the analysis of certain classes of fingerprints.

One sub-area of the analysis of patterns that has been extensively studied recently is that of parsing mathematical expressions. With subscripts, superscripts, etc., such an expression can be a relatively complex two-dimensional object. Suppose an on-line computer user wishes to input such expressions using a light pen or Rand tablet. Further, suppose there exists a suitable recognizer for the individual characters as they come in. Thus the result of this "preprocessing" is a list of characters and their x–y coordinates (and perhaps other information, such as size). Now one very often wants a linearized form of the mathematical expression suitable for, say, input to a conventional algebraic compiler. To do this, one needs to analyze the input to determine which characters go with which——in short, to determine the structure of the input pattern according to some concatenation rules. In the system of Klerer and May[22] (where input is by a special typewriter permitting combination of strokes to form symbols), the grammar is implicit; in work by Anderson[23] and Martin[24], explicit grammars and parsing procedures for this problem are discussed.

In general, in any of the work mentioned above in which a pattern parsing procedure was developed, this was carried out in terms of a fixed set of primitives. Thus the grammar rules could be changed relatively easily, but a change in the underlying primitives in terms of which the grammar is written would require extensive changes in the entire system. Work by the author[25] has been aimed in part at removing this restriction. The result is a pattern analysis system of considerable generality in which the inclusion of a new primitive object type (as long as the assumed preprocessor can find it) or a new primitive relationship is almost as easy as a change in the grammar itself. The analyses produced by most of the schemes we have described can be reproduced within this system by defining a few appropriate primitive relations (again, assuming the preprocessing to find the lowest-level objects mentioned in the grammar has been done). Of course, there is the possibility that this generality will be paid for by extremely inefficient parsing. In the present version, considerable attention has been paid, therefore, to optimization, with satisfactory results at least for research purposes (that is, interesting cases can be run in the time available). However, much remains to be done in this direction; it ought to be possible for the user to provide information to the parser about special properties of the primitives or of the input patterns in a much more general way and have it exploit such information to make a more efficient analysis. Work on some aspects of this problem is under way at present. As an example, recall the problem of parsing mathematical expressions. These expressions are "quasi-linear"; that is, they can be thought of as having a linear left-to-right structure with occasional exceptions, and the parsing procedures that have been developed specially for this problem take advantage of this fact to do more efficient parsing. It would be desirable to be able to state such information conveniently to a program and have it used. It is worth noting that, if one knows in sufficient detail the operation of a given parsing scheme, one can often achieve some of the desired effect of controlling the parsing by writing the grammar rules in one particular form rather than in another equivalent one.

Of course, the goal of combining the generality and "cleanness" of the grammar-driven analyzer with sufficiently efficient analysis for large-scale application may well turn out to be unattainable, at least in the relatively near future. In that case, the development may parallel that in the syntax-directed compiler field since it began around 1960, where one can discern a trend away from the "pure" formalisms first introduced toward something more like special-purpose programming languages for use in compiler writing, the loss in elegance and compactness of description being compensated for by the greatly increased flexibility of control placed in the hands of the (presumed expert) user.

Having sketched the present state of this branch of the pattern-recognition field, we pass on to examining (rather briefly) a number of issues raised by this work:

(i) Preprocessing

The syntax-directed approach assumes that a first stage intervenes between the "raw" pattern and the parser, turning the pattern into a set of primitive objects (perhaps with additional information gained during the preprocessing attached to them for later use) which are then passed to the parser. The work we have been discussing makes no contribution to the design of such preprocessing, just as most work on the classical classification scheme makes no contribution to the internal design of feature extractors. There has been considerable work on picture processing techniques (both digital and analog) which transform pictures into other pictures (with the goals of noise removal, contrast enhancement, etc.), but very little on systematically extracting from pictures the kind of information needed for the approach we have been discussing (with some exceptions, e.g., the MIT Robot Project mentioned earlier). At AFCRL Zschirnt[26] has designed a processing logic based on large-scale logic array hardware that should be capable of very rapidly finding and outputting line segments in a pattern input to the processor by photocell. This is a sample of the sort of preprocessing hardware that may ultimately make feasible for practical use pattern analysis methods of the sort we have been discussing. Incidentally, both Narasimhan and Clowes have considered grammars in which the lowest-level primitive objects are points in a quantized picture; thus there is no separate stage of preprocessing. While it is logically appealing to use the same machinery throughout, this approach appears to present formidable combinatorial difficulties, unless one is considering special purpose hardware—as was, in particular, Narasimhan, who was thinking in terms of the ILLIAC III picture-processing computer.

We have talked of a model in which preprocessing is completed, then syntactic analysis takes over. Presumably it would be more efficient to have an implementation in which the operations we have called preprocessing are available instead under the control of the analysis procedure, so that they can be called only as needed during the analysis. To the user (i.e., grammar writer) such a system could look exactly the same as the simpler version. The system described in [9] is organized in this way.

(ii) The Role of the Standard Classification Techniques

At each stage of the syntactic analysis of a pattern, a decision must be made as to whether a certain set of subpatterns can be regarded as the constituents of a pattern defined by a grammar rule. At each such juncture, all the techniques developed in statistical pattern classification theory can be put to use to aid in making such a decision. Also, if statistical machinery is used to produce a reliability estimate for each such decision in terms of the reliabilities associated with the component patterns, one could, for example, choose between alternate possible parsings according to such estimates or decide at some point during the analysis procedure that a parsing had become too implausible to continue. The fact that the research to date in pattern syntax has not made appreciable use of the classical work does not seem to reflect any fundamental difficulty in incorporating it, so much as a desire to concentrate on the novel syntactic aspects by dealing with "noiseless" idealized pattern classes.

(iii) Learning

In connection with the classification model, there exists a substantial body of work on learning schemes, that is, techniques for automatically improving the performance of the decision-making mechanism through exposure to a sequence of correctly-identified patterns, typically by modifying the weighting factors corresponding to the importance assigned in the decision-making process to the output of each feature extractor. We have said nothing of analogous learning techniques for syntax-directed pattern analysis, and in fact, there are no published methods or results. However, there exists the interesting possibility of developing methods to automatically construct a "best" grammar (in terms of given primitives) to "fit" a set of patterns. Such problems are quite difficult, even for string grammars of fairly simple kinds[27]. Some preliminary work on this grammatical induction problem has been carried out on a rather *ad hoc* basis by the author. This work will be continued, with emphasis on looking for more general techniques.

(iv) Overlap

Among the problems of picture analysis with which syntactic analysis techniques can help are difficulties of overlap and hidden lines. In the system of [25], a quite flexible facility is included to permit the grammar-writer to specify what information is to be attached to a newly-created object in terms of the information attached at an earlier stage to its constituents. Together with the "context-sensitivity" permitted in the rule formalism, this facility permits grammar rules to be written that can accomplish the effect of "filling in" plausible hidden lines, if desired. It is not yet very well understood how far this technique can be extended.

(v) Applications

The reader who concludes at this point that there has as yet been no significant application of the syntactic analysis techniques to a real-world problem in pattern analysis would be correct (with the marginal exceptions of parsing of two-dimensional mathematical expressions and some physics pictures). It seems reasonable to expect such application to at least limited cases of photointerpretation within, say, two years. The efficiency of the parsing procedures now available will certainly be improved, but presently-attainable efficiencies are probably not a real stumbling block. The most immediate prerequisite for testing these methods on real problems is pre-processing capable of reducing any real input pattern from some class to a combinatorially manageable collection of primitive elements for input to the syntactic analysis phase.

BIBLIOGRAPHY

1. M. Minsky, "Steps Toward Artificial Intelligence," *Proc. IRE,* Vol. 49, No. 1, January, 1961.
2. R. Grimsdale *et al,* "A System for the Automatic Recognition of Patterns," *Proc. IEEE,* 106B, pp. 210-221, 1959.
3. T. Evans, "A Program for the Solution of a Class of Geometric-Analogy Intelligence-Test Questions," Ph.D. Thesis, MIT Dept. of Mathematics, May, 1963. (Also available as AFCRL Phys. and Math. Sci. Res. Paper No. 64).
4. T. Marill *et al,* "CYCLOPS–1: A Second Generation Recognition System," *Proc. AFIPS Fall Joint Computer Conf.,* November, 1963.
5. R. Narasimhan, "Labeling Schemata and Syntactic Descriptions of Pictures," *Inf. and Control,* Vol. 7, No. 2, June, 1964.
6. R. Narasimhan, "Syntax-Directed Interpretation of Classes of Pictures," *Comm. ACM,* Vol. 9, No. 3, March, 1966.
7. R. Kirsch, "Computer Interpretation of English Text and Picture Patterns," *IEEE–TEC,* Vol. EC–13, No. 4, August, 1964.
8. A. Shaw, "A Proposed Language for the Formal Description of Pictures," CGS Memo. 28, Stanford University, February, 1967.
9. W. Miller and A. Shaw, "A Picture Calculus", Stanford Linear Accelerator Center report No. 358, October, 1967.
10. A. Guzmán, "Some Aspects of Pattern Recognition by Computer," M. S. Thesis, Dept. of Elect. Eng., MIT, February, 1967.
11. M. Clowes, "Aspects of the Syntax of Simple Pictorial Displays", Seminar Paper No. 3, Workshop on Complex Processes, Univ. of Sydney, Australia, May, 1966.
12. M. Clowes, "Perception, Picture Processing and Computers," in *Machine*

Intelligence I, N. Collins and D. Michie, Ed's., Oliver and Boyd, Ltd., London, 1967.
13. R. Sauvain, "An Adaptive Pattern Description Program," Inf. Proc. Working Paper, No. 5, Univ. of Michigan, June, 1966.
14. P. Knoke and R. Wiley, "A Linguistic Approach to Mechanical Pattern Recognition," IEEE Computer Conf., 1967.
15. V. Kovalevsky, "Application of Mathematical Programming for Character and Pattern Recognition," *Proc. Fifth Int. Conf. on Cybernetics,* Namur, Belgium, September, 1967.
16. W. Watt, "Morphology of the Nevada Cattlebrands and Their Blazons, Part One," National Bureau of Standards Report 9050, February, 1966.
17. W. Watt, "Morphology of the Nevada Cattlebrands and Their Blazons, Part Two," Carnegie-Mellon University, October, 1967.
18. R. Ledley *et al,* "Fidac:Film Input to a Computer and Associated Syntax-Directed Pattern Recognition Programming System," in *Optical and Electro-Optical Inf. Proc.,* MIT Press.
19. K. Rankin *et al,* "On the Pictorial Structure of the Chinese Character," NBS Technical Note 254; Washington, D.C., 1965.
20. M. Eden, "On the Formalization of Handwriting," in *Structure of Language and its Mathematical Aspect,* Amer. Math. Soc., Providence, R.I., 1961.
21. A. Grasselli, "On the Automatic Classification of Fingerprints," this proceedings.
22. M. Klerer and J. May, "Two-Dimensional Programming," *Proc. FJCC,* Las Vegas, Nevada, November, 1965.
23. R. Anderson, "Syntax-Directed Recognition of Hand-Printed Two-Dimensional Mathematics," Aiken Computation Laboratory, Harvard University, August, 1967.
24. W. Martin, "A Fast Parsing Scheme for Hand-Printed Mathematical Expressions," MIT Artif. Intell. Memo No. 145, October, 1967.
25. T. Evans, "A Formalism for the Description of Complex Objects and Its Implementation," *Proc. Fifth Int. Conf. on Cybernetics,* Namur, Belgium, September, 1967.
26. H. Zschirnt, personal communication.
27. J. Feldman, "First Thoughts on Grammatical Inference," Stanford Artif. Intell. Memo No. 55, August, 1967.

ON SEQUENTIAL PATTERN RECOGNITION SYSTEMS*

K. S. Fu

PURDUE UNIVERSITY
LAFAYETTE, INDIANA

Abstract

This paper is concerned with the application of sequential decision procedures to pattern recognition problems when the costs of feature measurements are of considerable importance. Three techniques are discussed, namely, the modified sequential probability ratio test (with time-varying stopping boundaries), the backward procedure using dynamic programming, and the nonparametric sequential ranking procedure. Two-class classification problems are first treated. Generalized procedures for multi-class problems are then given. In addition to classification problems, the backward procedure has also been applied to feature ordering and selection in sequential recognition processes. Computer simulated experiments in character recognition are presented to illustrate the proposed approaches.

I. Introduction

In the pattern classification systems using fixed-sample size Bayes decision rule, all the features are observed by the classifier at one stage[1-4]. As a matter of fact, the cost of feature measurements has not been taken into consideration. It is evident that an insufficient number of feature measurements will not be able to give satisfactory results in correct classification. On the other hand, an arbitrarily large number of features to be measured is impractical. If the cost of taking feature measurements is to be considered or if the features extracted from input patterns is sequential in nature, one is led to apply sequential decision procedures[5,6] to this class of pattern recognition problems. The problem is especially pertinent when the cost of taking feature measurements is high. For example, if some quantities in an industrial process are to be measured and the measurements require the process to be interrupted, or if elaborate equipments, excessive time, or a complicated operation (in biomedical applications) is required to perform the measurement. A trade-off between the error (misrecognition) and the number of features to be measured can be obtained by taking feature measurements sequentially and terminating the sequential process (making a

* This work was supported by the National Science Foundation under Grant GK-1970.

decision) when a sufficient or desirable accuracy of classification has been achieved. Since the feature measurements are to be taken sequentially the order of the features to be measured is important. It is expected that the features should be ordered such that measurements taken in such an order will cause the terminal decision earlier. The problem of feature ordering is a rather special problem in sequential recognition systems. It is an objective of this paper to cover the recent developments in the application of sequential decision procedures to feature ordering and pattern classification.

II. Sequential Decision Model for Pattern Classification

Application of sequential decision procedures to pattern classification was proposed in [7]. Assume that there are m possible pattern classes ω_1, $\omega_2, \ldots, \omega_m$ and there are N features, $f_1, f_2, \ldots, f_N$, to be extracted for classification. The problem of classification is formulated as a problem of hypotheses testing. Let the (noisy) measurements of the N feature be denoted by $x_1, x_2, \ldots, x_N$, where $x_j = f_j$ + noise. Each set of N feature measurements can be represented as an N-dimensional vector X or as a point in the N-dimensional feature space Ω_X. Let the a priori probability of each pattern class be $P(\omega_i)$, $i = 1, \ldots, m$. If there are two pattern classes to be recognized, m=2, Wald's sequential probability ratio test (SPRT) can be applied[5]. At n-th stage of the sequential process, that is, after n-th feature measurement is taken, the classifier computes the sequential probability ratio

$$\lambda_n = \frac{p_n(X/\omega_1)}{p_n(X/\omega_2)} \tag{2.1}$$

where $p_n(X/\omega_i)$, i = 1, 2, is the conditional probability density function of $X = [x_1, x_2, \ldots, x_n]^T$ for pattern class ω_i, and the superscript "T" indicates the transpose operation. The λ_n computed by (2.1) is then compared with two stopping boundaries A and B. If

$$\lambda_n \geqslant A, \text{ then } X \sim \omega_1, \text{ i.e., X is classified as from pattern class } \omega_1 \tag{2.2}$$

$$\text{and if } \lambda_n \leqslant B, \text{ then } X \sim \omega_2. \tag{2.3}$$

If $B < \lambda_n < A$, then an additional feature measurement will be taken and the process is proceeding to the (n+1)-th stage. The two stopping boundaries are related to the error (misrecognition) probabilities by following expressions

$$A = \frac{1 - e_{21}}{e_{12}}$$

and (2.4)

$$B = \frac{e_{21}}{1 - e_{12}}$$

where e_{ij} = probability of deciding $X \sim \omega_i$ when actually $X \sim \omega_j$ is true, i,j = 1,2. Following Wald's sequential analysis, it has been shown that a classifier, using the SPRT, has an optimal property for the case of two pattern classes, that is, for given e_{12} and e_{21}, there is not other procedure with at least as low error probabilities or expected risk and with shorter length of average number of feature measurements than the sequential classification procedure.

For more than two pattern classes, m > 2, the generalized sequential probability ratio test (GSPRT) can be used[8]. At n-th stage, the generalized sequential probability ratios for each pattern class are computed as

$$U_n(X/\omega_i) = \frac{p_n(X/\omega_i)}{\left[\prod_{q=1}^{m} p_n(X/\omega_q)\right]^{1/m}}, \quad i = 1, 2, \ldots, m \qquad (2.5)$$

The $U_n(X/\omega_i)$ is then compared with the stopping boundary of i-th pattern class, $A(\omega_i)$, and the decision procedure is to reject the pattern class ω_i from consideration, that is, X is not considered as in ω_i if

$$U_n(X/\omega_i) < A(\omega_i), \quad i = 1, 2, \ldots, m \qquad (2.6)$$

The stopping boundary is determined by the following relationship

$$A(\omega_i) = \frac{1 - e_{ii}}{\left[\prod_{q=1}^{m} (1-e_{iq})\right]^{1/m}}, \quad i = 1, 2, \ldots, m \qquad (2.7)$$

After the rejection of pattern class ω_i from consideration, the total number of pattern classes is reduced by one and a new set of generalized sequential probability ratios is formed. The pattern classes are rejected sequentially until only one is left which is accepted as the recognized class. The rejection criterion suggested, though somewhat conservative, will usually lead to a high percentage of correct recognition because of the fact that only the pattern classes which are the most unlikely to be true are rejected.

For two pattern classes, m=2, the classification procedure (2.6) is equivalent to Wald's SPRT and the optimality of SPRT holds. For m > 2, whether the optimal property is still valid remains to be justified. However, the classification procedure is close to optimal in that the average number of feature measurements required to reject a pattern class from consideration is nearly minimum when two hypotheses (the hypothesis of a pattern class to be rejected and the hypothesis of a class not rejected) are considered. A general block diagram for a sequential recognition system is shown in Figure 1.

A pattern classifier using a standard sequential decision procedure, SPRT or GSPRT, may be unsatisfactory because: *(i)* an individual classification may require more number of feature measurements than can be tolerated, and *(ii)* the average number of feature measurements may become extremely large, if e_{ij}'s are chosen to be very small. In practical situations, it may become virtually necessary to interrupt the standard procedure and resolve among various courses of decision. This can be achieved by truncating the sequential process at $n = N$, where N is the maximum number of features allowed. For example, the truncated sequential decision procedure for SPRT will be the following. Carry out the regular SPRT until either a terminal decision is made or stage N of the process is reached. If no decision has been reached at stage N, decide $X \sim \omega_1$ if $\lambda_n \geqslant 1$ and $X \sim \omega_2$ if $\lambda_n \leqslant 1$. In a pattern classifier using truncated GSPRT, at $n = N$ the input pattern is classified as belonging to the class with the largest generalized sequential probability ratio. Under the truncated procedure the process must terminate in at most N stages. Truncation is a compromise between an entirely sequential procedure and a classical, fixed-sample size decision procedure. It is an attempt to reconcile the good properties of both procedures: the sequential property of examining measurements as they accumulate and the classical property of guaranteeing that the tolerances will be met with a specified number of available measurements.

III. Forward Procedure for Finite Sequential Classification Using Modified Sequential Probability Ratio Test

3.1 MODIFIED SEQUENTIAL PROBABILITY RATIO TEST

As described in Section II, the error probabilities e_{ij} can be prespecified in SPRT and GSPRT. However, in this case, the number of feature measurements required for a terminal decision is a random variable which, in general, depends upon the specified e_{ij} and has a positive probability of being greater than any constant. Since it is impractical to allow an arbitrarily large number of feature measurements to terminate the sequential process, one is frequently interested in setting an upper bound for the number of feature measurements within which the pattern classifier must make a terminal decision. An abrupt truncation of the process as described in Section II is an answer. Instead of using abrupt truncation this problem is studied in this section by considering time-varying stopping boundaries for the sequential classification process[9-11]. The idea of varying the stopping boundaries as a function of time or number of feature measurements enables us to investigate the behavior of a modified SPRT (with time-varying stopping boundaries) as compared with the standard Wald's SPRT with constant stopping boundaries A and B. Since the stopping boundaries are constructed and employed in the direction of usual time sequence starting with the first feature measurement, the term "forward procedure" is emphasized here to distinguish from the "backward procedure" discussed in Section IV.

The modified SPRT is formulated as follows: Let $E_i(n)$ be the expected number of feature measurements when $X \sim \omega_i$, $i = 1, 2$, that is, a terminal decision is made. Subject to the requirement that when X is classified as from class ω_i, the probability of misrecognition will be at most $e_{ij} (i \neq j)$, the problem is to give a procedure with time-varying stopping boundaries for deciding between $X \sim \omega_1$ and $X \sim \omega_2$ such that $E_i(n)$ is minimum.

The procedure of modified SPRT can be stated as follows: Let $g_1(n)$ and $g_2(n)$ be either constants, or monotonically non-increasing and non-decreasing functions of n, respectively. The classifier continuously takes measurements as long as the sequential probability ratio λ_n lies between $e^{g_1(n)}$ and $e^{g_2(n)}$, that is, the sequential process continues by taking additional feature measurements as long as

$$e^{g_2(n)} < \lambda_n < e^{g_1(n)}, \quad n = 1, 2, \ldots \tag{3.1}$$

If $$\lambda_n \geqslant e^{g_1(n)}, \text{ then } X \sim \omega_1, \tag{3.2}$$

and if $$\lambda_n \leqslant e^{g_2(n)}, \text{ then } X \sim \omega_2 .$$

In this formulation, it is seen that the standard Wald's SPRT can be considered as a special case of the modified SPRT where $g_1(n)$ and $g_2(n)$ can be made functions of n enables us to design a sequential classifier such that the expected number of feature measurements in reaching a terminal decision and the probability of misrecognition may be controlled in advance.

Considered the modified sequential probability ratio test defined in (3.1) and (3.2) for which

$$g_1(n) = a' \left(1 - \frac{n}{N}\right)^{r_1} \tag{3.3}$$

$$g_2(n) = -b' \left(1 - \frac{n}{N}\right)^{r_2} \tag{3.4}$$

where $0 < r_1, r_2 \leqslant 1$, $a' > 0$, $b' > 0$, and N is the prespecified number of feature measurements where the truncation occurs and the classifier is forced to reach a terminal decision. The graphical representation of $g_1(n)$ and $g_2(n)$ as functions of n is shown in Figure 2. Let

$$L_n = \log \lambda_n = \log \frac{p_n(X/\omega_1)}{p_n(X/\omega_2)} \tag{3.5}$$

Then the modified sequential probability ratio test is defined in

$$-b' \left(1 - \frac{n}{N}\right)^{r_2} < L_n < a' \left(1 - \frac{n}{N}\right)^{r_1} \tag{3.6}$$

and the violation of either one of the inequalities is associated with the classification of $X \sim \omega_1$ or $X \sim \omega_2$. It is noted that as $N \to \infty$, (3.6) defines the standard Wald's SPRT where $a' = \log A$ and $b' = -\log B$. The derivatives of $g_1(n)$ and $g_2(n)$ at $n = 0$ are $-r_1 a'/N$ and $r_2 b'/N$ respectively; they characterize the initial slopes of the convergent boundaries and therefore determine the rate of convergence to N when the process is to be truncated.

Let $E_i(n)$, $i = 1, 2$, be the expected number of feature measurements for the modified SPRT when $X \sim \omega_i$, and let $E_i'^*(n)$ and $E_i'^{**}(n)$ be the corresponding expectations when the lower and upper stopping boundaries are violated respectively. Assume that e'_{12} and e'_{21}, the error probabilities upon the termination of the modified SPRT, are very small so that $1-e'_{12} \simeq 1$ and $1-e'_{21} \simeq 1$. This assumption is not necessary but it greatly simplifies the resulting expressions. Following this assumption the equation

$$E'_1(n) = e'_{21}\, E'_1{}^*(n) + (1-e'_{21})\, E'_1{}^{**}(n) \tag{3.7}$$

is replaced by

$$E'_1(n) = E'_1{}^{**}(n) \tag{3.8}$$

Assume that the feature measurements are independently and identically distributed. Let $u = \frac{n}{N}$ and $z_j = \log \frac{p(x_j/\omega_1)}{p(x_j/\omega_2)}$. By using a well-known result of sequential analysis,[5,6] together with often-mentioned neglect of excess over the boundaries, we obtain

$$E'_1(z_1 + \ldots + z_n) = E'_1(L_n) \simeq E'_1{}^{**}(n)\, E_1(L_n) \tag{3.9}$$

and

$$E'_1(z_1 + \ldots + z_n) = e'_{21}\, E'_1{}^*[-b'(1-u)^{r_2} + (1-e'_{21})\, E'_1{}^{**}[a'(1-u)^{r_1}] \tag{3.10}$$

When $e'_{21} \ll 1$, the first term on the right-hand side of (3.10) can be neglected, then by (3.9),

$$E'_1{}^{**}(n)\, E_1(L_n) \simeq E'_1{}^{**}[a'(1-u)^{r_1}] \simeq E'_1{}^{**}\{a'[1-r_1 u + \frac{r_1(r_1-1)}{2} u^2 \ldots]\} \tag{3.11}$$

Thus

$$E'_1{}^{**}(n) \simeq E'_1(n) \simeq \frac{a'}{E_1(L_n) + \frac{r_1 a'}{N}} \tag{3.12}$$

where all the conditional moments of u higher than the first are neglected.

To obtain the error probability e'_{12} the following relation is used

$$E'_1{}^{**}[e^{-g_1(n)}] \simeq \frac{e'_{12}}{1-e'_{21}} \tag{3.13}$$

Or, equivalently,

$$E'_1{}^{**}[e^{-a'(1-u)^{r_1}}] \simeq \frac{e'_{21}}{1-e'_{21}} \tag{3.14}$$

Taking into account $1-e'_{21} \simeq 1$, neglecting the conditional moments of u higher than the first in the Taylor series expansion about u = 0, and substituting (3.12) for $E_1'^{**}(n)$, we get

$$e'_{12} \simeq e^{-a'}\left[1 + \frac{r_1\, a'^2}{N\, E_1(L_n) + r_1\, a'}\right] \tag{3.15}$$

Equations (3.12) and (3.15) apply when $X \sim \omega_2$ is true, by replacing a′ by $-b'$, e'_{12} by e'_{21} and $E'_1(n)$ by $E'_2(n)$.

Now consider the standard Wald's SPRT with upper stopping boundary $A = e^a$ and lower stopping boundary $B = e^{-b}$. If e_{12} and e_{21} are very small, $E_1(n) \simeq a/E_1(L_n)$ and $e^{-a} \simeq e_{12}$. Suppose $a' = a$, that is, the boundary of the standard Wald's SPRT and the modified SPRT begin (n=0) at the same points. Then (3.12) and (3.15) can be rewritten as

$$E'_1(n) \simeq \frac{E_1(n)}{1 + \dfrac{r_1}{N} E_1(n)} \tag{3.16}$$

and

$$e'_{12} \simeq e_{12}\left[1 + \frac{r_1\, a\, E_1(n)}{N + r_1 E_1(n)}\right] \tag{3.17}$$

From (3.16) and (3.17), it is important to observe the following relationships:

(i) $$\frac{E_1(n)}{1 + r_1} < E'_1(n) \leqslant E_1(n) \tag{3.18}$$

This is to say that, because of the convergent property of the time-varying stopping boundaries, the modified SPRT requires less expected number of feature measurements. The amount of reduction is controlled by the design parameter r_1 as shown in the left inequality of (3.18).

(ii) e'_{12} is greater than e_{12} since $r_1 a\, E_1(n)/[N + r_1 E_1(n)]$ is a positive quantity. This result is to be expected due to the optimality of the standard Wald's SPRT. In fact, if e'_{12} were set equal to e_{12}, the modified SPRT will have a larger expected number of feature measurements than that of the Wald's SPRT. This in turn implies also that the modified SPRT must begin at $a' > a$.

With regard to the results obtained above, it becomes clear that, by properly constructing the time-varying stopping boundaries for the sequential classification process, the following purposes can be accomplished: *(i)* the classification process always terminates by a prespecified maximum number of feature measurements, *(ii)* the expected number of feature measurements is controllable and usually less than that required for the standard Wald's SPRT with fixed parallel stopping boundaries, and *(iii)* it is possible by adjusting the starting points of stopping boundaries to achieve error probabilities as low as those in Wald's SPRT. Similar results can also be obtained for the case of continuous time parameter[9].

3.2 PROCEDURE OF MODIFIED GENERALIZED SEQUENTIAL PROBABILITY RATIO TEST

Generally speaking, the principle of constructing the time-varying stopping boundaries for Wald's SPRT also applies to the generalized sequential probability ratio test when the number of pattern classes to be recognized is more than two. In the following, the procedure of modified GSPRT (with time-varying stopping boundaries) is described. The classifier takes feature measurements sequentially at its input and decide, as soon as possible, to classify the input as one of the m possible pattern classes. At n-th stage, the generalized sequential probability ratio for each pattern class is computed

$$U_n(X/\omega_i) = \frac{p_n(X/\omega_i)}{\left[\prod_{j=1}^{m} p_n(X/\omega_j)\right]^{1/m}}, \quad i = 1, \ldots, m \tag{3.19}$$

and is compared with the stopping boundary $g_i(n)$, $i = 1, \ldots, m$. As soon as

$$U_n(X/\omega_i) < g_i(n) \tag{3.20}$$

the pattern class ω_i is dropped from consideration, and the number of possible pattern classes is reduced by one for the next computation. The process of forming the generalized sequential probability ratio continues until there is only one pattern class retained, the pattern class would be assigned to the input. Note that the stopping boundaries $g_i(n)$, $i = 1, \ldots,$ m, are, in general, functions of n and need not be identical for all classes. Similar to the ones suggested for the modified SPRT, a simple class of convergent boundaries may assume the form as

$$g_i(n) = G_i'\left(1 - \frac{n}{N}\right)^{r_i}, \quad i = 1, \ldots, m \tag{3.21}$$

In fact, the spirit of the modified GSPRT relies on an optimal construction of these functions such that all the pattern classes but one are dropped from consideration by a prespecified number of feature measurements N. In Section VI, an algorithmic construction of the time-varying stopping boundaries will be given, and experimental results will be used to illustrate how the desirable performance resulting from the modified SPRT may also be achieved in the case of modified GSPRT.

IV. Backward Procedure for Finite Sequential Recognition Using Dynamic Programming

4.1 BASIC FORMULATION AND FUNCTIONAL EQUATION

As mentioned in Section II, many pattern recognition problems may be considered as sequential decision processes in which the number of observations is necessarily finite. The method of modifying the sequential probability ratio test described in Section III is certainly one approach of solving this class of decision problems. However, the optimality of the original decision procedure is frequently sacrificed, especially in the multiple decision case ($m > 2$). The optimal Bayes sequential decision procedure which minimizes the expected risk including the cost of observations is essentially a backward procedure[6,12]. It is intended to show in this section that, as an alternative approach to the modified sequential probability ratio test, the dynamic programming[13-18] provides a feasible computational technique for a class of sequential recognition systems with finite stopping rules[19-21]. The intuitive argument of using dynamic programming for finite sequential recognition problems can be stated as follows: Consider a sequential decision process. With observations taken one at a time, each stage of the process is a decision problem including both the choice of closing the sequence of observations and making a terminal decision, and the choice of taking an additional observation. It is easy to determine the expected risk involved in the decision when the procedure is terminated, but it is not easy to find the expected risk involved in taking an additional observation. For the case of taking one more observation, the expected risk is that of continuing and then doing the best possible from then on-wards. Consequently, in order to determine the best decision at the present stage (i.e., whether to continue the process or not) it is necessary to know the best decision in the future. In other words, as far as seeking the optimal decision procedure is concerned, the nature time order of working from the present to the future is of little use because the present optimum essentially involves the future optimum. The only alternative to keep the true optimality is to work backwards in time, i.e., from the optimal future behavior to deduce the optimal present behavior, and so on back into the past. The entire available future must be considered in deciding whether to continue the process or not, and the method of dynamic programming provides just such an optimization procedure, working backwards from a prespecified last stage to the very first stage. In the problems of sequential recognition where the decision procedure must terminate at a finite number of observations, the termination point can be used as a convenient starting point (i.e., the last stage)for backward computation.

The way in which the dynamic programming is carried out in the finite optimal sequential decision procedure is by applying the Principle of Optimality. As stated by Bellman[13], "An optimal policy has the property that whatever the initial state and initial decision are, the remaining decisions must constitute an optimal policy with regard to the state resulting from the first decision." In essence, it is equivalent to saying that if an optimal policy is pursued, then at each stage of the sequential process the remaining decisions must themselves form an optimal policy from the state reached to the terminal point of the process.

Consider the successive observations of feature measurements $x_1, x_2, \ldots, x_n$, $n = 1, 2, \ldots$, with known distribution function of x_{n+1} given the sequence $x_1, \ldots, x_n$, $P(x_{n+1} | x_1, \ldots, x_n)$. After the observation of each feature measurement, the decision made by the classifier includes both the choice of closing the sequence of feature measurements and making a terminal decision (to decide the pattern class based on the observed feature measurements), and the choice of making another observation of the next feature measurement before coming to a terminal decision. Let

$R_n(x_1, x_2, \ldots, x_n) =$ the minimum expected risk of the entire sequential decision process, having observed the sequence of feature measurements $x_1, x_2, \ldots, x_n$;

$C(x_1, x_2, \ldots, x_n) =$ the cost of continuing the sequential process at the n-th stage, i.e., taking an additional feature measurement, x_{n+1};

and

$G(x_1, x_2, \ldots, x_n; d_i) =$ the risk of making terminal decision d_i: $X \sim \omega_i$ (i.e., the i-th pattern class is accepted by the classifier), $i = 1, 2, \ldots, m$ on the basis of the feature measurements $x_1, x_2, \ldots, x_n$.

If the classifier decides to stop the process, the expected risk is $\underset{i}{\text{Min}}\ G(x_1, x_2, \ldots, x_n; d_i)$ by employing an optimal decision rule. If the classifier decides to continue the process and to take one more feature measurement x_{n+1}, the expected risk is $C(x_1, x_2, \ldots, x_n) + \int R_{n+1}(x_1, x_2, \ldots, x_n, x_{n+1})\, dP(x_{n+1} | x_1, \ldots, x_n)$ where the integration is carried over the admissible region of x_{n+1}. Hence, by the Principle of Optimality, the basic functional equation governing the infinite sequence of the expected risk $R_n(x_1, x_2, \ldots, x_n)$, $n = 1, 2, \ldots$, is

$$R_n(x_1, x_2, \ldots, x_n) = \text{Min} \left[\begin{array}{l} \text{Continue: } C(x_1, \ldots, x_n) \\ \quad + \int R_{n+1}(x_1, \ldots, x_n, x_{n+1})\, dP(x_{n+1} | x_1, \ldots, x_n) \\ \text{Stop: } \underset{i}{\text{Min}}\ G(x_1, \ldots, x_n; d_i) \end{array} \right. \tag{4.1}$$

In the case of finite sequential decision processes where a terminal decision has to be made at or before a preassigned stage number N, the optimal stopping rule can be determined backwards starting from the given risk function (or specified error probabilities) of the last stage. That is, let, at N-th stage,

$$R_N(x_1, x_2, \ldots, x_N) = \underset{i}{\text{Min}}\ G(x_1, x_2, \ldots, x_N; d_i) \tag{4.2}$$

and compute the expected risk for stage number less than N through the functional equation (4.1). Specifically, starting with the known (or given) value for $R_N(x_1, x_2, \ldots, x_N)$ in (4.2), we have at (N−1)-th stage,

$$R_{N-1}(x_1, x_2, \ldots, x_{N-1}) = \text{Min} \left[\begin{array}{l} \text{Continue: } C(x_1, x_2, \ldots, x_{N-1}) \\ + \int R_N(x_1, \ldots, x_N) dP(x_N | x_1, \ldots, x_{N-1}) \\ \\ \text{Stop: } \underset{i}{\text{Min}}\ G(x_1, \ldots, x_{N-1}; d_i) \end{array} \right. \quad (4.3)$$

in which $R_N(x_1, \ldots, x_N)$ is obtained from (4.2). At (N−2)-th stage,

$$R_{N-2}(x_1, x_2, \ldots, x_{N-2}) = \text{Min} \left[\begin{array}{l} \text{Continue: } C(x_1, x_2, \ldots, x_{N-2}) \\ + \int R_{N-1}(x_1, \ldots, x_{N-1}) dP(x_{N-1} | x_1, \ldots x_{N-2}) \\ \\ \text{Stop: } \underset{i}{\text{Min}}\ G(x_1, \ldots, x_{N-2}; d_i) \end{array} \right. \quad (4.4)$$

in which $R_{N-1}(x_1, \ldots, x_{N-1})$ is obtained from (4.3). At second stage

$$R_2(x_1, x_2) = \text{Min} \left[\begin{array}{l} \text{Continue: } C(x_1, x_2) + \int R_3(x_1, x_2, x_3) dP(x_3 | x_1, x_2) \\ \\ \text{Stop: } \underset{i}{\text{Min}}\ G(x_1, x_2; d_i) \end{array} \right. \quad (4.5)$$

in which $R_3(x_1, x_2, x_3)$ is obtained from the third stage. At first stage,

$$R_1(x_1) = \text{Min} \left[\begin{array}{l} \text{Continue: } C(x_1) + \int R_2(x_1, x_2) dP(x_2 | x_1) \\ \\ \text{Stop: } \underset{i}{\text{Min}}\ G(x_1; d_i) \end{array} \right. \quad (4.6)$$

in which $R_2(x_1, x_2)$ is obtained from (4.5).

One can easily see the computational difficulty arising from this formulation. Aside from the necessary memory locations for estimating the high order conditional probabilities, the storage in a computer required for calculating the risk functions alone is already enormous. For example, suppose there are eight feature measurements available for successive observations (N=8) and if each measurement can take on one of ten values (discrete case); in order to resolve (4.1) through the recursive equations just described, the total storage required for storing all the possible risk functions $R_n(x_1, x_2, \ldots, x_n)$, $n = 1, 2, \ldots, 8$, is $10 + 10^2 + \ldots + 10^8$. Because of this type of computational difficulties, methods toward the reduction of storage requirement are of major concern in designing a truly sequential recognition system with optimal stopping rule. This is the subject of discussion in the next section.

4.2 REDUCTION OF DIMENSIONALITY

(A) Use of Sufficient Statistics

The first possible solution to reduce the dimensionality is the use of sufficient statistics in describing the recognition process under consideration. Let each feature measurement assume one of the r discrete values $E_1, E_2, \ldots, E_r$ (a quantization of feature space). Assume that the features of each pattern class are characterized by a multinomial distribution, i.e., for each ω_i, $i = 1, \ldots, m$, there exists a probability function

$$P(x_1, x_2, \ldots, x_n | \omega_i) = P(k_1, k_2, \ldots, k_r | \omega_i) = \frac{n!}{k_1!\, k_2! \ldots k_r!} \prod_{j=1}^{r} (p_{ij})^{k_j} \tag{4.7}$$

where p_{ij} is the probability of occurrence of E_j for class ω_i, $\sum_{j=1}^{r} p_{ij} = 1$, and k_j is the number of occurrences of E_j, $\sum_{j=1}^{r} k_j = n$. Since the statistic $(k_1, k_2, \ldots, k_r; n)$ is sufficient to characterize the multinomial distribution, it is reasonable to assume that only the number of occurrences of E_j, k_j, $j = 1, 2, \ldots, r$, not its order, is important in making a decision. Then the functional equation (4.1) becomes

$$R_n(k_1, k_2, \ldots, k_r) = \text{Min} \begin{cases} \text{Continue: } C(k_1, k_2, \ldots, k_r) \\ \quad + \sum_{i=1}^{m} P(\omega_i)[p_{i1} R_{n+1}(k_1+1, k_2, \ldots, k_r) \\ \quad + p_{i2} R_{n+1}(k_1, k_2+1, \ldots, k_r) + \ldots \\ \quad + p_{ir} R_{n+1}(k_1, k_2, \ldots, k_r+1)] \\ \text{Stop: } \underset{i}{\text{Min}}\ G(k_1, k_2, \ldots, k_r; d_i) \end{cases} \tag{4.8}$$

where $P(\omega_i)$ is the a priori probability for class ω_i. Equation (4.8) can be solved by working backwards with the terminal condition to be

$$R_N(k_1, k_2, \ldots, k_r) = \underset{i}{\text{Min}}\ G(k_1, k_2, \ldots, k_r; d_i) \tag{4.9}$$

The risk function $R_n(k_1, k_2, \ldots, k_r)$ is then determined for each and every sequence of $k_1, k_2, \ldots, k_r$, where $\sum_{j=1}^{r} k_j = n$, $n = 1, 2, \ldots, N$. In addition, the optimal stopping rule is also determined at each stage. That is, if the risk of stopping is less than the expected risk of continuing for a given history of feature measurements, the sequential process is terminated. The actual optimal structure of the resulting procedure is obtained in the course of solving the functional equation (4.8).

In resolving (4.8), it is also required to compute the minimum termination risk $\underset{i}{\text{Min}}\, G(k_1, l_2, \ldots, k_r; d_i)$ at each stage. Bayes decision rule is employed here to illustrate the computation procedure, although in practice other proper optimal decision rules may be chosen according to the statistical knowledge at hand. Let $L(d_j, \omega_i)$ be the loss incurred by making the terminal decision d_j when the input pattern is really from class ω_i. Then the risk function of deciding that the pattern belongs to class ω_j, having observed the joint event $[k_1, k_2, \ldots, k_r]$, can be written as

$$G(k_1, k_2, \ldots, k_r; d_j) = \sum_{i=1}^{m} P(\omega_i) L(d_j, \omega_i) P(k_1, \ldots, k_r \mid \omega_i) \tag{4.10}$$

The quantity $\underset{i}{\text{Min}}\, G(k_1, k_2, \ldots, k_r; d_i)$ is in fact the risk attained when the sequential process stops. It is worth noting that in the case of (0,1) loss function, i.e.,

$$L(d_j, \omega_i) = \begin{cases} 0 & \text{if } i = j \\ 1 & \text{if } i \neq j \end{cases} \tag{4.11}$$

the decision procedure reduces to: decide d_j if

$$P(\omega_j) P(k_1, k_2, \ldots, k_r \mid \omega_j) > P(\omega_i) P(k_1, k_2, \ldots, k_r \mid \omega_i) \text{ for all } i \neq j \tag{4.12}$$

and the risk attained is $G(k_1, k_2, \ldots, k_r; d_j)$.

The way in which the reduction of dimensionally can be achieved is due to the assumption of independent measurements implied by the ignorance of the ordering of the occurrence of E_j. This assumption allows the reduction of storage requirement from $\sum_{n=1}^{N} r^n$ to $\sum_{n=1}^{N} \binom{r+n-1}{n}$ by simply realizing the constraints that $\sum_{j=1}^{r} k_j = n$ and $n \leqslant N$. Detailed results on this type of reduction are given in [19].

(B) Assumption of Markovian Dependence

In many pattern recognition problems, the assumption of independent measurements and the ignorance of measurements ordering cannot be made without leading to an intolerable rate of misrecognition. Frequently, a more feasible approximation to the true state of affairs is to consider the simple Markovian dependence among the feature measurements successively observed by the classifier (higher order Markovian dependence may also be assumed if it is relevant). The assumption of this type of dependence relation has the obvious advantage of providing a more sophisticated model for the physical process under consideration while still retaining a certain degree of mathematical simplicity. In the solution of recursive equation (4.1), a reduction in dimensionality can also be achieved by replacing the high order conditional probability $P(x_{n+1} | x_1, \ldots, x_n)$ by a set of first order transition probabilities, when the underlying Markov processes are properly defined. The procedure of this replacement is described as follows.

Let the feature measurements $x_1, x_2, \ldots, x_n$ be considered as a discrete-time homogeneous first order Markov chain, with the state space being the r quanta $E_1, E_2, \ldots, E_r$. The sequence $x_1, x_2, \ldots, x_n$ is known to be generated by one of the m possible pattern classes with transition probability matrices $[P_u(i,j)]$, $u = 1, 2, \ldots, m$ where

$$P_u(i,j) = \text{Prob}\{x_n = E_j | x_{n-1} = E_i \; ; \omega_u\}$$
$$n = 1, 2, \ldots, N \text{ and } u = 1, 2, \ldots, m \tag{4.13}$$

Let the risk function at the n-th stage be defined by $R_n(k_{11}, k_{12}, \ldots, k_{1r}; k_{21}, \ldots, k_{2r}; \ldots; k_{r1}, \ldots, k_{rr})$ as the expected risk after having observed $x_1, x_2, \ldots, x_n$ in which k_{ij} transitions have been made from state E_i to state E_j, $i,j = 1, \ldots, r$, and

$$\sum_{i=1}^{r} \sum_{j=1}^{r} k_{ij} = n-1 \tag{4.14}$$

The continuing risk in (4.1) is then computed as

$$\begin{aligned}
&C(x_1, x_2, \ldots, x_n) + \int R_{n+1}(x_1, \ldots, x_n, x_{n+1}) dP(x_{n+1} | x_1, \ldots, x_n) \\
&= C(k_{11}, \ldots, k_{1r}; k_{21}, \ldots, k_{2r}; \ldots; k_{r1}, \ldots, k_{rr}) \\
&+ \sum_{u=1}^{m} P(\omega_u)[P_u(1,1) R_{n+1}(k_{11}+1), \ldots, k_{1r}; \ldots; k_{r1}, \ldots, k_{rr}) \\
&+ \ldots + P_u(i,j) R_{n+1}(k_{11}, \ldots, k_{1r}; \ldots, k_{ij}+1, \ldots; k_{r1}, \ldots, k_{rr}) \\
&+ \ldots + P_u(r,r) R_{n+1}(k_{11}, \ldots, k_{1r}; \ldots, k_{r1}, \ldots, k_{rr}+1)]
\end{aligned} \tag{4.15}$$

The functional equation governing the Markovian sequence of feature measurements becomes

$$R_n(k_{11}, \ldots, k_{1r}, \ldots, k_{rr})$$

$$= \text{Min} \left[\begin{array}{ll} & \text{Continue: } C(k_{11}, \ldots, k_{1r}; \ldots; k_{r1}, \ldots, k_{rr}) \\ + \sum_{u=1}^{m} \sum_{i=1}^{r} \sum_{j=1}^{r} P(\omega_u) & P_u(i,j) R_{n+1}(k_{11}, \ldots, k_{1r}; \ldots, k_{ij}+1, \ldots; k_{r1}, \ldots, k_{rr}) \\ & \text{Stop: } \underset{u}{\text{Min}}\, G(k_{11}, \ldots, k_{1r}; \ldots; k_{r1}, \ldots, k_{rr}; d_u) \end{array} \right. \tag{4.16}$$

Equation (4.16) can be solved again by working backwards with the terminal condition to be

$$R_N(k_{11}, \ldots, k_{1r}; \ldots; k_{r1}, \ldots, k_{rr})$$

$$= \underset{u}{\text{Min}} \; G(k_{11}, \ldots, k_{1r}; \ldots; k_{r1}, \ldots, k_{rr}; d_u) \qquad (4.17)$$

where

$$\sum_{i=1}^{r} \sum_{j=1}^{r} k_{ij} = N-1$$

Notice that the price to be paid for considering the Markovian dependence is an increase of storage requirement from

$$\sum_{n=1}^{N} \binom{r+n-1}{n} \quad \text{to} \quad \sum_{n=1}^{N-1} \binom{r^2+n-1}{n}$$

when compared with the case of independent measurements assumed in (A). However, the required storage is still considerably reduced in comparison with the conventional method, where high order conditional probabilities and risk functions for all possible sequences of measurement history in the original feature space would have to be determined.

4.3 BACKWARD PROCEDURE FOR BOTH FEATURE ORDERING AND PATTERN CLASSIFICATION

In Section 4.1 and 4.2, the dynamic programming procedure has been applied to pattern classification problem without considering the ordering of feature measurements. However, as mentioned in Section I, in order to terminate the sequential recognition process earlier the ordering of feature measurements is often rather important. In this section, a more general sequential recognition system is considered. The system so designed has the additional capability of selecting the best feature for next measurement. In other words, in the process of sequential decisions, if the decision is to continue taking an additional measurement it also, in the meantime, selects the best feature for the next measurement.

Let $F_N = (f_1, \ldots, f_N)$ be the set of N features extracted by the feature extractor in their natural order. Let $F_{t_n} = (f_{t_1}, \ldots, f_{t_n})$, $n = 1, \ldots, N$ be a particular sequence of n features measured by the classifier at the n-th stage of the sequential recognition process. The remaining features available for further measurements at the n-th stage will be $F_n = F_N - F_{t_n}$. Note that the feature f_{t_i} may be any one of the element in F_N and the (noisy) feature measurement corresponding to f_{t_i} is represented by a random variable x_i as in the previous formulation. Similar to those in Section 4.1, the following terms are defined:

$R_n(x_1, \ldots, x_n | F_{t_n})$ = the minimum expected risk of the entire sequential recognition process, having observed the sequence of feature measurements $x_1, \ldots, x_n$ when the particular sequence of features F_{t_n} is selected.

$C(x_1, \ldots, x_n | F_{t_n})$ = the cost of continuing the sequential recognition process at the n-th stage.

$G(x_1, \ldots, x_n; d_i | F_{t_n})$ = the expected risk of making terminal decision d_i, $i = 1, \ldots, m$ on the basis of the feature measurements $x_1, \ldots, x_n$ when F_{t_n} is selected.

$P(x_{n+1}; f_{t_{n+1}} | x_1, \ldots, x_n; F_{t_n})$ = conditional probability distribution of x_{n+1} when $f_{t_{n+1}}$ is selected, given the sequence of measurements $x_1, \ldots, x_n$ on the sequence of features F_{t_n}.

When the classifier decides to stop the process and make a terminal decision at the n-th stage, the expected risk is simply $\min_i G(x_1, \ldots, x_n; d_i | F_{t_n})$. If the classifier decides to take an additional measurement, then the measurement must be optimally selected from the remaining features F_n in order to minimize the risk. That is, the expected risk of measuring the (n+1)-th feature

$$\min_{f_{t_{n+1}} \in F_n} \{C(x_1, \ldots, x_n | F_{t_n}) + \int R_{n+1}(x_1, \ldots, x_n, x_{n+1} | F_{t_n}, f_{t_{n+1}}) \cdot dP(x_{n+1}; f_{t_{n+1}} | x_1, \ldots, x_n; F_{t_n})\}$$

Therefore, by the principle of optimality the basic functional equation governing the sequential recognition process becomes

$$R_n(x_1, \ldots, x_n | F_{t_n}) = \text{Min} \begin{cases} \text{Continue: } \min_{f_{t_{n+1}} \in F_n} \{C(x_1, \ldots, x_n | F_{t_n}) \\ \quad + \int R_{n+1}(x_1, \ldots, x_n, x_{n+1} | F_{t_n}, f_{t_{n+1}}) dP(x_{n+1}; \\ \quad f_{t_{n+1}} | x_1, \ldots, x_n; F_{t_n}) \} \\ \text{Stop: } \min_i G(x_1, \ldots, x_n; d_i | F_{t_n}) \end{cases} \tag{4.18}$$

Again, (4.18) can be recursively solved by setting the terminal condition to be

$$R_N(x_1, \ldots, x_N | F_{t_N}) = \min_i G(x_1, \ldots, x_N; d_i | F_{t_N}) \tag{4.19}$$

and computing backwards for risk functions R_n, $n < N$. The major difference between the solution of (4.18) and that of (4.1) lies in the fact that the optimal stopping rules obtained from the present solution are automatically accompanied by a best sequence of features capable of minimizing the expected risk upon termination.

In general, the knowledge of the joint probability density functions of all the features and the a priori probabilities for each class are required in the computation of (4.18). From the computational point of view the procedure is often difficult to implement without large-scale computation facilities. If certain assumptions (e.g., independence of feature measurements) can be made in the practical recognition problems, the optimal procedure can be implemented as that described in Section 4.2. However, it will still be desirable to develop an approximation to the optimal procedure so the computations involved can be much simplified. The approximation made which leads to a suboptimal solution is that, at each stage, the classifier considers the next stage to be terminal, that is, a classification decision must be made at the next stage (one-stage ahead truncation). The following three different cases are chosen to illustrate the effectiveness of the suboptimal solution:

Case 1: Optimal solution when the feature measurements for each class are independent;

Case 2: Suboptimal (one-stage ahead truncation) solution when the feature measurements for each class are independent;

Case 3: Suboptimal solution when the feature measurements for each class have a first order Markov dependence.

A comparison of Cases 1 and 2 displays the effects of the truncation approximation. On the other hand, a comparison of Cases 1 and 3 allows a determination as to the relative advantage of increase the computational complexity either through *(i)* increasing the knowledge of the statistical dependence of the feature measurements while truncating the backward procedure, or *(ii)* simplifying the probability assumptions and carrying out the entire backward programming computation.

Case 1: In this case

$$P(x_{n+1}; f_{t_{n+1}} | x_1, \ldots, x_n; F_{t_n}) = P(x_{n+1}; f_{t_{n+1}}) \qquad (4.20)$$

Let P_n be the set of a posteriori probabilities of the occurrence of each class computed by (4.22), i.e.,

$$P_n = \{P(\omega_i | x_1, \ldots, x_n; F_{t_n}); \ i = 1, \ldots, m\} \qquad (4.21)$$

and

$$P(\omega_i | x_1, \ldots, x_n; F_{t_n}) = \frac{P(\omega_i | x_1, \ldots, x_{n-1}; F_{t_{n-1}}) P(x_n; f_{t_n} | \omega_i)}{\sum_{j=1}^{m} P(\omega_j | x_1, \ldots, x_{n-1}; F_{t_{n-1}}) P(x_n; f_{t_n} | \omega_j)} \qquad (4.22)$$

Then the basic recursive equation (4.18) using P_n as the sufficient statistic reduces to

$$R_n(P_n) = \text{Min} \begin{cases} \text{Continue:} & \underset{f_{t_{n+1}}}{\text{Min}} \{C(x_1, \ldots, x_n \mid F_{t_n}) \\ & + \int R_{n+1}(P_n) dP(x_{n+1}; f_{t_{n+1}})\} \\ \text{Stop:} & \underset{d_i}{\text{Min}} \{G(d_i \mid P_n)\} \end{cases} \tag{4.23}$$

Case 2: Equation (4.25), in this case, becomes

$$R_n(P_n) = \text{Min} \begin{cases} \text{Continue:} & \underset{f_{t_{n+1}}}{\text{Min}} \{C(x_1, \ldots, x_n \mid F_{t_n}) \\ & + \int R_N(P_n) dP(x_{n+1}; f_{t_{n+1}})\} \\ \text{Stop:} & \underset{d_i}{\text{Min}} \{G(d_i \mid P_n)\} \end{cases} \tag{4.24}$$

It is noted that, in (4.24), the averaging process is always over the terminal stage costs, and is easily performed as the sequential recognition process proceeds. In this way the requirement for the storage (i.e., the storage of the cost surfaces at each stage) is greatly reduced, and the resulting computations simplified.

Case 3: For this case,

$$P(x_{n+1}; f_{t_{n+1}} \mid x_1, \ldots, x_n; F_{t_n}) = P(x_{n+1}; f_{t_{n+1}} \mid x_n; f_{t_n}) \tag{4.25}$$

and the a posteriori probabilities are calculated by

$$P(\omega_i \mid x_1, \ldots, x_n; F_{t_n}) = \frac{P(\omega_i \mid x_1, \ldots, x_{n-1}; F_{t_{n-1}}) P(x_n; f_{t_n} \mid x_{n-1}; f_{t_{n-1}}; \omega_i)}{\sum_{j=1}^{m} P(\omega_j \mid x_1, \ldots, x_{n-1}; F_{t_{n-1}}) P(x_n; f_{t_n} \mid x_{n-1}; f_{t_{n-1}}; \omega_j)} \tag{4.26}$$

The sufficient statistic is then $(P_n; x_n; f_{t_n})$ and (4.18) becomes

$$R_n(P_n; x_n; f_{t_n}) = \text{Min} \begin{cases} \text{Continue:} & \underset{f_{t_{n+1}}}{\text{Min}} \{C(x_1, \ldots, x_n \mid F_{t_n}) \\ & + \int R_N(P_n) dP(x_{n+1}; f_{t_{n+1}} \mid x_n; f_{t_n})\} \\ \text{Stop:} & \underset{d_i}{\text{Min}} \{G(d_i \mid P_n)\} \end{cases} \tag{4.27}$$

It can be seen that for Cases 1 and 2, all information provided by the past history of feature selection and measurement outcomes up to and including the n-th stage is contained in the a posteriori probabilities calculated. All that need be done is to keep tracking what features have been measured, and the a posteriori probabilities calculated. Thus, the actual values of measurement outcomes and the order of features measured can be dropped from consideration, thereby allowing the reduction in computations and storage. In Case 3, additional storage is required in order to save the last feature measurement. More serious memory requirements are necessitated by the storage of the transition matrices, and by the added dimension of dependence of the cost function at each stage. Of course, the main computational advantage remains the fact that the expectation (averaging) in (4.27) is taken only over the terminal stage and can be easily computed at each stage of the process.

V. Nonparametric Procedure in Sequential Pattern Classification

5.1 INTRODUCTION TO SEQUENTIAL RANKING PROCEDURE

The design of a sequential pattern classification system for classifying patterns in a random environment (noise, distortion, etc.) has been primarily concerned with the case where the following assumptions are made: *(i)* a sufficient number of feature measurements is always available and thus the classification process can be prolonged forever if needed, and *(ii)* the statistical knowledge about the patterns in each class is either completely known a priori or can be estimated by the classification system through some learning processes. The first difficulty, which arises from the prolonged experimentation, can be avoided by either modifying the standard Wald's sequential probability ratio test so that the classification process will terminate at a prespecified finite number of feature measurements as described in Section III, or simply employing the dynamic programming procedure which determines the optimal stopping boundaries by computing backwards from the last feature measurement up to the first as discussed in Section IV. An equally important, but perhaps less explored, case of design is the one which will relax the constraint in *(ii)* so that no assumption or actual knowledge is needed on the form of the underlying probability distributions associated with each pattern class. The purpose of this section, therefore, is to introduce a nonparametric approach to the design of a sequential pattern classification system using Wald's SPRT.

It is noted that in order to carry out the computation in Wald's SPRT, an assumption or actual knowledge is needed on the specific forms of the probability density functions, $p_n(X/\omega_1)$ and $p_n(X/\omega_2)$. This is essentially what has been done in the experiments presented in Section VI where the feature vectors are assumed to be samples from known probability distributions describable within a set of parameters (for example, mean vectors and covariance matrices in gaussian distributions), known to or estimated by the classification system. It may frequently happen that this knowledge is not available or any simplified assumption cannot be justified due to the lack of a priori information about the random patterns, or due to the changing statistics of the operating environment. In either case, nonparametric methods would have to be pursued so as to obtain a more realistic mathematical model in approximating the physical situation. In statistical decision theory, many nonparametric schemes are based on the set of ranks determined by sample measurements. In the following sections, a sequential ranking procedure[22] is employed and the resulting performances analyzed in the design of a binary classifier so that the nonparametric setting of Wald's SPRT can be naturally applied. A generalized procedure capable of classifying patterns from more than two classes is also discussed.

In order to apply Wald's SPRT in the nonparametric setting, one would have to replace the feature measurement vector $X = [x_1, x_2. \ldots, x_n]^T$ by a vector of ranks $T = [T_1, T_2, \ldots, T_n]$. The rank T_i for x_i is Z, $Z = 1, 2, \ldots,$ n, if and only if x_i is the Z-th smallest measurement with respect to the set of measurements $x_1, x_2, \ldots, x_n$. Because of the sequential nature of taking the feature measurements in SPRT, one is naturally led to the idea of sequentially ranking the measurements every time a new measurement is taken, without having to rerank all the preceding measurements in the entire feature vector. To see exactly how such a procedure may be derived, it is beneficial to look into the ordinary (non-sequential) reranking process which is described as follows.

Suppose that the feature measurements $x_1, x_2, \ldots, x_n$ are taking successively, and each time a new measurement is taken the entire set of measurements is reranked. Let T_{ij} be the rank of x_j with respect to the entire set of measurements $(x_1, x_2, \ldots, x_i)$ at the i-th stage of measurement, where $i = 1, 2, \ldots, n$ and $j = 1, 2, \ldots, i$. Then the following two groups of vectors will describe the ordinary reranking process:

	Successive measurement set	Ordinary rank vector
First Stage	x_1	T_{11}
Second Stage	(x_1, x_2)	$[T_{21}, T_{22}]$
n-th Stage	$(x_1, x_2, \ldots, x_n)$	$[T_{n1}, T_{n2}, \ldots, T_{nn}]$

It should be pointed out that the vector $[T_{11}, T_{22}, \ldots, T_{nn}]$ alone completely determines the reranking process, in the sense that each ordinary rank vector listed above can be reconstructed given only the ranks T_{ii}, $i = 1, 2, \ldots, n$, where T_{ii} is the rank of x_i relative to the measurement set $(x_1, x_2, \ldots, x_i)$. In fact, it is easily seen that a feature measurement can be ranked as it is measured, relative to the entire preceding measurements, without reranking the previous measurements, and still retain the information which would come from reranking all the preceding measurements. This method of ranking the measurements is one which fits in naturally with the idea of sequential decision procedure, when the measurements are taken successively in accordance with a specified stopping rule. To formally present this idea which leads to the development of a nonparametric sequential classification procedure, the following definition and lemma are first given:

DEFINITION: The "Sequential Rank" of x_n relative to the set of measurements $(x_1,x_2, \ldots, x_n)$ is S_n if x_n is the S_n-th smallest in $(x_1,x_2, \ldots, x_n)$.

Thus the sequential rank of x_1 is always 1, the sequential rank of x_2 is either 1 or 2 depending on $x_2 < x_1$ or $x_1 < x_2$, and the sequential rank of x_3 is 1,2, or 3 according to that x_3 is the smallest, the next largest or the largest in the set of measurements (x_1,x_2,x_3), etc. In the sequel, the sequential rank vector for the feature measurement vector $X = [x_1,x_2, \ldots, x_n]^T$ will be denoted by $S(n) = [S_1,S_2, \ldots, S_n]$.

*Lemma**: There is a one-to-one correspondence between the set of n! possible orderings $x_{i_1} < x_{i_2} < \ldots < x_{i_n}$ and the n! possible sequential rank vectors $[S_1,S_2, \ldots, S_n]$ for the feature measurement vector $X = [x_1,x_2, \ldots, x_n]^T$.

The significance of this lemma, which will become clear later, may be summarized as follows: If one considers each ordering, say $x_{i_1} < x_{i_2} < \ldots < x_{i_n}$, of a feature measurement vector $X = [x_1,x_2, \ldots, x_n]^T$, and uses the definition given above to obtain the associated sequential ranks S_1, S_2, $\ldots$, S_n, the sequential rank vector will be uniquely determined. Conversely, the sequential rank vector uniquely determines the original ordering. Since a particularly ordering $x_{i_1} < x_{i_2} < \ldots < x_{i_n}$ also uniquely determines the ordinary rank vector $[T_{n1}, T_{n2}, \ldots, T_{nn}]$, there exists a one-to-one mapping between the set of sequential rank vectors and the set of ordinary rank vectors for all possible orderings.

In order to provide a smooth transition of the Wald's SPRT to its nonparametric setting, it is necessary to find the probability distribution for the sequential rank vectors. There are two significant findings in nonparametric statistics which can be used to obtain, respectively, the exact calculation of sequential rank distribution and a practical application in nonparametric testing problems. One is due to the fact that there exists a one-to-one correspondence between the ordered measurements (hence the ordinary rank vectors) and the sequential rank vectors. It follows that the distribution of the sequential ranks is completely determined since the distribution for the ordinary ranks can be easily calculated.[24] A second useful finding is the basic assumption of Lehmann alternatives frequently made in nonparametric tests. It will be shown that, later in Section 5.3, this assumption, although necessary, is not quite as restrictive as it appears to be when used in the nonparametric design of sequential classification systems.

Consider first the distribution of the sequential rank vectors. Using the fact that there is a unique relation between the ordered feature measurements and the sequential rank vectors, the distribution of the sequential rank vectors is also completely specified by

---

* The proof of the lemma can be found in Lemma 3.1 of Parent[22] or in Theorem 1.1 of Ole Barndorff-Nielsen.[23]

$$P(x_{i_1} \leqslant x_{i_2} \leqslant x_{i_n})$$
$$= \int_{-\infty \leqslant x_{i_1} \leqslant \ldots \leqslant x_{i_n} < \infty} \cdots \int \prod_{j=1}^{n} dP_{i_j}(x_{i_j}) \tag{5.1}$$

where $P_{i_j}(x_{i_j})$ indicates the distribution function of x_{i_j} and the x_{i_j}'s are assumed to be independent in this calculation. For the special case when the distribution functions $P_i(x_i)$ are taken to be Lehmann alternatives,[25] then

$$P_i(x_i) = P^{r_i}(x_i) = [P(x_i)]^{r_i}, \quad r_i > 0 \tag{5.2}$$

so that

$$dP_i(x_i) = dP^{r_i}(x_i) = r_i\, P^{r_i-1}(x_i)dP(x_i) \tag{5.3}$$

Using (5.1) and substituting (5.3), we obtain

$$P(x_1 \leqslant x_2 \leqslant \ldots \leqslant x_n)$$
$$= \int_{-\infty \leqslant x_1 \leqslant \ldots \leqslant x_n < \infty} \cdots \int \prod_{i=1}^{n} dP^{r_i}(x_i) \tag{5.4}$$

Let $y_i = P(x_i)$, (5.4) becomes[26]

$$P(x_1 \leqslant x_2 \leqslant \ldots \leqslant x_n)$$
$$= \int_{0 \leqslant y_1 \leqslant \ldots \leqslant y_n \leqslant 1} \cdots \int \prod_{i=1}^{n} dy_i^{r_i}$$
$$= \prod_{i=1}^{n} r_i \int \cdots \int \prod_{i=1}^{n} y_i^{r_i-1} dy_i$$
$$= \prod_{i=1}^{n} r_i [\int_0^1 y_n^{r_n-1} dy_n \int_0^{y_n} y_{n-1}^{r_{n-1}-1} dy_{n-1} \ldots \int_0^{y_3} y_2^{r_2-1} dy_2 \int_0^{y_2} y_1^{r_1-1} dy_1]$$
$$= \prod_{i=1}^{n} r_i [\int_0^1 y_n^{r_n-1} dy_n \ldots \int_0^{y_3} (\frac{1}{r_1}) y_2^{r_1+r_2-1} dy_2]$$
$$= \prod_{i=1}^{n} r_i [\int_0^1 y_n^{r_n-1} dy_n \ldots \int_0^{y_4} (\frac{1}{r_1})(\frac{1}{r_1+r_2}) y_3^{r_1+r_2+r_3-1} dy_3]$$
$$= \prod_{i=1}^{n} r_i \Big/ \prod_{i=1}^{n} (\sum_{j=1}^{i} r_j) \tag{5.5}$$

By relabeling the x_i's, the probability of any order of the x_i's can be found using (5.5), givin all the values needed in (5.1) to specify the distribution of the sequential rank vectors.

5.2 A SEQUENTIAL TWO-SAMPLE TEST PROBLEM

As a basic model for the nonparametric design of a sequential classification system, a sequential two-sample test problem is described in this section. Suppose there are available two measurement vectors of successive measurements $X = [x_1, x_2, \ldots, x_n]^T$ and $Y = [y_1, y_2, \ldots, y_n]^T$, each sampled from some probability distributions. The problem is to test the hypothesis that the two distributions are the same, against the alternative hypothesis that they are different, using as few measurements as possible. Let the successive measurements $x_1, x_2, \ldots, x_n$ and $y_1, y_2, \ldots, y_n$ be independent random variables, and assume that one wishes to test

$$\text{Hypothesis } H_0: G = P(X) \text{ against}$$
$$\text{Alternative } H_1: G = f(P(X))$$

with the assumption that $P(X)$ is the probability distribution of X and $f(P(X))$ the distribution of Y. In order to use the Wald's SPRT based on the sequential ranks, the measurements will be arranged so that they can be taken alternatively as $x_1, y_1, y_2, y_2, \ldots, x_n, y_n$. Let the combined measurements at the k-th stage be denoted by a vector $V(k) = [v_1, v_2, \ldots, v_k]$ where $v_1 = x_1$, $v_2 = y_1$, etc. Let $S(k) = [S_1, S_2, \ldots, S_k]$ be the sequential rank vector for $V(k)$, and let

$$\lambda_k = \frac{p_k(S(k)/H_1)}{p_k(S(k)/H_0)} \tag{5.6}$$

be the sequential probability ratio at the k-th stage of the process.

Under the hypothesis H_0, $p(S(k) = S/H_0) = 1/k!$ for a certain outcome vector S of S(k) and therefore, $p_k(S(k) = S/H_1)$ can be computed by noting that each outcome S corresponds, in a one-to-one manner, to a particular ordering of the combined measurements of the x_i's and y_j's. That is, it is sufficient to compute

$$P(v_1 \leqslant v_2 < \ldots \leqslant v_k/H_1)$$
$$= \int \ldots\ldots\ldots\ldots \int_{-\infty < t_1 \leqslant t_2 \leqslant \ldots \leqslant t_k < \infty} \prod_{i=1}^{k} df_i(P(t_i)) \tag{5.7}$$

where $f_i(P(t_i)) = P(t_i)$ when v_i is an x, and $f_i(P(t_i)) = f(P(t_i))$ when v_i is a y. Again in the case of Lehmann alternatives we have

$$H_0: G = P(X) \text{ against}$$
$$H_1: G = f(P(X)) = P^r(X)\ , \ r > 0.$$

Using (5.5) and (5.7) one obtains, for k even

$$p_k(S(k)/H_1) = p(S_1, S_2, \ldots, S_k/H_1)$$

$$= \frac{r^{k/2}}{\prod_{i=1}^{k} \left(\sum_{j=1}^{i} A_j \right)} \tag{5.8}$$

where

$$A_j = \begin{cases} 1 & \text{if } v_j \text{ is an } x \\ r & \text{if } v_j \text{ is a } y \end{cases} \tag{5.9}$$

The sequential probability ratio at the k-th stage then reduces to

$$\lambda_k = \frac{p_k(S(k)/H_1)}{p_k(S(k)/H_0)} = \frac{k!\ r^{k/2}}{\prod_{i=1}^{k} \left(\sum_{j=1}^{i} A_j \right)} \quad \text{for k even} \tag{5.10}$$

and

$$\lambda_k = \frac{p_k(S(k)/H_1)}{p_k(S(k)/H_0)} = \frac{k!\ r^{(k-1)/2}}{\prod_{i=1}^{k} \left(\sum_{j=1}^{i} A_j \right)} \quad \text{for k odd} \tag{5.11}$$

As the (k+1)-th measurement is taken, λ_k becomes λ_{k+1}. Using the sequential rank for the (k+1)-th observations, S_{k+1}, one can rewrite (5.10) and (5.11) to obtain λ_{k+1} as follows:

$$\lambda_{k+1} = \frac{(k+1)!\ r^{k/2}}{\prod_{i=1}^{S_{k+1}-1} \left(\sum_{j=1}^{i} A_j \right) \prod_{i=S_{k+1}+1}^{k} \left(1 + \sum_{j=1}^{i} A_j\right)} \quad \text{for k even} \tag{5.12}$$

$$\lambda_{k+1} = \frac{(k+1)!\ r^{(k+1)/2}}{\prod_{i=1}^{S_{k+1}-1} \left(\sum_{j=1}^{i} A_j \right) \prod_{i=S_{k+1}+1}^{k} \left(r + \sum_{j=1}^{i} A_j\right)} \quad \text{for k odd} \tag{5.13}$$

To complete the nonparametric SPRT procedure, it is only left to set the pair of stopping boundaries with which the sequential probability ratios are compared. The crossing of either one of the boundaries will result in a terminal decision as described previously. Note that in the process of forming the sequential probability ratio from one stage to another, one needs only to know the sequential rank S_{k+1} of the (k+1)-th measurement and the vector $A(k) = [A_1, A_2, \ldots, A_k]$ defined in (5.9). If S_{k+1} is determined to be Z, then the (k+1)-th measurement comes between the (Z−1)-th and the (Z+1)-th smallest measurement of the preceding measurements. In this way a new vector $A(k+1) = [A_1, A_2, \ldots, A_{Z-1}, A^*, A_{Z+1}, \ldots, A_k]$ with (k+1) element is formed with $A^* = 1$ if the (k+1)-th measurement is an x, and $A^* = r$ if it is a y. The sequential probability ratio λ_{k+1} is then obtained, through (5.12) or (5.13) using S_{k+1} and A(k+1). In summary, the nonparametric SPRT can be reduced to the following steps:

Step 1. Obtain the sequential rank for the (k+1)-th measurement.

Step 2. Form vector A(k+1) from A(k) and S_{k+1}.

Step. 3 Compute the sequential probability ratio λ_{k+1} by (5.12) or (5.13) and compare with stopping boundaries.

A natural question to ask here is the validity of assuming Lehmann alternatives to distinguish significant departures from a hypothesis in practical applications. While it is true that the proposed alternatives are primarily motivated by its simplicity in developing a useful test procedure, they are justifiable in many classification problems for the following reasons: *(i)* It seems that when nonparametric methods are appropriate, one usually does not have a very precise knowledge about the alternatives. What one would like to know is whether the alternatives are the representatives of the principal type of deviations from the hypothesis, in terms of which one can study the ability of various tests to detect such deviations. Lehmann alternatives have been found to provide the typical deviations which usually prevail in many probability distributions describing various pattern classes, *(ii)* While other types of alternatives are also readily available in nonparametric statistics, for example, $G = P(X \pm a)$ or $G = pP(X) + q\,P^2(X)$, they again depict alternatives with similar deviations without suggesting new measure of the difference between the hypothesis and the alternatives. In addition, the computation of the sequential probability ratio under these alternatives would be much more complicated than that under Lehmann alternatives, since the distribution of the ranks would depend not only on a (or p and q) but also on P(X). In Section 5.3, discussions will be centered on the application of the sequential two-sample test model to the design of a nonparametric classification system. Analysis of the classifier thus designed will then be made in terms of the performance criterion. Moreover, a selection rule will be found to determine a suitable Lehmann alternative when the statistics of the patterns is completely unknown, so that this seemingly unusual assumption may find its interpretation and appropriateness in practical applications.

5.3 NONPARAMETRIC DESIGN OF SEQUENTIAL PATTERN CLASSIFIERS[27]

It is assumed that the input pattern samples to the classifier are known to be taken from two distinct classes of nonparametric distributions, each of which represents a class of patterns. The problem is to seek a nonparametric design of a sequential pattern classifier which, for a pair of prespecified error probabilities, will classify the unknown patterns into one of the two pattern classes with the fewest expected number of feature measurements. Clearly, the assumption of nonparametric statistics and the requirement of optimal termination suggest that the solution be obtained by considering the classification procedure as a sequential two-sample test in the nonparametric setting.

Suppose there are available some classified pattern samples from each pattern class. Let these samples, each with n measurements, be denoted by two sets of feature vectors $\{X_1\} = \{[x_{11}, x_{12}, \ldots, x_{1n}]\}$ and $\{X_2\} = \{[x_{21}, x_{22}, \ldots, x_{2n}]\}$ belonging to class ω_1 and class ω_2 respectively. Let the input pattern to be presented for classification be denoted by a feature vector $Y = [y_1, y_2, \ldots, y_n]$ whose components are measured successively by the classifier. To determine which class the input pattern Y belongs to, it is sufficient to decide whether Y comes from a distribution to which $\{X_1\}$ belongs. Since in the case of binary classification, the acceptance of a pattern in one class implies the rejection in the other (once the terminal decision is made), it is sufficient for the classifier to decide whether Y and $\{X_1\}$ (or say, $\{X_2\}$) come from the same distribution. Furthermore, if the set of $\{X_1\}$ consists of samples which are representatives of pattern class ω_1, the classification process reduces to a sequential two-sample test problem in which the classifier performs the test of

$$\text{Hypothesis } H_0: G = P(X) \text{ against}$$
$$\text{Alternatives } H_1: G = P^r(X),\ r > 0$$

where P(X) is the probability distribution of the x_{1i}'s in X_1, and $G = P^r(X)$ is the probability distribution of the y_j's in Y. From the discussion in Section 5.2, it follows that a simple application of the sequential probability ratio test, based on the sequential ranks of the combined measurements, will result in the decision of either accepting or rejecting the hypothesis H_0, corresponding to the recognition of pattern class ω_1 or ω_2, respectively.

It is noted that, for any given value of r in the Lehmann alternatives to the hypothesis, the sequential classification procedure obtained above is optimum if two parallel stopping boundaries are used (standard Wald's SPRT). That is, the procedure requires, on the average, fewer measurements to make a terminal decision than any other test procedure, sequential or nonsequential, with at least as low error probabilities. From the practical design standpoint, the value of r can be freely chosen by the designer. However, any change of r is, in general, to affect the classifier in its structure as well as its performance. Therefore, it is desirable to analyze the system's performance by deriving an approximated relation between the parameter "r" in the Lehmann alternatives and the expected number of measurements required to make a terminal decision. The result of this derivation will establish a suitable way of choosing the value of r such that a more efficient design may be achieved without seriously increasing the system's complexity.

It can be shown that, under the hypothesis H_0[27],

$$E_r(k) = \frac{1}{\log \frac{1}{2}(r^{-1/2} + r^{1/2})} \left\{ e_{10} \log \frac{e_{10}}{1 - e_{01}} + (1 - e_{10}) \log \frac{1 - e_{10}}{e_{01}} \right\} \tag{5.14}$$

If e_{10} is chosen to be very small, i.e., $e_{10} << 1$, (5.14) can be written as

$$E_r(k) \simeq \frac{\log \dfrac{1-e_{10}}{e_{01}}}{\log \dfrac{1}{2}(r^{-1/2}+r^{1/2})} \tag{5.15}$$

which is an approximated relation between the expected number of measurements and the parameter value r, given e_{10} and e_{01}.

Consider the case when $r < 1$. It is clear that the denominator of $E_r(k)$ in (5.15) increases as r decreases. Since $\log [(1-e_{10})/e_{01}]$ is a constant for given e_{10} and e_{01}, $E_r(k)$ tends to decrease accordingly. On the other hand, when $r > 1$, the denominator increases as r increases, which, in turn, makes $E_r(k)$ decrease. It can be concluded that the expected number of measurements $E_r(k)$ decreases as the value of r departs from unity, regardless of whether $r < 1$ or $r > 1$. A qualitative plot of $E_r(k)$ vs. r, which depicts the functional relation of (5.15), is shown in Figure 3.

There is a natural generalization from the sequential two-sample test to the case where the number of pattern classes is more than two. Let $P(X/\omega_i)$, $i = 1, 2, \ldots, m$ be the probability distribution (unknown) for the m pattern classes, and let the set of learning samples from class ω_i be denoted by $\{X_i\} = \{[x_{i1}, x_{i2}, \ldots, x_{in}]\}$, $i = 1, 2, \ldots, m$. To determine the pattern class to which a pattern sample $Y = [y_1, y_2, \ldots, y_n]$ belongs, the two-sample test can be applied to each and every class ω_i to test

$$\begin{aligned} &\text{Hypothesis } H_0: G = P(X/\omega_i),\ i = 1,2, \ldots, m \text{ against} \\ &\text{Alternative } H_1: G = f(P(X/\omega_i)) = P^{r_i}(X/\omega_i),\ r > 0, \\ &\qquad i = 1, 2, \ldots, m. \end{aligned}$$

Consider the successive measurements of the m combined sample vector be

$$V_1(k) = [v_{11}, v_{12}, \ldots, v_{1k}] = [x_{11}, y_1, x_{12}, y_2, \ldots, x_{1n}, y_n]$$

$$V_2(k) = [v_{21}, v_{22}, \ldots, v_{2k}] = [x_{21}, y_1, x_{22}, y_2, \ldots, x_{2n}, y_n]$$

$$\vdots$$

$$V_m(k) = [v_{m1}, v_{m2}, \ldots, v_{mk}] = [x_{m1}, y_1, x_{m2}, y_2, \ldots, x_{mn}, y_n]$$

where $k = 1,2, \ldots, 2n$. The corresponding sequential rank vectors are determined as

$$S_1(k) = [S_{11}, S_{12}, \ldots, S_{1k}]$$

$$S_2(k) = [S_{21}, S_{22}, \ldots, S_{2k}]$$

$$\vdots$$

$$S_m(k) = [S_{m1}, S_{m2}, \ldots, S_{mk}]$$

where $k = 1, 2, \ldots, 2n$. At the k-th measurement of the m combined sample vectors $V_1(k), V_2(k), \ldots, V_m(k)$, the sequential probability ratios are computed, i.e.,

$$\lambda_{ik} = \frac{p_k(S_i(k)/H_1)}{p_k(S_i(k)/H_0)}, \quad i = 1, 2, \ldots, m \tag{5.16}$$

where $p_k(S_i(k)/H_0)$ or $p_k(S_i(k)/H_1)$ is the probability of the sequential rank vectors $S_i(k)$, given the hypothesis that Y belongs to the class ω_i, or the alternative that Y does not. Following (5,8), for k even, (5.16) becomes

$$\lambda_{ik} = \frac{k!\ r_i^{k/2}}{\prod_{q=1}^{k} \left(\sum_{j=1}^{q} A_{ij} \right)}, \quad i = 1, 2, \ldots, m \tag{5.17}$$

where

$$A_{ij} = \begin{cases} 1 & \text{if } v_{ij} \text{ is an x from } X_i \\ r_i & \text{if } v_{ij} \text{ is a y} \end{cases} \tag{5.18}$$

Adopting the rejection criterion of the GSPRT, the pattern class ω_i is dropped from consideration at the k-th measurement if

$$\lambda_{ik} \geqslant A_k(\omega_i) \tag{5.19}$$

The process of forming λ_{ik} continues until there is only one sequential probability ratio left not satisfying the above inequality, and its associated hypothesis is then accepted as the true pattern class to which Y belongs. Note that the upper stopping boundaries $A_k(\omega_i)$ in (5.19) are generally functions of both the hypothesis under test and the number of stage k under consideration. In practice, $A_k(\omega_i)$ may be set to $[1-(e_{01})_i]/(e_{10})_i$ where $(e_{10})_i$ and $(e_{01})_i$ are the two types of error probabilities for the hypothesis associated with class ω_i. As shown in (5.19), the lower stopping boundaries $B_k(\omega_i)$ have been made negligibly small, by setting $(e_{01})_i$ arbitrarily small, to prevent the test from accepting a hypothesis prematurely when the alternative H_1 is true. In any case, the stopping boundaries should be determined in such a way that they would minimize the effect of possible ambiguity, for example, a rejection in all pattern classes in a situation where it is known that the input sample is from one of the pattern classes, or an acceptance in more than one class.

VI. Illustrative Examples

The sequential pattern recognition techniques discussed in previous sections were applied to hand-printed and hand-written English character recognition. The pattern samples used for the experiments were obtained by asking subjects to write characters in a two-inch square (for hand-printed characters) or a circle with two-inch diameter (for hand-written characters). Eight features, $x_1, \ldots, x_8$, were selected for hand-printed characters, and eighteen features, $x_1, \ldots, x_{18}$, for hand-written characters, as shown in Figure 4. Each feature measurement is the distance measured along a predetermined path from the edge of the square or the circle to the edge of the character (also see Figure 4). These features were chosen somewhat arbitrarily with the hope that, for each pattern class, the distribution function of the feature was close to a multivariate gaussian distribution.* The mean vector and the covariance matrix were estimated from sixty test samples of each character by computing the sample mean vector and the sample covariance matrix.

Experiment 1 — MODIFIED SPRT AND GSPRT

The feature distributions for each pattern class is assumed to be multivariate gaussian.

Let $p_n(X/\omega_i)$, i = 1, 2, 3, represent the multivariate gaussian densities for characters a, b and c, respectively, at the n-th stage of the sequential classification process. X is an n-dimensional feature vector denoting the successive measurements of $(x_1, x_2, \ldots, x_n)$, $n \leqslant N = 18$. This is the case that the classification process terminates in no more than eighteen feature measurements. Specifically,

$$p_n(X/\omega_i) = \frac{1}{(2\pi)^{n/2} |K|^{1/2}} \exp[-\frac{1}{2}(X-M_i)^T K^{-1} (X-M_i)] , \quad i = 1, 2, 3 \tag{6.1}$$

where M_i is the mean vector for class ω_i, K is the nxn common covariance matrix for all three classes.

Case (a). Binary classification of characters a and b using the modified SPRT.

In this case, m = 2, the logarithm of sequential probability ratio computed at n-th stage is

$$L_n = X^T K^{-1} (M_2 - M_1) - \frac{1}{2} (M_2 + M_1)^T K^{-1} (M_2 - M_1) \tag{6.2}$$

The upper stopping boundary for the modified SPRT is chosen as

$$g_1(n) = a'(1 - \frac{n}{18}) , \quad n = 1, 2, \ldots, 18 \tag{6.3}$$

and the lower stopping boundary as

$$g_2(n) = -b'(1 - \frac{n}{18}) , \quad n = 1, 2, \ldots, 18 \tag{6.4}$$

*The gaussian assumption for feature distribution has been studied by many authors[2,28].

where a′ and −b′ are the starting boundaries adjusted in such a way that the various levels of error probabilities and the expected number of feature measurements were obtained. The result is shown in Figure 5 in which the trade-off between error and classification time (in terms of expected number of measurements) is demonstrated. On the same figure, the corresponding curve for the standard Wald's SPRT (by setting constant stopping boundaries of various levels) is shown for the purpose of comparison. It is noted that while the same power of classification between two characters may be achieved, the modified SPRT has shown its capability of reducing the classification time up to 40% for small error probabilities.

Case (b). Multi-classification of characters a, b and c using the modified GSPRT.

In this case, i = 1, 2, 3, the generalized sequential probability ratio for each class computed at n-th stage is

$$U_n(X/\omega_i) = \frac{p_n(X/\omega_i)}{\left[\prod_{j=1}^{m} p_n(X/\omega_j)\right]^{1/m}}, \quad \begin{array}{l} i = 1, 2, 3 \\ n = 1, 2, \ldots, 18 \end{array} \tag{6.5}$$

where m may assume the value 2, or 3, depending on the number of pattern classes under consideration at each stage. Let

$$g_i(n) = G'(1 - \frac{n}{18}) \quad , \quad n = 1, 2, \ldots, 18 \tag{6.6}$$

where $G' > 0$, and i = 1, 2, 3. The classification procedure of the modified GSPRT is to drop the class ω_i from consideration at n-th stage if $U_n(X/\omega_i) < g_i(n)$ for some i. As soon as there is only one class which does not satisfy the inequality, this class is assigned to the input pattern. In Figure 6, the relationship between error and classification time is obtained by setting different values for the starting boundary G′. The corresponding result for GSPRT with constant boundaries is also shown in the same figure. It is important to observe that by properly constructing the time-varying stopping boundaries, a better performance of reducing the classification time may also be achieved in the modified GSPRT without sacrificing the prespecified error probabilities.

Experiment 2 – BACKWARD PROCEDURE FOR PATTERN CLASSIFICATION

In order to test the formulation and procedure outlined in Section 4.1 and 4.2, a particular pattern recognition problem was taken. The pattern classes considered were the handprinted English characters D, J, P, and V (denoted as Class ω_1, ω_2, ω_3 and ω_4, respectively). Eight radial intersection measurements (taking on values from 1 to 20) were used as successive feature measurements as shown in Figure 4. To reduce the difficulty in computation, the method described in Section 4.2(A) was used, assuming that the feature measurements were statistically independent. Furthermore, each feature measurement was quantized into five levels, $E_1, E_2, \ldots, E_5$; and only events consisting of a feature measurement falling into a particular quantum were considered. Parameter values $(p_{i1}, p_{i2}, \ldots, p_{i5})$ characterizing the multinomial distribution of class ω_i were estimated by preparing a histogram and computing the frequency ratios for the occurrence of the quantized events. The approximate cumulative distribution function of feature measurements thus obtained is given in Table 1. F(i,j) represents the number of measurements from the class ω_i which falls below the integer value j; i = 1, 2, 3, 4 and j = 1, 2, . . . , 20. For example, if quantum 3 was chosen to be (6,10], then, for class ω_2, $p_{23} = [F(2,10)-F(2,6)]/36x8$.

In addition to the dynamic programming procedure, experiments were also run to determine the classification accuracies attainable using all the eight features identically quantized (nonsequential or fixed-sample size Bayes' classification procedure). The results then allowed a fair comparison of the expected number of feature measurements required and the correct classifications achieved for the sequential and nonsequential procedures.

Table 1

DISTRIBUTIONS OF FEATURE MEASUREMENTS FOR ENGLISH CHARACTERS D, J, P, AND V.

j	F(1,j)	F(2,j)	F(3,j)	F(4,j)
1	0	0	0	0
2	1	0	1	0
3	4	5	12	3
4	17	21	40	13
5	31	51	80	28
6	68	100	128	45
7	124	121	168	81
8	199	136	242	143
9	264	158	269	197
10	287	187	277	226
11	288	223	277	235
12	288	223	281	235
13	288	252	283	237
14	288	272	286	249
15	288	280	288	264
16	288	284	288	270
17	288	286	288	276
18	288	288	288	282
19	288	288	288	285
20	288	288	288	288

Case (a). Experimental conditions:

(i) All measurement costs are equal = 0.03/measurement

(ii) Loss function

$$L(d_j,\omega_i) = \begin{cases} 0, & i = j \\ A, \text{ (constant)}, & i \neq j \end{cases}$$

(iii) $P(\omega_1) = P(\omega_2) = P(\omega_3) = P(\omega_4) = 0.25$

(iv) Quantum partitions: $E_1 = (0,6]$, $E_2 = (6,7]$, $E_3 = (7,8]$
$E_4 = (8,11]$, $E_5 = (11,20]$.

Classification results:

(i) Dynamic programming procedure

True Class	No. of Patterns Classified as				% of Correct Recognition	Total No. of Required Measurements
	D	J	P	V		
D	26	2	8	0	72	240
J	0	27	6	3	75	137
P	13	3	19	1	53	226
V	0	9	2	25	70	129
						732

Overall accuracy: 67%

True Class	No. of Patterns Classified as				% of Correct Recognition	Total No. of Required Measurements
	D	J	P	V		
D	27	2	7	0	75	288
J	0	24	9	3	67	288
P	12	3	20	1	55	288
V	0	5	5	26	72	288
						1152

Overall accuracy: 67%

Case (b). Experimental conditions:

(i), (iii), (iv) same as in Case (a).

(ii) Loss function – the loss due to misrecognition when a pattern is true from class ω_3; i.e., character P, equals four times that of other misrecognitions.

Classification results – Dynamic programming procedure:

True Class	No. of Patterns Classified as				% of Correct Recognition	Total No. of Required Measurements
	D	J	P	V		
D	2	0	34	0	5	87
J	0	21	15	0	58	114
P	0	0	36	0	100	83
V	0	6	9	21	58	143
						427

Overall accuracy: 55%

The results of the experiments are summarized and discussed as follows:

(1) Case (a) shows a comparison of classification results between the dynamic programming procedure and a nonsequential classification procedure for two different quantizations of feature space. As expected, in each experiment the required number of measurements using the dynamic programming procedure is much less than that using the nonsequential procedure, without sacrificing significantly the percentage of correct classification.

(2) Case (b) shows the effect of employing an unsymmetric loss function. By weighting the misrecognitions most heavily on class ω_3, it is possible to achieve 100% correct classification for that class. While it is true that this result is accomplished at the expense of causing greater errors in classifying patterns from other classes, the change of loss functions does make the classification procedure more flexible and useful in distinguishing various errors.

Experiment 3 – FEATURE ORDERING AND PATTERN CLASSIFICATION

To test the formulation and the optimality of the procedure outlined in Section 4.3, the English character recognition problem described in Experiment 2 was again used. Only three pattern classes D, J, and P were considered. All feature measurements were assumed statistically independent. In order to reduce the computational difficulty, the Bayesian statistic (a posteriori probability) was used. At each stage of the process, the conditional probability that the sample was from each class was calculated by (4.22), given the past history of feature measurements. Thus, it can be seen that by using this procedure, all information provided by the past history of feature selection and measurement outcomes is contained in the a posteriori probabilities calculated by (4.22).

The classifying decision at the final stage depends on the a posteriori probability of occurrence of each class having measured all eight features in addition to the loss due to misrecognition. For computational purpose each a posteriori probability was quantized into twenty equal divisions. Thus the probability space was quantized into a total of 210 quanta. The loss due to misrecognition was assumed equal to one in all cases, i.e.,

$$L(d_j,\omega_i) = \begin{cases} 0 \,, & i = j \\ 1 \,, & i \neq j \end{cases}$$

The cost of feature measurement is 0.01/measurement. In all experiments the a priori probability of each class was taken to be equal to 1/3. The expected risk of making a decision for various a posteriori probabilities is associated with the corresponding quantum.

Three cases were considered. The purpose of these experiments was to allow a verification of the optimal properties of the proposed procedure and a comparison of results obtained from using the proposed procedure and other statistical classification procedures.

Case (a) – Sequential classification with feature ordering

Case (b) – Nonsequential Bayesian classification using all eight features

Case (c) – Sequential classification without feature ordering

Table 2 summarizes the results concerning the accuracy of recognition and the number of feature measurements required for classification.

The results of the experiments are summarized and discussed as follows:

(1) It is seen that the same percentage of correct recognition is obtained for all the three classification procedures. In fact, it turned out that the misrecognitions were made on exactly the same patterns.

(2) From Table 2, it should be noted that even though the sequential classification procedure without feature ordering required fewer feature measurements to classify patterns from class J than the sequential procedure with feature ordering, it did require more measurements for the entire process. It appears that the sequential procedure with feature ordering may cause poorer performance in some particular cases, but on the average over the entire process it produces better results. This is expected since the optimization was carried out over the entire process.

(3) The sequential procedure with feature ordering required about 60% less feature measurements than the nonsequential Bayesian procedure while the sequential procedure without feature ordering required about 50% less.

Experiment 4 – NONPARAMETRIC PROCEDURE

A computer simulation experiment was carried out to test the sequential ranking procedure discussed in Section 5.3. The experiment consisted in classifying the handwritten English characters a and b as described in Figure 4, with the exception that the probability distributions of patterns in each class were assumed to be nonparametric and unknown. Let the learning sample from character a be denoted by

$$X_a = [x_{a_1}, x_{a_2}, \ldots, x_{a_{18}}]$$

Table 2

ACCURACY OF CLASSIFICATION

Case (a)

True Class	No. of Patterns Classified as			% of Correct Recognition	Total No. of Required Measurements
	D	J	P		
D	33	0	3	91.6	147
J	0	36	0	100	82
P	7	0	29	80.6	135
					364

Overall accuracy: 90.7%

Case (b)

True Class	No. of Patterns Classified as			% of Correct Recognition	Total No. of Required Measurements
	D	J	P		
D	33	0	3	91.6	288
J	0	36	0	100	288
P	7	0	29	80.6	288
					864

Overall accuracy: 90.7%

Case (c)

True Class	No. of Patterns Classified as			% of Correct Recognition	Total No. of Required Measurements
	D	J	P		
D	33	0	3	91.6	187
J	0	36	0	100	61
P	7	0	29	80.6	189
					436

Overall accuracy: 90.7%

which was obtained, in this experiment, from the estimated mean vector of sixty samples from character a. The classification of an unknown input pattern Y was then based on the successive measurement of the combined sample vector denoted by

$$V(36) = [v_1, v_2, \ldots, v_{36}] = [x_{a_1}, y_1, x_{a_2}, y_2, \ldots, x_{a_{18}}, y_{18}]$$

Using (5.10) and (5.11), the classifier decides to accept the hypothesis that Y belongs to the class of character a, or the alternative that it does not (i.e., to accept that Y belongs to the class of character b). For the purpose of illustration, some sixty pattern samples of characters a and b were tested on the computer. The classification results are summarized in Figure 7 in which the error probability (average percentage of two types of misrecognition) is plotted against the average number of feature measurements required to make a terminal decision. The classification experiment was repeated with r in the Lehmann alternatives as a running parameter. It is seen that the experiment performed tends to verify the theoretical conclusions in two respects: *(i)* the sequential ranking procedure and the resulting two-sample test model to provide an effective nonparametric procedure for sequential classification in which the error probability decreases as the number of measurements increases, as usually expected in Wald's SPRT. *(ii)* For a specified error probability, fewer measurements are required to make a terminal decision by increasing the value of r if $r > 1$, or by decreasing the value of r if $r < 1$, which is the relation concluded in (5.15). This relation is particularly useful in selecting a desirable Lehmann alternative for a certain pattern class in the absence of any statistical knowledge about the pattern samples. Although no direct verification of the validity of the assumption of Lehmann alternatives was attempted in the experiment, the simulation result does indicate possible low error probabilities in the classification of character samples if proper Lehmann alternatives are chosen and a sufficient number of measurements are available.

VII. Conclusions and Further Remarks

Sequential decision procedures have been shown being applicable to the design of pattern recognition systems when the costs of taking feature measurements are important. The standard Wald's sequential probability ratio test and the generalized sequential probability ratio test are convenient in computation but difficult in controlling the number of feature measurements required for terminal decisions. These test procedures are modified by using time-varying stopping boundaries with which the sequential (or generalized) probability ratios are compared at each stage of the recognition process. The fact that the stopping boundaries are set monotonically convergent guarantees the finite termination and, in turn, the acceleration of the recognition process, but not without sacrificing the optimal properties of the original tests. Nevertheless, the resulting procedures are simple and efficient as demonstrated in the simulated experiments of character recognition.

When a truly optimal (and finite) sequential decision procedure is required, it is appropriate to employ the backward procedure – dynamic programming. The stopping rules are established by recursively minimizing the expected risk functions at each stage, starting at the termination stage. The resulting procedure is truly optimal, but it is much more complex in computation. Several methods of reducing the computational difficulties and storage requirement are suggested. In addition, the backward procedure has also been successfully applied to the problems of both feature ordering and pattern classification.

A nonparametric approach has been presented for the design of sequential classifiers in which no assumption is made as to the form of the underlying probability distributions characterizing the patterns in each class. For the case of two-class classification problems, a sequential ranking procedure is found useful in a two-sample problem in which a test is performed on the hypothesis against Lehmann alternatives based on the successively ranked feature measurements. The procedure has also been extended for multi-class classification. Computer simulated experiments in character recognition indicate satisfactory results in illustrating the proposed approaches.

Although the results of the study have given solutions to a number of problems in sequential recognition, they also suggest new problems for further investigations. Some of these problems are indicated below.

(1) The form of the time-varying stopping boundaries $g_i(n)$ is only a suggested one. The method of selecting an optimal form for $g_i(n)$ has not been studied.

(2) There has not been much quantitative comparison of performance between the forward and the backward procedure in terms of the simplicity in computation and the optimality in recognition. This lack of comparison makes it difficult to determine which procedure is more appropriate for a particular recognition problem on hand.

(3) The nonparametric approach proposed is rather a preliminary study and the approach appears to be based on the assumption of Lehmann alternatives which supposedly characterize the alternative pattern classes under consideration. More general nonparametric approaches and possible extensions with alternatives other than the Lehmann alternatives are certainly needed.

REFERENCES

1. C.K. Chow, "An Optimum Character Recognition System Using Decision Functions", IRE Trans. on Electronic Computers, Vol. EC–6, December, 1957, pp. 247–254.
2. T. Marill and D.M. Green, "Statistical Recognition Functions and the Design of Pattern Recognizers", IRE Trans. on Electronic Computers, Vol. EC–9, December, 1960, pp. 472–477.
3. G. Sebestyen, *Decision–making Processes in Pattern Recognition,* Macmillan, New York, 1962.
4. N.J. Nilsson, *Learning Machines–Foundations of Trainable Pattern Classifying Systems,* McGraw-Hill, 1965.
5. A. Wald, *Sequential Analysis,* Wiley, New York, 1947.
6. D. Blackwell and M.A. Girshick, *Theory of Games and Statistical Decisions,* Wiley, New York, 1954.
7. K.S. Fu, "A Sequential Decision Model for Optimum Recognition," *Biological Prototypes and Synthetic Systems,* Vol. I, Plenum Press, 1962.
8. F.C. Reed, "A Sequential Multi-decision Procedure", Proc. Symp. on Decision Theory and Application to Electronic Equipment Development, USAF Dev. Center, Rome, New York, April, 1960.
9. Y.T. Chien and K.S. Fu, "A Modified Sequential Recognition Machine Using Time-Varying Stopping Boundaries", IEEE Trans. on Information Theory, Vol. IT–12, No. 2, April, 1966, pp. 206–214.
10. T.W. Anderson, "A Modification of the Sequential Probability Ratio Test to Reduce the Sample Size", Ann. Math. Stat., Vol. 31, March, 1960.
11. J.J. Bussgang and M.B. Marcus, "Truncated Sequential Hypothesis Tests", Memo. RM–4268–APRA, The Rand Corporation, November, 1964.
12. G.B. Wetherrill, *Sequential Methods in Statistics,* Methuen and Co., and Wiley, 1966.
13. R. Bellman, *Dynamic Programming,* Princeton University Press, 1957.
14. R. Bellman, R. Kalaba and D. Middleton, "Dynamic Programming, Sequential Estimation and Sequential Detection Processes," Proc. National Academy of Sciences, Vol. 47, 1961, pp. 338–341.
15. D.V. Lindley, "Dynamic Programming and Decision Theory", Applied Statistics (10), 1961, pp. 39–51.
16. E.B. Dynkin, "The Optimum Choice of the Instant for Stopping a Markov Process", Soviet Mathematics, Vol. 4, No. 3, 1963, pp. 627–629.
17. R.A. Howard, *Dynamic Programming and Markov Processes,* Wiley, 1960.
18. P.C. Fishburn, "A General Theory of Finite Sequential Decision Processes", Tech. paper RAC–TP–143, Research Analysis Corporation, McLean, Virginia, February, 1965.
19. K.S. Fu, Y.T. Chien and G.P. Cardillo, "A Dynamic Programming Approach to Sequential Pattern Recognition", IEEE Trans. on Electronic Computers, December, 1967.
20. G.P. Cardillo and K.S. Fu, "A Dynamic Programming Procedure for Sequential Pattern Classification and Feature Selection," Mathematical Biosciences, Vol. 1, September 1967, pp. 463–491.
21. Y.T. Chien and K.S. Fu, "An Optimal Pattern Classification System Using Dynamic Programming", Mathematical Biosciences, Vol. 1, September 1967, pp. 439–461.

22. E.A. Parent, "Sequential Ranking Procedure", Tech. Rept. No. 880, Dept. of Statistics, Stanford University, 1965.
23. Ole Barndorff-Nielsen, "On the Limit Behavior of Extreme Order-Statistics", Ann. Math. Stat. Vol. 34, 1963, pp. 992–1002.
24. W. Hoeffding, "Optimum Nonparametric Tests", Proc. Second Berkeley Symp. on Math. Stat. and Probability, University of California Press, 1951, pp. 83–92.
25. E.L. Lehmann, "The Power of Rank Tests", Ann. Math. Stat., Vol. 24, 1953, pp. 23–43.
26. I.R. Savage and J. Sethuraman, "Stopping Time of a Rank-Order Sequential Probability Ratio Test Based on Lehmann Alternatives", Ann. Math. Stat., Vol. 37, No. 5, October, 1966, pp. 1154–1160.
27. K.S. Fu and Y.T. Chien, "Sequential Recognition Using a Nonparametric Ranking Procedure," IEEE Trans. on Information Theory, July, 1967.
28. J.A. Lebo, "On the Selection of Decision Criteria and the Estimation of Probabilities in Pattern Recognition", Ph.D. Thesis (Tech. Rept. TR–EE64–15), School of Electrical Engineering, Purdue University, September, 1964.
29. K.S. Fu and C.H. Chen, "Sequential Decisions, Pattern Recognition, and Machine Learning", Tech. Rept. TR–EE65–6, School of Electrical Engineering, Prudue University, April, 1965.
30. A. Dvoretzky, J. Kiefer and J. Wolfowitz, "Sequential Decision Problems for Processes with Continuous Time Parameter, Testing Hypotheses", Ann. Math. Stat., Vol. 24, June, 1953, pp. 87–93.
31. R.M. Phataford, "Large Sample Sequential Analysis of Markovian Observations", J. Indiana Stat. Assoc., 1963.
32. D.A.S. Frazer, *Nonparametric Methods in Statistics*, Wiley, 1957.

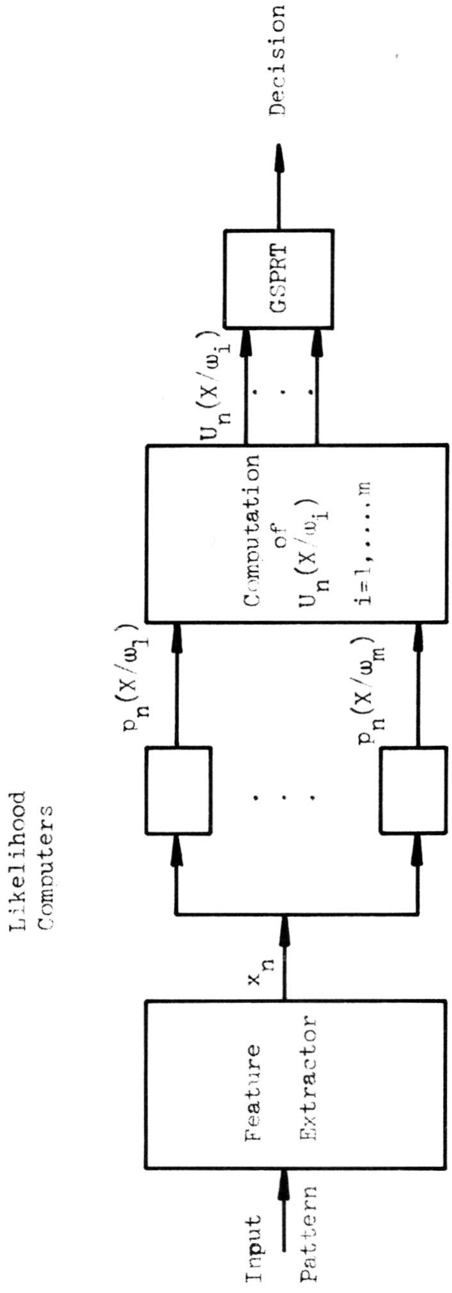
Input
Pattern
Feature
Extractor
x_n
Likelihood
Computers
$p_n(X/\omega_1)$
$p_n(X/\omega_m)$
Computation
of
$U_n(X/\omega_i)$
$i=1,\ldots,m$
$U_n(X/\omega_i)$
GSPRT
Decision

Figure 1

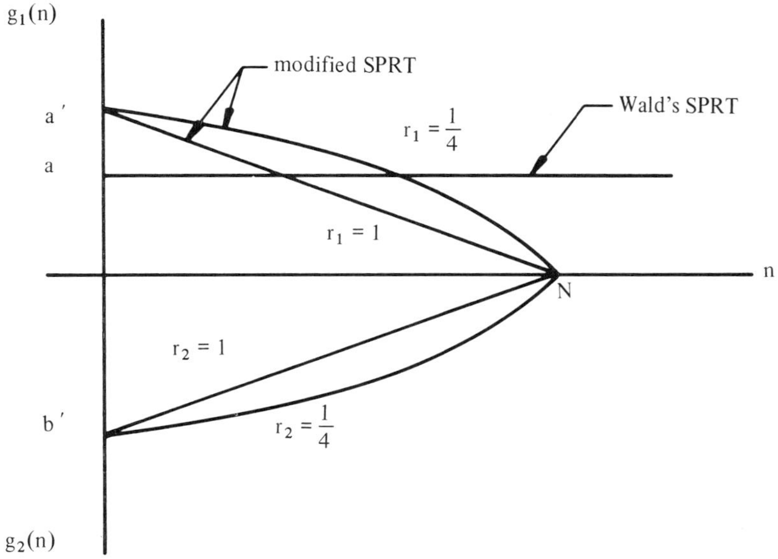

Figure 2

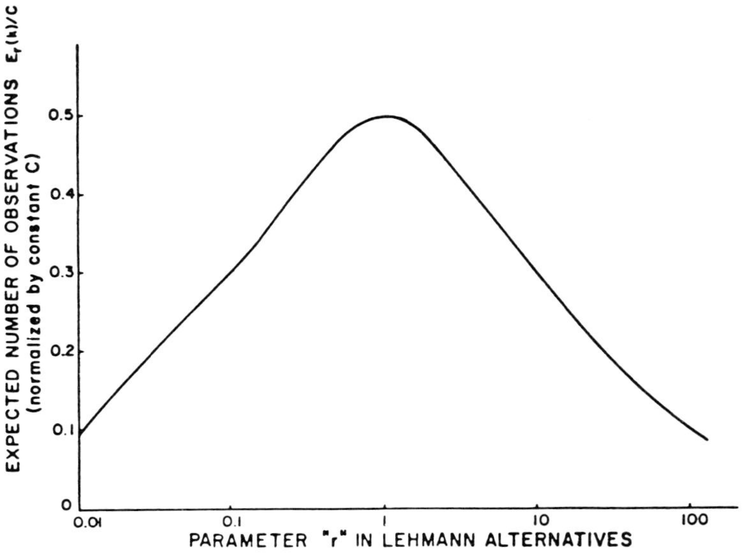

Figure 3: Plot of Equation (5.15) Showing the Relation Between the Expected Number of Observations and the Parameter "r" in the Lehman Alternatives

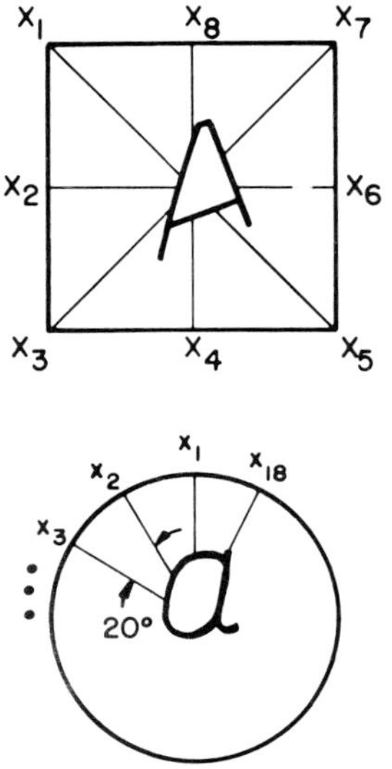

Figure 4: Typical Samples and Their Feature Measurements for Handwritten and Handprinted Character a and b

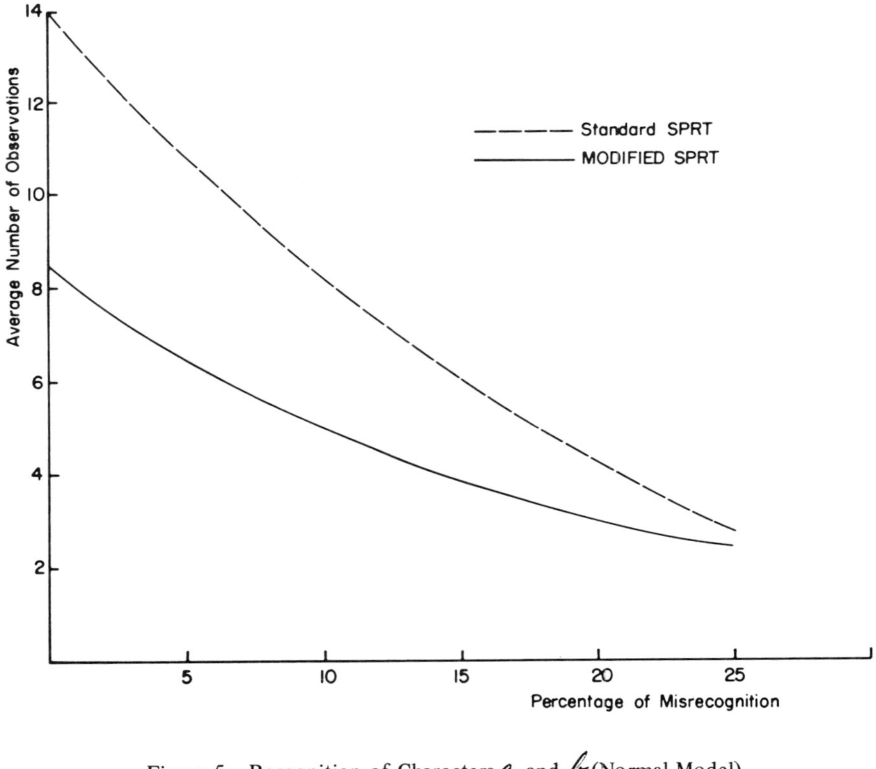

Figure 5: Recognition of Characters *a* and *b* (Normal Model)

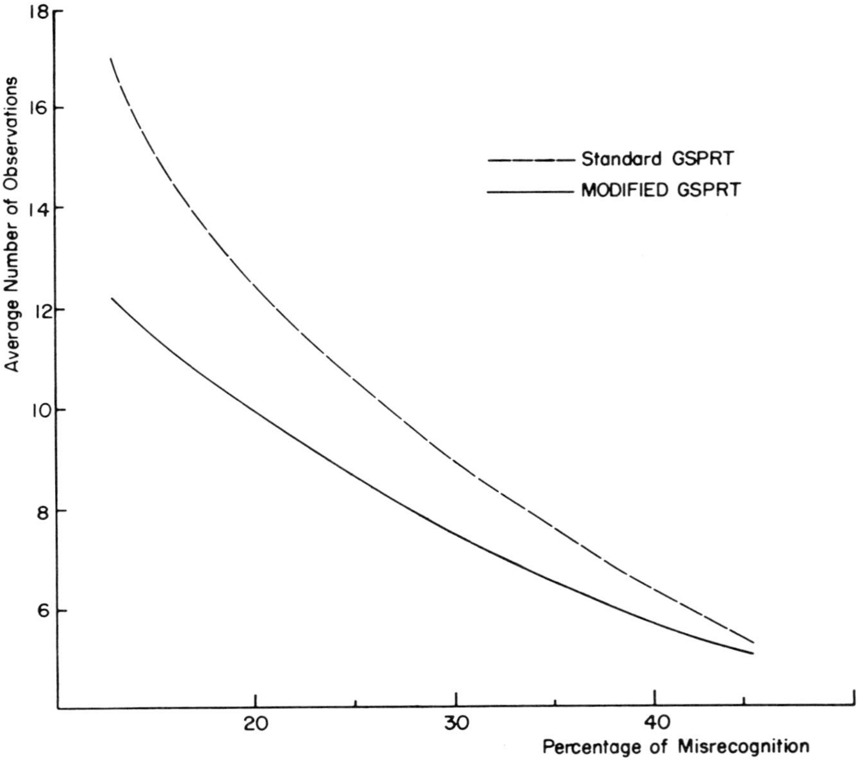

Figure 6: Recognition of Characters *a*, *b* and *c* (Normal Model)

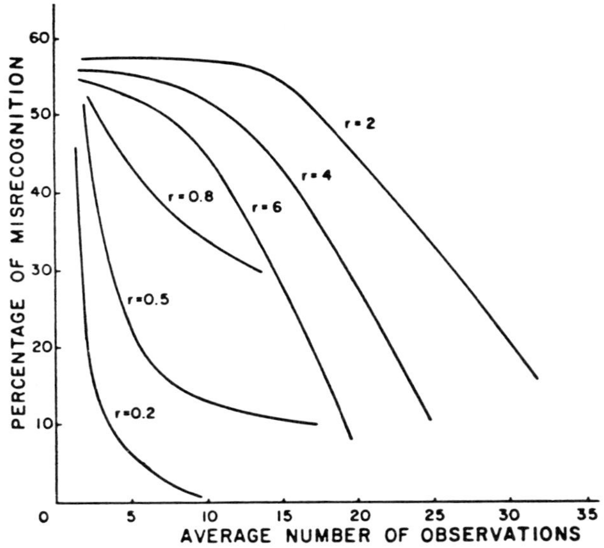

Figure 7: Performance Curves – Recognition of Characters a and b (Nonparametric Model)

INTRODUCTION TO BIOLOGICAL AND MECHANICAL PATTERN RECOGNITION

Earl E. Gose

INFORMATION ENGINEERING DEPARTMENT
UNIVERSITY OF ILLINOIS AT CHICAGO CIRCLE

Pattern recognition or classification is a process which groups input signals or stimuli (patterns) into categories according to their properties. The categories and properties may or may not be known in advance, and the system is usually required to generalize to stimuli which were not used in its design or training. The ability of animals to recognize patterns is one aspect of their intelligence, and the study of mechanical pattern recognition is a sub-division of the field of artificial intelligence[97, 106]. All of these fields fall into the general category of cybernetics, defined as the sciences of communication and control in animals and machines[157].

Because of the large amount of research that has been done in the field of pattern recognition, the present paper can only be a summary with examples rather than a comprehensive survey of the field. No attempt is made to trace the concepts and techniques in use today back to their original sources. The references have been selected from only a small fraction of the pertinent literature, but they will serve to guide the interested reader to the current work.

Pattern Recognition by Animals

The study of pattern recognition in animals is difficult because of their behavioral and neurophysiological complexity[95]. Behaviorally, one can never be certain to which stimuli an organism is responding. Neurophysiologically, we are limited to recording from only a few neurons simultaneously and we have no complete maps of their interconnections and no great knowledge of their functions. Direct investigation of the inner workings of the human nervous system is not permissible because of the injurious nature of the present measurement techniques, except in rare cases where data may be obtained without additional risk to the patient during brain operations. In view of these limitations, it is not surprising that detailed modeling of neural information processing is mainly of those most peripheral portions of the nervous system which seem to be involved with preprocessing the signals for later computation. More general information concerning the anatomical locations where various functions are performed is available from ablation studies in which portions of the brains of animals are removed or connections between them are cut[48,49]. Similar information on humans is available from cases of accidental injury.

This paper will consider only two of the most important senses involved in pattern recognition, vision and hearing. Of these, vision is probably the most studied, and informationally it is our largest input channel. Important though vision may be, the loss of hearing is often considered to be more of a handicap than the loss of vision, for it is through this sense that we carry out most of our day-to-day communication with our fellow man.

Vision

Knowledge of animal vision comes from both perceptual and neurophysiological experimentation. Perceptual experiments are based on the response of the entire organism to visual stimulation, so they cannot be explained on the basis of the structure of the visual neural tracts alone. Animals tend to base their responses on all the information available to them, so that other sensory modalities often influence their response to visual stimulation. Neurophysiological experiments measure the responses of single neurons during visual stimulation. Microelectrodes have been used to measure signals from fibers in the optic nerve and from fibers and cells in the lateral geniculate, the tectum, and the cortex. Some models which help to consolidate the results of both types of experiments will be described in a later section.

PERCEPTUAL EXPERIMENTS

All animals, from insects to primates, *generalize* on the basis of their visual sensations. For example, when animals are trained to respond to the larger or the brighter of two particular stimuli, they will still respond to the larger or brighter of two other stimuli from a completely different intensity or size range[82]. Each animal has its own bias or direction in which it tends to generalize. The Octopus is particularly sensitive to the horizontal or vertical extent of visual figures, as if it were projecting these figures onto horizontal and vertical visual axes[144].

Some patterns of response are *instinctive.* The reaction of inexperienced ducklings depends on the direction of motion of a moving silhouette. When moving in one direction, it resembles a long-necked duck and evokes no response, but when moving in the other direction, it resembles a long-tailed hawk and evokes strong flight reactions[110]. Human babies tend to look longer at drawings of faces than at randomly garbled drawings containing the same elements[41]. Chickens have an innate pecking preference for circles as compared to triangles or squares[143]. Many young animals pass through a period during which they are susceptible to *"imprinting"* of visual or other images, usually of a parent figure, which will then have much more significance to them than images learned later in life. Imprinting is guided by instinct and in ducks it is stronger and longer-lasting for some ways of painting decoys than others[79].

Learning is important in visual perception, particularly in the higher animals. People whose vision is restored by an operation after they have been blind from birth will be able to tell light from dark, but it typically takes several months before they can recognize objects easily. People who have worn special goggles which turn their visual world upside down, or produce a right-left inversion, found that the world looked normal again after wearing the goggles for a week or more. On removing these goggles, the world again appeared reversed, although the subsequent period of readaptation was shorter[55]. Goggles containing prisms produce yellow fringes on one side of an object and blue fringes on the other side. The side the yellow fringe is on depends upon whether the object is lighter or darker than its background. These fringes are not noticeable after adaptation, but when the goggles are removed, oppositely colored fringes are perceived.

The role of *activity* is important in adaptation. People wearing wedge prisms which deflect their field of view to the side adapt rather quickly when permitted to move objects around in their field of view with their hands, while those who are not allowed this experience do not adapt significantly. Other experiments were performed on kittens raised with deprivation of patterned visual stimuli except while in a training machine. In this machine, the passive kitten was held above the floor in a cradle attached to one end of a centrally pivoted rod. The active kitten was harnessed to the other end of the rod, which revolved as the active kitten walked in a circle. The apparatus was constructed in such a way that the two kittens had the same visual experience, but the active kitten learned considerably more than the passive one[60].

The lower animals are less adaptive. When wedge prisms were placed over the eyes of chicks they did not adapt, but pecked consistently at the wrong spot[143]. When the eye of the newt was rotated surgically by 180 degrees, it did not adapt. Even when the optic nerve was cut, the fibers regenerated according to their original plan and the animals' attempts at fly-catching were inverted. A similar operation on sufficiently young clawed toad larvae produced no inversion, or only right-left reversal, rather than rotation of the visual field[71] which indicates that the right-left coordinate of the map is specified at an earlier stage of development than the up-down coordinate. The chemical or other variables which enable the fibers to find their way to the appropriate terminations are unknown.

One category of *visual illusions*, the *ambiguous* figures, demonstrates that there is an instability in the perceptual mechanism which causes sudden changes in the perception of ambiguous figures. The figure may be perceived in one way or the other, but not both simultaneously. A common figure of this type is a drawing of the edges of a cube, which may be seen in two ways. An example of *figure-ground* ambiguity is shown in Figure 1. Some other static illusions are shown in Figures 2 and 3. Other illusions depend upon *motion*: a rotating spiral seems to shrink or expand, and a moving blurred edge appears to move faster than a sharp one. Self-luminous objects appear to move ahead of objects of equal velocity illuminated by a stroboscope flashing less than 15 times per second[4]. The world seems stationary during normal eye or head movement, but movement produced by tapping the head with the fist or the eyelid with the finger produces the impression that the world is moving. If the eye muscles are paralyzed, the world seems to move in the direction of intended eye movement when the subject tries to move his eyes. *Color illusions* are also common. The shadows of objects illuminated by red light appear green. Experiments[81] have shown that it is possible to produce the impression of full color in a scene which is produced by only two monochromatic sources of light. The effect exists even when each eye sees a single color[47], which indicates that interaction at a cortical level is involved.

Many visual illusions are produced as *after-effects* of other visual stimulation. Some of the most striking ones are motion after-effects. The *waterfall effect* can be produced by staring at a waterfall, after which other objects appear to be moving upward. A similar effect can be produced by staring at a spiral which is revolving in such a direction as to appear to shrink, after which other objects will appear to expand. These objects, however, do not appear to increase in size, which indicates that perceptions need not be logically consistent.

Figural after-effects[93, 94] are produced by stimuli such as those shown in Figure 4. After gazing intently at the circular figure on the left, if the gaze is directed at a blank surface, a perception similar to the radial figure on the right will be seen. The after-effect produced by the radial figure is a rosette. Experience with many other figures has produced the general conclusion that the lines making up the after-effect image are perpendicular to those in the original image. A type of vector addition also seems to hold: the after-effect produced by observing a set of vertical stripes and then the radial figure is a horizontal ellipse. These effects are also observed with stabilized images on the retina and thus are not due to eye movement, which could produce Moirée effects.

An interesting after-effect is produced by projecting black and orange vertical stripes alternating every few seconds with black and blue horizontal stripes. After watching this for two to four minutes, an uncolored scene consisting of black and white horizontal stripes on the left and black and white vertical stripes on the right will appear to be orange on the left and blue-green on the right. This effect persists for as long as one hour. The effect disappears when the testing scene is rotated 45 degrees. Tests made on the eyes separately show that interocular transfer does not take place[97].

When images are stabilized on the retina, they normally fade, sometimes in patches, and disappear. However, simple figures are sometimes more persistent. One experiment[91] showed that a stabilized line disappeared when an unstabilized background was added to the scene and reappeared when the background was removed.

The perception of *depth* is due to many separate cues. Some of the monocular cues are texture, covering of one object by another, perspective, and eye focussing. Convergence of the eyes, the principle used in range-finders, is a rather weak cue in comparison to binocular paralax, which produces different images on the two retinas. Experiments[72, 73] have shown that monocularly discernible objects are not necessary for depth perception. In one test, a random dot pattern was presented to one eye, while the pattern presented to the other eye was the same except that all the dots in a central square of the figure were shifted to one side, the gap being filled with more random dots. With monocular viewing, either of these fields appeared to be composed of random dots, but when the fields were observed binocularly, one with each eye, the appearance was that of a square covered with random dots floating above a plane, also covered with random dots. It was shown that rather complex three-dimensional objects, which were not discernible monocularly, could be perceived in this way. An example of one of these figures is shown in Figure 5. It may be seen in three dimensions by looking at one square with each eye, so that the two squares appear to be superimposed.

Interactions between visual perception and other sensory modalities can be demonstrated. For example, in a study of human acuity in ranking the weight of various objects, it was found that large objects were consistently perceived to be lighter than small objects of the same weight, even though they were both lifted with the same wire hook[130]. In another experiment[31], an after-effect of prolonged head tilt was demonstrated. After two or three minutes of 30 degree head tilt, the subject's head was positioned vertically and he was required to adjust a lighted bar to a vertical position in a dark room. The average bias was about 2 degrees in the direction opposite to the tilt. The same effect was found with the subject lying on his back, which shows that it is not a gravitational effect. A more cerebral type of interaction was found in an experiment[145] which compared human performance in detecting signals in noise with the optimal guessing that would result from an application of signal detection theory. The subjects were given visual or audible signals mixed with Gaussian noise. They were sometimes given the *a priori* probabilities of occurrence of the signals and the costs for both types of errors. It was found that the subjects could change their thresholds of detection by 3 db in vision and 6 db in hearing to meet various error penalty criteria. Models which explain some of the perceptual results will be presented after some neurophysiological experiments have been described.

NEUROPHYSIOLOGICAL EXPERIMENTS

First, the visual neuroanatomy will be summarized. In man and in some other animals, the central portion of the retina is more sensitive than the periphery. This region is called the *macula*, and its most central portion is the *fovea.* The human retina contains about 125 million rods and 5 million cones. The cones are responsible for human color vision and are most concentrated in the macula. The retinas of some animals contain only cones, some contain only rods, while others have both. A drawing of cells in the frog retina is shown in Figure 6. It is generally similar to the human retina, but it contains red- and green-sensitive rods, only one type of cone, and has no fovea. The vertebrate retina is composed of five types of cells: *photoreceptors, horizontal* cells, *bipolar* cells, *amacrine* cells, and *ganglion* cells, arranged in layers. The main direction of information flow is from the photoreceptors (rods and cones) through the bipolar cells to the ganglion cells, the axons of which make up the optic nerve. The flow of information is chiefly in this direction but some unknown source in the central nervous system sends signals *to* the primate retina. The fibers carrying these signals have their terminations between the bipolar and the ganglion cells. Their function is not known, but it has been suggested that they may carry feedback signals concerning selective attention or the tuning of filters.

The horizontal cells and the amacrine cells presumably send information perpendicular to the main direction of flow. The amacrine cells in particular are not well understood, but recent electron micrographs[34] show structures which appear to be synapses with both the bipolar and the ganglion cells. Generally the receptors, bipolars, and ganglion cells have dendritic fields with considerable overlap and intermixing, but in the human fovea there is a direct connection from each cone to a midget bipolar cell and then a midget ganglion cell, which maps each cone to a separate fiber in the optic nerve. In man, each optic nerve contains about one million fibers, of which about 35,000 carry signals from foveal cones.

The flow of information in man is from the retina to the *lateral geniculate* body via the optic nerve. From there, signals are sent to the *primary visual cortex* (area 17 of the brain) and then to the *visual association areas,* 18 and 19. (In the frog, which has no lateral geniculate or cortex, the optic nerve sends its signals to the *optic tectum*, also known as the *superior colliculus.*) A drawing of cells in the cortex is shown in Figure 7.

The cells of the cortex appear to be arranged in columns, about 100 cells deep, perpendicular to its surface[65,99]. The majority of cortical connections are between cells lying in the same column. The retina is mapped onto the primary visual cortex in a manner which preserves its topology, but the map is distorted so that the area corresponding to the fovea is made larger in the cortex. The primary visual cortex sends fibers only to the visual association areas, and here the mapping is apparently random. Electrical stimulation of the human primary visual cortex gives visual perceptions of light, shadows, and colors, while stimulation of the association areas produces the impression of contours of moving or stationary objects[5,48,49,100]. It has been conjectured[17] that much of the information processing in the higher centers such as the gray matter of the cortex is carried out by decremental conduction, possibly without synaptic contact, rather than by spike propagation with synaptic contact as is generally found in the more peripheral areas of the nervous system.

Animals such as insects and Crustacea have *compound* or "faceted" eyes, rather than retinas. The individual photoreceptors are known as *ommatidia*, each of which is equipped with a tiny lens which makes it sensitive to light coming from a small circular area of the visual field known as its receptive field. The receptive fields of neighboring ommatidia overlap considerably. The *Limulus* (Horseshoe Crab) eye contains approximately 700 ommatidia. Each ommatidium contains an eccentric cell. The axons of these cells form branches, some of which intertwine with their neighbors, while the others form the optic nerve. Signals from single fibers in the optic nerve of Limulus have been studied to determine their relationship to the illumination of the ommatidia[57]. It was found that increasing the illumination of the ommatidium that gives rise to a particular fiber increases its firing rate, but that illumination of the neighboring ommatidia decreases it. This effect, known as *lateral inhibition*, is proportional to the number and the firing rate of the stimulated neighboring ommatidia. The inhibiting effect of more distant ommatidia decreases with distance.

The term *receptive field* is used to describe the effects of light in the visual field on the activity of neurons at any level of the nervous system. Thus, the receptive field of an optic nerve fiber in the Limulus is considered to be a pair of concentric circles. The center circle is an *excitatory* region corresponding to the receptive field of the ommatidium, while the annulus is *inhibitory*. Light coming from a point source inside the excitatory circle tends to increase the firing rate of the cell, while light coming from an area in the inhibitory annulus tends to decrease the rate through lateral inhibition.

This *center-surround* receptive field is the most common type in all animals. Sometimes the center is inhibitory and the surround is excitatory. Of the fibers measured in the optic nerve of the squirrel[103], 63% were of the center-surround type, as were nearly all of those found in the lateral geniculate of the cat[65]. The size of these fields normally corresponds to a few degrees of visual angle, although 4% of those measured from ganglion cells in the cat had a center of only one-half degree and a surround of 15 degrees[141]. The boundaries of receptive fields are difficult to measure accurately, and may depend on the intensity of illumination.

Some center-surround fields show *selective color sensitivity*. Let red, green, blue, excitation, inhibition, center, and surround be abbreviated by R, G, B, +, –, C and S. The majority of ganglion cells measured in the goldfish retina were sensitive to *simultaneous* color contrasts[30]. Two types of cell, (RC+, GS+, GC–, RS–) and (GC+, RS+, RC–, GS–) were found equally commonly. These cells would respond maximally to red dots on green backgrounds, and green dots on red backgrounds, respectively. Other goldfish cells are sensitive to *successive* color contrasts and respond maximally when the illumination of the entire receptive field changes from red to green, or vice versa. Four types of these fields, (RC+, GS–), (GC+, RS–), (RC–, GS+), and (GC–, RS+) were also common in the lateral geniculate of the Rhesus monkey[156], where a few (BC+, GS–) were also found. Other cells showed opposite effects for green and blue light, but the receptive fields were the same for both. Another group showed green-red opposition with fields that appeared to differ somewhat, and a final group had center-surround fields with identical spectral sensitivities. Some of the monkey cells behaved as if they were effected by rods as well as red-, blue-, or green-sensitive cones. In the optic nerve of the squirrel, 19% of the fields measured were of a blue-green center-surround type[104]

The cells described above give steady *sustained* responses for stimulation in their receptive fields, but some cells respond only transiently, some when the light is turned on, some when it is turned off, and some respond to either. These *on-off* cells are found to the extent of about 50% in the frog retina, 30% in pigeons and rabbits, but only 8% in cats[141]. It must be pointed out that these systems are highly *non-linear*, and that testing with one type of stimulus does not allow one to predict the response to a different stimulus. Many of the on-off cells have been found to "really" be *motion* detectors. In the optic nerve of the squirrel, 18% of the fibers measured responded selectively to black or white spots, bars, or edges moving in a particular direction in any part of their receptive fields, and gave no response to motion in the opposite direction. Their *directional sensitivities* were equally prevalent and they were equally distributed throughout the retina. Their receptive fields were from one-half to one degree of visual angle in diameter. In the rabbit[9] one-third of the ganglion cells had directionally sensitive fields of about 5 degrees. In cats[65] some units responded only to motion slower than one degree per second, while other units responded only to motion faster than 10 degrees per second. One ganglion cell in the cat was found which was excited by motion towards the center of its receptive field and inhibited motion away from the center. The firing of two other cells was suppressed by any *contrast* in their visual fields[126].

In contrast to the center-surround fields at the level of the lateral geniculate, *non-circular* "simple" receptive fields were found in the primary visual cortex (striate cortex) of the cat[64, 65]. Eighty-four percent of these cells could be stimulated from either eye, with varying degrees of sensitivity. (Covering the right and the left eye on alternate days from birth until two months of age decreased the number of binocularly driven cells to 9%, but the same procedure had no effect on adult cats[67].) In all these cases, the type of receptive field was the same in both eyes, and the positions of the receptive fields on the two retinas were the same. A typical cortical cell had a 4 degree total receptive field with a 4 degree by 1 degree inhibitory center, the rest of the field being excitatory. Some fields had long, narrow central regions with extensive flanking areas, while others had large central areas and concentrated slit-shaped flanks. In many fields, the two flanking regions were asymmetrical, differing in size and in shape. In some units, only two regions could be found, one excitatory and one inhibitory, lying side by side. Excitatory and inhibitory centers were equally common. In most of these fields, excitation balanced inhibition, so that illumination of the entire field gave no response. Of the 303 cortical cell fields measured, 233 were of the "simple" types described above, with distinct excitatory and inhibitory regions. There was summing or antagonism between regions and the response to stationary or moving spots of various shapes was predictable from a map of the fields. For cells with elongated central fields, changing the *orientation* of a stripe by 5 or 10 degrees abolished or greatly reduced the response.

The remainder of the cat primary visual cortical cells had "complex" receptive fields and their responses could not be predicted by field maps made with small circular spots of light. Often these maps could not be made at all, because small spots were ineffective or gave mixed on-off responses throughout the receptive field. The most effective stimuli for these "complex" cells were *white slits, edges,* and *dark bars.* The stimulus was effective wherever it was placed in the receptive field, provided its orientation was correct. The receptive fields varied in diameter from one-half to 6 degrees and were generally larger than the "simple" fields. They were larger for peripheral than for central areas of the retina. The optimum stimulus width was about the same size as the centers of the circular receptive fields found in the geniculate, which also corresponds to the width of the long narrow central portions of the "simple" fields.

The striate cortex is organized into columns about one-half mm in diameter, extending from the surface to the white matter, each containing thousands of cells. Within each column, the cells had the same receptive field axis orientation and both "simple" and "complex" fields were found. They were usually overlapped, differing only slightly in retinal position, with varying relative influence of the two eyes. Some neighboring cells had common field areas; for example, an excitatory center of one field might correspond in position to an excitatory flank of another field. Eight of the

43 multiple recordings were of neighboring cells whose fields were opposite (with respect to excitation or inhibition) to each other with almost superimposed fields. The ratio of "simple" to "complex" fields in the six layers of the cortex, starting at the surface, were approximately 0, .2, 2, 30, 18, 3.

Two additional maps of the retina have been found in the areas lateral to the striate cortex, which have been called visual areas II and III of the cat[66]. In both these areas, "lower order hypercomplex" fields have been found which respond to slits, edges, or dark bars of appropriate orientation only if their *lengths* are limited in one or both directions. "Higher order hypercomplex" fields were also found in area III. These cells respond similarly to the lower order hypercomplex cells but have *two* preferred orientations differing by a 90 degree rotation, and the position of the end of the stimulus is not important. They are thus particularly sensitive to properly oriented *corners* anywhere in their fields.

In the cat, the receptive fields tend to be quite simple until the cortex is reached, but in the frog[84, 85] very complex operations are carried out in the retina itself. Five types of ganglion cell fields have been measured at the level of the optic nerve of the frog. Group 1 has a 2 to 4 degree receptive field and responds to any *sharp boundary* in its field. The response is enhanced by movement, often with directional sensitivity, and the cell is insensitive to overall illumination. Cells from Group 2 respond only to dark objects with convex sharp boundaries which are moving or have moved toward the centers of their fields of 3 to 5 degrees. A small dark object moved into this field and stopped before reaching the center creates a long-lasting discharge, which can be erased by a transient dimming of the illumination and will not recur until the object is moved again. Groups 1 and 2 can detect targets as small as three minutes of arc, and their fibers make up 97% of the optic nerve population. The Group 2 cells have been called "bug detectors."

Cells from Group 3 respond to moving or changing contrasts. Their receptive fields are from 7 to 11 degrees in diameter. They fire more rapidly when the boundary is moving fast or when its contrast is sharp and have no sustained response for static targets. Targets as small as 1 degree in diameter are effective throughout the receptive fields. Cells from Group 4 respond to any dimming in their receptive fields of about 15 degrees and are most sensitive near the centers of their fields. Cells of the fifth group are very rare and seem to respond inversely to the average illumination over the entire eye. In recording from the dendritic bushes in the tectum, which form the terminations of the optic nerve fibers, it was found that the first four types of fibers terminated at four different levels in the tectum, forming four maps of the retina, in registration. Fibers of the fifth group were mixed with those of the third.

The cells in the frog tectum[84] which receive impulses from the optic nerve respond in an even more complex manner. One type, called "newness" neurons have receptive fields of about 30 degrees. These neurons respond with an intensity which depends on the jerkiness, velocity, direction of movement, and size of an object moving in their visual fields. The response always stops when the motion stops. They adapt to motion along a path so that if the cell responds to motion along a particular path, it will not respond to motion along the same path for about 10 seconds, although it will be sensitive to motion along a different path during this time period. "Sameness" neurons have even more complex behavior. Each of these cells is responsive over almost the complete visual field. When a small dark object is moved around in its field, the cell will suddenly "notice" it, after which any motion, and particularly any discontinuity of motion, will increase the firing rate. Only if the object remains stationary for about two minutes will the firing cease. After this, the object can be moved around a bit without causing the cell to fire, but if the motion is sufficient to cause the cell to "notice" it again, even the smallest motion will be signaled. Newness or "novelty" neurons have also been found in *Crustacea*[154].

MODELS

The lateral inhibition observed in the eye of the Limulus produces a type of *spatial differentiation* which could be used to counteract the blurring due to the overlap of the receptive fields of the individual ommatidia. It has been shown[57] that the magnitude of this *sharpening filter* is sufficient to counteract the blur, with a little extra sharpening besides. This seems understandable in an animal which lives much of its life in muddy water. It has been conjectured[139] that each receptor inhibits itself, as well as its neighbors, giving rise to a sharpening of its *temporal* as well as its spatial discrimination. Certain aspects of this system seem to be well fitted by linear transfer functions. Experiments with blinking lights show that when large areas are illuminated the response has a rather sharp maximum in the vicinity of 3 cycles per second. When smaller areas are illuminated, the magnitude is less at the peak frequency, but greater at both high and low frequencies, a result which is consistent with the model of lateral inhibition[123]. The overshoot in firing rate in response to a step change in illumination is typical of *negative feedback* systems and is consistent with the self-inhibition model.

There is not sufficient genetic information to completely specify all the neural interconnections, so considerable attention has been given to network models which have *iterative* structures or which require only *statistical* specification[148,149,150]. One example is that of a layered network, the first layer of which sends out many excitatory and inhibitory fibers to the second layer. It is assumed that the locations of the connections from a given element are normally distributed around the corresponding element in the second layer, and that the variance of the distribution for the inhibitory fibers is greater than that for the excitatory fibers. This produces typical center-surround receptive fields at the second layer. Adding more layers of the same type produces successively higher spatial derivatives.

Figures 8 and 9 show how some of the more complex receptive fields could be built up from simpler ones. It has been suggested[65] that the "simple" cells in the cortex which have elongated receptive field centers might receive their afferents from the cells in the lateral geniculate with concentric center-surround fields, while the "complex" cells in the cortex which detect a line or an edge regardless of its position in the receptive field, receive their inputs from the "simple" cells in the same column of cortex. Similarly, the "hypercomplex" cells may produce transformations of the signals from the "complex" cells. It has been shown[85] that the four main groups of fields found in the optic nerve of the frog can be plausibly correlated with the different shapes of the dendritic fields of the ganglion cells, and mathematical network models[101,107] for Group 2, the bug detectors, have been proposed. The models agree with the observed responses to moving and stationary objects of various sizes and shapes.

A model explaining the tendency of the Octopus to classify objects as if it were projecting them onto horizontal and vertical axes is suggested by the fact that the dendrites in its optic lobe are not oriented randomly, but are polarized in the horizontal and vertical directions[159].

The illusions in Figure 3 may be produced because the figures do not have clear boundaries but are made up of a series of slanted lines. The apparent slopes of the long vertical broken "lines" corresponding to the loci of the short ones are biased in the direction of the short lines, as if the slopes of the long broken lines were partly computed by *averaging* the slopes of the short ones. This could be due to the stimulation of "complex" or "hyper-complex" edge or line detectors corresponding to the orientations of the short lines, and the system's tendency to automatically conclude that the slopes of the long broken "lines" are the same as those of the short ones. A similar error in estimating the slopes of the boundaries of the concentric circular patterns would produce the impression that the figure is a clockwise-inward spiral. Another type of averaging is indicated by the observation[93] that the accuracy of alignment of two straight lines by an individual can exceed the resolution of the retinal mosiac. Fisher's measure of the information content of the line increased linearly with the length of the line up to 50 cone diameters, and then more slowly.

A direction-sensitive *motion* detector could be produced by a neuron with inputs from two different locations, one of which has a greater delay than the other. If the input with the larger delay were stimulated before the other, the two signals could arrive at the neuron at the same time. If the threshold were so high that both impulses had to arrive at nearly the same time to cause firing, stimulation in the reverse order, or at too high or too low a speed, would not cause it to fire. The impression that self-luminous objects move ahead of stroboscopically illuminated ones can be explained by assuming that the perceived position of a moving object is at least partly determined as an integral of its apparent velocity, and that the velocity detectors are not well stimulated by the blinking light[4]. An explanation for the fact that a blurred edge appears to move faster than a sharp one has been based on a presumed non-linear characteristic of the motion detectors, but an alternative explanation is based simply on light adaptation[3]. When the dark blurred edge enters an area of the retina which is somewhat light adapted, the apparent darkening at that point will be greater than the actual darkening, which could give the impression that the edge had moved farther. If the edge moves in the other direction, it is allowing more light to fall on an area which is dark adapted, giving the impression of even greater lightening, and thus greater motion.

A study was made of the tendency of a beetle to walk to the right or to the left when placed inside a vertical revolving striped drum[125]. It was found that light stimuli sweeping across two neighboring or next-to-neighboring ommatidia could cause the optomotor turning response, but there was no interaction between ommatidia farther apart. It was found that the beetle's turning tendency for a constant drum rotation rate depended only on the amplitude of the Fourier spectrum of the stripes, and not the phase. A model which agreed with the observed behavior contained linear filters and multiplicative and subtractive elements, as shown in Figure 10.

The fact that the visual world does not appear to move in response to voluntary eye movement has been explained by the idea that the signals which are sent to the eye muscles are also sent to the neural location of the visual image, and that the perception of motion depends on both signals[61, 93]. When the eye muscles are temporarily paralyzed it is apparently "more believable" that the visual scene moves than that the eyes do not respond to an attempt to move them. The effects of prolonged head tilt on the apparent vertical could be caused by receptors in the joints and ligaments of the first three cervical vertebrae, which have been shown to affect the extra-ocular muscles.

Most of the other visual illusions can be explained by *adaptation* or *fatigue* of the appropriate neural elements, actual or hypothetical. The complimentary after-images produced by looking at Figure 4 can be explained by postulating edge detectors or line detectors in the human similar to those found in the cat. If it is assumed that the detectors have a finite output even in the absence of lines, the fatigue of the detectors corresponding to the directions of the lines in the viewed figures would allow the signals from detectors with perpendicular orientations to predominate when the gaze is transferred to a blank surface or to visual noise[93, 94]. A similar explanation will suffice for Figure 2 where the straight lines appear to be curved in such a way as to make them more nearly perpendicular to the other lines than they really are. An explanation for the experiment involving colored stripes calls for a more complex neural element. Figures 8 and 9 show how a color sensitive line detector could be made from the color sensitive center-surround fields found in squirrels, goldfish, and monkeys. Orange vertical stripes would fatigue these elements so that white vertical stripes would appear blue-green, and viewing horizontal blue stripes would make horizontal white stripes appear orange, as was found[97]. A somewhat similar mechanism could cause gray shadows cast by red light to appear green. The fatigue of downward-sensitive motion detectors by looking at a waterfall could create an imbalance which causes stationary objects to appear to move upwards. Similarly, viewing a "shrinking" rotating spiral would cause other objects to appear to expand.

At higher neural levels, the *recognition* of an object regardless of its size or position on the retina has been modeled by assuming that the image is shifted to all its possible translations, dillitations or rotations by a neural network and that the properties are averaged over this entire *group* of transformations[120]. The plausibility of a similar model based on cross-correlation has been suggested[74]. A model based on transformations that form Lie groups has been proposed[62], and the *computing power* of networks of threshold elements has been evaluated[98]. A semi-qualitative model of *learning* based on the growth of cell-assemblies in the association areas of the brain has also been proposed[59]. It has been suggested that network models which are *continuous* in their structure as well as in their signals should be investigated[92].

Hearing

The sense of hearing is less rich than that of vision from the information-theoretic point of view. The aural signal is well defined by the amplitude of its frequency spectrum while phase information is relatively unimportant. At least two types of codes are used for sonic information in the lower parts of the nervous system. "Place" coding involves receptors which are sensitive to particular frequencies, while "frequency" coding requires receptors which track the stimulus with a firing rate which rises and falls according to the instantaneous sound pressure[29]. Models of sharpening filters analogous to the spatial sharpening filters produced by lateral inhibition in the eye of the Limulus have been proposed. The sharpness of tuning of a series of "place" receptors can be increased if each of them tends to inhibit the neighboring receptors which are sensitive to higher and lower frequencies[56].

Some moths can hear the high-pitched sonar pulses used by bats to locate their prey. Although their ears contain only a few neurons, they are able to estimate the direction and distance of a bat, and take appropriate evasive action. It was found that bullfrogs responded to a synthetic mating call only if there was sufficient energy in two bands centered at 20 cps and 1400 cps and the ratio of energy in the 500 cps band to that in the 20 cps band was sufficiently low. Two types of neurons in the 8th nerve of the bullfrog were found. The first was sensitive in the 1000-1500 cps range and was not inhibited by other sounds, while the second type was inhibited by 500 cps sound[20].

The behavior of cells in the primary auditory cortex of the cat is somewhat reminiscent of those found in the optic cortex. Measurements on 163 cells[36,37] showed 20% to be unresponsive to auditory, visual, or tactile stimulation. Twenty-one percent responded only to clicks, jangling keys, or other "novel" sounds, and did not respond to frequency modulated tones, while 24% gave sustained excitation, 10% gave sustained inhibition, 6% had *on* responses, 6% had *off* responses, and 2.5% had *on-off* responses for tones. Four percent of the cells responded only when a gilding tone of changing frequency passed through their receptive frequency ranges. About equal numbers responded to ascending and descending tones. Two and one-half percent responded only to visual stimulation, and 0.5% responded both to sound and vision. The average frequency bandwidth was about one octave for signals 15 db above threshold, but there was considerable variation about this value. Half of the cells were sensitive to frequencies above 20 kc, with a maximum of 45 kc. Cells which were excited by sound in one frequency range and inhibited by sound in another range were extremely rare in the cortex, although they are commonly found in the lower centers. There was a rough progression of low to high frequency sensitivity as the recording site ranged from the posterior to the anterior portions of the primary cortex, but low frequency units were found everywhere. Many of the units showed strong adaptation and it was sometimes difficult to hold the "attention" of those cells responding to odd or novel stimuli.

When sounds are presented to the two human ears by earphones, the perceived location of the sound tends to be in the direction of the ear which receives the first or the louder signal. Neural models for this effect, some of which take the known anatomy into account, have been proposed[23, 56]. The "cocktail party effect" refers to the ability of humans to listen to only one of a number of simultaneous conversations, even though it may not be the loudest.

Pattern Recognition by Machines

The field of mechanical pattern recognition is still in its infancy. Many applications have been attempted, some successfully, but the great variety of problems and techniques has prevented the emergence of a coherent strategy for the attack of new problems as yet. The literature consists mainly of reports of the results of applying a single technique to a single body of data (which is usually not reported) and of theoretic analyses of techniques. More comprehensive investigations using several techniques on standard data sets are needed in the near future if the field is to mature[14]. However, there still will remain a great deal of art in the field, as there is in other engineering fields, because many of the basic problems involved are metamathematical.

Pattern recognition techniques are data transformations which operate on the patterns to produce decisions as to their class memberships. Sometimes a list of possible classes and the confidence of each is produced, rather than a single decision. Usually the transformation contains parameters which are adjusted to perform as well as possible on a group of patterns of known classification, sometimes called the *training set*. Any appropriate transformation with a sufficient number of adjustable parameters can be made to classify the training set properly, but this success does not mean that it will generalize well to patterns that were not used in its design. Thus the transformation should next be tried on a separate *testing set* of patterns to measure its generalizing ability. Many experiments reported in the literature have overlooked this important step.

Pattern recognition techniques have also been applied to cases where the classes are not known in advance. In these cases, the problem is to find natural groupings of the data that will serve to define the classes. An example of a problem of this type would be that of finding a reasonable way of classifying dogs into various breeds, unspecified in advance, given a set of measurements on a large number of dogs. This problem of *class discovery* is sometimes called "learning without a teacher"[25].

Most pattern recognition procedures can be considered to consist of three steps. First the signals are *preprocessed* in some way to improve their quality, after which *properties* of the signals are measured and *decisions* of class membership are made on the basis of these properties. The preprocessing operations are normally used to make the property measurement step easier or more reliable, and thus are quite dependent on the properties to be measured. Rigorous mathematical techniques are available for some preprocessing operations such as noise reduction, but the assumptions underlying these techniques are not usually known to be true of the data being analysed, so the applicability of the techniques must be determined empirically. Similarly, there are no mathematical techniques for the important problem of determining what properties of a signal should be measured, although there are methods for comparing the utility of properties once they have been chosen and measured. No useful decisions can be made on the basis of irrelevant properties. Mathematical decision making techniques are also based on uncertain assumptions, so the decision as to which technique is appropriate for a given problem must be made on the basis of intuition and experience. From a philosophical point of view, all the techniques reduce to intelligent guessing, for no procedure for logical induction or abduction can guarantee its applicability[153]. The costs of writing and of running computer programs, as well as their performance, are important engineering considerations.

Pattern recognition techniques have been applied to many classes of data including pictures, continuous waves, and more abstract measurements. Examples of pictorial pattern recognition include the recognition of armored tanks, airplanes, and oil tanks in aerial photographs, blood cells and chromosomes on microscope slides, fingerprints, cloud patterns, and tracks produced by nuclear particles in bubble, cloud, or spark chambers. Handwriting, signatures[96], handprinting, and mechanically printed material have also been analyzed. Examples of continuous signals include electrocardiograms, electroencelphalograms, and voice signals[86, 87]. Examples of the more abstract areas include computer diagnosis of disease from a list of symptoms and weather forecasting from wind, pressure, humidity, and temperature measurements[155]. Applications to automatic process control and the prediction of tsunami waves[39] have also been made. Simple pattern recognition should be distinguished from *scene analysis*, a description of all the elements in a picture and the relationships between them. Little work of this type has been done but the problems have been discussed to some extent and some special languages for picture processing are under development[38, 77, 89, 109, 111].

PREPROCESSING

Preprocessing operations include data smoothing, the reduction of various types of random or predictable noise or distortion, and contrast improvement[70, 146]. For example, sampling at a rate of 233 per second, followed by a seven-point least square error parabolic fit smoothing technique, puts the first zero amplitude point of the frequency response spectrum at 60 cps, and has been successful in eliminating both 60 cps and high frequency noise from electrocardiographic signals.

Blurring of photographs due to such factors as poor focus or atmospheric turbulence can be partly corrected by a transformation similar to that used by the Limulus to reduce the blur produced by its overlapping receptive fields. This transformation produces a new picture, each element of which has an intensity which is a weighted sum of the intensity of the corresponding element in the original picture minus the intensities of the neighboring elements[80]. Blur can be considered to be a loss of high frequency information and its elimination can be considered to be an operation on the frequency spectrum of the signal. One approach is to calculate the two-dimensional Fourier spectrum of the signal, multiply this spectrum by some function of frequency which increases the high frequency content of the signal, and then invert the transformation to produce a sharpened image. A consideration of this transformation in the signal domain shows that the lateral inhibition transformation produces only an approximate correction if the blur is caused by poor focus. The more rigorous procedure produces a new picture element which is a weighted sum of all the elements in the original picture. The magnitudes of the weights decrease with distance from the element being transformed.

Operations such as this sharpening transformation can be considered to be a *convolution* of the original image with a weight matrix, a linear digital filtering transformation. The matrix of weights is shifted to each possible position over the original image, multiplied by the corresponding original picture elements, and these products are summed to give the element for the new picture. This multiplication and addition is equivalent to a vector dot product. Considerable computation can be saved if the digital filter can be *decomposed* into a number of simpler filters. For example, consider a smoothing filter in which each element of the new picture is the average of the 25 elements in a 5 x 5 grid surrounding the corresponding element in the original picture. A straightforward approach would be to calculate the convolution of a 5 x 5 filter, each element having a weight of 1/25, with the original picture. Each new point would require 25 multiplications and additions so that the application of the transformation to a N by N picture would require $25N^2$ additions and multiplications. Computation could be saved if this convolution operation were carried out in two stages: first, a convolution with a 5 x 1 vertical filter with weights of 1/5 to produce an intermediate picture; then, a convolution of this intermediate picture with a 1 x 5 horizontal filter with weights of 1/5 to produce the final picture. The number of multiplications and additions in this procedure is $5N^2$ for each of the two steps, giving a value of $10N^2$ for the complete transformation[68].

This decomposition technique is applicable to other than uniform filters and should be considered in all cases where the filter matrix can be factored into a product or a sum of products of a number of other matrices, the elements of which are mostly zeros. When the filters are large, this procedure can save a tremendous amount of computation. It is interesting to note that this decomposition technique is analogous to the model of information processing in the visual system presented in Figures 8 and 9. The factoring of matrices is also the basis of the new fast techniques for computing Fourier transforms, which decrease the number of computational steps from M^2 to $M \ln_2 M$, where M is the number of sample points[15]. The use of this technique can determine the practicability of Fourier transform techniques in some cases. For example, a 1000 x 1000 element picture contains one million elements, so the computation speed will be increased by a factor of 50,000 with the new technique.

Several types of preprocessing operations were carried out to improve the quality of pictures taken by the Ranger Satellites[112]. When more than one picture of the same scene was available, they were not simply averaged, but for each picture element an average was first made and then all of the points which deviated too much from this average were eliminated in forming a new average intensity for the element. An additive noise was found in scans of these photographs. Superficially it was of a single frequency, but its phase drifted slowly throughout the picture. It was eliminated by cross-correlating a sine wave of appropriate frequency with various portions of the picture scan to determine the phase, after which the noise could be subtracted from the picture. *Scan line noise* which had a high frequency in the direction perpendicular to the scan and a low frequency along the direction of scan was also found. It was eliminated by convolution of the picture with a filter which was 21 elements wide perpendicular to the scan, and 41 elements long, as shown in Figure 11. The filter was found to resonate in regions of high contrast so it was turned off in areas where the picture contrast exceeded some threshold. The attenuation of the high frequency components of a signal from a flying spot scanner, due to the finite spot size, was also corrected by convolution with a two-dimensional filter. Since the scanning spot was elliptical in shape, the filter was not symmetric in its two dimensions. The filter was designed to have a frequency characteristic which was the inverse of the attenuation of high frequencies found in calibration, but a maximum enhancement factor of five was used to avoid the magnification of high frequency noise. *Geometric distortion* was corrected by linear interpolation based on calibration with a rectangular grid.

The techniques mentioned above are useful not only in reducing distortion or noise but also can be used to emphasize the features of a scene which are of interest. For example, a *high frequency emphasis filter* has been used to increase the visibility of small blood vessels in x-rays of the brain[133], as is shown in Figure 12. The *gray scale* of photographs can also be changed to improve the visibility of objects of interest. For example, if the interesting objects constitute the darkest 10% of a picture, the gray scale can be warped so that the range of grays of these objects make up 90% of the gray range in the transformed picture[118].

The convolution of a picture with a filter to produce a new picture can be accomplished in a single step by optical *holographic* techniques employing coherent sources of light such as lasers. These techniques can also produce one or two dimensional Fourier transforms of pictures or cross-correlations between two pictures[142].

PROPERTY SELECTION

The choice of properties is completely dependent upon the types of patterns and the classes into which they are to be categorized. An attempt is made to find properties which are characteristic of the classes or of the differences between classes. If a property can be found which has one range of values for the members of one particular class and a non-overlapping range of values for the members of all other classes, then that property will be *sufficient* for determining whether or not an unknown sample is a member of the particular class. Similarly, *necessary* properties can determine non-membership but not membership in a particular class. Most single properties used in pattern recognition are neither necessary nor sufficient, so that decisions must be based on combinations of properties. A common technique for property selection is to try to determine what properties are used by humans in distinguishing between members of the different classes and then to write computer programs which measure approximations of these properties. However, some properties which are easily measured by humans can be extremely difficult to measure by computer, and vice versa, so measurement costs must be considered.

Another technique is to use appropriately defined *random* properties. For a given quality of decision making, more properties will be required if they are chosen randomly than if they are well chosen by intuition guided by a thorough study of the problem. If the random properties are easy to measure, their use may still be efficient for some problems. In one theoretical study it was found that only twice as many random binary properties would be required to classify objects into a number of classes than would be required if the properties had been chosen optimally[63]. In an empirical study of the classification of objects in photographs it was found that about 15 random masks were equivalent to one well chosen mask[138]. The probability of correctly separating patterns into two arbitrary groups by a hyperplane in property space on the basis of random properties has been found theoretically to be 0.5 when the number of patterns is twice the number of properties[113]. It has been found empirically that LP/L-1 patterns can be correctly classified into L classes by L-1 parallel hyperplanes, where P is the number of random properties[16]. A theoretical analysis has been made of the effects of the number of noisy properties and their standard deviations on the reduction of uncertainty of class membership when the number of classes is large[11].

Factor analysis is a classical technique for the generation of new properties which are linear combinations of the old ones. It may be thought of as a linear transformation of the axes of the vector space containing the original measurements which places the origin at the center of the cloud of data and selects new coordinate axes in such a way as to minimize the variance of the data in the new system while keeping the volume of the cloud of data constant[131, 151, 152]. The first coordinate axis is chosen in the direction of maximum variance of the data while the second axis is placed perpendicular to the first in the direction of the next largest variance, etc. If only some of the best coordinates in this new space are used, they will be better able to approximate the position of a sample point than an equal number of dimensions in the original space. Thus the dimensionality or number of properties can be reduced with less loss of information in the new space than in the old one. However, class membership is not considered in this transformation, so the information discarded could be that which is most vital to the subsequent classification process.

Evolutionary techniques have also been used for property selection. One technique, based on adaptive discriminant functions, maintained a constant number of properties. In each "generation", some of the least valuable properties were replaced by randomly chosen new ones. The values of the properties were estimated by the magnitude of their contributions to the discriminant function[108, 109]. Other value estimation criteria have been investigated[54, 78] and a theory for determining the optimum replacement schedule has been derived[53]. An application to character recognition used evolution of a population of masks according to their values in the decisions to which they contributed[147]. Another program used an evolutionary technique to determine which conditional probabilities between a number of binary properties were to be considered in making decisions[24]. An approach to the modeling of a dynamic process started with six competing blocks of transfer functions. The adjustable parameters in each block of transfer functions were adjusted to give its best fit to the unknown process by a hill-climbing technique. The two blocks giving the worst fits to the unknown process were than eliminated and replaced by new blocks formed by selecting randomly from the transfer functions in the four best blocks. The parameters in these new blocks were then adjusted and the cycle was repeated[76]. A similar approach in automaton theory formed new state diagrams by cutting apart and patching together nodes from those state transition diagrams which scored best at predicting the next member of a string of inputs[42].

SOME USEFUL PROPERTIES

The simplest properties are the input variables themselves, such as the symptoms and test-outcomes used as the basis of a medical diagnosis. A simple binary property can be based upon whether or not a sample of printing passes through a particular section of the surface on which it is printed. Slightly more complex properties are typified by the example shown in Figure 13, where an electrocardiogram is first analyzed to find the positions of its characteristic waves and then their various time intervals and voltages are used as properties. These are the most common properties used in electrocardiogram diagnosis[8, 119, 135].

Probably the next simplest type of property is based on *masks*. The employment of a mask is equivalent to forming a weighted sum of the original picture elements, although the weights are usually restricted to the values 0, 1. If the mask resembles the object to be detected, the process is called *template* matching. In the recognition of Chinese characters, two levels of masks were used to reduce computing time[21]. There were 1000 individual masks, each corresponding to a different Chinese character, and 58 group masks. In analyzing an unknown character, first the group masks were used to determine which group of characters the unknown fell into, after which the appropriate individual masks were used to determine which character it was. Masks have been designed randomly, intuitively, by extracting pieces of the pictures to be analyzed, and from the statistics of the classes and their samples[32, 127, 134, 147]. Sometimes the location of the mask is fixed and in other cases it is scanned over the entire picture in search for a match.

One of the most common types of property involves the expansion of a signal as an orthogonal or non-orthogonal *series*. The coefficients of the series expansion are the new properties. Fourier series are particularly valuable in speech recognition[40, 69, 86] and in the analysis of the sounds produced by the beating heart[25]. These properties are often measured by sending the signal through a bank of analog tuned filters, which saves computation. An example of the spectrum of a spoken word is shown in Figure 14. An orthogonal series of damped sinusoids has also been used in speech recognition[33]. Properties of letters which were invariant with respect to translation and rotation were obtained by first representing the outer boundary of the letter in a tangent angle vs. contour position (arc length) coordinate system and then expanding this curve as a Fourier series[124]. Fourier series as well as a series of orthonormal exponentials have been used to represent electrocardiograms[19, 160]. Hermite-Laguerre series[13] n′th order auto-correlation functions[102], and series of orthogonal Boolean functions[1, 51, 52, 58] have also been used in pattern recognition. Human chromosomes have been characterized by the first seven geometric moments about their centers[18]. Series expansions can be very useful, but experience has shown that an expansion which is not well suited to the data can easily lead to a *degradation* of the information content of the new parameters in comparison to the original data.

Images have been *projected* onto their horizontal or vertical axes, which reduces the dimensionality of the data. This technique has been used for character recognition and in the automatic measurement of the cardio-thoracic ratio from chest x-rays[10]. In this case, the image was projected onto the horizontal axis, giving a curve of average intensity vs. horizontal distance. The maximum found near the center of this curve was produced by the heart and spinal column. The distance between the two minima lying on either side of this maximum was taken to be the diameter of the heart, and the distance between the maxima lying outside these two points (produced by the ribs) was taken to be the diameter of the thorax.

Shrinking and *expanding* operations which subtract or add elements to the boundaries of objects in pictures have been used to eliminate specks and fill gaps in images[114]. They have also been used to derive measures of the elongation and other properties of images and to detect blood cells having multiple nuclei, a property related to radiation damage[12, 121, 128].

The number of *intersections* of an object with a straight line has been used as a property in character recognition[35, 132, 152]. A similar approach based on integral geometry has been used to classify objects[6, 158]. Jigsaw puzzles have been solved by computer programs using properties based on the representation of the outlines of the pieces in terms of tangent angle vs. arc length[43]. The variation of the apparent *texture* of objects with position has been used to determine the slopes of their surfaces[22]. Textures have been described in terms of piece size, auto-correlation functions, conditional probabilities, two-dimensional Fourier transforms, and covariance[129].

The classification of types of white blood cells was based on properties of the histogram of the frequency of occurrence of each of 256 optical density levels, measured over the whole cell picture[122]. It was found that the background, the cytoplasm, and the nucleus gave three separate peaks in the histogram which allowed estimates of their areas and other properties to be made without measurements on the actual image. These useful properties are easily measured by computers but not by humans. Some other specialized measurements include the arm lengths of chromosomes[83, 150] and the measurements of cusps, closures, and retrograde motions in the recognition of cursive script[44, 88]. *Topological* properties based on branching were used in the recognition of hand-printed numerals[105]. A character recognition scheme was based on the absence or presence of filled-in areas when "waves" were propagated from the four sides of an area surrounding the letter[50]. These waves propagate, filling in area, until they reach a line boundary. For example, an H will be completely filled in by waves propagating from the top and the bottom of the area but not from the sides, while an E would be filled in by waves from the sides.

DECISION MAKING

The set of measurements or property values of a pattern can be considered to be a vector, so that each pattern or sample can be represented as a point in a vector space, the axes of which correspond to the individual properties. If the properties are well chosen the samples for a given class will tend to be near each other in the space. Decisions are then based on a *partitioning* of the space into distinct regions, each of which corresponds to a single class. A sample of unknown class will thus be categorized as belonging to the class associated with the region of space in which it lies. In general each class may be associated with one or more separate regions of space, which may be of any shape or size. The boundaries of the regions, across which the decision changes, are called *decision boundaries*. Much of the art of decision making is involved with finding reasonable techniques for placing decision boundaries, based on a finite number of samples of known class[28, 113, 131]. If the actual *probability distribution functions* of the classes in the space are known, rigorous statements about the optimal decision boundaries according to various criteria such as minimizing the probability of error are possible. Strictly speaking, the distributions are never known because this would require an infinity of samples, but in practice they can be approximated with confidence by measurements on a reasonable number of known samples if the distributions are not too complex and the dimensionality of the space is not too great.

Consider the example shown in Figure 15, where the curves represent the distribution functions for the three classes A, B, and C. The samples are to be categorized according to the value of a single property, x. The Bayesian technique which minimizes the probability of the decision being in error is simply to find the value of x for the unknown sample and choose the class which has the greatest value of p at that value of x, if the *a priori* probabilities of membership in each of the three classes are equal. The decision boundaries are the points x' to x''''. If the *a priori* probabilities are unequal or if the costs of deciding on a class erroneously are different, each distribution must be multiplied by the ratio of its *a priori* probability to its cost of error before the maximum is chosen to minimize the expected cost.

Normally, the probability distributions must be approximated from a number of known samples such as those represented by points on the three lines at the bottom of Figure 15. One method is to first plot the cumulative distribution of the samples in each class and then approximate these points by a smooth curve. The approximate probability distribution is then found by taking the derivative of this smooth curve. Choosing this curve is an art: too much smoothing will obliterate the fine structure of the data and would, for example, eliminate the sharp peak in the B distribution of Figure 15, while too little smoothing will result in distributions containing an intolerable amount of noise due to the discrete and random nature of the known samples. Another method for approximating the probability distributions is to assume that they belong to a certain *family*, such as Gaussian, and then assign those values for the *parameters* of the distributions which best fit the data[131].

In many decision making techniques a consideration of the probability distributions is bypassed and the problem of where to draw the decision boundaries is attacked directly. For example, in Figure 16, the classes, A, B, and C can be separated perfectly by the decision boundaries $(x_1-4)^2-x_2+3=0$ and $x_1-x_2-5=0$, yielding the decision rule: if $(x_1-4)^2-x_2+3<0$ decide A; if $x_1-x_2-5>0$ decide C; otherwise decide B. In many real problems the classes cannot be separated perfectly by simple surfaces. Complex surfaces which separate the classes perfectly can always be found, but their use will often not result in good generalization to unknown samples. This problem is analogous to that of curve-fitting for the purpose of interpolation: n given points on a curve can always be fit exactly by a $n-1$ degree polynomial, but the resulting curve may fluctuate wildly between the known points, so a polynomial of smaller degree which only approximates the known points must be used.

Linear decision boundaries are *hyperplanes* when the number of properties is greater than three, and can be represented by the equation $\Sigma\, w_i x_i = w_o$, where the x_i are the property values and the w_i are weights. The weight w_o is often called a *threshold.* Its variation produces translation but not rotation of the hyperplane. *Adaptive* or *learning* techniques for finding hyperplane decision boundaries[2,113,127] are based on a stepwise adjustment of the weights and do not require storage of the sample points. This makes them useful for training adaptive electronic networks. To start the adaptive process, the w_i are set at arbitrary values and the result of classifying the first known sample is determined. If it is incorrect, all the w_i are changed by some increment, each in the direction which tends to correct the decision, and the next sample is presented. No changes in the w_i are made when a sample is classified correctly. It may be necessary to present the training set several times to arrive at a solution, but it has been shown that procedures of this type will converge to a solution with zero error if one exists, and to a solution which minimizes the loss based on the distances between the misclassified pattern vectors and the decision boundary if the average risk function is unimodal in the parameter space.

In cases where two classes can be separated perfectly by a hyperplane there is generally some freedom in its selection. One technique of choice is to consider two parallel hyperplanes, either of which achieves perfect separation, with a "dead zone" containing no samples between them. The planes are placed so that the size of the dead zone is maximized and then the decision surface is placed half-way between them[152]. For cases where the known samples cannot be perfectly separated by hyperplanes, techniques for finding the "best" hyperplane are available. The most natural criterion for defining the best one would be that one which minimizes the number of misclassified training samples, but this criterion yields a discontinuous function of the parameters w_i and leads to problems solvable only by combinatorial mathematics, such as large sets of linear programming problems. Approximate techniques are thus normally used.

Analyses of the trade-off of *speed vs. stability* of these hill-climbing adaptive techniques as a function of the correction increment have been made[2]. A useful technique is to use a large increment at the beginning of training to obtain a fast approximation to the optimum values, and a small increment near the end of the training cycle to improve the accuracy of the result. Adaptive techniques for finding the parameters in *multithreshold* functions which produce a number of parallel hyperplane decision boundaries have also been proven to converge to an exact solution when one exists[16, 108]. Studies of the effects of component imperfections in adaptive networks have been made[90, 115]. Networks for pattern recognition have also been "grown" by electro-deposition of iron, gold, silver, and tin fibers from liquid solutions[117, 140].

Non-linear decision boundaries can always be represented as linear decision boundaries (hyperplanes) in a higher dimensional space. For example, the separation of the three classes in Figure 16 required a non-linear boundary in x_1, x_2 space, but if a new "property" x_3 were defined as $x_3 = x_1{}^2$, the three classes could be separated perfectly by two hyperplanes in x_1, x_2, x_3 space. Any boundary of the form $\Sigma\ w_j \phi_j(x_1, x_2, \ldots, x_n) = 0$, which may be non-linear in the x_i space, will be linear in a space the coordinates of which are the variables ϕ_j. The weights w_j may be found by the techniques mentioned above for finding the parameters for hyperplanes. This simplification is possible because the non-linear boundaries are linear in the weights w_j. No general techniques exist which are guaranteed to find the best values for adjustable parameters which make non-linear contributions to the decision boundary.

Another approach to decision making is based on *discriminant functions*[113, 131]. Corresponding to each class there is a separate discriminant function, which may be of the form $f_i = \Sigma\ w_{ij}\phi_j(\underline{x})$. The decision is made by substituting $\underline{x}$ into each of these functions and choosing the class corresponding to the largest value of f_i. The resulting decision boundaries are composed of segments of hyperplanes in ϕ_j space. The values for the w_{ij} may be found by procedures similar to those for finding the parameters of hyperplane decision boundaries. For example, an adaptive technique increments the w_{ij} in the functions corresponding to the class that was chosen and the class that should have been chosen, each in the direction which tends to decrease the error, whenever a classification error is made. A more powerful approach uses a separate discriminant function for each *pair* of classes. The tests are applied sequentially, one class being ruled out at each step.

The *nearest neighbor* decision rule decides that the class of an unknown sample is the same as that of the nearest known sample in the property space[27]. The resulting decision boundaries are composed of segments of hyperplanes. This rule is valuable when the samples of each class form relatively separate clusters in property space, particularly if the number of clusters is large or if their shapes are complex. It is a simple rule and does not require the pre-calculation or optimization of decision boundaries. One disadvantage is that it requires the continual storage of a large number of known samples and the calculation of a large number of distances for each sample to be classified. Another disadvantage may be seen from Figure 15. The optimal decision would be B whenever x were between x′ and x″, but this rule would often choose A or C as the class. A modification which overcomes this disadvantage chooses the class that is most represented by the *k nearest neighbors*. This rule is asymptotically optimum as the number of samples approaches infinity and k approaches infinity more slowly.

Other modifications weight the contributions from the k neighbors according to their *proximity* to the unknown point. One approach considers all the points in the space to be neighbors and weights their contributions by a Gaussian function of their distance from the unknown sample[136, 137]. This is equivalent to approximating the probability density function by the sum of a number of Gaussian distributions, one centered at each known sample point. The variance of these distributions is used as a variable smoothing factor. The equation of the decision boundary for this rule was expanded as a Taylor series in which the contribution of each sample to each term could be found independently.

A method for combating the large storage and calculation requirements of nearest neighbor techniques is to form *clusters* of points. Separate possibly overlapping clusters are formed for each class. Each cluster, which may be due to a large number of points, can be represented by the location of its center and its size (possibly in each dimension). As each new known sample is introduced, its location relative to the existing clusters is calculated. If it falls in or near an existing cluster of its class, it is merged with it and appropriate adjustments of the cluster parameters are made. If it does not fall near an existing cluster, it can be the basis of formation of a new cluster. An unknown point is classified according to the nearest cluster, weighted by its size[7, 131]. Clustering techniques can also be very useful in the problem of class discovery.

Clustering techniques using *cross-correlation* rather than distance as a measure of similarity have also been used[116]. The normalization process maps all the points in the vector space onto a hypersphere centered at the origin, so that their positions are determined by a number of angles while the lengths of the vectors are disregarded. In general this loss of information is a disadvantage. But, for example, if the vector components represent time samples of a waveform and its shape but not its size is important, then the normalization is desirable.

Sequential decision theory is valuable when the costs or risks involved in making tests (measuring properties) is considerable. The tests are made in an order which may be fixed or may depend upon the previous test outcomes. A classification decision is made when the trade-off between the probable error costs and the costs for new tests is favorable[45,46].

A *decision tree* is a tree structure with a question at each node. The answer to the question or test in the first node of the tree determines which branch is to be taken from that node, and thus determines the next question. The path is continued through the tree until it exits. Each exit corresponds to a decision. An example of a decision tree for the recognition of cursive script is shown in Figure 17. The result of applying a decision tree with n branches from each node is representable by an n-ary logical function of all the questions in the tree, but the use of the tree has the advantage that not all the tests are needed to arrive at any particular decision. Trees are also relatively easy to remember, which makes them valuable as human decision making techniques. A disadvantage is that the number of branches from each node is usually rather limited. If the measurements are continuous variables, this results in a rather coarse quantization of the decision space. Another disadvantage is that a single error made in passing through the tree will generally result in an erroneous decision while in other techniques a single error in property measurement will often be offset by a number of other correct measurements.

Conclusion

Information processing in the nervous system is carried out by parallel multi-level networks of neurons. It is known that networks of even simple threshold elements are capable of computing any function computable by a finite machine. But it is not known what functions are computed by most real neurons, or how these functions vary with the number and placement of synapses on the three-dimensional surfaces of the neurons. Non-synaptic interactions may also be present. Although the directions of the interactive effects (excitation or inhibition) are known in many cases, this information is not sufficient to predict the behavior of a richly connected network.

In the lower levels of the visual system, various operations are carried out which may be conveniently considered to be transformations of the original image to produce new images with different properties. Many of these transformations are differencing operations which report spatial or temporal variation. Objects are not detected by their absolute light intensities, but by the variation in intensity found at their boundaries. Colors of objects are not measured absolutely, but are relative to the colors of surrounding objects. The nature of these transformations tends to free the system from errors due to variation in the intensity and color of illumination and in the behavior of some of the neurons.

The transformed images flow in parallel through the network. Thus, the optic nerve does not carry a single image, but many. The fibers carrying the separate images can be sorted out again to form separate layers for each image, as is done in the frog tectum. It seems possible that the few relatively simple transformations already found in the frog are used to compute measures of how threatening the scene is, how "buggy" it is, etc., and that these simple measures are fed to a decision making system which also considers other variables, much as the state of hunger, and commits the animal to a mode of behavior. If that mode is bug-catching, the motor system could then use the information from the bug-filtered image to guide its attack. The mind of the frog may thus be capable of having only a small number of concepts.

The question of how many parallel images there are in the higher animals may not be legitimate, because of the variety of transformations that take place. Cells have been grouped into many classes according to their responses to stimuli, and one approach would be to consider that each class of cells corresponds to a separate transformed image. One possible objection to this idea is that the variability of cells within a class may allow it to be broken into sub-classes an arbitrary number of times. Another objection is that the test stimuli used to determine the class of a cell really *define* the class, and that the possible combinations and orderings of stimuli are arbitrary and essentially infinite. Tests reported in the literature range from the cell's response to very simple geometric stimuli, to how easy it is to get the cell to "notice" an erratically moving object. However, there is still hope that the cells can be grouped into meaningful coherent classes by their behavior, their biochemical properties, or by finding that their outputs are treated equivalently by neurons at a higher level, in spite of individual variation.

Almost nothing is known about the techniques used by neural networks to recognize objects on the basis of the properties of the transformed images. The cortex appears to employ complex reverberating loops, but the nature of their calculations is unknown, as are the anatomical bases of learning, memory, and concept formation. The development of transducers which could non-destructively measure the responses of large numbers of neurons simultaneously would be extremely valuable. If they were bidirectional, they could make direct interaction between living and artificial networks possible.

Mechanical pattern recognition techniques have been successful in solving many problems. Preprocessing, property measurement and selection, and decision making techniques have been developed. They have been most successful in cases such as printed character recognition where the variability of the patterns is not intrinsic, but is due only to noise. The classification of "natural" patterns such as voices, clouds, cells, or electrocardiograms is much more difficult. Success has generally been achieved in these areas only when the number of classes is small and the dimensionality of the data has been greatly reduced by discovering a small set of important properties.

Some problems appear to be so difficult that they can only be solved by increasing the computing effort by orders of magnitude over that which is available today. The recognition of normal spoken speech without restrictions on the vocabularies or accents of the speakers seems to be one of these problems. Studies of speech recognition by humans show that context and familarity of the accent are quite important clues as to what was said. Building similar features into a program would require guessing where a word began and ended, a comparison with words in a very large dictionary to determine potential candidates, and analysis of the context to select among them. Long term measurements to compensate for accents would also be required. Advances in the efficiency of computing techniques may allow the solution of some new classes of problems. Methods are needed to aid in the selection of decision making techniques for new problems. The use of computer graphics to allow the visual exploration of multi-dimensional property spaces should be of help both in property selection and in the selection of decision making techniques.

Many of the preprocessing, property measurement, and decision making operations used in mechanical pattern recognition are most conveniently described in terms of information processing networks. For example, a comparison of three ways of describing essentially the same transformation shows that "lateral inhibition" is a much simpler concept than linear digital filtering by convolution with a matrix, or Fourier transformation, multiplication by a weighting function, and inverse transformation. Several important classes of networks are well understood, including those with a single level of adaptive weights, but very little is known about multilevel adaptive networks. The success of the nervous system in recognizing patterns and the limitations of shallow networks indicate that multilevel networks could also be of value in mechanical systems. The first levels of a network could carry out preprocessing operations while later stages computed properties with successively higher orders of semantic abstraction and the final layers were involved with decision making. It would probably be efficient to allow feedback loops so that the decision making levels could adjust the lower levels to provide the best possible information concerning the most probable decisions.

Such systems can be simulated on general purpose computers, but if they are used extensively it may be desirable to build new classes of microelectronic information processing networks. Their structures could resemble those of the nervous system, with appropriate modifications due to the differing natures of the network elements. Because of their short interconnections, large numbers of elements, and parallel organization, they would not be so subject to the speed-of-light limitations currently being approached by general purpose serial digital computers. The parallel processing computers currently under construction represent a step in this direction.

Although the study of animal pattern recognition is primarily motivated by scientific interest and the design of mechanical systems is primarily an engineering activity, interaction between workers in these areas is of considerable potential value. The mathematics of information processing in networks is the same whether the network elements are natural or artificial. Transformations which are common to both areas, such as sharpening filters and edge detectors, have already been found. Experimentation and theoretical analysis of artificial networks has suggested models for natural systems, and the implications of these and other models have been investigated both by building artificial networks and by simulating their behavior on general purpose computers. The study of living systems has also led to new useful properties and transformations for mechanical systems. As more is learned about these areas, the value of interaction between them can be expected to increase.

Acknowledgement

This research was supported in part by the Air Force Office of Scientific Research, under grant number AF-AFOSR-1341-68.

REFERENCES

1. Abend, K., T. J. Harley, and L. N. Kanal, "Classification of Binary Random Patterns," Technical Report No. PR339, Philco Applied Research Laboratory. (January 1965).
2. Amari, S., "A Theory of Adaptive Pattern Classifiers," IEEE TRANSACTIONS ON ELECTRONIC COMPUTERS, Vol. EC–16, No. 3, pp. 299–307. (1967).
3. Andrews, D. P., D. M. MacKay, and J. P. Wilson, "Apparent Relative Movement of 'Unsharp' and 'Sharp' Visual Patterns," NATURE, Vol. 199, No. 4889, p. 161. (1963).
4. Anstis, S. M., R. L. Gregory, N.DeM. Rudolf, and D. M. MacKay, "Influence of Stroboscopic Illumination on the After-effect of Seen Movement," NATURE. Vol. 199, No. 4888, pp. 99–100. (1963).
5. Bailey, P., G. Bonin, and W. S. McCulloch, THE ISOCORTEX OF THE CHIMPANZEE University of Illinois, Urbana. (1950).
6. Ball, G. H., "An Application of Integral Geometry to Pattern Recognition," Stanford Research Institute Project No. 3605, (February 1962).
7. Ball, G. H., "Data Analysis in the Social Sciences: What About the Details?" PROCEEDINGS–FALL JOINT COMPUTER CONFERENCE, pp. 533–59. (1965).
8. Balm, G. J., "Crosscorrelation Techniques Applied to the Electrocardiogram Interpretation Problem," IEEE TRANSACTIONS ON BIO-MEDICAL ENGINEERING, Vol. BME–14, No. 4, pp. 258–62. (1967).
9. Barlow, H. B., and R. M. Hill, "Selective Sensitivity to Direction of Movement in Ganglion Cells of the Rabbit Retina," SCIENCE, Vol. 139, No. 3553, pp. 412–14. (1963).
10. Becker, H. C., W. J. Nettleton, Jr., P. H. Meyers, J. W. Sweeney, and C. M. Nice, Jr., "Digital Computer Determination of a Medical Diagnostic Index Directly from Chest X-ray Images," IEEE TRANSACTIONS ON BIO-MEDICAL ENGINEERING, Vol. BME–11, No. 3, pp. 67–72. (1964).
11. Bledsoe, W. W., "Some Results on Multicategory Pattern Recognition," JOURNAL OF THE ASSOCIATION FOR COMPUTING MACHINERY, Vol. 3, No. 2, pp. 304–16. (1966).
12. Blum, H., "A Transformation for Extracting New Descriptors of Shape," MODELS FOR THE PERCEPTION OF SPEECH AND VISUAL FORM, Weiant Wathen-Dunn, Editor, M.I.T. Press, pp. 362–79. (1967).
13. Brick, D. B., "On the Applicability of Wiener's Canonical Expansions," BIO-MEDICAL ENGINEERING, HUMAN FACTORS, AND SYSTEMS SCIENCE AND CYBERNETICS, Part 9, IEEE INTERNATIONAL CONVENTION RECORD, New York, pp. 36–47. (1967).
14. Brick, D. B., "Pattern Recognition, The Challenge, Are We Meeting It?" In this volume.
15. Brigham, E. O., and R. E. Morrow, "The Fast Fourier Transform," IEEE SPECTRUM, Vol. 4, No. 12, pp. 63–70. (1967).
16. Brown, R. J., "Adaptive Multiple-Output Threshold Systems and Their Storage Capacities," Systems Theory Laboratory, Stanford Electronics Laboratories, Technical Report No. 6771-1. (June 1964).
17. Bullock, T. H., "Neuron Doctrine and Electrophysiology," SCIENCE, Vol. 129, No. 3355, pp. 997–1002. (1959).
18. Butler, J. W., and M. K. Butler, "Computer Analysis of Photographic Images," NUCLEONICS, pp. 44–50. (February 1967).
19. Cady, L. D., M. A. Woodbury, L. J. Tick, and M. N. Gertler, "A Method for Electrocardiogram Wave Pattern Estimation," CIRCULATION RESEARCH, Vol. 9 pp. 1078–82. (1961).
20. Capranica, R., L. Frishkopf, and M. H. Goldstein, Jr., "Voice and Hearing in the Bullfrog," MODELS FOR THE PERCEPTION OF SPEECH AND VISUAL FORM, Weiant Wathen-Dunn, editor, M.I.T. Press, pp. 244–45. (1967).

21. Casey, R. and G. Nagy, "Recognition of Printed Chinese Characters," IEEE TRANSACTIONS ON ELECTRONIC COMPUTERS , Vol. EC–15, No. 1, pp. 91–101. (1966).
22. Charton, P. W. and E. E. Ferris, "The Visilog: A Synthetic Eye," Technical Documentary Report AL–TDR–64–185, General Electric Company. (January 1965).
23. Cherry, C., "Two Ears–But One World," SENSORY COMMUNICATION, Walter A. Rosenblith, editor, M.I.T. Press and John Wiley & Sons, Inc., pp. 99–117. (1961).
24. Chow, C. K. and C. N. Liu, "An Approach to Structure Adaptation in Pattern Recognition," IEEE TRANSACTIONS ON SYSTEMS SCIENCE AND CYBERNETICS, Vol. SSC–2, No. 2, pp. 73–80. (1966).
25. Coleman, D. J. and C. A. Caceres, "The Acoustic Vibrations of the Heart and Computer Analysis," THE THEORY AND PRACTICE OF AUSCULTATION, F. A. Davis Company, pp. 102–09. (1963).
26. Cooper, P. W., "Non-supervised Learning in Statistical Pattern Recognition," In this volume.
27. Cover, T. M. and P. E. Hart, "Nearest-Neighbor Pattern Classification," IEEE TRANSACTIONS ON INFORMATION THEORY, Vol. IT–13, pp. 21–7. (January 1967)
28. Cover, T. M., "Learning in Pattern Recognition." In this volume.
29. Davis, H., "Peripheral Coding of Auditory Information," SENSORY COMMUNICATION, Walter A. Rosenblith, editor, M.I.T. Press and John Wiley & Sons, Inc., pp. 119–41. (1961).
30. Daw, N. W., "Goldfish Retina: Organization for Simultaneous Color Contrast," SCIENCE, Vol. 158, No. 3803, pp. 942–4. (1967).
31. Day, R. H. and N. J. Wade, "Visual Spatial Aftereffect from Prolonged Head-Tilt," SCIENCE, Vol. 154, No. 3753, pp. 1201–2. (1966).
32. Deutsch, S., "Conjectures on Mammalian Neuron Networks for Visual Pattern Recognition," IEEE TRANSACTIONS ON SYSTEMS SCIENCE AND CYBERNETICS, Vol. SSC–2, No. 2, pp. 81–5. (1966).
33. Dolansky, L. O., "Novel Method of Speech-Sound Analysis and Synthesis," Ph.D. Dissertation, Harvard University, Cambridge, Mass. (1959).
34. Dowling, J. E., "The Site of Visual Adaptation," SCIENCE, Vol. 155, No. 3760, pp. 273–9. (1967).
35. Doyle, W., "Recognition of Sloppy, Hand-Printed Characters," Lincoln Laboratory, Group Report 54–12. (December 1959).
36. Evans, E. F., and I. C. Whitfield, "Classification of Unit Responses in the Auditory Cortex of the Unanaesthetized and Unrestrained Cat," JOURNAL OF PHYSIOLOGY, 171, pp. 476–93. (1964).
37. Evans, E. F., and I. C. Whitfield, "Response of Cortical Neurons to Acoustic Stimuli Varying Periodically in Frequency," JOURNAL OF PHYSIOLOGY, 172, pp. 52–3. (1964).
38. Evans, T. G., "Descriptive Pattern-Analysis Techniques: Potentialities and Problems." In this volume.
39. Ewald, A. T., and T. Kaminuma, "Classification and Prediction of Tsunami Waves by Clustering and Threshold Techniques," IEEE International Symposium on Information Theory, San Remo, Italy, September 11–15, 1967.
40. Fant, G., "Auditory Patterns of Speech," MODELS FOR THE PERCEPTION OF SPEECH AND VISUAL FORM, Weiant Wathen-Dunn, editor, M.I.T. Press, pp. 111–25. (1967).
41. Fantz, R. L., "Origin of Form Perception," SCIENTIFIC AMERICAN, 204, No. 5, p. 66. (May 1961).
42. Fogel, L. J., A. J. Owens, and M. J. Walsh, ARTIFICIAL INTELLIGENCE THROUGH SIMULATED EVOLUTION, John Wiley & Sons, Inc. (1966).
43. Freeman, H., and L. Garder, "Apictorial Jigsaw Puzzles: The Computer Solution of a Problem in Pattern Recognition," IEEE TRANSACTIONS ON ELECTRONIC COMPUTERS, Vol. EC–13, No. 2, pp. 118–27. (1964).

44. Frishkopf, L. S., and L. D. Harmon, "Machine Reading of Cursive Script," INFORMATION THEORY, Colin Cherry, editor, Butterworth & Co., Ltd., pp. 300–16. (1961).
45. Fu, K. S., and Y. T. Chien, "Sequential Recognition Using a Non-parametric Ranking Procedure," IEEE TRANSACTIONS ON INFORMATION THEORY, Vol. IT–13, No. 3, pp. 484–92. (1967).
46. Fu, K. S., "On Sequential Pattern Recognition Systems." In this volume.
47. Geschwind, N., and J. R. Segal, "Colors of All Hues from Binocular Mixing of Two Colors," SCIENCE, Vol. 131:608. (1960).
48. Geschwind, N., "Disconnexion Syndromes in Animals and Man, Part I," BRAIN, Vol. 88, Part II, pp. 237–94. (1965).
49. Geschwind, N., "Disconnexion Syndromes in Animals and Man, Part II," BRAIN, Vol. 88, Part III, pp. 585–644. (1965).
50. Glucksman, H. A., "A Parapropagation Pattern Classifier," IEEE TRANSACTIONS ON ELECTRONIC COMPUTERS, Vol. EC–14, No. 3, pp. 434–43. (1965).
51. Gose, E. E., "An Adaptive Network for Producing Real Functions of Binary Inputs," INFORMATION AND CONTROL, Vol. 8, No. 2, pp. 111–23. (April 1965).
52. Gose, E. E., "A Synthesis Technique for Networks Consisting of Logical Functions Feeding a Linear Summation Element," IEEE TRANSACTIONS ON ELECTRONIC COMPUTERS, Vol. EC–14, No. 2, pp. 254–6. (April 1965).
53. Gose, E. E., "Improving the Population of Elements in a Pattern Recognition Network," IEEE International Symposium on Information Theory, San Remo, Italy, September 11–15, 1967.
54. Gose, E. E., and A. H. Klopf, "Evolutionary Pattern Recognition Networks," Hawaii International Conference on Systems Science, Honolulu, Hawaii, January 29–31, 1968.
55. Gregory, R. L., "Human Perception," BRITISH MEDICAL BULLETIN, Vol. 20, No. 1 (Experimental Psychology), pp. 21–6. (1964).
56. Harmon, L. D., and E. R. Lewis, "Neural Modeling," PHYSIOLOGICAL REVIEWS, Vol. 46, No. 3, pp. 513–91. (1966).
57. Hartline, H. K., H. G. Wagner, and F. Ratliff, "Inhibition in the Eye of Limulus and the Mutual Interaction of Receptor Units," JOURNAL OF GENERAL PHYSIOLOGY, Vol. 41, p. 1049. (1958).
58. Hawkins, J. K., "Self-Organizing Systems—A Review and Commentary," PROCEEDINGS OF THE IRE, pp. 31–48. (January 1961).
59. Hebb, D. O., THE ORGANIZATION OF BEHAVIOR: A NEUROPSYCHOLOGICAL THEORY, John Wiley & Sons, Inc., London. (1949).
60. Held, R. and A. Hein, "On the Modifiability of Form Perception," MODELS FOR THE PERCEPTION OF SPEECH AND VISUAL FORM, Weiant Wathen-Dunn, editor, M.I.T. Press, pp. 296–303. (1967).
61. Helmholtz, H. von, HELMHOLTZ'S TREATISE ON PHYSIOLOGICAL OPTICS, 3 vols., translated from the third German edition and edited by J. P. C. Southall, The Optical Society of America, pp. 1924–25. (1909–10).
62. Hoffman, W. C., "The Lie Algebra of Visual Perception," Mathematics Research Report D1–82–432, Boeing Scientific Research Laboratories. (April 1965).
63. Hsieh, H. S., and G. W. Zopf, Jr., "Determination of Equivalence Classes of Orthogonal Properties," Electrical Engineering Research Laboratory, Engineering Experimental Station, University of Illinois, Urbana, Technical Report No. 2, (February 1962).
64. Hubel, D. H., and T. N. Wiesel, "Receptive Fields of Single Neurones in the Cat's Striate Cortex," JOURNAL OF PHYSIOLOGY, 148, pp. 574–91. (1959).
65. Hubel, D. H., and T. N. Wiesel, "Receptive Fields, Binocular Interaction and Functional Architecture in the Cat's Visual Cortex," JOURNAL OF PHYSIOLOGY, 160, pp. 106–54. (1962).
66. Hubel, D. H., and T. N. Wiesel, "Receptive Fields and Functional Architecture in Two Nonstriate Visual Areas (18 and 19) of the Cat," JOURNAL OF NEUROPHYSIOLOGY, Vol. XXVIII, pp. 229–89. (1965).

67. Hubel, D. H., and T. N. Wiesel, "Binocular Interaction in Striate Cortex of Kittens Reared with Artificial Squint," JOURNAL OF NEUROPHYSIOLOGY, Vol. XXVIII, pp. 1040–72. (1965).
68. Huang, T. S. and H. L. Kasnitz, "The Combined Use of Digital Computers and Coherent Optics in Image Processing," PROCEEDINGS: COMPUTERIZED IMAGING TECHNIQUES SEMINAR, Society of Photo-optical Instrumentation Engineers. (June 1967).
69. Hughes, G. W., "The Recognition of Speech by Machine, " M.I.T. Research Laboratory of Electronics Technical Report No. 395. (May 1961).
70. Inselberg, A., and H. Von Foerster, "Linear Property Filters," Electrical Engineering Research Laboratory, University of Illinois, Urbana, Technical Report No. 2. (July 1962).
71. Jacobson, M., "Retinal Ganglion Cells: Specification of Central Connections in Larval Xenopus laevis," SCIENCE , Vol. 155, No. 3766, pp. 1106–8. (1967).
72. Julesz, B., "Binocular Depth Perception of Computer-Generated Patterns," BELL SYSTEM TECHNICAL JOURNAL, Vol. 39, pp. 1125–62. (1960).
73. Julesz, B., "Texture and Visual Perception," SCIENTIFIC AMERICAN, Vol. 212, No. 2, pp. 38–55. (1965).
74. Kabrisky, M., A PROPOSED MODEL FOR VISUAL INFORMATION PROCESSING IN THE HUMAN BRAIN, University of Illinois Press. (1966).
75. Kanal, L. and B. Chandrasekaran, "Recognition, Machine 'Recognition', and Statistical Approaches." In this volume.
76. Kaufman, H., "An Experimental Investigation of Process Identification by Competitive Evolution," IEEE TRANSACTIONS ON SYSTEMS SCIENCE AND CYBERNETICS, Vol. SSC–3, No. 1, pp. 11–16. (June 1967).
77. Kirsch, R. A., "Computer Interpretation of English Text and Picture Patterns," IEEE TRANSACTIONS ON ELECTRONIC COMPUTERS, Vol. EC–13, No. 4, pp. 363–76. (August 1964).
78. Klopf, A. H., "Evolutionary Pattern Recognition Systems," M. S. Thesis, Case Institute of Technology, Cleveland, Ohio, June 1966. (Defense Documentation Center, Rep. No. AD–637 492.)
79. Klopfer, P. H., "Stimulus Preferences and Imprinting," SCIENCE, Vol. 156, No. 3780, pp. 1394–96. (1967).
80. Kulikowski, J. J., "Adaptive Visual Signal Preprocessor with a Finite Number of States," IEEE TRANSACTIONS ON SYSTEMS SCIENCE AND CYBERNETICS, Vol. SSC–2, No. 2, pp. 90–101. (1966).
81. Land, E. H., "The Retinex," AMERICAN SCIENTIST, Vol. 52, No. 2, pp. 247–64. (June 1964).
82. Lashley, K. S., "The Problem of Cerebral Organization in Vision," BIOLOGICAL SYMPOSIA, Vol. VII, pp. 301–22. (1942).
83. Ledley, R. S., "High-Speed Automatic Analysis of Biomedical Pictures," SCIENCE, Vol. 146, No. 3641, pp. 216–23. (October 1964).
84. Lettvin, J. Y., H. R. Maturana, W. H. Pitts, and W. S. McCulloch, "Two Remarks on the Visual System of the Frog," SENSORY COMMUNICATION, Walter A. Rosenblith, editor, M.I.T. Press and John Wiley & Sons, Inc., pp. 757–76. (1961).
85. Lettvin, J. Y., H. R. Maturana, W. S. McCulloch, and W. H. Pitts, "What the Frog's Eye Tells the Frog's Brain," PROCEEDINGS OF THE IRE, Vol. 47, No. 11, pp. 1940–59, November 1959. Reprinted in EMBODIMENTS OF MIND by W. S. McCulloch, M.I.T. Press, pp. 230–55. (1965).
86. Lindgren, N., "Machine Recognition of Human Language–Part I," IEEE SPECTRUM Vol. 2, No. 3, pp. 114–36. (1965).
87. Lindgren, N., "Machine Recognition of Human Language–Part II," IEEE SPECTRUM, Vol. 2, No. 4, pp. 44–59. (1965).
88. Lindgren, N., "Machine Recognition of Human Language, Part III–Cursive Script Recognition," IEEE SPECTRUM, Vol. 2, No. 5, pp. 104–16. (May 1965).

89. Lipkin, L. E., W. C. Watt, and R. A. Kirsch, "The Analysis, Synthesis, and Description of Biological Images," ANNALS OF THE NEW YORK ACADEMY OF SCIENCES, Vol. 128, Article 3, pp. 984–1012. (January 1966).
90. Low, P. R., "Influence of Component Imperfections on Performance of Trainable Systems," Western Electronic Show and Convention, San Francisco, California, August 20–23, 1963.
91. MacKay, D. M., "Monocular 'Rivalry' Between Stablized and Unstablized Retinal Images," NATURE, Vol. 185, No. 4716, p. 834. (1960).
92. MacKay, D. M., "Modeling of Large-Scale Nervous Activity," SYMPOSIA OF THE SOCIETY FOR EXPERIMENTAL BIOLOGY, No. XIV, Models and Analogues in Biology, pp. 192–8. (1960).
93. MacKay, D. M., "Interactive Processes in Visual Perception," SENSORY COMMUNICATION, Walter A. Rosenblith, editor, M.I.T. Press and John Wiley & Sons., Inc., pp. 339–55. (1961).
94. MacKay, D. M., "Ways of Looking at Perception," MODELS FOR THE PERCEPTION OF SPEECH AND VISUAL FORM, Weiant Wathen-Dunn, editor, M.I.T. Press, pp. 24–43. (1967).
95. MacKay, D. M., "Neural Communications: Experiment and Theory," SCIENCE, Vol. 159, No. 3812, pp. 335–53. (19 January 1968).
96. Mauceri, A. J., "Feasibility Study of Personnel Identification by Signature Verification," Technical Report No. RADC–TR–65–33, Display Techniques Branch, Rome Air Development Center, Research and Technology Division, Griffiss Air Force Base, New York. (April 1965).
97. McCollough, C., "Color Adaptation of Edge-Detectors in the Human Visual System," SCIENCE, Vol. 149, pp. 1115–6. (3 September 1965).
98. McCulloch, W. S., and W. H. Pitts, "A Logical Calculus of the Ideas Immanent in Nervous Activity," BULLETIN OF MATHEMATICAL BIOPHYSICS, Vol. 5, pp. 115–33, University of Chicago Press, 1945. Reprinted in EMBODIMENTS OF MIND by W. S. McCulloch, M.I.T. Press, pp. 19–36. (1965).
99. McCulloch, W. S., "Modes of Functional Organization of the Cerebral Cortex," FEDERATION PROCEEDINGS, Vol. 6, pp. 448–52, Federation of American Societies for Experimental Biology, 1947. Reprinted in EMBODIMENTS OF MIND by W. S. McCulloch, M.I.T. Press, pp. 67–71. (1965).
100. McCulloch, W. S., "Machines That Think and Want," originally entitled "Brain and Behavior," in COMPARATIVE PSYCHOLOGY MONOGRAPH 20, No. 1, Series 103, W. C. Halstead, editor, University of California Press, pp. 39–50, 1950, Reprinted in EMBODIMENTS OF MIND by W. S. McCulloch, M.I.T. Press, pp. 307–18. (1965).
101. McCulloch, W. S., *et. al.*, Group report (untitled), Research Laboratory for Electronics, Neurophysiology Group, QUARTERLY PROGRESS REPORT, No. 81, pp. 227–52, M.I.T.
102. McLaughlin, J. A., and J. Raviv, "Nth Order Autocorrelations in Pattern Recognition," Research Report, IBM Watson Research Center, Yorktown Heights, New York. (March 1967).
103. Michael, C. R., "Receptive Fields of Directionally Selective Units in the Optic Nerve of the Ground Squirrel," SCIENCE, Vol. 152, No. 3725, pp. 1092–94. (1966).
104. Michael, C. R., "Receptive Fields of Opponent Color Units in the Optic Nerve of the Ground Squirrel," SCIENCE, Vol. 152, No. 3725, pp. 1095–97.(1966).
105. Minneman, M. J., "Handwritten Character Recognition Employing Topology, Cross Correlation, and Decision Theory," IEEE TRANSACTIONS ON SYSTEMS SCIENCE AND CYBERNETICS, Vol. SSC–2, No. 2, pp. 86–96. (1966).
106. Minsky, M., "Steps Toward Artificial Intelligence," PROCEEDINGS OF THE INSTITUTE OF RADIO ENGINEERS, 49, pp. 8–30, January 1961. Reprinted in COMPUTERS AND THOUGHT, E. A. Feigenbaum and J. Feldman, editors, McGraw-Hill Book Company, pp. 406–60. (1963).

107. Moreno-Diaz, R., "An Analytical Model of the Group 2 Ganglion Cell in the Frog's Retina," Technical Report E–1858, M.I.T. Instrumentation Laboratory. (October 1965).
108. Mucciardi, A. N., "Adaptive Pattern Recognition Using Non-Linear Elements," M.S. Thesis, Case Institute of Technology, Cleveland, Ohio, October 1964. (Systems Research Center Report SRC–65–A–64–22.)
109. Mucciardi, A. N. and E. E. Gose, "Evolutionary Pattern Recognition in Incomplete Nonlinear Multithreshold Networks," IEEE TRANSACTIONS ON ELECTRONIC COMPUTERS, Vol. EC–15, No. 2, pp. 257–61. (April 1966).
110. Muntz, W. R. A., "Mechanisms of Visual Form Recognition in Animals," MODELS FOR THE PERCEPTION OF SPEECH AND VISUAL FORM, Weiant Wathen-Dunn, editor, M.I.T. Press, pp. 126–135. (1967).
111. Narasimhan, R., "Syntax-directed interpretation of classes of pictures," COMMUNICATIONS OF THE ASSOCIATION OF COMPUTING MACHINERY, Vol. 9, No. 3, pp. 166–173. (March 1966).
112. Nathan, R., "Digital Video-Data Handling," Technical Report No. 32–877, Jet Propulsion Laboratory. (January 1966).
113. Nilsson, N. J., LEARNING MACHINES , McGraw-Hill Book Company, (1965).
114. Nilsson, N. J., "Adaptive Pattern Recognition: A Survey," Bionics Symposium, Dayton, Ohio, May 1966.
115. Offner, F., "Limitations on Complexity of Random Learning Networks," BIOPHYSICAL JOURNAL, Vol. 5, No. 2, pp. 195–200. (1965).
116. Okajima, M., L. Stark, G. Whipple, and S. Yasui, "Computer Pattern Recognition Techniques: Some Results with Real Electrocardiographic Data," IEEE TRANSACTIONS ON BIO-MEDICAL ELECTRONICS, Vol. BME–10, No. 3, pp. 106–14. (July 1963).
117. Pask, G., "The Natural History of Networks," SELF-ORGANIZING SYSTEMS, M. Yovits and S. Cameron, editors, Pergamon Press, pp. 232–63. (1960).
118. Pike, W. S., "Some Television Image Enhancement Techniques," ANNALS OF THE NEW YORK ACADEMY OF SCIENCES, Vol. 97, pp. 395–407. (1962).
119. Pipberger, H. V., F. W. Stallmann, K. Yano, and H. W. Draper, "Digital Computer Analysis of the Normal and Abnormal Electrocardiogram," PROGRESS IN CARDIOVASCULAR DISEASES, Vol. 5, No. 4, pp. 378–92. (January 1963).
120. Pitts, W. and W. S. McCulloch, "How We Know Universals: The Perception of Auditory and Visual Forms," BULLETIN OF MATHEMATICAL BIOPHYSICS, Vol. 9, pp. 127–47, University of Chicago Press, 1947. Reprinted in EMBODIMENTS OF MIND by W. S. McCulloch, M.I.T. Press, pp. 46–66. (1965).
121. Preston, Jr., K., "Machine Techniques for Automatic Leukocyte Pattern Analysis," ANNALS OF THE NEW YORK ACADEMY OF SCIENCES, Vol. 115, pp. 482–90. (1964).
122. Prewitt, J. M. S., and M. L. Mendelsohn, "The Analysis of Cell Images," ANNALS OF THE NEW YORK ACADEMY OF SCIENCES, Vol. 128, pp. 1035–53. (1966).
123. Ratliff, F., B. W. Knight, J-I. Toyoda, and H. K. Hartline, "Enhancement of Flicker by Lateral Inhibition," SCIENCE, Vol. 158, No. 3799, pp. 392–3. (1967).
124. Raudseps, J. G., "Some Aspects of the Tangent-Angle Vs. Arc Length Representation of Contours," Technical Report 1801–6, Ohio State University Research Foundation. (March 1965).
125. Reichardt, W., "Autocorrelation, A Principle for the Evaluation of Sensory Information by the Central Nervous System," SENSORY COMMUNICATION, W. A. Rosenblith, editor, M.I.T. Press, John Wiley & Sons, pp. 303–17, 1961. Reprinted in PATTERN RECOGNITION, Leonard Uhr, editor, John Wiley & Sons, pp. 212–23. (1966).
126. Rodieck, R. W., "Receptive Fields in the Cat Retina: A New Type, " SCIENCE, Vol. 157, No. 3784, pp. 90–2. (1967).
127. Rosenblatt, F., PRINCIPLES OF NEURODYNAMICS, Spartan Books. (1962).

128. Rosenfeld, A., and J. L. Pfaltz, "Sequential Operations in Digital Picture Processing," JOURNAL OF THE ASSOCIATION FOR COMPUTING MACHINERY, Vol. 13, No. 4, pp. 471–94. (1966).
129. Rosenfeld, A., "On Models for the Perception of Visual Texture," MODELS FOR THE PERCEPTION OF SPEECH AND VISUAL FORM, Weiant Wathen-Dunn, editor, M.I.T. Press, pp. 219–223. (1967).
130. Ross, H. E., and R. L. Gregory, "Is the Weber Fraction a Function of Physical or Perceived Input," QUARTERLY JOURNAL OF EXPERIMENTAL PSYCHOLOGY, Vol. XVI, Part 2, pp. 116–122. (1964).
131. Sebestyen, G. S., DECISION-MAKING PROCESSES IN PATTERN RECOGNITION, The Macmillan Company. (1962).
132. Selfridge, O. G., "Pandemonium: A Paradigm For Learning," Session 3, Paper 6, pp. 511–31, MECHANISATION OF THOUGHT PROCESSES, Vol. 1, National Physical Laboratory Symposium No. 10, London: Her Majesty's Stationery Office. (1959).
133. Selzer, R. H., "Digital Computer Processing of X-ray Photographs," Technical Report No. 32–1028, Jet Propulsion Laboratory, Pasadena. (November 1966).
134. Simek, J. G., and C. J. Tunis, "Handprinting Input Device for Computer Systems," IEEE SPECTRUM, Vol. 4, No. 7, pp. 72–81. (1967).
135. Smith, R. E., and C. M. Hyde, "A Computer System for Electrocardiographic Analysis," IBM Engineering Publications, Systems Development Division Laboratory, Rochester, Minn. (May 1966).
136. Specht, D. F., "Generation of Polynomial Discriminant Functions for Pattern Recognition," IEEE TRANSACTIONS ON DIGITAL COMPUTERS, Vol. EC–16, No. 3, pp. 308–19. (1967).
137. Specht, D. F., "Vectorcardiographic Diagnosis Using the Polynomial Discriminant Method of Pattern Recognition," IEEE TRANSACTIONS ON BIO-MEDICAL ENGINEERING, Vol. BME–14, No. 2, pp. 90–5. (1967).
138. Spooner, M. G., C. W. Swonger and J. B. Beach, "An Evaluation of Certain Property Formation Techniques for Pattern Recognition," Western Electronics Show and Convention, Los Angeles, August 25–27, 1964.
139. Stevens, C. F., "Methods Used by a Simple Eye to Improve Its Spatial and Temporal Resolving Power," Western Electronic Show and Convention, San Francisco, August 20–23, 1963.
140. Stewart, R. M., G. I. Hickey, and J. R. Milne, "Field-Trainable Electrochemical Dipole Arrays," Technical Report SGC No. 485FR–2, Research on Adaptive Devices, Space-General Corp., Los Angeles. (February 1966).
141. Stone, J. and M. Fabian, "Specialized Receptive Fields of the Cat's Retina," SCIENCE, Vol. 152, No. 3726, pp. 1277–9. (1966).
142. Stroke, G. W., and R. G. Zech, "A Posteriori Image-Correcting 'Deconvolution' by Holographic Fourier-Transform Division," PHYSICS LETTERS, Vol. 25A, No. 2, pp. 89–90. (1967).
143. Sutherland, N. S., "Stimulus Analysing Mechanisms," MECHANISATION OF THOUGHT PROCESSES, Proceedings of a Symposium held at the National Physical Laboratory November 24–27, Vol. 2, pp. 575. London: Her Majesty's Stationery Office. (1961).
144. Sutherland, N. S., "Shape discrimination and receptive fields," NATURE (London), Vol. 197, pp. 118–122, 1963.
145. Swets, J. A., W. P. Tanner, Jr., and T. G. Birdsall, "Decision Processes in Perception," PSYCHOLOGICAL REVIEW, Vol. 68, No. 5, pp. 301–40. (1961).
146. Tippett, J. T., D. A. Berkowitz, L. C. Clapp, C. J. Koester, and A. Vanderburgh, Jr., editors, OPTICAL AND ELECTRO-OPTICAL INFORMATION PROCESSING, M.I.T. Press. (1965).
147. Uhr, L., and C. Vossler, "A Pattern-Recognition Program that Generates, Evaluates, and Adjusts Its Own Operators," PROCEEDINGS OF THE WESTERN JOINT COMPUTER CONFERENCE, 19, pp. 555–70, 1961. Reprinted in COMPUTERS AND THOUGHT, E. A. Feigenbaum and J. Feldman, editors, McGraw-Hill Book Company,

pp. 251–68, 1963; and in PATTERN RECOGNITION, L. Uhr, editor, John Wiley & Sons, pp. 349–64. (1966).
148. Von Foerster, H., "Circuitry of Clues to Platonic Ideation," ASPECTS OF THE THEORY OF ARTIFICIAL INTELLIGENCE, C. A. Muses, editor, Proceedings of the First International Symposium on Biosimulation, Locarno, June 29–July 5, Plenum Press, pp. 43–81. (1960).
149. Von Foerster, H., "Structural Models of Functional Interactions," EXCERPTA MEDICA INTERNATIONAL CONGRESS SERIES NO. 49, pp. 370–83. (1962).
150. Von Foerster, H., "Computation in Neural Nets," CURRENTS IN MODERN BIOLOGY, Vol. 1, North-Holland Publishing Company, Amsterdam, pp. 47–93. (1967).
151. Watanabe, M.S., "Karhunen-Loeve Expansion and Factor Analysis," TRANSACTIONS OF THE FOURTH PRAGUE CONFERENCE ON INFORMATION THEORY, STATISTICAL DECISION FUNCTIONS, RANDOM PROCESSES, Prague, August 31–September 11, 1965, The Czechosolvak Academy of Sciences, pp. 635–60. (1967).
152. Watanabe, S., P.F. Lambert, C.A. Kulikowski, J.L. Buxton, and R. Walker, "Evaluation and Selection of Variables in Pattern Recognition," COMPUTER AND INFORMATION SCIENCES–II, Academic Press, Inc., pp. 91–122. (1967).
153. Watanabe, S., "Pattern Recognition as an Inductive Process." In this volume.
154. Waterman, T.H. and C.A.G. Wiersma, "Electrical Responses in Decapod Crustacean Visual Systems," JOURNAL OF CELLULAR AND COMPARATIVE PHYSIOLOGY, Vol. 61, No. 1, pp. 1–16. (1963).
155. Widrow, B., G.F. Groner, M.J.C. Hu, F.W. Smith, D.F. Specht and L.R. Talbert, "Practical Applications for Adaptive Data-Processing Systems," Western Electronic Show and Convention, San Francisco, August 20–23, 1963.
156. Wiesel, T.N., and D.H. Hubel, "Spatial and Chromatic Interactions in the Lateral Geniculate Body of the Rhesus Monkey," JOURNAL OF NEUROPHYSIOLOGY, Vol. XXIX, No. 4, pp. 1115–56. (July 1966).
157. Wiener, N., CYBERNETICS , John Wiley & Sons. (1958).
158. Wong, E., and A.J. Steppe, "Invariant Recognition of Geometric Shapes." In this volume.
159. Young, J.Z., A MODEL OF THE BRAIN, Oxford Press, 1964.
160. Young, T.Y. and W.H. Huggins, "Computer Analysis of Electrocardiograms Using a Linear Regression Technique," IEEE TRANSACTIONS ON BIO-MEDICAL ENGINEERING, Vol. BME–11, No. 3, pp. 60–7. (July 1964).

Figure 1: An example of figure-ground ambiguity in which a white face in profile with a black background or an old woman with a white background may be seen.[55]

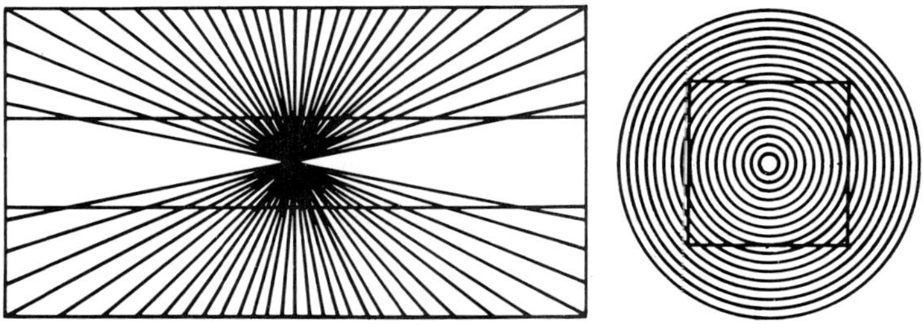

Figure 2: The parallel lines on the left appear to bow outward and the sides of the square on the right appear to curve inward.

Figure 3: The vertical straight lines on the left appear to be bent and the circles on the right look like spirals.

Figure 4: Two figures which produce complementary after-images.[94]

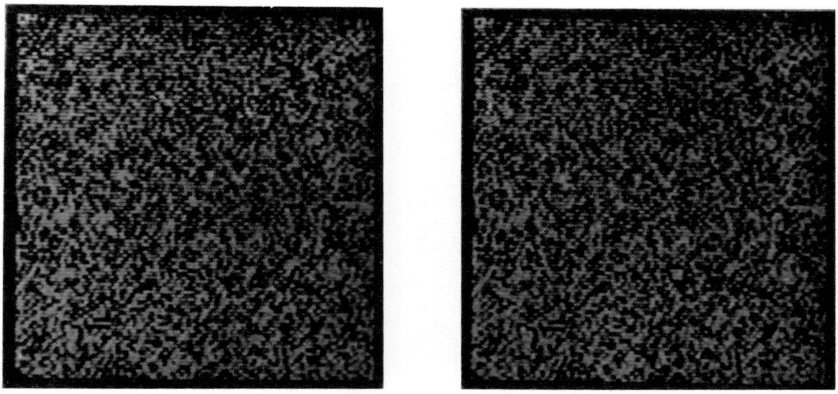

Figure 5: When viewed sterioscopically, planes at three distances are seen.[72]

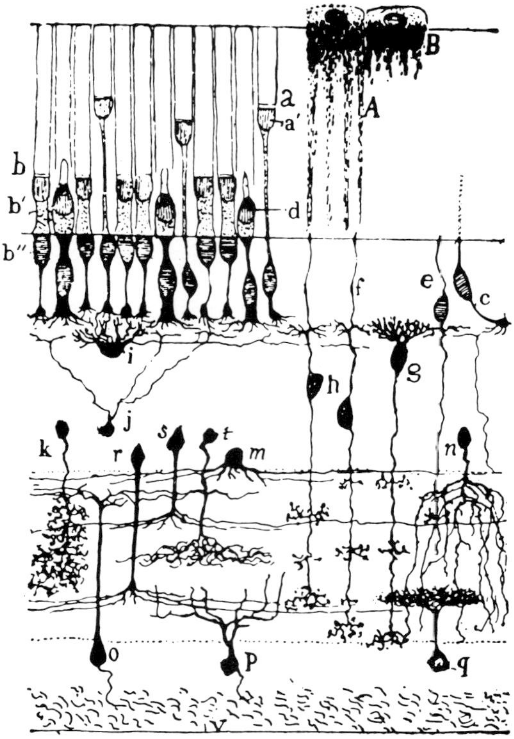

Figure 6: A drawing by Ramon y Cajal of some of the types of cells in the frog retina, stained with Golgi stain. a and b are photoreceptors; i is a horizontal cell; f,g, and h are bipolar cells; k,r,s,t, and m are amacrine cells; o,p, and q are ganglion cells. From *Histology du Système Nerveux* (Paris: Maloine, 1909–11).

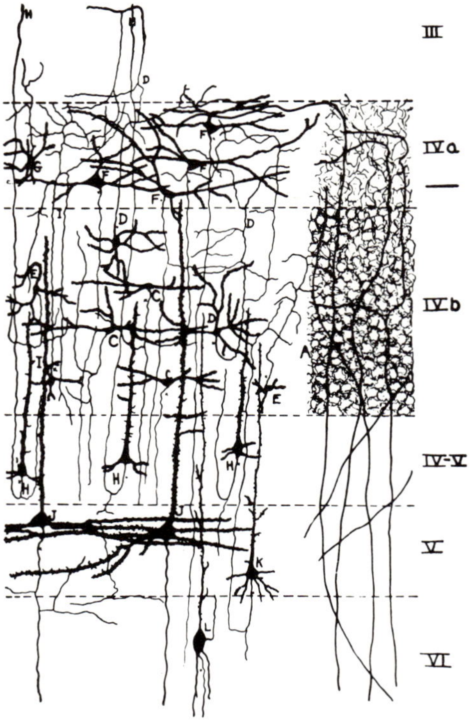

Figure 7: A drawing of some cell types in the human visual cortex, from Cajal.

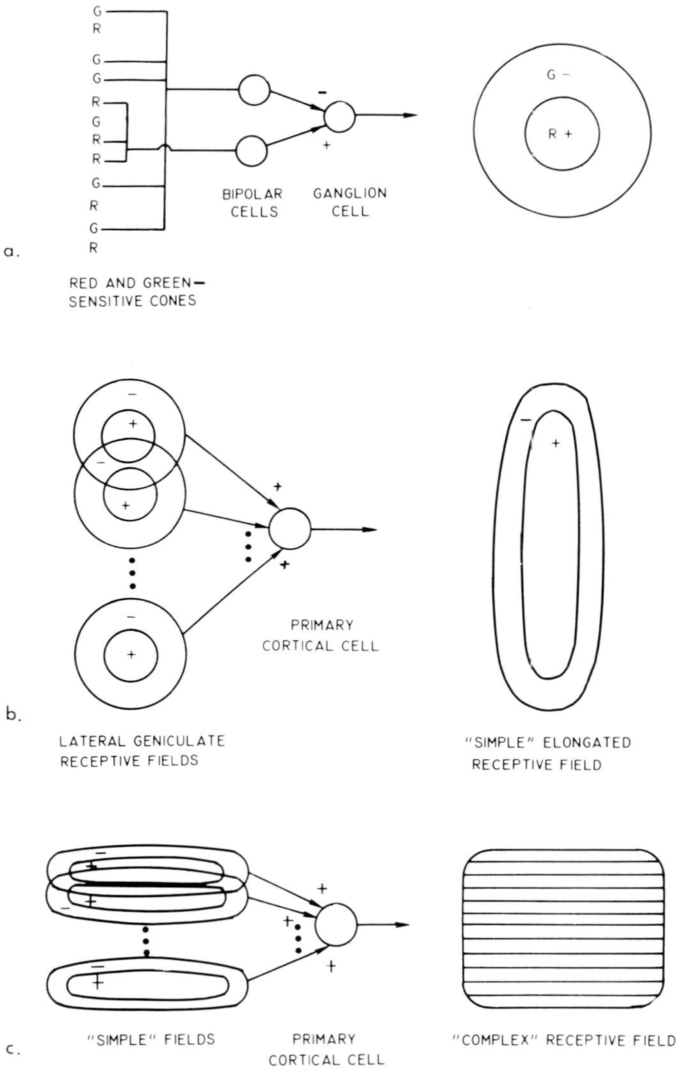

Figure 8: Some very simplified models which suggest ways in which some observed receptive fields could be produced. (a) A color-selective center-surround receptive field which is stimulated by red light in the central region and inhibited by green light in the periphery. (b) The elongated "simple" receptive field is produced by a cell which fires only if stimulated by many of the center-surround cells feeding it. (c) A "complex" receptive field which responds to a properly oriented line anywhere in the field.

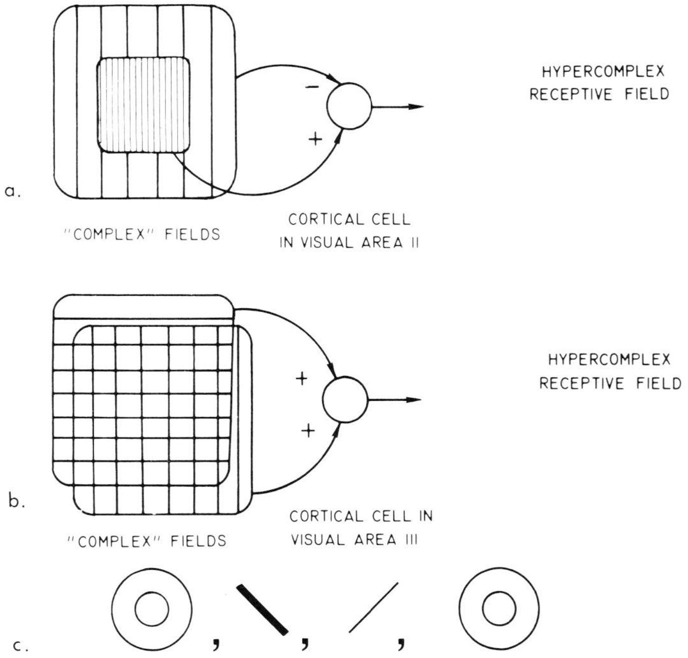

Figure 9: Further simple models for receptive fields. (a) Model for a terminated line detector or "lower order hypercomplex" receptive field which responds to a vertical line only if it does not enter the peripheral region. (b) Model for a "higher order hypercomplex" receptive field which responds to lines in either of two positions 90° apart. (c) A symbolic notation which summarizes the sequence of operations in the model for the terminated line detector of 9a. The sequence consists of a center-surround operation, followed by a one-dimensional spread operation with a high threshold, followed by a one-dimensional spread in a different direction with a low threshold, followed by another center-surround operation.

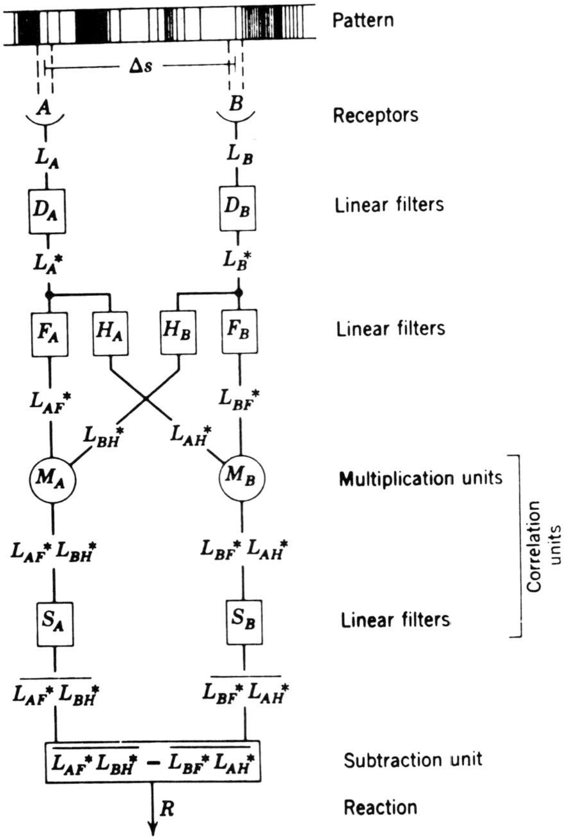

Figure 10: Model of optomotor responses in the beetle Chlorophanus.[125]

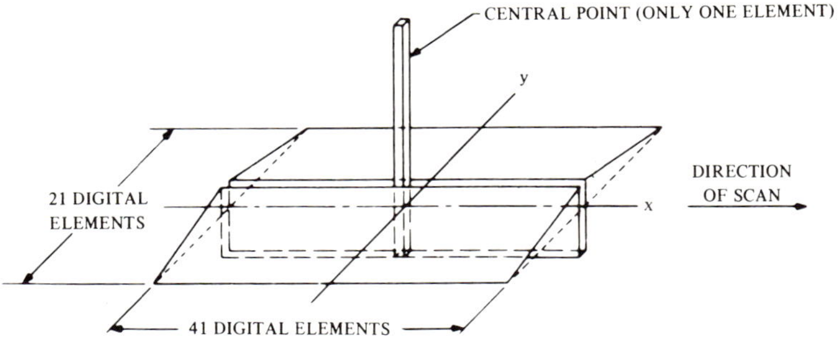

Figure 11: Scan-line filter used on Ranger photographs.[112]

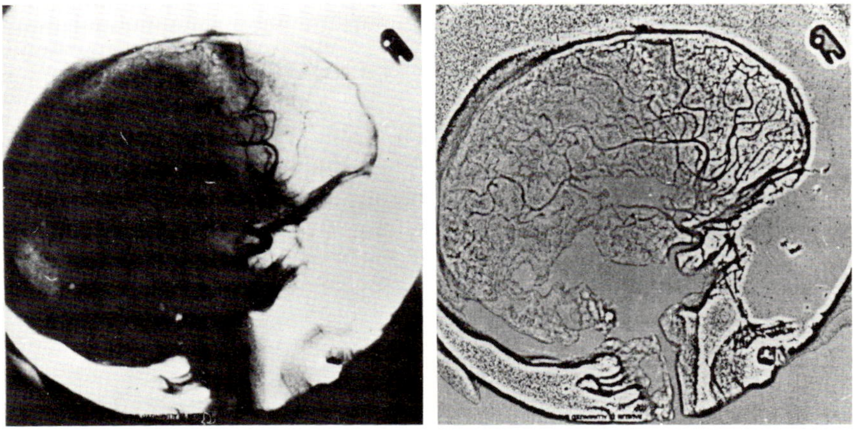

Figure 12: Angiogram of skull before and after high-pass filtering.[133]

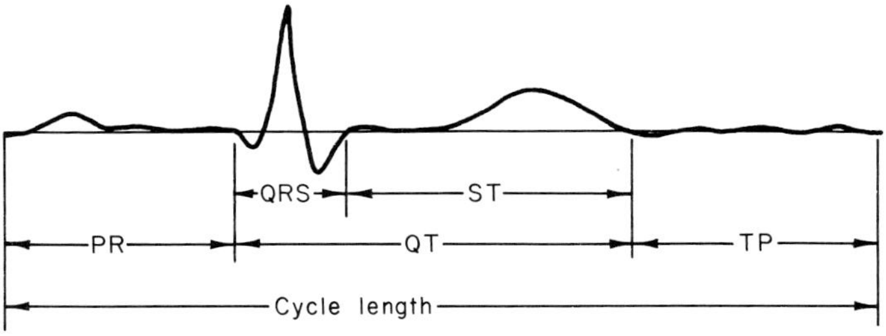

Figure 13: A typical electrocardiogram with P wave, QRS complex, and T wave.[8]

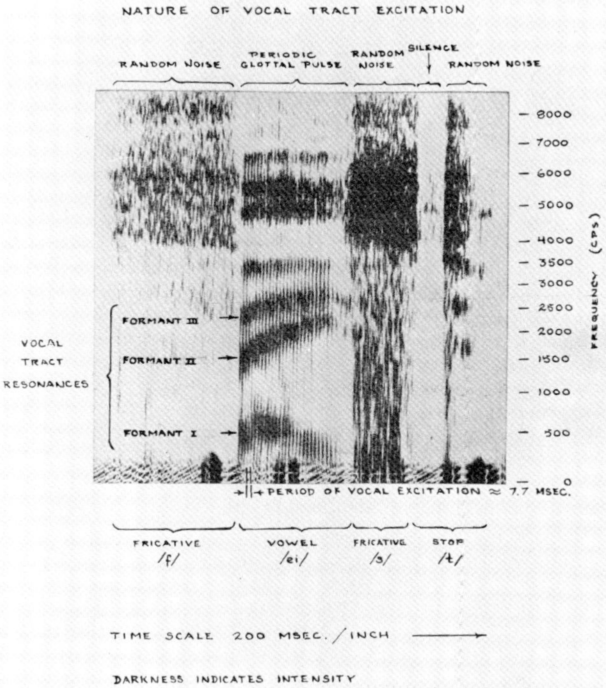

Figure 14: Sonogram of the word "faced". The darkest areas correspond to those frequency bands in which the power is most concentrated.[69]

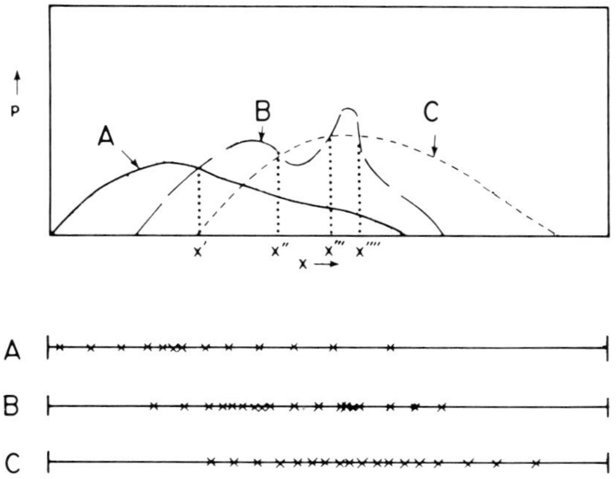

Figure 15: Probability distributions and samples from three classes.

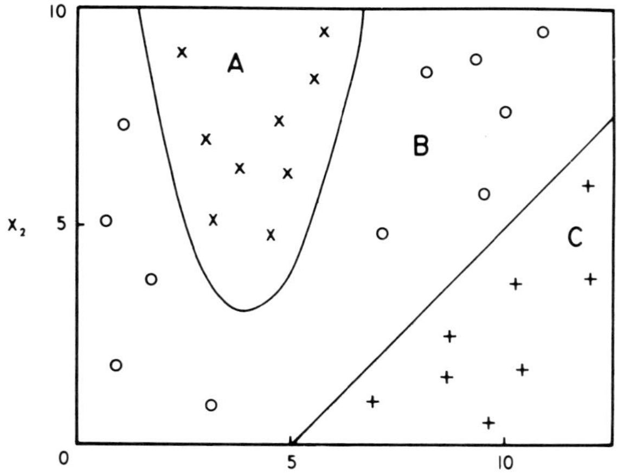

Figure 16: Two-dimensional property space showing samples and decision boundaries.

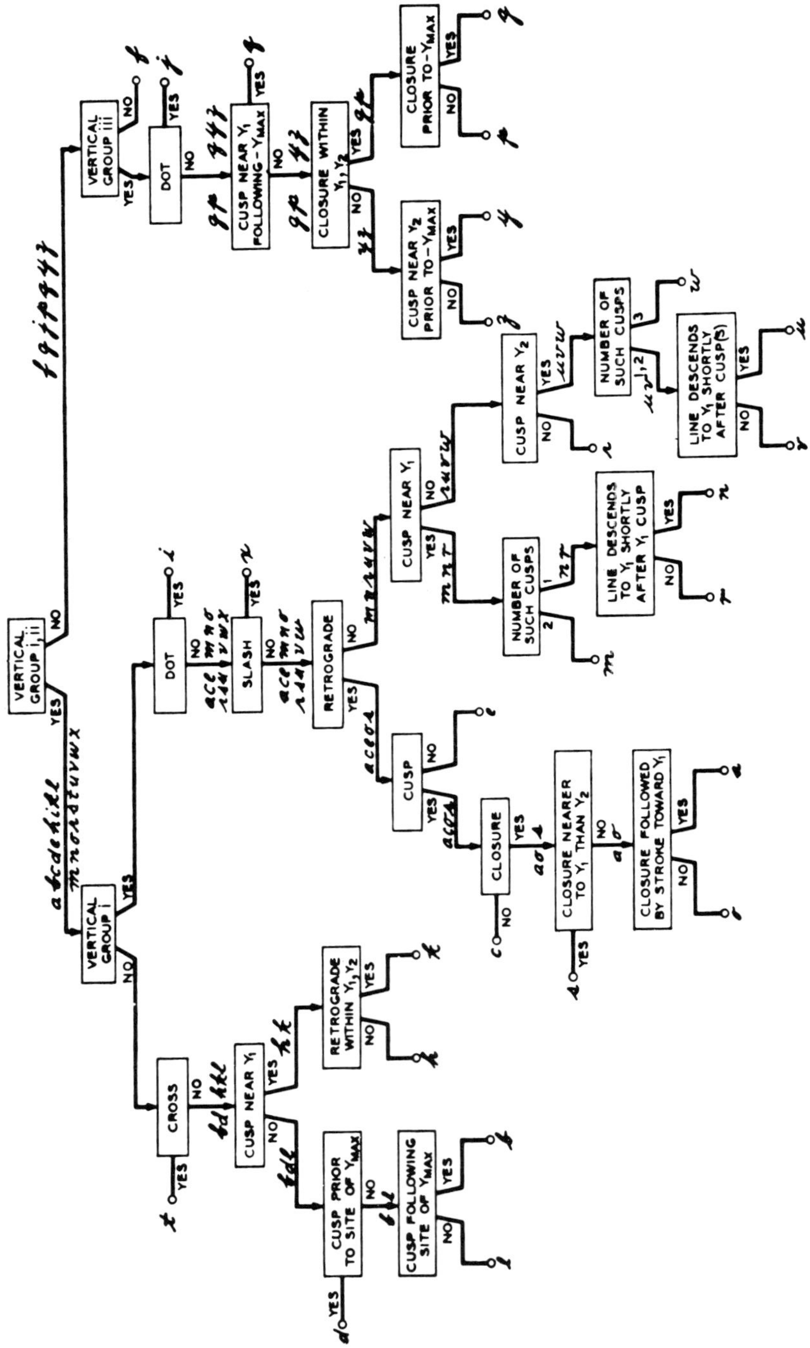

Figure 17: A decision tree for cursive script.[44]

ON THE AUTOMATIC CLASSIFICATION OF FINGERPRINTS – SOME CONSIDERATIONS ON THE LINGUISTIC INTERPRETATION OF PICTURES

Antonio Grasselli

CENTRO STUDI CALCOLATRICI ELETTRONICHE
CONSIGLIO NAZIONALE DELLE RICERCHE
UNIVERSITA DI PISA, PISA, ITALY

1. Introduction

A linguistic approach to pattern recognition in pictorial sources has been proposed by Kirsch[1] and Narasimhan[2], and has received a great deal of attention from research workers in the past few years [3-11]. This line of attack has undoubtedly some appeal, since it casts the problem of picture processing into a comfortable unifying theoretical framework, giving the possibility of generalizing methods which were developed for the syntactic analysis of string languages.

Several questions need however to be answered before one can definitely assess the importance and usefulness of linguistic methods in picture processing. The purpose of this paper is to ask some of these questions in the light of a specific example.

2. The Analysis of Dermatoglyphics in Medecine

The usefulness of fingerprints for personal identification was recognized long ago, following the work of Galton[12]: this author had not only pointed out that *minutiae** of fingerprints remain unchanged throughout the life of an individual, but had also observed the heritability of finger- and palm-prints. Until recently, however, the study of these patterns (currently called dermatoglyphics) had relevance only in police work and in anthropological studies.

There is presently overwhelming evidence on the significance of dermatoglyphics in medecine: in particular, there is an abundance of results on pattern distortions caused by chromosomal aberrations; congenital heart

---

* The term *minutia* is used to indicate either a branch or an interruption of dermal ridges.

diseases have also been studied.*

The systematic classification of fingerprints, as used in medical studies[15], is still very crude, and depends fundamentally on the recognition of *triradii:* a triradius, shown in Figure 1, is the meeting point of three lines, which demarcate three fields of almost parallel ridges. Thus, the number of triradii allows the classification in three main patterns: arch, loop and whorl, which have respectively 0, 1 or 2 triradii. These three main patterns are shown in the drawings of Figure 2; triradii are indicated by solid arrows. Three examples are given in Figures 3, 4 and 5, which show respectively an arch, a loop and a whorl.

A quantitative parameter which is also of interest in the classification of fingerprints is the *ridge count*: this number is conventionally zero for an arch, it is equal to the number of ridges between the core** of the pattern and the triradius for a loop, and to the sum of the number of ridges between the core** and each of the triradii for a whorl.

Between the three main patterns, there exist figures which can be seen as transitional stages. A loop of low ridge count (see Figure 6) is very similar to an arch; likewise, the pattern in Figure 7 (*central pocket*) is classified as a whorl, but has a stronger resemblance to a loop. A third example is that of Figure 8 (*twin loops,* again classified as a whorl because of two triradii).

The number and position of triradii is also the fundamental criterion for studying palm-prints: for the sake of brevity, these will not be discussed in this paper.

3. The Automatic Classification of Dermatoglyphics

The classification scheme illustrated in the previous section is still that of Galton. Patterns very different from one another are in this scheme in the same class: as an example, consider the very different appearance of the arches and whorls in Figures 3 and 9, 4 and 10 respectively.

There is presently a trend in the medical world to believe that dermatoglyphics can tell us more about the individual as they do now. A more careful analysis would require the examination of large masses of data and a more elaborate classification scheme: this means that structural parameters other than the easily observable ridge counts will have to be identified in the prints. It seems therefore worthwhile to provide the medical experimenter with a facility to test hypothesis and to try out new classification schemes, freeing him from the bottlenecks of hand examination.

* We will not attempt to give here a complete bibliography; see, for example [13,14,16].

** The core of the patterns is indicated by a dotted arrow in Figures 2(b) and 2(c).

We* are presently developing an automatic analysis procedure, with the present limited goal of classifying fingerprints**; later, we intend to work with palm-prints also. A detailed description of the physical device used to digitize the prints is out of order here: we will only say that it consists of a random-access flying-spot scanner for 24 x 36 mm. negatives; the scanner digitizes the picture in an array of 512 x 512 points, in 8 grey levels. The scanner is coupled through a PDP–8 computer to the (medium size) computer CEP. Initial experiments, due to the unavailability of the scanner, presently in the completion stage, have been carried out by digitizing the negatives on the FIDAC scanner of the Clinical Effects of Radiation Research Unit of the Medical Research Council in London.

4. A Classification Algorithm

Fingerprints seem to offer an almost ideal ground for trying out linguistically-oriented methods. We have however resisted the temptation of writing down at once a bidimensional grammar to describe the pictures, and rather we have concentrated on the problem of finding an efficient algorithm.

Let us suppose, for simplicity, that patterns be classified in arches, loops, whorls and their transitional figures. For this classification, it is sufficient to determine triradii, pattern cores, and ridge counts. By looking at the pictures in the paper, one sees immediately that there is an high amount of redundancy in the patterns. It would seem quite wasteful to recognize individually each ridge in the pattern: in fact, as can be seen by looking at the examples in the paper, the patterns are quite noisy***, and this recognition would require a substantial preprocessing for noise elimination.

Instead, we have tried to take advantage of the redundancy in the patterns by the following method. The picture is subdivided into a certain number of squares, called *samples*. We will use here the picture in Figure 11 as a running example: in this case the picture has been subdivided into 360 samples, as shown in Figure 12. For each sample, the "predominant" slope of the ridge segments in the picture is determined, and digitized in one of eight possible values. The predominant slope can be obtained by various algorithm, which will not be discussed here: we will simply say that the

* This work is carried out in collaboration with Dr. M. Ceccarelli, Prof. P. Giorgi and Prof. A. Paci (of the Paediatric Clynic of the University of Pisa) and Mr. G. Levi (of the Centro Studi Calcolatrici Elettroniche).

**The author is aware of only one other effort in this direction, by Tou and Hankley[17]: at the time of writing, he has been unable to obtain their paper or any report on their activity.

***The quality of the pictures could be much improved by a more careful print-taking technique,but one must think that these prints were taken on children,and it is quite difficult to convince them to collaborate to a scientific enterprise.

actual algorithm which we employ consists in plotting density profiles in the eight directions, and in looking for peaks in these profiles. The value obtained will be called *sampled slope*, and the picture obtained by recording the sampled slopes in each sample will be called *sampling matrix*. The sampling matrix derived from the picture in Figure 11 is shown in Figure 12; an encoded version of the sampling matrix is shown in Figure 13.

Observe that, while the fine structure of the original picture is obviously lost, the sampling matrix still allows a fairly good structural description of the pattern. Clearly, the choice of sample dimension is critical: if the sample is too small, there is an intolerable deterioration of the pattern, since the distortion introduced by the process of sampled slope determination is the predominant factor. If the sample is too large, too much of the pattern structure is lost to afford reliable classification. The matter is further complicated by marked differences in the aspect of different pictures, for example in ridge widths (compare Figures 3 and 11). From our experience, however, the acceptable range is not too narrow, and it is possible to decide on sample dimensions in each specific instance by carrying out simple processes such as for example the determination of average picture density.

Clearly, zones of interest in the pictures (triradii and pattern cores) are among those where there exist discontinuities in the slope of ridges. On the sampling matrix in Figure 13, we have encircled the value of a sample whenever this value differs from the value of an adjacent sample by 2 or more: a comparison of the original picture with the encoded matrix will show at a glance that the triradius and core zones correspond to regions of encircled samples.

Let us now call *component* of the sampling matrix a connected region of samples of equal slope value. Further processing of the picture can be seen as the application of syntactic rules to components, with the ultimate goal of finding systems of parallel ridges. We have found it useful to perform some smoothing of components before combining them. For example, with reference to Figure 13, there are two samples of value 4 immersed in a large component of value 5: the value of these samples will be transformed to 5. A set of satisfactory smoothing rules can be easily established.

Without illustrating here in a detailed fashion the rules of component combination (while these rules are intuitively simple, their precise description requires a lengthy explanation beyond the scope of this paper), we will note that their end results can be pictorially represented in the sketch in Figure 14: it is relatively unimportant to describe the data structure which encodes this sketch, but one can certainly appreciate, by looking at the sketch, the fact that the pattern structure can be correctly identified. At this point, to complete the analysis, it will certainly be necessary to take a second look into the shaded region, since the sketch does not provide enough information to localize with sufficient accuracy the position of the triradius. The (relatively small) shaded region can be examined now by ridge-following algorithms as precisely as possible.

5. Some Questions on the Linguistic Approach

The process sketched in the previous section is naturally subdivided into several phases:

(a) determination of sample size;
(b) construction of the sampling matrix;
(c) component delineation and component smoothing;
(d) combination of components;
(e) careful examination of selected regions.

The first two steps are of the "cookbook recipe" type, and could hardly be cast into the linguistic framework: from the linguistic viewpoint, these steps have as goal that of defining *primitive symbols.* The third,fourth and fifth steps are certainly linguistically-oriented, and a bidimensional grammar expressing these transformations can be written down.

The difficulty in starting with the original picture as the primitive linguistic object derives from the difficulty of expressing formally metric attributes, while it is certainly not so hard to implement various ad-hoc algorithms based on metric properties. To be sure, in principle it is certainly possible to frame the process of sampling matrix construction as a linguistic process; while this could probably be seen as an useful exercise in formal description methods, it would most certainly have as a result poor efficiency of the recognition algorithm.

Note that the first two stages are a substantial portion of the global process, and certainly its most critical part. While the implementation of the remaining stages is certainly not trivial, one can be reasonably sure that reliable classification will be achieved if "good" sampling matrices are obtained. Therefore, whether or not the rest of the process is linguistically oriented does not seem to be of capital importance, since the hard problem has been solved upstream. While no general conclusions can be drawn at this point, it seems however pertinent to ask the following question: how often is the hardest problem the one that must necessarily be solved by ad-hoc methods (if one wants to preserve processing efficiency), while the remaining parts can be nicely theorized upon? There is some experience on this very question in the field of programming languages: all the work on string grammars notwithstanding, the most central problems in compiler writing still defy theorization.

We will note further that it seems capital to us, in practical application, to concentrate first in defining good processing algorithms rather than trying out a linguistic description at the first onset. Establishing a bidimensional grammar for a class of pictures has not yet become a routine problem: thus, the creation of a description outside the guidelines of a processing algorithm may give a result which has both formal elegance and adequate descriptive power, but suffers from fabulous processing inadequacies. The fact that the algorithm is focused first may result in the implicit definition of a language which can be later on be rendered explicit provided that one can find a suitable metalanguage. It is questionable, at this point, whether this late formalization is very useful.

A third question which needs to be answered is about the applicability of linguistic methods in processing pictures of natural objects. As yet, there is certainly a lack of experimental results to substantiate an answer. We will recall that while Kirsch[1] had excluded these pictures from the scope of its proposal, other authors (for example Clowes[6]) have worked on languages whose scope embraces also natural pictures. It is important that evidence be gained on this point, since the great majority of picture processing problems lies in this area.

The foregoing observations should not be taken as a negative appraisal of linguistic methods: rather, they have the purpose of pointing out some of its limits. Further work needs certainly to be done to remove them totally or partially. For the time being, the linguistic approach seems to offer more an underlying operating philosophy (in the line of the early work by Grimsdale[18] and Eden[19]) than a complete theory and a set of useful specific operational techniques.

BIBLIOGRAPHY

1. Kirsch, R. A., Computer interpretation of English text and picture patterns, *IEEE Trans. on Electronic Computers,* 13, 363–376 (1964).
2. Narasimhan, R., Labeling schemata and syntactic description of pictures, *Information and Control, 7,* 151–179 (1964).
3. Ledley, R. S., High-speed automatic analysis of biomedical pictures, *Science, 146,* 216–233 (1964).
4. Clowes, M. B., Perception, picture processing and computers, Medical Research Council Psycholinguistic Research Unit, Oxford, Report PLU/65/17 (1965).
5. Narasimhan, R., Syntax-directed interpretation of classes of pictures, *Comm. ACM, 9,* 166–173 (1966).
6. Clowes, M. B., Aspects of the syntax of simple pictorial displays, Seminar Paper No. 3, Workshop on Complex Processes, 22–23 May 1966.
7. Lipkin, L. E., W. C. Watt and R. A. Kirsch, The analysis, synthesis and description of biological images, *Annals New York Acad. Sci., 128,* 984–1012 (1966).
8. Watt, W. C., Morphology of the Nevada cattlebrands and their blazoons, National Bureau of Standards, Applied Math. Div. Rept. 9050 (1966).
9. Narasimhan, R. and V. N. S. Reddy, A generative model for English letters and its computer implementation, Tata Institute for Fundamental Research, Computer Group Rept. No. 12 (1966).
10. Shaw, A. C., A proposed language for the formal description of pictures, Stanford University, Memo. GSG–28 (1967).

11. Miller, W. F. and A. C. Shaw, A picture calculus, Conf. on Emerging Concepts in Computer Graphics, Urbana, 5–8 November 1967, available as Stanford University SLAC Publication 358.
12. Galton, F., Finger Prints (MacMillan, London 1892).
13. Penrose, L. S., Fingerprints, palms and chromosomes, *Nature, 197,* 933–938 (1963).
14. Forbes, A. P., Fingerprints and palm prints (dermatoglyphics) and palmar-flexion creases in gonadal dysgenesis, pseudohypoparathyroidism and Klinefelter's syndrome, *New England J. of Medecine,* 270, 1268–1277 (1964).
15. Penrose, L. S., Dermatoglyphic topology, *Nature, 205,* 544–546 (1965).
16. Sanchez Cascos, A., Finger-print patterns in congenital heart disease, *British Heart J., 26,* 524–527 (1964).
17. Tou, J. T. and W. J. Hankley, Automatic fingerprint interpretation and classification via topological coding and contextual analysis, presented at Symp. on Automatic Photointerpretation, Washington, May 31–June 2, 1967.
18. Grimsdale, R. L., *et al.,* A system for the automatic recognition of patterns, *Proc. IEE, 106,* part B, 210–221 (1959).
19. Eden, M., Handwriting and pattern recognition, *IRE Trans. on Information Theory, 8,* 160–166 (1962).

Figure 1: A Triradius

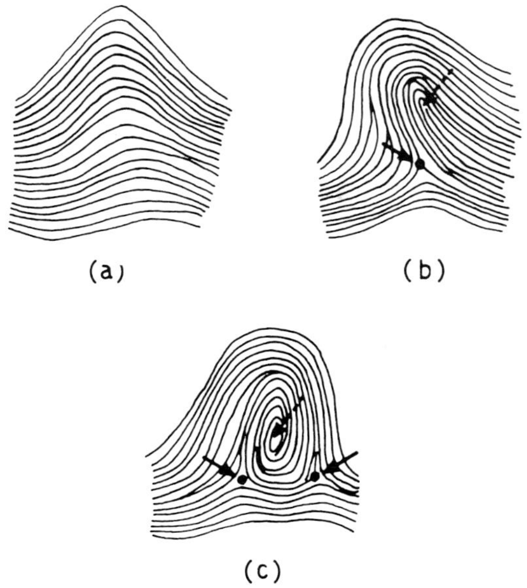

Figure 2: Schemes of the Three Main Patterns: (a) Arch, (b) Loop, (c) Whorl. Solid arrows indicate triradii, dotted arrows the cores of the patterns.

Figure 3: Arch

Figure 4: Loop

Figure 5: Whorl

Figure 6: Loop of Low Ridge Count

Figure 7: Central Pocket

Figure 8: Twin Loops

Figure 9: Another Arch

Figure 10: Another Whorl

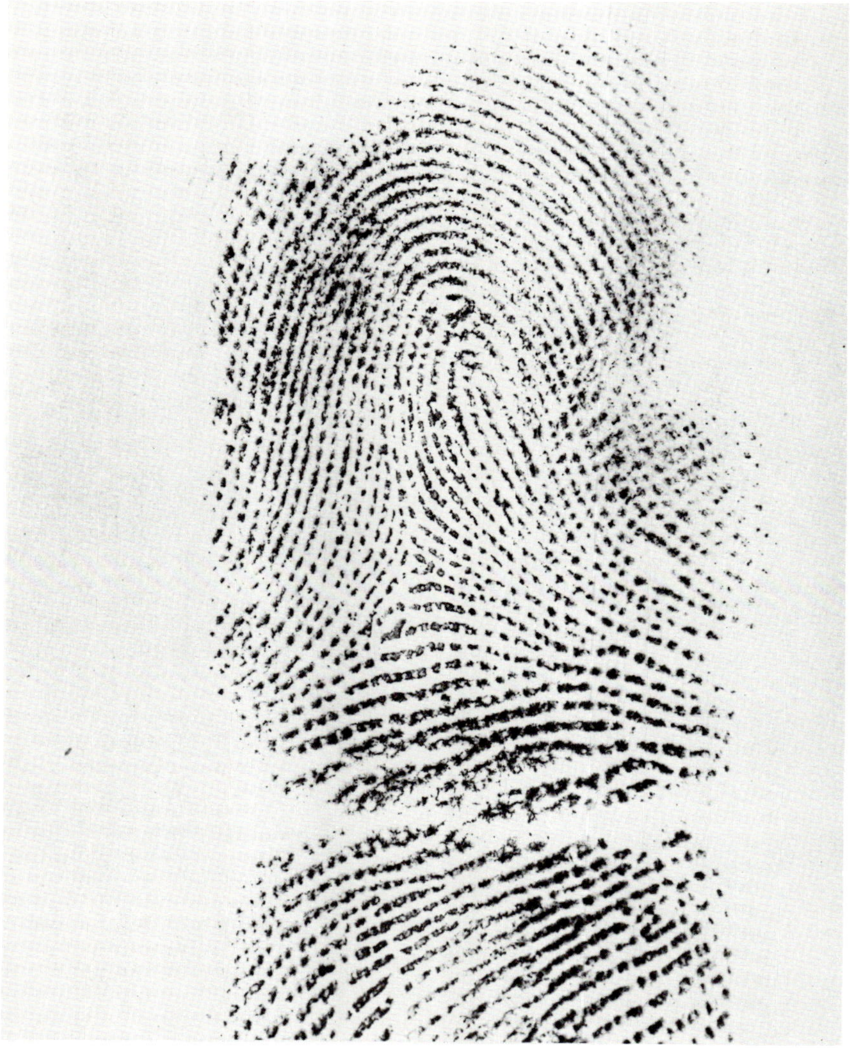

Figure 11: Pattern Employed in the Description of the Classification Algorithm

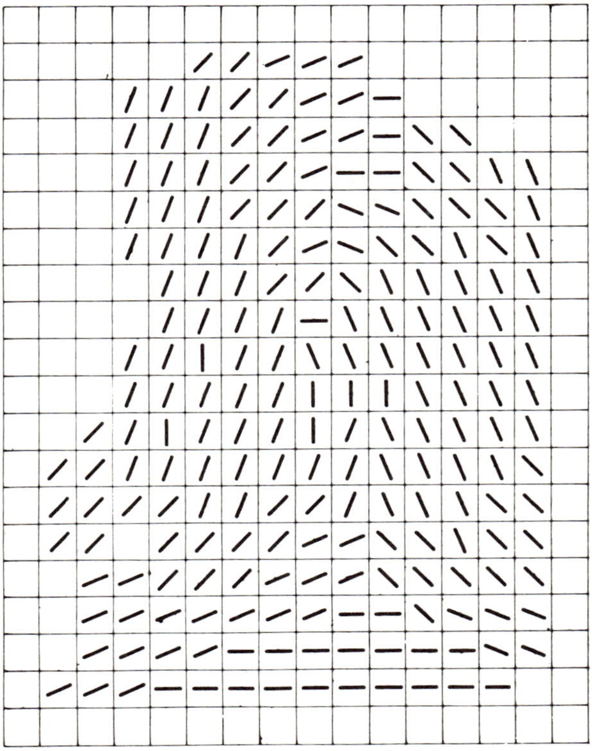

Figure 12: Sampling Matrix

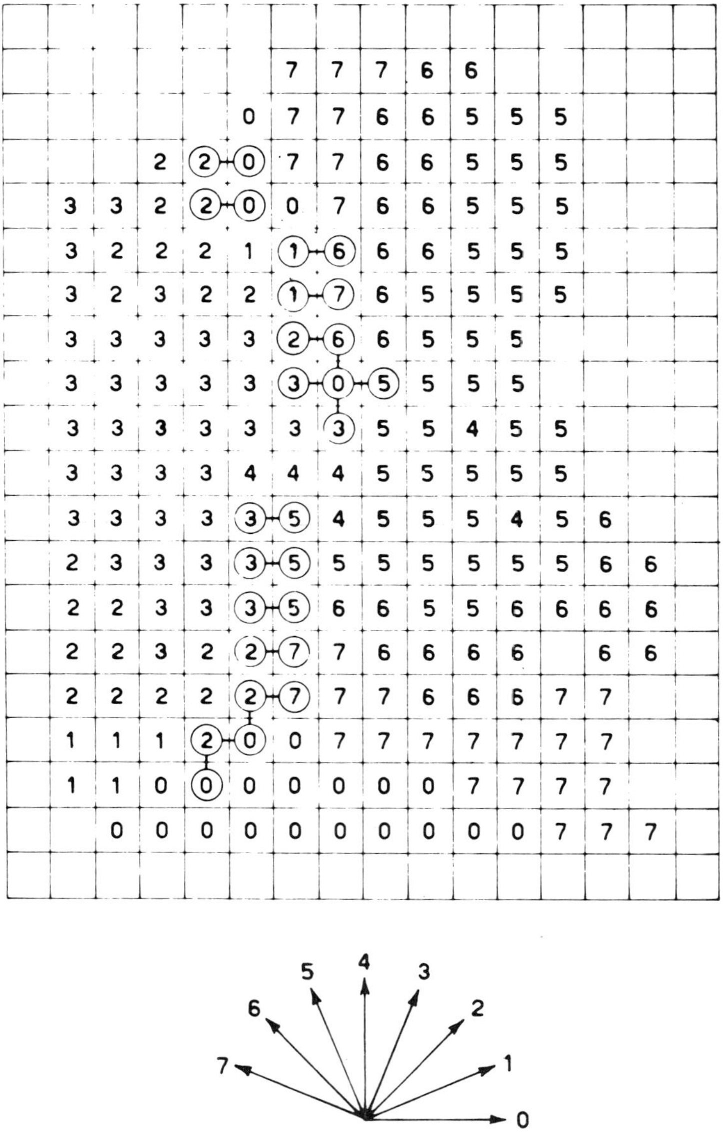

Figure 13: Encoded Sampling Matrix

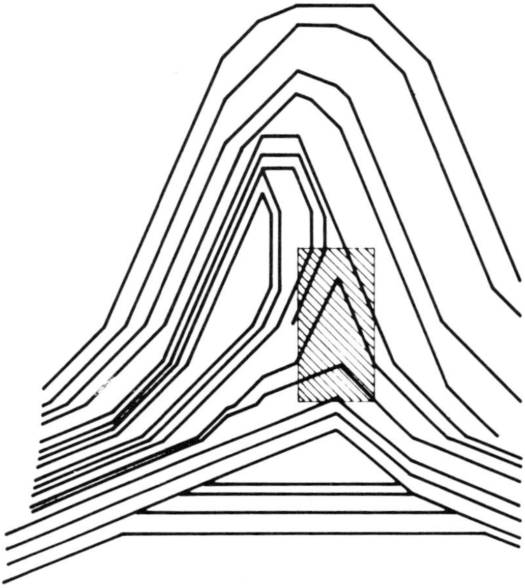

Figure 14: Sketch of the Pattern in Figure 11

NETWORK PROPERTIES FOR PATTERN RECOGNITION

Joseph K. Hawkins

ROBOT RESEARCH
LA JOLLA, CALIFORNIA

1. Introduction

Although great strides have been made in the field of automatic pattern recognition, a large gap remains to be bridged before many of the pressing problems of the day can be solved. Both theory and hardware must make significant advances if such complex applications as automatic photographic reading are to be realistically achieved.

In the realm of theory, present mathematical techniques barely go beyond the level of linear systems. The enormous amount of computation required to go to higher-order approaches has virtually been precluded by the present state of the computer art, impressive as it is. A much more powerful computational ability is no doubt required if, as suggested by von Neumann[1], heuristic experiments conducted on large, complex systems are needed to give mathematics the intuitive base for formulating concepts dealing with the massive non-linear problems encountered in pattern recognition.

In the field of hardware, five or six orders of magnitude in processing rates separate present approaches both from the requirements of specific applications and from the biological competition. The enormous data processing load imposed by a typical automatic image screening task has been documented[2] and evaluated in terms of parallel vs. serial network approaches[3]. Only unimaginably expensive and massive computers even larger than those presently contemplated[4], can hope to accomplish such tasks with present components. On the other hand man, the biological competition, easily processes million–element pictures in full color at reasonable speeds, is priced at a mere $20,000 by industry[5], and requires relatively few hours of on-the-job programming.

In the face of these large disparities in both theory and hardware, it is time to re-evaluate directions. The viewpoint adopted here is that the key to progress lies in the area of improved hardware. It is presumed that such improvements will themselves reveal new theoretical principles, or will at least open the computational door to more sophisticated mathematical experimentation. Consider, then, the present alternatives.

Large scale integrated circuit technology is presently at the level of several hundred components on a chip, with simple interconnections. We can probably look forward to thousands on a chip. But soon the wavelength of light employed in fabrication and the demands of yield and reliability will impose a limit. Even if this is overcome by electron-beam deposition and machining, the sticky interconnection problem remains.

Optical techniques have been very attractive because of their high degree of parallelism[6]. But suitable non-linear, amplifying optical materials have been slow to appear. These are mandatory if interconnections (filter functions) and non-linear decisions are to be made readily.

Parallel electro-optical approaches[7] involving image intensifier-like components offer modest parallelism on the order of millions of elements, and speed. Again, interconnection remains a problem since information transfers can only be made at the expense of large power loss in the optical domain. Although direct electron transfer may be feasible, such information transfers are difficult to control.

These problems suggest that man's tools, while marvelous, are still too large and clumsy to perform the type of network fabrication required. It is the author's belief that these problems can only be overcome by some form of self-constructing and self-repairing network. It is probable that organic chemistry will play the dominant role in developing such networks. Nature long ago discovered this solution, no doubt because only these materials offer sufficiently complex interaction behavior to permit the fabrication program to occur.

The remainder of this paper is therefore devoted to the concept that highly parallel, richly interconnected data processing networks can be constructed from organic materials. It is well understood that before such a concept can be realized, a number of severe technical problems must be overcome, and it is the purpose of the following sections to point to possible avenues of approach.

Not only must we learn how information can be processed in networks composed of rather unconventional components, we must also devise methods for constructing the networks with minimum outside intervention. Thus the principles of structural computing must be mastered, along with the attendent automatic structural repair. Finally, we must pay attention to the factor of time, since both data processing and self-construction activities need to be based upon economic reality.

2. Signal Amplification

The network concept under consideration here is that of large, highly parallel arrays of elements. The network is conceived as consisting of many layers of such arrays, interconnected richly, with each array containing a modest number of element types. Each element computes some logic function of its input signals, and passes the result to its multiple outputs.

Focusing attention first upon individual elements, the question is: what properties of organic materials can we take advantage of to implement a signal-processing or logic function? Or more generally, what properties are required of nature in order to produce signal processing, and can these be found in organic materials?

The crucial property needed to implement a logic function is that of amplification. Since at the rudimentary level amplifiers are inherently single-input, functions of multiple inputs can always be generated by a trivial analog linear or non-linear summation process at the input.

Amplification, in turn, appears to rest upon the existence of certain fundamental structural and energetic conditions. First, there must be a container for storing the input signal. This implies a structure which can maintain strong material or charge concentration gradients against a hostile thermal world, as in the transistor. Second, there must be a pump or energy source which can repeatedly interrogate the contents of the store. The gain of the amplifier is then the average number of times the structure can be interrogated before its stored information is inadvertently destroyed. The results of the interrogation are of course made available elsewhere to other units, and are known as the output. To be useful, the output must be available to more than one other unit–fanout–and the gain must exceed the fanout if information is not to be lost.

This rudimentary description appears to fit a wide variety of both conventional solid-state components and others, including photographic[9], chemical[8], and electron-optical[7]. These properties also appear to exist in organic structures.

The living membrane is an outstanding example of a structure capable of maintaining a concentration gradient against the environment. In a recent article, Katchalsky[10] points this out, and emphasizes the fact that space must be anisotropic for the phenomenon of transport against a gradient to occur. That is, there must be boundaries (storage walls) or at least differential resistance to flow.

Katchalsky also brings up the important point––to which we will refer later––that dynamic processes must be coupled for the desired behavior to occur. The coupling for two flows, J_d and J_r, is written in terms of the driving forces, X_d and X_r, as

$$X_d = R_d J_d + R_{dr} J_r$$

$$X_r = R_{rd} J_d + R_r J_r$$

in which the R's are constants. An important and universal restriction on the coupling term is that $R_{dr} = R_{rd}$. It is fascinating to note that the canonical equations of the junction transistor[11] can be written in a similar form, for collector and emitter currents I_c and I_e,

$$X_c = A_{11} I_c + A_{12} I_e$$

$$X_e = A_{21} I_c + A_{22} I_e$$

in which the A's are constants. The X's represent the exponential junction potential, [exp(V) – 1], with V the appropriate junction voltage divided by the thermal potential, kT/q. Again, the coupling restriction holds that $A_{12} = A_{21}$.

Interesting amplifying behavior in biological membranes has long been known. It is also known that similar behavior occurs in artificial membranes. Teorell[12] describes processes in macroscopic membranes of collodion, cellophane or sintered glass in virtually the same terms of concentration gradients and flows as one would describe a transistor. More recently[13], membranes formed of lipids similar to those found in biological material, doped with proteins, have been shown to exhibit negative resistance characteristics inherent in any amplifying phenomenon.

It is clear, then, that the amplification necessary for signal processing can exist in structures as thin as 100 Å. But what is the minimum useful area? Or to put it another way, if the above analogies suggest that the principles of amplification are the same throughout the physical world, how small a unit can still exhibit the necessary properties?

Ling[14] proposes that the phenomenon occurs at the molecular level. In a chapter entitled, "The transmission, amplification, and mixing of biological signals at the molecular level", he points to zipperlike all-or-none processes in charged hydrocarbon groups. Models of these processes, which depend upon strong coupling between adjacent charged groups, are presented. These models offer a realistic degree of plausibility to some of the conjectures of Pattee[15] regarding structural computations in molecular strings.

The notion that information processing can occur by rearrangement of charged groups at the molecular level suggests that our conventional distinction between signals and the structures doing the signal processing may be undesirable. Perhaps all signal processing depends ultimately upon structural changes. Thus the storage of charge in the base region of a transistor–resulting in an output signal–might better be described as a rearrangement of the structural distribution of energy states. In any case, it appears that further understanding of the charge distributions in molecular groups[16] will help to elucidate those conditions under which logic functions can be implemented at this level. Note again the importance of strong local coupling for producing interesting behavior.

3. Structural Amplification

At an incredibly early stage of the computer industry, von Neumann[1] recognized the drawbacks of existing components, noting that it is the "mechanical instability of our materials which prevents us from reducing sizes further". He saw clearly the need for self-constructing and self-repairing networks if interesting artificial behavior was to be achieved, and proceeded to construct an existence proof that self-reproduction by automata is possible. His basic unit turned out to be a 29-state machine in a two-dimensional space[17]. The problem posed was only that the machine produce copies of itself which were themselves capable of reproduction, but it could clearly be extended to include other information processing functions as well.

An important point regarding "Complexity" was observed by von Neumann, namely, "This fact, that complication, as well as organization, below a certain minimum level is degenerative, and beyond that level can become self-supporting and even increasing, will clearly play an important role in any future theory of the subject". Note the interesting analogy to typical amplifier behavior. That is, small input signals have little effect upon the output signal, but as the input increases linearly the output increases exponentially until saturation sets in. This threshold effect, present in all devices, apparently resembles a typical structural growth process.

In work closely allied to the viewpoint taken in this paper, von Foerster[18] also points out the similarity between signal processing and structural amplification by saying, "Of course, the bio-chemist would probably use the terms 'to form' or 'to synthesize', instead of 'to compute', but in an abstract sense these terms are equivalent." He goes on to model the growth of a highly parallel network requiring only one bit of genetic information (and some noise) to specify. The result is an array of Laplacian operators which are, however, formed in a way that might be described as "unusualness computing", whereby structural growth drives to zero all responses to commonly occurring stimuli, but allows responses to uncommon stimuli. This seems to be a clear illustration of how environmental signals might modify the structures of incompletely specified networks.

The notion that order can grow from disorder is given plausibility by idealized molecular models developed by Pattee[15]. Noting that evolution has not lasted long enough to generate living matter by a random process, he investigated how order lying somewhere between the level of amino acid groups and the level of self-replicating molecules could occur naturally. He pointed out that molecules which exhibit local coupling among groups, and feedback (by twists in the growing string) are equivalent to feedback shift registers capable of producing long strings of symbols with a relatively few elements. In the binary case, the periodicity of symbols is limited by the length, n, of the feedback loop to at most $2^n - 1$. Thus, short-range order can produce long-range order under conditions of tight coupling and growth.

While the above studies indicate that the replication of structure is possible under quite general conditions, the question remains as to whether we can identify similar processes, which can be put to useful work, in non-living organic material. The evidence is scattered but intriguing.

Pattee's conjecture regarding the formation of group sequences appears to be supported by recent comparisons of amino acid sequences in proteolytic enzymes[19]. Sequences of amino acids were found to be similar in a variety of proteases, reflecting a "phylogenetic" relationship.

Relatively simple structural replication under the control of an input "signal" is now believed to be responsible for stereospecific polymerization[20]. In this case, the monomer added to the growing end of a polypropylene oxide crystal can be either of two types, dependent upon the geometry—the structural signal—around the catalyst site on an enzyme.

At a higher level of complexity, Spiegelman[21] has recently reported on what appears to be the smallest known self-duplicating entity. The entity in this case was a viral RNA molecule known as Q_β. An enzyme generated in response to this bacteriophage proved highly selective to its template, producing a twenty-fold increase when seeded by the Q_β – RNA, while leaving other RNA templates virtually untouched. It was further found that fragments of the molecule did not produce replicative behavior. Spiegelman suggests a model in which both the local molecular group sequence and the "intactness" of a linear heteropolymer can be determined by the enzyme by causing the molecule to form a circle and by "recognizing" the resulting double stranded region. He also reports on an evolutionary sequence performed outside of a living cell. By selecting successive generations of Q_β – RNA on the basis of speed of replication, by the 75th generation a highly efficient replicating product was produced which retained only 17% of the length of the original molecule.

At an even higher level of structural organization, Fox[22,23] has investigated the properties of microspheres formed by protenoids——substances which resemble proteins but are synthetic and not derived from living material. These substances automatically form double-walled microspheres when heated in water and allowed to cool. The microspheres so formed exhibit a number of suggestive characteristics, including fission under the influence of raised pH, chemical selectivity of the microsphere wall, formation and liberation of "buds" which themselves enlarge and form new buds.

These and other studies certainly indicate that structures can increase in degree of order under the influence of external control and in the presence of a source of energy or prior order. They do not yet, however, permit the engineer to construct networks of arbitrary geometry and function.

4. Time

Time is important from an engineering standpoint, in the formation of networks, and in the gain of an amplifier. It is desirable, in fact, if a figure of merit similar to the gain-bandwidth product in electronics can be identify and used to evaluate alternative implementations.

The speed of molecular interactions is enormously high. But this does not tell the whole story, since slower processes such as drift and diffusion are apt to control the cycle time in any chemical amplification[8].

Few figures on this subject are known to the author. Gerard[24] reports that each molecule of enzyme catalyzes the oxidation of 10^5 molecules of substrate per second. Cowan[25] reports an estimate that something like 10^{19} bits per second are processed in macromolecular synthesis.

In any case it is clear that structural amplifiers, unlike most electronic amplifiers, are producing more than a single bit with each unit generated. The gain-bandwidth in a transistor amplifier is simply the numerical gain divided by the time to achieve it. In a structural replicating amplifier, we must multiply the number of unit structures produced by the number of bits of information represented by each structure.

It is not at all clear how a quantity of information should be assigned to natural structures. In axiomatic structures represented by a limited number of possible states, s, at each of n positions in space[26], it is possible to place the upper bound s^n on the number of possible structures. In natural structures, however, many internal constraints exist among atoms and molecules, and the information content of a given structural message is not immediately apparent.

This situation is compounded by the viewpoint that it is precisely the close coupling or internal constraints that make an organism what it is. Gerard[24] points out that, "Electrons, neutrons and protons become organized into atoms, which are, therefore, organisms." Perhaps when looked at in a different way, the approach and bonding of two atoms can be described from the standpoint of gain and bandwidth.

Pattee's[15] observation that the term feedback should "include the entire circuit of information used in the memory, growth, and replication cycle, and not necessarily only one twin of a helix", is important in this regard. Electronic gain-bandwidth should also be thought of as a cyclic process, since in all cases it is proportional to the reciprocal of the transit time of a unit of information around a closed loop which includes the message storage region[26]. In the transport of ions across a living membrane, a cyclic process apparently including both structural and electronic changes, a rate of 20 cycles per second is reported[10] for each carrier molecule.

Cyclic or feedback processes suggest the possibility both of multi-stable states in overall systems and of oscillation. Cowan[27] points out that the consequence of strongly interconnecting switching networks is that of producing multi-stable states, the simplest form being represented by the familiar S–curve of any typical amplifier. This results from positive feedback alone, while positive and negative feedback together can produce more complex transfer functions and more than two stable states.

In the area of macroscopic membranes, Teorell[28] has demonstrated spontaneous oscillation in systems using porous porcelain membranes and including hydrostatic energy storage.

All of the foregoing suggests that concepts of time, feedback and bandwidth in structural information processing are still far from clear. The notion of structural degradation with time[26] – an important corollary of self-repair[1] – also needs to be factored into the complete explanation.

5. Theoretical Background

Most of the mathematical proofs and simulation experience in the field of complex interacting or reproducing networks comes from the field of automata theory. Two early reviews, by McNaughton[29] and by Moore[30], cover much of the known field at that time, while a more recent one by Stahl[31] bears specifically on the area of machine self-reproduction. Eden[32] reports on computer-simulated two-dimensional growth processes, and more recently Arbib[33] describes a program for one-dimensional reproduction. Work currently under way by Rubinoff[34] deals with the two-dimensional array problem.

From the author's engineering viewpoint, all of this prior work seems to say the following. First, self-reproducing networks can indeed be constructed in principle, based upon a great variety of rather arbitrary algorithms, and giving rise to an equally large variety of network properties. Second, there does not at present appear to exist any principle on the basis of which one can select or synthesize the simplest or minimum basic unit which will still exhibit the property of autonomous network construction. Third, relatively little attention appears to have been given to the problem of devising components which can both replicate themselves into a two-dimensional network, and which, having done so, will be able to perform useful information processing. Fourth, with some exceptions the notion of a network as a dynamic entity with continuous or cyclic self-repair appears to have been given little attention. Fifth, the possible connections between axiomatic elements with well-defined logic behavior, and the real molecular elements of the physical world appear to this author to be tenuous at best, despite the obvious inspiration most axiomatic models draw from the world of organic chemistry.

With regard to the second point above, perhaps the author is looking for a logical calculus similar to that so useful to computer engineers. In this connection, concepts involving a calculus of triadic relationships such as those outlined by Moreno-Diaz and McCulloch[35] may prove to be important starting points.

With regard to the third and fourth points above, it appears to the author that rather basic approaches, such as that taken by Cowan[27], may be required. He is able, for example, to relate the parameters of a set of interacting species to such concepts as free energy, internal energy and entropy. He also sees clearly the important role of strong coupling, and the idea that complication or order is a regenerative phenomenon, being degenerative below a certain level, and self-amplifying above it. The key appears to be that of many elements, locally interacting, and he suggests, "The greater the number of cooperating symbio-organisms present, the greater is the probability of survival."

With regard to the fifth point above, it appears to the author that attempting to cast molecular interactions in terms of some manipulable logic is worthy of a serious effort at this time. Further detailed knowledge of molecular structures[16], and analyses of group interactions[14] will continue to be of great assistance in this connection.

6. Pattern Recognition

To his co-workers in the practical field of pattern recognition, the author would like to suggest that the directions of approach suggested above may not constitute such a diversion from the main stream of effort as might at first appear. After all, a molecule which selects out of a myriad of candidates only that one or few which it will replicate is surely recognizing a pattern in the very sense that this term has been used in image, voice or waveform recognition. Even simpler molecules, which can only react with certain classes of others, are also dichotomizing the world into classes in precisely the same sense that mathematical or hardware decision elements are placing hyperplanes into multidimensional space to separate it into classes.

The author would further like to suggest that when molecular interactions are thought of in terms of pattern recognition, the latter viewpoint may also benefit from some of the concepts of the former. For example, when "recognition" occurs at the molecular level, not only does the pattern produce an effect upon the recognition circuit, but the act of recognition produces an effect upon the pattern. In the case of two molecules, the act of bonding produces a redistribution of the charge around both. Does not this same effect occur in conventional pattern recognition? The answer of course depends on the system, but we know that nothing can be observed without disturbing it. This feedback effect is negligible in many practical recognition applications, for example when the pattern is recorded photographically, simply because such as small fraction of the optical energy leaving the pattern is collected. In very small networks, however, the effect of recognition upon the pattern recognized must no longer be neglected.

Chemical recognition suggests another viewpoint which may prove useful. It is clear that the act of recognition of one molecule by another is accompanied by a transition from a high energy state to a lower one. A crude analogy in our present computers lies in the flip-flop. We might say that one half of the flip-flop recognizes the condition of the other half, and acts accordingly. The result is a condition of low power dissipation. If the flip-flop is artificially forced into an intermediate state, power dissipation rises dramatically. Thus we might say that an undecided network is in a state of excessive energy dissipation, or tension, and is "relieved" when it can perform the act of recognition.

It may be that this phenomenon provides the driving force for adaptation, and growth in complexity. As long as a network has a satisfactory way of classifying the world—the simpler the scheme the better, in accordance with accepted scientific philosophy—little exertion is required. If the network is unable to decide on an appropriate classification, however, presumably energy dissipation goes up. The result must either be additional growth just sufficient to perform the required classification, or self-destruction if no solution can be found. Von Foerster's[18] model of elements which attempt to minimize their own responses smacks of this type of behavior, and deserves extension to more complex cases.

A closely related concept is suggested by Blum[36], who describes a spatially-propagating signaling system with inhibitory or quenching feedback from simultaneity detectors. He points out that the presence of quenching "leads to a coding for acceptance of stimulus meaning, the aim of the system being the quieting of the stimulus . . . such a process is a minimal abstractor of the stimulus since any acceptable representation removes the stimulus". Thus we may say that the act of recognition or classification "relieves tension", while indecision leaves a network open to further prodding either by the stimulus or by internal energy dissipation. Again, the need for coupling or feedback is significant.

BIBLIOGRAPHY

1. J. von Neumann, "The general and logical theory of automata", in *Cerebral Mechanisms in Behavior* (L. E. Jefress, Ed.), John Wiley & Sons, Inc., New York 1951, pp. 1–41.
2. T. J. Harley, L. Kanal, N. C. Randall, "System considerations for automatic imagery screening", in *Pictorial Pattern Recognition,* Thompson Book Co., Wash., D.C., 1968.
3. J. K. Hawkins, "Parallel electro-optical picture processing , Ibid.
4. D. L. Slotnick, W. C. Borck, R. C. McReynolds, "The Solomon computer", 1962 Fall Joint Computer Conf., *AFIPS Proc.,* Vol. 22, pp. 97–107.
5. J. F. Engelberger, "Role of industrial robots in improving production operations", Automation, June, 1964, pp. 62–67.
6. A. Vander Lugt, F. B. Rotz, A. Klooster, Jr., "Character reading by optical

spatial filtering", in *Optical and Electro-Optical Information Processing* (J. Tippett *et al*, Ed.), MIT Press, Cambridge, Mass., 1965, pp. 125–141.

7. J. K. Hawkins, C. J. Munsey, "Image Processing by Electron-Optical Techniques", *Journ. Optical Soc. Amer., Vol. 57,* No. 7, July, 1967, pp. 914–918.
8. J. K. Hawkins, PMW Navé, "Large Signal and Transient Characteristics of Electrochemical Amplifiers", *Proc. IEEE,* Vol. 53, No. 11, Nov., 1965, pp. 1707–1713.
9. J. K. Hawkins, C. J. Munsey, "Eulogismographic nonlinear optical image processing for pattern recognition", *Jour. Optical Soc. Amer.,* Vol. 54, No. 8, Aug., 1964, pp. 889–1003.
10. A. Katchalsky, "Living membranes", *Science & Technology*, Dec., 1967, pp. 52–60.
11. J. J. Ebers, J. L. Moll, "Large signal behavior of junction transistors", *Proc. IRE,* Vol. 42, Dec., 1954, pp. 1761–1772.
12. T. Teorell, "Transport processes and electrical phenomena in ionic membranes", in *Progress in Biophysics* (J. A. V. Butler and R. T. Randall, Eds.), Pergamon Press Ltd., London, 1953.
13. C. D'Agostino, L. Smith, Jr., "Bimolecular lipid membranes", in *Proc. Second Cybernetic Sciences Symposium*, (M. Maxfield *et al*, Eds.), Spartan Books, Wash., D. C., 1965.
14. G. N. Ling, *A Physical Theory of the Living State*, Blaisdell Publishing Co., New York, 1962.
15. H. H. Pattee, "On the origin of macromolecular sequences", *Biophysical Journal,* Vol. 1, 1961, pp. 683–710.
16. R. S. Mulliken, "Spectroscopy, molecular orbitals and chemical bonding", *Science,* Vol. 157, No. 3784, July, 1967, pp. 13–24.
17. J. von Neumann, *Theory of Self-Reproducing Automata* (A. W. Burks, Ed.), U. of Ill. Press, Urbana, 1966.
18. H. von Foerster, "Memory without record", Artorga, Communication 97–98, Jan.–Feb., 1967, pp. 388–433.
19. H. Neurath, K. A. Walsh, W. P. Winter, "Evolution of structure and function of proteases", *Science*, Vol. 158, Dec., 1967, pp. 1638–1644.
20. T. Tsuruta, S. Inoue, "Well-ordered polymers", *Science & Technology*, Nov., 1967, pp. 66–76.
21. S. Spiegelman, "An in vitro analysis of a replicating molecule", *Amer. Scientist,* Vol. 55, No. 3, Sept., 1967, pp. 221–264.
22. S. W. Fox, "Radiation and the first biopolymers", in *Radiation Research 1966,* North Holland Publishing Co., Amsterdam, 1967.
23. ——————, "A model of primitive heterotrophic proliferation", *Comp. Biochem. Physiol.,* Vol. 20, pp. 773–778, Pergamon Press (Great Britain), 1967.
24. R. W. Gerard, *Unresting Cells,* Harper & Brothers, New York, 1940.
25. J. D. Cowan, "The engineering approach to the problem of biological integration", in *Nerve, Brain and Memory Models* (N. Wiener, J. Schade, Eds.), Elsevier & Co., Amsterdam, 1963.
26. J. K. Hawkins, "Amplification", *IEEE Student Journal*, Vol. 5, No. 4, July, 1967, pp. 12–16.

27. J. D. Cowan, "The problem of organismic reliability", in *Progress in Brain Research,* (N. Wiener, J. Schade, Eds.), Elsevier Publishing Co., Amsterdam, 1965.
28. T. Teorell, "Electrokinetic membrane processes in relation to properties of excitable tissues," *Jour. General Physiology,* Vol. 42, 1959, pp. 831–863.
29. R. McNaughton, "The Theory of Automata, a Survey", in *Advances in Computers* (F. L. Alt, Ed.), Vol. 2, Academic Press, New York, 1961, pp. 379–421.
30. E. F. Moore, "Machine models of self-reproduction", in *Proc. Symp. on Applied Math., Amer. Math. Soc.,* Providence, Vol. 14, 1961, pp. 17–33.
31. W. R. Stahl, "Self-reproducing automata", in *Perspectives in Biology and Medicine*, Vol. 8, No. 3, U. of Chicago Press, 1965, pp. 373–393.
32. M. Eden, "A two-dimensional growth process", in *Fourth Berkeley Symposium on Mathematical Statistics and Probability*, U. of Calif. Press., Berkeley, 1961.
33. M. A. Arbib. "Simple self-reproducing universal automata", *Information Control,* Vol. 9, 1966, pp. 177–189.
34. M. Rubinoff, A. L. Eliasoff, J. Korsh, D. Shillady, "Mathematical studies for self-organizing systems", DOD report AD 627 795, Jan., 1966.
35. R. Moreno-Diaz, W. S. McCulloch, "On a calculus for triadas", Artorga, Communication 101, May, 1967.
36. H. Blum, "A new model of global brain function", in *Perspectives in Biology and Medicine*, Vol. 10, No. 3, U. of Chicago Press, 1967, pp. 381–408.

GOAL-DIRECTED PATTERN RECOGNITION

John H. Holland

DEPARTMENT OF COMMUNICATION SCIENCES
THE UNIVERSITY OF MICHIGAN

In theoretical investigations of pattern recognition it is common practice to represent the system-environment context minimally, usually by a partitioned set indicating the pattern categories. While this can be fruitful, as it has been for some kinds of character recognition, both thought and practice point up its limitations. It is particularly inadequate in goal-directed situations where the patterns to be recognized depend heavily on those features of the environment relevant to attainment of the system's goals. When the environment is unknown to the system in some essential aspects, such features must be discovered in the process of attempting to attain the goals. Different environments or different goals will determine different sets of critical features. That is, the critical features are defined implicitly by the system-environment context, rather than by being given explicitly. The object, then, of a goal-directed pattern recognition system is to discover, consistently recognize, and utilize critical features of any environmental situation within its competence. In terms more familiar to the pattern recognition field: the system, when confronted with any environment within its competence, must be able to classify each environment state according to the goal-directed response to be made to it. Thus the system must develop a set of detectors appropriate to the particular environment confronting it while simultaneously developing a procedure for deciding the appropriate response to each input configuration presented by the detectors.

This paper is concerned with the problems entailed in constructing such systems and with ways of resolving these problems. Section 1 examines relevant aspects of Samuel's well-known work, with the intent of exhibiting some features of goal-directed pattern recognition in a familiar context. Then in Section 2 several critical problems are delineated. A general organizational plan which takes these problems into account is proposed in Section 3. Finally, in Section 4, this plan is examined in the guise of a sampling procedure, with suggestions as to how its performance should be analyzed.

1. Samuel's Checker Player as a Pattern Recognizer

Samuel's checkerplayer[1] provides a familiar system employing goal-directed pattern recognition, though the pattern recognition aspect is usually not emphasized. The goal is clearcut: to win games. The input space in this case is the set B of possible checkerboard configurations. The candidates for critical features are functions θ_j from set B into the set of real numbers R. In Samuel's case, these functions are chosen initially. For the most part, they correspond to features an experienced checker player might look for, such as "pieces ahead", "penetration beyond the center-line", "control of the center", etc. For example, the function which measures "pieces ahead" assigns to each configuration $b \in B$ the difference in the number of pieces available to each side. It is significant for later discussion that these functions are actually defined by sequences of instructions for a digital computer and that the exact function defined does not seem to be overly critical. Once these functions have been chosen, they are combined in a weighted linear form, $V(b) = \Sigma_j a_{ij} \theta_j(b)$, in an attempt to assign a value (relatedness to the goal of winning) to each board configuration $b \in B$.[2] Via a sophisticated "lookahead" procedure involving a model of the environment (including the opponent) an anticipated future configuration is assigned to each possible response (move). The *anticipated* configuration assigned by the model to each (immediate) response, is then evaluated by V and the response associated with the highest-valued anticipated configuration is chosen. The use of a model as an integral part of the recognition process is a central concern of this paper.

The linear form $\Sigma_j a_{ij} \theta_j(b)$ used by Samuel is akin to the much-studied "adaptive threshold device": the functions θ_j correspond to the input functions of the threshold device, with the difference that their range is the reals rather than $\{0,1\}$; the threshold in effect varies from one set of move alternatives to another, being adjusted to select the highest-valued alternative in each set. It is important to note that the set of all possible arrays of values for the θ_j (i.e., the set $\Pi_j R_j$, where R_j is the range of θ_j)

---

[1] Samuel, A.L., "Some Studies of Machine Learning Using the Game of Checkers," *IBM J. Res. and Dev. 3,* 211–229 (1959).

[2] A later version ["Some Studies of Machine Learning Using the Game of Checkers. II-Recent Progress," *IBM J. Res. and Dev. 11,* 601–617 (1967)] uses a more sophisticated technique for calculating V(b): a hierarchy of signature tables. Each signature table amounts to a multivalued truth table and the hierarchy results from using the values from one set of tables as arguments for another (higher-level) table. This section will concentrate on the earlier linear technique because of its closer relation to familiar techniques and because the value-estimator/model organization is more easily introduced on this basis. In Section 3, the method of signature tables provides a concrete (though restricted) matrix for the suggestions there.

constitutes the set of states of the checkerplayer's model of its environment. It has no way of distinguishing two boards b and b′ if $[\theta_1(b), \ldots, \theta_m(b)] = [\theta_1(b'), \ldots, \theta_m(b')]$. Thus the adequacy of its model will depend in part upon whether or not distinctions which are critical to goal-attainment can in fact be made in the model.

The way in which Samuel adjusts and uses this linear form is not at all typical. The usual way is to provide an initial "training period" for adjusting the weights on the basis of information supplied by a referee capable of correctly classifying each test pattern presented. For the checkerplayer, on the other hand, a long sequence of patterns must be acted upon during the play of a game before a criterion (a "win" or a "loss") becomes available. The configurations underlying these patterns provide a great deal of relevant information, information which should be used in adjusting the weights. If it is not so used the checkerplayer encounters great difficulty in deciding which configurations were correctly, or incorrectly, handled in the course of play. It is here that the use of the linear form as a predictor opens up possibilities in just the right directions. A prediction about features of a configuration anticipated x moves hence can be checked as soon as x moves have elapsed. If the prediction is borne out, fine; if not, some adjustment of the linear form is called for. If, as suggested earlier, the prediction concerns the value of the expected configuration, then a heuristic for handling the adjustment of the linear form quickly presents itself. When the predicted value is off by an amount δ, the weight a_{ij} of function θ_j is modified to $a_{ij}-\Delta$, where $\Delta = c\delta a_{ij}\theta_j(b)$, b is the configuration at the time the prediction was made, and c is a constant of proportionality. (The algorithm actually used is more involved, particularly when the checkerplayer has an inexpert opponent, but the principle holds.) The result is a constant pressure for relevance and consistency in the prediction—relevance in the sense that the features recognized genuinely presage an opportunity (or difficulty), and consistency in the sense that the features are associated with the response appropriate to realizing (or avoiding) the prediction.[3] Irrelevant θ_j eventually acquire very low weights and hence are effectively eliminated from the linear form. Relevant θ_j acquire weights which, in conjunction with other θ_i, contribute to the choice of a goal-directed response. (Determination of an appropriate set of weights may be

[3] In other words: a set of detectors has sufficient relevance if all the distinctions critical to goal-attainment can be made within the set of model states $\Pi_j R_j$ determined by the detectors. A transition function τ: $0 \times \Pi_j R_j \rightarrow \Pi_j R_j$, where 0 is the set of responses, yields a model based on the states $\Pi_j R_j$; a model is consistent (with observation) if the observed state $[\theta_1(b'), \ldots, \theta_m(b')]$ after each response o is in fact the state $\tau[o, \theta_1(b), \ldots, \theta_m(b)]$ predicted by the transition function (where the environment goes from state b to state b′ when response o is made). It is of course only necessary that the model be consistent for situations actually encountered.

quite complicated since a given weighted θ_j may, without harm, take a moderate value in the "wrong direction" if at the same time other θ_i override it with large values in the "right direction"; this arrangement will be favored if there are other situations in which the same weighted θ_j proves to be the critical guide to an appropriate response.) At the end of each play of the game, the consistency of the value estimator will be checked against the outcome, thus tying the consistency requirement to the goal. The use of the linear form as a predictor enables the checkerplayer to assimilate the large amount of information it is receiving, continually sharpening its ability to recognize and use critical features.

2. Problems of Goal-Directed Pattern Recognition

In Samuel's checkerplayer we see a particular case of an interesting organization for goal-directed pattern recognition: the combination of modifiable feature detectors with a "lookahead" model based on these detectors. Just how general and efficacious is this organization? Any attempt to answer this question leads almost inevitably to two subsidiary questions which can be broadly phrased as follows: Can a system be supplied with procedures for generating extensive classes of feature detectors relevant to the environment confronting it? Are there reasonably general plans for constructing, modifying and using models on the basis of information supplied by the detectors?

Let us look more closely at the first of these questions. Samuel has already encountered a particular form of the problem presented by this question, designating it "the parameter problem." It arises when the set of detectors available to the system proves inadequate, in some circumstances, for prediction (i.e., the set has insufficient relevance). Since Samuel's detectors are defined by subroutines in a computer, new detectors can of course be generated by making random changes in the subroutines. However, by itself, this procedure is as little likely to prove effective as would an attempt to solve non-trivial problems by trying randomly modified programs one after another (cf. Friedberg).[4] Somehow, the detectors generated must be related to the needs of the system. Since the environment confronting the system will generally be unknown to it in several critical aspects, the system's needs and the detectors required must be discovered in the process of goal attainment. If the unknown aspects of the environment are at all complex, the detectors initially supplied can at best give the system a basis for discovering its further requirements. One fact uncovered by Samuel (and already alluded to) offers some hope. Fairly extensive alterations of the subroutines defining the basis functions θ_j did not much affect the performance of the checkerplayer. This indicates, at least in the case of the checkerplayer, that an exact hit is not necessary in order to find a new,

[4]Friedberg, R.M.,"A Learning Machine:Part 1," *IBM J. Res. and Dev. 2,* 2–13 (1958).

relevant function. Each candidate function apparently belongs to a large class, each element of which is a usable alternative. What features of the checker-playing situation make this so; i.e., what are the general conditions underlying this phenomenon? How can they be exploited?

To properly treat these questions we must return to the second of the subsidiary questions posed earlier. In any realistic situation the flow of information (in the formal sense) is overwhelming. It is so overwhelming that it is not reasonable to think of producing a model which will predict the flow in all its detail. Still, for typical goal-oriented systems, most of the details of the flow are only marginally relevant. Herein lies the justification of critical feature detectors and at the same time the possibility of models relevant to goal attainment. The major purpose of the model, already exemplified in Samuel's case, is prediction of the relative value of the response open to the system at any point in time. If the detectors are adequate (i.e., not only relevant but sufficient) to the particular goal-environment combination, reliable predictions can be based on the much-reduced flow of information from the detectors. Given the adequacy of the detectors, the major problem is that of assuring consistency of predictions by continually checking the model against the information supplied by the detectors. The modifications required to improve consistency are straight-forward in Samuel's case because of the linear form. Since the contributions of the individual weighted functions (detectors) are linearly superposed, credit ("debit") for errors can be apportioned accordingly. (This is strictly analogous to the technique for sharpening the separation of pattern categories with an "adaptive threshold device.") However, even in those cases where the detectors adequately signal all critical information, it is questionable that they will behave in such a quasi-orthogonal fashion. How is apportionment of credit to be made when the detectors enter into the predictor in more complicated fashion? This question is difficult enough but there is another as difficult. How is the system to determine whether or not the detectors it has are adequate?

The questions posed, to this point, are quite interdependent. The adequacy of a set of detectors for prediction cannot be determined in the absence of some assumptions about the predictor using them. The procedures for improving the predictor will depend upon the ease of generating and modifying detectors. The generation of relevant detectors will be contingent upon the way in which inadequacies in the extant set are discovered. And all depends upon the goals of the system and upon the environments the system may encounter.

3. A Value-Estimator/Model Procedure

One thread through this labyrinth appears when the model-predictor relation is examined more closely.

In the usual case the system will be initially primed with a set of detectors and a provisional model of the environment based on the detectors. In effect these detectors constitute an initial representation of the environment, embodying relevant prior information. Each possible configuration of values for the set of detectors constitutes a state of the environment from the system's viewpoint. The initial model incorporates conjectures about changes of state which can be effected by system responses. In other words, the initial model specifies a transition function (conjectured and partial) for the environmental representation. By iterating this transition function it is possible to make predictions about future detector state-configurations. (If the representation is adequate and the model is both complete with respect to the responses and deterministic, then the state-configuration attained by a given sequence of responses can be determined by tracing the state transition diagram corresponding to the model, as for a finite automaton.) Given this basis, a major technique for response selection uses an estimation procedure to assign each detector state-configuration a measure of its relatedness to goals. This measure is intended to reflect the best that can be attained from each configuration under the most propitious selection of subsequent responses. In order to select a current response the model is used to look as far ahead as practicable, taking into account time available and reliability of the model. Typically this lookahead will be co-ordinated with the value estimator so that only responses or sequences of responses leading to highly-valued configurations are further explored. At the conclusion of the lookahead, that response is chosen which initiates the sequence leading to the highest-valued anticipated outcome.

The foregoing organization suggests an overall plan for tackling the problems outlined earlier. The two objectives remain: relevance of the detectors and consistency of the model and value-estimator.

The analogy which likens the model to a finite automaton suggests a procedure for detecting inadequacies in the set of detectors. In the case of a finite automaton the outcome of any input-state internal-state combination is always the same. In the case of the goal-directed system each detector state-configuration is supposed to designate a state of the environment. Thus, if the system is to have a strictly deterministic model of the environment, a given response should not, on successive occasions, produce different outcomes (detector state-configurations) from a given configuration. Any time such an aberration does occur an inadequacy of the set of detectors is indicated. Of course in many circumstances a strictly deterministic model will not be required; it will suffice if the outcomes of the response-state pair fall within some set of admissible variants. (E.g., if the environment is stochastic it may suffice that the variance of the outcomes not increase beyond some bound.) However, this just weakens the condition for aberration—the principle still holds.

Consider now the detectors as employed in a linear form. Assume that each time an aberration does occur the accompanying complete (unfiltered) input state is added to a collection of such instances. Any procedure which assigns a high value to instances in the collection, while assigning a low value to most other input states, would be a good candidate for a new detector. We see here some indication of why the exact definition of the detector is not critical, in part answering the earlier question based on Samuel's observations. If the set of situations to which the new detector assigns a high value contains a "low density" of non-aberrant situations, then there is a good opportunity for the other detectors to override the new detector on the non-aberrant situations (when it signals falsely). This suggests a plan for automatically generating relevant new detectors as the need arises, a plan closely related to recent observations in genetics concerning *intra*-chromosomal duplication.[5] As implemented here this would amount to adding to the set of detectors extensively modified versions of detectors which have high values at the time an aberration occurs. If the modification procedure is not too narrowly conceived, some of these new detectors will still take high values on the aberrant situations, while taking low values on other situations which the "parent" detector confused with the aberrant situations. They will enable the goal-directed system to enlarge the state-set of its model in a relevant fashion. Other new detectors, so generated, which are irrelevant will acquire near-zero weights, effectively eliminating them as earlier.

When the system uses a linear form, aberrations involving detectors taking on relatively low values can be ignored since these detectors will have little effect on the value estimator. In effect, the detectors taking on low values are "inactive." However, the problem with the linear form is that an "active" (high-valued) detector is constrained to affect the value estimate strongly, and with the same sign, in all situations in which it is "active." A more general procedure would have the value estimator take different values for each distinct *configuration* of "active" and "inactive" detectors. But then the problem is one of determining which aberrations are important. The "active"--"inactive" dichotomy gives a hint as to how to proceed. Let the detectors be restricted to the range $\{0,1\}$, "inactive" or "active," and let the value estimation procedure be formulated as an independent subroutine which has the set of all possible detector value configurations as its domain. An aberration can then be handled as in the linear case, the *active* detectors at the time serving as the "parents" from which the new candidates are generated. Just as before, modifications of the detectors responsible for the aberrations have the best chance of distinguishing critical situations previously confused, thereby increasing the relevance of the set of detectors. At the same time, even for quite complex estimation functions,

[5] *Carnegie Institution of Washington Year Book 64*, 331–333 (1965).

it will generally be easy to modify the function so that it assigns a lower (higher) value to a particular detector configuration.[6] Therefore (with a caveat yet to be discussed) the Δ–procedure earlier used with the linear form to improve its consistency can also be used with a more complex value estimator. Thus, there are procedures for increasing both relevance and consistency even in badly nonlinear situations.

4. The Procedure as a Sampling Plan

As with other types of pattern recognition, the procedure just described can be looked upon as a sampling procedure. On this view, the purpose of the detectors is to project the environment on a set of dimensions relevant to goal attainment. It is the resulting (reduced) sample space which makes feasible the construction of a goal-oriented model. One of the two main objectives of the system, then, is to produce a relevant model on the basis of samples drawn from the space. This it does by assigning to observed elements of the sample space the successor element produced by a chosen response. (Responses are chosen on the hypothesis that they lead toward goals.) Here an element new to most pattern recognition studies enters. The initially chosen dimensions may permit a model with aberrations–a model with inadmissible multiple consequences of a given response at a given sample point. Under such conditions the dimensioning must be changed. This requires sampling in a new and distinct sample space, the space of all admissible detectors (say, all subroutines of a certain class). The object of this second sampling plan is to use information obtained on the extant dimensions to discover "neighborhoods" which contain detectors likely to improve the dimensioning. (Our previous discussion indicates the likelihood of such "neighborhoods" vis-a-vis a model-predictor organization of the system.) These "neighborhoods" can then be exploited by an increased density of sampling therein. (The plan analogous to intrachromosomal duplication does just this–responding to a dimensioning "crisis" by acting upon just those dimensions relevant to the crisis.) In so-doing the second plan seeks to resolve the counterpart of Samuel's parameter problem by locating new, relevant detectors.

Simultaneously with these two sampling procedures a third is carried out, aimed at building up a consistent value estimator. This constitutes the second major objective of the system. At each stage a candidate estimator is tested against the model for the consistency of its predictions. When a prediction is not verified the object is to select a new estimator which preserves the good features of the failed estimator while correcting for its inadequacy. This objective will be facilitated if credit for the error can be apportioned to the parts of the estimator, but this requires a suitable

---

6 See Samuel's discussion of the signature table procedure (ref. in footnote 2).

decomposition theory for the estimators. With a linear estimator there is a direct decomposition in terms of weighted detector functions. No such obvious decomposition exists for more sophisticated estimators, but there is a useful approach stemming from mathematical genetics. It is based on the assignment of "average excesses" as a measure of the average contribution of a given detector to the overall value estimate.[7] One can thus use the average excesses to apportion credit for errors and proceed as in the linear case. (There is the additional advantage of an interesting mathematical theory related to the rate of convergence of this technique.)[8]

Given enough time the system will acquire a relevant set of detectors and a consistent estimator. At that point a response can be rated immediately, without any further lookahead, by looking at the estimated value of the detector configuration it will lead to (according to the model). The effect is that of responding directly to the critical features detected.

The fundamental idea underlying all phases of the sampling plan's operation can be expressed as a testing of schema. In this context a schema results when a part of some structure (a detector, an estimator) is deleted and the resulting vacancy is treated as a slot in which any other structure satisfying the interface conditions can be substituted. If the structure is a program, then any subroutine with the proper entries and exits would be a candidate for filling the vacancy. The favored schema preserve critical pieces of goal-relevant information accumulated in past tests; the substitution instances are sampled on the basis of a probability distribution skewed according to past results. Apportionment of credit provides one way of determining what schema should be favored and what probabilities should be assigned to different instances. The distributions so determined play a role much like that of a simplicity ordering in inductive inference. It is important to note that each test of a particular structure, if properly exploited, constitutes a (simultaneous) test of all the schema which can be formed from that structure. This inherent parallelism provides a greatly increased sampling rate in the space of schema, with all the advantages attendant thereon.

— * —

The fundamental problem of goal-directed pattern recognition is to discover plans for generating and testing schema, plans which are demonstrably good over a broad spectrum of environments. In this paper we have looked at a general organization for accomplishing this end and some

---

[7] Kimura, M., "On the Change of Population Fitness by Natural Selection." *Heredity 12,* 145–167 (1958).

[8] *Idem.*

operators for implementing the organization.[9] On one hand the organization generalizes a successful, empirically-tested approach; on the other, it makes contact with some important aspects of genetics and mathematical genetics. We have looked at only one genetic-related operator but there are many candidates. Crossover, inversion, operon-operator concatenations, and others, all have meaning here, and some versions offer demonstrable improvements over techniques currently used to attain the same ends (see Bagley[10] and Rosenberg[11]). To date, these operators and the attendant theory have been little studied or exploited in a goal-directed sampling format. In my opinion a greater effort would be amply repaid, both by an increased sophistication in sampling plans for goal-directed pattern recognition and by an enlarged understanding of the action of genetic operators.

Acknowledgements

I would like to thank Professor Donald F. Stanat for a careful reading of the first draft of this paper and for many helpful suggestions. I would also like to thank the Office of Naval Research for its continued financial support (currently under Contract No. N00014-67-A-0181-0011) in areas relevant to the present paper.

---

[9] A more mathematical discussion of this organization can be found in Holland, J.H., "Nonlinear Environments Permitting Efficient Adaptation" in *Computer and Information Sciences–II* (ed. J. T. Tou) Academic Press (1967).

[10] Bagley, J. D., *The Behavior of Adaptive Systems Which Employ Genetic and Correlation Algorithms*. U. of Michigan Ph.D. Dissertation (1967).

[11] Rosenberg, R. S., *Simulation of Genetic Populations with Biochemical Properties.* U. of Michigan Ph.D. Dissertation (1967).

CLUSTER FORMATION AT VARIOUS PERCEPTUAL LEVELS*

Bela Julesz

BELL TELEPHONE LABORATORIES, INCORPORATED
MURRAY HILL, NEW JERSEY

1. Cluster Formation in Monocular Vision

In essence perception is equivalent to the unequal weighting of certain patterns in favor of others. One simple unequal weighting, also called feature extraction occurs in the visual system of the frog (1). Only moving targets of certain size and curvatures are detected, while still objects in general pass unnoticed. (There are exceptions, e.g., the blue color receptors which are probably signaling a pond (2)). These "bug" and "snake" detectors seem to explain adequately the behavioral repertoire of frog, and it seems unlikely that more than one moving object of specified geometry would enter its visual field at a time. Our peripheral vision is reminiscent of this antique organization. Without being able to resolve and recognize a small object a few degrees outside the center axis of the eye we are still aware of its presence provided it is moving or flickering. Many researchers in vision claim that even central vision behaves similarly when the saccadic movements of the eyes are compensated for. Indeed low contrast targets of low spatial complexity fade out after retinal stabilization (2,4) similarly entoptic images (e.g., retinal blood vessels) are never seen except during special manipulations. (I am quoting these examples for central (foveal) vision with some caution since the fragmentation phenomenon (5) in which certain perceptual units fade out differently from the rest and our own results with complex and high-contrast targets which resist fade out after retinal stabilization (6) indicate some complex processes at work.)

The next level of feature extraction occurs in the figure-ground phenomenon which according to Hebb (7) is the basic perceptual process. Here both figure and ground can be stationary, yet certain patterns tend to be seen as the "thing" while the rest is perceived as the "substance". In more modern

* International Conference on Methodologies of Pattern Recognition, Honolulu, Hawaii, January 24–26, 1968.

terminology we might call this perceptual process the "signal-noise" separation. It should be noted that here figure (signal) is a misleading term. The pattern need not be a familiar one, but can be of an abstract or amorphic design. Figure refers to the fact that we *attend* to this perceptual organization while other organizations pass unnoticed. The Gestalt school of psychology studied extensively those factors which influenced the emergence of a figure. These studies were usually carried out on line-drawings of relatively simple design and the terminology used (such as good-gestalt, closure, good-continuation) was more qualitative than quantitative. (For an up-to-date brief review see Ref. 8). Figure 1 shows, for instance, how outlined drawings of the smaller area tend to become the figure.

The advent of digital computers and high quality displaying devices permitted the use of controlled complex textures in visual perception (9). Instead of the classical figure-ground dichotomy another fundamental one could be studied, that is the discrimination between two textures (9). Two textures of different statistics are presented side-by-side and subjects are asked to discriminate between them. The discrimination must not be based on scrutiny (like in Figure 2) but rather on a spontaneous and effortless performance (like in Figure 3). My original efforts have been oriented towards textures which had the same k-order statistics (and of course all lower than k-order) but differed in their (k+1)-order probability distribution (9). Such stochastic processes can be always constructed if the event space has three or more members (e.g., black, gray and white brightness levels) (10). I wanted to know the maximum k-order for which texture discrimination is still possible and a perceptual quality remains attached to it. For instance, in Figure 3 the first-order statistics (tonal quality) is identical but the textures differ in their second-order probability distribution. Discrimination is effortless, and the perceived difference is in granularity (9). Figure 4 shows two textures of four brightness levels (having uniform first-and second-order statistics) that differ in their third-order statistics. (Of the 64 possible trigrams the left half field contains 32, the right half field the *complementary* 32.) Discrimination is impossible (9). The next experiment of Figure 5 unfortunately shows that n-order statistics are poor descriptors of perceptual performance (9). Here the quadrant in the lower right corner is random, while the rest is made up of the six equally probable staircase-like patterns shown in Figure 5B. In spite of the fact that each of these micropatterns has the same occurrence only the white triangles are perceived, while the rest pass unnoticed (9). Thus, only *clusters* of *proximate* points of *similar* brightness values lead to discrimination (9). Here proximate means closeness in an Euclidean distance sense while similar means adjacent brightness levels. Furthermore it was shown that the visual system works like a slicer; that is, white and light gray dots form a bright cluster and dark gray and black dots form a dark cluster. Similarly red and yellow proximate dots (of equal brightness) form an orange cluster and blue and green dots form a blue-green cluster, but it is impossible to organize nonadjacent brightness or hue values into clusters (10). Thus red and green will not form a cluster neither will blue and yellow. This finding indicates again that conscious effort cannot override some of the early processings by the visual system.

The moral of these first studies is as follows. There is a cluster-detector operating in the visual system probably at the earliest levels and only those statistical descriptors that describe cluster formations can have some perceptual significance. Thus, the usual joint probability distributions are inadequate descriptors in perception. There are at least two ways to handle this difficulty. One solution is to define some single cluster-formation rule and give probability distributions of the clusters and of some cluster parameters (orientation, compactness, etc.). The trouble with this solution is the arbitrariness of the cluster parameters selected. The second solution is the use of constructs of random geometry. Novikoff (11) suggested such a solution first. Frisch and I tried to use the generalized Buffon-needle problem in perceptual studies (12). If we throw over a two-tone image n-gons according a well specified random-throwing and collect the statistics of all the vertices falling on a black (or white) domain, we obtain a most useful n-order descriptor (12). For n=1 (points being thrown) the area fraction of white-black domains is obtained. The n=2 (line throwing) case determines the perimeter-area fraction. The n=3 case (triangles being thrown) extracts the notion of convexity and so on. The advantage of this technique is that the n-gon statistics (and the lower order terms in their Taylor-series expansion) often have excellent geometrical and perceptual interpretations.

We used this technique for studying figure-ground reversal (12). Random-dot stimuli were generated with various area fractions between black and white dots using various tesselations. Thus, the black and white dots were randomly selected with various area fractions (densities) on a Cartesian grid, a triangular grid, etc. Subjects were asked to judge the stimulus as being a black table top with white specks on it or vice versa. Since the n-gon statistics always differ for the various tesselations used, except for the first-order throwing, we wanted to know whether figure-ground perception depends on the tesselations used. According to our findings only the area fraction between black and white dots affects figure-ground perception and is independent of the tesselations used. Thus, for figure-ground perception of unfamiliar images the visual system incorporates only first-order statistics. This result is quite important in the light of recent neurophysiological findings. The concentric Kuffler units in the retinae of cat and monkey (13,14) could be regarded as the dot-throwing, while the edge and slit detectors in the visual cortex in cat and monkey (15) are probably not used for figure-ground perception when random-dot stimuli are used. (Of course a human face or other familiar pattern will resist attempts to be seen as the ground. Nevertheless, it is easy to imagine a wall-paper of a periodically repeated familiar shape with some amorphic discontinuity, for instance, a crack in it. In this case the shape merges into ground and the crack will probably stand out as the figure.) These experiments show, that with proper stimulus control and restricted perceptual task the visual system can be greatly simplified and studied.

The finding that only the area fraction of clusters affects figure-ground perception is of course restricted to this phenomenon. For texture discrimination more complex cluster parameters such as perimeter area fraction and orientation enter. In the multidimensional scaling of visual texture discrimination composed of random 2 x 2 arrays the most important factor was brightness and the next factor was orientation (16). Some recent studies (17) of the multidimensional scaling of random polygonal figures of Attnaeve and Arnoult (18) using some geometrical criterion of similarity reveal a dozen complex cluster parameters of compactness, jaggedness, skewness, rotation, etc., each being highly correlated with low order moments of interior angles, side lengths, perimeter and area measures. Which of these parameters is actually used by humans is hard to determine primarily because of shifts in human attention. These shifts in the parameters used and their large number greatly hamper the development of a psychophysics of form. Nevertheless, recent work indicates that human discrimination of random polygons can be represented in a 2-dimensional space of complexity and symmetry (38).

2. Clusters in Repetition and Symmetry Perception

The importance of cluster prèprocessing is more apparent the higher we go in the visual system. Recently I studied this question with regard to periodicity (repetition) and symmetry perception (19,20). A century ago Ernst Mach (21) studied the perception of simple amorphic clusters having repetitive and various symmetrical structures. He concluded that periodicity, bilateral symmetry across a vertical axis and centric symmetry can be perceived effortlessly; bilateral symmetry across a horizontal axis requires effort. These observations are valid for random textures too, provided some large clusters are present. For instance Figure 6 shows a periodic random texture which can be effortlessly perceived. Figure 7 shows a similar design except that in place of black and white picture elements, two diagonal line segments of ±45 and −45 degree orientations were used. Because of this, no macroclusters of black and white areas can form and the periodicity cannot be perceived without effort and scrutiny. Even with black and white picture elements if the complexity is high, (that is the periodicity is large compared to the picture element size) periodicities cannot be perceived. Figures 8 and 9 contain four identical quadrants which in Figure 8 are identically repeated while in Figure 9 are mirrored across the horizontal and vertical axis. While the two-fold summetry is well perceived, the periodic organization is not, The centric symmetry is also not apparent in complex textures as shown in Ref. 19. Bilateral symmetry across a vertical axis is more apparent than across a horizontal one as the viewing the left image of Figure 14 and then rotating it by 90 degrees illustrates. Yet symmetry perception also depends on cluster size. When the clusters are broken up symmetry perception is greatly reduced. Figures 10 and 11 show two images with two-fold symmetry, but a four picture element wide column around the symmetry axes are selected at random. In Figure 10 in which clusters are retained the symmetry is still apparent, yet in Figure 11 in which no macroclusters are retained only scrutinizing the stimulus reveals some traces of symmetry.

In summary, for the perception of repetitions and symmetries the periodicities and the distances from the symmetry axes have to be commensurable with the average cluster sizes. If the average cluster dimensions are much smaller than the dimensions of the global organization, then no repetition or symmetry can be perceived. Thus, for both texture discrimination and the perception of a global organization clusters play a decisive role. Whatever organization exists on a local level can be only perceived if this organization is retained at the cluster level too. In the next sections a method will be discussed in which the local and global organizations are separated monocularly and binocularly.

3. Cluster Formation in Binocular Depth Perception

Since the demonstration in 1959 that binocular shapes can be obtained from monocularly shapeless and contourless images many problems of stereoscopic depth perception (stereopsis) have been clarified (22,23). Figure 12 shows the schematic way such stereograms are produced and Figure 13 shows an actual computer-generated random-dot stereogram. Here the local organization is completely random, but binocularly certain areas are identical with various amounts of horizontal shifts (binocular disparity) in the left and right images. When monocularly viewed these images are seen as uniformly random, but when stereoscopically fused the shifted central square is seen in vivid depth in front of the surround. Of course, any surface can be portrayed by this technique (24).

These displays clarified many problems of stereopsis (25,26) which are too specific to be dwelt on at this occasion. But the demonstration that no monocular pattern recognition is necessary has more than psychological importance. Prior to this demonstration, it was commonly assumed that in order to establish binocular disparity the corresponding patterns in the two eyes view had to be recognized. That a much simpler pattern matching operation could give satisfactory results is not at all obvious. Some early devices for automatic contour-map plotting used zone-matching techniques with poor results. If the zone was small, the slightest noise destroyed matching, on the other hand, if the zone was large, the accuracy was limited to the zone size. Of course, if the zone had had the shape of the object to be matched, an ideal matching could have been achieved, but this necessitated the solution of the enigmatic problem of pattern recognition.

Results with random-dot stereograms helped to formulate and computer simulate a model of stereopsis (called AUTOMAP–1) which solved some of the difficulties (27). The differences between the left and right fields of the stereogram were computed point-by-point. Prior to subtraction the two fields were shifted horizontally by increasing amounts and staggered above each other in depth. In these difference fields proximate points of zero (or local minima) form *clusters* and these correspond to the cross sections of an object (having constant binocular disparity). Thus searching for clusters of minima inthe various difference fields is equivalent of localizing each point of the object in depth. Without recognition the visible surfaces of the object are determined. The only step necessary was a slight generalization of the notion of a cluster. Instead of connecting proximate points of similar brightness values into clumps, proximate points of minimum values (in a difference field) are connected together.

It is interesting to note that the random-dot stereograms of two brightness levels have a 50 percent probability that a black or white dot in the left image will coincide with the same brightness points in the right field by chance alone. Thus the difference field of zero-shift contains 50 percent zero valued picture elements. The fact that we do not perceive such a lacelike (transparent) center square at the same depth level as the surround (zero disparity) but instead a *solid* square at *larger disparity* values is very revealing. It demonstrates, that stereopsis selects the *densest* clusters even if this organization occurs at larger disparity values.

This example shows that a slight generalization of the powerful cluster notion yields some insights into binocular depth perception. Similar models can be developed for stroboscopic movement perception, in which the point-by-point difference between two images in temporal succession is determined. I would like to demonstrate a movie in which each frame is random, but areas of dynamic and static noise (both still or moving) give a strong perceptual effect. The difference field model with various amounts of shifts is a good model if we extend the horizontal shifts to vector shifts of any direction and extent.

Of course simple subtraction for binocular combination is an oversimplification. The real phenomena of stereopsis and movement perception are much more complex. Expansions of one image by 15 percent yield stereopsis, similarly ±6 degree rotation (22,28). Recently with Fender (29) we found great plasticity in stereopsis under binocular retinal stabilization. If the random-dot stereograms are stabilized with respect to the retinae (by using close fitting contact lenses with attached stalks and mirrors) the images have to be brought within 6 minutes of arc registration (called Panum's fusional area) to obtain fusion. Yet *after* fusion occurs the images can be slowly pulled apart by as much as 120 minutes of arc before they break away. After breaking, the images have to be brought into 6 minutes of arc registration to obtain fusion again. This area of hysteresis is much larger for random-dot stereograms than for classical line targets. This is well expected since hysteretic phenomena belong to the larger class of cooperative phenomena in which many constituents are simultaneously coupled. The more elements stimulated, the greater the lag between cause and effect. Indeed the simple line targets stimulate only a few edge or slit detectors while the complex random-dot stereograms stimulate a very large number of neural units. This hysteresis constitutes an elementary memory process and it is interesting, that as early in the processing chain as for stereopsis such processes are at work.

4. Juxtaposition of Local Global Organization

An extension of the random-dot stereogram techniques permits the reversal of the original paradigm. Originally it was shown that monocularly shapeless images can produce binocular shapes. In these recent experiments a monocular global organization (such as symmetry or readable text) can be made to disappear in the binocular view (19). Figure 14 shows such a stereogram, in which binocularly each local element is correlated (and produce horizontal stripes at two depth levels) yet the monocular organization in the form of bilateral symmetry is suppressed in the binocular percept. The more clusters the monocular images contain, the less successful this binocular suppression is. If the monocular clusters are further broken up even octal symmetries can be suppressed (19).

The interpretation of these findings might be as follows: First, a monocular process searches for clusters. Second, if such clusters do not exist, a binocular pattern matching process organizes point-by-point the images into a cyclopean view. Third, the higher order processes of symmetry perception or form recognition operate on the cluster processed field or on the cyclopean view.

5. Clusters in Higher Mental Processes

We have seen the importance of clusters in visual perception. It is customary in Nature that after a powerful solution has been developed, the same solution is then applied for more elaborate situations after a step of generalization has been found. Indeed, we are witnessing recently the birth of psychophysics of higher mental activities in which clusters play an important role. With the advent of fast digital computation nonmetric multidimensional scaling (factor analysis) (29,30) revealed some hidden internal structures in problems varying from Morse code perception to interpreting facial expressions, from phonemic confusions to problems of clinical and social psychology. Much work along these lines has gone under the name "numerical taxonomy" (31). The "objects" under study might be visual or auditory patterns presented to subjects. Psychological measurements are obtained on the similarities (or confusions) among these objects. The problem is then one of discovering whether there is any inherent structure (number of most important dimensions, metric and grouping) in the data themselves. The two main algorithms for achieving this goal are multidimensional scaling and clustering schemes. The first tries to find an abstract space of minimal dimensions in which the distances between objects preserve the psychologically determined similarities (29,30). The clustering schemes try to arrange the objects into optimally homogeneous groups (32). The problem with all these methods is the vast number of measurements necessary to determine the similarity between the objects. For n=100 objects $n(n-1)/2 \approx 5000$ object pairs have to be measured or rank ordered with respect to their psychological similarity (confusability). Such numbers defy the most motivated researchers. Interestingly, there seems to be one way out of this dilemma. Humans are exceedingly fast and accurate in sorting objects into clumps. For instance, the experimenter might suggest the number of clusters the objects should be sorted into and the subjects usually are able very quickly to perform the task. If the majority of subjects arrive at the same clustering primarily the data presentation is already solved. If the subjects' sortings differ, similarity measures can be defined on the basis of the sortings. Each pair of objects is assigned weight one if the pair is assigned to the same cluster by a given subject and weight zero otherwise, and then these weights for each object pair are averaged over subjects. This procedure assigns a similarity value between zero and one to each pair and the multidimensional scaling can be carried out.

While this similarity measure (the relative frequency of co-occurrence of items) has a strong intuitive appeal, and may be very useful in many cases, a refinement of this measure has been found, in at least one context (33), to provide a significant improvement. This refinement involves computing a measure of profile similarity (34) based on this co-occurrence measure. If we think of rows of the co-occurrence matrix as vectors in n-dimensional space, this measure of profile similarity is simply the squared Euclidean distance between these vectors. The rationale for this similarity measure is that, while similar items may not co-occur frequently they should have similar patterns of co-occurrence with other items. In practice, similarity matrices have been determined between several hundred objects, based solely on our ability to sort complex patterns into clusters.

Whether the data has been collected by asking subjects to clamp them or rank order the similarities of item pairs, the ultimate analysis can be either multidimensional scaling, cluster schemes or both. As an example, Figure 15 shows the results of both multidimensional scaling and clustering as developed by Shepard (35). In addition to his multidimensional technique (29) he superimposed the clustering technique of Johnson (36) using the data collected by Miller and Nicely on the confusability of 16 English consonants (37). The items (consonants) are presented in a two-dimensional abstract space as the result of multidimensional scaling. The contour lines around the items give the hierarchical clustering of Johnson, where to each contour a numerical value (similarity) is attached. When this value is zero, all items are separate clusters, when it is one, all items form a single cluster. Each clustering contains as elements clusters of a smaller similarity value. This hierarchical clustering provides a revealing insight into human phonemic recognition. Of course, the proximity metrics and similarity measures are much more complex than in the previous examples in vision.* Yet the basic concept of a cluster, a homogeneous grouping, is retained.

6. Conclusion

The visual examples given in this article (primarily the work of co-workers and myself) try to convey the importance of cluster processing in visual perception. Proximate points of similar brightness values form clusters. With some simple extensions of similarity and proximity, cluster detection can clarify many complicated psychological phenomena from texture discrimination to binocular depth perception and stroboscopic movement perception. These cluster processings are so fundamental that they affect the workings of the higher perceptual processes. For instance, the breaking up of clusters reduces the perception of symmetries and repetitions. Finally it was noted, that at a higher level of mental activity humans are very efficient in clumping complex items into clusters. The further generalization of similarity and proximity measures extends the usefulness of cluster notions into cognitive processes.

* It should be mentioned that in the multidimensional scaling literature proximity and similarity are often oppositely used to the one in this paper. "Psychological proximity" corresponds to my use of similarity, and "metric distance" corresponds to my use of proximity.

REFERENCES

1. Lettvin, J. Y., Maturana, H. R., McCulloch, W. S. and Pitts, W. H. (1959), What the frog's eye tells the frog's brain, *Proc. IRE*, 47, pp. 1940–1951.
2. Muntz, W. R. A. (1962), Microelectrode recordings from the diencephalon of the frog (Rana pipiens) and a blue-sensitive system. *J. Neurophysiol.,25,* pp. 699–671.
3. Ditchburn, R. W. and Ginsborg, B. L. (1952), Vision with a stabilized retinal image, *Nature, 170,* pp. 36–37.
4. Riggs, L. A., Ratliff, F., Cornsweet, J. C. and Cornsweet, T. N. (1953), *J. Opt. Soc. Amer., 43,* pp. 495–501.
5. Pritchard, R. M. and Hebb, D. O. (1960), Visual Perception Approached by the Method of Stabilized Images, *Canad. J. Pscyh d., 14,* pp. 67–77.
6. Fender, D. and Julesz, B. (1967), Extension of Panum's Fusional Area in Binocularly Stabilized Vision; *J. Opt. Soc. Am.,* 57, pp. 819–830.
7. Hebb, D. O. (1949), The organization of behavior, (New York, Wiley).
8. Hochberg, J. E. (1964), Perception (Prentice Hall, N. J.).
9. Julesz, B. (1962), Visual Pattern Discrimination; IRE Transactions on Information Theory, *IT–8,* pp. 84–92; and Julesz, B. (1965), Texture and Visual Perception, *Scientific American, 212,* pp. 38–48.
10. Rosenblatt, M., and Slepian, D. (1962), N*th* order Markov chains with any set of N variables independent. J. Soc. Indust. Appl. Math. *10,* p. 537.
11. Novikoff, A. B. J. (1962), Integral geometry as a tool in pattern perception. In H. von Foerster and G. W. Fopf (eds.), *Principles of self organization,* New York: Pergamon Press, p. 11.
12. Frisch, H. and Julesz, B. (1966), Figure-Ground Perception and Random Geometry; *Perception and Psychophysics, 1,* pp. 389–398.
13. Kuffler, S. W. (1953), Discharge patterns and functional organization of mamalian retina, *J. Neurophysiol., 16,* pp. 37–68.
14. Hubel, D. H. and Wiesel, T. N. (1960), Receptive fields of optic nerve fibers in the spider monkey; *J. Physiol., 154,* pp. 572–580.
15. Hubel, D. H. and Wiesel, T. N. (1962), Receptive Fields, Binocular Interaction and Functional Architecture in the Cat's Visual Cortex, *J. Physiol., 160,* pp. 106–154.
16. Julesz, B. (1964), Some Recent Studies in Vision Relevant to Form Perception, (ed. Wathen-Dunn, W. Models for the Perception of Speech and Visual Form, the MIT Press, 1967), pp. 136–154.
17. Brown, D. R. and Owen, D. H. (1967), The Metrics of Visual Form: Methodological Dyspepsia, Psychol. Bulletin, *68,* pp. 243–259.
18. Attneave, F. and Arnoult, M. D. (1956), The quantitative study of shape and pattern perception, Psychol. Bulletin, *53,*pp. 452–471.
19. Julesz, B. (1967), Suppression of Monocular Symmetry during Binocular Fusion without Rivalry; *Bell System Technical Journal, 46,* pp. 1203–1221.
20. Julesz, B. (1967), Visual Perception and Repetition, Rotation, Mirror and Centric Symmetry in Random Textures; International Information Theory Symposium, San Remo, Italy.
21. Mach, E. (1897) (republished by Dover, N. Y., 1959), Analysis of Sensations.

22. Julesz, B. (1960), Binocular Depth Perception of Computer-Generated Patterns, *Bell System Technical Journal, 39,* pp. 1125–1162.
23. Julesz, B. (1960), Binocular Depth Perception and Pattern Recognition; *Information Theory,* Fourth London Symposium, edited by C. Cherry (Butterworth & Co.; London), pp. 212–224.
24. Julesz, B., Miller, J. E. (1962), Automatic Stereoscopic Presentation of Functions of Two Variables, *Bell System Technical Journal, 41,* pp. 663–676.
25. Julesz, B. (1964), Binocular Depth Perception without Familiarity Cues; *Science, 145,* pp. 356–362.
26. Julesz, B., Spivack, J. (1967), Stereopsis Based on Vernier Acuity Cues Alone; *Science, 157,* pp. 563–565.
27. Julesz, B. (1962), Towards the Automation of Binocular Depth Perception; IFIPS Proceedings (ed. Popplewell North-Holland Publ., Amsterdam).
28. Fender, D. and Julesz, B. (1967), Extension of Panum's Fusional Area in Binocularly Stabilized Vision; *J. Opt. Soc. Am., 57,* pp. 819–830.
29. Shepard, R. N. (1962), The analysis of proximities: multidimensional scaling with an unknown distance function, 1 and 11. *Psychometrics,* 27, p. 125 and p. 219.
30. Kruskal, J. B. (1964), Multidimensional Scaling by Optimizing Goodness of Fit to a Nonmetric Hypothesis, *Psychometrica, 29,* p. 1 and p. 115.
31. Sokal, R. R. and Sneath, P. H. A. (1963), *Principles of Numerical Taxonomy* (Freeman, W. M., San Francisco).
32. Ward, J. H., Jr. (1963), Hierarchical grouping to optimize an objective function; *J. Am. Statistical Assoc., 58,* pp. 236–244.
33. Rosenberg, S., Nelson, C. and Vivekananthan, P. S., A multidimensional approach to the structure of personality impressions, to be published.
34. Shepard, R. N. and Carroll, J. D. (1966), Parametric Representation of Nonlinear Data Structures, Multivariate Analysis (ed., Krishnaiah, P. R., Academic Press, N. Y.) pp. 561–592.
35. Shepard, R. N., Psychological Representation of Speech Sounds (Human Communication, a Unified View, eds. David, E. E., Jr. and Denes, P., McGraw-Hill, to be published).
36. Johnson, S. C. (1967), Hierarchical Clustering Schemes, *32,* pp. 241–254.
37. Miller, G. A. and Nicely, P. E. (1955), An analysis of perceptual confusions among some English consonants, *27,* pp. 338–352.
38. Thomas, H. (1967), Multidimensional Analysis of Similarities Judgments to Twenty Visual Forms, (1967 Fall Meeting, Psychonomic Soc., Chicago).

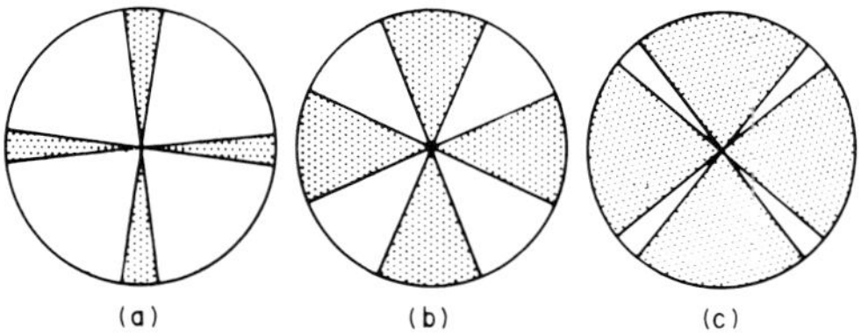

Figure 1: The role of area in figure-ground perception. The smaller area tends to be perceived as the figure; thus in (a) the figure is a wheel with black spokes, in (c) a wheel with white spokes and (b) is ambiguous. (Ref. 8)

METHODS	SCIENCE	COLUMNS	NIATREC	YLKCIUQ	DEHCNUP
SUBJECT	MERCURY	GOVERNS	ECNEICS	YFICEPS	ESICERP
COLUMNS	CERTAIN	QUICKLY	SDOHTEM	SDROCER	EZIDIXO
RECORDS	EXAMPLE	SCIENCE	STCIPED	HSILGNE	NIATREC
MERCURY	SPECIFY	PRECISE	TCEJBUS	DEHCNUP	SNREVOG
METHODS	COLUMNS	MERCURY	ELPMAXE	YLKCIUQ	YFICEPS
CERTAIN	DEPICTS	ENGLISH	ECNEICS	ESICERP	ELPMAXE
QUICKLY	METHODS	EXAMPLE	YFICEPS	YRUCREM	DEHCNUP
ENGLISH	SUBJECT	RECORDS	ELPMAXE	SNREVOG	EZIDIXO
MERCURY	PUNCHED	CERTAIN	SNMULOC	TCEJBUS	ESICERP
SUBJECT	OXIDIZE	GOVERNS	HSILGNE	SDROCER	ELPMAXE
METHODS	ENGLISH	COLUMNS	NIATREC	ESICERP	DEHCNUP
DEPICTS	SPECIFY	PRECISE	EZIDIXO	YLKCIUQ	ECNEICS
CERTAIN	RECORDS	SCIENCE	STCIPED	ELPMAXE	HSILGNE
PRECISE	QUICKLY	METHODS	YFICEPS	YRUCREM	SNREVOG

Figure 2: Display of English and nonsense half fields to illustrate a case of discrimination solely based on pattern recognition. (Ref. 9)

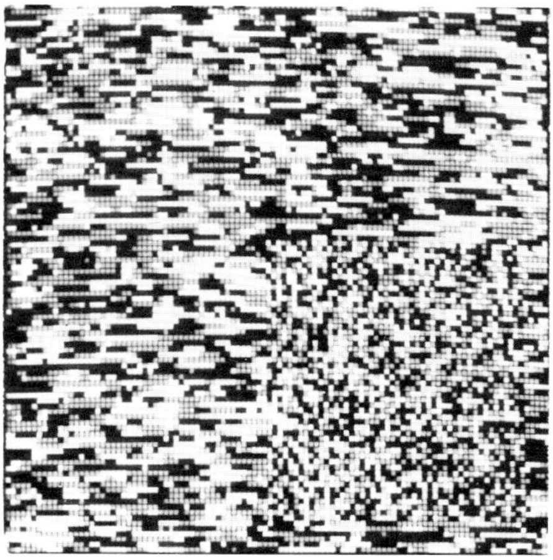

Figure 3: Two random fields with different second-order probability distribution but identical first order distribution. Texture discrimination occurs effortlessly. (Ref. 9)

Figure 4: Two random half-fields with identical first-and second-order probability distribution but different third-order distribution. (Ref. 9)

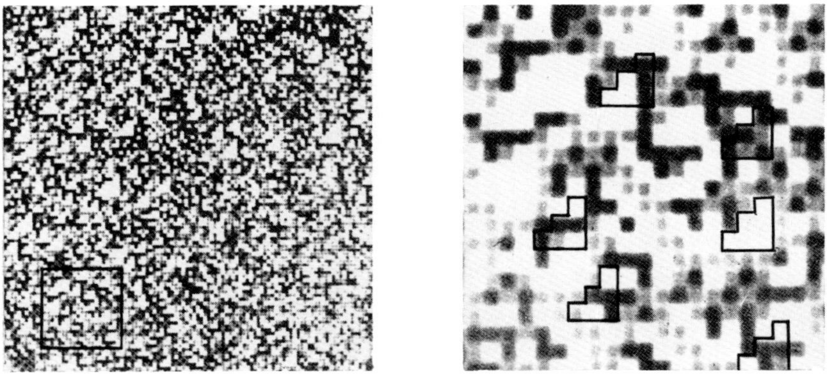

Figure 5: Two random fields to illustrate that of six equally probable triangular structures (B); only the uniformly black ones can be noticed. (Ref. 10)

Figure 6: Periodic random-dot texture of black and white dots. Repetition effortlessly perceived. (Ref. 20)

Figure 7: Similar to Figure 6, except that in place of black and white dots +45 and −45 degree diagonal line segments are selected. Repetition cannot be effortlessly perceived. (Ref. 20)

Figure 8: Four identical random quadrants. Perception of repetition requires scrutiny. (Ref. 20)

Figure 9: Similar to Figure 8 but mirrored across horizontal and vertical axes. Two-fold symmetry is effortlessly perceived. (Ref. 20)

Figure 10: Two-fold symmetry with random stripes along symmetry axes. Influence of points close to symmetry axes important. (Ref. 20)

Figure 11: Similar to Figure 10 except that the macroclusters are broken up. Perception of symmetry greatly reduced. (Ref. 20)

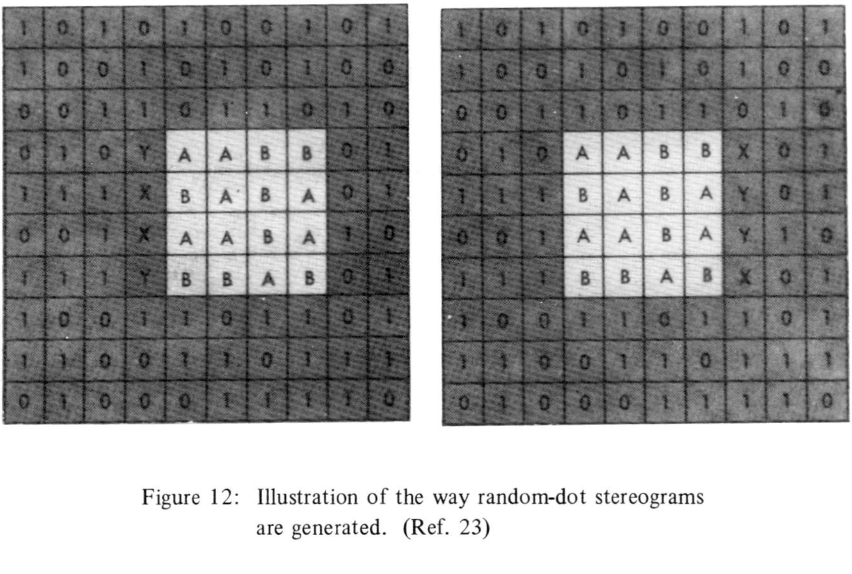

Figure 12: Illustration of the way random-dot stereograms are generated. (Ref. 23)

Figure 13: Random-dot stereogram. When monocularly viewed the two images are perceived as being random. When binocularly fused a center square is seen in front of a surround. (Ref. 23)

Figure 14: Random-dot stereogram which when monocularly viewed contains pattern of bilateral symmetry across horizontal axis. When binocularly fused horizontal stripes are seen in depth and monocular symmetry is suppressed. (Ref.19)

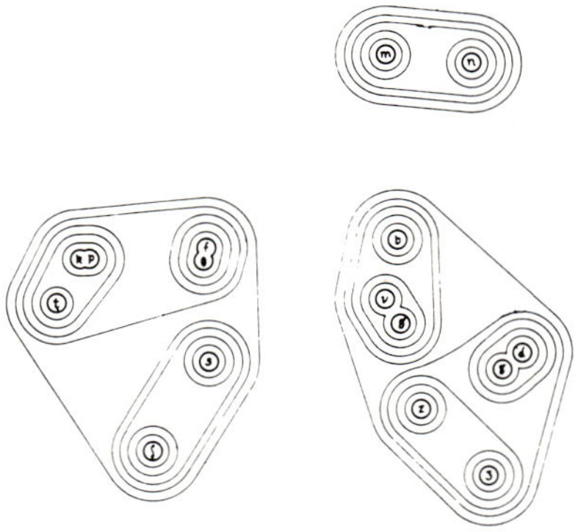

Figure 15: Confusability between 16 English consonants using a clustering algorithm. (Refs. 34 and 35)

RECOGNITION, MACHINE "RECOGNITION", AND STATISTICAL APPROACHES

Laveen Kanal and B. Chandrasekaran***

BLUE BELL, PENNSYLVANIA†

Introduction

Although perception and recognition, the logic of classification and statistical methodology have each been studied for decades, automatic pattern recognition is a new field. It is the recent emergence of computer related technology and needs that has led to serious attempts to synthesize various aspects of pattern recognition into machine recognition systems.

The past years have been years of exciting growth for the field of pattern recognition. However, this growth has not been orderly; advances in basic theoretical understanding have not preceded advances in technology and applications. Rather, we have a jumble of published and unpublished experimental and theoretical results, engineering successes and failures, comments, criticisms and philosophical arguments out of which, hopefully, will emerge some order and maturing of the field.

In Automatic Pattern Recognition there is a confusion between the goals of: (1) mechanical simulation of human perception and recognition; and (2) machine systems to automate certain data handling processes by

---

* Work partially supported by Contract AF30(602)–3623 with the Systems and Information Sciences Section, RADC, Griffiss Air Force Base, N. Y.

** Work supported by Contract F33(615)–67–C–1836 with the 6570th Aerospace Medical Research Labs, Aerospace Medical Division Air Force Systems Command, Wright-Patterson Air Force Base, Ohio.

† The authors are with the Communications and Electronics Division of Philco-Ford Corporation, Blue Bell, Pa. L. Kanal is also associated with the University of Pennsylvania's Wharton School and the Department of Electrical Engineering of Lehigh University.

performing some pattern classification tasks. While in some situations these goals are related, they are nevertheless distinct.

It must be admitted that much of the glamour in this area is due to the intentional or unintentional association with aspects of artificial intelligence. This depends on the original predilections with which each of us entered the field. It has been long recognized that Pattern Recognition is an important aspect of almost all activities to which the appellation 'intelligent' can be added confidently. Long before the emergence of the pattern recognition technology, psychologists have concerned themselves with the phenomena of perception, and concept formation (patterns cannot be recognized without the concept of the patterns). In view of all this, there has been a justified belief that if complex pattern recognition problems can be solved, a giant stride towards modeling human intelligence would have been achieved.

On the other hand, quite a few of us entered this field without such grand themes in mind. Technology was producing problems which needed solution. Someone needed a print reader, particle physics needed a cloud chamber track analyzer, and the growing computer technology needed a system to recognize spoken and written instructions; engineers have taken up these problems and have tackled them with varying degrees of success. Much of this has been done without a general theory to guide them. In any case, they have not particularly cared whether their systems can be considered models of human recognition systems.

This dichotomy between simulation of human perception and automation of certain data handling processes by performing pattern classification has been useful. It has at least produced many working systems: zip code readers, reasonably reliable aerial imagery screening machines, etc., and there is considerable hope that many more such systems can be designed. If we had waited to learn which neurons in the brain fire and which impulses occur when a human recognizes the letter A, zip code readers would have been long in coming. This is not cynicism, but a reminder that at least some kinds of so-called intelligent activities can be mechanized without any correspondence to human apparatus. Clearly there are activities which have needed a human to perform them until now, but now it has been demonstrated that machines can do them by the simple expedient of constructing machines that perform them.

Obviously, the engineering approach has built-in limitations. There is a certain level of complexity above which the engineer's bag of tricks fails to produce results. As an example while even multifont printed character recognition has been successfully handled, a satisfactory solution of cursive script recognition defies all attempts. Similarly there seems to be a fairly big jump between isolated speech recognition and continuous speech recognition. Those who have been hoping to model human recognition processes have also reached an impasse. It is probable that those problems which the engineers have found difficult to handle are precisely those which have to await more detailed understanding of human recognition systems. In any case, these feelings of crisis are intimately related to those in other aspects of artificial intelligence: game playing and mechanical translation. It is just possible that modelers of the human mind are in the game too early. It may be that a greater understanding of human perceptual phenomena will aid in mechanical model making rather than that the present attempts at modeling will throw any light on human perceptual performance.

With the above statements, we find ourselves squarely in the midst of the current controversy in artificial intelligence. It is not our role to take sides in the issue, if only because we believe it is not going to be settled convincingly one way or the other in the near future. However, insofar as it is relevant to pattern recognition in the next few years we can make some suggestions about possible avenues for progress, if by progress we mean the solution of some previously unsolved problems.

Recognition and Classification

The human sensory system is capable of responding only to selected parts of the electromagnetic spectrum and to restricted classes of patterns; perhaps the evolution of this system was related to survival. The evolution of intelligence has led through the development of machines, to the extension of human perception beyond that biologically available. This has been done either by transforming stimuli outside the range of the human sensory apparatus to within the range – e.g., the use of infrared sensors to enable night vision – and then using human perception and recognition, or by transforming an apparently complex perception-recognition problem into a classification problem which can then be automated.

Through an abuse of the language, words such as recognition and learning have been applied to machine systems which implement classification and estimation algorithms. Unfortunately this abuse of the language is here to stay and we shall also speak of machine recognition. Kenneth Sayre[1] hammers upon the insidious effects of this confusion between recognition and classification. Basing his thesis on the linguistic school of philosophy, he says, "classification of a group of objects is a matter either of sorting them according to a given set of categories or of devising a set of categories by which they can be sorted. Either procedure is a process and not itself an attainment" which according to his analysis is what recognition is. He goes on to say, "Even though I could not recognize a strange flower found among the flowers in my backyard, I could easily identify it – i.e., point it out for my neighbour when he arrives to inspect it". Further, "If I recognize an object it is something I could not have done more effectively, more thoroughly or more satisfactorily", all of which do apply to classification. Finally, "It may be the case that when one recognizes them, indeed by that token one is able both to classify and to identify the object one recognizes. But to classify an object is not thereby to recognize it, nor is recognition merely a matter of identification".

So much for linguistic philosophy. Our objection to the forced synonymity of recognition and classification and learning and estimation is based on less esoteric, more pragmatic considerations. Recognition and learning are poorly understood, apparently fairly complex capabilities of humans and animals. The aura of magic and mystery associated with these little understood capabilities was transferred to devices which implemented fairly simple classification and iterative estimation algorithms. Also, various classification network developers claimed to be modeling the brain and heuristic programmers spoke of simulating human perception all of which led to great expectations which were bound to be deflated sooner or later. Because of lack of adequate knowledge, the very foundations for the simulation of human perception and recognition are non-existent. To claim otherwise at this juncture, we believe, is to mislead.

Sometimes, however, we can solve specific problems and make models for specific acts of human perception; e.g., the attempts to explain the figure-ground perception problem. But that is not the simulation of human perception. Nevertheless, the optimistic thesis of this paper is that this need not prevent the development of machines and man-machine systems which "recognize" patterns both of the symbols and signs and signals recognized by humans and of other patterns not easily recognized by humans. The way this has been done and is going to be done – probably there is only a class of problems which can be solved in this way, though at the moment we do not know how to characterize that class – is by the transformation of an apparent perception-recognition problem into a classification problem. Studies of how humans perceive vowel sounds led our colleague Louis Focht[2] to a transform called the Single Equivalent Formant which has resulted in a compact isolated speech recognition device. However, such transformations may not always be possible. A few "non-existence theorems" will be of inestimable value in this enterprise, though none are in the horizon.

Indeed, this is the real sticky point for anyone working on automatic pattern recognition: a priori, given a real word pattern recognition problem task, we have no way of knowing what its complexity is for machine recognition – unless we have solved something very similar before and know which abstractions and algorithms are applicable. Thus, the multifont typed character recognition problem was considered very difficult if not impossible at one time in the history of automatic pattern recognition. A subset of the problem was tackled and solved well enough to automate a process of data sorting. Similarly, there was considerable doubt as to the feasibility of machine recognition of certain objects in nominally vertical, real aerial photography. These doubts having been removed they are now centered on hitherto unconsidered aspects of the problem.

Within the constraints of our limited capability, not knowing ahead of time what it takes to solve a problem, we can nevertheless go a long way in eliminating competing techniques if we take a problem oriented approach. One of us (L.K.) and associates gave an example of how this is done in our paper on "System Considerations for Automatic Imagery Screening".[3]

Transforming a recognition problem into a classification problem involves the generation and selection of features which form the inputs to the decision device in pattern recognition systems. The difficult problems in the field are those in which the generation of suitable complete sets of features has been formidable. There is also some doubt that the feature selection problem is really the only impediment to the development of true recognition systems. Hubert Dreyfus[4] points out that there are at least three other important requirements which mechanical systems aren't capable of fulfilling now if ever in the future they can. They are, essence-accident discrimination, fringe consciousness and ambiguity tolerance. A good case can be made that in a truly complex pattern recognition problem, these others are of vital importance in making the difference between what is practical and what is not. For instance, these last mentioned attributes will enable the recognition system not to waste time on an elaborate search. But in the absence of these attributes we just have to build this search into the recognition systems.

The reader will note that we have been at considerable pains to keep to the middle road. This middle road can be summarized as follows: We have quite an arsenal of solutions for classification problems under various conditions. But we do not have a general theory for recognition aspects of these problems. Whatever successes we have had in the field have been a result of an effective transformation of a perception-recognition problem into just such a classification problem. We are interested in knowing whether there is a general methodology, if not a theory, to effect this transformation in future problems, when they are solvable. We next turn our attention to these problems.

Data Analysis and Decision Theory

One important application of statistics in pattern recognition has been the use of decision theoretic procedures for classification purposes. By its very nature, decision theory does not concern itself with questions on what kind of variables to consider. The most that it can say is that the observables constitute an n-dimensional vector with assumed probability distributions or in nonparametric cases, without them. This is not to deny the importance of statistical decision theory in pattern recognition problems; undoubtedly, sophistication of decision procedures is useful. But the vital difference to the performance is going to be made by the appropriateness of the features selected. For all practical purposes the theory of pattern recognition has become identical to the statistical theory of classification. The reason for this lopsided development is that theorizing on the essentially heuristic job of feature formation is extremely difficult, even if formalizing heuristics is not a contradiction in terms.

The quality of decisions we make depends on the quality of questions we ask. The questions in this case correspond to the observables we choose to measure. In problems where the formalization of human recognition is not obvious, experimentation to determine suitable features is the only worthwhile route. This being the case, every attempt must be made to routinize this experimentation, and to develop new types of tools. For those aspects which cannot be routinized because they depend upon not understood human perceptual phenomena, making human interaction in the design process easy represents the best hope for progress. An example of this kind of system is provided by the On–line Pattern Analysis and Recognition System (OLPARS) being developed by the System Information Sciences group at Rome Air Development Center.[5] This system is being developed so as to be particularly suited for experimentation with respect to feature generation and selection purposes. It consists of a general purpose computer with a display console and the necessary computer software to enable a user to communicate on-line with the computer through the use of a keyboard and a light pen on the display console. The software capability consists of overlays which provide facilities for projection on a line and also for more general data analysis.

The above approach can be said to be in the spirit of the new trend in statistics, viz., Computer Data Analysis. To quote John Tukey[6]

> "Data analysis (consists of) among other things: procedures for analyzing data, techniques for interpreting the results of such procedures, ways of planning the gathering of data to make analysis easier . . . " and ". . . Large parts of data analysis are incisive, laying bare indications which we could not perceive by simple and direct examination of the raw data . . . Some parts of data analysis, as the term is here stretched beyond its philology, are allocation, in the sense that they guide us in the distribution of effort and other valuable considerations in observation, experimentation, or analysis."

In the design of automatic pattern recognition the methodology of on-line experimentation and interaction with computers seems most promising for feature generation and evaluation.

Statistical Approaches

There are instances of pattern recognition problems where feature selection is straightforward, and much of the theory of decision procedures can be directly applied. There are also problems for which machines are superior classification devices than humans. Many of the problems in signal detection are of this type and for these statistical approaches provide powerful tools.

More generally, however, routinizing the testing of our hypotheses concerning data through computer data analysis, requires that we incorporate a variety of statistical procedures and understand their theoretical properties.

At recent conferences such as the Puerto Rico Workshop[7] and this Hawaii meeting, when builders of pattern recognition devices have confronted people working on theoretical aspects of pattern recognition, especially on statistical approaches, there has been a tendency to question, in the name of practicality and simplicity, the need for theoretical studies in this area. While no engineer will quarrel with the emphasis on practicality and simplicity, the philosophy which says "if it works it's fine – there is no need for concern with its theoretical properties, convergence theorems etc.", leads to a deemphasis of all optimality criteria and makes it difficult to select between competing techniques without extensive experimentation. A suitable criterion can be used to analytically decide on the best technique among a set of *ad hoc* methods. Thus, in a stochastic context, the property of consistency, an optimality criterion of sorts, can be and is often used to select one from among a set of *ad hoc* estimates. Similar roles are played by optimality criteria such as asymptotic normality, asymptotic unbiasedness and asymptotic relative efficiency. These criteria are by no means irrelevant since asymptotic conditions could obtain rather quickly in high data rate situations.

As a concrete example of the above consider the *ad hoc* techniques of robust estimation. Within a class of simple and practical estimators, e.g., the class of estimators which are linear functions of the order statistics, we can in fact consider asymptotically best linear unbiased estimators, or estimators which are most robust according to some other analytical criterion. This allows a selection of one intuitive procedure from a class of intuitive procedures. Furthermore, as Gastwirth[8] and others have shown, we can use analytical procedures as constructive approaches; we can construct an asymptotically best linear unbiased estimator corresponding to an asymptotically most powerful rank test.

Our point, that it cannot hurt if we help our intuition with some analytical criteria is an obvious one, but one which tends to be forgotten. On the other hand, in these times when regretfully, even "engineering" journals are full of papers written in the dry "theorem-proof, theorem-proof" style, we find, all too often, workers in pattern recognition being carried away by the elegant mathematical aspects of a technique. For example, numerous papers in the Pattern Recognition literature have been devoted to variations of a small class of deterministic or stochastic iterative algorithms. In many cases the emphasis has been to show convergence on known samples. In practice, in most cases, the overall performance of these techniques has turned out to be not even as good as Fisher's linear discriminant function. Indeed in many cases the iterative techniques which are offered, asymptotically approach this very simple linear discriminant function. The early interest[9, 10] of one of us (L.K.) in deterministic iterative algorithms and in stochastic approximation methods was dampened considerably as a result of this understanding and experience. Since that period, although various iterative or "learning" pattern classification algorithms are included in our bag of tools for designing classification networks, usually when faced with a fixed set of samples of known classification, iterative algorithms occupy a low position in the order of approaches we try out. On this point refer also to the discussion in[3].

In the above context it is interesting to note that Peter Lambert's results presented at this conference[11] also show that Fisher's discriminant function compares very favorably with his algorithms based on mathematical programming techniques. Conversations a few years back with Arthur Albert who had worked on a learning algorithm for pattern classification[12] and Harold Kushner who had experimented with stochastic approximation methods for estimation[13] confirmed that the nice limit theorems for these techniques were not always a good guide to their performance in practice.

The development and extension of theoretical procedures as a result of critical experiments and the specification of critical experiments to test alternative theoretical approaches – a common approach in many areas of science, especially physics, has yet to occur on any scale in the field of automatic pattern recognition. This is in part because of the diversity of the applications, the presence of proprietary interests, and the very nature and infancy of the field. To a large extent, until recently, theoretical developments and practical implementation have taken independent paths with little interaction. Thus although one of the early applications of the decision theoretic model to automatic pattern recognition was that presented by Chow for character recognition,[14] most of the commercially available optical character readers have used heuristic techniques almost exclusively. Part of the reason for this is that commercial readers have been developed by hardware oriented engineers not familiar with or convinced about statistical classification theory. The fact remains that classical statistical decision theory is not by itself adequate for the solution of pattern recognition problems. It has had an impact on practical recognition systems only when it has been supplemented by a substantial amount of heuristic thinking. Thus, we have had some success in applying statistical classification techniques to the difficult problem of photographic pattern recognition[15, 3] (specific results have not been published because of security regulations); the success of this application can be traced to the combining of some heuristic approaches with the decision theoretic methodology.

Even as a model for classification, classical statistical decision theory has not been entirely satisfactory since it is applicable only when a single decision must be made. When the same decision problem occurs many times advantages can be gained by considering the whole collection of problems as a totality. Since a machine that classifiers pattern vectors is not expected to be used only once, we can identify the problem of pattern classification with what is called Compound Decision Theory. Thus we and our associates, along with others, have sought to relate, extend and apply compound decision theory to pattern recognition. Its appeal lies in that it provides an integrated theoretical framework for many problems in statistical pattern classification viz, learning with a teacher, learning without a teacher, automatic threshold adjustment, taking context into account, intersymbol interference, subminimax procedures, classification of nonstationary time series and distribution free learning. In the spirit of this conference we eschew most of the mathematics and dwell on the philosophy underlying the work in compound decision theory.

The General Compound Decision Problem

In a compound decision problem we have a sequence of states-of-nature (pattern classes), and a corresponding sequence of random variables (patterns). Let $\underline{\theta}_n = \{\theta_1, \theta_2, \ldots, \theta_n\}$ denote a sequence of elements from a set $\Omega = \{\omega_1, \omega_2, \ldots, \omega_m\}$ of pattern classes (states-of-nature). Associated with each possible sequence $\underline{\theta}_n$, is a cumulative distribution function $P(\underline{x}_n|\underline{\theta}_n)$ on a sequence of vector valued random variables $\underline{X}_n = \{X_1, X_2, \ldots, X_n\}$. A single observed value x_k of an element X_k of the sequence $\underline{X}_n$ is called a pattern. There is a space of possible actions $A = \{\alpha_1, \alpha_2, \ldots, \alpha_s\}$ and a loss function defined on $\Omega \times A$. For the problem of pattern classification we assume that $A \equiv \Omega$. We must choose a sequence of actions $\underline{a}_n = \{a_1, a_2, \ldots, a_n\}$.

The loss function is a matrix $L_{ij}(k) = L_k(\alpha_j|\omega_i)$ which specifies the loss for the kth decision if we choose action $a_k = \alpha_j$, when the true state-of-nature is $\theta_k = \omega_i$. We will denote the elements of the loss matrix by $L(\alpha_j, \theta_k)$. The loss for the compound problem is taken to be the average of the losses incurred at each of the n decisions and the compound risk is defined as the average of the risks for each of the "component" decision problems of the compound problem.

If all observations $\underline{x}_n$ are at hand before individual decisions must be made, we can use a *compound decision rule* $\underline{t}_n = (t_1, \ldots, t_n)$ where the kth component $t_k = t_k(\alpha_j|\underline{x}_n)$ is for each sequence $\underline{x}_n$, a distribution over the action space according to which the kth action is chosen. If only the first k observations $\underline{x}_k$ are available when the kth decision must be made, we can use a *sequential compound decision rule,* where $t_k = t_k(\alpha_j|\underline{x}_k)$. If the first k + r observations $\underline{x}_{k+r}$, $r \geqslant 1$, are at hand when the kth decision must be made, one can use a sequential compound decision rule

$t_k = t_k(\alpha_j|\underline{x}_{k+r})$ *deferred* "r units of time". A *simple rule* is one where the decision about the kth element θ_k, in the sequence of pattern classes depends only on the kth observation x_k, i.e., $t_k = t_k(\alpha_j|x_k)$. For a *simple symmetric rule,* the probability of taking action α_j given the observation x_k, is independent of k, i.e., $t_k = t(\alpha_j|x_k)$. Classical decision theory is restricted to using only simple symmetric rules.

The risk for the compound decision rule $\underline{t}_n$, called the *compound risk,* is the average of the component risks

$$R(\underline{\theta}_n, \underline{t}_n) = \frac{1}{n} \sum_{k=1}^{n} R(\underline{\theta}_n, t_k)$$

where

$$R(\underline{\theta}_n, t_k) = \int \sum_{j=1}^{s} L(\alpha_j, \theta_k)\, t_k(\alpha_j|\underline{x}_n)\, p(\underline{x}_n|\underline{\theta}_n)\, dx^n$$

is the risk for the kth problem and is referred to as the kth component risk. The integration is over the n-fold cartesian product of the pattern space.

If we assume the existence of an a priori probability function $G(\underline{\theta}_n)$ over the n-fold cartesian product Ω^n of the set of states-of-nature, then we can define a *compound Bayes risk:*

$$\overline{R}(G, \underline{t}_n) = \sum_{\underline{\theta}_n \in \Omega^n} R(\underline{\theta}_n, \underline{t}_n)\, G(\underline{\theta}_n)$$

$$= \frac{1}{n} \sum_{k=1}^{n} \overline{R}(G, t_k)$$

where

$$\overline{R}(G, t_k) = \sum_{\underline{\theta}_n \in \Omega^n} R(\underline{\theta}_n, t_k)\, G(\underline{\theta}_n)$$

is the kth *component Bayes risk.* A procedure is said to be *compound Bayes* against the a priori probability function G, if it minimizes the Compound Bayes risk $R(G, \underline{t}_n)$. It is easily seen that the Compound Bayes procedure is the decision function that for every k, minimizes the kth component Bayes risk, and for the special case of a zero-one loss matrix this is equivalent to maximizing the a posteriori probability $G(\theta_k|\underline{x}_n)$.

Empirical Bayes, Non-Bayesian Compound and Bayesian Compound Procedures

In most of the early work on compound decision theory and in much of the contemporary work, the assumption is made that the patterns are conditionally independent and that the classes are also independent, i.e.,

$$p(\underline{x}_n|\underline{\theta}_n) = \prod_{k=1}^{n} p_k(x_k|\theta_k)$$

and

$$G(\underline{\theta}_n) = \prod_{k=1}^{n} G_k(\theta_k)$$

Under these assumptions a *simple rule,* $t_k = t_k(\alpha_j|x_k)$ in which the kth decision is dependent only on the kth observation, will be compound Bayes against the a priori distribution G. A simple symmetric rule $t_k = t(\alpha_j|x_k)$ will be compound Bayes against G when the probabilities are independent of k, i.e., $G_k(\theta_k) = G(\theta_k)$ and $p_k(x_k|\theta_k) = p(x_k|\theta_k)$. However even in these cases, non-simple, i.e., compound, rules have merit.

Suppose we assume that the densities $p(x_k|\theta_k)$ are known but the a priori distribution G is unknown. Two approaches which have been put forth for this case are the following. The *empirical Bayes* approach of Robbins[16] assumes that the elements θ , in the sequence of states-of-nature, are independent and identically distributed according to an a priori distribution $g(\theta)$ over Ω . Robbins shows that if we use a procedure which is Bayes against a consistent estimate of $G(\theta)$ based on the first $(n-1)$ observations, then the Bayes risk of the nth decision in the sequence converges to the risk for a simple Bayes decision against known $G(\theta)$.

If we do not assume the existence of an a priori distribution $G(\underline{\theta}_n)$ and are unwilling to assume independence of the elements θ_k in the sequence of states-of-nature $\underline{\theta}_n$, then we can consider the *non-Bayesian compound* approach of Hannan and Robbins.[17] Without assuming the existence of an a priori probability distribution $G(\theta)$, let $G^n(\omega_i)$ be the true fraction of the θ's in $\underline{\theta}_n$, which are equal to ω_i . This is called the empirical a priori probability distribution of Ω . Hannan and Robbins show that if we use a procedure that is Bayes against a consistent estimate of G^n , then the compound risk converges uniformly for any sequence $\underline{\theta}_n$, to the risk for a simple Bayes decision against known G^n. The uniform convergence means that the compound risk is minimized even in the face of a malevolent nature which chooses a sequence $\underline{\theta}_n$ in the worst possible, non-random way. Thus, in addition to the assumption of independence of the states-of-nature, the empirical Bayes and non-Bayesian compound approaches differ in fundamental philosophy. The non-Bayesians are unwilling to grant the existence of an a priori $G(\theta)$, while the empirical

Bayesians assume the existence of a $G(\theta)$ of unknown value. Note however, that if indeed $G(\theta)$ exists, then the estimate $G^n(\theta)$ is itself a consistent estimate of $G(\theta)$. Therefore a consistent estimate of $G^n(\theta)$ is also a consistent estimate of $G(\theta)$ and vice versa. Therefore one finds that although the philosophies differ the estimation techniques and decision rules employed are the same.

The modern Bayesians go further. They assume not only the existence of an a priori distribution $G(\theta)$ which is of unknown value, but they also assume an a priori distribution function F(G) on the values of $G(\theta)$. This leads to a decision rule which is Bayes against an a posteriori estimate of $G(\theta)$ based on the observations. The same limit theorems holds, of course, because the Bayes estimate of $G(\theta)$ is consistent. Thus for the case where the pattern classes are independently and identically distributed but $G(\theta)$ is unknown, the three techniques give the same basic result, except that any consistent estimator may be used in the first two approaches.

Nonparametric Empirical Bayes Approaches

In problems of interest to us in pattern recognition, we are of course concerned with more than just unknown $G(\theta)$'s. We are interested in cases where the conditional probabilities of the pattern are unknown; where the patterns are not class conditionally independent; where the pattern classes are not independent. Also, we are interested in cases where the statistics of the patterns and the classes vary with time – the nonstationary case. We consider briefly some of the work based on compound decision theory which attempts to tackle these problems.

For unknown densities $p(x|\theta_k)$, with the a priori probability function G also unknown, two approaches have been put forth by Johns and Van Ryzin. The nonparametric empirical Bayes approach of Johns assumes that the θ's are independently and identically distributed and examines convergence of the component Bayes risk to its minimum value. It also assumes that when the kth decision must be made, there are at hand the true values of all previous states-of-nature and uses a sequential compound decision rule with $t_k = t_k(\alpha_j|\underline{\theta}_{k-1}, \underline{x}_k)$. One may use $\underline{\theta}_{k-1}$ and $\underline{x}_{k-1}$ to obtain consistent estimates of $p(x|\omega_i)$ for all $\omega_i \in \Omega$, and act as if these were the true densities to define a procedure "Bayes" against the known empirical a priori distribution G^{k-1}. Examples of such a consistent estimation procedure are the Fix-Hodges nearest neighbor method[18,19] which is used by Johns for this problem and the "Window Carpentry" procedure[20,21] used by Van Ryzin.[22] The procedure is asymptotically optimum in the empirical Bayes sense.

Van Ryzin[23] has shown that the above mentioned procedure is also optimum in the limit in the sense that the compound risk coverges to the minimum Bayes risk, i.e., the Bayes risk for known G^n, for *any* sequence $\underline{\theta}_n$. Thus the θ's do not have to be independent and identically distributed.

However, the assumption is that the true value of θ_k is given to us after each decision is made and Van Ryzin examines convergence of the average of the component risks. In a nonparametric pattern recognition problem we usually will have "training samples" from which to estimate the densities but we should not be concerned with whether or not the risk of a rule, applied to these samples, converges. What must be examined is convergence of the risk applied to the samples we wish to test and whose true classification is never known. This is done in the empirical Bayes approach in that one investigates convergence of the nth component Bayes risk given (n−1) training samples. However, this approach has two major limitations. It assumes that the states-of-nature are independent and it assumes that only one pattern need really be classified.

Some Pattern Recognition Applications of Compound Decision Theory

In our laboratory, Compound Decision Theory has been applied to the problems of adaptive threshold adjustment and taking context into account[24], the problem of intersymbol interference[25] and the sequential classification of nonstationary time series[26].

Note that even when the probability densities $p(x|\omega_i)$ are known, there are two distinct situations in which compound decision rules are needed. First when the a priori distribution $G(\underline{\theta}_n)$ is not known or assumed not to exist. Secondly when the states-of-nature are not independent as for example in the case of English text in which context may be helpful in recognizing characters.

For the case of two pattern classes with known densities but unknown a priori probabilities, Abend[24] presents compound procedures, including a two-threshold procedure on the likelihood ratio, involving a fixed threshold and an adjustable decision threshold. The fixed threshold is set to give a minimax probability of error and the fraction of times the fixed threshold is exceeded, is used in a truncated sequential estimate of the a priori probability to provide an adjustable decision threshold on the likelihood ratio.

For the case where both the probability densities and the a priori distribution are known but the states-of-nature are dependent he presents the optimum Bayes sequential compound procedure and analyses it in detail for special assumptions about the nature of the dependence between the states-of-nature, and the form of the probability density functions.

Harley[26] has noted that the general statement of the compound decision problem does not impose any assumptions of stationarity and neither does the expression for the optimum decision rule for the kth element of the sequence $\underline{\theta}_n$. Thus, classification of nonstationary time series fits within compound decision theory and the general classification problem for nonstationary time series is identical to the general compound decision problem.

Now, a nonstationary time series is, by definition, a time series which is not wide sense stationary, i.e., a time series is nonstationary if either the mean x_t or the autocovariance function $R(t, \tau) = E\{(x_t - \bar{x}_t)(x_{t-\tau} - x_{t-\tau})\}$ depends on t. In the cases of interest we are dealing with sequences of vector random variables $\{x_t;\ t = 1, 2, \ldots, n\}$ and therefore the mean $\bar{x}_t$ is a vector and the autocovariance function $R(t, \tau)$ is a matrix of covariance functions where the diagonal elements are the autocovariance functions of the elements of the vector x_t and the off-diagonal elements are the cross-covariance functions between terms of the vectors. Harley formulates the problem of unsupervised sequential classification of nonstationary time series as a compound decision problem. His paper directly extends the work of Patrick and Hancock[27]. In his treatment, the a priori class probabilities are assumed to be stochastically independent, time-varying and unknown. The class-conditional cumulative distribution functions of the observables x are assumed to be of known parametric form but with the parameter values unknown and time varying. A Bayesian approach is taken, employing an a priori distribution on the unknown parameters and class probabilities, which leads to a solution in terms of minimizing the sample conditional risk. If the unknown parameters and class probabilities are assumed to have Markov time dependence, then the nonstationary problem can be reformulated in terms of the problem of classifying stationary time series with known parameters and with known Markov dependence on the states-of-nature. Harley presents detailed results for two examples of nonstationary: time varying a priori class probabilities and time varying class means. Results for stationary time series are derived as special cases of the problem of time varying a priori class probabilities. In the case of time varying means, the solution is equivalent to that for a problem involving conditionally dependent stationary patterns.

The idea of converting a nonstationary estimation problem to a stationary one by assuming the nature of the time variation is not new, although usually the assumption is of a deterministic time variation. Harley's Bayesian formulation is more general and provides a neat illustration of the application of compound decision theory and suggests that a reasonable thing to do with a nonstationary problem is to convert it into a structurally equivalent stationary problem.

Recently we have learnt about independent work by various people, including Patrick and his students at Purdue, Lainiotis and his students at Texas[28] and Cover and his students at Stanford[29] on topics in Compound Decision Theory applied to pattern recognition.

Concluding Remarks

We have attempted to place the relationship between recognition and classification on the one hand and between theory and application of statistical classification on the other, in proper perspective. Compound decision theory is the latest step in the evolution of the most general model in which to imbed statistical classification problems arising in recognition system design. For the nonformalizable aspects of design, interactive approaches, namely those in which the human is part of the loop in the design process, with different classification and heuristic algorithms at his call, seem to be most promising.

REFERENCES

1. Sayre, K. M., *Recognition: A Study in the Philosophy of Artificial Intelligence,* University of Notre Dame Press, 1965.
2. Focht, L. R., "The Single Equivalent Formant – A New Parameter Useful in Speech Bandwidth Compression and Recognition", IEEE International Communications Conference, Philadelphia, June 1966.
3. Harley, T.J., Kanal, L. N., and Randall, N. C., "System Considerations for Automatic Imagery Screening" presented at the Symposium on Automatic Photo-interpretation, Washington, D. C., May 1967; appears in the *Proceedings* of Symposium published by Thompson Book Co., 1967.
4. Dreyfus, H., "Alchemy and Artificial Intelligence", Informal lectures delivered at Rand Corporation, Santa Monica, California, 1966.
5. Sammon, J. W., Jr., "On Line Pattern Analysis and Recognition System–OLPARS" RADC Report, TR–68–263, August 1968.
6. Tukey, J. W., "The Future of Data Analysis", *Ann. Math. Stat.,* Vol. 33, No. 1, pp. 1–67, 1962.
7. Kanal, L. N., (Editor), *Pattern Recognition: Proc. of the IEEE Puerto Rico Workshop,* Thompson Book Co., Washington, D. C., 1968.
8. Gastwirth, J. L., "On Robust Procedures", *J. Ann. Stat. Asso.,* Vol. 61, No. 316, pp. 929–948, 1966.
9. Kanal, L. N., "Evaluation of a Class of Pattern Recognition Networks", in Bernard and Kare (Editors), *Biological Prototypes and Synthetic Systems,* Vol. 1, pp. 261–269, Plenum Press, New York, 1962.
10. Kanal, L. N., Slaymaker, F., Smith, D., and Walker, W., "Basic Principles of Some Pattern Recognition Networks", *Proceedings Nat. Elect. Conf.*, Vol. 18, pp. 279–295, Oct., 1962.
11. Lambert, P. F., "Designing Pattern Categorizers with Extremal Paradigm Information", presented at the International Conference on Methodologies of Pattern Recognition, Honolulu, January 1968.
12. Albert, A., "A Mathematical Theory of Pattern Recognition", *Ann. Math. Stat.,* Vol. 34, No. 1, pp. 284–299, 1963.
13. Kushner, H., "Efficient Iterative Methods for Optimizing the Performance of Multi-Parameter Noisy Systems", M.I.T. Lincoln Lab. Report. AD245802, 20 October 1960.

14. Chow, C. K., "An Optimum Character Recognition System Using Decision Functions", *IRE Transaction,* Vol. PGEC–6, pp. 247–254, December 1957.
15. Kanal, L. N., and Randall, N., "Recognition System Design Using Statistical Analysis", Proceedings of the 19th National Conference of Assoc. for Computing Machinery, pp. D2·5–1 to D2·5–10, Pub. Association for Computing Machinery, New York, 1964.
16. Robbins, H., "An Empirical Bayes Approach to Statistics", *Proc. Third Berkeley Symposium on Math. Stat. and Prob.,* University of California Press, 1956.
17. Hannan, J. F., and Robbins, H., "Asymptotic Solutions of the Compound Decision Problem for Two Completely Specified Distributions", *Ann. Math. Stat.,* Vol. 26, No. 1, pp. 37–51, 1955.
18. Fix, E., and Hodges, J. L., Discriminatory Analysis; Non-Parametric Discrimination: Consistency Properties; USAF SAM Series in Statistics, Project No. 21–49–004, Report No. 4., USAF School of Aviation Medicine, Randolph Field, Texas, February, 1951.
19. Cover, T. M. and Hart, P. E., "Nearest Neighbor Pattern Classification", *IEEE Trans. on Information Theory,* Vol. IT–13, No. 1, pp. 21–27, 1967.
20. Parzen, E., "On Estimation of a Probability Density Function and Mode", *Ann. Math. Stat.,* Vol. 33, No. 3, pp. 1065–1076, 1962.
21. Murthy, V. K., "Nonparametric Estimation of Multivariate Densities with Applications", International Symposium on Multivariate Analysis, Aerospace Research Labs, Wright-Patterson AFB, Ohio, June, 1965.
22. Van Ryzin, J. R., "Bayes Risk Consistency of Classification Procedures Using Density Estimation" (to be published).
23. Van Ryzin, J. R., "Repetitive Play in Finite Statistical Games with Unknown Distributions", *Ann. Math. Stat.*, Vol. 37, No. 4, pp. 976–994, 1966.
24. Abend, K., "Sequential Compound Decision Procedures for Dependent States of Nature", *Pattern Recognition,* Proc. of the IEEE Puerto Rico Workshop, L. Kanal (Editor), Thompson Book Company, Washington, D. C., 1968.
25. Abend, K., Harley, T. J., Jr., Fritchman, B. D., Gumacos, G., "On Optimum Receivers for Channels Having Memory" submitted to *IEEE Transactions on Information Theory.*
26. Harley, T. J., "Sequential Classification of Nonstationary Time Series", Technical Report, Philco-Ford Corporation, Blue Bell, Pa., 1967.
27. Patrick, E. A., and Hancock, J. C., "Nonsupervised Sequential Classification and Recognition of Patterns", *IEEE Trans. on Information Theory,* Vol. IT–12, pp. 362–372, July 1966.
28. Lainiotis, D. G., and Hilborn, C. G., "Learning Systems" for Minimum Risk Adaptive Pattern Classification and Optimal Adaptive Estimation", Communication Systems Research Group Technical Report No. 9, November 1, 1967.
29. Alens, N., "Compound Bayes Learning Without a Teacher", Technical Report No. 6151–2, Systems Theory Laboratory, Stanford Electronics Laboratories, Stanford University, Stanford, Calif., Aug., 1967.

PATTERN RECOGNITION APPLIED TO THE COUNTING OF NERVE FIBER CROSS-SECTIONS AND WATER DROPLETS

T. Kasvand

NATIONAL RESEARCH COUNCIL
CONTROL SYSTEMS LABORATORY
OTTAWA, CANADA

Abstract

Very simple recognition algorithms for black and white pictures containing many simple objects of any size, position, orientation and shape are described. The techniques are simple to implement as computer programs, and have been applied to the histogramming of nerve fiber cross-sections and masses of water droplets.

Definition of the Problem

The problem that has been studied and solved under certain simplifying assumptions has consisted of black and white pictures (see Appendix for definition of certain terms) where: Any number of objects of any size or shape may be present. The objects may be in any position or orientation with respect to each other, i.e., translation and rotation of objects is allowed. The objects may touch or partially merge into each other or some parts of the objects may be missing. The objects may change their size and shape by undergoing plastic transformation, i.e., the objects do not have to be "perfect". Noise may be present in the picture. These will be called "allowable transformation". If any of the above properties, for example, rotation is the only separating variable between objects, this fact has to be accounted for.

The Processing Philosophy

The picture is processed gradually. In the beginning no attempts are made to recognize anything at all but rather to try to extract variables from the picture which are invariant with respect to as many of the allowable transformations as possible. If invariance cannot be achieved, it must be known how a given variable depends on any one of the allowable transformations. At the same time a minimum set of variables should be selected.

In the black and white picture the contour is independent of any of the transformations. The curvature of the contour is an inverse function only of the size of the object, except that it may be difficult to compute in noisy pictures. Obviously, the detection of the existence of a contour, and the computation of its curvature both in magnitude and direction can be performed irrespective of what the picture contains. This stage of the processing (preliminary processing) is independent of the contents of the picture.

A body in the picture will occupy a certain neighborhood (N). The inter-relationship of contours in N defines the body. However, since N is unknown we do not know which contours belong to what body. This can only be known if the body is known, but by that time recognition is no longer required. To avoid this paradox, it is advisable to identify regions (M) in the picture where most coherent discriptions of the neighbouring contours may be expected for the purposes of recognition. The center of such a region will be called a "center of interest" or "COFI". The algorithms for obtaining the center of interest should be relatively independent of size, rotation, plastic deformation and noise, since they are used to "pin down" the locations of the objects. The processing of the picture with COFI algorithms is called secondary processing, since it is object dependent to a certain degree.

The neighbourhood (M) around the COFI is to be represented in a form where the effects of the remaining allowable transformations are as decoupled from each other as possible. In this way the effects of size, rotation and plastic deformations of contours can be handled on an individual basis, if required, or eliminated if any of these variables do not constitute the separating variables in the recognition process.

Only in case of very simple bodies like circles, triangles, squares, etc., the body and the object may become identical. For more complicated bodies, the initial object (O) is only a part of the body (B) since the neighbourhood M is less than the neighbourhood N, but M need not be contained in N. The recognition algorithm consequently needs feedback to ascertain that the initial object (O) is a part of the body (B). In this process M approaches N. In other words, the initial hypothesis that O is a part of B is either accepted or rejected by referring to the memory for B. These problems are being studied.

With the exception of the feedback effect, the stages outlined above were tried out in a computer simulation where the picture contained black circles, squares, triangles, stars, etc. These elementary objects were recognized irrespective of size, orientation, position and numbers present. See Reference 1.

Practical Processing Stages

The philosophy of processing can become considerably modified and shortened in practice since it may not be necessary to go through all the steps to arrive at a stage where the picture is sufficiently processed (filtered) for recognition to be attempted. This, however, depends very much on the nature of the problem.

In the present black and white pictures very simple filters have been found satisfactory. Figure 1 shows an assembly of hexagonally placed cells. The center cell (o,o) may be anywhere in the picture L. The preprocessing normally consists of the following steps:

(1) Smoothing; to minimize microscopic noise:

$$a'_{oo} = (Wo\ a_{oo} + \sum_{j=1}^{6} a_{1j})/(Wo + 6)$$

where: a_{ij} ($i = 0, 1; j = 0, 1, \ldots 6$) is the illumination and Wo is a weight, a'_{oo} = smoothed illumination at the center cell (o,o).

(2) Quantization, to change the picture into a black and white representation:

if $a'_{oo} \geqslant$ quantization level, then $a'_{oo} = 1$ = black cell; if $a'_{oo} <$ quantization level, then $a'_{oo} = 0$ = white cell.

(3) Detection of contours:

if $a'_{oo} = 1$ and $0 < \sum_{j=1}^{6} a'_{1j} \leqslant 5$ then cell (o,o) or a'_{oo} is on a contour.

(4) Computation of curvatures of contours: A measure of curvature (Coo) at cell (o,o) is computed from

$$Coo = a'_{oo} + \sum_{j=1}^{6} a'_{1j} + \sum_{j=1}^{12} a'_{2j}$$

(5) Smoothing of curvature values:

$$C'oo = (Wo\ Coo + \sum_{j=1}^{6} C_{1j})/(Wo + n)$$

where: n = number of cells with curvature. Wo = a weight. C′oo = smoothed curvature at (o,o).

(6) The direction of the curvature $\psi(o,o)$ at the cell (o,o) is an important variable, but is not required in the present problems.

(7) The center of interest (COFI): The COFI is generally defined as the location (cell (i^*, j^*)) of the extremum value of a function (F) defined over a neighbourhood K in L. Thus cell $(i^*, j^*) = \underset{i,j \text{ in } K}{\text{extremum}}\, F$;
F may depend on all variables in K, which have been found during preliminary processing. The secondary processing stage in the practical cases has always been object-dependent and so far only relatively simple cases have been studied.

In the first case, the center of interest (cell (i^*, j^*)) was obtained as follows: Let D(i,j) = the distance to the closest contour at cell (i,j) in L, then

$$\text{(7a) cell } (i^*, j^*) = \text{local maximum of } D(i,j).$$

The principal directions of D(i,j) form the skeleton of the figure (Reference 2,3). For a simple body there is only one isolated COFI. A more complicated body has several isolated COFI's and may thus be considered to have been broken down into separate objects.

A computationally faster method is obtained by computing the distances $D(i^n, j^n, \theta)$ from a cell (i^n, j^n) to the contours in several angular directions (θ) and correcting the cell position to cell (i^{n+1}, j^{n+1}) with an adaptive algorithm, where:

$$D_x\,(i^{n+1}, j^{n+1}) = \sum_{\theta} D\,(i^n, j^n, \theta) \cos\theta;\; i^{n+1} = i^n + cD_x\,(i^{n+1}, j^{n+1})$$

$$D_y\,(i^{n+1}, j^{n+1}) = \sum_{\theta} D\,(i^n, j^n, \theta) \sin\theta;\; j^{n+1} = j^n + cD_y\,(i^{n+1}, j^{n+1})$$

(7b)

$n = 0, 1, 2, \ldots m$; c = a constant; until $D_x\,(i^m, j^m) \to 0$ and $D_y\,(i^m, j^m) \to 0$ which implies that cell (i^m, j^m) approaches the center of interest.

The formulation of a decision space has been problem-dependent in all practical cases.

Example 1

Figure 2 shows a microscope photograph of water droplets captured in oil. The problem is to recognize these droplets and to form a histogram of their masses.

The solution to this problem contains steps 1, 2, 3 and 7b. For each center of interest, the radii ($r_1(\theta)$, $r_2(\theta)$) (as functions of angular directions (θ)) are measured to the first and second contours, as seen from the center of interest. The standard deviation (δr_1)of r_1 is computed. The one dimensional decision space in the recognition process is given by $\delta r_1/r_1 = K$. If $K <$ some limit, the center of interest is in the middle of the drop in the white area, since this area is fairly round. The mass of the droplet is computed from the average value of $r_2(\theta)$. Some logic is used to select only those measurements or $r_2(\theta)$ where the drop is not in contact with other drops. The "new moon" shaped reflection inside the drop may be eliminated during photographing. For very small droplets only $r_2(\theta)$ can be used.

Example 2 – Reference 4

Figure 3 shows a microphotograph of nerve fiber cross-sections. The problem is to form a histogram of the sizes of the fibers.

The solution required steps 1, 2, 3, 4, 5 and 7b. Again the radii from the center of interest to the first ($r_1(\theta)$) and to the second($r_2(\theta)$) contour were measured. The curvature values at these points ($c_1(\theta)$), $c_2(\theta)$) were also obtained. The standard deviation (δr_1) and average values r_1 and c_1 of $r_1(\theta)$ and $c_1(\theta)$ were used in a two-dimensional decision space with axes $\delta r_1/r_1$ and $r_1 c_1$, since the fibers are essentially circular. Preliminary logic eliminated all objects that were partially outside the picture or had too thick walls. The remaining objects were separated manually into fibers and non-fibers (usually inter-fiber spaces). Figure 4a shows the fibers and 4b shows the non-fibers when plotted in the decision space. The rectangular area was sub-divided and to each sub-division a confidence level of recognition assigned. The mistakes consisted of very symmetrical inter-fiber spaces, which were recognized as fibers, and in rejecting very thin or small fibers. Both types of errors depend greatly on the resolution of the scanner. By eliminating the wall-thickness test, this program recognizes the water droplets in Example 1.

Conclusions

The general black and white problem, as defined, can be solved relatively easily if the bodies to be recognized are not much different from the objects located by the center of interest algorithms. More complicated problems are under study.

Acknowledgements

The author gratefully acknowledges the support from the National Research Council of Canada.

Appendix

In order to avoid ambiguities, a few definitions are required. The definitions here will be given under the assumption that the pattern recognition procedure is simulated in a computer.

A PICTURE: A two-dimensional array L of numbers. Each number is proportional to the illumination at the corresponding picture element. The elements of L are in the same relative position to each other as the original picture elements.

A CELL: An alternate name for a picture element or a number in the array L.

AN OBJECT: Anything in the picture on which a recognition algorithm will be applied.

CONTOUR: A black cell is on a contour if any one of its immediate neighbours is white, and vice versa.

A BLACK CELL: A black picture element.

A WHITE CELL: A white picture element.

CURVATURE OF A CONTOUR: $\Delta\theta/\Delta s$. The change of the angle $\Delta\theta$ of the tangent to a contour within a cell-assembly (of size Δs).

BODY: The "things" to be recognized in a picture, for example, water drops, fiber cross-sections, etc.

THE FIRST CONTOUR: The contour that is encountered first in any search for contours, starting from the center of interest outwards in a radial direction.

REFERENCES

1. T. Kasvand, Computer Simulation of Pattern Recognition by Using Cell-Assemblies and Contour Projection. Proceedings of the IFAC Tokyo Symposium on Systems Engineering for Control System Design, 1965, pp. 203–210.

2. H. Blum, A machine for performing visual Recognition by use of antenna-propagation concepts. Wescon 1962. August 21–24, 1962. Paper 6.4.

3. A. Rosenfeld and J. L. Pfaltz, Sequential Operations in Digital Picture Processing. Journal of the Assoc. of Computing Machinery, Vol. 13, No. 4, October 1966, pp. 471–494.

4. T. Kasvand, Pattern Recognition Applied to the Measurement of Nerve Fiber Cross-Sections. National Research Council Report (LTR–CS–2).

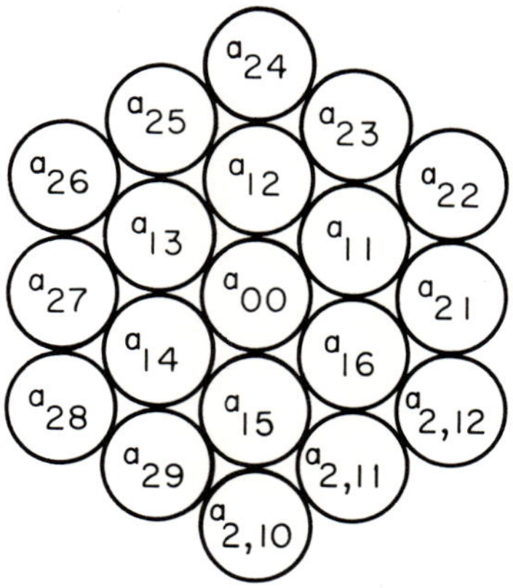

Figure 1: An Assembly of Hexagonally Placed Cells

a_{oo} = Center Cell

a_{1j} ($j = 1,2, \ldots, 6$) Cells on First Layer

$a_{2,j}$ ($j = 1,2, \ldots, 12$) Cells on Second Layer

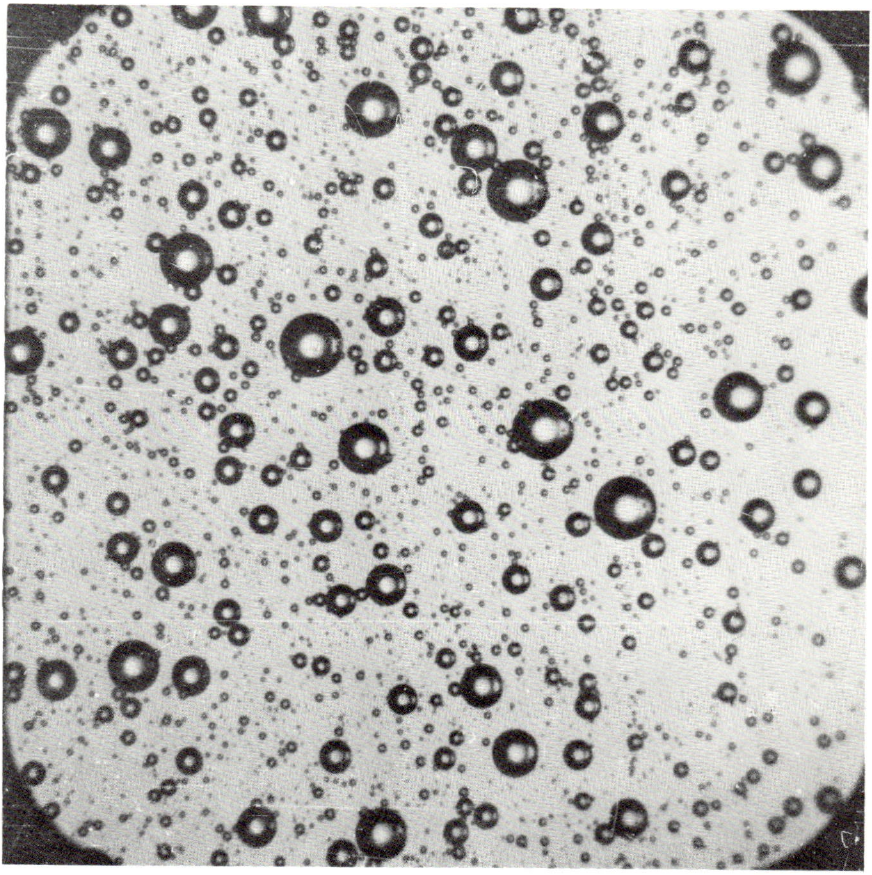

Figure 2: Picture of Microscopic Water Droplets

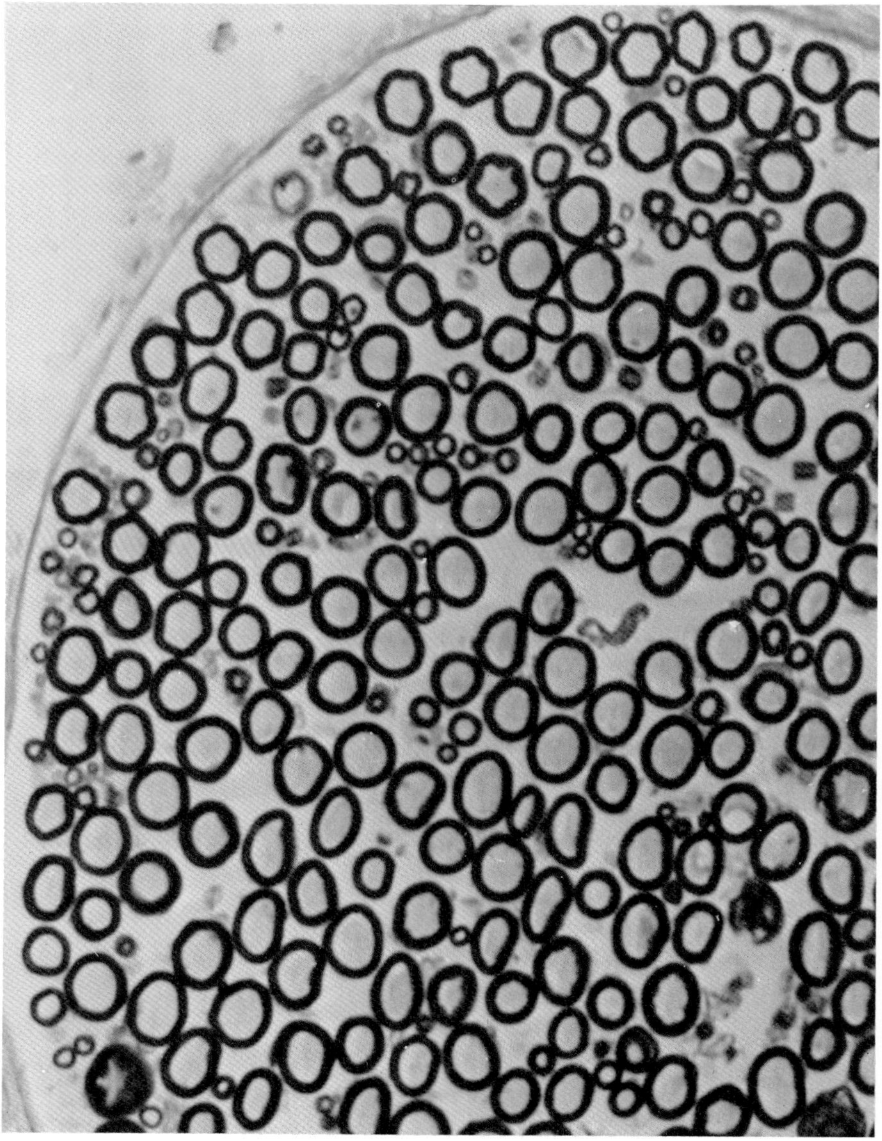

Figure 3: Picture of Nerve Fiber Cross-Sections

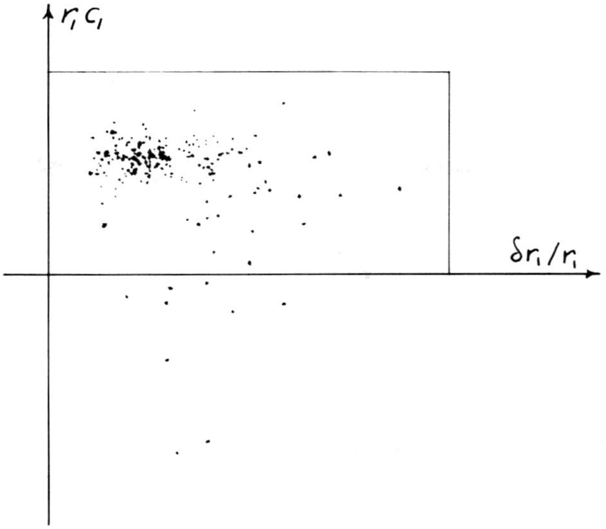

Figure 4a: Decision Space Plot of Nerve Fiber Cross-Sections After Manual Separation

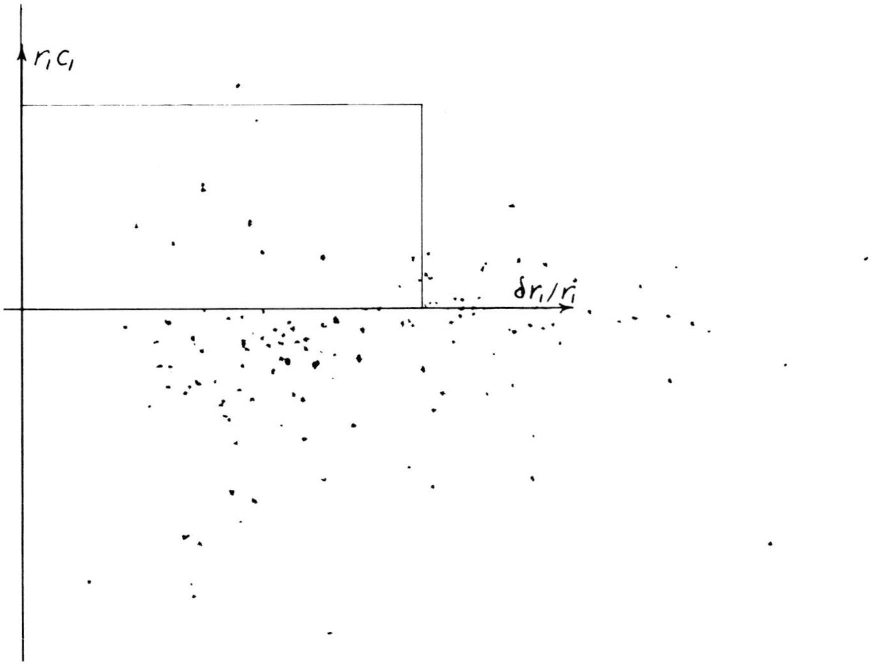

Figure 4b: Decision space plot of non-fibers which were passed by preliminary recognition logic.

RECOGNITION BY IMITATING THE PROCESS OF PATTERN GENERATION

V. A. Kovalevsky

INSTITUTE OF CYBERNETICS
UKRAINIAN ACADEMY OF SCIENCES
KIEV, U. S. S. R.

The main result of studying the pattern recognition problem at present is the conclusion of its great difficulty. This difficulty originates from the very intricate structure of the pattern sets in most practical tasks.

To exemplify this intricacy let us consider the set of signals arising at the outputs of a lightsensitive mosaic or a retina when projecting characters on it. Such signals will be referred to as multidimensional vectors. The set of signals arising at various translations of one and the same character along the retina cannot be described by analytical equations or by a sufficiently simple and well-studied probability distribution.

The analysis of properties of this set shows that in geometrical terms it must be conceived as a broken hypersurface winding in the multidimensional space in a whimsical manner. To confirm this it is sufficient to mention that in this space no three points associated with three translations of the same character lie on one straight line. Indeed, by averaging the brightness distributions of two translations of the same character we can never obtain a third translation of it (Figure 1). The multidimensional distance between two patterns of the same character depends upon a translation parameter not monotonically. As an instance one can consider vertical translations of a character E against another fixed one of the same shape starting from the coincidence position. The number of black and white retina meshes which agree for both patterns is firstly decreasing but later on it increases again. This non-monotony is an argument in favour of conceiving the set under consideration as a surface bent like a spiral.

Thus the pattern sets cannot be considered as convex ones even approximately. Therefore the illustrations accompanying many works on pattern recognition and representing either convex sets or unions of a few convex sets are absolutely not suitable even for the simplest problem of recognition of one-font characters at arbitrary translations.

In fact the set of such patterns may be satisfactorily approximated by a union of as many convex sets as the number of different retina meshes entered by a fixed point of the pattern at all possible translations. Some arguments in favour of this statement are given by Shlesinger and Svjatogor[1].

If the patterns differ besides translation also by scale, rotation, proportions, etc., then the corresponding sets have a still more intricate structure. Therefore, neither the known statistical methods nor the numerous heuristical approaches, most of which use separation of convex sets by hyperplanes, yield a satisfactory truth of recognition. All the known experiments on automatic recognition show an error probability much greater than that of recognizing the same patterns by human. Only for printed characters of fixed shape the truth of recognition is satisfactory.

Two Statements of the Problem

There are two known statements of the recognition-with-learning-problem. One of them proceeds from a given set of decision functions; the second one from a model describing the sets of signals for each of the distinguished classes.

The first of the said statements is as follows. A set F of possible decision functions $f_i(v)$ is given, each of which defines a certain classification of the signals v, i.e., the value of $f_i(v)$ for a given signal v indicates the class to which v must belong. Also, a learning sample is given which consists of 1 values v_j of the signal v ($j = 1, 2, \ldots, 1$), each v_j being associated with a corresponding value of $f(v_j)$. It is necessary to select from the given set F that function $f_s(v)$ which assumes the given values for all v_j from the learning sample.

It is supposed the set F and the learning sample to be such that the values of $f_s(v)$ are "true" also for that v which are not present in the sample.

This statement of the problem is considered in many works on recognition. In some of them it is clearly formulated[2], in some other[3] it is only implicit. (A much greater number of authors gives no statement at all, and no one knows what problem they solve).

The cited statement has some material shortcomings. The first one consists in the necessity of complying the power of the set F of decision functions with the volume of learning sample. In fact, it is easy to notice the analogy between the formulated problem and one of extrapolating a function from a given class. If we claim the sought-for function to be assuming some exactly defined values at given points, then the problem is in principle equivalent to solving a system of equations. If the number of parameters defining a certain function in the set F is smaller than the number of independent signals v_j in the sample, the equations are incompatible. But if, on the contrary, the set F is too extensive, the problem has no definite solution. The second case is the most frequent: because of lack of a priori information no essential restrictions are imposed on the functions $f_i(v)$ and the restoration of a function of a multidimensional argument encounters unsurmountable computational difficulties[4].

The second shortcoming is that one does not know how to choose the class of possible decision functions to insure correct decisions for the signals not presented in the learning sample. Numerous attempts have been made to overcome this difficulty by finding the so-called informative features, i.e., some functions of v which are a priori known to keep more or less constant values for one class, and hence suitable to be a base for extrapolation. It is felt intuitively that such features exist and that human recognition uses something like that. However the attempts to find them are not a success up till now. And what is more the problem of finding informative features as some kind of functions of v has even no definite statement, i.e., it is not clear what is to be found. All statements familiar to the author are not satisfactory since the function of v most suitable from the standpoint of these statements always turns out to be the optimal decision function f(v) itself.

To find a suitable set of decision functions which gives the hope that a function selected by a learning sample will be proper also for the signals not participating in learning, it is necessary to know the properties of the sets of signals to be recognized. These properties are exactly the point which the second statement proceeds from. The statement is close to that of statistical decision theory.

Let us consider the second statement firstly not in the most general form. We shall assume as known that the observed signals v may be represented as values of a known multidimensional (i.e., vectorial) function E(k,a,b) of some parameters these values being perturbed by random interference or noise r:

$$v = E(k,a,b) + r \qquad (1)$$

The parameters which E(k,a,b) depends on are of three kinds. One of them denoted by k is to be estimated as a result of the recognition (or description) process. The values of two other parameters a and b are of no interest for us but nevertheless they must be taken into account because the signal depends on them. The parameter a keeps a constant but unknown value for a given problem and b changes from one observation to another. The quantity E(k,a,b) can be interpreted as a *reference signal* or *reference pattern* which might appear in the absence of noise. The probability density $p_n(r)$ of noise is supposed to be known.

Given a learning sample, it is necessary to estimate the constant parameter a and then to find an optimal in a certain sense rule which associates to each observed value of v a certain value of the sought-for parameter k.

Such statement may seem to possess the same shortcomings as the first one does because if the function (1) and the probability distribution

$p_n(r)$ are unknown, the same difficulty arises as in the case when the class of decision functions is unknown. It would be true if one should rely only upon the empirical data of learning when looking for the said unknown functions. Indeed, the same reasons which render the restoration of a multidimensional argument decision function practically impossible without material a priori data, make also impossible to restore multivariate probability distribution. Even for a very rough description of an arbitrary N-dimensional distribution one has to define at least 2^N numbers. It is impracticable if N is greater than 50.

However, the second statement implies the use of all the stock of knowledge about the nature and properties of the signals to be recognized. The use of the model (1) does not require studying unknown distributions, since on the base of available information about the nature of the random interference it can be satisfactorily described in most cases by some known distribution, for instance by a normal one. In fact, if a recognition system is optimal with Gaussian noise it can be easily conceived that the system will work well enough also at any other noise distribution having not very great dispersion. Thus, the whole intricacy of the signal set is contained not in the distribution $p_n(r)$ but in the parametric dependence E(k,a,b).

The parameters k, a and b define various conditions under which the signal is generated. Hence the object of learning the signal model (1) can be attained by studying the process of signal generation. Such a study must be based on using the knowledge accumulated by the branch of science which the practical task to be solved relates to. Though being beyond formalization the said study is a very usual process in natural sciences and engineering.

The distinction between the two statements consists in the following. The available data should be expressed in the first statement in a form of a suitable collection of possible boundary surfaces enveloping each set. These surfaces are to be described by functions defined on the space V of observed signals v. This is difficult to perform in the case of non-convex intricate sets.

The second statement expects the same sets to be described by defining some under-dimensional skeletons or “regression lines” which the sets are threaded on. Such a skeleton is to be described in a parametric form, the parameters being interpreted as factors effecting the process of signal generation.

The most substantial is the methodological distinction of both statements: the second statement shows a way directly to solving concrete practical tasks by studying the signal generation process. The way to solve a problem formulated in terms of the first statement is the same, but we arrive at this conclusion only on the base of all arguments given above, and after arriving at it we have essentially to reject the first statement and to replace it by the second one, since the deduction of a class of suitable decision functions from a model of signals just means to solve the problem in terms of the second statement.

The Parametric Model with Non-Additive Noise

In practical tasks one often has to consider non-additive noise. For instance, when using binary quantization of the signal components it is not convenient to describe the noise as a random summand. A more general way to state random interference, which way retains the concept of reference pattern and hence holds the possibility to describe distributions with complex spatial configuration is as follows.

Let $p(v/E)$ be a multivariate distribution defined on the N-dimensional space V of signals v and depending on an N-dimensional parameter E. The possible values of E belong to the same space V. Assume the parameter E to be either equal to the mathematical expectation of $p(v/E)$ or bound with it by a simple linear dependence. Such parameter E we shall call a *reference pattern* for the signals v distributed according to $p(v/E)$. By varying the reference E we can, speaking figuratively, put the cloud of the distribution $p(v/E)$ in any place of the space V. If the reference depends, as before, on the parameters k, a and b, the signals appearing at certain values of these parameters have the distribution

$$p(v/E(k,a,b)) \qquad (2)$$

Defining this distribution in the form (2) instead of the most general form $p(v/k,a,b)$, one can describe by usual analytical means very complex distributions having a shape of a cloud enveloping the trajectory of the point $E(k,a,b)$ which it traces while the parameter b is varying. This parameter may be multidimensional and then the trajectory will be a multidimensional variety in the space V, although the number of its dimensions is, as a rule, much less than that of the space V.

The model (1) is a particular case of the model (2) corresponding to

$$p(v/E(k,a,b)) = p_n(v-E(k,a,b)) \, .$$

If, for instance, the distribution (2) is multivariate normal having the $E(k,a,b)$ as its mean, we have the case of Gaussian additive noise.

Consider as another example the case of a binary space V when each component of v assumes only two numbers: $v_m=0,1$ $(m = 1, 2, \ldots, N)$ and is irrelevant to other components. Distribution (2) can then be expressed by a product of distributions of individual components:

$$p(v/E(k,a,b)) = \prod_{m=1}^{N} p^*(v_m/E_m(k,a,b)). \qquad (3)$$

The individual distribution p* is defined by two numbers:

$$p^*(1/0) = \alpha \quad \text{and} \quad p^*(0/1) = \beta \quad , \qquad (4)$$

where α is the probability of a reference zero component to be converted to a unity component of the signal; β – analogous probability of distortion of a unity component.

If the probabilities α and β are equal the probability (2) is expressed through the Hamming distance h:

$$p(v/E(k,a,b)) = (1-\alpha)^{N-h}\, \alpha^h \quad ,$$

where N is the total number of components, h is the Hamming distance between the binary vectors v and E(k,a,b), i.e., the number of out-of-step components of these vectors.

To summarize the aforesaid, let us formulate the basic hypothesis of the present work.

For the most applied recognition problems, it is possible after studying the process of signal generation to describe the latter by means of a parametric set of reference patterns and some simple and well-studied probability distribution of interference, i.e., to design a model of signals like that of (2). The parameters which the reference pattern depends on are subdivided into sought-for, constant and varying. Then the problem of learning consists in estimating the constant parameters on the base of a learning sample. The recognition problem implies the finding of a decision rule, optimal in some sense, which assigns to each possible signal a certain estimate of the sought-for parameter.

Composite Hypotheses and Maximum Likelihood

The presented formulation of the recognition problem makes it possible to consider this problem as testing composite statistical hypotheses[5]. Really, on learning, when an estimate is put in place of the parameter a, the model (2) defines a probability distribution for the signal v depending on parameters k and b. Each hypothesis on the sought-for parameter k is associated with many distributions corresponding to different values of b.

It is known[5], that such problem can be solved by the maximum likelihood method. The probability density (2) for the observed signal v, being considered as a function of parameters, is called the likelihood function. The values of k and b which maximize the likelihood function (2) for a given v are called the maximum-likelihood estimates of those parameters.

The likelihood function (2) which depends on the signal v and the reference E can be interpreted as a quantitative measure of their *resemblance*. Using the formal concepts of reference pattern and resemblance, the recognition problem can be considered as the finding among a given parametric set of reference patterns that one which has the greatest resemblance to the given signal.

Generally the reference depends on many parameters and hence the finding of the maximum resemblance is confronted with great computational difficulties. Only in the simplest case of recognition of fixed shape printed characters the problem can be solved in a rather simple way[6]. Indeed, in this case a reference is characterized only by four parameters: contrast, mean brightness and translations along two perpendicular axes. The maximum resemblance can be found by calculating the correlation which is invariant with respect to the first two parameters and by scanning all possible translations.

If the number of parameters is greater, modern optimization methods should be employed deriving benefit from particular properties of the functions which describe the dependence of resemblance on the reference parameters.

There are many applied recognition problems for which the set of references can be defined by a constructive procedure consisting in composing the reference patterns of some elementary parts. If the resemblance function meets certain conditions as, for instance, to be represented as a sum of functions each depending on a single elementary part, the global maximum of resemblance can be found by dynamic programming without the scanning of all possible reference patterns. In this case the finding of the most resembling reference pattern is similar to the optimal control of the process of composing such a pattern.

Recognition of Handprinted Characters

Consider as an example a somewhat simplified problem of handprinted character recognition. A general scheme for solving problems of that kind has been stated by the author before[7].

Let the process of composing a reference character on a rectangular retina of N meshes be a sequence of elementary steps each of which consists in blackening one mesh of the retina. A subsequent mesh to be blackened can be chosen from a set D of meshes allowed at that step. This set depends on the process state conditioned by the shape of the character part already constructed and by that which mesh has been blackened last. Thus, to specify the state of the process after i elementary steps it is necessary to name the coordinate vector ρ_i of the last blackened mesh and the type z_i of the shape constructed before.

After blackening one of the meshes allowed in a given state, a transition to a new state is performed. The new state (z_{i+1}, ρ_{i+1}) is dependent on the previous one (z_i, ρ_i) and on the choice of one of the allowed meshes:

$$z_{i+1} = Z(z_i , \Delta\rho_{i+1}) , \tag{6}$$

$$\Delta\rho_{i+1} \in D(z_i) , \tag{7}$$

$$\rho_{i+1} = \rho_i + \Delta\rho_{i+1} \tag{8}$$

The relations (6) and (7) can be conveniently represented by an oriented graph the vertices of which correspond to different values of z and the edges or arrows—to different $\Delta\rho$. The set of arrows starting from a vertex z_i determines the set $D(z_i)$ in (7). The vertex z_{i+1} which an arrow $\Delta\rho_{i+1}$ starting from z_i is passing to, indicates the value of the function $Z(z_i ,$ $\Delta\rho_{i+1})$ in (6).

To simplify the explanation, let us take only that characters which can be composed of straight lines and by a single stroke. Such characters are Russian Б , Г ,И , Л ,М, П , Р ,С , Ь , and others. The process of constructing these characters (not taking into account the restrictions imposed on the length of segments)can be explained by the simplified graphs shown in Figure 2. These graphs show the successive change in the segment directions. The origin of a next segment is attached to the end of a previous one. Each graph has several initial points marked by circles and a single final point marked by a cross. A straight segment is constructed by adding black meshes in a necessary direction. This procedure has been described in detail before[7]. It is allowed at each step either to continue the construction of a segment having a chosen direction, or to pass over to the next direction allowed by the graph. To construct an admitted reference pattern of some character, it is necessary to pass along one of the graphs from an initial state to the final one.

We shall use the simplest model of noise (5) prescribing the finding of the admitted reference pattern which is the closest in the sense of Hamming to the pattern to be recognized. The Hamming distance can be expressed through the components v_m of the given pattern and the components E_m of the references:

$$h = \sum_{m=1}^{N} (v_m(1-E_m) + (1-v_m)E_m), \tag{9}$$

where N is the number of retina meshes. The components v_m and E_m assume only two values: 0 for the white meshes and 1 for the black ones. The expression (9) can be transformed to single out a term being calculated by summation over the black meshes of the reference pattern only.

$$h = \sum_{m=1}^{N} v_m - \sum_{m=1}^{N} (2v_m-1)E_m = B(v) - \phi(v,E) ,$$

$$\text{where } B(v) = \sum_{m=1}^{N} v_m$$

$$\text{and } \phi(v,E) = \sum_{m=1}^{N} (2v_m - 1)E_m \; . \qquad (10)$$

The first summand B(v) does not depend on the reference pattern and is equal to the number of black meshes of the given pattern. The second term $\phi(v,E)$ is calculated by summing the quantity $(2v_m - 1)$ over all black meshes of the reference pattern, i.e., over all elementary parts which the latter consists of. Hence, the quantity $\phi(v,E)$ meets the said conditions which make possible the use of dynamic programming. We name this quantity the resemblance of the patterns v and E. Such a name does not contradict the definition of resemblance proposed above, since the likelihood function (5) depends on $\phi(v,E)$ monotonically (if $h \leqslant N/2$).

Consequently, the problem is as follows. Given a binary pattern v, it is necessary to construct in accordance with the rules (6), (7) and (8) such a sequence of black meshes which maximizes the sum (10). This problem can be solved by dynamic programming[8]. The computational procedure in application to pattern recognition is described in detail in a said work of the author[7].

Experiments have been conducted by means of a computer equipped with an optical scanner. The graphs defining the admitted reference patterns were complicated to some degree so that the segments which a character consisted of might be not strictly rectilinear. They could deviate rather materially from an ideal straight line keeping a certain direction only on an average. The size of the retina was 20 x 20 meshes.

Figure 3 shows a quantized pattern put into the computer, and the references Б , Р and П closest to that pattern. Each reference is accompanied by the corresponding value of the resemblance function $\phi(v,E)$.

A decision is taken in favour of that reference which has the greatest resemblance. The time consumed by the computer to recognize one character is equal to the duration of 250 thousand two-address operations.

About 50 such experiments were carried out up till now. They did not pursue the accumulation of data for error statistics. "Difficult" patterns were intentionally selected to discover the weak points of the algorithm. Such weak points turned out to be: the fixed thickness of the reference lines which sometimes badly disagreed with the line thickness of a given pattern; too much freedom in deviation from the main direction when constructing a segment; no restrictions which could insure true size proportions of some parts of the character.

It is obvious that the first two shortcomings can be eliminated. Due to the third shortcoming some patterns having quite extraordinary proportions of parts may appear among the reference patterns constructed in accordance with the graphs of Figure 2. We fail to introduce necessary restrictions since the complexity of the solution increases very much. Therefore, after finding the most resembling reference pattern, it is necessary to check the proportions of its parts and, if they do not meet certain restrictions, to come to the reject decision. If, however, the restrictions are met, then the found solution evidently coincides with one of the problem including the restrictions. Thus, the neglection of the proportion restrictions in constructing a reference increases the probability of rejection but not that of errors.

Conclusion

There are two main difficulties in the field of recognition. The first one originates from a great variety of the observed signals; the second from the presence of interference. Most methods of recognition proposed up till now are designed to overcome only one of them (at the best).

The recognition method suggested here combines efficient noise-proofness with great versatility. The noise-proofness is insured due to calculation of the resemblance carried out instead of checking the exact coincidence of the observed signal with one of the references. High versatility is achieved by defining a vast number of various reference patterns which nevertheless are not to be completely scanned to find the most resembling one. The formal statement of the problem enables one to judge of the range of the method applicability.

It should be noted that the suggested approach is rather general. Character recognition was described as an example only. By this approach a problem of separating a typed line without distinct blanks between characters has been solved[9]. T.K. Vintsjuk has achieved high probability in spoken word recognition[10]. Some theoretical premises for recognition of telegraph signals of non-standard duration are obtained by the author[11]. There is a hope for successful solution of the problem of bubble chamber photograph analysis.

The proposed approach may prove useful to obtain syntactic descriptions of pictures, i.e., to solve the problem set by R. Narasimhan[12]. One should use as a description of a noisy picture the parameters of the reference pattern most resembling this picture. The syntactic description rules are exactly the rules of reference pattern construction expressed here by relations (6), (7) and (8). For instance, the list of the segments which the reference pattern of Figure 3b consists of and the coordinates of their ends form a description of the character Б shown in Figure 3a.

The present work is not to be regarded as a description of a completed recognition method. It presents rather a methodological approach to the problem. To arrive at complete solutions even of the small number of the particular problems mentioned here many difficulties are still to be overcome.

Acknowledgement

The author wishes to thank his colleague V.M. Sharypanov for programming the computer, performing the experiments and making some improvements in the recognition algorithm.

REFERENCES

1. M.I. Schlesinger, L.A. Svjatogor, "On the Construction of References for Correlating Reading Automata," Information Processing Systems (Conference Proceedings), Vol. 3, pp. 129–139, Moscow, VINITI,1967.
2. M.A. Aiserman, Y.M. Braverman, L.I. Rozonoer, "Theoretical Foundations of the Method of Potential Functions for the Problem of Training Automata to Divide Input Situations into Classes," Automatika & Telemekhanika, Vol. 25, No. 6, Moscow, 1964.
3. F. Rosenblatt, "Principles of Neurodynamics," New York, 1962.
4. V.A. Kovalevsky, "Present and Future of Pattern Recognition Theory," Proceedings of IFIP Congress, v. 1, pp. 37–43, New York, 1965.
5. E.L. Lehmann, "Testing Statistical Hypotheses," New York, 1959.
6. V.A. Kovalevsky, "Pattern Recognition Method Based on Reference Pattern Transformations," Proceedings of IFIP Congress, v. 2, pp. 566–567, New York, 1965.
7. V.A. Kovalevsky, "Sequential Optimization in Pattern Recognition and Pattern Description," paper submitted for IFIP Congress, 1968 (Edinburgh).
8. R. Bellman, "Dynamic Programming," New York, 1957.
9. V.A. Kovalevsky, "Optimal Algorithm for the Recognition of Certain Sequences of Patterns," Journal Kibernetika, No. 4, pp. 75–80, Kiev, 1967.
10. T.K. Vintsjuk, "Recognition of Words in Verbal Speech by the Methods of Dynamic Programming," Journal Kibernetika, No. 1, pp. 81–88, Kiev, 1968.
11. V.A. Kovalevsky, "Application of Mathematical Programming for Character and Pattern Recognition," Proceedings of Vth International Congress on Cybernetics, Namur, 1967 (to be published).
12. R. Narasimhan, "Syntax-Directed Interpretation of Class of Pictures," Communications of the ACM, v. 9, No. 3, pp. 166–173, 1966.

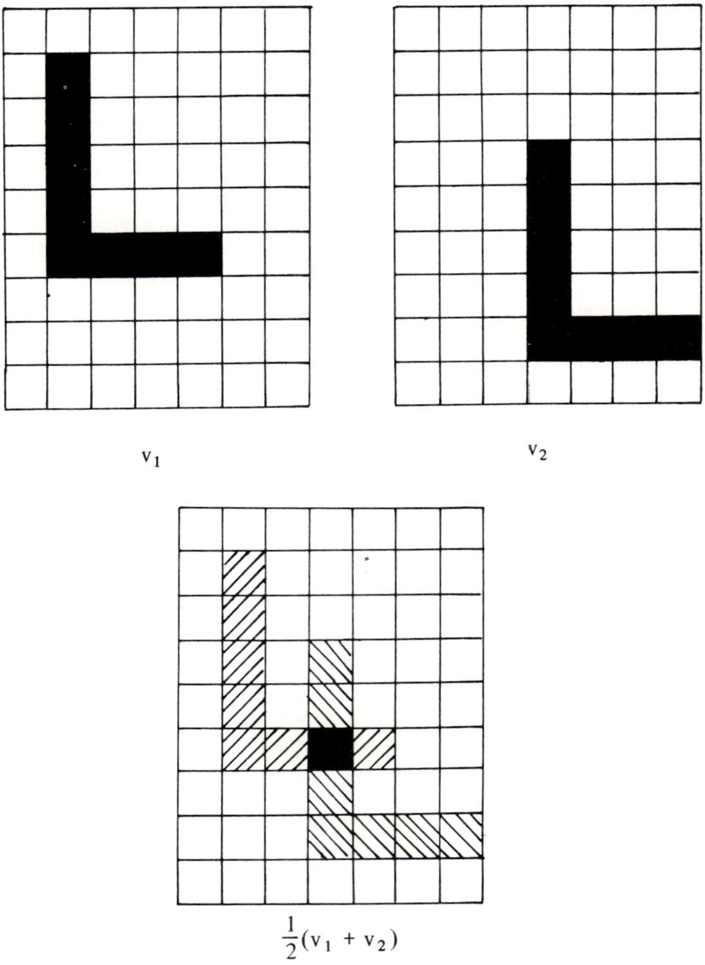

Figure 1: A linear combination of two translations of one and the same character does not produce a third translation of it.

Figure 2: Three graphs describing the sequence of directions when drawing different characters.

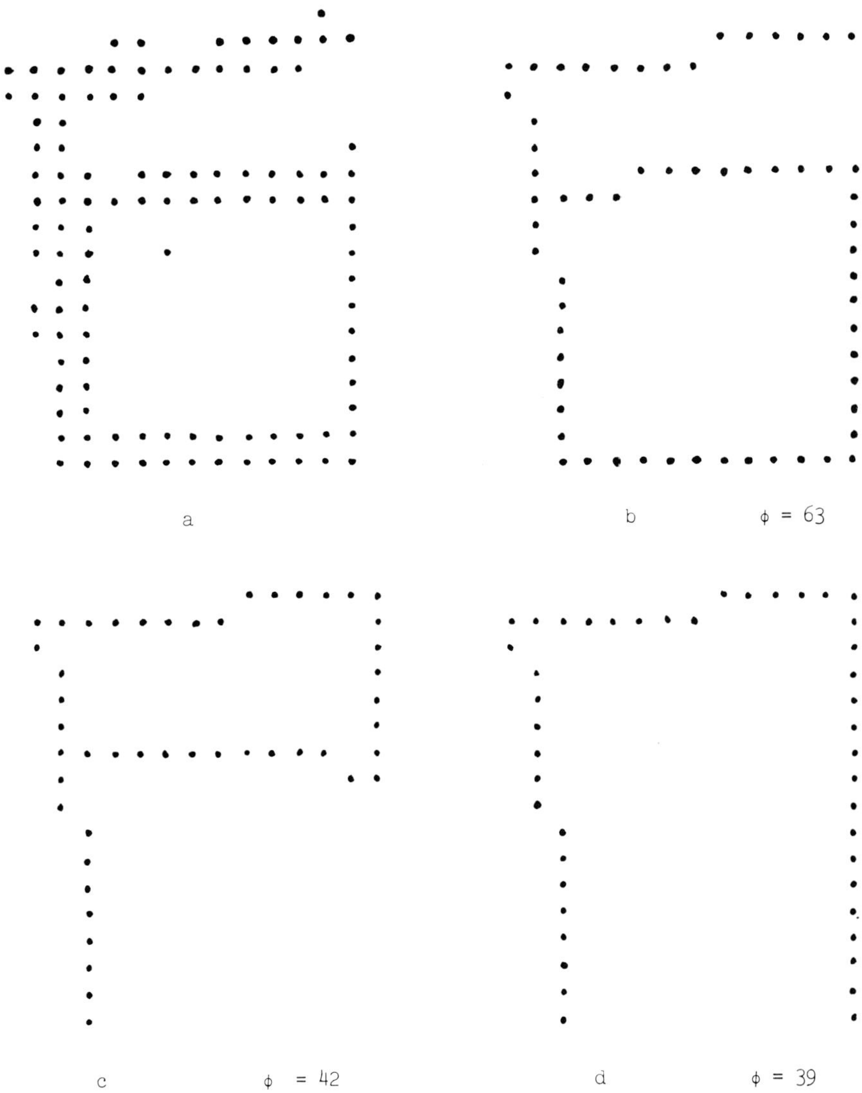

Figure 3: An input character (a), three most resembling reference patterns (b,c,d) found by the computer and the corresponding values of the resemblance function $\phi(v,E)$.

DESIGNING PATTERN CATEGORIZERS WITH EXTREMAL PARADIGM INFORMATION *

Peter F. Lambert †

1. Introduction

A pattern classification system can usually be considered to be comprised of two basic subsystems, (1) the receptor, which, by means of sensors, interacts with the physical representation of a pattern to produce a set of measurements $X = (x_1, \ldots, x_n)$ called the pattern measurement vector, and, (2) the categorizer, which makes a classificatory decision about each of the pattern measurement vectors transmitted to it by the receptor. If we assume that each pattern measurement vector is comprised of n real, continuous valued components, then the function of the receptor can be viewed as a mapping of each pattern into a single point in an n-dimensional Euclidean space R^n. If there are m pattern classes of interest, C_i, $i = 1, 2, \ldots, m$, the function of the categorizer is essentially to partition the space R^n by means of "decision surfaces" into m subspaces or "decision regions" R_j, $j = 1, 2, \ldots, m$ such that if a particular pattern measurement vector falls in R_j, then the associated pattern is assigned to pattern class C_j. A rejection decision and rejection region R_0 can be included for generality.

An important problem in pattern recognition system design concerns synthesis of the multi-dimensional decision surfaces of the pattern categorizer from given sets of previously identified sample pattern measurement vectors, or paradigms, representing each of the pattern classes to be distinguished. The purpose of this paper is to discuss the feasibility and implementation of two particular nonparametric design procedures for pattern categorizers employing hyperplane surfaces. The first of these procedures, called "Dead Zone Maximization", or DZM for brevity, assumes a class-pair

---

* The majority of this work was performed at Dunham Laboratory, Yale University, New Haven, Conn. and represents a condensation of portions of the author's doctoral dissertation. The work was supported in part by contract AF 19(628)–4804 with the Decision Science Laboratory, Electronic Systems Division, United States Air Force, L.G. Hanscom Field, Bedford, Mass.

† The author is presently with Bell Telephone Laboratories, Whippany, N. J.

dichotomization approach to the synthesis of the categorizer and is based on certain conditions for the orientation of a hyperplane decision surface dichotomizing the paradigms representing two pattern classes. These conditions apply to pairs of paradigm sets which are either linearly separable or linearly inseparable. In the linearly separable case, implementation of the DZM conditions results in a pair of parallel hyperplanes each of which perfectly separates the two paradigm sets in such a way that the half-spaces bounded by these hyperplanes and containing the paradigm sets are separated by a slab, or "dead zone", of maximal thickness. In the linearly inseparable case there is no separating hyperplane, however, implementation of the DZM conditions for this case results in a pair of parallel hyperplanes, each of which supports one of the paradigm sets in such a way that the half-spaces bounded by these hyperplanes and containing the paradigm sets intersect in a slab, or "negative dead zone", of minimal thickness.

The second procedure, called the "Method of Hyperparallelepipeds", (MHP) seeks to construct a "box" around each paradigm set in such a way that the box has a very close fit to the convex hull of the paradigm set. The simplified representation of a paradigm set by such a box facilitates certain decision procedures which can lead to final decision surfaces which are piecewise linear and quadric and decision regions which may be nonconvex and unconnected.

The mathematical problems posed by the DZM and MHP procedures are similar types of nonlinear programming problems and, hence, solution techniques based on nonlinear mathematical programming algorithms are feasible. These solution techniques are discussed and some experimental results are presented.

One of the common underlying characteristics of both the DZM and MHP procedures is that they are based on hyperplanes that support and/or separate the convex hulls of the paradigm sets. Since the convex hull of a point set is completely specified by its extreme points, then these procedures are relying essentially on the information contained in the extreme points, or extremal paradigms, of the paradigm sets. The dependence of categorizer design on extremal paradigm information is a central theme of this paper and its implications are discussed at several points. Before proceeding with a discussion of the two design criteria, therefore, let us develop some important concepts about extremal paradigms.

2. Extremal Paradigms

Let us assume that the categorizer is to be synthesized using a set Ω, of r paradigms. The set Ω consists of m subsets, Ω_i, each of which contains r_i paradigms representing pattern class C_i. Each of the sets Ω_i is assumed to span the space R^n, i.e. Ω_i is not contained in a deficient subspace of R^n. The set Ω_i^*, which is the convex hull of the paradigm set Ω_i, is comprised of all points X^* which are of the form,

$$X^* = \mathbf{M}_i V \quad (1a)$$

where

$$U^T V = 1 \quad (1b)$$

$$V \geqslant 0 \quad (1c)$$

In the above expressions, $\mathbf{M}_i$ is the $(n \times r_i)$ matrix whose r_i columns are the n-dimensional paradigms of the set Ω_i, V is an r_i-dimensional vector of "convex multipliers", U is an r_i-dimensional vector of ones, and 0 is an r_i-dimensional null vector. It should be noted here that all vectors are assumed to be column vectors and vector equalities or inequalities such as (1a) and (1c) are assumed to hold for each element of the vectors involved. The relations of (1) are simply mathematically compact expressions of the fact that X^* is a convex combination of all the paradigms, X, in the set Ω_i. A point $X_e^* \in \Omega_i^*$ is an "extreme point" of Ω_i^* if and only if it cannot be expressed as a convex combination of any other points in Ω_i^*. We will define a paradigm $X_e \in \Omega_i$ to be an "extremal paradigm" of Ω_i if and only if it is an extreme point of Ω_i^*. This definition can be stated mathematically as follows; X_e is an extremal paradigm of Ω_i if and only if the problem,

Minimize: $f(V) = v_e$ = convex multiplier in V which multiplies X_e (2a)

Subject to: $\mathbf{M}_i V = X_e$ (2b)

$$U^T V = 1 \quad (2c)$$

$$V \geqslant 0 \quad (2d)$$

has the solution, $f(V) = 1$. The problem of (2) is a linear programming problem and is a compact mathematical expression of the fact that a point X_e is an extreme point of the set Ω_i if and only if it cannot be expressed as a convex combination of any other points in that set. The quantities $\mathbf{M}_i$, V, U and 0 are identical to those in (1). Since $X_e \in \Omega_i$, then it appears as one column in the matrix $\mathbf{M}_i$ and the quantity v_e is the convex multiplier in V which multiplies X_e. We will define the matrix $\mathbf{M}_i^*$ as the matrix whose columns are the extremal paradigms of Ω_i.

If Ω_i consists of a finite number of points, then the convex hull Ω_i^* is a convex polyhedron and, hence, has a finite number of extreme points. In addition, the convex hull Ω_i^* is identical to the convex hull of the extreme points of Ω_i^*. This means that economy of expression or "information compression" can be obtained if the convex hull Ω_i^* is specified by using only the set of extreme points $\{X_e^*\}$ in (1) instead of the entire set of paradigms Ω_i, i.e. by using the matrix $\mathbf{M}_i^*$ instead of $\mathbf{M}_i$.

Our major interest in extremal paradigms is not motivated by the fact that they can provide economy of expression (at the expense of computation) in the specification of the convex hulls, but rather by the fact that when one deals with categorizer surfaces which bound, support, or separate convex hulls of paradigm sets, one is dealing strictly with the information contained in the extremal paradigms of those sets. The adaptive algorithms described by Rosenblatt [1], Mays [2], and Nilsson [3, Chap. 4], for example, are essentially iterative techniques for determining separating hyperplanes for pairs of convex hulls. Although the complete set of paradigms is used to determine the final separating hyperplane in these algorithms, a similar result could be achieved by iterating through only the extremal paradigms. The linear programming technique of Mangasarian [4] for determining a separating hyperplane for two paradigm sets would yield identical results if only the extremal paradigms were used. Even the technique described by Highleyman [5] for determining a hyperplane decision surface which dichotomizes two paradigm sets with minimum sample error reduces to finding a separating hyperplane for the convex hulls if one exists.

The dependence of separating hyperplanes on a particular subset of paradigms was recognized by Mays [6] and Cover [7] who noted that for any two point sets Ω_i and Ω_j there exists a minimal point set $Z_{ij} \subset (\Omega_i \cup \Omega_j)$ such that any hyperplane correctly separating the subsets $(Z_{ij} \cap \Omega_i)$ and $(Z_{ij} \cap \Omega_j)$ also correctly separates the sets Ω_i and Ω_j. The point set Z_{ij} was called the "boundary matrix" by Mays and the "set of extreme patterns" by Cover. It should be noted that the definition given above for extremal paradigms of a set Ω_i depends only on the geometry of the points making up that one set while the point set Z_{ij} is defined with respect to a linearly separable dichotomy of two sets Ω_i and Ω_j. Clearly the set Z_{ij} is contained in the set of extremal paradigms of Ω_i and Ω_j.

In the context of categorizer design we are concerned with such questions as; How reliable are design results which are based on the extreme point geometry of a random sampling of points? Can we expect reasonably similar results from two sets of paradigms obtained by random sampling from a given pattern class? These are difficult questions and the answer must be obtained in part by experimentation in real pattern situations. From a qualitative standpoint, it may be possible to answer these questions by isolating those extremal paradigms that are "instrumental" or "active" in determining the design result, eliminating them from the set and resolving the design problem with a "reduced" set of paradigms. If the design results are reasonably similar after one or more such eliminations, then we may feel reassured that the sensitivity of the design solution to a particular subset of extremal paradigms is low and hence that the solutions are relatively stable. It is shown in Section 3 that the determination of those extremal paradigms that are instrumental in the design result can be readily accomplished by several means.

3. The Dead Zone Maximization Criterion

Consider a categorizer which is to distinguish between m pattern classes by means of a complete set of $m(m-1)/2$ class-pair dichotomies. Each of these dichotomies is to be implemented by means of a hyperplane $H(W,w_0)$ with normal vector $W = (w_1, \ldots, w_n)$ and threshold constant w_0. These hyperplanes are to be synthesized using the set Ω of available paradigms.

Let $H = H(W,w_0)$ be a hyperplane which is to dichotomize pattern classes C_i and C_j. The decision procedure to be employed with H is the following,

$$\text{If } X^T W - w_0 \geqslant 0 \quad \text{then } X \in C_i \tag{3a}$$

$$\text{If } X^T W - w_0 < 0 \quad \text{then } X \in C_j \tag{3b}$$

Hence, all points in +HS, the positive half-space bounded by H, will be assigned to pattern class C_i while all points in −HS, the negative half-space bounded by H, will be assigned to pattern class C_j. All points in the hyperplane H are arbitrarily assigned to C_i.

The Dead Zone Maximization criterion for the hyperplane H is the following [8,9],

$$\text{Maximize:} \quad D = (\alpha-\beta)/\gamma \tag{4a}$$

$$\text{Subject to:} \quad \mathbf{M}_i^T W - \alpha U_i \geqslant 0_i \tag{4b}$$

$$-\mathbf{M}_j^T W + \beta U_j \geqslant 0_j \tag{4c}$$

$$W^T W = \gamma^2 \tag{4d}$$

where,

r_i = number of paradigms in the set Ω_i representing pattern class C_i

r_j = number of paradigms in the set Ω_j representing pattern class C_j

$\mathbf{M}_i$ = $(n \times r_i)$ matrix whose r_i columns are the n-dimensional paradigms of the set Ω_i

$\mathbf{M}_j$ = $(n \times r_j)$ matrix whose r_j columns are the n-dimensional paradigms of the set Ω_j

W = n-dimensional column vector representing the normal to the decision hyperplane H

U_i, U_j = r_i and r_j-dimensional column vectors of ones

$0_i, 0_j$ = r_i and r_j-dimensional column vectors of zeros

α, β = scalars

γ = positive constant

$W^T W = \|W\|^2$ = square of norm of W

The inequalities (4b) and (4c) are simply mathematically compact expressions of the conditions,

$$X^T W - \alpha \geqslant 0 \qquad \text{all } X \in \Omega_i \tag{5a}$$

$$X^T W - \beta \leqslant 0 \qquad \text{all } X \in \Omega_j \tag{5b}$$

By comparison with (3) it can be seen that (4b) defines a hyperplane $H_\alpha = H(W,\alpha)$ which is parallel to H and which is positioned such that the paradigm set Ω_i is completely contained in $+HS_\alpha$, the positive half-space bounded by H_α. Similarly, (4c) defines a hyperplane $H_\beta = H(W,\beta)$ which is parallel to both H and H_α and which is positioned such that the paradigm set Ω_j is completely contained in $-HS_\beta$, the negative half-space bounded by H_β. Constraint (4c) insures that $\|W\| = \gamma > 0$ and hence the quantity D of (4a) is the directed distance from H_β to H_α. The directed distance has a magnitude equal to the actual Euclidean distance between H_α and H_β but its sign is positive if $\alpha > \beta$ and negative if $\alpha < \beta$. Figure 1 gives examples of the directed distance geometry in 2-space. Clearly, if $\alpha > \beta$ then $+HS_\alpha$ and $-HS_\beta$ do not intersect while if $\alpha < \beta$ then $+HS_\alpha$ and $-HS_\beta$ do intersect as indicated by the shaded region in (c) and (d) of Figure 1.

Figure 2 gives examples in 2-space of two parallel hyperplanes, H_α and H_β, which satisfy the inequalities of (4b) and (4c) for paradigm sets which are either linearly separable or inseparable. The individual paradigms are represented by the black dots.

As the above discussion indicates, the DZM criterion is a formal mathematical statement of the problem of determining a pair of parallel hyperplanes H_α and H_β such that $\Omega_i \subset +HS_\alpha$ and $\Omega_j \subset -HS_\beta$ and such that the directed distance from H_β to H_α is maximized. This maximum directed distance will hereafter be called the DZM maximum and will be denoted by D^*. The solution (W^*, α^*, β^*) which maximizes D^* will be called the DZM optimal solution and any pair of hyperplanes $H_\alpha^* = H(W^*,\alpha^*)$ and $H_\beta^* = H(W^*,\beta^*)$ satisfying the DZM criterion will be called DZM optimal. The hyperplanes of Figure 2 illustrate typical examples of DZM optimal hyperplanes in 2-space. It should be noted that the maximization of (4a) is to be understood in the positive sense and not in the sense of magnitude without regard to sign. Thus, if Ω_i and Ω_j are linearly separable, then the half-spaces $+HS_\alpha^*$ and $-HS_\beta^*$, bounded by a pair of DZM optimal hyperplanes, should be disjoint and separated by a slab of maximum thickness D^*. Since this slab has no paradigms from either Ω_i or Ω_j in its interior, it is a buffer slab or "dead zone region". If Ω_i and Ω_j are linearly inseparable, then the half-spaces $+HS_\alpha^*$ and $-HS_\beta^*$ must, of necessity, intersect and share a common slab, which, in general, contains paradigms from both Ω_i and Ω_j in its interior. Under the DZM criterion, this common slab should be of minimal thickness. If, for the sake of symmetry, we consider this common slab as a "negative dead zone region", then it becomes reasonable to call the criterion of (4) the Dead Zone Maximization criterion.

Since the convex hulls of the paradigm sets Ω_i and Ω_j are closed convex sets it is always possible to construct a pair of bounding hyperplanes such as H_α and H_β. Hence, a solution to the DZM problem is always realizable and it can be readily shown [4] that D* serves as a test for linear separability, D* being positive when Ω_i^* and Ω_j^* are linearly separable and negative or zero when Ω_i^* and Ω_j^* are linearly inseparable.

We can easily see from configurations of the type shown in Figure 3 that the DZM optimal solution, is not necessarily unique in the linearly inseparable case. It should be noted, however, that although easily constructed, the shaded intersections shown in Figure 3 represent rather specific geometrical situations, i.e. regular or symmetric polygons, which, in general, would have a low probability of occurrence in a random sampling situation. In general, one must make provision in the solution techniques for the possibility that the DZM solution is not unique.

In the linearly separable case it can be readily shown [8] that the DZM maximum D* must equal the distance between the convex hulls Ω_i^* and Ω_j^* and that the DZM optimal normal is unique and must have detection cosines which are identical to L*, the minimum length connector of Ω_i^* and Ω_j^*. The significance of this fact is made use of in Section 5.

A problem of the type being considered was first proposed by Pervozvanskii [10] as a means for obtaining a nonarbitrary solution to the problem of determining hyperplane decision surfaces by means of linear programming. The constraint (4d) on the norm of W, however, clearly implies that the problem is not a linear but a nonlinear programming problem and, hence, nonlinear mathematical programming solution techniques are needed. These techniques are discussed in Section 5.

It is instructive to examine the necessary conditions for a DZM optimal solution. The necessary conditions for a solution to an inequality constrained maximization of the type under consideration were developed in general form by Kuhn and Tucker [11] and are frequently called the Kuhn-Tucker necessary conditions. For the DZM problem these conditions can be normalized with respect to γ and written in the form [8],

$$M_i^T W^* - \alpha^* U_i \geqslant 0_i \tag{6a}$$

$$-M_j^T W^* + \beta^* U_j \geqslant 0_j \tag{6b}$$

$$W^{*T} W^* = 1 \tag{6c}$$

$$M_i\Lambda_i^* - M_j\Lambda_j^* = -2\gamma\lambda_0^* W^* \tag{6d}$$

$$U_i^T\Lambda_i^* = 1 \tag{6e}$$

$$U_j^T\Lambda_j^* = 1 \tag{6f}$$

$$\Lambda_i^* \geqslant 0_i \tag{6g}$$

$$\Lambda_j^* \geqslant 0_j \tag{6h}$$

$$[M_i^T W^* - \alpha^* U_i]^T \Lambda_i^* = 0 \tag{6i}$$

$$[M_j^T W^* - \beta^* U_j]^T \Lambda_j^* = 0 \tag{6j}$$

where λ_0^* is the Lagrange multiplier associated with the equality constraint (4d), Λ_i^* is the r_i-dimensional vector of Lagrange multipliers associated with the r_i inequalities of (4b ,) and Λ_j^* is the r_j-dimensional vector of Lagrange multipliers associated with the r_j inequalities of (4c). For this normalized case, D^* is given by $D^* = (\alpha^* - \beta^*)$.

The following important points can be ascertained from these conditions.

(1) The arbitrary constant, γ , in constraint (4d) represents only a scale factor for the DZM problem. This is evident from the fact that it can be lumped into the Lagrange multiplier λ_0^* of (6d) and can thereby be completely eliminated from the necessary conditions for a solution.

(2) The conditions (6d)–(6h) indicate that the DZM optimal normal W^* must be representable as the difference of two points, one of which is contained in Ω_i^* and the other of which is contained in Ω_j^*. This is evident since from (6d),

$$W^* = -\frac{1}{2\gamma\lambda_0^*}(X_i^* - X_j^*) \tag{7a}$$

where

$$X_i^* = M_i\Lambda_i^* \tag{7b}$$

$$X_j^* = M_j\Lambda_j^* \tag{7c}$$

Relations (7b), (6e), and (6g) are identical in form to (1a)–(1c) which are the necessary and sufficient conditions for X_i^* to be a point in Ω_i^*. Similarly $X_j^* \in \Omega_j^*$. This also points up the interesting fact that the vector of Lagrange multipliers Λ_i^* is equivalent to the vector of convex multipliers V in (1) and similarly for Λ_j^*. This fact is further demonstrated in Section 5 when the DZM problem is posed as a dual-form quadratic programming problem for the linearly separable case.

(3) Condition (6i) indicates that for all $k = 1, 2, \ldots, r_i$, either the paradigm $X_k \in \Omega_i$ satisfies

$$X_k W^* - a^* = 0 \tag{8}$$

or else $\lambda_{ik} = 0$, i.e. the Lagrange multiplier for that paradigm is zero. Since all λ_{ik} cannot be zero due to condition (6e) then at least one X_k must satisfy (8). Equation (8) signifies however that X_k lies in the hyperplane $H_a^* = H(W^*, a^*)$. Thus, there must be at least one or more paradigms of Ω_i which lie in H_a^* and only these paradigms will have nonzero Lagrange multipliers associated with them. A similar argument can be made for Ω_j and H_β^*. This result indicates that H_a^* must support Ω_i and H_β^* must support Ω_j. This fact, in conjunction with condition (7a), also indicates that the DZM optimal normal is expressible as a function of only those paradigms which lie in the DZM optimal hyperplanes. This latter set of paradigms will, in general, be comprised solely of extremal paradigms. This gives a direct indication of the dependence of the DZM solution on the extremal paradigms. In addition, it is these paradigms which, in Section 2, we called the "active" or instrumental extremal paradigms. Thus, to check the sensitivity of a DZM solution by means of iterative solution on "reduced" sets we may identify the active extremal paradigms by the fact that they lie in DZM optimal hyperplanes or else by the fact that they have nonzero convex multipliers associated with them.

4. The Method of Hyperparallelepipeds

Consider now the following iterative constrained maximization problem involving the paradigms from just the set Ω_i,

$$\text{Maximize:} \quad D_k = (a_k - \beta_k)/\gamma \tag{9a}$$

$$\text{Subject to:} \quad \mathbf{M}_i^T W_k - a_k U_i \geq 0_i \tag{9b}$$

$$-\mathbf{M}_i^T W_k + \beta_k U_i \geq 0_i \tag{9c}$$

$$W_k^T W_k = \gamma^2 \tag{9d}$$

$$W_{k-\ell}^T W_k = 0 \tag{9e}$$

$$\ell = 1, 2, \ldots, k-2, k-1$$

where (W_k, a_k, β_k) is the solution sought on the kth or most current iteration and $W_{k-\ell}$ is the vector obtained on the $(k-\ell)^{th}$ iteration of the problem. The quantities D, a, β, $\mathbf{M}_i$, W, U_i, and 0_i are identical to those discussed in connection with the DZM problem.

The problem of (9) has the following interpretation. On the first iteration, only constraints (9b)–(9d) are applicable. From our previous discussion of the DZM problem we can see that we are looking for a pair of parallel hyperplanes, $H_\alpha^{(1)} = H(W_1, \alpha_1)$ and $H_\beta^{(1)} = H(W_1, \beta_1)$, such that $\Omega_i \subset +HS_\alpha^{(1)}$ and, at the same time, $\Omega_i \subset -HS_\beta^{(1)}$ with D_k the directed distance from $H_\beta^{(k)}$ to $H_\alpha^{(k)}$ as before.

Figure 4 gives an example of the desired geometry for this first pair of hyperplanes. The maximization of D_1 under the constraints amounts to determining a solution $(W_1^*, \alpha_1^*, \beta_1^*)$ such that the hyperplanes $H_\alpha^{(1)}$ and $H_\beta^{(1)}$ are separated by a slab of minimum thickness, i.e., they are separated by minimum distance subject to the constraint that Ω_i lies between them. This problem is essentially identical in form and significance to the DZM problem for the linearly inseparable case. Let us assume that the first iteration has been completed and that a solution set $(D_1, W_1, \alpha_1, \beta_1)$ has been obtained. The vector W_1 is now used in a linear constraint of type (9e) and a new solution $(D_2, W_2, \alpha_2, \beta_2)$ is sought. It should be noticed that the constraints (9e) are orthogonality constraints on the current solution vector W_k, i.e. they require the current solution vector to be orthogonal to all previous solution vectors. Thus the solution hyperplanes $H_\alpha^{(2)}$ and $H_\beta^{(2)}$ must end up as close together as possible subject to the constraint that Ω_i lie between them and subject to the additional constraint that W_2 be orthogonal to W_1. Figure 4 indicates the desired geometry for this second pair of hyperplanes. It can be seen that as k goes from 1 to n, the pairs of parallel hyperplanes $(H_\alpha^{(1)}, H_\beta^{(1)}), (H_\alpha^{(2)}, H_\beta^{(2)}), \ldots, (H_\alpha^{(n)}, H_\beta^{(n)})$ will generate an n-dimensional hyperparallelepiped with orthogonal sides. We will call this orthogonal hyperparallelepiped a "box" for brevity. If a true constrained maximum of D_k is obtained at each iteration then the directed distance will be a monotonically decreasing function of the iteration index k, i.e.

$$D_1 > D_2 > \ldots D_k \tag{10}$$

Since $D_k < 0$ for all k, then this means that the actual distance between each pair of hyperplanes increases monotonically with the iteration index k. The volume v_b^i of the final box is given by

$$v_b^i = \prod_{k=1}^{n} -D_k = \prod_{k=1}^{n} |D_k| \tag{11}$$

Since the convex hull Ω_i^* is the smallest convex set containing the point set Ω_i, then we know that the volume, v_i^*, of Ω_i^* is a lower bound for the volume of any other convex body which contains Ω_i and Ω_i^*. Hence, the relation $v_b^i \geqslant v_i^*$ must be satisfied since a hyperparallelepiped is a convex body. Similarly, the difference $(v_b^i - v_i^*)$ must always be non-negative and if v_i^* were known, it would be a measure of the closeness of fit of the box to the convex hull Ω_i^*.

It is possible to generalize the problem of (9) so as to produce an n-dimensional hyperparallelepiped with sides which are not necessarily orthogonal. This can be done by replacing each of the orthogonality constraints of (9e) by the pair of linear inequalities,

$$c \geqslant W_{k-\ell}^T W_k \geqslant -c \tag{12}$$

where c is some positive constant less than γ^2. The pair of constraints of (12) requires that $\theta_{k\ell}$, the angle between $W_{k-\ell}$ and W_k satisfy,

$$0 < \cos^{-1}\left(\frac{c}{\gamma^2}\right) \leqslant \theta_{k\ell} \leqslant \cos^{-1}\left(-\frac{c}{\gamma^2}\right) < \pi \tag{13}$$

It is not completely clear whether the use of the more general constraint of (12) will lead to a hyperparallelepiped with a closer fit to the convex hull of the paradigm set Ω_i. In general, from Hadamard's inequality [12] we know that the volume of a hyperparallelepiped with side lengths D_k does not exceed the product of these side lengths, and it equals this product if and only if its sides are orthogonal as indicated by (11). If the final product of solutions D_k obtained at each iteration of the generalized problem is less than or equal to the final product of the orthogonality constrained solutions, then from Hadamard's inequality we know that the volume of the nonorthogonal hyperparallelepiped will be less than v_b^i and hence will yield a closer fit to the convex hull Ω_i^*.

As will be noted in Section 6, the orthogonal hyperparallelepiped offers some distinct advantages for simple specification of relatively complicated decision surfaces and, hence, in the remainder of the discussion we will presuppose the use of the orthogonality constrained problem of (9).

It should be noted here that the above method is not the only way to construct a box which contains Ω_i. One may, for example, determine the extreme values of Ω_i along each of the coordinate axes of the space R^n and define the box with faces orthogonal to these axes and intersecting them at the extreme values. One may also use a technique such as the Karhunen-Loève expansion discussed by Watanabe [13,14] to determine an orthogonal coordinate system whose axes are parallel to the eigenvectors of the sample covariance matrix of Ω_i. The extreme values of Ω_i along each of these axes may then be used to specify a box as above. Our interest in the method of (9) lies in the fact that it looks like a promising technique for generating a box which contains Ω_i and has a close fit to Ω_i^*. The close fit is important since in the decision procedures described in Section 5, each paradigm set is characterized in the space R^n by its enclosing box.

The discussion about the realizability and uniqueness of the DZM solution for the linearly inseparable case holds also for the solution to the problem of (9) at each iteration. It should be noted however that at each iteration of problem (9) there are always two possible normals, 180° apart, which will yield the same value of D. Hence, even though Max $\{D_k\}$ may be unique at the kth iteration the solution may be either (W_k, α_k, β_k) or $(-W_k, -\alpha_k, -\beta_k)$.

5. Implementation Procedures

Before proceeding with a discussion of general nonlinear programming solution techniques for the DZM and MHP problems, let us consider a solution technique which is valid for the DZM problem when the paradigm sets are linearly separable. It will be recalled that for the linearly separable case the DZM problem is identical to the problem of finding a minimum connector for the convex hulls of the sets Ω_i and Ω_j. Let L be any n-dimensional vector connecting a point $X_i^* \epsilon \Omega_i^*$ to a point $X_j^* \epsilon \Omega_j^*$. From (1), we know that L can be defined as follows,

$$L = X_i^* - X_j^* = \mathbf{M}_i V_i - \mathbf{M}_j V_j \tag{14}$$

where V_i and V_j, the vectors of convex multipliers, each satisfy (1b) and (1c).

The distance d between Ω_i^* and Ω_j^* is by definition,

$$d = \|L^*\| \tag{15}$$

where L^* is the minimum connector of Ω_i^* and Ω_j^*. Since L^* and d are unique for any given pair of linearly separable convex hulls, we may determine L^* by solving the following quadratic programming problem,

$$\text{Maximize:} \quad g(L, V_i, V_j) = -\tfrac{1}{2} L^T \mathbf{I}_n L \tag{16a}$$

$$\text{Subject to:} \quad \mathbf{M}_i V_i - \mathbf{M}_j V_j - L = 0_n \tag{16b}$$

$$U_i^T V_i = 1 \tag{16c}$$

$$U_j^T V_j = 1 \tag{16d}$$

$$V_i \geqslant 0_i \tag{16e}$$

$$V_j \geqslant 0_j \tag{16f}$$

where $\mathbf{I}_n$ is an n-dimensional identity matrix and where the quadratic form $L^T \mathbf{I}_n L = \|L\|^2$ is clearly positive definite. The problem of (16) is in the form of what Dorn [15] has called a Type II dual form quadratic programming problem. These types are summarized in Table 1. The corresponding primal form problem can be put in the form,

$$\text{Minimize:} \quad f(W,\alpha,\beta) = \tfrac{1}{2}W^T \mathbf{I}_n W - (\alpha - \beta) \tag{17a}$$

$$\text{Subject to:} \quad \mathbf{M}_i^T W - \alpha U_i > 0_i \tag{17b}$$

$$-\mathbf{M}_j^T W + \beta U_j \geqslant 0_j \tag{17c}$$

which is equivalent to the DZM problem of (4). Dorn's duality theorem [15] for quadratic programs tells us that if a solution, $(W,\alpha,\beta) = (W^*,\alpha^*,\beta^*)$ exists for the primal problem of (17), then a solution $(L,V_i,V_j) = (L^*,V_i^*, V_j^*)$ exists for the dual problem of (16). Conversely, if a solution, $(L,V_i, V_j) = (L^*,V_i^*V_j^*)$ to the dual problem exists, then a solution $(W,\alpha,\beta) = (W^*,\alpha^*,\beta^*)$ for the primal problem which satisfies

$$W^* = \mathbf{I}_n W^* = \mathbf{I}_n L^* = L^* \tag{18}$$

also exists and in either case,

$$g(L^*,V_i^*,V_j^*) = \text{Max}\{g(L,V_i,V_j)\} = \text{Min}\{f(W,\alpha,\beta)\} = f(W^*,\alpha^*,\beta^*) \tag{19}$$

From this result and the above definitions we get,

$$(\alpha^* - \beta^*) = \tfrac{1}{2}W^{*T}W^* + \tfrac{1}{2}L^{*T}L^* = ||L^*||^2 = d^2 \tag{20}$$

and hence,

$$D^* = (\alpha^* - \beta^*)/||W^*|| = \frac{d^2}{||L^*||} = d \tag{21}$$

thus corroborating the earlier statement in Section 3 that the DZM maximum D^* must equal d, the distance between the convex hulls Ω_i^* and Ω_j^*. The significance of the primal problem of (17) has also been discussed by Rosen [16].

If the quantity $||L||^2$ is expanded using the identity of (14) we get,

$$||L||^2 = L^T L = V_i^T \mathbf{M}_i^T \mathbf{M}_i V_i - V_i^T \mathbf{M}_i^T \mathbf{M}_j V_j - V_j^T \mathbf{M}_j^T \mathbf{M}_i V_i + V_j^T \mathbf{M}_j^T \mathbf{M}_j V_j \tag{22}$$

This expansion can then be used to express the minimization of $||L||^2$ as a Type III primal form quadratic programming problem as follows,

$$\text{Minimize:} \quad f(V_i,V_j) = ||L||^2 = V^T \mathbf{Q} V > 0 \tag{23a}$$

$$\text{Subject to:} \quad U_i^T V_i = 1 \tag{23b}$$

$$U_j^T V_j = 1 \tag{23c}$$

$$V_i \geqslant 0_i \tag{23d}$$

$$V_j \geqslant 0_j \tag{23e}$$

where V and **Q** are given by,

$$V = \begin{bmatrix} V_i \\ \\ V_j \end{bmatrix} \tag{24a}$$

$$Q = \left[\begin{array}{c|c} \mathbf{M}_i^T \mathbf{M}_i & -\mathbf{M}_i^T \mathbf{M}_j \\ \hline -\mathbf{M}_j^T \mathbf{M}_i & \mathbf{M}_j^T \mathbf{M}_j \end{array}\right] \tag{24b}$$

The quadratic form $V^T\mathbf{Q}V$ is positive definite from (23a) and the matrix **Q** of (24b) is symmetric since $\mathbf{M}_i^T\mathbf{M}_i$ and $\mathbf{M}_j^T\mathbf{M}_j$ are symmetric and since $-\mathbf{M}_i^T\mathbf{M}_j$ is the transpose of $-\mathbf{M}_j^T\mathbf{M}_i$.

Solution of problem (23) yields the two sets of convex multipliers V_i^* and V_j^* which specify the end points X_i^{**} and X_j^{**} of the minimum connector L*. Additional calculations must then be made to determine L* from (14). The scalars α^* and β^* are obtained as follows,

$$\alpha^* = (X_i^{**})^T L^*/\|L^*\| \tag{25a}$$

$$\beta^* = (X_j^{**})^T L^*/\|L^*\| \tag{25b}$$

The additional calculations required to determine the DZM optimal solution from the solution of problem (23) represent a drawback to the use of this particular formulation. Another drawback is that the matrix **Q** becomes quite large for moderately large numbers of paradigms (r_i+r_j), although the formulation of (23) has advantages if $n \gg (r_i+r_j)$.

The quadratic programming solution techniques discussed above apply only to the DZM problem for the linearly separable case. The general solution of the DZM and MHP problems requires the use of a more general type of nonlinear programming algorithm. We will discuss next a particular nonlinear programming algorithm called the Method of Approximation Programming (MAP) which was introduced by Griffith and Stewart [17]. This algorithm was used to obtain the experimental results described in Section 7. For a discussion of other general nonlinear programming algorithms which might be applicable to solution of the DZM and MHP problems the reader is referred to the surveys of Dorn [18] and Zoutendijk [19].

The Method of Approximation Programming (MAP) is a differential technique in which all nonlinear constraints are linearized by means of a first order Taylor's series expansion about some point and a linear programming algorithm is used repetitively in such a way that the solution of the linearized problem converges to a solution of the original nonlinear programming problem. The MAP formulation of the DZM problem is obtained by replacing the nonlinear constraint (4d) by its linearized version,

$$W_{k-1}^T W_k = \tfrac{1}{2}(\gamma^2 + W_{k-1}^T W_{k-1}) \qquad (26)$$

where W_k is the solution vector sought on the kth or most current iteration of the MAP algorithm and W_{k-1} is the solution obtained on the previous iteration. A detailed discussion of the use of this algorithm is rather lengthy and will not be included here. We will only note the following points relating to the MAP solution technique.

(1) The constraint of (4d) can be decomposed into the pair of simultaneous inequalities,

$$W_k^T W_k \geqslant \gamma^2 \qquad (27a)$$

$$W_k^T W_k \leqslant \gamma^2 \qquad (27b)$$

and it can be shown [8, Appendix II] that if only (27a) is used in the linearly inseparable case while only (27b) is used in the linearly separable case, then the resulting solutions will still satisfy the Kuhn-Tucker necessary conditions of the original DZM problem.

(2) If only constraint (27a) is imposed, the MAP algorithm will converge to a solution which satisfies the Kuhn-Tucker conditions of the original DZM problem. This was proven by Rosen [20] in another context.

(3) A constraint of the type (27a) implies that the solution region is nonconvex and, hence, the Kuhn-Tucker conditions are only necessary and not sufficient conditions for a global maximum of the DZM problem for the linearly inseparable case. Thus the MAP algorithm will converge to a DZM solution which yields a constrained relative maximum which may or may not be global.

(4) If only (27b) is used, the solution region is convex and the Kuhn-Tucker conditions are therefore both necessary and sufficient for a global maximum. However, it has not yet been proven for this case that the MAP algorithm will converge to a solution satisfying the Kuhn-Tucker conditions. *If* a solution satisfying these conditions is obtained, then this solution is, in fact, a global maximum. For more details the reader is referred to [8,17, 20].

6. Decision Procedures

In this section we will discuss ways to use the results obtained from the DZM and MHP criteria defined in Sections 3 and 4.

It should be noted that the DZM criterion of (4) specifies a normal W^* and a *pair* of hyperplanes H_α^* and H_β^*. It does not specify how these hyperplanes should be used to implement the final decision surfaces of the categorizer. In this case, we have several alternatives. One alternative is to use both H_α^* and H_β^* as decision surfaces and to classify an unknown pattern vector X as follows, $X \epsilon C_i$ if $X \epsilon +HS_\alpha^*$, $X \epsilon C_j$ if $X \epsilon -HS_\beta^*$, X rejected if X lies between H_α^* and H_β^* . Another alternative is to define a single decision hyperplane, $H = H(W^*, w_0)$, by determining a threshold constant w_0. In general, if $D^* > 0$, i.e. if Ω_i and Ω_j are linearly separable, then any w_0 which satisfies $\alpha \geqslant w_0 \geqslant \beta$ will result in a decision hyperplane H which separates Ω_i and Ω_j with zero sample error. If $D^* < 0$, i.e., if Ω_i and Ω_j are inseparable, then some w_0 which satisfies $\beta \geqslant w_0 \geqslant \alpha$ will produce the minimum sample error given the normal W^*. The paradigms of Ω_i and Ω_j can be projected orthogonally onto the normal W^* by simply evaluating the quantity $X^T W^*/\gamma$ for each paradigm. This projection operation produces the marginal distribution of the paradigms of Ω_i and Ω_j on an axis parallel to W^*. Given this distribution, we may search the interval $(\alpha^*/\gamma, \beta^*/\gamma)$ along this axis to find the value or values of w_0 which minimize the sample error. In the experimental study described in Section 7 the value of w_0 was arbitrarily set equal to $.5(\alpha^* + \beta^*)$ since linear separability was achieved in nearly every dichotomy.

If only one hyperplane, $H^{ij} = H(W^{ij*}, w_0^{ij})$, is used per dichotomy, and it is arbitrarily assumed that W^{ij*} is established such that $\Omega_i \epsilon +HS_\alpha^{ij*}$ and $\Omega_j \epsilon -HS_\beta^{ij*}$ whenever $i < j$ then the decision region R_k associated with pattern class C_k is defined by,

$$R_k = \left(\bigcap_{i=1}^{k-1} -HS^{ik}\right) \cap \left(\bigcap_{j=k+1}^{m} +HS^{kj}\right) \quad k = 1, 2, \ldots, m \tag{28}$$

There are a number of ways in which we can use the orthogonal hyperparallelepipeds, or "boxes", generated by the MHP criterion of (9) to generate decision surfaces. We will describe only two of them here. The first procedure assigns an unknown pattern vector X to class C_i if and only if it lies within the box generated from the paradigms of Ω_i . The decision region R_i corresponding to class C_i is defined as follows for this procedure,

$$R_i = \bigcap_{k=1}^{n} \left(+HS_\alpha^{(k)} \cap -HS_\beta^{(k)}\right) \quad i = 1, 2, \ldots, m \tag{29}$$

where $+HS_\alpha^{(k)}$ and $-HS_\beta^{(k)}$ are the half-spaces associated with the kth solution of the problem of (9) for paradigm set Ω_i. Clearly the decision regions R_i are not necessarily disjoint even if all the paradigm sets are mutually linearly separable. Hence a "priority rule" must be established to determine which class has priority in case two or more decision regions intersect. Such a rule may be set up by determining for each set Ω_i how many paradigms lie in the box associated with some other set Ω_j, $j = 1, 2, \ldots, m$, $j \neq i$. A set of pair-wise priorities can then be constructed by letting R_i have priority over R_j if there are more paradigms of R_j in R_i than there are paradigms of R_i in R_j.

The result of a pair-wise priority rule such as the above is that the intersection region $R_i \cap R_j$ is assigned to one class or the other depending on the relative representation of the two paradigm sets Ω_i and Ω_j in this intersection region. Such a priority rule can lead to decision regions which are nonconvex and not necessarily connected as shown by Figure 5. The dotted lines in Figure 5 show the original box outlines. Any point not satisfying (29) for some value of i = 1, 2, . . . , m is rejected, i.e. it is assumed to belong to the rejection region R_0 as indicated in Figure 5. More complicated priority rules can be established for cases in which three or more boxes share a common intersection region.

The "in-the-box" decision procedure described above would be expected to generate relatively large numbers of rejections since any point not falling inside a box is assigned to R_0 and, hence, rejected. In addition, since the size of the boxes will generally be related to the number of paradigms used, the resulting decision regions will generally be sensitive to the size of the design sample. These undesirable aspects can be reduced if a "minimum-distance-to-the-box" (MDTB) decision procedure is used. In this case the decision regions are defined with respect to the boxes B_ℓ, $\ell = 1, 2, \ldots, m$ as follows,

$$R_i = (X \mid d(X,B_i) = \min_{\ell}\{d(X,B_\ell)\}) \tag{30}$$

where $d(X,B_i)$, the distance from point X to box B_i, is defined by,

$$d(X,B_i) = \begin{cases} 0 & \text{if} \quad X \in B_i \\ \left[\sum\limits_{k\epsilon K_a} (X^T W_k^i - a_k^i)^2 + \sum\limits_{k \epsilon K_\beta} (X^T W_k^i - \beta_k^i)^2 \right]^{1/2} & \\ & \text{if} \quad X \notin B_i \end{cases} \tag{31}$$

and where K_a and K_β are the sets of indexes k for which the following hold,

$$k \in K_a: \quad X^T W_k^i - a_k^i < 0 \tag{32a}$$

$$k \in K_\beta: \quad X^T W_k^i - \beta_k^i > 0 \tag{32b}$$

It should be noted that (32a) and (32b) are inconsistent for any given X and k since $\beta_k^i > a_k^i$. Hence, K_a and K_β are disjoint.

Although formidable looking, the above relations have a simple interpretation and are very easy to compute. In fact, the MDTB decision procedure involves only slightly more computation than the in-the-box procedure. In order to determine if a pattern vector X lies in a particular box B_i, one must form each of the n scalar products $X^T W_k^i$, k = 1, 2, . . . , n and compare them to the appropriate threshold constants α_k^i and β_k^i. If either (32a) or (32b) is satisfied for some index k, then X does not lie in the box B_i. For the in-the-box procedure the computation involving box B_i would end here and another box would be examined to see if it contained X. The left-hand-side of (32a) or (32b), however, is the distance of X from the kth face of the box. In the MDTB procedure the distance to the box is the square root of the sum of the squares of these distances (32) since the faces of the box are orthogonal. Hence, the distances $d(X,B_\ell)$ can be computed as a by-product of the in-the-box computation. Figure 6 shows the decision surfaces resulting from an MDTB procedure applied to the boxes of Figure 5. It should be noted that these surfaces are piece-wise linear and quadric. The quadric portions arise when the surfaces are the loci of all points equidistant from a point (corner of a box) and a hyperplane (face of a box). In two-space such a locus defines a parabola.

7. Experimental Results

The DZM procedure was implemented experimentally in the design of a categorizer to classify certain selected groups of multi-font (9 fonts) impact printed characters. The character data were obtained from the Thomas J. Watson Research Center, IBM Corporation, Yorktown Heights, New York. The data have been used in studies by IBM personnel and are described in detail in a recent paper by Liu and Shelton [21]. The raw data consisted of a series of binary video images of the type illustrated in Figure 7 in which the asterisks represent logical ones and blanks represent logical zeros. Prior to use in the experiment, the raw data were subjected to feature extraction processing in which a set of 22 normalized central moments were generated for each character.

A normalized central moment of order (i+j) is defined as follows,

$$M_{ij} = \frac{1}{n_b} \sum_k (x_k^*)^i (y_k^*)^j \qquad (33)$$

where n_b is the number of logical ones in the binary video image of the character and where (x_k^*, y_k^*) is the normalized coordinate of the k-th bit in the ordered array of bits making up the video image . The sum over k; the bit index, is assumed to apply only to logical one bits. The actual coordinates x_k^* and y_k^* are normalized as follows,

$$x_k^* = (x_k - \bar{x})/\sigma_x \qquad (34a)$$

$$y_k^* = (y_k - \bar{y}) / \sigma_y \qquad (34b)$$

where x_k and y_k are the original, (unnormalized) integer cartesian coordinates of the bit location, $\bar{x}$ and $\bar{y}$ are the x and y centroids of the binary video image, and σ_x^2 and σ_y^2 are the second central moments of the binary video image, i.e.

$$\bar{x} = \frac{1}{n_b} \sum_k x_k \qquad \bar{y} = \frac{1}{n_b} \sum_k y_k \qquad (35)$$

$$\sigma_x^2 = \frac{1}{n_b} \sum_k (x_k - \bar{x})^2 \qquad \sigma_y^2 = \frac{1}{n_b} \sum_k (y_k - \bar{y})^2 \qquad (36)$$

Again, the sum over k applies only to the logical one bits. The use of normalized central moments as pattern features was proposed by Hu [22] and Alt [23], and a detailed discussion of the invariance properties of these features can be found in the references cited.

In the experimental study only the 22 moments of order 3 through 6 were used. These moments are listed schematically in Table 2.

Table 3 gives the composition of the experimental design and test groups. The prefixes "L" and "U" in Table 3 indicate "lower case" and "upper case" respectively. The particular choice of character classes and the grouping of these classes was based on the idea of trying to dichotomize only those characters which are generally the most difficult to distinguish from one another. Accordingly, dichotomies were obtained of only those character classes contained in the same group. Thus, $4(4-1)/2 = 6$ decision hyperplanes were needed for each of the three groups. In the design sample, 10 paradigms of each font, 90 in all, were used for those classes involving only lower or upper case characters and 14 paradigms of each font, 7 upper and 7 lower case, 126 in all, were used for those classes involving both upper and lower case characters. The fonts were approximately evenly distributed in the test sample.

For purposes of comparison, decision hyperplanes based on the Fisher criterion and the Minimum Distance criterion were also synthesized. In the context of dichotomization, the Fisher criterion [24] seeks that normal W which maximizes the ratio of the between set variance to the within set variance when the two paradigm sets are projected orthogonally onto W. This criterion is the basis for what statisticians call Linear Discriminant Analysis and it has been proposed in several forms as a categorizer design criterion [25,26,27]. The Fisher optimal normal, W_F^*, is given by,

$$W_F^* = S_{ij}^{-1} [\bar{X}_i - \bar{X}_j] \qquad (37)$$

where $\overline{X}_i$ and $\overline{X}_j$ are the sample mean vectors of the paradigm sets Ω_i and Ω_j, i.e.

$$X_\ell = \frac{1}{r_\ell} \sum_{k=1}^{r_\ell} X_k \qquad X_k \in \Omega_\ell \qquad \ell = i,j \tag{38}$$

and where S_{ij}^{-1} is the inverse of the within-sample scatter matrix. This matrix is defined by,

$$S_{ij} = S_i + S_j \tag{39}$$

where S_i and S_j are the internal scatter matrices of Ω_i and Ω_j. The mnth element of S_i is defined by,

$$s_{mn} = \sum_{k=1}^{r_i} (x_{km} - \overline{x}_{im})(x_{kn} - \overline{x}_{in}) \tag{40}$$

where x_{km} is the mth component of $X_k \in \Omega_i$ and $\overline{x}_{in}$ is the nth component of $\overline{X}_i$. The threshold constant w_{oF} used with the normal W_F^* was the following

$$w_{oF} = .5(\pi_i + \pi_j) \tag{41}$$

where π_i and π_j are the means of the projections of the sample clusters Ω_i and Ω_j on W_F^*.

The minimum distance criterion is based on the idea that each pattern class can be represented by a single "template" or prototype pattern vector. The criterion calls for the establishment of a hyperplane decision surface which assigns an unknown pattern vector to that class whose prototype vector lies the least distance from the unknown vector. In the experiments the sample mean vector $\overline{X}_i$ of each paradigm set Ω_i was chosen as the prototype vector. The required decision hyperplane for each pair of classes C_i and C_j can be readily shown [3, p. 18] to have a normal W_D^* and threshold constant w_{oD}^* given by

$$W_D^* = (\overline{X}_i - \overline{X}_j) \tag{42a}$$

$$w_{oD}^* = .5(\overline{X}_i^T \overline{X}_i - \overline{X}_j^T \overline{X}_j) \tag{42b}$$

Table 4 lists the dead zone values,

$$D = \frac{1}{\|W\|} \left(\underset{X \in \Omega_i}{\text{Min}} \{X^T W\} - \underset{X \in \Omega_j}{\text{Max}} \{X^T W\} \right) \tag{43}$$

obtained on the design data under the DZM, Fisher, and Minimum Distance criteria. As expected, the DZM criterion yielded the largest dead zone in every case followed in uniform succession by the Fisher and Minimum Distance criteria. As noted in Section 3, a positive value for D indicates linear separability of two paradigm sets. A classification test on the design data verified that all class-pairs except I–LL were linearly separable. These results are tabulated in Table 5. It should be noted that even though a decision hyperplane implementing linear separability of class pairs is not an explicit objective of the Fisher criterion as it is for the DZM criterion, the Fisher designed hyperplanes achieved linear separability in 16 of the 17 possible linearly separable cases. The linear inseparability of the I–LL class pairs probably resulted from the fact that sans-serif upper case "I" and lower case "L" were included in the design data and these characters have an identical video image.

Table 6 summarizes the classification performance of the categorizers on the test data. It is apparent from both Tables 5 and 6 that the minimum distance criterion produces inferior results. The differences in performance between the DZM and Fisher categorizers on the test data were statistically significant only for Group II. The inferior performance of the DZM categorizer for this group was due in large part to the I–LL class pair and can probably be attributed to the somewhat artificial inseparability of this pair and the sensitivity of the DZM solution for that pair to the relatively few sans-serif UI and LL characters that emerged as extremal paradigms during the design phase.

8. Acknowledgments

I wish to thank Professor Michael S. Watanabe and Professors Kumpati Narendra, Peter Schultheiss and Conrad Wogrin for their valuable comments during the development of the above material. I also wish to thank Dr. Stephen D. Shapiro for suggesting orthogonal hyperparallelepipeds as decision aids and Dr. Richard H. McCullough for suggesting generalization to the nonorthogonal case. I am indebted to Dr. George Nagy of the Thomas J. Watson Research Center, IBM Corporation, for his generosity in providing the character data used in the experimental portions of this study.

REFERENCES

1. Rosenblatt, F., "The Perceptron—A Theory of Statistical Separability in Cognitive Systems," *Cornell Aero. Labs. Rept. VG-1196-6-1,* Jan. 1958.
2. Mays, C.H., "Adaptive Threshold Logic," *Stanford Electronics Labs. Tech. Rep.* 1557-1, April, 1963.
3. Nilsson, N.J., *Learning Machines,* McGraw-Hill Book Co., N.Y., 1965.
4. Mangasarian, O.L., "Linear and Nonlinear Separation of Patterns by Linear Programming," *Operations Research,* Vol. 13, 444–452, 1965.
5. Highleyman, W.H., "Linear Decision Functions, with Application to Pattern Recognition," *Proc. IRE,* Vol. 50, 1501–1514, June, 1962.
6. Mays, C.H., "The Boundary Matrix of Threshold Functions," *IEEE Trans. on Elect. Comp.,* Vol. 14, 65–66, Feb., 1965.
7. Cover, T.M., "Geometrical and Statistical Properties of Systems of Linear Inequalities with Applications in Pattern Recognition," *IEEE Trans. on Elect. Comp.,* Vol. 14, 326–334, June, 1965.
8. Lambert, P.F., "Study of a Design Criterion for Linear Pattern Categorizers," D. Eng. Dissertation, Yale School of Engineering, New Haven, Conn., 1968.
9. Watanabe, M.S., Lambert, P.F., Kulikowski, C.A., Buxton, J.L., and Walker, R., "Evaluation and Selection of Variables in Pattern Recognition," in *Computer and Information Sciences–II,* Ed. by J.T. Tou, Academic Press, N.Y., 91–122, 1967.
10. Pervozvanskii, A.A., "Abstract Pattern Recognition as a Problem in Linear Programming," *Engineering Cybernetics,* Vol. 4, 1965.
11; Kuhn, H.W., and Tucker, A.W., "Nonlinear Programming," *Proc. 2nd Berkeley Symposium on Math. Statistics and Probability,* University of California Press, 481–492, 1951.
12. Shilov, G.E., *An Introduction to the Theory of Linear Spaces,* Prentice-Hall Inc., Englewood Cliffs, N.J., p. 173, 1961.
13. Watanabe, M.S., "Karhunen-Loeve Expansion and Factor Analysis—Theoretical Remarks and Application," *Proc. 4th Conf. Information Theory, Prague, 1965.*
14. Watanabe, M.S., "A Method of Self-Featuring Information Compression in Pattern Recognition," *Proc. BIONICS Conf.,* 1966.
15. Dorn, W.S., "Duality in Quadratic Programming," *Quarterly of Applied Mathematics,* Vol. 18, 155–162, 1960.
16. Rosen, J.B., "Pattern Separation by Convex Programming," *J. Math. Anal. and Applications,* Vol. 10, 123–134, 1965.
17. Griffith, R.E., and Stewart, R.A., "A Nonlinear Programming Technique for the Optimization of Continuous Processing Systems," *Management Science,* Vol. 7, 379–392, 1961.
18. Dorn, W.S., "Nonlinear Programming—A Survey," *Management Science,* Vol. 9, 171–208, 1963.
19. Zoutendijk, G., "Nonlinear Programming: A Numerical Survey," *J. SIAM Control,* Vol. 4, 194–210, 1966.
20. Rosen, J.B., "Iterative Solution of Nonlinear Optimal Control Problems," *J. SIAM Control,* Vol. 4, 223–244, 1966.
21. Liu, C.N., and Shelton, G.L., "An Experimental Investigation of a Mixed-Font Print Recognition System", *IEEE Trans. on Elect. Comp.,* Vol. 15, 916–925, 1966.

22. Hu, M.K., "Visual Pattern Recognition by Moment Invariants," *IRE Trans. on Info. Theory,* Vol. 8, 179–187, 1962.
23. Alt, F.L., "Digital Pattern Recognition by Moments," *J. Assoc. Comp. Machinery,* Vol. 9, 240–258, 1962.
24. Fisher, R.A., "The Use of Multiple Measurements in Taxionomic Problems," in *Contributions to Mathematical Statistics,* 32.179–32.188, John Wiley, New York, 1950.
25. Sebestyen, G.S., *Decision Making Procedures in Pattern Recognition,* Macmillan Co., N.Y., 1962.
26. Widrow, B., "Generalization and Information Storage in Networks of Adaline 'Neurons'," in *Self-Organizing Systems 1962,* M.C. Yovits, G.T. Jacobi, G.D. Goldstein Eds., Spartan Books, Washington, D.C., 435–461, 1962.
27. Peterson, D.W., and Mattson, R.L., "A Method of Finding Linear Discriminant Functions for a Class of Performance Criteria," *IEEE Trans. on Info. Theory,* Vol. 12, 380–387, 1966.

TABLE 1

Primal and Dual Forms for Several Types of Quadratic Programming Problems

PRIMAL PROBLEM	DUAL PROBLEM
TYPE I	
MIN: $\frac{1}{2}X^T\underline{Q}X + P^TX$ $\underline{A}X \geqq B$ $X \geqq 0$	MAX: $-\frac{1}{2}Y^T\underline{Q}Y + B^TV$ $\underline{A}^TV - \underline{Q}Y \leqq P$ $V \geqq 0$
TYPE II	
MIN: $\frac{1}{2}X^T\underline{Q}X + P^TX$ $\underline{A}X \geqq B$	MAX: $-\frac{1}{2}Y^T\underline{Q}Y + B^TV$ $\underline{A}^TV - \underline{Q}Y = P$ $V \geqq 0$
TYPE III	
MIN: $\frac{1}{2}X^T\underline{Q}X + P^TX$ $\underline{A}X = B$ $X \geqq 0$	MAX: $-\frac{1}{2}Y^T\underline{Q}Y + B^TV$ $\underline{A}^TV - \underline{Q}Y \leqq P$
TYPE IV	
MIN: $\frac{1}{2}X^T\underline{Q}X + P^TX$ $\underline{A}X = B$	MAX: $-\frac{1}{2}Y^T\underline{Q}Y + B^TV$ $\underline{A}^TV - \underline{Q}Y = P$

TABLE 2

Schematic Listing of Moments

i \ j	0	1	2	3	4	5	6
0				M_{03}	M_{04}	M_{05}	M_{06}
1			M_{12}	M_{13}	M_{14}	M_{15}	
2		M_{21}	M_{22}	M_{23}	M_{24}		
3	M_{30}	M_{31}	M_{32}	M_{33}			
4	M_{40}	M_{41}	M_{42}				
5	M_{50}	M_{51}					
6	M_{60}						

TABLE 3

Composition of Experimental Groups

GROUP	ORDER				DESIGN	TEST
	1	2	3	4		
I	LA	UB	LE	US LS		
DESIGN	90	90	90	126	396	
TEST	85	77	83	228		473
II	UI LI	UJ LJ	LL	LT		
DESIGN	126	126	90	90	432	
TEST	226	222	88	83		619
III	UC LC	UG	UO LO	UQ		
DESIGN	126	90	126	90	432	
TEST	220	82	221	85		608
TOTAL					1260	1700

TABLE 4

Experimental Dead Zone Values

		CRITERION		
GROUP	DICHOTOMY	DZM	FISHER	MINIMUM DISTANCE
I	LA–UB	.680	.090	−7.275
	LA–LE	1.870	.323	−2.569
	LA–S	.556	.276	−10.887
	UB–LE	1.430	.166	−7.338
	UB–S	.471	.208	−16.454
	LE–S	.719	.193	−3.764
II	I–J	1.898	.377	−14.378
	I–LL	−.012	−.197	−3.360
	I–LT	1.230	.254	−4.584
	J–LL	1.498	.241	−9.072
	J–LT	5.528	.931	−2.636
	LL–LT	2.190	.210	−4.905
III	C–UG	.559	.159	−10.078
	C–O	.643	.076	−11.718
	C–UQ	1.265	.010	−4.968
	UG–O	.594	.065	−8.287
	UG–UQ	.946	.055	−4.212
	O–UQ	.164	−.158	−10.854
AVERAGE		1.234	.182	−7.622

TABLE 5

Classification Performance on Design Data

DESIGN CRITERION	GROUP	PERCENTAGES RIGHT	PERCENTAGES WRONG	PERCENTAGES REJECT
DZM	I	100.00	.00	.00
	II	92.82	6.94	.23
	III	100.00	.00	.00
	AVE	97.61	2.31	.08
FISHER	I	100.00	.00	.00
	II	96.99	3.01	.00
	III	99.31	.69	.00
	AVE	98.77	1.23	.00
MINIMUM DISTANCE	I	65.91	34.09	.00
	II	76.62	23.38	.00
	III	72.45	27.55	.00
	AVE	71.66	28.34	.00

TABLE 6

Classification Performance on Test Data

DESIGN CRITERION	GROUP	PERCENTAGES RIGHT	PERCENTAGES WRONG	PERCENTAGES REJECT
DZM	I	96.83	1.69	1.48
	II	92.41	7.27	.32
	III	97.04	2.63	.33
	AVE	95.43	3.86	.71
FISHER	I	97.89	1.48	.63
	II	97.09	2.91	.00
	III	98.36	1.48	.16
	AVE	97.78	1.96	.26
MINIMUM DISTANCE	I	65.54	34.46	.00
	II	76.90	23.10	.00
	III	74.01	25.99	.00
	AVE	72.15	27.85	.00

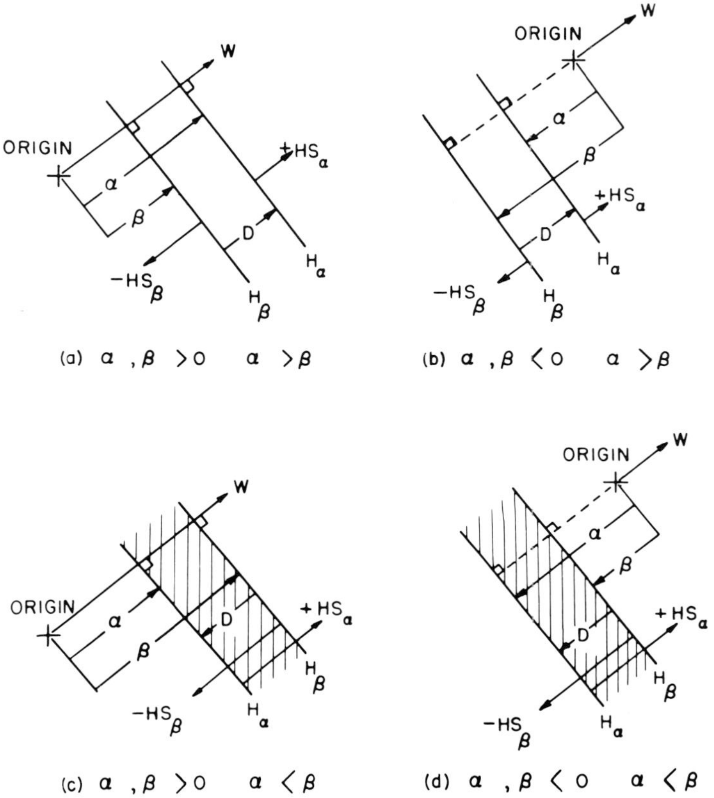

Figure 1: Directed Distance Geometry

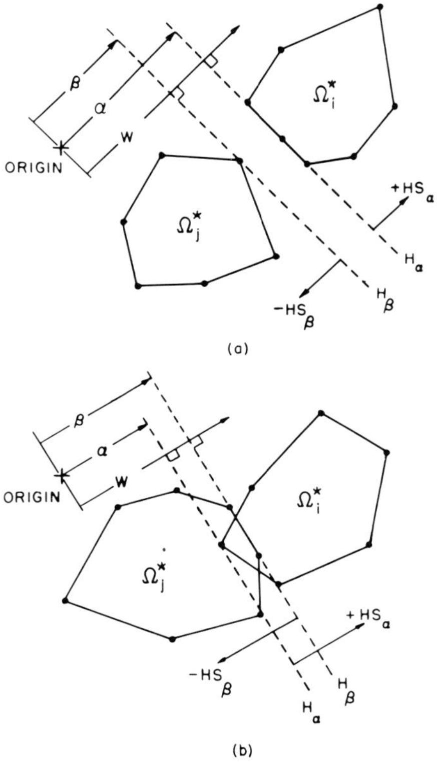

Figure 2: Example of Parallel Hyperplane Geometry

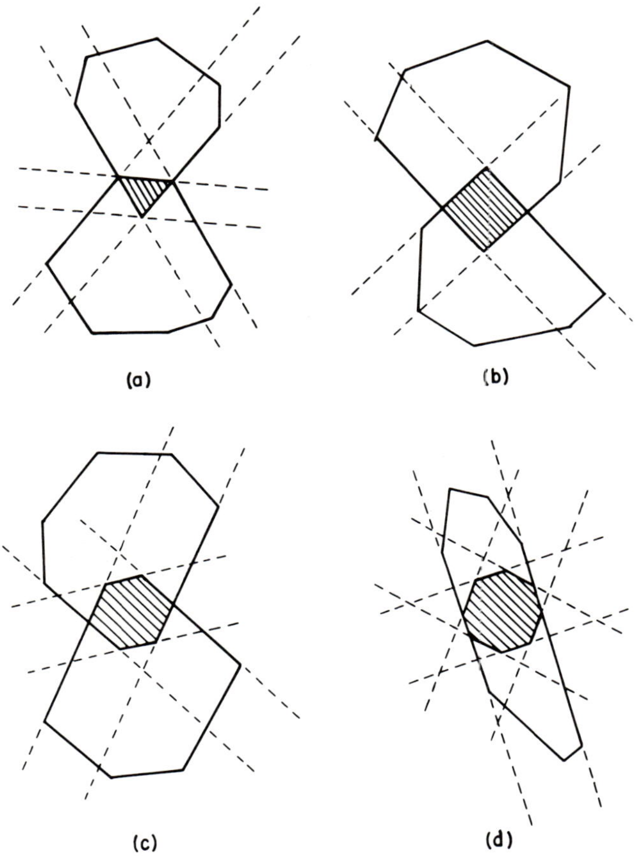

Figure 3: Examples of Inseparable Situations in Which the DZM Solution Is Not Unique

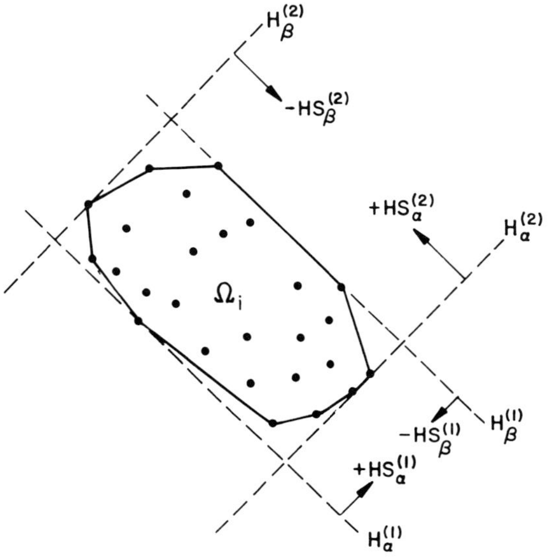

Figure 4: Sample Geometry for Method of Hyperparallelepipeds

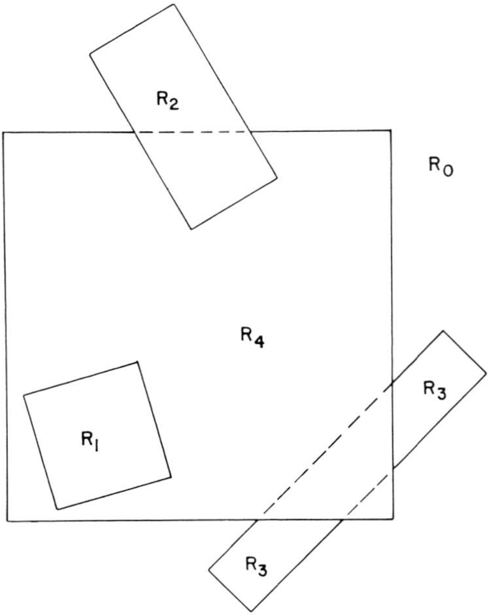

Figure 5: Decision Surfaces for "In-the-Box" Decision Procedure

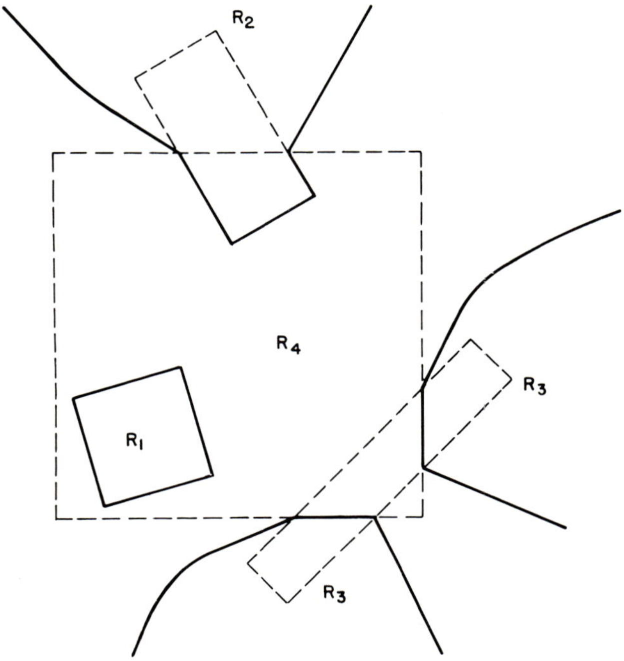

Figure 6: Decision Surfaces for "Minimum-Distance-to-the Box" Decision Procedure

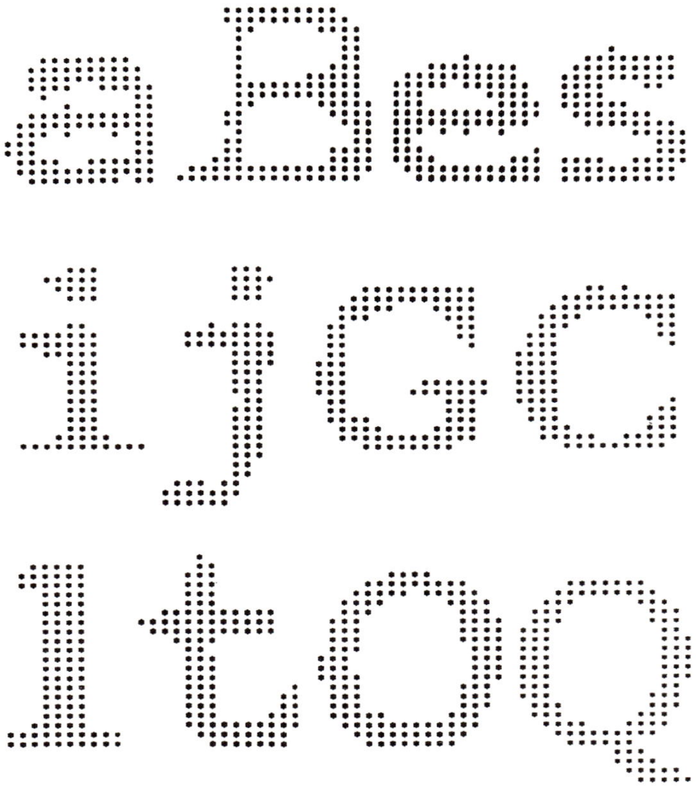

Figure 7: Binary Video Representations of Some Characters Used

THE IMPORTANCE OF PATTERN RECOGNITION FOR GENERAL PURPOSE ADJUSTMENT SYSTEMS

Hans Martin Lipp

INSTITUTE FOR PROCESSING AND TRANSMISSION
OF INFORMATION
UNIVERSITY OF KARLSRUHE

In the past many papers have been published concerning topics of artificial intelligence like programs for games, problem-solving, learning systems, adaptive structures etc. The common criterion of most of these problems always was the existence of two systems arranged in a closed loop connection. Otherwise these processes had very little in common. The investigators mainly were concerned with special problems; the formal description and the tools used for their solution primarily were based on properties of these special subjects. Therefore it was nearly impossible to use the same procedures when solving other somewhat different tasks. The required a priori knowledge and the special constraints did not allow such transfers. Although these investigations often led to very impressive results, no common theory had really been established.

This paper now treats the problem of using a more general description for adaptive or adjustment processes and of developing more general pattern recognition methods that are not based on properties of a special problem.

To achieve more general descriptions and solution algorithms, there is the need for abstraction from a priori knowledge and special properties and to use only a few general relations. Figure 1 shows the principle of the problem. A first system should be adjusted by a second system in a given sense by interaction in a closed loop arrangement. Necessarily each adjustment process needs an appropriate adjustment criterion which enables system 2 to evaluate its trials with regard to the goal to be achieved. This criterion in most cases is not directly accessible to the adjusting system.

In a first study, the results of which will be presented here, methods coming from the theory of automatons were chosen for describing the system to be adjusted (system 1). To avoid a pure mathematical study and to ensure the applicability to technical tasks the study is more heuristic than an exact one.

For this first investigation a clear, well understood model – the finite, discrete, deterministic and completely defined automaton – was chosen. Thus, a quintuple

$$(X, Y, Z, \delta, \lambda)$$

is sufficient to represent the behavior: three sets of symbols, X, Y, and Z (related to input-, output-, and state-variables of the system) and two mappings δ and λ for the transient behavior and the output relations. They are defined as follows (see also Figure 2): δ maps the Cartesian product of the sets X and Z into set Z

$$X \times Z \xrightarrow{\delta} Z$$

and with respect to time relations

$$z^{(t+1)} = \delta\ (z^{(t)}, x^{(t)})\ .$$

λ maps the same product into set Y

$$X \times Z \xrightarrow{\lambda} Y$$

and with respect to time relations

$$y^{(t+1)} = \lambda\ (z^{(t)}, x^{(t)})\ .$$

Mapping δ is not limited in any way; that means: transitions are possible between all states. However, it should be mentioned that reversible transitions are not necessarily given in real systems. Therefore, the transient function may show such restrictions.

In many technical systems the output function λ can be reduced to a very simple one. Often there exists a one-to-one relation between states and output symbols, and for simplicity's sake one may reduce λ here to

$$\lambda : Z \xleftrightarrow{1:1} Y \quad \text{MEDWEDEW automaton}$$

In consequence set Y will be replaced by set Z and therefore mapping λ will be omitted further on.

All adjustment processes need an adjustment criterion, which may be defined implicitly or explicitly. When using the given abstraction principle one has to detach the criterion from special problems and to construct a new basis for it. With regard to many technical and other systems it seems to be sufficient to define a new function ω mapping uniquely the states of system 1 into the set of (positive) real numbers:

$$\omega : Z \rightarrow W$$

with

$$0 \leqslant w(z) \leqslant w_{max}$$

It is now possible to replace the goal of the special adjustment process in such a way that it will be related to the new mapping. Several levels of complexity then are possible. The most complex one defines the goal by the statement, that the final state of system 1 (called goal) shows the highest value ($w(goal) \leqslant w_{max}$) of all states, and that neither the state nor the value are explicitly known.

Now the only assumptions made in this study can be given in a generalized form (see Figure 3): The a priori knowledge available for system 2 is the number of symbols in the two finite sets X and Z, the value of w_{max}, and the type of goal to be reached. Functions δ and ω are completely unknown to system 2 and have to be built up during the adjustment process by observation.

A description of system 1 by mappings and automaton tables is very clear but not too concrete. Therefore, it is preferably used for formal definitions and computer simulation. For showing the principle of the investigation here, it seems to be better to use the automaton graph. Figure 4 shows the relations between the states z, their values w(z), the input symbols, and the elements of the graph. Representation of the system by automaton mappings and by automaton graph is naturally completely equivalent.

Then – using the graph – the adjustment process corresponds to a hike through a (not necessarily two-dimensional) maze, of which only the number of vertices and edges but not the structure is known. Evidently the adjustment process will be under these generalized circumstances a random search with very small efficiency. It is out of interest to use such a simple adjustment system.

The main problem of investigation, therefore, is to get information during the process about system 1, its behavior, and the trend of the evaluation function ω. Figure 5 gives by means of a randomly chosen example an idea of the difficulties arising during the search. There are some areas that cannot be left anymore; other parts of the graph and some transitions are not of advantageous influence to the amount of steps the system needs to reach the goal. On the other hand the weights of the vertices may be distributed randomly or in some ordered way over the parts of the graph.

Naturally the two functions δ and ω are very important for receiving interesting information. The investigation yields some typical patterns that are easily detected during the process and on the other hand strongly influence the adjustment process. The recognition of these patterns enables system 2 to shorten the path to the goal and to avoid search in such areas of the graph that have already been passed through without successfully reaching the goal.

The influence of information about the two functions is quite different with regard to the process. Whereas the detected patterns established by δ only avoid search with repeated ineffective steps, the patterns of function ω in many cases lead to very progressive steps towards the goal. It seems not very desirable to use a lot of different patterns due to special circumstances. For this reason the patterns to be defined should comply with some general requirements:

1. They have to be based only on general relations as used in the description of system 1.
2. The number of different basic patterns should be as small as possible.
3. The detection of a pattern should directly influence the decisions of the process.
4. The detection should be done by a computer program and not by a "superior observer".

With these four basic types of patterns in the transient behavior seem to be sufficient to describe ineffective steps. Because the amount of information about function δ depends on the observation time, the pattern recognition procedure itself depends on the results of the search. Thus, an additional criterion is necessary to distinguish the detected patterns with regard to the consequences for further steps of the adjustment process:

1. Momentary type of a pattern(m-type):
   It is the random result of the used transitions and further on can be avoided using other already known input symbols.
2. Stationary type of a pattern (s-type):
   The structure of δ itself necessary forces this pattern. There is no possibility to avoid it using all other input symbols of this area. Some of the stationary patterns do not allow the search to be continued in the graph.
3. Temporary type of a pattern (t-type):
   Lack of information about this area does not allow a decision as to whether the pattern is of momentary or stationary type.

Figures 6 and 7[1] show the four basic structures – sling, blind alley,

[1] Upper ones: m-type; lower ones: s-type

loop and cycle-with the two possible configurations, either momentary or stationary, in each case.

Rules can be established for the decomposition of more complex patterns or structures into these basic ones (e.g. see Figure 5).

The structures already detected can be identically characterized by a small number of parameters. This compressed information may be stored and used later on in the process to increase the efficiency in reaching the goal.

The complete procedure for detecting these typical patterns and their more complex groupings consists of a larger set of rules. In this context, however, there is no advantage in describing perfectly this procedure. It is sufficient only to explain the principle. The information about system 1 (which system 2 gains during the progress of the adjustment process) at first is embedded in the strings of states, values, and respective input symbols related to each transition. Therefore, the pattern recognition procedure has to be based on this information. Figure 8 shows with some randomly chosen examples the structures of the four basic patterns as they are embodied in the string of states. When comparing the present state $z^{(t)}$ with all earlier observed states, the position, the distance (in time units) and the sequence of the identical states is characteristic for each of these patterns.

The structures to be detected in the evaluation function ω depend on the structure of the transient behavior. The string of values as observed during the process is not sufficient information about the function ω. Relations between several values can only be established regarding the relations of the corresponding states.

With steadily working adaptive systems the structure called maximum (respectively minimum) of a function is easy to define and to compute. Because of the discrete behavior of system 1 used here, that definition has to be generalized in an appropriate manner. To do this, first a measure for the "distance" between states of system 1 will be introduced as follows: The number of transitions to bring system 1 from state z_i into state z_j seems to be an adequate measure for the distance of these two states, which, therefore, is called "edge-distance" ED .

$$ED_{i,j} = \text{number of transitions between } z_i \text{ and } z_j$$

The edge-distance normally depends on the direction of the transitions if no reversible ones are present. That means

$$ED_{i,j} \neq ED_{j,i}$$

and thus two types of environment are to be distinguished – a forward and a backward one. Using this distance, the structure "hill" as the wanted generalization is defined by the statement: If z_i is the state with the maximum value of the hill, then for all other states z_j of the hill with

$$ED_{i,j} < ED_{i,j+1} \quad \text{resp.} \qquad ED = 1, 2, \ldots$$
$$ED_{j,i} < ED_{j+1,i}$$

the inequality

$$w_j \geqslant w_{j+1}$$

must hold for all strings. Figure 9 illustrates by an example the so defined hill structure. This definition is very flexible and also encloses things like mesas, crests, etc.

Besides these relations between states and their values one may propose to use also those between input signals and the change of value caused by them. This will be called "tendency" of an input signal. Simulations have shown that the average value of all changes taken over an interval of a given number of transitions is a very helpful structure to shorten the search for the goal. Figure 10 shall give an idea of this structure.

The principles of this pattern recognition procedure for the functions δ and ω require sufficient stored information. The extent of storage determines the possibility of detecting more or less complex patterns and of influencing the adjustment process.

Each of these generally defined basic patterns results in a specific decision to choose new steps which will be assumed to be more efficient for the way towards the goal than other ones. In detail these relations are as follows:

1. Identification of the goal stops the process successfully.
2. After the detection of an m-type structure such steps should be chosen that enable system 1 to leave that structure. Later on, all steps are to be neglected that lead into it.
3. The detection of a t-type pattern is related to a lack of information about the corresponding structures. Thus, such steps are preferred, by which system 2 expects to get essential data.
4. If system 1 shows an s-type pattern, there are two different decisions:
   - 4.1 Blind alleys and loops should be left at the exit state.
   - 4.2 Slings and cycles cannot be left any more. Consequently system 2 should finish its trials to reach the goal and stop the process without success.

5. The decision of a hill structure also results in two different decisions with regard to available information about it:
   5.1 If the hill area is completely known, system 2 will leave this region and avoid all steps returning to it. Search continues in unknown parts of the graph. By this principle, system 1 will not remain in submaximas.
   5.2 If not all transitions in the hill area are known, system 2 should try to gain information about them.

The concept of hill structures led to an additional more heuristic assumption on the behavior of system 1. If all other possibilities seem to be inefficient, unknown steps will be made from that state with the highest value of all states in the known area. The underlying principle is that with regard to hills, this state may have the smallest edge-distance to the goal of all states. Consequently the goal should be reached more easily from this state than from others.

6. The observation of tendencies with the input symbols results in the application of that symbol showing the highest value of tendency, hoping this trend will hold also for the next step.

There are several possibilities to arrange the mentioned decisions in a hierarchy. Figure 11 shows a very simplified scheme of the solution used with the computer simulations. Numbers indicated level of decisions in the hierarchy with number 1 as the highest level. The complete diagram, however, is much more complicated than the demonstrated one.

To conclude this paper, some other aspects of the given design will be discussed. The whole procedures had been programmed in the computer language ALGOL and simulation was done using a medium-size computer. Very different types of problems like some simpler games, optimization processes, and search in complex mazes proved the procedures to be efficient when using the described pattern recognition. It should, however, be mentioned that there are some hard difficulties for applying such a generalized adaptive system. The pattern recognition depends on a sufficient amount of information about system 1 and the evaluation criterion. The difficulties do not arise mainly because of lack of large storage units, but principally because the organization of the available units does not allow effective search in list structures. The computing time, for this reason, was high due to storage operations and not to calculation. Content decoded storage units would strongly increase the efficiency of the procedures.

A second limitation for the application of the described adaptive system is the assumption of deterministic behavior of system 1. The results of current, but still unfinished investigations show, however, that the procedures may be extended to use with indeterministic problems without great difficulties.

BIBLIOGRAPHY

Basic Literature [0] – [15]

[0] Lipp, H. M., Entwurf eines geschlossenen adaptiven Systems für diskrete deterministische Prozesse. Dissertation, Universität (TH), Karlsruhe, 1967.

[1] Minsky, M., Steps Toward Artificial Intelligence. Proc. IRE *49* (1961) S. 8–30.

[2] Steinbuch, K., Adaptive Networks Using Learning Matrices. Kybernetik *2* (1965) S. 148–152.

[3] Lipp, H. M., An Application of the Learning Matrix Dipole. (Bionics Symposium Dayton/Ohio, 1966).

[4] Gluschkow, W. M., Theorie der abstrakten Automaten. Berlin 1963, VEB Deutscher Verlag der Wissenschaften.

[5] Behnke, H. und Tietz, H. (eds.), FISCHER-Lexikon Mathematik II. Frankfurt 1966, Fischer-Bücherei KG.

[6] Busacker, H. G.; Saaty, T. L., Finite Graphs and Networks. (International Series in Pure and Applied Mathematics). New York 1965, McGraw-Hill, Inc.

[7] Behnke, H., *u.a. (eds.)*, FISCHER-Lexikon Mathematik I. Frankfurt 1964, Fischer-Bücherei KG.

[8] Wiener, Chr., Über eine Aufgabe aus der Geometria situs. Math. Ann. *6* (1873) S. 29–30.

[9] König, D., Theorie der endlichen und unendlichen Graphen. New York 1950, Chelsea Publ. Comp.

[10] Eier, R.; Zemanek, H., Automatische Orientierung im Labyrinth. Elektron. Rechenanl. *2* (1960) S. 23–31.

[11] Wolf, F.; Schmitt, A., Modelle lernender Automaten. Elektron. Datenverarb., Beiheft *8*, Braunschweig 1966, Vieweg & Sohn.

[12] Zemanek, H., Elementare Informationstheorie. Wien und München 1959, R. Oldenbourg.

[13] Hammersley, J. M.; Handscomb, D. C., Monte Carlo Methods. London 1964, Methuen & Co. Ltd.

[14] Wendt, S., Prüfung der Gleichverteilung und der statistischen Bindungen bei Pseudozufallszahlenfolgen. (Unveröffentlichtes Manuskript).

[15] Sties, M., Für ein adaptives Einstellsystem sollen vorgegebene Algorithmen in Form von ALGOL-Prozeduren programmiert und zu einem Gesamtprogramm zusammengesetzt werden. Diplomarbeit am Institut für Nachrichtenverarbeitung und -übertragung der TH Karlsruhe, WS 1966/67.

[16] Amarel, S., On the Automatic Formation of a Computer Program which represents a Theory. Yovits-Jacobi-Goldstein; edts. Self Organizing Systems. Washington 1962, Spartan Books, S. 107–175.

[17] Baumann, R., ALGOL-Manual der ALCOR-Gruppe. München-Wien 1965, R. Oldenbourg.

[18] Burks, A. W.; and Wang, H., The Logic of Automata. J. Assoc. Computing Mach. *4* (1957) S. 193–218 und S. 279–297.

[19] Citrenbaum, R. L., The Concept of Strategy and its Application to Three Dimensional TIC-TAC-TOE. System Research Center 72-A-65-26 (1965).

[20] Cooper, D. B.; Cooper, P. W., Non-supervised Adaptive Signal Detection and Pattern Recognition. Information and Control 7 (1964) H. 3, S. 416–444.
[21] Florio, G. P., Intelligent Automata and Man-Automaton Combinations. A Critique and Review. Electr. Engng. (1963) H. 82(3), S. 200–203.
[22] Ginsburg, S., An Introduction to Mathematical Machine Theory. Addison-Wesley Publ. Company (1962).
[23] Hawkings, J. K., Self-Organizing Features – A Review and Commentary. Proc. IRE *49* (1961) H. 1, S. 31–48.
[24] Henze, E., Räumlich homogene Irrfahrten im Gitter. Math. Ann. *147* (1962) S. 347–366 und S. 422–444.
[25] Holland, J. H., Cycles in Logical Nets. J. Franklin Inst. *270* (1960) S. 202–226.
[26] Holland, J. H., Outline for a Logical Theory of Adaptive Systems. J. Assoc. Computing Mach. *9* (1962) S. 297–314.
[27] Hormann, A. M., Programs for Machine Learning. Information and Control *5* (1962) S. 347–367 und *7* (1964) S. 55–77.
[28] Kämmerer, W., Über die Existenz kybernetischer Teilsysteme. ZAMM *44* (1964) H. 4/5, S. 183–192.
[29] Kelly, J. L. jr.; Selfridge, O. G., Sophistication in Computers: A Disagreement. IRE Trans. Inform. Theory *IT8* (1962) S. 78–80.
[30] Lin, Shen, Computer Studies of Turing Machine Problems. J. Assoc. Computing Mach. *12* (1965) H. 2, S. 196–212.
[31] McMurtry, G. J., A Study of Stochastic Automata as Models of Adaptive and Learning Controllers. Sonderdruck Dr.-Arbeit Purdue University (1965) S. 103.
[32] Mental Health Research Institute, Tenth Annual Report. University of Michigan Ann Arbor (1965).
[33] Mesarovic, M. D., Toward a Formal Theory of Problem Solving. ONR Conference of Computer Augmentation of Human Reasoning (1964).
[34] Minsky, M.; Selfridge, O. G., Learning in Random Nets. Information Theory London Symposium (1961) S. 335–347 (Ed. C. Cherry).
[35] Nawarecki, E., Self-Learning Modell of Multi-Parameter Controlled Objects. IFAC-Kongress 1966, Sonderdruck (preprint) 41 E.1.
[36] Pask, G., Learning Machines (Survey Paper). IFAC-Kongress 1963, Sonderdruck.
[37] Pearson, J. D., Decomposition, Coordination, and Multilevel Systems. IEEE Trans. System Science and Cybernetics *2* (1966) H. 1, S. 36–40.
[38] Pollack, M.; Wiebenson, W., Solutions of the Shortest-Route Problem: A Review. Operations Res. (1960) H. 8, S. 224–230.
[39] Trucal, J. G., Computers in Automatic Control Systems. Proc. IRE *49* (1961) S. 305–314.
[40] Unger, H., Elektronische Datenverarbeitung und Automatentheorie. Köln und Opladen 1965, Westdeutscher Verlag.
[41] Walker, C. C., A Study of a Family of Complex Systems, an Approach to the Investigation of Organisms Behaviour. AF-Grant 7–64, Techn. Report No 5, June 1965.

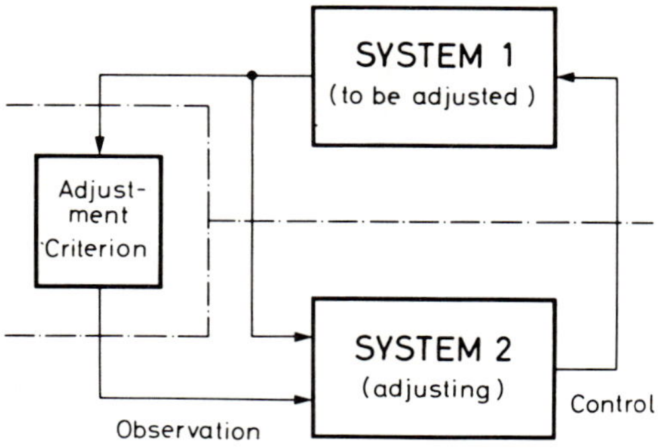

Figure 1: Basic Structure of the Adjustment Process

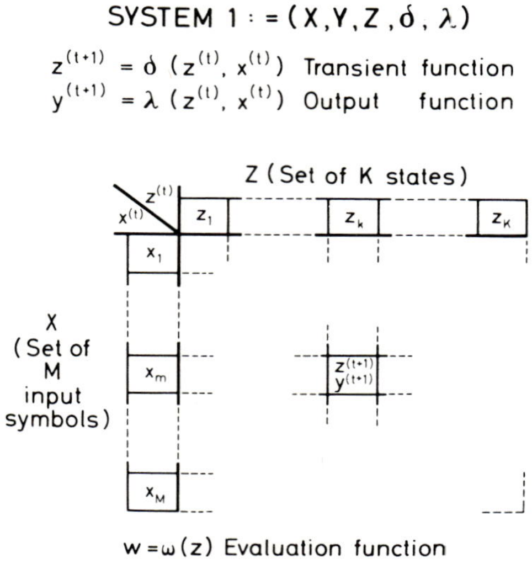

Figure 2: Representation of System 1 by an Automaton

1. Finite, deterministic, discrete and completely defined automaton

2. Transient function δ without limitation
   $z_{k'} = \delta(z_k, x_m)$ $k, k' = 1 \ldots K$; $m = 1 \ldots M$
   Transition between z_k and z_k' not necessarily reversible.

3. Output function λ one-to-one mapping
   $Z \xleftrightarrow{1:1} Y$ (MEDWEDEW-automaton)

4. Evaluation function ω unique mapping
   $Z \longrightarrow W$; W set of real numbers w
   with $0 \leq w(z) \leq w_{max}$

Figure 3: Assumption on System 1

States of system 1 ≙ vertices
value $w(z)$ system 1 ≙ weight of vertices
input symbols system 1 ≙ edges

e.g.

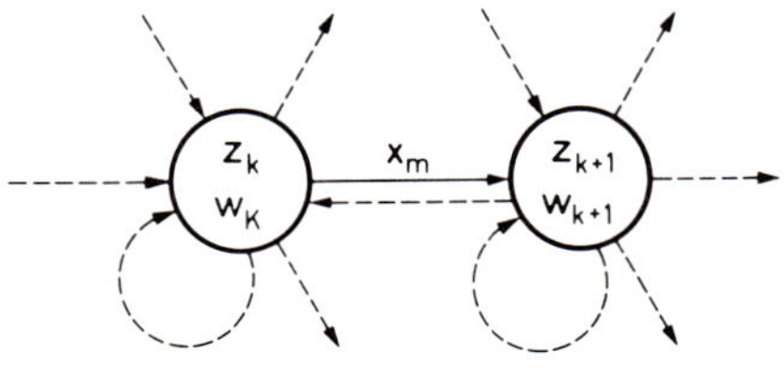

Sum of all edges / vertex = M = const.

Figure 4: Representation of System 1 by a Finite Graph

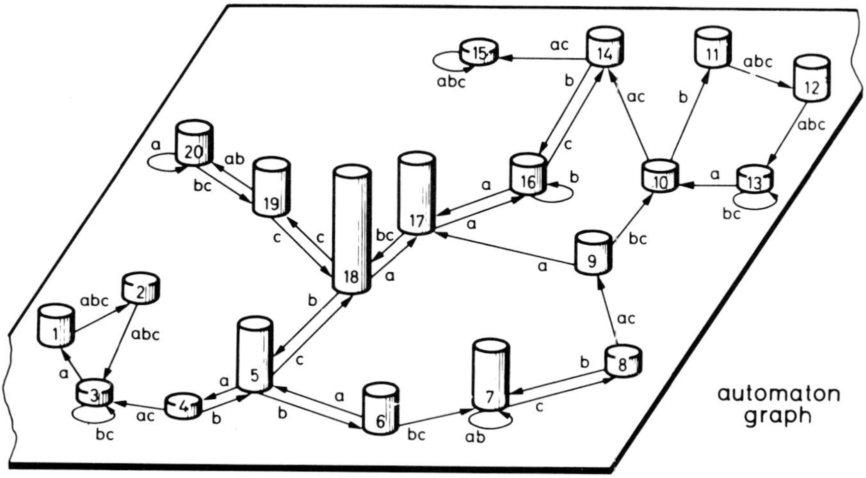

Transition table with evaluation of the states

state z		1	2	3	4	5	6	7	8	9	10	11	12	13	14	15	16	17	18	19	20
value w		11	7	5	4	24	15	22	7	12	7	10	12	5	9	4	11	27	47	18	12
input signal x	a	2	3	1	3	4	5	7	9	17	14	12	13	10	15	15	17	16	17	20	20
	b	2	3	3	5	6	7	7	7	10	11	12	13	13	16	15	16	18	5	20	19
	c	2	3	3	3	18	7	8	9	10	14	12	13	13	15	15	14	18	19	18	19

Figure 5: Random Chosen Example for the Behavior of System 1

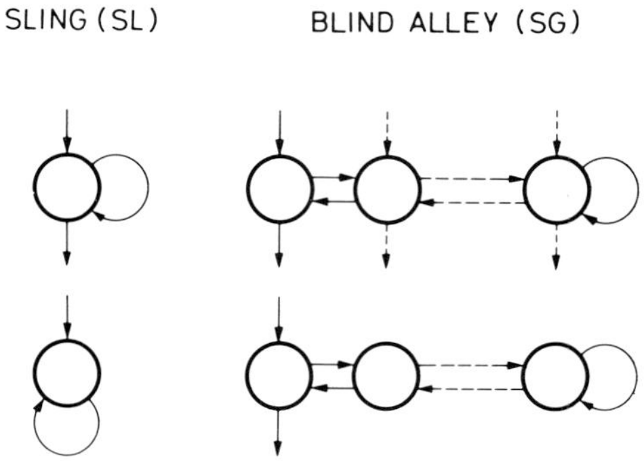

Figure 6: Basic Structures Sling and Blind Alley

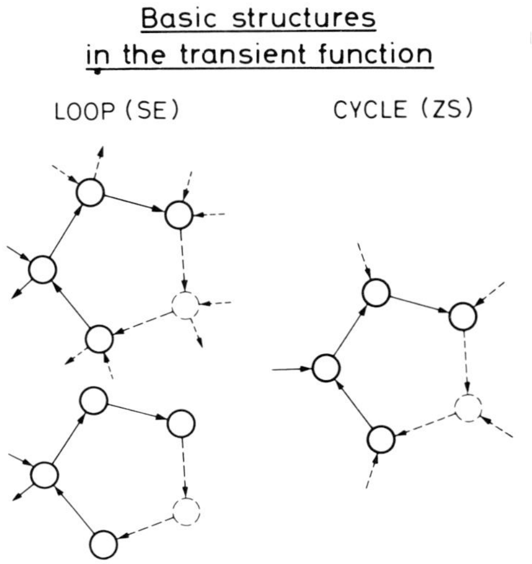

Figure 7: Basic Structures Loop and Cycle

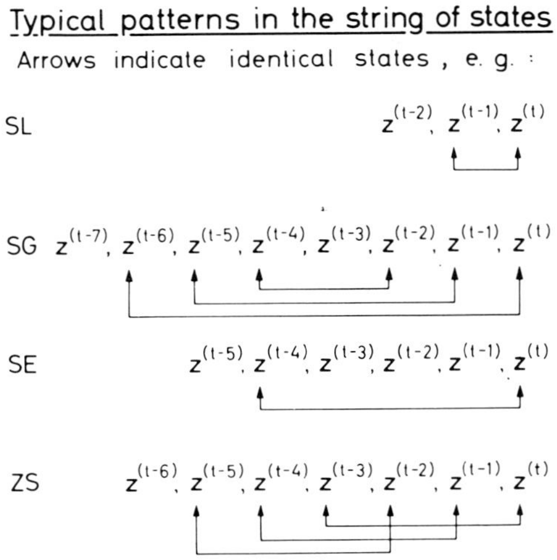

Figure 8: Principle of Detecting Patterns

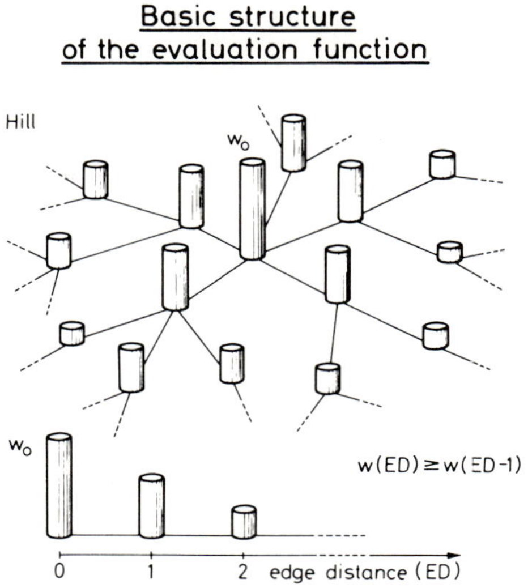

Figure 9: Basic Structure Hill

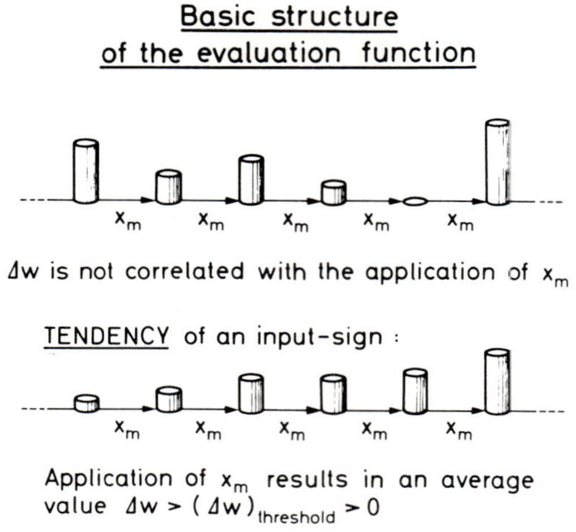

Figure 10: Basic Structure Tendency

Pattern recognition →	Adjustment process
1. Goal identification	Stop with success
2. Stationary pattern	Stop without success
3. Lack of information (t -Type structure)	Steps with unknown transitions in this structure
4. Hill area	
not completely known	Steps with unknown transitions in this area
completely known	Steps leaving hill area
5. Tendency	Steps with input symbol, showing the highest average + Δw
6. No pattern	Random steps

Figure 11: Hierarchy of Pattern Recognition and Related Decisions

RECOGNITION AND ACTION

Donald M. MacKay

RESEARCH DEPARTMENT OF COMMUNICATION
UNIVERSITY OF KEELE
STAFFORDSHIRE, ENGLAND

1. What Makes a Pattern?

The problem of pattern recognition cannot ultimately be separated from that of the organization of action: activity in view of ends.[1] Without this overall view of the context in which the notion of 'pattern' arises, we are liable to find ourselves floundering in inconclusive disputes as to what makes a pattern, whether pattern recognition entails classification, how to measure the success of a 'pattern recognizer' and so forth, sometimes generating more heat than light in the process. The key to some at least of these problems, I suggest, is to recognize that the concept of pattern is essentially relative. What we are concerned with is always the notion of pattern-for-an-agent; and the problem of pattern-recognition is always ill-defined until the class of agents in question, and their repertoire, have been specified in relevant detail.

The organization of action in a structured world can be thought of as a process of running selection (in series-parallel) from the repertoire of modes of action at the agent's disposal. Whether the elements of that repertoire are discrete or continuous need not now concern us. The point is that the structure of the field of action imposes restrictions on the range of possible activity that could be 'successful' (as currently evaluated by the agent) at any given time. If successful action in this sense is to be carried on, the organization of the running selective process must reflect correspondingly the structure of the field. Any predictability or stability in that structure will be reflected by informational *redundancy* in the selective process. This implies the possibility of *pre-fabricating* some components of that process, either in the sense of statistically weighting the conditional probabilities of selection or, when the local structure of the field has sufficiently stable or recurrent features, by constructing complete subroutines which can be triggered off as wholes as required to mould the selective process to match those features.[2]

Such internal activity, goal-directed towards matching the conditional probabilities of the selective process to the restrictions imposed by the structure of the field, we may call *organizing activity*. From this standpoint, we can define a pattern (for the agent) as a structural feature that can be matched in the foregoing sense by an organizing subroutine. This brings us close to the primary use of the term 'pattern', to signify an original after which something else could be replicated or 'patterned'. What is patterned after the original here is the conditional organization for any action whose form will have to take account of it.

Thus, to take just one example, a schoolboy fumbling his way along an unfamiliar maze may successfully adapt to each twist and turn; but if we enquire whether he has perceived any pattern in the required path, we mean to ask something more than whether he has negotiated the maze successfully. We want to know whether he has developed any *internal organization to match* the form of the successful path. If this path shows a regular alternation of left and right bends, for example, he may develop an appropriate 'conditional readiness' to turn right after left and vice versa, so that he needs less information per turn, or proceeds more rapidly, than before he did so. Even if the required path is quite irregular, he may be found on a later occasion to have retained the information gained on his earlier run in the form of a matching subroutine. In either case the path now has a pattern-for-him, regardless of the degree of randomness in the specification from which it may have been constructed.

Notice however that although our notion of pattern is essentially relative, it is not on that account subjective. On the contrary, to claim that something has a pattern for an agent is to imply an objective fact about the relation between it and the agent, which could in principle be demonstrated in terms of the organization of his brain without asking the agent how he views the situation. The agent indeed could be an automaton without nullifying the basis of our definition—which in the present context is just as well.

In these terms it is easy to distinguish between different levels of recognition of given stimuli. Thus recognizing "8" as a geometrical form involves making a selection out of a clearly different set of 'conditional readinesses' from those employed in recognizing it as a numeral. Recognizing a 3-dimensional object in a stereoscopic pair entails selecting from a range of conditional readinesses for action-in-depth, quite other than those affected by recognition of the two images as an optical array.

2. Alternative Principles of Organization

How can the internal organizing process most effectively be guided by incoming stimuli? To summarize discussions presented elsewhere[3], there are two extremes between which our solution can locate itself: (a) The one extreme would be to install a bank of 'feature filters' covering the whole range of possible inputs, so that each input became internally identifiable by the distribution of excitation, and appropriate logical networks could be installed to set up an appropriate state of readiness for each distribution. (b) The other extreme would be to install a single self-adjusting 'imitator' of the input or some transform of the input, and allow it to fumble its way into balance with each input change, under the guidance of a comparator or error-indicator. Its setting could then determine the state of readiness. Suffice it here to say that whereas the first is wasteful of equipment unless all combinations of inputs are equally likely, the second is wasteful of time unless most combinations of inputs are highly unlikely. The best solution would seem to lie in a combination of the two principles, whereby 'feed-forward' from relatively few key feature-filters is used to preselect or mould the repertoire of the matching generator, on the basis of filtrates from both the incoming signals and the (multidimensional) error signals from the comparator.[4]

The process of filtering and matching with comparison and error-feedback will of course be recognized as typical of much scientific investigation. Selected data suggest a hypothesis which generates a prediction; this prediction is then compared with data (usually including fresh material) and the discrepancies should ideally suggest refinements of the generative hypothesis. The parallel between artificial pattern recognition and the practice of experimental science seems particularly suggestive in connection with what can be called the problem of inspection, where patterns of a certain class have to be sought among or against a background of other forms. Methodical scanning of the field with a matched filter, which may be feasible when the variety of possible patterns is small, becomes rapidly uneconomical where many varieties of wanted pattern may exist, embedded in a background containing many rather similar forms which do not belong to the required class.

The experimental scientist frequently faces an analogous problem. He has a measurement to make against a background which is not wholly unpredictable; or he has a theory, say of planetary motion, and he wants to refine it by looking for anomalies. He may have little idea what kind of signal or anomaly to expect; but he knows what to expect if no signal or anomaly is present. In such a case he uses a 'null method'. Generating locally a prediction based on the null hypothesis (that no signal, or no anomaly, is present) he *subtracts* this from the input in order that any difference may stand out clearly. His task then becomes to generate a prediction of the *difference*; and it is crucial to the easy operation of the method that the degrees of freedom of the second operation should be as far as possible independent of those used in the first.

Ideally, subtraction of the second approximation should now enable a finer adjustment to be made to the first, and so on by successive approximation, with as few generators being added as possible.

A simple example is afforded by the balancing of an A. C. Wheatstone bridge, where two A. C. signals are matched in amplitude and phase so as to reduce to zero the difference between them. The chief attraction of such a null method in physics is the high sensitivity it offers without requiring correspondingly high linearity, or even any calibration at all, in the measuring instrument. Discrimination of 1 part in 1000, for example, can be achieved with the help of a simple yes/no indicator of imbalance.

On the other hand, the principle of 'nothing for nothing' holds here as elsewhere. The requirement for high accuracy is of course transferred to the generators instead. The method presupposes that it is easier to generate a match for a signal with a given accuracy than it is to analyse and measure it with the same accuracy.

Where the contents of a complex field have to be recognized artificially, there would seem to be corresponding advantages in *subtracting out what is known* in order to facilitate spotting and identifying what remains. To mention only one, it would facilitate the use of holographic methods, which are normally liable to treat the spaces between figures as recognizable forms on the same footing as the figures themselves. If each figure were subtracted from the input configuration as soon as it was identified, these spurious 'gap figures' would automatically be identified as such and would in any case progressively disappear.

3. Evidence from Human Pattern-Perception

The papers by Drs. Gose and Julesz have sketched the main outlines of our still meagre knowledge of human perceptual mechanisms, and I would add only a few notes relevant to the foregoing theme. There are several features of human pattern-perception which I think invite interpretation in terms of an internal matching or nulling process of the kind we have discussed.

Perhaps the chief of these is the *exclusiveness* of perceptual interpretation. The well-known ambiguous drawing of Figure 1a can be seen as *either* a pair of faces *or* a candlestick, perhaps in rapid alternation, but not both at the same time. Each can be felt to 'exhaust' the drawing in its turn. With a simple scanning filter or holographic pattern-detector, on the other hand, all three figures (two faces and a candlestick) would be signaled as simultaneously present.

The same point emerges in relation to the familiar 'reversible' perspective drawings typified by Figure 1b, where a 'filtering-and-classifying' system would required *ad hoc* machinery to prevent it from giving two output signals, whereas a 'null' system could of course balance out the input in only one way at a time.

An important qualification, however, is thrust on us by other evidence such as the optical illusion of Figure 2. Here the perception of spirality is irresistible; yet the twisted cords are all in fact circular. Thus whatever the internal process involved in recognition (whether filtering or matching) it clearly does not depend upon comparison of the overall input figure with a global template. For the only templates that could match the total figure would be circular, and circles are not what we see. Instead, we may infer that any analysis and matching is carried out on a local basis, the final integration being represented by the overall 'state of conditional readiness' for interaction with the pattern, set up in the perceiver on the basis of all the local clues. Since Fraser designed his figure to contain many local areas in which directional contrast gives rise to spurious signals as if from portions of a spiral, it would not be surprising on the foregoing basis that the overall state of readiness is set up to match a spiral figure.

A similar moral can be drawn from the ancient 'waterfall effect' known to the Greeks, whereby after viewing a moving textured surface (such as a waterfall) for some time, one's perception adapts so that stationary objects imaged on the same retinal region seem to have a backward *velocity* with *no resulting displacement*. No real figure, of course, could meet these paradoxical conditions, so that we are driven once again to think of the internal state as matching itself to filtrates of the input – in this case to the output of filters sensitive to the 'brushing' of the retina by the optical image, which react to prolonged 'brushing' in one direction by producing an after-discharge in the opposite sense. Such filters have not yet been identified physiologically in man, but their existence has been rendered more plausible by the discovery of velocity-sensitive cells in the retina of the rabbit.[5]

Perhaps the most significant feature of a null-method of pattern recognition from a philosophical standpoint is that it could enable a perfectly definite act of recognition to take place without necessarily enabling the recognizer to *specify* what features of the input were critical. In the limit, a mechanism could (with luck) grope its way into a matching response without any preprocessing and feature-classification of the input at all. Its only internal label for the input would then be its generative matching-response configuration, which might be partly or wholly 'analogue' in character; but this for many purposes could be adequate, and even advantageous.[6] The parallel with the human recognition of faces and common objects, which philosophers consider to be irreducible to the enumeration of definitive features, is at least suggestive. I have argued elsewhere[7] that if ever we are to reproduce the characteristic features of the human intellect, and indeed of information itself, a combination of digital and analogue processes would seem to be necessary. Although a few American writers are now beginning to echo this idea,[8] it has so far had little attention from those engaged in artificial pattern recognition. It would seem worthy of more exploration in this connection.

4. Conclusion

It is no part of my purpose to suggest that for all pattern recognition tasks our best course will be to learn from and imitate nature. This extreme form of the 'bionic' credo seems manifestly false. We have always to remember that human or animal sense organs are special-purpose devices developed as part of an integrated system, and that the principles on which they analyse and process information must be expected to reflect the specific needs of the particular organizing hierarchy and repertoire of the organism. Even if we want an artefact to replace a human being in some limited function, we must still ask which features of the human perceptual system, if any, are appropriate to that restricted task.

The general point is that any method of analysing input tends to carry penalties in the form of blind spots or Procrustean distortions. There is thus everything to be said for postponing our choice of pre-processing methods until the needs are clear. Why should we blind our automata with our own prejudices? To take just one example, human beings are very bad at recognizing complex patterns of waves or clouds which a machine could be 'trained' to identify fairly easily. There is therefore no reason to suppose that for such a task we should gain anything from imitating specifically the human visual system; on the contrary, some of its features might be expected to be a positive hindrance.

In terms of our earlier discussion the most fundamental way to start would be to specify the *repertoire* of the automaton in question (including its subroutines) in order to see what kind of 'descriptive space' it offers. Patterns could then be operationally defined in terms of the organizing matching-response they require from the repertoire, and preprocessing devised to facilitate (by feed-forward) the achievement of this.

Finally, in seeking to learn from nature's tricks we should beware of assuming too readily that the 'feature filters' we find in the nervous system are acting as classifiers of input patterns. They may have to do with quite other functions such as the control of eye movements and accommodation; and even when they supply the perceptual system their job may be only to initiate or guide the exploratory matching activity whose successful achievement is the act of recognition.

Summary

The concept of 'pattern' is essentially relative; ambiguity can be removed only by talking of pattern-for-an-agent. The significance of a pattern for an agent lies in the conditional demands it makes on his organizing system. It is suggested that the best general solution to the pattern-recognition problem may be to use 'feed-forward' from feature filters to guide a self-moulding internal matching response at the appropriate level of the organizing system, using a combination of digital and analogue techniques.

The parallel between this process and the hypothetico-deductive procedure in science is noted, and the advantages of 'null methods' in pattern recognition briefly explored, especially in connection with the problem of inspection. Evidence suggesting an analogous process in human perception is mentioned; but reasons are advanced for doubting whether imitation of nature will necessarily provide the best solutions to all problems in artificial pattern recognition.

REFERENCES

1. MacKay, D. M., Cerebral Organization and the Conscious Control of Action in *Brain and Conscious Experience* (John C. Eccles, ed.), Springer-Verlag, New York, 1966.
2. MacKay, D. M., Towards an Information-Flow Model of Human Behaviour, *Brit. J. Psychol., 47,* 30–43, 1956.
3. (a) MacKay, D. M., Mindlike Behaviour in Artefacts, *Brit. J. Phil. of Sci., II,* 105–121, Also *III,* 352–3, 1953.
   Also in *The Modeling of Mind* (K. R. Sayre & F. J. Crosson, eds.), University of Notre Dame Press, 225–241, 1963.

   (b) MacKay, D. M., The Epistemological Problem for Automata, *Automata Studies,* (C. E. Shannon & J. McCarthy, eds.), Princeton University Press, 235–251, 1955.
4. MacKay, D. M., Ways of Looking at Perception, in *Models for the Perception of Speech and Visual Form* (Weiant Wathen-Dunn, ed.), 25–43, M.I.T. Press, Boston, 1967.
5 (a) Barlow, H. B., Hill, R. M. and Levick, W. R., Retinal Ganglion Cells Responding Selectively to Direction and Speed of Image Motion in the Rabbit, *J. Physiol., 173,* 377–407, 1964.

   (b) Barlow, H. B. and Levick, W. R., The Mechanism of Directionally Selective Units in Rabbit's Retina, *J. Physiol., 178,* 477–504, 1965.
6. MacKay, D. M., Mentality in Machines, *Proc. Aristot. Soc. Suppt. XXVI,* 61–86, 1952.
7. (a) MacKay, D. M., On the Combination of Digital and Analogue Computing Techniques in the Design of Analytical Engines, Mimeographed, 20.5.49., Reprinted as Appendix to ref. 7 (c).

   (b) MacKay, D. M., In Search of Basic Symbols, *Proc. 8th Conf. on Cybernetics* (H. von Foerster, ed.), Josiah Macy, Jr. Foundation, New York, 181–221, 1951.

   (c) MacKay, D. M., Operational Aspects of Intellect in *Mechanization of Thought Processes* (N. P. L. Symp. No. 10, 1958), H. M. S. O., 37–52, 1959.
8. Dreyfus, H. L., Alchemy and Artificial Intelligence, RAND paper P-3244, 1965.

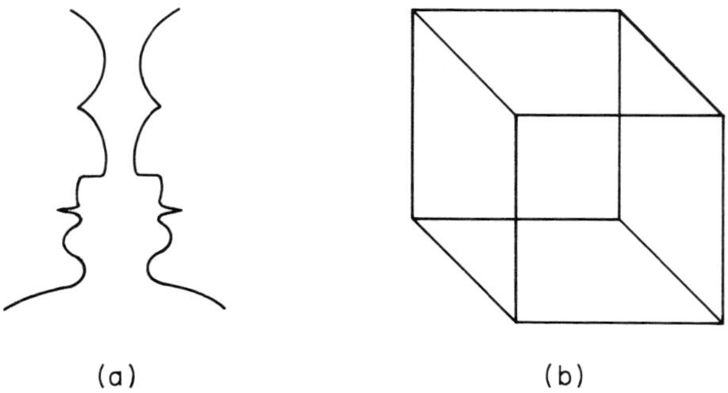

Figure 1 (a) An Ambiguous Picture: Faces or Candlestick?
(b) Ambiguous Depth Perspective: The Necker Cube

Figure 2: The Fraser 'pseudospiral'. The twisted cords all lie on concentric circles.

SOME VIEWS ON PATTERN—RECOGNITION METHODOLOGY

John H. Munson

STANFORD RESEARCH INSTITUTE
MENLO PARK, CALIFORNIA

Introduction

This paper presents the author's views on various topics in the field of pattern recognition. The views were largely developed in the context of research in hand-printed text recognition, and the examples are drawn primarily from that area.[1] * However, research in other areas and many discussions on the philosophy and methodology of pattern recognition have contributed in large measure to the development of these ideas. The views expressed should be applicable to all areas of pattern recognition, when expressed in terms appropriate to each individual area.

The author is indebted to his many colleagues at Stanford Research Institute, and especially to Drs. Richard O. Duda, Peter E. Hart, and Nils J. Nilsson, for many stimulating and penetrating discussions on these topics.

An Infinity of Problems

In the pattern-recognition field, we often speak of the character-recognition problem, the problem of analyzing electrocardiograms, the photointerpretation problem, and so on. Yet each of these is in reality not a single problem but a problem area, an entire ensemble of problems. The problems within an area are generally governed by a number of important parameters. Each proposed application, each choice of parameters, specifies a new problem from the ensemble—there are literally an infinity of problems.

For the designer who wishes to create a practical system, this multiplicity of problems presents a very serious difficulty. A system that performs well, for example, on any number of handwriting samples gathered

* References are given at the end of this paper.

in the designer's laboratory, may prove embarrassingly poor when confronted with the writing of the general public on bank checks, envelopes, or credit cards. A designer might work long and hard on an electrocardiogram-classifying or speech-recognizing system, and achieve excellent results using design data and independent test data from a large random sampling of adult males, only to find that his classifying system gets nowhere with data from children and females—or from hearts acclimatized to high altitudes or voices from a part of the country not covered in the experimental samples.

To cite a current example, the United States Post Office is presently facing the difficult problem of generating data sets against which to test various address-reading systems. The distributions of the problem parameters (inks, typefaces, abbreviations, etc.) are different among first-class collection letter mail, metered mail, second-class mail, package mail, and so on.

In short, it is hard to evaluate a system developed for a particular application without data gathered under precisely specified system conditions. The alternative is to extrapolate from the available experimental data, paying extremely diligent attention to the possible experimental variables.

The situation is complicated by the fact that the methods applied to one problem may not extrapolate to another, seemingly similar problem. For example, a system that extracts feature information from printed characters and classifies them on the basis of this information may perform adequately on the 26 upper-case letters. If the ten numerals are added, however, the system may entirely lack provision for the necessary feature information to discriminate between 5 and S, even if design data for these two classes are made available. Again, if the common punctuation symbols are added, the system may be unable to discriminate between the slash and the numeral 1, and between the left parenthesis and the letter C. Although these examples may seem a little forced, it is the author's contention that the influence of the particular problem at hand does unavoidably creep into the design of a recognition system in various large and small ways, and that the system becomes tailored to the specifics of the problem.

Let us now consider what the multiplicity of problems means to the researcher reporting his experimental results. If a paper describes experimental procedures and concludes with a section on "Results" which merely reports, in effect, that N test patterns were gathered and the performance on them was X percent, then it has said next to nothing to aid in evaluating performance. The problem at hand has not been specified. Without knowledge of the problem, a numerical measure of recognition success is meaningless.

There are two ways to convey the degree of difficulty of a particular pattern-recognition problem. One way is to describe the subject matter of the problem itself fully enough that one's audience can *judge in their own minds* the nature of the problem and the significance of results on that problem. Because of the multiplicity of problems, the parameters of the problem must be carefully specified, and an idea must be given of the *quality* of the data. Liberal presentation of sample data is an important aid here, if the data are in human-recognizable form.

The other, and more quantitative, way to convey the degree of difficulty of a problem is to describe the performance of various systems, and human subjects, on the problem. If a set of data for a particular problem is processed by several recognition systems, it may acquire the status of a "standard data set." However, in view of the multiplicity of problems of potential interest, there can be no single *standard* data set. In practice, there will be available from the infinity of possible problem data sets those few that experimenters have taken the trouble to gather and make available. These few sets still serve an important purpose by providing the only benchmarks of relative performance among various systems. Thus, the evaluation of problems and the evaluation of systems are interrelated.

The pattern-recognition performance of human subjects on a problem whose subject matter is familiar to humans is often the most useful benchmark of the problem's difficulty, because it allows the audience to form an intuitive ranking of the difficulty. Furthermore, devices proposed for pattern-recognition applications are often competing with humans who perform the recognition task in existing systems. It is sometimes said that human performance provides an "existence proof" for the performance that we can expect of a recognition system on a given task, and human performance is often taken as an implicit upper limit. The effort a designer spends in improving his system may be largely determined by the gap between the system's performance and that of humans. In one case which occurred in the author's laboratory, however, considerable effort was being spent to improve the performance of a system on a problem, when it was decided to test human performance on the problem. The test showed that the system was already significantly outperforming humans, even though the subject matter of the problem was familiar to humans.

Let us consider the parameters that determine the different problems in the area of off-line hand-printed character recognition. First, the area of off-line recognition (from a printed page) should be sharply distinguished from that of on-line recognition (from a light pen, RAND tablet, or similar device).[2] The on-line source data provide a nearly exact trace of the path of the writing instrument and give accurate stroke-position and time-sequence information. The blob of ink or graphite that constitutes an off-line source image yields no time information, and it is virtually impossible to reconstruct the path of the writing instrument throughout much of the image. The natural system requirements for the two classes of recognition problems are also different. In the on-line environment, a character can be classified by the system, displayed, and corrected immediately by the writer if it is wrong. Off-line, it may be better to avoid absolute classifications, and to make use of the contextual relations among characters. This topic will be discussed below.

The recognition of hand-printed characters should also be distinguished from that of cursive (connected) script.[3] The separation of the printed characters and the fact that each belongs in a well-specified category obviate the "segmentation problem" that makes cursive-script recognition much more difficult.

Within the framework of off-line block hand printing, then, what makes one problem different from another? We may list these factors: the size of the alphabet; the "standard" forms of the individual characters and the degree of constraint placed on their formation; the size, spacing, and arrangement of text on the page; the writing instrument(s); the number of writers to be accommodated; the training and motivation of the writers; and the characteristics of each individual writer. This last factor changes from day to day and even from minute to minute.

Although applications exist for limited alphabets, such as the ten digits, a broader goal is the recognition of an alphabet containing at least the fifty-odd letters, digits, and basic punctuation marks, and preferably one the size of the full BCD or ASCII alphabets. The difficulty of an alphabet, in some reasonable measure, increases with its size. The removal of the archaic letter-number similarities (0 and zero, I and one) leads to an obvious reduction in difficulty. The enforcement of explicit shape differences between such character pairs as Z–2, S–5, and 4–9, similarly lightens the problems.

Even given a specific alphabet and prototype character forms, the legibility of a hand-printed document and the difficulty of the problem it represents will vary greatly as a result of the other factors listed above. Figures 1–3 show quantized samples of the hand-printed numeral 8 from different data sets. The data in Figure 1 are from a well-known set of hand-printed numerals and letters collected and made available by W. H. Highleyman. The characters in Figure 2 were gathered in the course of the author's research. Those in Figure 3 were gathered during the development that led to the IBM 1287 Optical Reader. Great differences may be observed in the legibility and uniformity of the characters in the three groups.

The document scanner will make its own contribution to the task facing the remainder of the recognition system, a contribution that may be hard to unravel from that of the original image.

The nature of the writing instrument, the hardness of the lead if a pencil is used, the character cell size, and so on, all contribute to the nature of the problem. It appears that a particularly important parameter is the ratio of stroke width to character size, with a smaller ratio yielding more easily recognized characters.

Contraints on the formation of characters may be applied over a wide range. The coders may be instructed to write carefully, to write in boxes, to write filling the boxes, to write around dots or other markers, etc. More stringent constraints can lead to great increases in legibility, but they will be acceptable in diminishing areas of application.

Closely allied to the question of applicable constraints is the nature of the coding population. Is it the general public, a widespread sales force, or a few specialists? To what degree are the users educated in printing for the system? Under what conditions is the printing done? What motivations for better printing are applied, and how is the motivation feedback loop closed? It is in this area that the designer wishing to test a system for a specific application will face the greatest difficulty in controlling his experiments to ensure meaningful results.

Preprocessing and Classification

The generic pattern-recognition problem, in its simplest form, is this: A number of test patterns (which may be entities in any domain) are each to be assigned to one of N classes, or categories. We shall consider here only the commonest case, in which there is no a priori relationship among the N classes. (An example of an opposite case is a problem in which the classes correspond to the ranges of a numeric variable, such as the next day's temperature in a weather-prediction problem. In this case one might wish to use a recognition system whose structure forced continuity between the nth and $(n+1)$th classes.)

We also assume that a separate set of *training patterns* are used, in some way, as the means of adjusting the recognition system to classify the test patterns, after its general form has been specified by the designer. Depending on the nature of the system, this adjustment may take the form of estimating parameters of statistical distributions, accepting training patterns as prototypes, modifying adjustable weights during the presentation of the training patterns, etc. The adjustment process might even involve human intervention. In any case, the system is considered to be *pattern designed* as opposed to being designed on the basis of knowledge obtained outside the set of training patterns.

To provide a framework for this discussion, we may describe the pattern-recognition system in terms of three stages, transducer, preprocessor, and classifier (Figure 4).

A transducer is usually employed in the front end of a recognition system to transform patterns from their original domain in the "real world" to a representation acceptable to the remainder of the system, generally an electronic signal or a collection of digital information. Although the transducer has some effect on the problem presented to the remainder of the system, it is often more or less ignored, and the transduced pattern is considered to contain essentially the same information for the problem at hand as the original pattern. We shall take this attitude, and ignore the distinction between the original pattern and the transduced one that is presented to the preprocessor.

The remainder of a typical recognition system may be thought of as consisting of a preprocessor (or feature extractor) and a classifier. Although the boundary between the two is not always well defined, we claim that it generally takes the following form: The preprocessor extracts from the pattern a *feature vector* consisting of a limited number of features, which are invariably represented as numerical quantities (binary, multiple-valued, or continuous-valued). The classifier is given the task of assigning the feature vectors among the N classes. In the large majority of cases, *the classifier assumes no a priori relations among the components (features) of the feature vector.*

We can now proceed to develop two arguments: first, that the theory and practice of classification are much farther advanced than those of preprocessing, and second, that there is much similarity among the various well-known families of classifiers and the performance they can achieve. On the basis of these arguments, we would suggest that the major future advances in pattern-recognition capability should come from improvements in preprocessing rather than from the refinement of classifiers.

Let us first consider the problem facing the classifier. In the framework that has been postulated, a preprocessed pattern is a point (equivalently, a vector from the origin) in feature space. The coordinates of the feature space are the individual features, and they may be taken as a set of orthogonal Euclidean coordinates without loss of generality. Furthermore, we have assumed that there is no a priori relation among the features. In this framework, the classification problem we have formulated becomes the following: Given a Euclidean hyperspace (the feature space), and given a set of points in the space (the training feature vectors) whose true mapping into a set of N elements (the classes) is known, find a mapping from the hyperspace into the N classes that will minimize the expected misclassification of new points (the test feature vectors) drawn from the same ensemble as the training feature vectors.

Thus stated, the "classification problem" is abstracted completely into the realm of mathematics, and appears as a family of problems in statistical decision theory. And, indeed, this abstraction or formalization of the classification problem has allowed it to be well explored on a theoritical as well as a pragmatic basis. Nilsson's book,[4] for example, evidences the degree of organization to which the field has been subjected.

By contrast, preprocessing seems to be still as much of an art as a science. Although one can speculate on a generalized preprocessor that can extract valuable features with equal ease from aerial photographs, printed characters, radio signals, neural recordings, etc., such a device or method seems remote. Preprocessors are currently developed through familiarity with a given problem, inspiration, and a great deal of hard work.

Now let us look in more detail at a classification problem. We may distinguish between an *asymptotic problem*, characterized by arbitrarily large training and test samples from a given set of class distributions, and a *specific problem* represented by a specific pair of finite training and test sets.

An asymptotic problem has a definite Bayes risk, which depends on the overlapping of the class distributions and on the a priori class probabilities. For a specific problem, however, the performance level that a classifier can attain depends not only on the asymptotic Bayes risk (and on the vagaries of the test set) but also on the interrelation of three factors: the complexity of the underlying distributions in feature space, the degree to which the training feature vectors adequately represent the distributions, and the complexity or flexibility of the decision surfaces the classifier can implement.

Figure 5, for example, illustrates a schematic feature space with a very simple four-category classification problem. (We would credit the preprocessor with having done an excellent job in this case.) Most types of classifier should be able to achieve perfect classification on the basis of even one training sample in each class (because, roughly speaking, the sizes of the distributions are less than the distances separating them).

In Figure 6, we can again expect even the simplest classifiers to solve the problem completely, but only if they are given enough training vectors to map out the boundaries between distributions adequately. In Figure 7, fewer training samples might suffice, but now the classifier must be capable of implementing nonlinear decision boundaries. A polynomial boundary would separate Class III from Class IV; a "multimodal" capability would probably be required to separate Class I from the others.* These represent two of the extensions commonly made to the basic classifiers of each family.

I believe that one's conceptualization of the classification problem often extends to include multimodality, as suggested in Figure 7, but often stops there. However, I would propose that Figure 8 is a more suggestive model for a problem in which preprocessing has not succeeded in unscrambling the categories. It is hard, in a two-dimensional sketch, to even suggest the situation in hyperspace, where intuition is quite unreliable. The impression might be better conveyed by saying that the distributions resemble a "ball of hyperworms." The critical aspect of this situation is that the distributions are tenuous: They wind through hyperspace for distances large compared with their thickness and their separation from each other.

Figure 9, for example, shows four block capital letters as they might appear in the output of a transducer that performed binary quantization on an 8 x 10 matrix. If these patterns were treated by a translation-invariant preprocessor, the resulting feature vectors for the two L's would be

---

* Polynomial functions can, of course, describe highly convoluted regions, but the number of terms required and the difficulty of adjusting them simultaneously make this approach impractical as the complexity of the distributions increases.

identical, as would those for the two U's. As an opposite extreme, we may consider a preprocessor that does no processing at all. Its output feature vector consists of 80 binary features directly representing the elements of the matrix. For this preprocessor, the Hamming distance between the feature vectors for the two L's would be 22 units, and between the two U's, 32 units. The Hamming distance between the L of Figure 9(a) and the U of Figure 9(c), however, is only six units, and the same is true between the L of Figure 9(b) and the U of Figure 9(d). It can be seen that translations such as the one shown here, rotations, changes of scale, and distortions all spread the class distributions around the feature hyperspace in a manner more suggestive of intertwined tentacles than of the multiple modes of Figure 7.

The asymptotic problem represented by the situation we have just described may have a low Bayes risk; in fact, if the class distributions in feature space are disjoint, as in Figure 8, the asymptotic risk is zero. The performance on a specific problem, however, will be limited both by the number of training patterns and by the complexity attainable by the classifier. Loosely, we can say that there must be enough training samples so that every point within a class distribution in feature space is nearest a training point from that class. Similarly, because none of the usual classifiers has the ability to cover at one stroke a tentacle-like region, the classifier must generally be capable of establishing enough modes to form a *convex covering* of each distribution, as one would cover the regions of Figure 8 with collections of overlapping circles or polygons.

Most of the well-known families of pattern classifiers have members capable of multimodal operation. The nearest-neighbor classifiers[5] and the clustering algorithms[6] are inherently multimodal. Parametric statistical estimation methods, and the various nonparametric methods of the iterative adaptation type,[4] can be made multimodal by the explicit assignment of more than one statistical distribution or adaptive element to each class. However, it is not an easy problem to cause the assigned units to distribute themselves properly to cover the class distributions.

Any of these multimodal classifiers can handle an inherently tenuous distribution, given enough modes and enough training samples. To the extent that each classifier implements a convex covering of the asymptotic distributions, their performance will be rather similar. If the training patterns are inadequate to represent the distributions, or if memory limits or computation times restrict the various classifiers to a given number of modes, the performance of all the classifiers should be degraded in approximately the same way. Solving these problems then depends not on the choice of a particular classifier but on an improvement in preprocessing to make the classification task more manageable.

Context and Continuity

In the preceding sections of this paper, we have taken the viewpoint that the goal in a pattern-classification problem is the achievement of a minimum error rate in the assignment of a set of test patterns among a number of classes. We now reexamine this viewpoint in the light of the larger goals of a recognition system.

Although examples can be drawn from almost any field, text recognition provides one of the clearest examples. By text recognition we mean the problem (more precisely, the family of problems) of processing text on a printed document and creating a copy of the text in a computer or information system with maximum accuracy. Text recognition provides an excellent vehicle for this discussion because each element of the text, i.e., a character, belongs to a clearly defined class. Thus, we can speak of the character-recognition problem, as before. Our first observation is that the real goal of text recognition is not the recognition of characters per se, but the creation of the computer text copy *at minimum total system cost,* including the cost of proof-reading and correcting errors.

Let us illustrate this point with an example of the recognition of text in the FORTRAN programming language. One of the well-known FORTRAN statement types is the DIMENSION statement, which must begin with the nine characters

DIMENSION

Suppose that these characters are scanned from the document, preprocessed, and classified, yielding

DINEN$ION

Any person or system performing a post-analysis or context analysis on the outputs of the classifier should be able to reach two conclusions: First, that the character string shown is syntactically impossible within the FORTRAN language; second, that the probability is overwhelming that the correct string is DIMENSION. (Although many other alternatives, such as

DINEN(ION . . .

are syntactically possible, the a priori probability of occurrence of DIMENSION is overwhelming.) This example illustrates, at the simplest level, the role of context analysis in improving text-recognition performance.

We next observe that information in addition to the simple character classifications is required for the best use of context analysis. Consider the conditional branching statement

IF(SENSE SWITCH 2)7, 12

which might come out of the character classifier as

IF(SENSE SWITCH 2)7112

The context analyzer can determine that the character string contains an error, because this statement form must have two numerical statement labels separated by a comma. Clearly, however, there is no way for the analyzer to choose the correct form over the form

IF(SENSE SWITCH 2)71,2

The situation is different if the analyzer has access to ranking information generated by the classifier. In other words, let the classifier report not only its first choice for each character, but also its second choice, third choice, etc. In this case, the classifier output for the last four characters of the example might take the form

```
7 T L 9 0 . . .
1 , ) T 3 . . .
1 L 7 ( A . . .
2 Z 3 S N . . .
```

Scanning this information, the analyzer can determine that the correct character string almost unquestionably ended in 7, 12 rather than 71, 2.

In practice, the classifier not only ranks the alternatives for a character in order of preference, but it also assigns a confidence measure to each alternative. This allows finer judgments on the part of the analyzer. For example, the analyzer can determine whether a second choice ranks almost on a par with the first choice or whether its confidence is so low that it should be ignored.

As an example, the classifier might output the following first-choice character strings at different locations in the text, where the context marks them as occurrences of variable names: INX, INY, IMX, INX, JNX, INY, INX, INX, and so on. How many actual names are involved, and how many have been formed by the misclassification of characters? It is impossible to answer this question on the basis of the first choices alone, but by considering the other leading alternatives and their confidence measures the analyzer may be able to make a reasonable guess.

We thus see that, when a body of related information is to be "recognized" through classification of its constituent elements and subsequent context analysis, the alternative choices of the classifier and their confidences contain vital information. This information is lost if the classifier reports only its first choice. In this light, we can say that the classifier should not classify; it should estimate as best it can and let the context analyzer finalize the decisions.

What classifiers can produce confidence information? One broad group of classifiers, which we may call decision-tree classifiers, proceeds by successive dichotomization of the output classes. A printed character might first be tested to determine whether it has any loops, then whether it is concave to the right, and so on. Each test removes a number of possible classes from contention, until only one is left. A decision-tree classifier cannot reasonably yield confidence information, owing to the binary nature of the tests.

Most of the common families of classifiers fall into the other group, which we may call one-in-many classifiers. A classifier of this type generates for each class a measure of the confidence that the pattern under test falls into that class, and the output class is selected by taking the maximum of these measures. These measures are natural confidence measures for the classes. They are thrown away if the pattern is explicitly classified. Depending on the family, the confidence measure may be the distance of the test feature vector from a prototype vector (nearest-neighbor classifier), the dot product of the test vector with a stored weight vector (linear learning machine), the estimated probability that a point was drawn from a given statistical distribution (Bayes classifier), etc. In a multimodal classifier, a number of measurements are made for each class, and the largest of these is taken to represent the class.

The decision-tree type of classifier is not only at a disadvantage with respect to the one-in-many classifier for the purpose of producing confidence information, but in the author's experience it is also at a disadvantage in terms of classification performance. Each test in a decision tree is crucial, yet in dealing with off-line hand-printed characters it has appeared difficult if not impossible to devise *any* truly reliable tests. Take, for example, the basic question of whether or not a character has enclosures (loops). Examination of data of "moderate" quality discloses many characters in which loops have been blacked in or broken open, and many others in which micro-enclosures have been formed in the transducing process. Thus a separation of characters on the basis of enclosures will not perform the desired dichotomy of classes.

Let us look at the failure of the decision-tree classifier in the following light: The classifier (or the preprocessor that precedes it) is forced to decide whether a character has a feature (such as an enclosure), yes or no, and the classifier is forced to commit itself on the basis of this information. The one-in-many classifier, by contrast, can combine the enclosure feature with a multitude of other features, given various weights, in order to arrive at a confidence measure for a particular category. Furthermore, in this combining process, nonbinary, many-valued features can be employed. Thus, the enclosure feature can indicate *with what confidence* there appears to be or not to be a significant enclosure.

Let us go one step further and suggest that the points just noted (the advisability of producing class confidence information in the classifier, and the advisability of producing many-valued features in the preprocessor) are both reflections of a general principle—that of retaining full information at each intermediate stage of the pattern-recognition process.

Another way of stating the principle is this: Never make a firm decision unnecessarily. Only at the last stage of the recognition process, where a final decision is required, should the transformation be made to a discrete space of unqualified alternatives.

The argument for this principle may be summarized as follows: Each stage of the pattern-recognition process operates with a wider field of view (a broader context) than the preceding stages. On the basis of the broader context, it may see fit to adjust or to overrule the decisions made by an earlier stage. The confidence, or firmness, assigned to an earlier decision is information important to this adjustment process. If the outputs of the earlier stage are chopped into binary decisions, too much information is lost.

In the "ultimate" pattern-recognition system for reading printed or handwritten texts, for example, each stage of the system would have the ability to refer back to previous stages to acquire further information in cases of uncertainty. This is a feature of human reading, performed so naturally that it is on an unconscious level most of the time. One comes to a sentence that seems wrong, and rescans the text to look for alternative word interpretations that may have been overlooked. Occasionally, especially in handwritten texts, the problem is difficult enough to rise to the conscious level, and one may spend several seconds looking at a scrawled image and trying to fit alternative letter shapes into portions of it as a clue to guessing at the word. This is a case in which the request for review is made back through several levels of organization.

It is impossible, however, to provide such general back-referencing capability in a recognition system within the present state of the art. Systems must be segmented to be manageable. We contend that the use of many-valued coordinates and multiple confidence measures provides a partial compensation for the lack of back-referencing. By providing graded responses and alternative confidence measures, each stage of the recognition system has prepared in advance an answer to the question that may be asked by a higher-order stage, "What can you tell me if I don't accept your first-choice response?"

Another principle, corollary to the one just discussed, is that of providing a smooth transformation between data spaces. The preprocessor may be thought of as performing a mathematical transformation of the data from its representation in "transduced space" (the output of the transducer) to feature space (Figure 4). The classifier transforms the data from feature space to the "class space" of class confidence measures. Other stages of the recognition process may be regarded as performing similar transformations.

The idea of a smooth transformation is, loosely speaking, that of a continuous transformation in the mathematical sense. In the same vein that many-valued coordinates are used to approximate the ideal of continuous confidence measures, the smooth transformation is not truly continuous but might be called a quasi-continuous transformation between one space of multivalued coordinates and another.

The argument for the principle of smooth transformations is perhaps most readily made by an example. Consider two pattern classes, hand-printed numeral 8 and letter B. As the original pattern is continuously transformed from a "good" 8 to a "good" B, it will pass through a transition region where the probability of its being a B increases and that of its being an 8 decreases. The features from the preprocessor (for example, the feature of having a concavity on the left side) and the confidences of the two classes output by the classifier should reflect this continuous change. It is clearly undesirable to place some arbitrary infinitesimal change in the pattern in the position of being the straw that breaks the camel's back—suddenly creating a concavity, or changing a definite 8 to a definite B—if there is a higher order of contextual analysis to which close decisions can be applied.

We have argued above that each intermediate stage of a pattern-recognition system should produce many-valued output coordinates reflecting the confidences attached to its decisions, so that the confidence information can be utilized by subsequent stages. It is worth noting that in many systems of practical interest the ultimate decisions, or the ultimate verifications of decisions made by the machine part of the system, are performed by a human. Thus, even the final machine stage in such a system is intermediate in the overall system. Its output should reflect the confidences of its decisions and the possible alternatives. This principle should have a considerable influence on the design of the output displays of an automatic text-recognition system, at which a human is to proofread the text. One can think of many aids to proofreading that the system might provide, based on its analysis of the confidences of its own outputs. These include the simple marking of characters in doubt or regions where difficulties were encountered, the displaying of the original character classifications where the system made a spelling change or a syntax substitution in which it was not highly confident, the presentation of possible alternatives in a kind of multiple-choice format for rapid decision-making by the human and so on. The economy of various aids will be determined by the trade-off between the cost of their implementation and the reduction in proof-reading costs that they provide, remembering that the minimization of total system cost is the ultimate objective. This fact can lead to some curious results, such as the fact that it is more worthwhile to track down and flag subtle errors than glaring ones.

Every type of text—programming languages, natural languages, accounting forms—in fact, every area of pattern recognition that involves a hierarchy of organization has its own contextual structure. The rules of context may differ almost completely from one application to another. In many cases, of which FORTRAN text recognition is an example, the more sophisticated aspects of context analysis are probably economically unattractive at the present time. However, we can expect future recognition systems to employ an increasing hierarchy of analysis procedures and to carry the overall recognition process more nearly to completion.

REFERENCES

1. John H. Munson, "The Recognition of Hand-Printed Text," *Proc. IEEE Pattern Recognition Workshop,* Puerto Rico, October 24–26, 1966 (Thompson Book Company, Washington, D.C., 1968).
2. Gabriel F. Groner, "Real-Time Recognition of Hand-Printed Text," *AFIPS Conf. Proc., 1966 Fall Joint Computer Conference,* Vol. 29, pp. 591–601 (Spartan Books, Washington, D.C., 1966). Also, references therein.
3. Nilo Lindgren, "Machine Recognition of Human Language, Part III–Cursive Script Recognition," *IEEE Spectrum,* pp. 104–116 (May 1965).
4. Nils J. Nilsson, Learning Machines (McGraw-Hill Book Company , New York, N. Y., 1965).
5. T. M. Cover and P. E. Hart, "Nearest-Neighbor Pattern Classification," *IEEE Trans. on Info. Theory,* Vol. IT–13, pp. 21–27 (January 1967).
6. G. H. Ball, "Data Analysis in the Social Sciences–What About the Details?" *AFIPS Conf. Proc., 1965 Fall Joint Computer Conference,* Vol. 27, Part I, pp. 533–559 (Spartan Books, Washington, D.C., 1965).

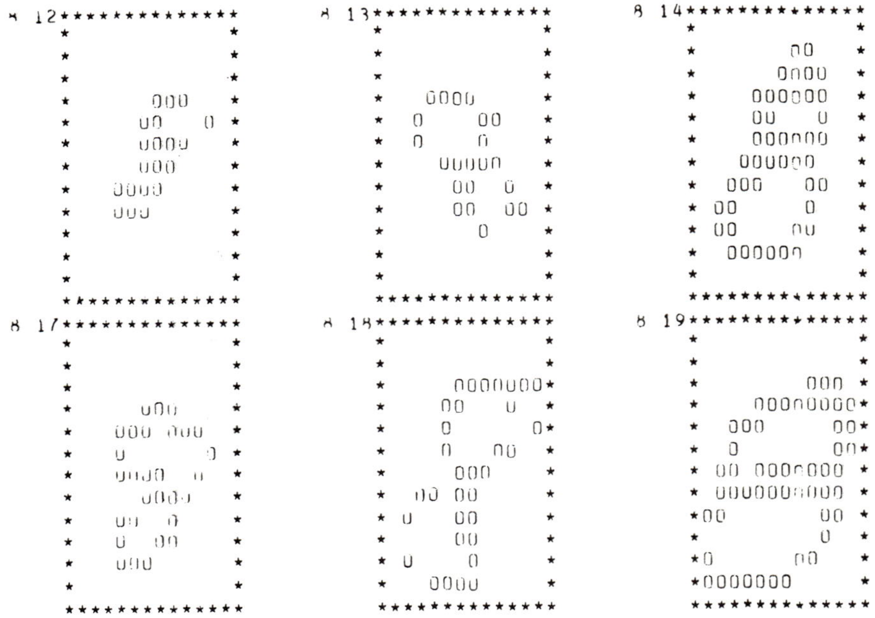

Figure 1

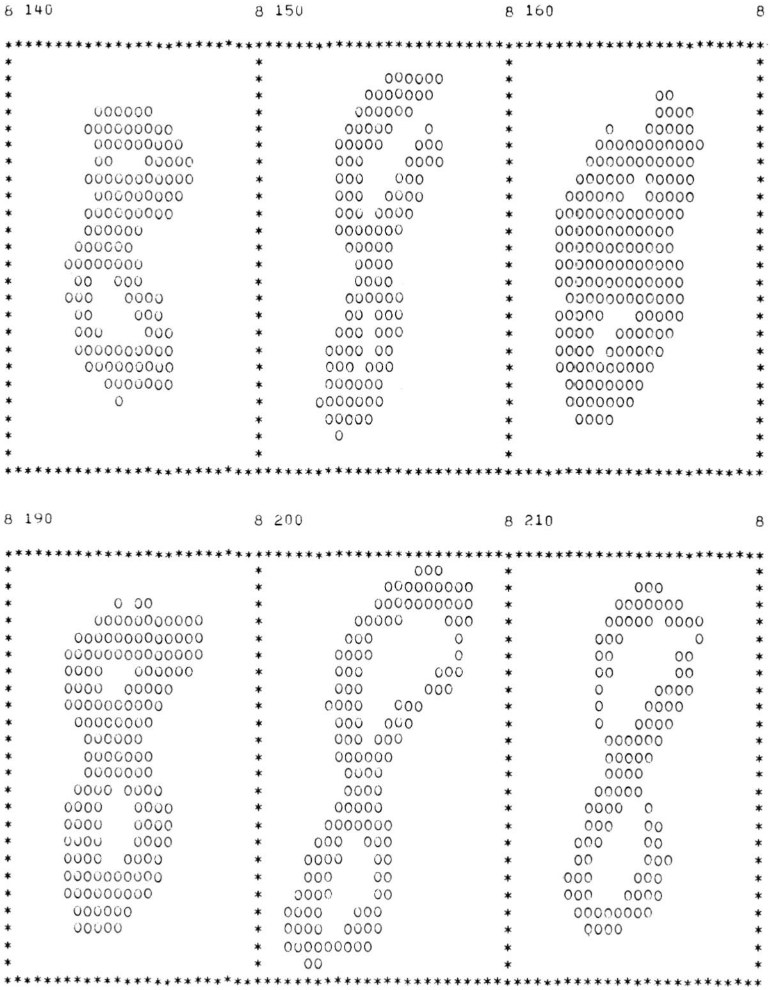

Figure 2

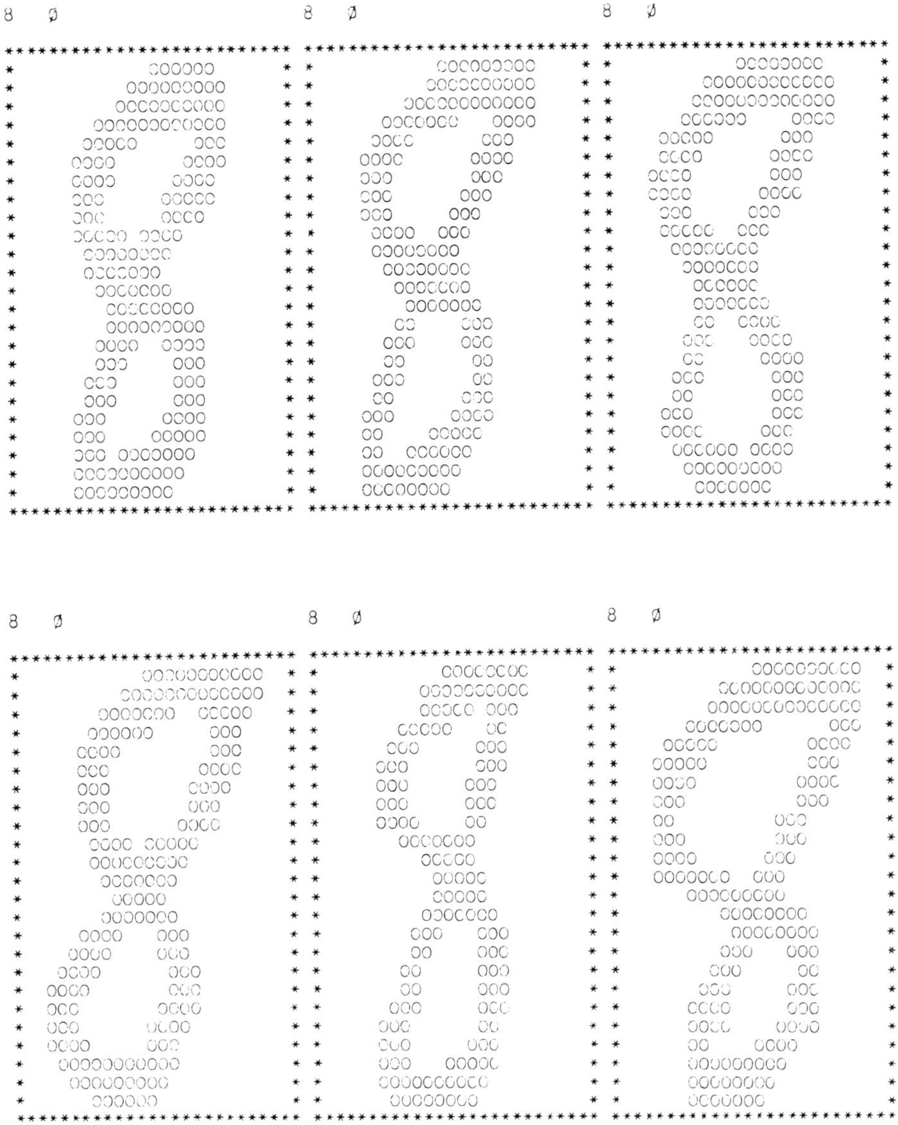

Figure 3

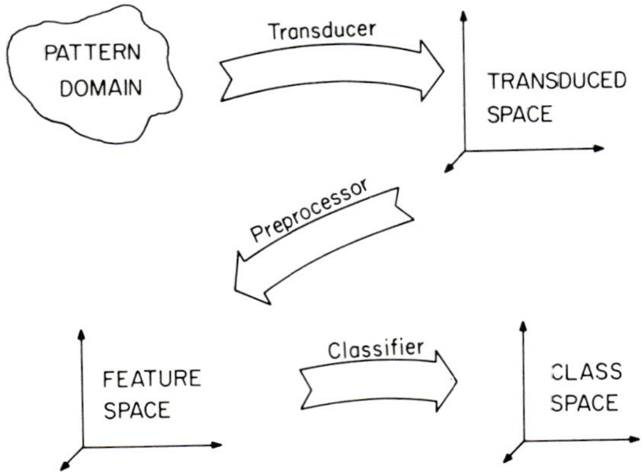

Figure 4

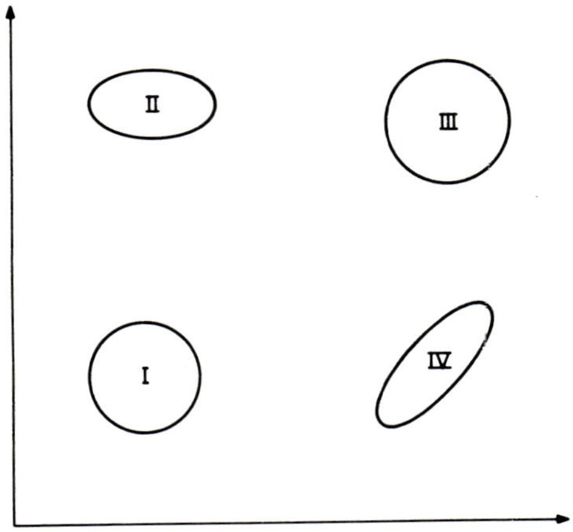

Figure 5

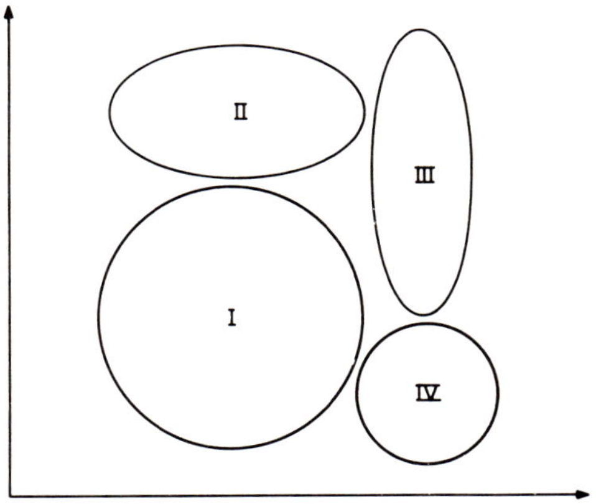

Figure 6

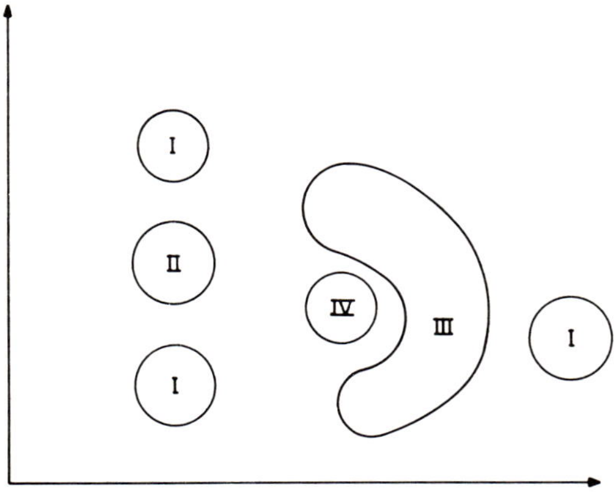

Figure 7

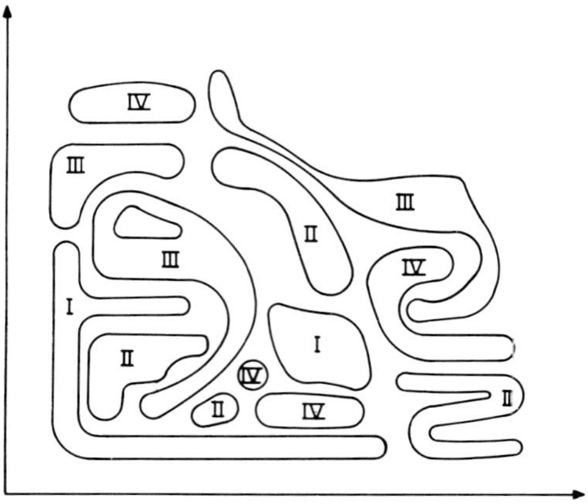

Figure 8

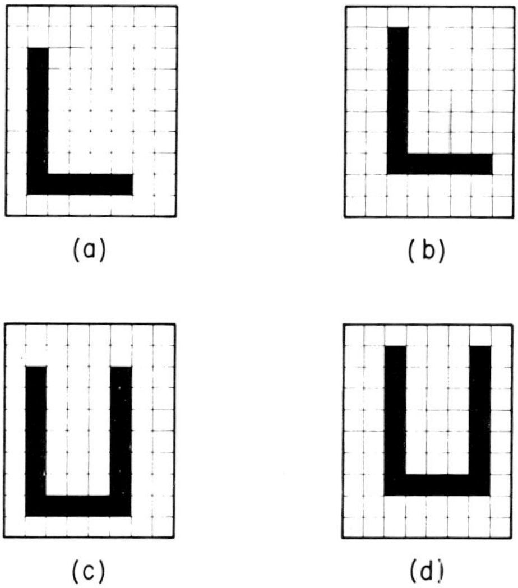

Figure 9

THE EVALUATION OF THE STATISTICAL CLASSIFIER

Shoichi Noguchi, Kazuyuki Nagasawa,
and Juro Oizumi

RESEARCH INSTITUTE OF ELECTRICAL COMMUNICATION
TOHOKU UNIVERSITY, SENDAI, JAPAN

Synopsis

The recognition ability of the typical statistical classifiers, the minimum distance classifier, the Bayes classifier and the regression classifier is evaluated under the assumption that the patterns are distributed according to $N(\mu_\ell, \underline{\Sigma})$. $(\ell = A, B)$.

New concepts, that is, the information processing capacity and the a% information processing capacity are introduced.

The evaluation of the recognition ability of each classifier is obtained by these new concepts.

The Bayes classifier and the regression classifier show the same classification ability, but the minimum distance classifier is somewhat different.

Several kinds of computer simulations are obtained to check the theoretical results. These results coincide well with the theoretical results.

1. Introduction

The models of the pattern recognition are generally classified into two types; (1) the dynamic model and (2) the static model. The dynamic model is represented by the reverberations in the network. Although this model has many attractive features for the pattern recognition, it still has many problems to be solved in order to be utilized. From this standpoint, we only discuss the static model. In this model, the input patterns are processed sequentially while they are passing through the several units: (1) the sensory unit, (2) the normalizing unit, (3) the feature extracting unit, (4) the associative unit, (5) the decision unit and (6) the response unit.

In order to design the powerful pattern recognizer, we should make the theoretical researches on the recognition system and utilize each unit in the synthetic way. But as the first stage of research, it is important to analyze and get enough information on the characteristics of each unit. It is not necessary here to mention the normalization and the feature extracting processes. We have made some important theoretical and practical researches in these aspects.

The associative unit is a very important part for the pattern recognizer, because it organizes the classifier and decides the capability of the information processing and the complexity of the system. Well-known typical organizers of this unit are: (1) the statistical organizer and (2) the nonstatistical organizer. The nonstatistical organizer is represented by Perception type procedure. The capability of the information processing and the concrete method for the organization of this system are reported in several papers[1,2,3]. Although this system shows high capability in information processing, it has some disadvantages as follows: (1) If the patterns are not linearly separable, the organizing procedure does not converge and in order to check the linear separability, it sometimes requires a lot of trials. (2) Even though the patterns are linearly separable, it also sometimes requires a lot of trials and large memories.

In contrast to the disadvantages of non-statistical method, the statistical method has many merits from the practical point of view. These merits are summarized as follows: (1) it is not necessary to consider the linear separability of the input patterns and the system can organize the recognizer in optimal way even when the pattern are not linearly separable, (2) the organization of the system can be made quickly by the analogue technique. For these reasons, several kinds of the statistical organizers have been developed[4]. But we have not made the theoretical research yet on the capability of the information processing which is the most important characteristics of the classifier. From this standpoint, we took the theoretical evaluation of the statistical classifier into consideration. We introduced the new concepts of the information processing capacity and the α% information processing capacity as in the case of the nonstatistical case. The recognition ability of each classifier is evaluated by these concepts.

2. The Statistical Classifier

In the following analysis, our basic assumptions are as follows: (1) The patterns are classified into two categories A and B. (2) Both categories have a member of M/2 sample patterns respectively. (We can also extend our analysis with slight modification to the various cases of different sample patterns in each category.) (3) Each pattern is represented by an N dimensional vector $\mathbf{X}_\alpha$ and each $\mathbf{X}_\alpha$ is distributed according to multivariate normal distribution $N(\underline{\mu}_\ell, \underline{\Sigma})$ (ℓ = A, B) respectively ($\underline{\mu}_\ell$ and $\underline{\Sigma}$ are unknown parameters). (4) The sample covariance matrix is assumed to be full rank.

As the basic statistical classifier, we compared three types: (1) the minimum distance classifier, (2) the Bayes classifier and (3) the regression classifier.

2.1 THE MINIMUM DISTANCE CLASSIFIER

We define the distance D between two vectors $\mathbf{X}$ and $\mathbf{Y}$ by

$$D = \|\mathbf{X}-\mathbf{Y}\| = \sqrt{\mathbf{X}^t\,\mathbf{Y}}\,, \tag{1}$$

where $\mathbf{X}^t$ means the transpose of $\mathbf{X}$. In this system, we classify patterns as follows: if

$$\|\mathbf{X}-\underline{\mu}_A\| - \|\mathbf{X}-\underline{\mu}_B\| \leqslant 0, \qquad \mathbf{X} \in A \tag{2}$$

and if

$$\|\mathbf{X}-\underline{\mu}_A\| - \|\mathbf{X}-\underline{\mu}_B\| > 0, \qquad \mathbf{X} \in B\,.$$

Because parameters $\underline{\mu}_A$ and $\underline{\mu}_B$ are unknown, we estimate them by the sample means

$$\overline{\mathbf{X}}^{(\ell)} = \frac{2}{M} \sum_{a} \mathbf{X}_a^{(\ell)} \quad (\ell = A, B) \tag{3}$$

By the above procedure, the final decision function which decides the region of classification into A, R_1, and into B, R_2 is obtained as follows:

$$R_1 ; \underline{\delta}^t \mathbf{X} - \frac{1}{2} \underline{\delta}^t (\overline{\mathbf{X}}^A + \overline{\mathbf{X}}^B) \geqslant 0$$
$$R_2 ; \underline{\delta}^t \mathbf{X} - \frac{1}{2} \underline{\delta}^t (\overline{\mathbf{X}}^A + \overline{\mathbf{X}}^B) < 0 \tag{4}$$

where

$$\underline{\delta} = \overline{\mathbf{X}}^{(A)} - \overline{\mathbf{X}}^{(B)} \tag{5}$$

2.2 THE BAYES CLASSIFIER

In this model, the fundamental principle is to find i which minimizes $C_{X(i)}$ when the input pattern $\mathbf{X}$ is applied;
where

$$C_{\mathbf{X}(i)} = \sum_{j}^{A,B} \lambda(i|j) P(\mathbf{X}|j) P(j) \tag{6}$$

and $\lambda(i|j)$ is a loss function assigned to this system. For simplicity, we assume $\lambda(i|j)$ by

$$\lambda(i|j) = 1 - \delta_{i,j} \quad . \tag{7}$$

In this case, the decision function $g(\mathbf{X})$ is obtained by

$$g(\mathbf{X}) = \mathbf{X}^t \underline{\Sigma}^{-1} (\underline{\mu}_A - \underline{\mu}_B) - \frac{1}{2} (\underline{\mu}_A + \underline{\mu}_B)^t \underline{\Sigma}^{-1} (\underline{\mu}_A - \underline{\mu}_B) \tag{8}$$

We estimate unknown parameters $\underline{\mu}_A$, $\underline{\mu}_B$, and $\underline{\Sigma}$ by unbiased estimators $\overline{\mathbf{X}}^{(\ell)}$ and $\mathbf{S}$ in the following way;

$$\overline{\mathbf{X}}^{(\ell)} = \frac{2}{M} \sum_{a} \mathbf{X}_a^{(\ell)} \quad (\ell = A, B) \tag{9}$$

$$\mathbf{S} = \frac{1}{M-2} \sum_{\ell} \sum_{a} (\mathbf{X}_a^{(\ell)} - \overline{\mathbf{X}}^{(\ell)})(\mathbf{X}_a^{(\ell)} - \overline{\mathbf{X}}^{(\ell)})^t. \tag{10}$$

The final decision function which decides the region of classification into A, R_1 and into B, R_2 is obtained by

$$R_1;\ \mathbf{X}^t\mathbf{S}^{-1}\underline{\delta} - \frac{1}{2}(\overline{\mathbf{X}}^{(A)} + \overline{\mathbf{X}}^{(B)})^t\mathbf{S}^{-1}\underline{\delta} \geqslant 0$$

$$R_2;\ \mathbf{X}^t\mathbf{S}^{-1}\underline{\delta} - \frac{1}{2}(\overline{\mathbf{X}}^{A} + \overline{\mathbf{X}}^{(B)})^t\mathbf{S}^{-1}\underline{\delta} < 0\ . \tag{11}$$

2.3 THE REGRESSION CLASSIFIER[5]

In this system, we assign the desired output $Y_a^{(\ell)}$ to each pattern $\mathbf{X}_a^{(\ell)}$ (ℓ = A, B, a = 1 ~ M/2) and organize the weight vector W and the threshold W_o so as to minimize the following Q function;

$$Q = \sum_{\ell} \sum_{a} \{Y_a^{(\ell)} - \mathbf{W}^t\mathbf{X}_a^{(\ell)} - W_o\}^2\ . \tag{12}$$

The optimum values, $\widetilde{\mathbf{W}}$ and $\widetilde{\mathbf{W}}_o$ are obtained by

$$\widetilde{\mathbf{W}} = \mathbf{V}^{-1}\mathbf{U}\ ,\ \widetilde{W}_o = \overline{Y} - \widetilde{\mathbf{W}}^t\overline{\mathbf{X}} \tag{13}$$

where $\mathbf{V} = \mathbf{S}_o + \frac{M}{4}\underline{\delta}\underline{\delta}^t$, $\mathbf{U} = \sum_{\ell}\sum_{a}(Y_a^{(\ell)} - \overline{Y})(\mathbf{X}_a^{(\ell)} - \overline{\mathbf{X}})$, $\overline{Y} = \frac{1}{M}\sum_{\ell}\sum_{a} Y_a^{(\ell)}$,

$\overline{\mathbf{X}} = \frac{1}{M}\sum_{\ell}\sum_{a}\mathbf{X}_a^{(\ell)}$ and

$$\mathbf{S}_o = \sum_{\ell}\sum_{a}(\mathbf{X}_a^{(\ell)} - \overline{\mathbf{X}}^{(\ell)})(\mathbf{X}_a^{(\ell)} - \overline{\mathbf{X}}^{(\ell)})^t\ . \tag{14}$$

The final decision function which decides the region of classification into A, R_1 and into B, R_2 is obtained by

$$R_1\ ;\ \widetilde{\mathbf{W}}^t\mathbf{X} + \widetilde{W}_o \geqslant 0$$

$$R_2\ ;\ \widetilde{\mathbf{W}}^t\mathbf{X} + \widetilde{W}_o < 0\ . \tag{15}$$

3. The Characteristics of the Classifier

3.1 THE MINIMUM DISTANCE CLASSIFIER

If the sample patterns are applied to the linear equation (3), the distribution of the output of this equation is approximated by the uninormal distribution $N(\mu_\ell, T)$ (ℓ = A, B) where

$$\mu_A = \frac{1}{2}\underline{\delta}^t\underline{\delta} \qquad \mu_B = -\frac{1}{2}\underline{\delta}^t\underline{\delta} \qquad \text{and } T = \underline{\delta}^t\underline{\Sigma}\underline{\delta} \tag{16}$$

The parameters μ_A, μ_B and T are the random variables. μ_A and μ_B are distributed as the non-central χ^2 distribution, and T, the Wishart distribution. For simplicity, we consider the input patterns distributed according to $N(\underline{\mu}_\ell, \text{II})$; where $\underline{\text{II}}$ is the identity matrix.

In this case, $\sqrt{M/4}\ \underline{\delta}$ is distributed as $N(\sqrt{M/4}\ (\underline{\mu}_A - \underline{\mu}_B), \text{II})$, and $\underline{\delta}^t\underline{\delta}$ as the non-central χ^2 distribution with N degree of freedom and the non-centrality parameter λ by

$$\lambda = \frac{M}{8}(\underline{\mu}_A - \underline{\mu}_B)^t(\underline{\mu}_A - \underline{\mu}_B)\ . \tag{17}$$

If $\underline{\mu}_A = \underline{\mu}_B$, the distribution is the χ^2 distribution with N degree of freedom. Putting $\underline{\delta}^t\underline{\delta} = d_m$, we obtain

$$\mu_A = \frac{1}{2} d_m, \qquad \mu_B = -\frac{1}{2} d_m \qquad \text{and} \qquad T = d_m\ . \tag{18}$$

This parameter d_b expresses the measure of the separations of two categories and the probability density function of d_m is expressed by[6]

$$f_{N(\lambda)}(d_m) = \frac{M}{4}\sum_{k=0}^{\infty}\frac{e^{-\lambda}\lambda^k}{k!}\ \frac{(\frac{M}{8}d_m)^{\frac{N}{2}+k-1}}{\Gamma(\frac{N}{2}+k)}\exp(-\frac{M}{8}d_m) \tag{19}$$

The relation between the correct recognition probability R_m and the parameter d_m is obtained easily by

$$R_m = \Phi(\frac{1}{2}\sqrt{d_m}\ ) \tag{20}$$

where $\Phi(x)$ is an error function. The probability density function of R_m is obtained by two equations (19) and (20).

3.2 THE BAYES CLASSIFIER

If the sample pattern is applied to the linear equation (11), the distribution of this output is approximated by the uninormal distribution.*

$$N(\bar{\mu}_\ell, \bar{T}) \quad (\ell = A, B)$$

where

$$\bar{\mu}_A = \frac{1}{2}\,\underline{\delta}^t S^{-1}\underline{\delta},\ \bar{\mu}_B = -\frac{1}{2}\,\underline{\delta}^t S^{-1}\underline{\delta},\ \text{and } \bar{T} = \underline{\delta}^t S^{-1}\underline{\delta} \quad . \tag{21}$$

We define a new parameter d_b by

$$d_b = \bar{\mu}_A - \bar{\mu}_B = \underline{\delta}^t S^{-1}\underline{\delta} \ . \tag{22}$$

This parameter d_b means the measure of the separation of two categories. The distribution of this parameter is a kind of T^2 distribution derived by Hotelling. It is easily proved that $\underline{\delta}_o = \sqrt{M/4}\,\underline{\delta}$ is distributed as $N(\mathbf{V}, \underline{\Sigma})$, and $S_o = (M-2)\mathbf{S}$ independently as

$$\sum_{a=1}^{M-2} Z_a Z_a^t$$

with the $\mathbf{Z}_a$ independent and each with distribution $N(\underline{0}, \underline{\Sigma})$; where

$$\mathbf{V} = \sqrt{\frac{M}{4}}\,(\underline{\mu}_A - \underline{\mu}_B) \tag{23}$$

Then $\dfrac{m_2}{m_1}\,\dfrac{M}{4(M-2)}\,d_b$ [6] is distributed as a non-central F distribution with m_1 and m_2 degrees of freedom and the non-centrality parameter λ, where

$$m_1 = N,\ m_2 = M-N-1 \ \text{and}\ \lambda = \frac{1}{2}\mathbf{V}^t\underline{\Sigma}^{-1}\mathbf{V} \ . \tag{24}$$

If $\underline{\mu}_A = \underline{\mu}_B$, the distribution is the central F-distribution.

The probability density function of d_b is obtained by

$$f_{N(\lambda)}(d_b) = \sum_{k=o}^{\infty} \frac{e^{-\lambda}\lambda^k}{k!} \frac{\Gamma(\frac{m_1+m_2}{2}+k)}{\Gamma(\frac{m_1}{2}+k)\,\Gamma(\frac{m_2}{2})} \frac{1}{4} \left(\frac{d_b}{4}\right)^{\frac{m_1}{2}+k-1}$$

$$\left(1+\frac{d_b}{4}\right)^{-\left(\frac{m_1+m_2}{2}+k\right)} \ . \tag{25}$$

* In this case, we consider only M patterns, so the number of patterns in this population is finite with the mean $\underline{\mu}_\ell$ and the covariance matrix $\mathbf{S}$. We approximate this distribution by $N(\underline{\mu}_\ell, \mathbf{S})$.

The relation between the correct recognition probability R_b and d_b is obtained before and given by

$$R_b = \Phi(\frac{1}{2}\sqrt{d_b}) \ . \tag{26}$$

3.3 THE REGRESSION CLASSIFIER

If the input patterns are applied to this system, the distribution of the output is approximated by the uninormal distribution $N(\tilde{\mu}_\ell , \tilde{T})$. ($\ell$ = A, B), where

$$\tilde{\mu}_A = \frac{1}{2} U^t V^{-1} \underline{\delta} + \bar{Y} \ , \ \tilde{\mu}_B = -\frac{1}{2} U^t V^{-1} \underline{\delta} + \bar{Y}$$

and (27)

$$\tilde{v} = \frac{1}{(M-2)} \{U^t V^{-1} U - \frac{M}{4} U^t V^{-1} \underline{\delta}\, \underline{\delta}^t V^{-1} U\} \ .$$

In order to attain the maximum correct classification probability, it is necessary to maximize the following function F;

$$F = \frac{\frac{(M-2)}{4} U^t V^{-1} \underline{\delta}\, \underline{\delta}^t V^{-1} U}{U^t V^{-1} U - \frac{M}{4} U^t V^{-1} \underline{\delta}\, \underline{\delta}^t V^{-1} U}$$

$$\simeq \frac{U^t V^{-1} \underline{\delta}_o \underline{\delta}_o{}^t V^{-1} U}{U^t V^{-1} S_o V^{-1} U} \ . \tag{28}$$

The problem is reduced to find the eigen value of the following equation

$$| \underline{\delta}_o \underline{\delta}_o{}^t - \tilde{\lambda}\, S_o | = 0 \ . \tag{29}$$

The optimum correct recognition probability R is obtained by

$$R = \Phi (\frac{1}{2}\sqrt{\tilde{\lambda}}) \ . \tag{30}$$

We have the following theory:[6] If **Y** is an N dimensional vector, and **A** is a non-singular N dimensional matrix, $\mathbf{Y}^t \mathbf{A}^{-1} \mathbf{Y}$ is only one non-zero eigen value of the following equation,

$$| \mathbf{Y}\, \mathbf{Y}^t - \lambda\, \mathbf{A} | = 0 \ . \tag{31}$$

By this relation, we obtain the optimum eigen value $\tilde{\lambda}$ by

$$\tilde{\lambda} = \underline{\delta}_o{}^t \, \mathbf{S}_o{}^{-1} \underline{\delta}_o \quad . \tag{32}$$

The assignment of the desired output $Y_a{}^{(\ell)}$ is an important problem in this system. It is shown here that the assignment $Y_a{}^{(A)} = 1$ and $Y_a{}^{(B)} = -1$ is one of the optimum solution.

By the above assignment, equation (27) is replaced by

$$\tilde{\mu}_A = \frac{M}{4} \underline{\delta}^t \mathbf{V}^{-1} \underline{\delta} \; , \; \tilde{\mu}_B = -\frac{M}{4} \underline{\delta}^t \mathbf{V}^{-1} \underline{\delta}$$

and (33)

$$\tilde{T} = \frac{M}{8} \underline{\delta}^t \mathbf{V}^{-1} \underline{\delta} \left(2 - \frac{M}{2} \underline{\delta}^t \mathbf{V}^{-1} \underline{\delta}\right) \; .$$

We define a new parameter d_r by

$$d_r = \frac{M}{2} \underline{\delta}^t \mathbf{V}^{-1} \underline{\delta} = 2 \underline{\delta}_o^t \mathbf{V}^{-1} \underline{\delta}_o \quad . \tag{34}$$

It is clear that d_r is the eigen value of the

$$| \underline{\delta}_o \underline{\delta}_o{}^t - f \frac{\mathbf{V}}{2} | = | (1 - \frac{f}{2}) \underline{\delta}_o \underline{\delta}_o{}^t - \frac{f}{2} \mathbf{S}_o | = 0 \; . \tag{35}$$

By equation (35), we obtain the relation $\tilde{\lambda}$ and f by

$$\tilde{\lambda} = \frac{f}{2-f} \quad . \tag{36}$$

By equation (33), the correct recognition probability of this case is obtained by

$$R_r = \Phi\left(\sqrt{\frac{d_r}{2-d_r}}\right) = \Phi\left(\sqrt{\frac{f}{2-f}}\right) \; . \tag{37}$$

Equation (37) shows the same probability as that of (30) and attains the optimum classification on the average.

By equation (22), we notice more important relations between d_b and d_r by

$$d_b \simeq \frac{4 d_r}{2 - d_r} \tag{38}$$

Substituting this relation in (25), we obtain the probability density function of d_r as follows when $Y_a{}^{(A)} = 1$ and $Y_a{}^{(B)} = -1$;

$$f(d_r) = \sum_{k=o}^{\infty} \frac{e^{-\lambda}\lambda^k}{k!} \frac{2^{(1-k-\frac{m_1+m_2}{2})}}{B(\frac{m_1}{2}+k, \frac{m_2}{2})} d_r^{\frac{m_1}{2}+k-1} (2-d_r)^{\frac{m_2}{2}-1} \tag{39}$$

where

$$B(m, n) = \frac{\Gamma(m)\ \Gamma(n)}{\Gamma(m+n)} \quad . \tag{40}$$

This is a kind of noncentral Beta distribution.

4. The Classification Ability and the Pattern Processing Capacity of the Classifiers

The probability density function of the correct classification is determined theoretically as the function of M, N, $(\mu_A - \mu_B)$ and Σ for each classifier. But in order to have an insight in the gross, we simplify the problem by considering the representative parameters of the distribution. We define R_m, R_b, and R_r by

$$\bar{R}_m = \Phi(\frac{1}{2}\sqrt{\bar{d}_m}) \ , \ \bar{R}_b = \Phi(\frac{1}{2}\sqrt{\bar{d}_b}) \text{ and } \bar{d}_r = \Phi(\sqrt{\frac{\bar{d}_r}{2-\bar{d}_r}}) \tag{41}$$

where $\bar{d}_m$, $\bar{d}_b$ and $\bar{d}_r$ are the mean value of each distribution d_m, d_b, and d_r respectively.

We define two concepts, pattern processing capacity $I_n^{(m)}$ and the $a\%$ processing capacity $I_n^{(m)}$ $(a\%)$ in the minimum distance classifier by

$$I_n^{(m)} \triangleq (\frac{M}{N}) \ , \text{ when } \bar{R}_m = 1 \tag{42}$$

and

$$I_n^{(m)}\ (a\%) \triangleq (\frac{M}{N}) \ , \text{ when } \bar{R}_m = a\% \ . \tag{43}$$

This means the pattern processing capacity for one dimension. The same definition is also adopted in other classifiers.

4.1 THE MINIMUM DISTANCE CLASSIFIER

The probability density function of d_m is given by (19). We obtain the following relation;

$$E[d_m{}^n] = \left(\frac{M}{8}\right)^n \sum_{k=o}^{\infty} \frac{e^{-\lambda}\lambda^k}{k!} \frac{\Gamma\left(\frac{N}{2}+n+k\right)}{\Gamma\left(\frac{N}{2}+k\right)} \tag{44}$$

$$E[d_m] = \frac{4}{M}\,(N + 2\lambda) \tag{45}$$

In order to make clear the meaning of the information processing capacity, the model with the following assumptions is considered: (1) The pattern is distributed according to N(0,II). (2) The pattern is distributed according to N(1/2 ΔI, II) for A category and to N(– 1/2 ΔI, II) for B respectively; where I is a vector with all component 1 and II is the unit matrix. For the first case, we obtain

$$\lambda = 0 \quad \text{and} \quad \bar{d}_m = \frac{4N}{M} \ . \tag{46}$$

By this result, we get

$$\bar{R}_m = \Phi\left(\frac{1}{2}\sqrt{\bar{d}_m}\right) \ . \tag{47}$$

This relation is given in Figure (1). We have

$$I_n{}^{(m)} = 0 \tag{48}$$

and for the 99% information capacity,

$$I_n{}^{(m)}\ (99\%) \simeq 0.184 \tag{49}$$

For the second case, we obtain noncentrality λ and $\bar{d}_{m(\lambda)}$ by

$$\lambda = \frac{M}{8}\, N\Delta^2 \tag{50}$$

and

$$\bar{d}_{m(\lambda)} = 4\,\frac{N}{M}\left(1+\frac{M}{4}\,\Delta^2\right) \ . \tag{51}$$

By this relation, $I_n{}^{(m)}$ (99%) is obtained by

$$I_n{}^{(m)}\ (99\%) \simeq 0.184\left(1+\frac{M}{4}\,\Delta^2\right) \ . \tag{52}$$

$\bar{R}_{m(\lambda)}$ is defined by

$$\bar{R}_{m(\lambda)} = \Phi(\frac{1}{2}\sqrt{\bar{d}_{m(\lambda)}}) \quad . \tag{47'}$$

The relation of the mean recognition rate $\bar{R}_{m(\lambda)}$ vs. M/N ratio is given in Figure 2.

The probability of the correct classification of the total patterns $P_{m(\lambda)}$ is defined by

$$P_{m(\lambda)} = (\bar{R}_{m(\lambda)})^M \tag{53}$$

The relation of $P_{m(\lambda)}$ vs. M/N is given for some parameters in Figure (3).

4.2 THE BAYES CLASSIFIER

The probability density function of d_b is given by (25). We obtain

$$E[d_b{}^n] = 4n \sum_{k=o}^{\infty} \frac{e^{-\lambda}\lambda^k}{k!} \frac{\Gamma(\frac{m_1}{2} + k + n)\,\Gamma(\frac{m_2}{2} - n)}{\Gamma(\frac{m_1}{2} + k)\,\Gamma(\frac{m_2}{2})} \tag{54}$$

and

$$E[d_1] = 4 \sum_{k=o}^{\infty} \frac{e^{-\lambda}\lambda^k}{k!} (\frac{m_1 + 2k}{m_2 - 2}) = 4\frac{N+2}{M-N-3} \quad . \tag{55}$$

As in the case of [4.1], we consider the following problems. (1) The pattern is distributed according to $N(\underline{0}, \Sigma)$. (2) The pattern is distributed according to $N(1/2\ \Delta I, \underline{\Sigma}_1)$ for A categories and to $N(-1/2\ \Delta I, \underline{\Sigma}_1)$ for B respectively;

where
$$\underline{\Sigma}_1 = \begin{bmatrix} 1 & \rho & \cdots & \rho \\ \rho & 1 & \cdot & \cdot \\ \cdot & & \cdot & \cdot \\ \cdot & & \cdot & \cdot \\ \rho & \rho & \cdots & 1 \end{bmatrix} \tag{56}$$

The eigen values of the matrix $\underline{\Sigma}_1$ are $(1-\rho)$ and $[1 + (N-1)\rho]$. As to $\underline{\Sigma}_1$ which is the covariance matrix, and is of full rank, we have the following limitation on the value of ρ;

$$-\frac{1}{N-1} < \rho < 1 \quad . \tag{57}$$

For the first case, we obtain

$$\lambda = 0 \quad \text{and} \quad \bar{d}_b = \frac{4N}{M-N-3} \simeq \frac{4}{\frac{M}{N} - 1} \qquad (M-N>3) \tag{58}$$

We obtain

$$\bar{R}_b = \Phi\left(\sqrt{\frac{1}{\frac{M}{N} - 1}}\right) . \tag{59}$$

and

$$R_b = 1 \qquad \text{if } M \simeq N \ . \tag{60}$$

In this classifier, the information processing capacity and the 99% information processing capacity are given by

$$I_n{}^{(b)} = 1 \tag{61}$$

and

$$I_n{}^{(b)}\,(99\%) \simeq 1 + 0.184 \ . \tag{62}$$

The relation between $\bar{R}_b$ and M/N is given in Figure (4).

For the second case, we obtain noncentrality λ and $\bar{d}_{b(\lambda)}$ as follows;

$$\lambda = \frac{M}{4} \, \frac{N\Delta^2}{1+(N-1)\rho} \tag{63}$$

and

$$\bar{d}_{b(\lambda)} \simeq 4\left(\frac{1 + \frac{M\Delta^2}{4(1+(N-1)\rho)}}{\frac{M}{N} - 1}\right) . \tag{64}$$

By equation (64), we obtain

$$I_n{}^{(b)} = 1 \ . \tag{65}$$

and

$$I_n{}^{(b)}\,(99\%) \simeq 1 + 0.184 \left(1 + \frac{M}{4} \, \frac{\Delta^2}{1+(N-1)\rho}\right) \tag{66}$$

$\bar{R}_{b(\lambda)}$ is defined by

$$\bar{R}_{b(\lambda)} = \Phi \sqrt{\frac{1}{2}\, \bar{d}_{b(\lambda)}} \tag{59'}$$

The relation of $\bar{R}_b(\lambda)$ vs. M/N is given in Figure (5). By equation (55), it is known that $I_n^{(b)} = 1$ in any distribution. The probability of the correct classification of the total patterns $P_b(\lambda)$ is defined by

$$P_b(\lambda) = (\bar{R}_b(\lambda))^M \; . \tag{67}$$

The relation of $\bar{R}_b(\lambda)$ and $P_b(\lambda)$ vs. M/N when $\rho = 0$, is given in Figure (6) and (7).

4.3 THE REGRESSION CLASSIFIER

The probability density function of d_r is given by (39). We obtain

$$E[d_r^n] = 2^n \sum_{k=o}^{\infty} \frac{e^{-\lambda}\lambda^k}{k!} \frac{B(\frac{m_1}{2} + k + n, \frac{m_2}{2})}{B(\frac{m_1}{2} + k, \frac{m_2}{2})} \tag{68}$$

$$E[d_r] = 2 \sum_{k=o}^{\infty} \frac{e^{-\lambda}\lambda^k}{k!} \left(\frac{N+2k}{M-1+2k}\right) \; . \tag{69}$$

In this classifier, the same problems are considered as in the case of [4.2]. For the first case, we obtain

$$\lambda = 0 \text{ and } \bar{d}_r = \frac{2N}{M} \tag{70}$$

and

$$\bar{R}_r = \Phi\left(\sqrt{\frac{1}{\frac{M}{N} - 1}}\right) \tag{71}$$

(71) is the same result as (59). By this consideration, we obtain

$$I_n^{(r)} = 1 \tag{72}$$

and

$$I_n^{(r)} (99\%) \simeq 1 + 0.184 \tag{73}$$

For the second case, the procedure is quite the same and we obtain

$$I_n^{(r)} (99\%) \simeq 1 + 0.184 \left(1 + \frac{M}{4} \frac{\Delta^2}{1+(N-1)\rho}\right) \; . \tag{74}$$

By equation (69), we also obtain

$$I_n^{(r)} = 1 \tag{75}$$

in any distribution. $\bar{R}_r(\lambda)$ is also defined in the same way. The relations between $\bar{R}_r$ and M/N, $\bar{R}_r(\lambda)$ and M/N and $P_r(\lambda)$ and M/N are expressed by the same curves as in Figures (4), (5), (6) and (7).

5. Computer Simulations

In our simulations, the normal random patterns distributed according to $N(\underline{0}, I)$ are adopted first. Every point on the curve is obtained by the mean value of the ten trials. Figures (8), (9) and (10) also show the theoretical curves and the experimental results of the mean recognition rate vs. M/N for the minimum distance classifier, the Bayes classifier and the regression classifier respectively. The results of the computer simulations show good agreement with those of the theoretical curves. Figure (11) shows the relation between theoretical curve and the experimental results of the 99% information processing capacity vs. Δ for the Bayes classifier. In Figure (12), the relation between the theoretical curve and the experimental results of the mean recognition rate vs. M/N for the Bayes rule classifier is obtained when the patterns are distributed according to $N(1/2\ \Delta \underline{I}, \Sigma_1)$ for A category and to $N(-1/2\ \Delta \underline{I}, \Sigma_1)$ for B respectively. The difference between the theoretical curve and the experimental results must have come from the fact that the mean recognition rate $R_b(\lambda)$ does not express the real mean value of the correct classification probability. This problem is now under study.

6. Conclusion

The fundamental consideration of the evaluation of the statistical classifier is given under the assumption that the patterns are distributed according to $N(\underline{\mu}_\ell, \Sigma)$ (ℓ = A, B).

New concepts, the information processing capacity and the *a*% information processing capacity are introduced. The recognition ability of each classifier is discussed in terms of these concepts. So far as these concepts are concerned, we found that the Bayes classifier and the regression classifier show the same ability in the first stage approximation, but the minimum distance classifier shows some difference.

The important points obtained in this paper are summarized as follows: (1) The information processing capacity of the minimum distance classifier is zero. (2) The information processing capacity of the Bayes classifier and the regression classifier is 1. (3) The *a*% information processing capacity of each classifier depends upon the parameters, and shows the remarkable increase with the increase of the difference of the mean value between two distributions. In order to check the theoretical results, several kinds of the computer simulations are made for the classification ability and the information processing capacity using the normal random patterns. These results coincide well with our theoretical results.

REFERENCES

(1) F. Rosenblatt, "Principle of Neurodynamics", Spartan Books.

(2) T.M. Cover, "Geometrical and statistical properties of linear threshold device", T. R. No. 6107–1, Stanford Univ., May 1964.

(3) S. Noguchi, A. Suzuki and J. Oizumi, "The recognition ability of the Self-organized Random Networks", Jour. Inst. Electronics Comm. Engrs., Japan, May 1966.

(4) G.S. Sebestyen, "Decision-Making Processes in Pattern Recognition", The Macmillan Comp., 1962.

(5) K. Nagasawa, S. Noguchi and J. Oizumi, "Fundamental Consideration on the Statistical Classifier", Jour. Inst. Electronics Comm. Engrs., Japan, Dec. 1966.

(6) T.W. Anderson, "An Introduction to Multivariate Statistical Analysis", Wiley Book, 1958.

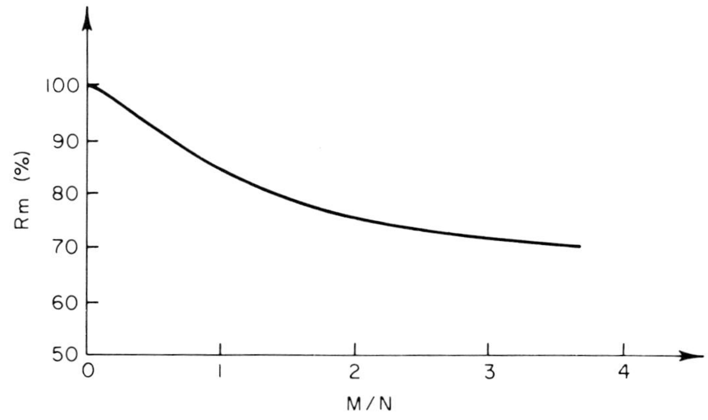

Figure 1: The Relation of $\bar{R}m$ vs. M/N

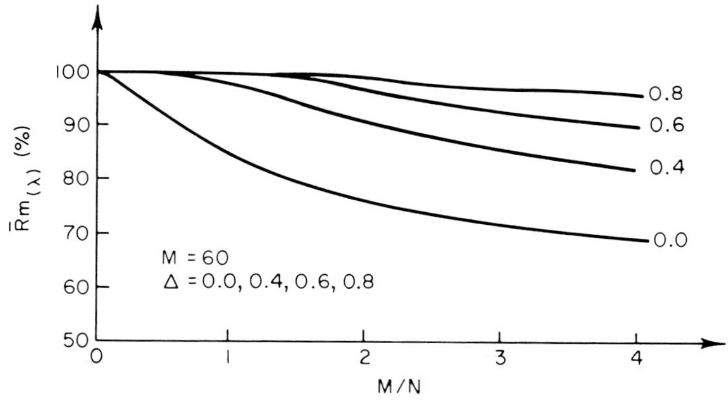

Figure 2: The Relation of $\bar{R}m_{(\lambda)}$ vs. M/N

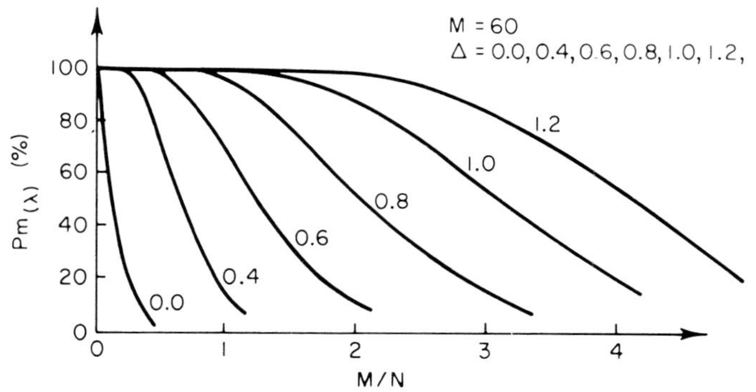

Figure 3: The Relation $Pm_{(\lambda)}$ vs. M/N

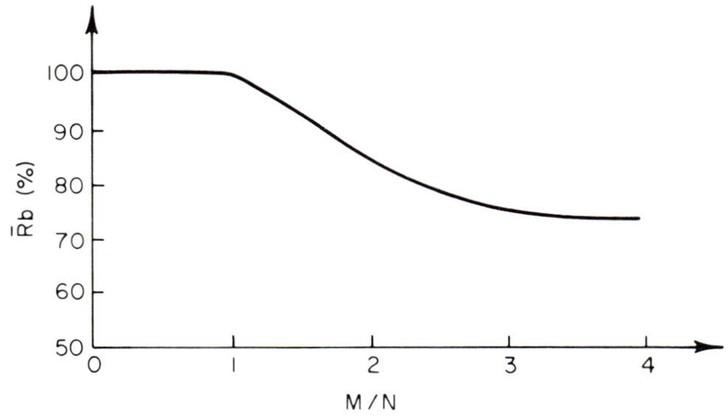

Figure 4: The Relation of $\overline{R}b$ vs. M/N

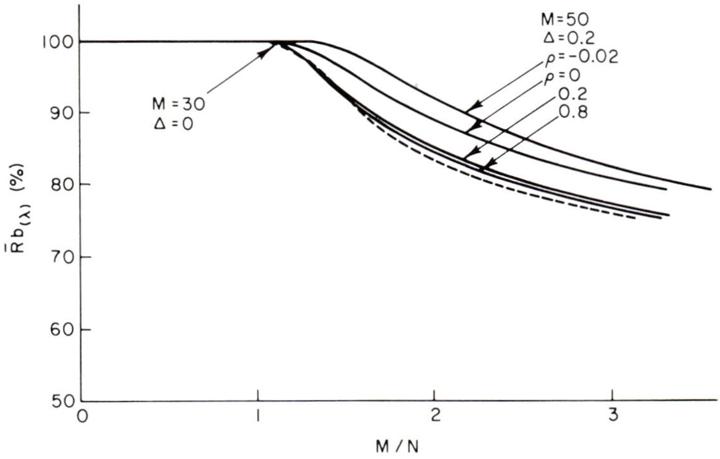

Figure 5: The Relation of $\overline{R}b_{(\lambda)}$ vs. M/N

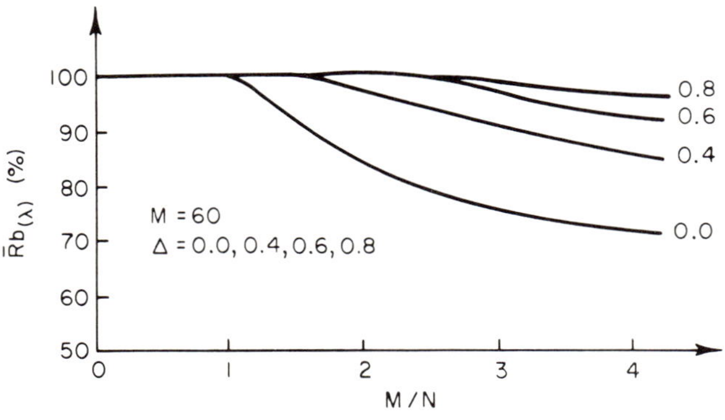

Figure 6: The Relation of $\overline{R}b_{(\lambda)}$ vs. M/N when $\rho = 0$

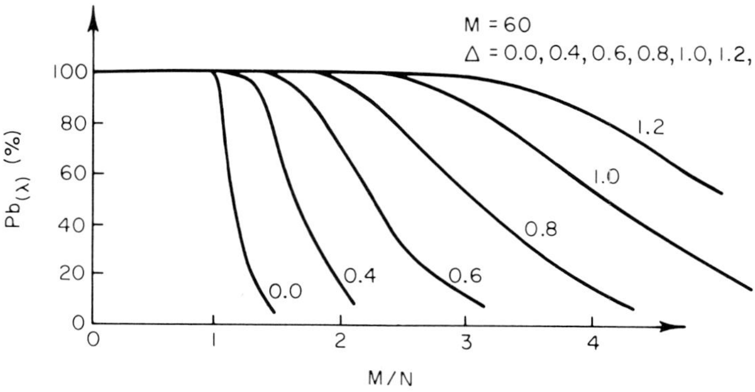

Figure 7: The Relation of $Pb_{(\lambda)}$ vs. M/N when $\rho = 0$

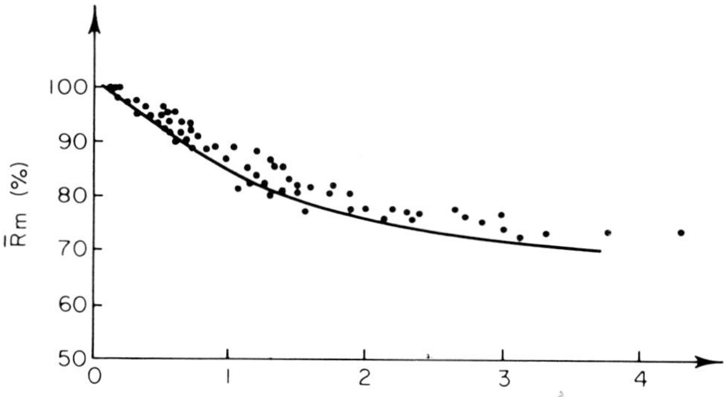

Figure 8: The Theoretical Curve and the Experimental Results of $\overline{Rm}$ vs. M/N

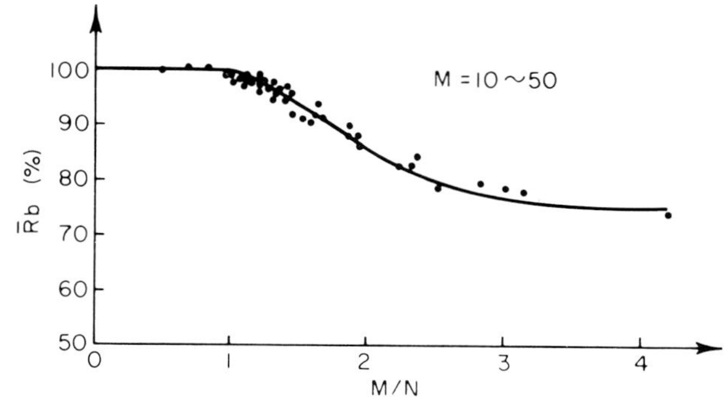

Figure 9: The Theoretical Curve and the Experimental Results of $\overline{Rb}$ vs. M/N

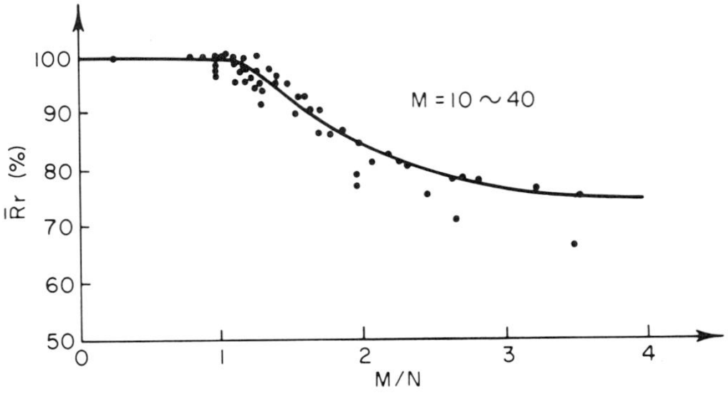

Figure 10: The Theoretical Curve and the Experimental Results of $\overline{\mathrm{R}}\mathrm{r}$ vs. M/N

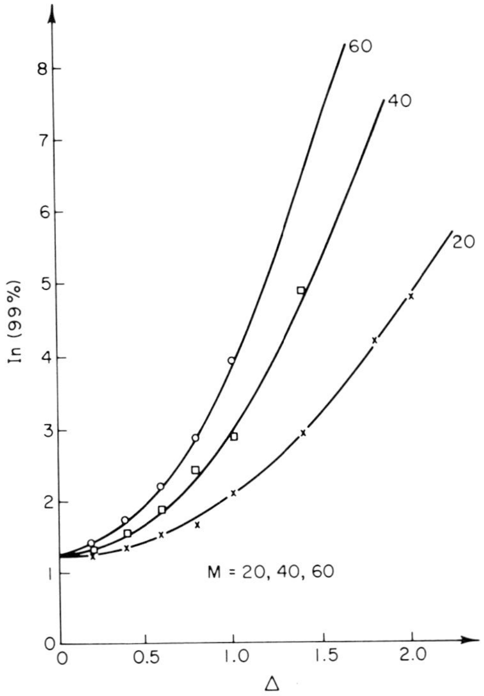

Figure 11: The Theoretical Curves and the Experimental Results of In (99%) vs. Δ

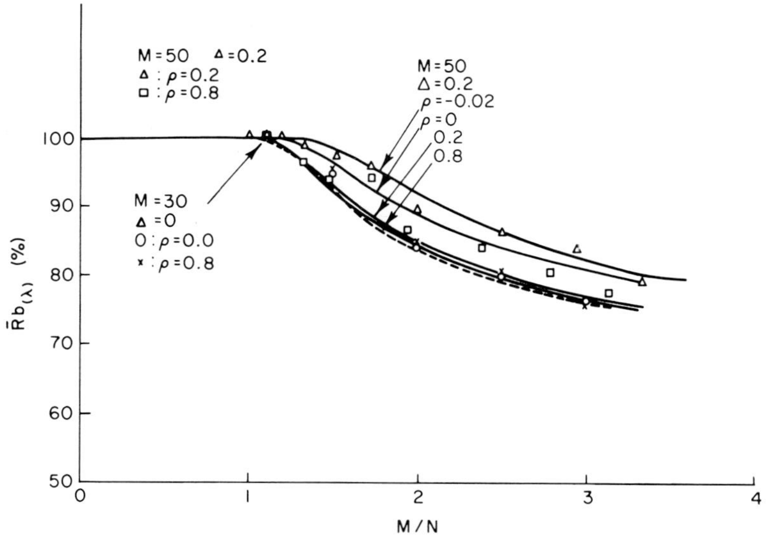

Figure 12: The Theoretical Curves and the Experimental Results of $\overline{Rb}_{(\lambda)}$ vs. M/N

ADAPTIVE SYSTEM OF PATTERN RECOGNITION

Toshiyuki Sakai

DEPARTMENT OF ELECTRICAL ENGINEERING
KYOTO UNIVERSITY, KYOTO, JAPAN

1. Introduction

The researches and developments on pattern recognition have recently resulted in the announcement of commercial reading machines one after another, such as MICR and OCR, which can deal with both printed characters and hand written letters. This may seem to be a great advancement to the study of pattern recognition. However, the intrinsic ability of pattern recognition by human being has not been clarified yet. It is far from the situation that it is introduced to the mechanical recognition systems. It still remains to be solved in front of us.

The display systems for the output of the processed data from the information processing machines also have progressed very rapidly, for example, graphic displays, audio responses and so on. But the interface between man and the information processing machines, has a lot of troubles and problems, all of which are related to the ability of pattern recognition. Typical examples are character input, figure input and speech input. The light pen input system on the CRT display are useful only for the simple instructions at present, and it may be hard to be regarded as a truely powerful input device.

A scanning device for the input of graphs or general photographs in the same principle with the ordinary TV system cannot be a candidate for the widespread use as a terminal to the information processing machines, because of its high scanning speed, of its requirement of large channel capacity of the transmission lines, and of the cost for the memory capacity necessary for the machines.

The speech input has also the similar difficulties. The problems of pattern recognition must be solved in the first place for the realization of the speech input.

One of the compromise by the side of technology for this intrinsic difficulty of pattern recognition is to use the controlled patterns (stylized characters). This, however, can only be applicable to the characters. The situation is completely different for the general patterns, which may be accepted by human being as meaningful ones but has no guarantee of the standardizations and mathematical descriptions.

When the application of the pattern recognition is directed to the automatic classifications in post office businesses, which allow a certain degree of error or rejection, the present reading systems may be enough. When it is directed to the computer input, the error and the rejection rates must be decreased drastically to the extent that is comparable to the reliability of the computer or its related data transmission systems. At present by the computer systems reliable code systems are adopted, where several error check bits are included as redundant elements, such as parity check for a code, group count check for a group code, etc.. Furthermore system checks are often built in for the overall reliability.

Even with these check systems attached to the data transmission line, there happens errors when the noise or distortion is sporadically large on some parts of the line. In this case the correct signals cannot be recovered at the receiver terminal, so that the received information may have considerably different pattern compared to the original signal pattern.

These error detection systems applied to codes may not be simply applied to the general patterns, but the similar idea must be introduced into the pattern recognition system if its reliability and high accuracy is to be desired.

Here let us clarify the meaning of the word "adaptive" used in this paper. The pattern recognition system in general is composed of the following elements; input pattern, environment, parameter extraction, decision algorithm, and the adaptive or learning mechanism. As is well known, the logical circuit is either combinational or sequential. The former is the circuit, the output of which is determined by the combination of the input signals at the moment, while the latter is the circuit, determined by the present input signals and the sequence of the past input signals. The effect of the past input sequence is stored in the memory of the sequential circuit. The "adaptive" in the pattern recognition is here used as the strategy of parameter extraction and decision algorithms which can be changed flexibly according to the state of the input patterns and its environment, with the additional function of the learning, the effect of which is very similar to the change of the internal state of the sequential machine, and has considerably long duration.

The selection of the effective parameters and decision algorithms are among many of them, and the change of their threshold levels is also included in the usage of the word "adaptive".

For the effective adaptive system we have a general purpose computer, which backs up several information processing machines. This paper describes our information processing system, the global decision mechanism for the adaptive situations, the selection strategy suitable for a lot of specific situations, and the pattern matching in actual implementations in several of our research works.

2. Pattern Matching

In this section several examples of information processings are described, which present various kinds of problems aroused in "pattern matching" used in a broad sense.

2.1 DECODING MODEL OF TELEGRAPH CODE

This subject treats a problem which occurs in decoding cryptographically encoded telegraph by using a knowledge of a statistic feature of natural languages, that is, an emergency frequency of alphabets or probability of digram and trigram of alphabets. This aims to study to what extent the simple statistic knowledge of language works effectively in information processing, especially to investigate the weighting function for matching which finds out a change over of code-table in decoding telegraphs encoded by using several code-tables in mixture.

In our experiment, the original information is supposed to be English sentences (Burnett's "Little Load Fauntleroy" was used) and composed of 31 symbols including all alphabets and several signs.

These sentences are encoded using one of three code-tables in turn and transmitted to the communication channel in five-bits-code (See Figure 1). The encoding is carried out in the same way as a three shift teletype coding using H, R, and L as shift codes, which are selected from the frequency table of alphabets and are common to the three code-tables. If these shift codes appear in the sequence of source sentences, the code-table for encoding of them is changed automatically to ϕ_1, ϕ_2, and ϕ_3 according to H, R, and L.

The decoding model infers the original sentences by decoding the transmitted codes using an adequate code-table which is discovered through the statistical knowledge of natural languages. This simulation was performed by digital computer resulting in inferring correctly no more than 93 percent of original sentences, using the frequency table of digram and trigram and the conditional probability of certain alphabets as an inference rule.

The result showed that the weighting function should be applied adaptively; that is, if the decoding of a certain code is correct, the digram table is to be on a set value for decoding the next code. On the other hand, if the decoding of a certain code is wrong, the digram table is lessened in weight.

EXAMPLE

Original sentence	:	CEDRIC HIMSELF KNEW NOTHING WHATEVER ABOUT IT. IT HAD NEVER BEEN EVEN MENTI . . . .
Transmitted sentence	:	'INRFQKHEOZILIXQJ'YXJ,BHEDWQGHXFIJIRKTDGYA KFA,KFAKHXNQDIJIRKDZZMKZ?ZMKNMAF . . . .

ϕ_1^{-1}	:	CEDRT , HIMSELEA VC.AVK?HING WHATEVER,FNW. X,TXK,TX,HAD NEVER,NSSO,SBSO,DSOXT . . . .
ϕ_2^{-1}	:	EFJRIKQH'.SFLF KNEW NOTH'GYKDH IFNFRQBGDWM QIMOQIMQH JKGFNFRQGSSAQA.SAQJSAMI . . . .
ϕ_3^{-1}	:	JFMRIC HZGEFLFPC'JUP'.DHZBSCOHPIF'FR ABOUT IT. IT HPMCBF'FR BEEN EVEN MENTI . . . .
Decoded sentence	:	
(1)*		CEDRT HIMEELE KNJUANOTHING WHATEVER ANDUT I T. IT HAD NEVER BESO SVEN MENTI . . . .
(2)**	:	CEDRIC HIMSELE KNEW NOTHING WHATEVER ABOUT IT. IT HAD NEVER BEEN EVEN MENTI . . . .
ϕ_1^{-1} , ϕ_2^{-1} , ϕ_3^{-1}	:	decoded sentence by each code table
*	:	decoded sentence using a digram table
**	:	decoded sentence using a trigram table

2.2 PATTERN MATCHING IN AUTOMATIC SPEECH RECOGNITION

We constructed an automatic speech recognition machine which accepts speech sound analyzed in short time as an input pattern. The short time analysis in our case was performed by a zero crossing wave analysis.

Speech sound is complex as same as general patterns. And it is impossible in case of speech to stylize or control the pattern. The manner of articulation is classified into three categories: (1) a voiced sound which is quasi-periodic, (2) an unvoiced sound which is aperiodic and continuous noise, and (3) a plosive sound whose wave form is a single pulse. Their beginning point and ending point are to be determined asynchronously in conversational speech.

One of the problems in recognizing speech sound automatically is how to cut each segment of different manner of articulation from the input sound pattern. Another problem is how to describe effectively such sound segments. Suppose a frequency band for speech sound is 4 kc, and sampling frequency is 8 kc according to the sampling theorem, and sampled data for a vowel of a quasi periodic wave are too bothersome as a description of the sound.

Therefore, we take short time interval (5 ~ 10 ms) pattern of analyzed speech sound as a unit of segmentation. And if the successive segments are judged to be the same pattern (which is represented by 5 channels for the first formant and nine channels for the second formant) by the pre-determined criterion (Hamming distance between two patterns), the repetition number of the pattern is set in the counter (weighting pattern ω_j) (See Figure 2).

If the successive segments are different, the pattern (sequence pattern f_j) and its repetition number (weighting pattern) are stored in the shift register. This expression is equivalent to the regular expression in mathematics.

Pattern matching of sequence patterns must be adaptively adjusted according to the context of the sound, personality of speakers, or utterance speed. This adaptive control of the matching criterion and also the selection of parameters for an analyzed pattern are apt instances for making an adaptive system.

2.3 PATTERN MATCHING IN LINE DRAWING PATTERNS

When the engineering drawings and the graphs are to be sent via long transmission lines to the computer and to be stored in the computer's large file, the usual scanning form of the commercial TV system is not preferable because of its requirement of the wide frequency band width and the very wasteful package density in the memory file. Therefore a line figure is segmented into several parts, each of which is matched to one of the circular portion, straight line, and some other simple curves. The maximum displacement between the figure and the reference curves are kept within a certain value. The transmission and the storage of the figure are done by the codes of these references. We are examining by a digital computer the most suitable algorithm for the automatic segmentation and coding of the line figures in this sense.

The evaluation of possible coding algorithms are done both by the maximum allowable displacement between the figure and the reference and by the smoothness of the joint of the segments judged by the human eyes. The strictness of this evaluation, of course, depends entirely on the purpose of the utilization of the figure after it is stored in the computer.

This treatment of the line figures can be utilized in the quantitative measurement of the quality of printed characters having dots or voids as noise.

2.4 PATTERN MATCHING IN SYNTAX ANALYSIS OF NATURAL LANGUAGES

Here is shown an example of pattern matching technique applied to mechanical translation from English into Japanese. Natural languages, as is generally known, are not wholly context-free, but rather context-sensitive.

Therefore it is difficult to analyze syntactic structures of them only by treating restricted strings of parts of speech in the given sentences. For the effective analysis, wider context must be taken into consideration not only by giving special terminal symbols to each word, but also by introducing adequate cluster symbols which characterize the function of phrases or clauses (patterns). If these symbols, both terminal and cluster symbols, are determined adequately, they constitute partially ordered patterns having context-free forms. We have been studying the hierarchy in these patterns and have reduced the processing time by simplifying the stored form of these patterns in the computer. Further studies are being carried out through computer experiments to investigate to what extent these ordered patterns which are classified into several hierarchies work well in analyzing syntactic structures of the natural languages.

We have obtained several information from these experiments to refine the hierarchies in patterns and to make matching algorithm more effective for various kinds of input sentences.

An example is shown in Figure 3. A brief explanation is given below.

The input sentence shown below, which is punched on the paper tape, is fed into the computer from PTR.

> "WE ARE VERY GLAD TO BE ABLE TO SHOW YOU THE RESULTS OF MACHINE TRANSLATION WHICH WERE OBTAINED BY THE DIGITAL COMPUTER IN OUR LABORATORY."

At first, an idiomatic expression is substituted with a single word using an Idiom Dictionary, for example, in the above sentence "BE ABLE TO" is substituted with "CAN" . Then, a Word Dictionary is consulted for each word. The symbols (or parts of speech) given to each word are shown below.

**	=	N4	VL	B1	AI	TO	VA	VD	N4	DT	N1	P2
											VI	
N1	N1	R1	PL	VT	P2	DT	N1	N1	P1	DT	N1	=

The mnemonic name of them are:

** Boundary mark	VA Auxiliary verb	PL Past of VL	B1 Adverb
= Beginning mark	VD Dative verb	PT Past of VT	N1 Noun
= Ending mark	VI Intransitive verb	DT Determinar	N4 Pronoun
P1 Preposition–1	VL Linking verb	AI Adjective–I	TO to
P2 Preposition–2	VT Transitive verb	R1 Relatives	

Our translation system has 59 symbols which correspond to pre-terminal symbols and 27 non-terminal symbols. They are classified by considering syntactic structures of both English and Japanese.

In the Word Dictionary each English word is stored in 5 characters (30 bits) compressed by a cut-sum method, special letters at word end being taken off.

Next, parts of speech which is found in the word dictionary are altered, if necessary, according to the word ending mark and the syntactic context. In the example, a symbol N1 is chosen from two parts of speech N1 and VI for a word "RESULTS" because it comes just behind a determiner (DT). As for the word "OBTAINED", its symbol (VT), which corresponds to the word "OBTAIN", is changed to PT because word ending mark "D" possessed by VT (verb) means that the word is probably a past form of the verb. The object string for the pattern matching is shown in Figure 3–(3).

The pattern matching (or syntax-analysis) in English-Japanese mechanical translation is begun at the end of the string using "pattern" whose structure is shown in Figure 4. The patterns are classified into four groups according to their syntactic functions and length of pattern. The number of symbols (length) on the left side of arrow in pattern structure in Figure 4 is limited to 3 and 2.

They are [A–3], [A–2], [B–3], and [B–2]; [A–3] and [A–2] groups mainly contain noun phrases and prepositional phrases, [B–3] and [B–2] contain mainly verb phrases and clauses. The first priority in pattern matching is given to [A–3], the next is to [A–2], [B–3], and [B–2] in this order.

A tree structure presented in Figure 3–(4), which was printed out at the same time with the pattern matching, shows in what way the pattern matching is carried out. Some examples of patterns used in this example are shown below.

= · SS · =	→ SS(2 · ∅ · ∅ ' ∅ · ∅ · ∅)	A–3	PL · PT→PI(2 · ∅,RARE ∅)	A–2
N4 · R1 · PE	→ N4(3 · 1 · ∅ ,IMASITA·∅ · ∅)	A–3	VD ·N4 · N4→VE(2 · 3 · 1,NI ·0 ·RU)	B–3
DT · N1	→ N4(1 · 2, ∅ · ∅)	A–2	PI · PB→PE(2 · 1, ∅ · ∅)	B–2
P1 · N4	→ PA(2 · 1, ∅ · ∅)	A–2	N4· VE→SS(1 · 2, WA · ∅)	B–2
P2 · N4	→ PB(2 · 1, ∅ · ∅)	A–2		

When the pattern matching is successed, the Japanese which corresponds to the sub-string of English is synthesized, as shown in Figure 4 or in the tree structure in Figure 3–(5).

Our present program consists of about 1200 instructions, and accepts any sentences, and translates them within 1 minute using magnetic tapes as auxiliary memories.

2.5 PATTERN MATCHING IN TRAFFIC CONTROL SYSTEM

Traffic control is a new research area rapidly developed recently. The traffic information such as speed and density of the traffic flows is sent to the computer from car detectors placed on the main streets and intersections. The computer determines the best signal system from the obtained traffic data and controls the traffic signals according to this results. On and off of the traffic signal is specified by the cycle, split and offset. Cycle is the time of the repetition of the signal. Split is the ratio of the green and red times. The offset is the phase difference of the on–time of the greens between adjacent traffic signals. The evaluation standards of the optimal signal setting is the minimum journey time, the minimum waiting time by the red signal, or the maximum increment of total traffic volume in the area.

Usually a lot of optimum signal patterns are prepared beforehand for a lot of traffic situations. (The preparation of these optimum signal patterns is an important and difficult task. This can only be done by the time consuming simulation experiments in the computer.)

Therefore a problem is how to select a most suitable traffic signal patterns from the incoming traffic data. The signal patterns are usually prepared for several sub-areas, which however are in some cases recombined to form another sub-area division by the incoming data.

Thus the determination of an optimum signal system (i.e., cycle, split and offset of all the signals) among many candidates corresponding to the traffic information of the controlled area is considered as a pattern matching. In this case it is very important to evaluate the incoming traffic information if it is stable, or if it is sporadic and noisy. The determination algorithm therefore must be flexible and adaptive to the situations. Without this facility the computer control of the traffic flows of wide area cannot be successful.

2.6 PATTERN MATCHING IN CHARACTER RECOGNITION

As in the case of the automatic recognition of printed characters where standard type font can be used, the pattern matching is most effective. There are many kinds of pattern matching also in this case, such as the maximum or minimum of the analogue quantity obtained by the superposition of the input pattern and the references, logical concordance, the measurement of the distances between the input pattern and the references, cross-correlations , etc..

3. Experimental System of On-line Computer

Figure 5 shows a computer and several on-line I/0 devices we have in our laboratory. This middle size computer is introduced mainly for the study of several on-line uses, for the experiments of the man-machine communications, and for the study in question-answering and information retrieval . The outline of this computer is as follows: The access time of the core memory: 2μ sec; the capacity of the core memory: 16 k characters (will be increased up to 32 k char. in the near future); a quick access drum memory: 8 msec, 327 k characters; magnetic tape: 5 units (20 kc), a line printer, a paper tape reader, and a paper tape punch (See Figure 6).

The peripheral adaptor was designed and attached to the computer for our research objects and has on-line connections to the display panels of the traffic simulation, the terminal of the synthesized speech, traffic data exchange unit, vidicon camera input device, and the XY recorder and write-pen input.

The computer is NEAC 2200 Model 200 and is the same as Honeywell 200 Series. This computer has no instructions of the floating arithmetic, but is suited to the character operations. The computer accepts any kind of 6 bits code so that not only character codes but also data from analogue–digital converter can be read in very easily.

Therefore we are processing in the computer the paper tape data of sign + 10 bits which are obtained from the A–D converter of 20 kc sampling of speech wave, and the video signal data of 3 bits which are obtained from the vidicon scanner by 50 kc sampling. This latter is read in on-line to the drum memory under the program control of the vidicon scanning. The computer has several interruption facilities, by which the I/0 devices can be connected to the computer efficiently.

The research works related to this computer may be classified as follows:

1. The works incapable for human beings in efficiency and cost, but suited for the computer:

The AD converter output of both the speech sound and the analyzed speech sound by multi channel filters. Its input to the computer, the storage and processing of the traffic data.

2. Development of I/0 devices as man-machine interface:

I/0 systems such as automatic speech recognition device, on-line speech synthesizer as an audio response, character recognition machine, general pattern scanner.

3. The trials to bring nearer the natural and machine languages:

Natural language is often semantically ambiguous and implicit. Human beings often make mistakes and are weak at repeating the same behavior (speech utterance, handwriting, etc.) again.

The computer on the other hand memorizes and can reproduce the same thing very correctly but is very weak at conjecture and the utilization of implicit redundancy. Therefore man-machine communication is very important.

We are investigating the specifications for a language which serves smooth communication and cooperation between man and machine.

4. Adaptive System of Pattern Recognition

This system aims at the well balance between hardware and software, the decrease of the error rate in the pattern recognition, and the development of a flexible decision-making strategy. We have an asynchronous optical character reader as a special purpose machine, which reads printed characters in high speed.

If this OCR cannot recognize an input character, it sends the interruption signal to the back-up computer. Then the computer takes the control of the vidicon scanner and reads the video data under the program control. If the cause of the reject by the OCR is not serious, the computer tells the OCR the threshold level of the video signal, or the vertical position of the input characters, and the computer returns the scanner control to the OCR. If the cause of the rejection is too serious for the OCR, the computer itself performs the recognition. These several operations are unified under the adaptive principle for the character recognition.

4.1 ASYNCHRONOUS CHARACTER READER

A character-recognition machine has been designed, built, and tested. It aims at fast reading of document paper and economical compactness in performing the business data processing. The machine can read a whole document page at a considerably high speed. The recognition logic circuits employed are the asynchronous ones, so that the uniformity of the reading speed of a document is not intrinsic to the recognition principle which is the most profitable point of the machine. The outline of the machine is as follows:

The characters accepted are numerals, alphabet, and a few special characters. The height of characters is to be adjusted to the prescribed length by the telescope mechanism of the input part. The recognition logics are so marginally designed to accept several kinds of font. The machine optically scans the characters aligned horizontally and magnifies the reflected light signals from the document paper about three times. This enlarged optical pattern is transformed by 22 vertically aligned photo-transistors to the electrical signals of the same number of channels which are connected to the circuit detecting the position of the line.

The scanning mechanism we are now utilizing is an electric typewriter whose tabulator and carriage return operations are controlled from the central timing circuit of the machine.

When many lines are to be read sequentially, the allowance of the line spacing should be limited. However, there exists a certain amount of deviation of the line position at the bottom of a page when a page is scanned from the top by the automatic carriage return function of an electric typewriter. The height of a character is set to that of 16 photo-transistor channels and these are selected from the 22 photo-transistor acceptors provided for the deviation of the printed lines.

When the typewriter carriage reaches the end point, it returns on a new line, and during this preliminary scanning period the line position is sensed among the 22 channels. If the line position deviates more than 6 channels, an alarm signal appears. When the line position is determined, the proper 16 channels are selected and are led into the recognition logics. This is done by simple combinatorial logical circuits. These selected channels are held unchanged during the forward-scanning period which is realized by the tabulator function of a typewriter.

When the characters to be recognized are restricted to only numerals, alphabet and some other special ones, it is sufficient to check only three time points of 16 input channels as a character goes by. This recognition scheme is explained by the numeral "2". As Figure 7 indicates, the numeral "2" can be reasonably expressed by the hatched parts. These characteristic features are expressed by 16 Boolean variables:

$$A, B, \ldots G, H, h, g, \ldots c, b, a$$

which are named from the top to bottom channels:

$$Q_1 = \overline{A}(B + C + D)\overline{F}\overline{G}\overline{H}h(e + d + c)\ (b + a)$$
$$Q_2 = (A + B + C)\overline{E}\overline{F}\overline{G}(H + h + g)\overline{e}\overline{d}(b + a)$$
$$Q_3 = \overline{A}E(D + F)\overline{g}\overline{f}\overline{e}(c + b + a)$$

When a character "2" passes under the acceptor, first, the logic Q_1 is satisfied at the time t_1, second, the logic Q_2 at t_2, and finally the logic Q_3 at t_3. Only when the logics Q_1, Q_2, and Q_3 are sequentially realized in this order, the system recognizes that the pattern now appearing is "2". This final recognition is done at the moment the character has passed completely through the acceptor and there are no signals in any channel. As the input pattern is thus judged by the sequence of four logical states, the two internal memories are sufficient for the recognition of a character.

The reading speed of this system is now restricted to about 100 characters/sec by the speed of the tabulator and the carriage return of the electric typewriter, but the speed can be increased to about 2,000 characters/sec or more as far as the transistor switching speed allows.

The installed logics for the system of experimental purpose are for 10 numerals (also includes the ISO standard characters proposed in May 1964), 10 alphabet characters, and five special symbols. The number of recognition logics such as Q_1, Q_2, and Q_3 illustrated above is about 50.

The correct reading rate is 99.6 percent, rejection rate is 0.3 percent, and misreading rate is 0.1 percent for normally typed characters.

4.2 CONNECTION DIAGRAM OF ADAPTIVE OCR SYSTEM

Figure 8 is a block diagram of adaptive OCR system, which is composed of a digital computer, vidicon scanner, data exchange, video monitor and the OCR mentioned in 4.1. Usually the serial data output from the vidicon scanner is transferred to the OCR, where serial signal is converted to the parallel one with the same effect of the parallel photo-transistor scanning.

The vidicon scanner is specially designed to accept the signals such as scan start, scan stop, the change of scan mode, etc. from the computer and the OCR. For the control of the vidicon camera and the data transmission between the scanner and the computer, 53 coaxial cables are laid about 100 meters. The video monitor is for the ease of the fine adjustment of the video scanner.

The vidicon tube is the ordinary 7038, the resolution of which is about 200 lines. Two scanning modes are possible as shown in Figure 9. The one is the picture scan mode, which is similar to the ordinary TV scanning, and sends the digitized video data to the computer. This horizontal scanning can be halted at any vertical position by the record mark in computer memory area. The other is the character scan mode.

This first scans horizontally until there appear characters, then vertical scanning is automatically initiated between the top and bottom of the characters. For this scanning there are three counters, A, B and C. The top and bottom lines are memorized in A and B counters (each 8 bits). The horizontal position of the vertical scan is directed by C counter. These counters are triggered by every scanning end of the vidicon deflection, and the values of the counters are converted into analogue voltage by DA converter, which is supplied on the deflection coils of the scanner. The video signal output is digitized in 3 bits by AD converter shown in Figure 8 and is sent to the OCR or the computer by parallel lines.

When it is necessary to read again the same character, the vertical deflection is to be done backwards from right to left. In this case the scanner is in the V backward scan mode. V forward scan mode is the ordinary scanning mode from left to right and in this case the video signal is transferred into the OCR. Therefore C counter is the reversible counter, according to which the horizontal position is determined.

The character reading is performed from left to right along a line of characters. When the scanning reaches to the right end, the horizontal scanning is resumed from the next position to find a next line. The top and bottom of a line are determined as shown in Figure 9. That is, the top position is the maximum level of all the tops of characters in a line, and the bottom position is the minimum level of all the bottoms. These positions are detected automatically in the scan mode control from the scanned video signal.

The region of a character in a line can be determined by the vertical scanning with the similar algorithm mentioned above. The V scan is done from the bottom to the top of a line. A vertical scanning corresponds to a line of photo-transistors in 4.1. When the scanning is done for a character, the OCR outputs the recognition result. If it is the rejection, the OCR sends the interruption signal to the computer.

Then the computer takes the control of the scanner and V backward scan is done for the unknown character. The video output at this time is sent to the computer. The computer judges if the unknown character can be recognized by the OCR with the change of parameters or not. If it were, the computer sends the proper value to the threshold circuit in which 3 bits video signal is to be changed in white or black. The computer also tells the channel selection circuit of the OCR the vertical displacement of the unknown character. Then the control is returned to the OCR and the unknown character is read again by the OCR. If the unknown character is too deteriorated for the OCR, the elaborate recognition program is called out in the computer main memory and the recognition is done by the computer. Thus the change of the parameters in the OCR is done adaptively to the input patterns.

How to decrease the OCR rejection and error rates with this back-up system compared to the OCR alone depends entirely on the way the rejection and error detection is done in the OCR.

For the decrease of the error rate, it is not enough to make strict the decision logic. This strictness increases the rejection and the interruption to the computer becomes frequent. Ordinarily, the computer back-up takes much time and the balance between hardware and software breaks and the overall efficiency will fall down.

For the decrease of the rejection and error rate, techniques in data transmission give suggestions. That is, the following techniques may be useful: the repetitive scanning of a character, the comparison between the results of the OCR recognition logics obtained by the V forward and backward scannings, the system check by the recognition results with different decision strategies, the special algorithms for the characters which are apt to be rejected or to cause errors, the check of the number of characters in a line and that of the actually read ones, etc.. Which of these is effective must be examined by a further experiment with this system.

5. Automatic Speech Recognition

The automatic speech recognition mentioned in section 2.2 is an example of pattern matching experimented by a hardware.

In this section a more complicated and powerful system for automatic speech recognition under planning by general purpose digital computer is described.

First, speech sound is analyzed into quasi-zero crossing wave. This analyzed wave coincides with original speech sound only in zero crossing interval, and its wave form and amplitude are different from the so-called zero crossing wave whose amplitude is quantized into two levels and whose wave form is rectangular pulse.

The speech sound obtained by quantizing these zero crossing intervals into 26, 19, or 14 discrete intervals (we call symbols) after computer processing is certified to have sufficient articulation by human hearing-test.

Further, redundant characters contained in speech sound patterns are effectively utilized. That is, as for quasi-periodic sound, one pitch interval wave in periodic interval is sampled as a standard wave unit, and quasi-periodic sound is expressed by repeating this standard wave unit. As for noise-like sound, we established an expression method by use of the sequences of above mentioned symbols, preserving analyzed spectrum pattern of noisy sound in the same fashion.

It has become possible to synthesize speech sound using digital computer of medium size. The processing to be carried out is as follows: a standard sequence expression of smallest speech elements in terms of prescribed symbols, an adaptive modification for co-articulation, accent, a calculation of onset and offset frequencies in transient part from one phoneme to the next. Any Japanese speech sounds can be produced by this synthesis method when the input are introduced into the computer in the form of Roman letters or phoneme expression.

For the synthesis, the program include the instruction of the arrangement of symbols (26, 19 or 14), amplitude information, wave form information, repetition number of speech element, minor modification in speech element (this corresponds to slight change in accent in Japanese), etc.

These synthesized speech sound is looked upon as a standard speech pattern or idealized speech sound from the point of automatic recognition because human voice has a largely different pattern from these synthesized sound and is much complex in wave form. It is very important to evaluate that the synthesized sound may be described in Kleene's regular expression, since it is composed of finite numbers of symbols.

An automaton model for speech recognition, therefore, becomes as follows: Unknown speech is analyzed into a regular expression of the symbols, after short-time automatic pattern matching, and long-time pattern matching is performed using a transition matrix (Shannon) prepared by a large number of speech sound analyses.

We have already completed a programming system which simulates these automata written in block diagrams, and now we are going to investigate whether it is possible or not to perform automatic recognition of speech by fairly complex pattern matching between synthesized sound and analyzed one.

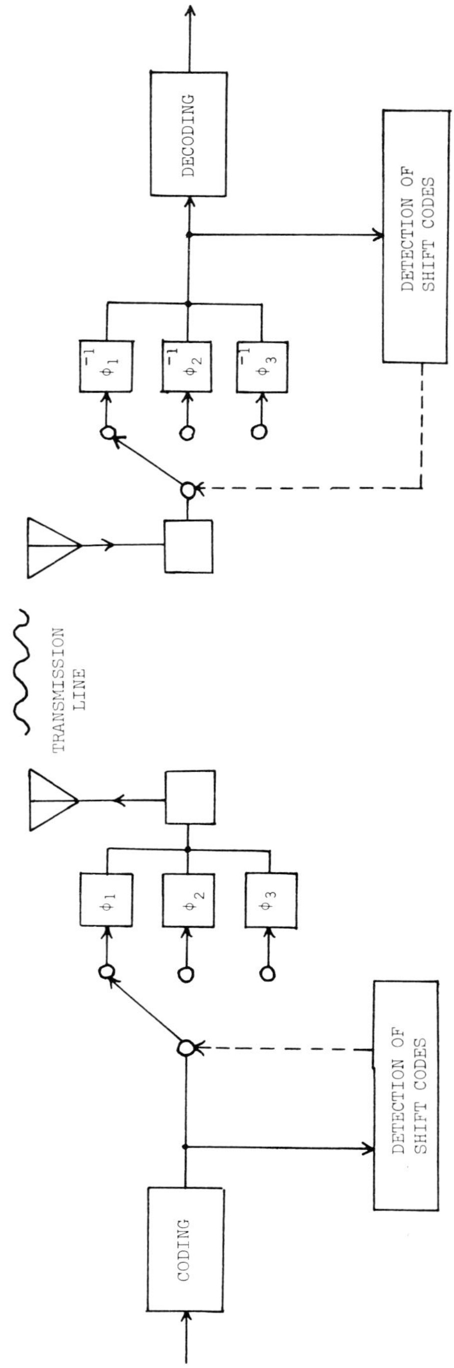

Figure 1: Digital Code Transmission System

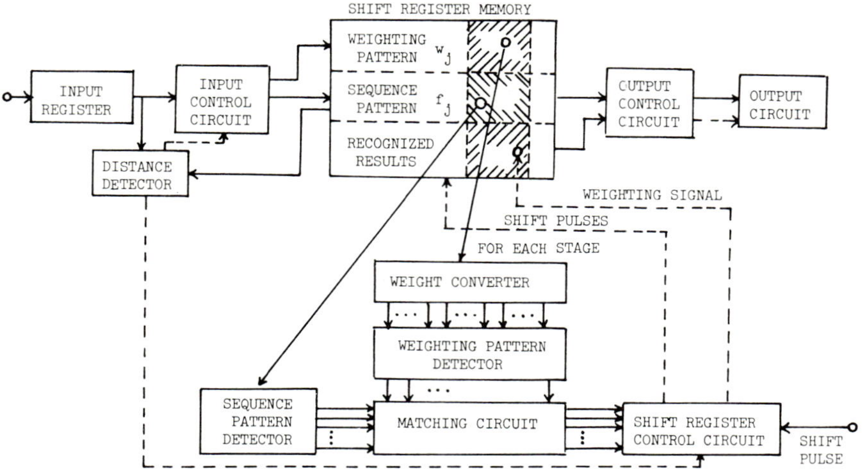

Figure 2: Block Diagram of Speech Recognition System, Considering the Phonetic Contextual Effect. ←: Flow of Information, ← – – : Flow of Control Signal

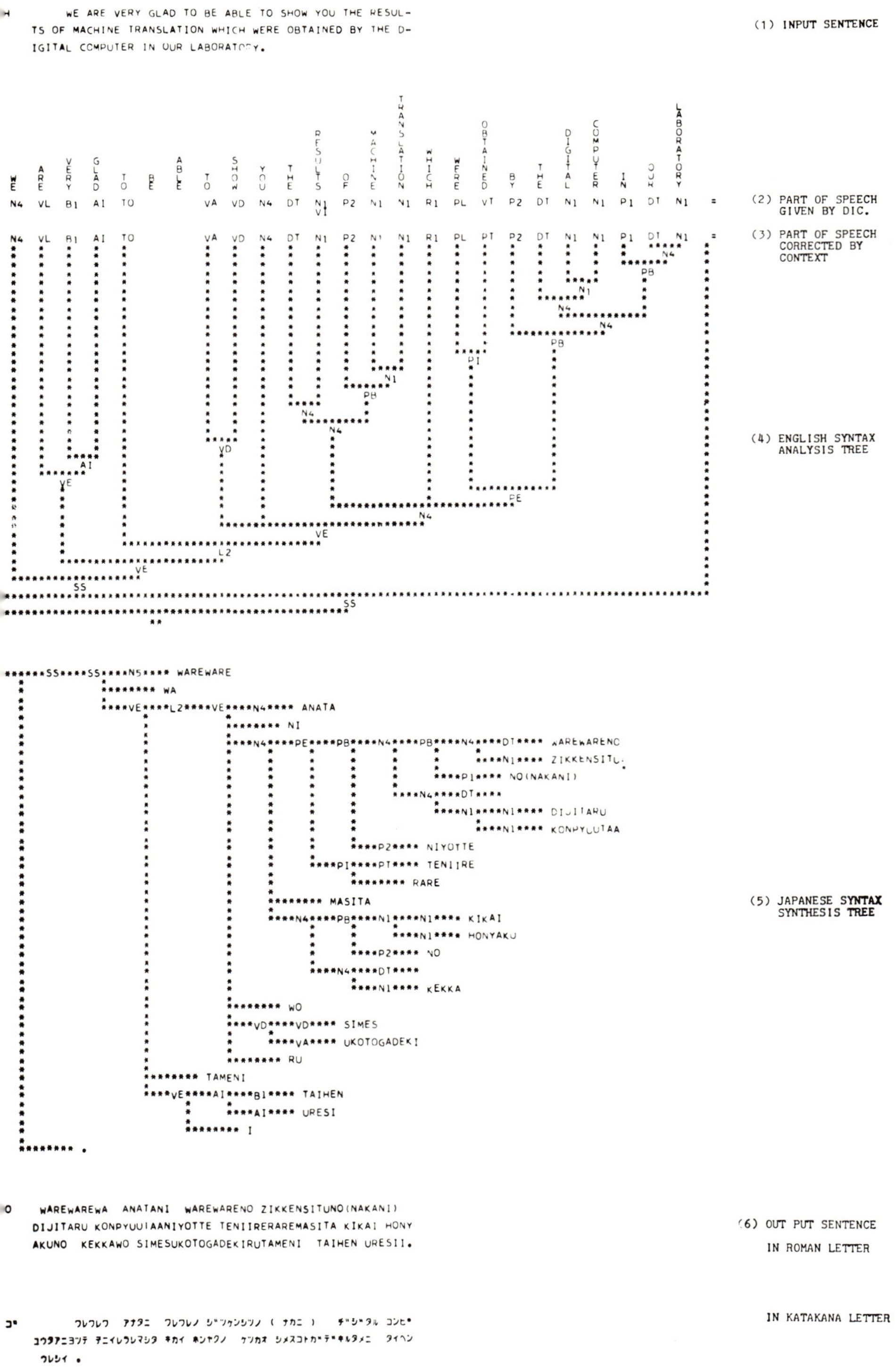

Figure 3: An Example of English into Japanese Translation

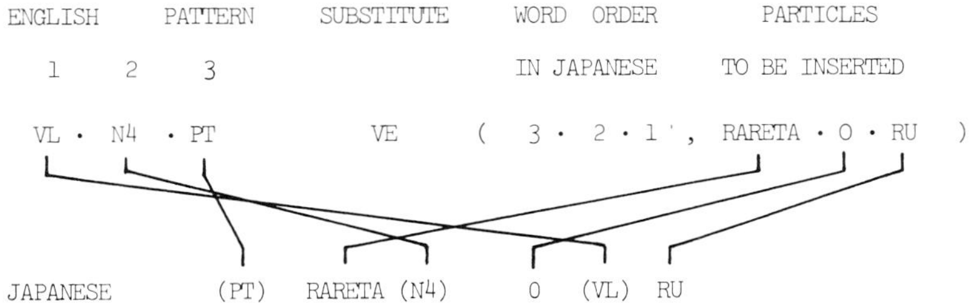

Figure 4: Structure of "pattern" in Mechanical Translation

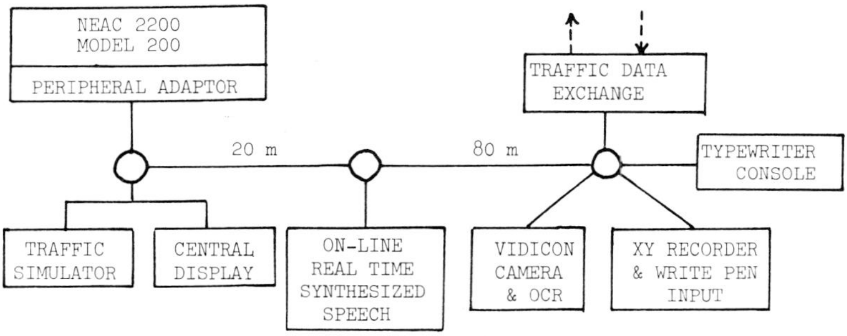

Figure 5: System of On-Line Devices

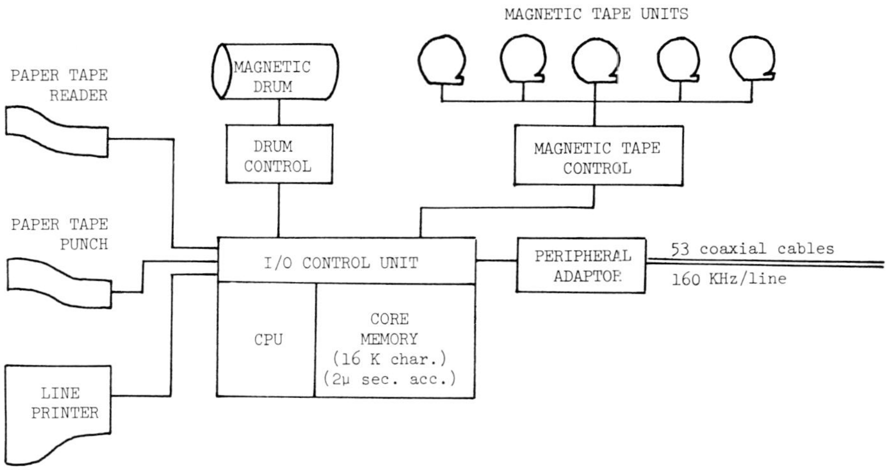

Figure 6: Computer System (NEAC 2200 Model 200)

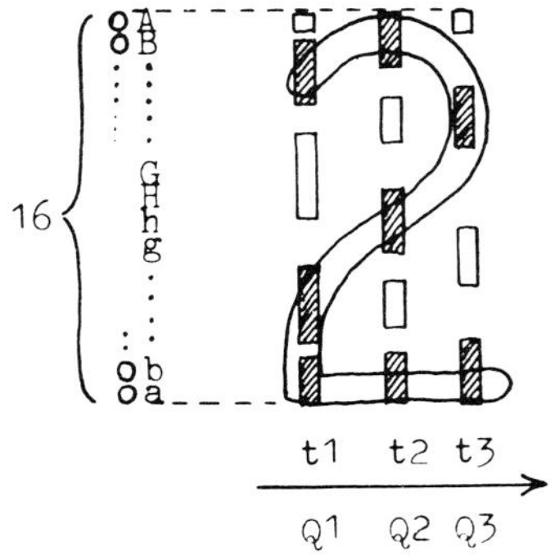

Figure 7: Characteristic Features of "2"

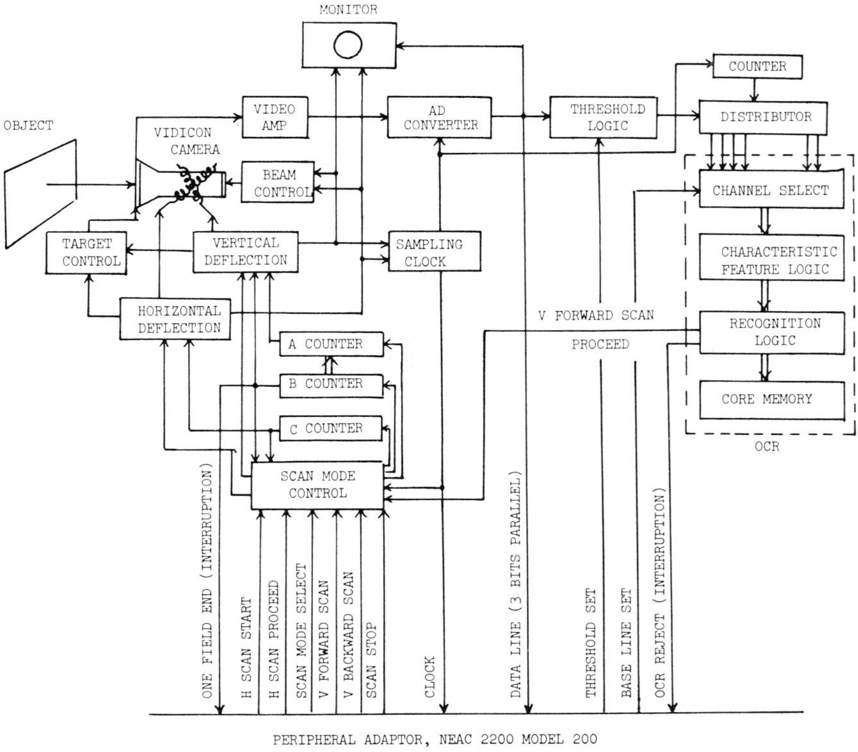

Figure 8: Adaptive System Composed of Vidicon Camera, OCR, and Computer

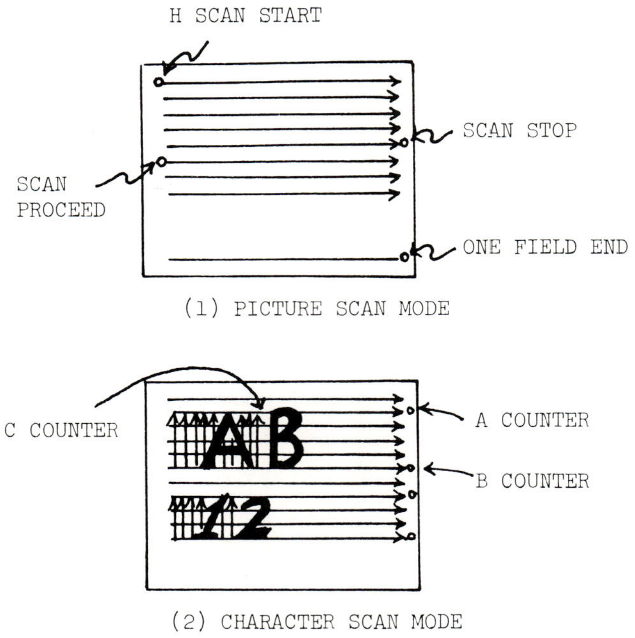

Figure 9: Scanning Modes of a Vidicon Camera

Equipments related to speech processing. A data recorder, an AD and DA converter, a paper tape puncher (left), a speech synthesizer (middle), a bank of filters and CRT display unit (right).

An optical character reader (left), a vidicon camera input scanner, and its control device with monitor display.

Computer system (NEAC 2200 Model 200) from left printer, paper tape reader, magnetic tape unit (5).

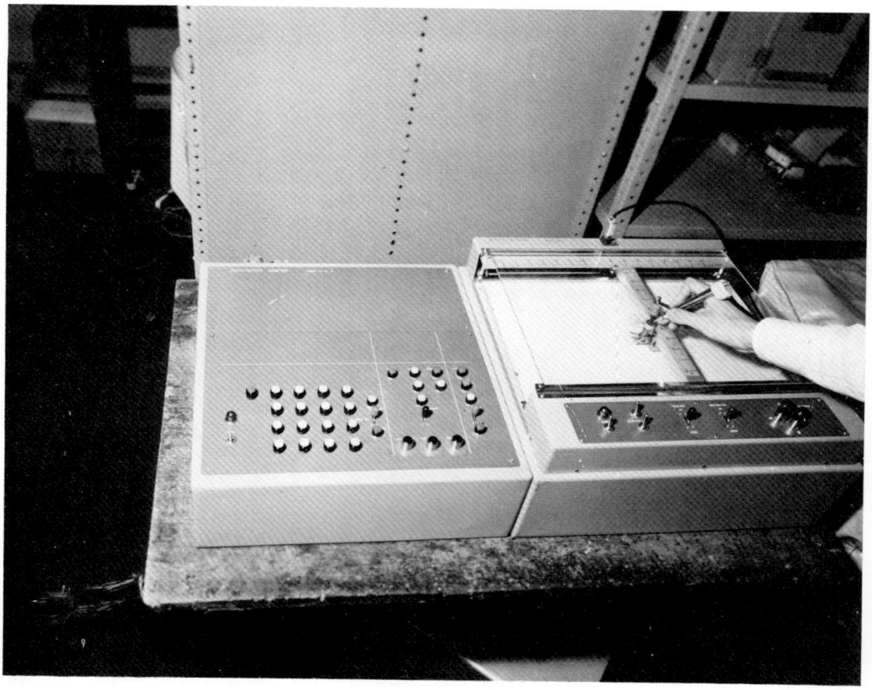

XY recorder and Write-pen input, left: function keys.

NONPARAMETRIC LEARNING AND PATTERN RECOGNITION USING A FINITE NUMBER OF STATES

Stephen D. Shapiro

BELL TELEPHONE LABORATORIES, INC.
WHIPPANY, NEW JERSEY

Abstract

Pattern recognition techniques are often based primarily on the efficient utilization of geometric and a priori statistical characteristics of measurement vectors associated with various classes. Of secondary consideration is the question of implementation which is usually treated subsequently as a separate matter.

The opposite approach may be taken: the structure of the recognition system itself may be used as a starting point. In particular, the restricted class consisting of those structures having a small number of states may be explored.

A theoretical example of this approach is described in terms of a nonparametric recognition system for the case of two hypotheses in which nothing is known about the underlying statistics but time independence. A learning procedure for training sequences in which the hypotheses associated with the measurement vectors appear mixed in accordance with their unknown a priori probabilities is treated.

A clustering method is described which generates v volumes and a central property called the "gradation of clusters" is shown. This property is used to suggest various decision procedures. Expressions are given for the mean of the resulting error probabilities after an infinite training period and bounds are obtained for training by a finite number of inputs.

Introduction

Pattern recognition techniques are often based primarily on the efficient utilization of geometric and a priori statistical characteristics of measurement vectors associated with various classes. Of secondary consideration is the question of implementation which is usually treated subsequently as a separate matter.

The opposite approach may be taken: the structure of the recognition system itself may be used as a starting point. In particular, the restricted class consisting of those structures having a small number of states may be explored.

A theoretical example of this approach is described in terms of a nonparametric recognition system for the case of two hypotheses, H_1 and H_2, in which nothing is known about the underlying statistics but time independence. A learning procedure for training sequences in which the hypotheses associated with the measurement vectors appear mixed in accordance with their unknown a priori probabilities, $P(H_1)$ and $P(H_2)$, is described and analyzed.

Structure of the System and Training Procedure

Let X be a pattern vector and let the volume which contains all of the possible pattern vectors be called the pattern space. We partition the pattern space into disjoint volumes $V_1, V_2, \ldots, V_w$ and it is upon these volumes that the system acts. The volumes may be selected in an arbitrary manner when no a priori information is available about H_1 and H_2. If any such information is available, the volumes should be selected to produce either a large or small likelihood ratio over each V_k to improve the overall performance.

We associate with each V_k a finite set S_k of v states which are to be used for training the pattern recognition system. The states of each S_k are labeled 1, 2, . . . , v. There are many possible training procedures given this partition of the pattern space and the corresponding sets. We treat one such procedure which is quite direct since it involves no computations such as divisions or matrix multiplication and no explicit storage of the pattern vectors used for training. However, it will be seen that, unlike many recognition systems, the formation of the decision surfaces is based on a random process which does not converge to a single value as the length of the training sequence is increased – with the result that the probability of error of the system always remains random regardless of the number of training inputs.

Denote by $C_k^{(n)}$ the state occupied on S_k after the nth training input to the system. Thus $C_k^{(n)} = 1, 2, \ldots, v$ for each k. A sequence of X vectors is applied to the system and accompanying each of these vectors is a statement indicating whether it is a sample under H_1 or H_2. For the nth training sample the systems finds that k for which $X \epsilon V_k$ and changes $C_k^{(n-1)}$ according to the following: ($C_k^{(0)}$ arbitrary)

$C_k^{(n)} = C_k^{(n-1)} + 1$	$C_k^{(n-1)} = 1, 2, \ldots, v-1$	if X is a sample under H_2
$= C_k^{(n-1)}$	$C_k^{(n-1)} = v$	
$C_k^{(n)} = C_k^{(n-1)} - 1$	$C_k^{(n-1)} = 2, 3, \ldots, v$	if X is a sample under H_1
$= C_k^{(n-1)}$	$C_k^{(n-1)} = 1$	

For $j \neq k$, $C_j^{(n)} = C_j^{(n-1)}$.

We observe that $C_k^{(n)}$ carries the only information retained about the relative frequencies of H_1 and H_2 for each V_k and, for a string of X vectors contained in V_k , can only register an excess of v in the number of occurrences of one hypothesis over another. So that even for a very large number of vectors $X \epsilon V_k$, a string of v vectors under (say) H_1 can force $C_k^{(n)}$ down to 1 even though $P(H_2 | X \epsilon V_k)$ might be much greater than $P(H_1 | X \epsilon V_k)$. Clearly this would not be the case if $C_k^{(n)}$ were related to the ratio of occurrences of H_1 and H_2 for $X \epsilon V_k$. The decision procedure implied above, of associating low values of $C_k^{(n)}$ with H_1 and high values with H_2, will be discussed in more detail.

Analysis of State Transitions

The behavior of the system may be described by means of w first order Markov chains relating successive states on each S_k under the assumption that the inputs to the system, each of which is one of the 2w events $\{X \epsilon V_k, H_1\}$ or $\{X \epsilon V_k, H_2\}$ $k = 1, 2, \ldots, w$, have stationary probabilities and occur independently. The probabilities of these events are unknown but let us call them a_k and b_k ; i.e.,

$$a_k = P(X \epsilon V_k, H_1) \qquad k = 1, 2, \ldots, w$$

$$b_k = P(X \epsilon V_k, H_2)$$

where

$$a_k + b_k > 0.$$

The transition matrix π_k for each S_k may now be expressed in terms of the unknowns a_k and b_k.

Let us define $C_k(n)$ for $X \epsilon V_k$ in analogy with the previously defined $C_k^{(n)}$:

$C_k(n)$ = state on S_k after the nth training input of $X \epsilon V_k$. We may now consider

$$\pi_k = [P_{kij}]$$

where $P_{kij} = P(C_k(n) = j | C_k(n-1) = i)$. The values of the P_{kij} are:

$$P_{k11} = \frac{a_k}{a_k + b_k}, \quad P_{kvv} = \frac{b_k}{a_k + b_k}, \quad P_{ki,\, i+1} = \frac{b_k}{a_k + b_k} \qquad i \neq v \ ,$$

$$P_{ki,\, i-1} = \frac{a_k}{a_k + b_k} \qquad i \neq 1 \ , \qquad P_{kij} = 0 \qquad \text{Otherwise.}$$

To examine the operation and performance of the learning procedure consider an infinite training sequence in which an infinite number of vectors $X \in V_k$ are present for all k. As $n \to \infty$, the random variable $C_k(\infty)$ has a density, obtained from the steady state value of π_k^n as $n \to \infty$, of

$$P_{kj} = P(C_k(\infty) = j) = \frac{1-r_k}{1-r_k^v} r_k^{j-1} \qquad \begin{array}{l} j = 1, 2, \ldots, v \\ k = 1, 2, \ \ldots, w \end{array}$$

where

$$r_k = \frac{b_k}{a_k} \ .$$

That is, when the value of state on S_k is sampled in the steady state, the probability of its being j is P_{kj}.

We make the following key observation; form the ratio P_{kv}/P_{k1} :

$$\frac{P_{kv}}{P_{k1}} = r_k^{v-1}$$

When the steady state learning process is sampled, if r_k is large, $b_k > a_k$, very likely $C_k(\infty)$ will be near v, and, if r_k is small, $C_k(\infty)$ will tend to be near state 1. In the decision making scheme for a vector X with an unknown H_k, we say H_1 is the underlying hypothesis if $C_k(\infty)$ is near 1 where $X \in V_k$. Similarly, we associate H_2 with $\{X \in V_k\}$ if $C_k(\infty)$ is near v. We see that the effectiveness of this kind of decision making procedure becomes more pronounced as v increases. We also note that $C_k(\infty)$ and $C_k^{(\infty)}$ have the same distribution.

Clustering

We will base the overall decision procedure on a set of clusters. These clusters form a second partition of the pattern space. After n training inputs to the system, we form v clusters, $\Xi^{(n)}$ as follows:

$$\Xi_k^{(n)} = \bigcup_{C_j^{(n)} = k} V_j \qquad k = 1, 2, \ldots, v$$

As the training is taking place, n increasing, the volumes V_k are shifting from cluster to cluster producing a moving boundary for each cluster. In the steady state the clusters are random: their boundaries change with each new training input and their structure is described by a nondegenerate density function stemming from the P_{kj}. That is, whenever the steady state process is sampled the $C_j^{(n)}$ take on one of their possible values.

A set of events $\{X \epsilon \Xi_1\}$, $\{X \epsilon \Xi_2\}$, . . . , $\{X \epsilon \Xi_v\}$ may be considered. The event $\{X \epsilon \Xi_k\}$ is the event that X, a nontraining sample which is to be classified, is contained in that cluster for which all of the states are k when the states are sampled as $n \to \infty$.

In the steady state, the clusters form an average ordering of regions in the pattern space with respect to the probability of occurrence of H_1 and H_2 when X is given:

$$R_1 \geqslant R_2 \geqslant \ldots \geqslant R_v$$

where

$$R_k = \frac{P(H_1 \mid X \epsilon \Xi_k)}{P(H_2 \mid X \epsilon \Xi_k)} \qquad k = 1, 2, \ldots, v$$

This property follows directly from a stronger set of conditions to be called the gradation of clusters:

$$P(H_1 \mid X \epsilon \Xi_i) \geqslant P(H_1 \mid X \epsilon \Xi_j) \quad 1 \leqslant i \leqslant j \leqslant v$$

$$P(H_2 \mid X \epsilon \Xi_i) \geqslant P(H_2 \mid X \epsilon \Xi_j) \quad 1 \leqslant j \leqslant i \leqslant v$$

The derivation of these relations appears in the Appendix.

Decision Procedure

Based on these properties of $P(H_k \mid X \epsilon \Xi_j)$, we select a decision procedure which is somewhat analogous to the likelihood ratio test. The quantities α and β correspond to the threshold on the likelihood ratio. Suppose that n inputs have been used for training; then

$$\text{Accept } H_1 \quad \text{if} \quad X \epsilon \bigcup_{k=1}^{\alpha} \Xi_k^{(n)} \quad (\text{reject } H_2)$$

$$\text{Accept } H_2 \quad \text{if} \quad X \epsilon \bigcup_{k=v-\beta+1}^{v} \Xi_k^{(n)} \quad (\text{reject } H_1)$$

$$\text{No decision} \quad \text{if} \quad X \in \bigcup_{k=\alpha+1}^{v-\beta} \Xi_k(n)$$

The resulting probability of error is a random variable since it depends on values of the $C_k(n)$ and is given by

$$P_n(\text{Error}) = \sum_{k=v-\beta+1}^{v} \sum_{C_j(n)^k=k} a_j + \sum_{k=1}^{\alpha} \sum_{C_j(n)^k=k} b_j$$

As before, when $n \to \infty$ we see that $P_\infty(\text{Error})$ is still random since it depends on the $C_k(\infty)$.

The minimum probability of error that is realizable by any decision method which is based solely on membership in the V_k is

$$P^M = \sum_{k=1}^{w} \text{Min}(P(\text{Error}, X \in V_k))$$

$$= \sum_{k=1}^{w} \text{Min}(a_k , b_k)$$

under the condition that a decision is always made. It will be seen below that as v increases, the steady state average value of the error probability approaches P^M.

The mean value of the error probability may be obtained from equation (4) of the Appendix and the analogous relation under H_2 as $n \to \infty$ We thus consider the average taken over the $C_k(\infty)$:

$$E(P_\infty(\text{Error})) = \sum_{k=1}^{w} a_k \frac{1-r_k{}^{-\beta}}{1-r_k{}^{-v}} + b_k \frac{1-r_k{}^{\alpha}}{1-r_k^{v}}$$

When a decision is always to be made and we do not favor either hypothesis, $\alpha = \beta = v/2$. As the number of states in each S_k is increased we have for this case

$$\lim_{v \to \infty} E(P_\infty(\text{Error})) = \sum_{\substack{k \\ r_k \geqslant 1}} a_k + \sum_{\substack{k \\ r_k < 1}} b_k = P^M$$

which is the probability of error when the best decision is made for each V_k.

The better the choice of V_k, i.e. the greater the deviation of r_k from 1, the smaller the average error. It may be seen that average error goes to zero as the $r_k \to 0$ or $r_k \to \infty$ for α and $\beta < v$. This corresponds to the case where the volumes "separate" the hypothesis in the pattern space.

Finite Training

When the system has been trained by n inputs, the transition probabilities for S_k may be expressed in terms of the conditional probabilities

$$P(C^{(n)} = j \mid C^{(0)} = i, n_k) = P_{kij}(n_k)$$

$$[P_{k\ell m}(n)] = \pi_k^n$$

where n_k = the number of samples $X \epsilon V_k$ in a training sequence of length n.

The expression giving $P_{kij}(n_k)$ is very difficult to deal with directly when seeking the analytical properties of the system. However bounds on the performance may be given since it may be shown that

$$B_k(m) = \underset{i,j}{\text{Max}} \mid P_{kij}(m) - P_{kj} \mid$$

is a monotone decreasing function of m for all values of r_k.

The bounds are obtained by selecting a value of δ and for each S_k finding the smallest value of m such that

$$B_k(m) \leqslant \delta$$

Since $B_k(m)$ is a function of r_k, because the transition probabilities are a function of r_k, this value of m also depends on r_k. We call this value d_k. Table 1 shows d_k for various values of r_k and δ. It may be seen that $B_k(m)$ is unchanged when r_k is replaced by $1/r_k$ so the same d_k holds for both values.

If nothing is known about r_k in advance, we let

$$d_k = d = \underset{r_k}{\text{Max}} \; d_k(r_k).$$

Based on this notion of d_k and δ, we will say the system is trained when the distribution over each S_k is within δ of the steady state. This is equivalent to requiring the effect of the initial conditions on the state, after training has been completed, to be small. Hence we seek that minimum number of inputs N which assures, with probability $1-\epsilon$, at least d_k samples of $X \epsilon V_k$ for each k. Let P_n = P (training occurs in n inputs); i.e.

$$P_n = P(n_1 \geqslant d_1, n_2 \geqslant d_2, \ldots, n_w \geqslant d_w)$$

where

$$\sum_{k=1}^{w} n_k = n .$$

We then require the smallest N such that

$$P_n \geqslant 1 - \epsilon$$

for $n \geqslant N$. Thus N is a function of δ and ϵ.

For example, we may consider this equation in ϵ when nothing is known about the r_k, in which case, $d_k = d$ and when the a priori probability of $X \epsilon V_k$ is assumed equal for all k. A conservative estimate of N may then be found from the equation

$$(d-1) \log n + n \log(1 - \frac{1}{w}) = f(w,d,\epsilon)$$

where

$$f(w,d,\epsilon) = \log(\frac{\epsilon}{d}) + (d-2)\log w + \log((d-1)!) + (d-1)\log(1 - \frac{1}{w})$$

which can be derived by means of Boole's inequality[1]. This equation usually has two roots, the estimate of N is the integer part of the larger root.

We note that

$$N \geqslant \sum_{k=1}^{w} d_k$$

For $w \leqslant 100$, $d \leqslant 20$, and $\epsilon = 10^{-8}$, N is usually less than 4dw under the specified conditions.

After training by $n \geqslant N$ inputs, the average error probabilities obey the following inequalities, not shown here,

$$| E(P_n(I)) - E(P_\infty(I)) | \leqslant \beta\delta C(\epsilon,\delta)$$

$$| E(P_n(II)) - E(P_\infty(II)) | \leqslant a\delta C(\epsilon,\delta)$$

$$| E(P_n(Error)) - E(P_\infty(Error)) | \leqslant \mathrm{Max}(a,\beta)\ \delta C(\epsilon,\delta)$$

where

$P_n(I)$ = P(type 1 error after a training sequence of length n) ,

$P_n(II)$ = P(type 2 error after a training sequence of length n), and

$C(\epsilon,\delta) = 1-\epsilon + \frac{\epsilon}{\delta} \cong 1$ for $\epsilon << 1$ and $\epsilon << \delta$.

The inequalities have several applications. When there is partial a priori knowledge about the r_k it may be utilized by means of the expressions for the average steady state error probabilities to determine properties after finite training. For example, if it is known that the V_k have been moderately well chosen so that for all r_k either $r_k \geqslant r_+ > 1$ or $r_k \leqslant r_- < 1$ the influence on the error after finite training may be seen as a function of r_+ and r_-.

Acknowledgment

The author wishes to thank R. H. McCullough for his useful comments.

REFERENCE

[1] W. Feller, *An Introduction to Probability Theory and Its Applications,* New York: John Wiley, Vol. 1, 2nd ed., 1957, p. 23.

Table 1

Values of d_k as a function of r_k and δ for $v = 4$

r_k and	$\frac{1}{r_k}$	10^{-1}	10^{-2}	10^{-3}	10^{-4}
1.00	1.00	5	11	17	25
.900	1.11	5	11	19	25
.800	1.25	5	11	19	25
.700	1.43	5	13	19	25
.600	1.67	7	13	19	25
.500	2.00	7	11	17	23
.400	2.50	7	11	17	21
.300	3.33	5	11	15	19
.200	5.00	5	9	13	17
.100	10.0	5	7	9	13
10^{-2}	10^{2}	3	5	7	7
10^{-3}	10^{3}	3	3	5	5
10^{-4}	10^{4}	3	3	3	5

Appendix

GRADATION AND ORDERING OF CLUSTERS

We first derive the gradation of clusters property from which the ordering $R_1 \geqslant R_2 \geqslant \ldots \geqslant R_v$ follows directly. Proof: Using the definition of conditional probability, we have

$$P(H_k \mid X \epsilon \Xi_i) = \frac{P(X \epsilon \Xi_i \mid H_k)P(H_k)}{P(X \epsilon \Xi_i)} \quad k = 1, 2 \tag{1}$$

where $P(H_k) = \rho_k$ = a priori probability of H_k. The first inequality becomes

$$\frac{P(X \epsilon \Xi_i \mid H_1)}{P(X \epsilon \Xi_i)} \geqslant \frac{P(X \epsilon \Xi_j \mid H_1)}{P(X \epsilon \Xi_j)} \quad 1 \leqslant i \leqslant j \leqslant v \tag{2}$$

The probability $P(X \epsilon \Xi_i \mid H_1)$ is obtained by conditioning on the disjoint events $\{X \epsilon V_k\}$ and using the theorem of total probability:

$$P(X \epsilon \Xi_i \mid H_1) = \sum_{k=1}^{w} P(X \epsilon \Xi_i \mid X \epsilon V_k, H_1)\, P(X \epsilon V_k \mid H_1). \tag{3}$$

However, $P(X \epsilon \Xi_i \mid X \epsilon V_k, H_1)$ does not depend on H_1 given $\{X \epsilon V_k\}$ when the training is sampled in the steady state and is equal to $P(V_k \subseteq \Xi_i) = P(C_k^{(\infty)} = i) = P_{ki}$. The $P(X \epsilon V_k \mid H_1) = a_k/\rho_1$; hence

$$P(X \epsilon \Xi_i \mid H_1) = \frac{1}{\rho_1} \sum_{k=1}^{w} P_{ki} a_k \tag{4}$$

and, after applying the same argument under H_2, we obtain

$$P(X \epsilon \Xi_i) = \sum_{k=1}^{w} P_{ki}(a_k + b_k) \tag{5}$$

Substituting (4) in (2) and rearranging yields

$$\sum_{k=1}^{w} P_{ki} a_k\, P(X \epsilon \Xi_j) - P_{kj} a_k\, P(X \epsilon \Xi_i) \geqslant 0 \tag{6}$$

$$1 \leqslant i \leqslant j \leqslant v$$

Substituting (5) in (6) gives

$$\sum_{k=1}^{w} \sum_{\ell=1}^{w} a_k(a_\ell + b_\ell)\, \Delta_{k\ell}^{ij} \geqslant 0 \qquad 1 \leqslant i \leqslant j \leqslant v \tag{7}$$

where

$$\Delta_{k\ell}^{ij} = P_{ki}P_{\ell j} - P_{kj}P_{\ell i}\,. \tag{8}$$

We observe that $\Delta_{k\ell}^{ij}$ has the property

$$\Delta_{k\ell}^{ij} = -\Delta_{\ell k}^{ij} \quad (\text{hence } \Delta_{kk}^{ij} = 0)$$

Therefore (7) may be written:

$$\sum_{k=2}^{w} \sum_{\ell=1}^{k-1} (a_k b_\ell - a_\ell b_k)\, \Delta_{k\ell}^{ij} \tag{9}$$

Since $a_k b_\ell - a_\ell b_k = a_k a_\ell (r_\ell - r_k)$, (9) is non-negative for $1 \leqslant i \leqslant j \leqslant v$ if $\Delta_{k\ell}^{ij} \geqslant 0$ for $r_\ell \geqslant r_k$ and $\Delta_{k\ell}^{ij} \leqslant 0$ for $r_\ell < r_k$.

Substituting the expression for P_{kj} in (8) results in

$$\Delta_{k\ell}^{ij} = \frac{1-r_k}{1-r_k^v}\,\frac{1-r_\ell}{1-r_\ell^v}\,(r_k^{i-1} r_\ell^{j-1} - r_k^{j-1} r_\ell^{i-1}). \tag{10}$$

For $1 \leqslant i \leqslant j \leqslant v$, the sign of $\Delta_{k\ell}^{ij}$ is determined by the sign of $r_\ell^{j-i} - r_k^{j-i}$ or

$$\begin{aligned} r_\ell^{j-i} - r_k^{j-i} &\geqslant 0 \qquad & r_\ell \geqslant r_k \\ &\leqslant 0 \qquad & r_\ell \leqslant r_k\,. \end{aligned}$$

Consequently, the sum (9) is non-negative.

Under H_2, the expression corresponding to (9) is

$$\sum_{k=2}^{w} \sum_{\ell=1}^{k-1} (a_\ell b_k - b_\ell a_k)\, \Delta_{k\ell}^{ij} \tag{11}$$

which is shown in the same way to be non-negative.

The ordering property follows by comparing R_i and R_{i+1}, $i = 1, 2, \ldots, v-1$, using the gradation of clusters; i.e.

$$R_i = \frac{P(H_1 \mid X \in \Xi_i)}{P(H_2 \mid X \in \Xi_i)} \geqslant \frac{P(H_1 \mid X \in \Xi_{i+1})}{P(H_2 \mid X \in \Xi_i)} \geqslant \frac{P(H_1 \mid X \in \Xi_{i+1})}{P(H_2 \mid X \in \Xi_{i+1})} = R_{i+1}\,. \tag{12}$$

FEATURE SELECTION FOR PATTERN RECOGNITION SYSTEMS

Julius T. Tou

UNIVERSITY OF FLORIDA
GAINESVILLE, FLORIDA

Introduction

Recognition is regarded as a basic attribute of human beings as well as living organisms. Based upon laboratory and clinic experiments, we may make the conjecture that human recognition involves mainly statistical association, search for features, and adaptive template matching. The major problem of pattern recognition is essentially the discrimination of the input data between statistical populations via the search for features among members of a population. This paper presents several approaches for the extraction of features in pattern recognition systems.

We perform the acts of recognition every instant of our waking lives. We recognize the objects around us and we move and act in relation to them. We can spot a friend in a crowd and recognize what he says; we can read handwritings; we can distinguish smiles from gestures of anger. Recognition of patterns by humans may be considered as a psycho-physiological problem which involves a relationship between a person and a physical stimulus. When a person perceives a pattern, he is making an inductive inference and associating that perception with some general concept or clues which he has derived from his past experience. Human recognition would be a question of estimating the relative odds that the input data are to be associated with one of a set of known statistical populations which depend upon our past experience and which form the clues and a priori information for recognition. Thus, the problem of recognition may be regarded as one of discriminating the input data not between individual patterns but between populations via the search for features or invariants among members of a population.

The design of pattern recognition systems generally involves several major problem areas. The first problem is concerned with the representation of input data which can be measured from the objects of a pattern class. This is the sensing problem. The second problem is concerned with the selection of characteristic features or attributes from the received input data. This is often referred to as the feature extraction or selection problem. The third problem deals with the determination of optimum decision procedures which are needed in the process of identification and classification. This is the optimum decision problem. In solving the feature selection problem and the optimum decision problem, there is generally involved a set of parameters to be estimated and optimized. This gives rise to the parameter estimation problem. Both the feature selection and the decision process may be improved by making use of contextual information in the patterns. When we wish to design a pattern recognition system which is resistant to distortion, flexible with pattern deviations, and capable of self-adjusting, we are confronted with the adaptation problem. A block diagram describing a basic pattern recognition system is shown in Figure 1.

The features of an object from a pattern class may be described in one of four different forms: physical features, topological features, mathematical features, and statistical features. This paper emphasizes the latter two types of features. Often it is more convenient to design pattern recognition machines to select mathematical or statistical features than to construct machines to extract physical and topological features of patterns. Furthermore, when mathematical and statistical features are considered, the feature selection problem is more amenable to a unified mathematical solution.

Feature Selection Via Entropy Minimization

The selection of features has been recognized as an important process in a pattern recognition system. When the complete set of discriminatory features for each pattern class can be determined from the measurement, the recognition and classification of the patterns will present no problem and automatic classification may be reduced to a simple matching procedure. However, in all pattern recognition systems in practice, with the exception of some very simple cases, the determination of complete discriminatory features is extremely difficult if not impossible. Automatic classification is by no means a trivial problem.

Frequently, we may be able to find some of the discriminatory features from the observed data. These features can be used to advantage in the simplification of the recognition process. For instance, we can reduce the dimensionality of the measurement vectors via a transformation with minimum loss of information. The transformation matrix consists of the feature vectors which are selected from the property vectors. The optimum feature selection is carried out by the process of minimizing the population entropy which is used as a measure of the intraset dispersion.

Consider a pattern recognition system which is designed to recognize N pattern classes $\{\omega_i, i = 1, 2, \ldots, N\}$. For each pattern class, the feature extractor of the system determines the set of discriminating features which are necessary for correct classification and recognition. Assume that the pattern components are normally distributed random variables. The joint probability density of n components of the pattern vector is described by a multivariate normal distribution. For the *ith* pattern class under consideration, the normal probability-density function is completely specified by the mean vector $\mathbf{M}_i$ and covariance matrix $\underline{\Sigma}_i$ and is often expressed as

$$p_i(x) \sim N(\mathbf{M}_i, \underline{\Sigma}_i) \tag{1}$$

The normal probability-density function is important because it offers computational simplicity and represents a realistic model of many pattern recognition situations. In the following discussions, we assume that all of the N covariance matrices $\underline{\Sigma}_i$ describing the statistics of the pattern classes are identical and equal to $\underline{\Sigma}$. This situation arises when each pattern belonging to the *ith* class is a random vector given by the sum of a fixed, non-random vector and a random vector. The additive random vectors are drawn from the same normal distribution. This is a reasonable assumption for many practical applications.

The feature selection process involves the transformation of the received data $\mathbf{x}$ from the input patterns of the class by a linear transformation

$$\mathbf{y} = \mathbf{A}\,\mathbf{x} \tag{2}$$

so that the intraset dispersion of the image patterns $\mathbf{y}$ is a minimum. In the above equation, $\mathbf{x}$ is an n-vector, $\mathbf{y}$ is an m-vector, $m<n$, and $\mathbf{A}$ is an $m \times n$ matrix whose rows form the m feature vectors of the pattern class.

$$\mathbf{A} = \text{col}\,[a_1'\ a_2'\ \ldots\ a_m'] \tag{3}$$

The problem can now be stated as the determination of the m feature vectors so that the intraset dispersion of the image patterns is minimized.

The multivariate normal population is characterized by the mean vector and the covariance matrix which is, in turn, characterized by eigenvalues and eigenvectors. These eigenvectors carry the information describing the properties of the pattern class under consideration. The eigenvectors may be regarded as the property vectors of the pattern class. However, some of the property vectors bear more information than the others, and are therefore more important in pattern recognition. This phenomenon suggests a feature extraction procedure by selecting the most significant property vectors which we will call feature vectors. These feature vectors may be used to construct the transformation matrix $\mathbf{A}$. The following paragraphs will discuss an approach to the selection of feature vectors on the basis of minimum entropy concept.

The population entropy for the original pattern vectors $\mathbf{x}$ of the *ith* category is given by

$$H_i = -\int p_i(x)\,[\log p_i(x)]\,dx \tag{4}$$

where the multivariate normal probability density function $p_i(x)$ is

$$p_i(x) = \frac{1}{(2\pi)^{n/2}\,[\det \underline{\Sigma}]^{1/2}} \exp[-\tfrac{1}{2}(x-M_i)'\,\underline{\Sigma}^{-1}(x-M_i)] \tag{5}$$

The covariance matrix for the image patterns $\mathbf{y}$ is

$$\underline{\Sigma}^{\nu} = \mathbf{A}\,\underline{\Sigma}\,\mathbf{A}' \tag{6}$$

and the transformed mean is

$$\mathbf{M}_i^{\nu} = \mathbf{A}\,\mathbf{M}_i \tag{7}$$

Using the above equations and the relationship that the determinant of a matrix is equal to the product of its eigenvalues, we obtain the probability density of the image patterns for category ω_i as

$$p_i(y) = \frac{1}{[\prod_{k=1}^{m} (2\pi)^m \beta_k]^{1/2}} \exp\{-\tfrac{1}{2}\,\mathrm{tr}\,[(\mathbf{A}\,\underline{\Sigma}\,\mathbf{A}')^{-1}(y-\mathbf{M}_i^{\nu})(y-\mathbf{M}_i^{\nu})']\} \tag{8}$$

in which β_k, $(k = 1, 2, \ldots, m)$, are the eigenvalues of the covariance matrix $\underline{\Sigma}^{\nu}$.

Then the population entropy for the image patterns $\mathbf{y}$ is given by

$$H_i = \frac{1}{2}\sum_{k=1}^{m} \log \beta_k + \frac{m}{2}(1 + \log 2\pi) \tag{9}$$

We wish to determine the feature vectors $\mathbf{a}_k$ so that the population entropy is minimized. To carry out the minimization, we determine the differential entropy dH_i,

$$dH_i = \frac{1}{2}\sum_{k=1}^{m} \frac{1}{\beta_k}(d\beta_k) \tag{10}$$

It can be shown that

$$d\beta_k = 2\,\mathbf{b}_k'\,[(d\mathbf{A})\,\underline{\Sigma}\,\mathbf{A}']\,\mathbf{b}_k \tag{11}$$

Combining Eqs. (10) and (11) yields

$$dH_i = \mathrm{tr}\left[(d\mathbf{A}) \sum_{k=1}^{m} \frac{\underline{\Sigma}\, \mathbf{A}'\mathbf{b}_k\, \mathbf{b}_k'}{\beta_k}\right] \qquad (12)$$

Using the constraint

$$\mathbf{a}_k'\, \mathbf{a}_k = 1 \qquad (13)$$

where $\mathbf{a}_k$, $(k = 1, 2, \ldots, n)$, are the eigenvalues of covariance matrix $\underline{\Sigma}$, it can be shown that the condition for the population entropy H_i to be a minimum is

$$\underline{\Sigma}\, \mathbf{A}' \sum_{k=1}^{m} \frac{\mathbf{b}_k\, \mathbf{b}_k'}{\beta_k} - \mathbf{A}'\underline{\Gamma} = \mathbf{0} \qquad (14)$$

where $\underline{\Gamma}$ is the Lagrange multiplier matrix.

Since the feature vectors are selected from the orthonormal eigenvectors of $\underline{\Sigma}$, we derive the relationship

$$\mathbf{A}\, \underline{\Sigma}\, \mathbf{A}' = \underline{\alpha} \qquad (15)$$

where the matrix $\underline{\alpha}$ is the diagonal matrix given by

$$\underline{\alpha} = \begin{bmatrix} \alpha_1 & 0 & . & . & . & 0 \\ 0 & \alpha_2 & & & & . \\ . & & \ddots & & & . \\ . & & & \alpha_k & & . \\ . & & & & \ddots & 0 \\ 0 & . & . & . & 0 & \alpha_m \end{bmatrix} \qquad (16)$$

in which the elements on the principal diagonal are the corresponding eigenvalues of $\underline{\Sigma}$. Making use of the properties of the eigenvalues, it can readily be shown that

$$\beta_k = \alpha_k, \quad k = 1, 2, \ldots, m \qquad (17)$$

Furthermore, it can be shown that

$$\sum_{k=1}^{m} \frac{\mathbf{b}_k\, \mathbf{b}_k'}{\beta_k} = \underline{\alpha}^{-1} \qquad (18)$$

Consequently, by letting $\underline{\Gamma} = \mathbf{I}$, Eq. (15) satisfies the local minimum condition given in Eq. (14).

Thus, for a specified m the population entropy H_i will assume a global minimum equal to

$$H_i = \frac{1}{2} \sum_{k=1}^{m} \log \alpha_k + \frac{m}{2}(1 + \log 2\pi) \tag{19}$$

if m smallest eigenvalues are chosen from the n eigenvalues of the covariance matrix $\underline{\Sigma}$, and the eigenvectors associated with the m smallest eigenvalues α_k are chosen as the m feature vectors. The number of feature vectors may be so determined that the minimum population entropy for all the N pattern classes satisfies a lower bound and the image patterns retain sufficient discriminatory information.

The above analysis provides a simple algorithm for performing feature selection. The covariance matrices for the pattern classes under consideration are first determined. Then we compute the eigenvalues α_k for the covariance matrix $\underline{\Sigma}$ and the corresponding eigenvectors $\mathbf{a}_k$. From the n eigenvectors we select m eigenvectors associated with m smallest eigenvalues. These m eigenvectors are used to represent the feature vectors, which form the rows of the transformation matrix **A**. The image patterns obtained through the linear transformation serve as the inputs to a discriminating device. The size of the image pattern vector can be determined through learning by an adaptive scheme. Shown in Figure 2 is a flow chart for this feature selection process.

Formation of α-tuples as Basic Features

A two-dimensional pattern, such as an alphabet, a numeral, or a character, can be readily measured by a scanning device. Such measurement displays the pattern in a two-dimensional discrete coordinate system as a matrix with n pattern points. This measurement can also be expressed as a column vector **x** of dimension n. The value of n is usually very large, and the measurement vector **x** has a dimension which gets to be too high to handle. Assume that the measured values are quantized to yield binary numbers. If n = 100, it would require the availability of 2^{100} computer addresses, and successful recognition would be restricted to those patterns which had been learned before. To train a linear machine to classify pattern vectors of very high dimension we may run into the problems with separability and convergence. The complexity of the recognition system may grow exponentially in proportion to the dimensionality of pattern vectors.

When the sensory device displays the pattern as a matrix with n elements, we can accomplish feature selection by suitable formation of α-tuples from the pattern elements. The entire set of n pattern elements is replaced by a smaller set of m α-tuples which characterize the basic features of the pattern. This approach to feature selection is conceptually simple, but it involves two major problems. The first problem is concerned with what characteristic information should be stored during the training phase. The second problem is how to select the best α-tuples for a specified recognition task and how to adapt the selection scheme for performing different recognition tasks.

Let the input pattern matrix with n pattern points be expressed as a measurement vector

$$x = \text{col}(x_1, x_2, \ldots, x_k, \ldots, x_n) \quad (20)$$

where the elements x_k are equal to 0 or 1 if the input is in the form of a binary matrix. By grouping x_k's to form α-tuples, we may transform the x-vector to a y-vector

$$y = \text{col}(y_1, y_2, \ldots, y_j, \ldots, y_m) \quad (21)$$

where the elements y_j are determined from the α-tuples which describe pattern features. The y-vector may be referred to as the image pattern vector, which is generated from the α-tuples through a feature coding procedure as shown in Figure 3. For the binary case, each α-tuple has 2^α possible values corresponding to the 2^α possible binary patterns. Thus, the image pattern vector y has m 2^α valued components. Now, we define f_{jk} as the *kth* feature value ($k = 1, 2, \ldots, 2^\alpha$) of the *jth* feature element ($j = 1, 2, \ldots, m$). One way to implement the feature selection by α-tuples is to code the image pattern vector elements in binary form. The *jth* element y_j is equal to 1, if the feature value f_{jk} is found in the input pattern, and it is equal to zero if f_{jk} is not found in the input pattern. An alternative way is to let y_j equal the feature value of the corresponding α-tuple. In calculating the feature values, we may use a decoding rule to enhance the discriminatory ability of the image pattern vectors. After the image pattern vectors are established, we may determine the discriminant function for each category.

The α-tuples may be formed in a number of ways. They may be selected in a random manner as long as the α-tuples will represent independent pattern characteristics. The elements in each row of the pattern matrix may be grouped to form an α-tuple, or the elements in each diagonal of the pattern matrix may be grouped to form the α-tuples. A zig-zag selection of pattern points is another way of constructing the α-tuples. With no priori knowledge of the patterns to be recognized, it is difficult to say which scheme will lead to the best α-tuple formation, and random selection may be a better compromise. If we have a priori knowledge on the pattern classes, human's feature extraction strategies may be built into the pattern recognition system for pre-selection of features.

Consider the automatic recognition of hand-written numerals or printed characters. Since we know the general shape of these patterns, we may locate several strategic points on the pattern grid or binary matrix and form α-tuples around these points. Maximum information could be conveyed by proper selection of the α-tuples. As an illustration, consider the pattern grid shown in Figure 4. Two strategic points p_1 and p_2 are located on the grid as shown. Then we may form the α-tuples by grouping the boxes (or 0's and l's) from these two points to the four edges of the grid. The box is represented by a 1 if the numeral passes through or touches that box, and it is represented by a 0 otherwise. Following this grouping rule, we obtain the α-tuples for a hand-written 3 as

$$a_3 = 000, \quad b_3 = 001, \quad c_3 = 0100, \quad d_3 = 00001$$

$$e_3 = 0000, \quad f_3 = 01101, \quad g_3 = 010, \quad h_3 = 001$$

These α-tuples describe the important attributes of the hand-written numeral 3. The elements of the image vector $\mathbf{y}$ are determined by counting the number of 1's in the corresponding α-tuple. For this hand-written 3, the image vector is

$$\mathbf{y} = \mathrm{col}(0\ 1\ 1\ 1\ 0\ 3\ 1\ 1) \tag{22}$$

For a hand-written 8, we obtain the α-tuples as

$$a_8 = 010, \quad b_8 = 001, \quad c_8 = 0100, \quad d_8 = 01101$$

$$e_8 = 0100, \quad f_8 = 01101, \quad g_8 = 001, \quad h_8 = 001$$

The corresponding image vector is

$$\mathbf{y} = \mathrm{col}(1\ 1\ 1\ 3\ 1\ 3\ 1\ 1) \tag{23}$$

The image vectors for other numerals can be determined by coding the α-tuple features in the same manner. Because of the variability of each numeral, the elements of the corresponding image vector may vary between an upper and a lower bound. Taking into account the threshold of variations we may encode the image vector into a string of alphabets. The recognition process can then be carried out by using a decoding scheme.

The above feature selection process results in a data string which contains much less data than is initially available in the binary matrix. It is the intent of the feature selection process to remove the information which will not necessarily effect the final decoding of the pattern string into a single unique symbol. In general, the determination of whether or not an alphabet in the data string is necessary to the recognition process depends upon what other alphabets surround it. Contextual analysis plays an important role in this scheme. In generating a string of alphabets for the description of a binary pattern matrix, we may convert each row of the binary matrix into an alphabet. All the consecutive rows with the same topological properties can be represented by one alphabet, thus reducing the length of a data string and simplifying the recognition process.

In the early version of the Bledsoe-Browning machine, only the 1 and 0 or their joint frequency of occurrences were stored. This stored information appeared to be insufficient, and it did not produce good results. An alternative way is to store the information describing the joint probability of occurrence of the category ω_i and the feature value f_{jk}. The feature value is different for different α-tuples, and it takes into consideration the ordering of the pattern points. It has been shown that such storage scheme can produce better results in recognizing distorted patterns.

Feature Extraction Through Approximation

The statistical features of a pattern class can be described by a function f(x) which is determined on the basis of a set of observed data from the pattern class. The process of feature extraction can then be viewed as a problem of approximation. Assume that during the training phase we have obtained the values of the feature function f(x) at the points $x = x_1, x_2, \ldots, x_N$. We wish to seek an approximation $\hat{f}(x)$ to f(x) such that certain performance criterion is optimized. A convenient criterion for such approximation is that the weighted sum of the squares of the errors at these observed data points is a minimum.

Now let $w(x_k)$ be some positive weights, where $k = 1, 2, \ldots, N$. Using the above criterion, we want to minimize

$$R = \sum_{k=1}^{N} \{w(x_k)[f(x_k)-\hat{f}(x_k)]^2\} \tag{24}$$

The approximation function $\hat{f}(x)$ may be expressed in the form

$$\hat{f}(x) = \underline{\gamma}'\underline{\phi}(x) \tag{25}$$

where

$$\underline{\phi}(x) = \mathrm{col}[\varphi_1(x), \varphi_2(x), \ldots, \varphi_i(x), \ldots, \varphi_r(x)] \tag{26}$$

and

$$\underline{\gamma} = \mathrm{col}[\gamma_1, \gamma_2, \ldots, \gamma_i, \ldots, \gamma_r] \tag{27}$$

The coefficients γ_i appear linearly in the approximation, and the function $\varphi_i(x)$ are independent elements of a linear vector space of dimension N of functions on the point set $x_1, x_2, \ldots, x_N$.

In view of Eq. (25), $\hat{f}(x_k)$ contains the coefficients γ_i (i = 1, 2, . . . , r with r<N) and the minimum of R may be evaluated by taking the partial derivatives with respect to γ_i. The conditions for a minimum

$$\frac{\partial R}{\partial \gamma_i} = 0 , \qquad i = 1, 2, \ldots, r \tag{28}$$

provide a set of algebraic equations for the determination of the coefficients γ_i.

Carrying out the partial differentiation, we obtain the matrix equation relating the coefficient vector $\underline{\gamma}$ to $w(x_k)$ and $\varphi_i(x_k)$

$$\mathbf{A}\,\underline{\gamma} = \mathbf{v} \tag{29}$$

In Eq. (29), **A** is a r×r positive definite symmetric matrix with elements

$$a_{ij} = \sum_{k=1}^{N} w(x_k)\, \varphi_i(x_k)\, \varphi_j(x_k)$$

and **v** is a r-vector with elements

$$v_i = \sum_{k=1}^{N} w(x_k)\, \varphi_i(x_k)\, f(x_k) \tag{30}$$

To simplify computation, we may choose the functions $\varphi_i(x)$ which are orthogonal with respect to the weight factors for summation over the observed data points x_k. Then the functions $\varphi_i(x)$ satisfy the condition

$$\sum_{k=1}^{N} w(x_k)\, \varphi_i(x_k)\, \varphi_j(x_k) = 0 , \quad i \neq j \tag{31}$$

and the matrix **A** is diagonal. The coefficients γ_i which are required for the determination of the approximation function $\hat{f}(x)$ are given by

$$\gamma_i = \frac{\sum_{k=1}^{N} w(x_k)\, \varphi_i(x_k)\, f(x_k)}{\sum_{k=1}^{N} w(x_k)\, \varphi_i^2(x_k)} \tag{32}$$

When the functions $\varphi_i(x)$ are orthonormal with respect to the weight factors, Eq. (32) reduces to

$$\gamma_i = \sum_{k=1}^{N} w(x_k)\, \varphi_i(x_k)\, f(x_k) \tag{33}$$

The above approach to statistical feature extraction is motivated by the Weierstrass Approximation Theorem. We choose orthogonal functions for the following additional reasons. If the sum of the squares of the errors at the observed data points is not small enough, we may obtain a higher-order approximation $\hat{f}_{r+1}(x)$ by adding an extra term $\gamma_{r+1}\,\varphi_{r+1}(x)$ where $\varphi_{r+1}(x)$ is another independent element of the vector space. Furthermore, all the previously determined coefficients $\gamma_1, \gamma_2, \ldots, \gamma_r$ in the approximation function $\hat{f}_r(x)$ remain unchanged. We merely add the new term both in the new approximation function and in the new error estimates. These properties of orthogonal functions simplify greatly the computational procedure.

The statistical features of the patterns of a class may be determined from the observed samples of the pattern class by the method of kernel approximation. Let f(x) be a statistical feature function which is to be determined from a set of observed data, $(x^1, x^2, \ldots, x^k)$. It can be shown that an approximation $\hat{f}(x)$ to f(x) is given by

$$f(x) \sim \hat{f}(x) = \int K_n(x,y) f(y)\, dy \tag{34}$$

Where $K_n(x,y)$ is a known kernel which satisfies the following conditions:

(a) $\int_a^b K_n(x,y)\, dy = 1$

(b) $\lim_{n \to \infty} \int_{x-\epsilon}^{x+\epsilon} K_n(x,y)\, dy = 1$

(c) $\lim_{n \to \infty} K_n(x,y) = \delta(x,y)$

(d) $K_n(x,y) \geqslant 0$

(e) $K_n(x,y) = K_n(y,x)$

Then by the strong law of large number, the approximation function $\hat{f}(x)$ can be estimated from the k independent samples by using the relationship

$$\hat{f}_k(x) = \frac{1}{k} \sum_{i=1}^{k} K_n(x,x^i) \tag{35}$$

For each x, $\hat{f}_k(x)$ converges to $\hat{f}(x)$ with probability 1 as $k \to \infty$; and $\hat{f}(x)$ converges to f(x) uniformly as $n \to \infty$. Needless to say, the quality of approximation given in Eq. (34) depends upon the nature of the kernel $K_n(x,y)$. The statistical features determined from Eq. (35) can then be used as the basis for pattern classification and recognition. A simple classification scheme is to determine the m statistical features $\hat{f}_k(x/\omega_j)$, $j = 1, 2, \ldots, m$. Since the statistical feature functions are highly tuned, a maximum detector can be used to examine the values of these functions. The machine decides that x belongs to class ω_j, if $\hat{f}_k(x/\omega_j)$ has the largest value.

Assume that from the population of a pattern class ω_ℓ we observe a sequence of random variables $(x^1, x^2, \ldots, x^k)$ which are independent and identically distributed with unknown probability density $p(x/\omega_\ell)$. The probability density can be considered as a statistical feature function for this pattern class, and the kernel approximation method can be applied to determine the statistical features. Let the probability density $p(x/\omega_\ell)$ for pattern class ω_ℓ be represented by a linear combination of N orthonormal functions $\varphi_i(x/\omega_\ell)$,

$$p(x/\omega_\ell) = \sum_{i=1}^{N} c_i \, \varphi_i(x/\omega_\ell) \tag{36}$$

and the kernel $K(x,y/\omega_\ell)$ be given by

$$K(x,y/\omega_\ell) = \sum_{j=1}^{N} \varphi_j(x/\omega_\ell) \, \varphi_j(y/\omega_\ell) \tag{37}$$

where the functions $\varphi_j(x/\omega_\ell)$ are bounded and satisfy the orthonormality condition

$$\int_X \varphi_j(x/\omega_\ell) \, \varphi_k(x/\omega_\ell) dx = \delta_{jk} \tag{38}$$

In Eq. (38), δ_{jk} is the Kronecker function. It follows from Eq. (35) that

$$\hat{p}_k(x/\omega_\ell) = \frac{1}{k} \sum_{i=1}^{k} K(x,x^i/\omega_\ell) \tag{39}$$

which is used to determine an approximation to the statistical feature function from an observation of the k samples $x^1, x^2, \ldots, x^k$.

Using Eqs. (36) and (37), we have

$$\int K(x,y/\omega_\ell)p(y/\omega_\ell)dy = \int \sum_{j=1}^{N} \varphi_j(x/\omega_\ell) \, \varphi_j(y/\omega_\ell) \sum_{i=1}^{N} c_i \, \varphi_i(y/\omega_\ell)dy \tag{40}$$

$$= \sum_{j=1}^{N} \varphi_j(x/\omega_\ell) \sum_{i=1}^{N} c_i \int \varphi_j(y/\omega_\ell) \, \varphi_i(y/\omega_\ell)dy$$

In view of Eq. (38), the above equation reduces to

$$\int K(x,y/\omega_\ell)p(y/\omega_\ell)dy = \sum_{j=1}^{N} c_j \, \varphi_j(x/\omega_\ell) \tag{41}$$

Hence, we have

$$\int K(x,y/\omega_\ell)p(y/\omega_\ell)dy = p(x/\omega_\ell) \tag{42}$$

At each sample point $x \in X$, the approximate probability density function $\hat{p}(x/\omega_\ell)$ tends in probability to $p(x/\omega_\ell)$ as $k \to \infty$.

Conclusions

Pattern recognition is one of the major areas of endeavor in the design of intelligent automata. In fact, it is a necessary prerequisite to fruitful development of intelligent machines and sophisticated information processing systems. The major problem areas involved in the design of adaptive pattern recognition schemes are the input representation problem, the feature selection problem, the contextual analysis problem, the optimum decision problem, the parameter estimation problem, and the adaptation and learning problem. Among these problems, feature selection has been considered as a key to the classification and recognition of patterns. Pattern recognition can be regarded as the categorization of input data into identifiable classes via extraction of the significant features of the data from a background of irrelevant detail.

Automatic classification is reduced to a simple matching task when the complete set of discriminatory features for each pattern class can be determined from the observed data. Unfortunately, for practical pattern recognition systems, the determination of complete discriminatory features is extremely difficult, if not impossible. In general, only some of these features can be found. The classification scheme can be simplified by making use of these features and the available contextual information.

This paper presents several methods of feature selection for pattern recognition systems. The feature selection process may be carried out through the minimization of population entropy. The significant features may be represented by α-tuples. Finally, we treat the feature extraction as an approximation problem and we introduce the method of kernel approximation for the determination of the statistical feature from observed sample data.

BIBLIOGRAPHY

1. Kullback, S., *Information Theory and Statistics,* John Wiley & Sons, Inc., New York, 1958.
2. Bledsoe, W.W. and Browning, I., "Pattern Recognition and Reading by Machine," *Proceedings of the Eastern Joint Computer Conference,* 1959.
3. Steck, G.P., "Stochastic Model for the Browning-Bledsoe Pattern Recognition Scheme," *IRE Transactions on Electronic Computers,* April 1962.
4. Sebestyen, G., *Decision-making Processes in Pattern Recognition,* The Macmillan Company, New York, 1962.
5. Watanabe, M.S., "A Method of Self-featuring Information Compression," *Proceedings of Bionics Symposium,* May, 1966.

6. Tou, J.T. and Heydorn, R.P., "Some Approaches to Optimum Feature Extraction," in *Computer and Information Sciences–II* (edited by J.T. Tou) Academic Press Inc., New York, 1967.
7. Szego, G., *Orthogonal Polynomials,* American Mathematical Society, 1959.
8. Aronszajn, N., "Theory of Reproducing Kernels," Translation American Mathematical Society, pp. 337–404, 1950.
9. Aizerman, M.A., Braverman, E.M., and Rozonoer, L.I., "Theoretical Foundations of the Potential Function Method in Pattern Recognition Learning," *Automation & Remote Control,* Vol. 25, No. 6, 1964.
10. Block, H.E., Nilsson, N.J., and Duda, R.O., "Determination and Detection of Features in Patterns," in *Computer and Information Sciences–I* (edited by J.T. Tou and R.H. Wilcox), Spartan Books, 1964.
11. Watanabe, S., *et al,* "Evaluation and Selection of Variables in Pattern Recognition," in *Computer and Information Sciences–II* (edited by J.T. Tou), Academic Press, Inc., New York, 1967.

Acknowledgment

The work reported in this paper was supported in part by the Office of Naval Research under contract N00014-68-A-0173.

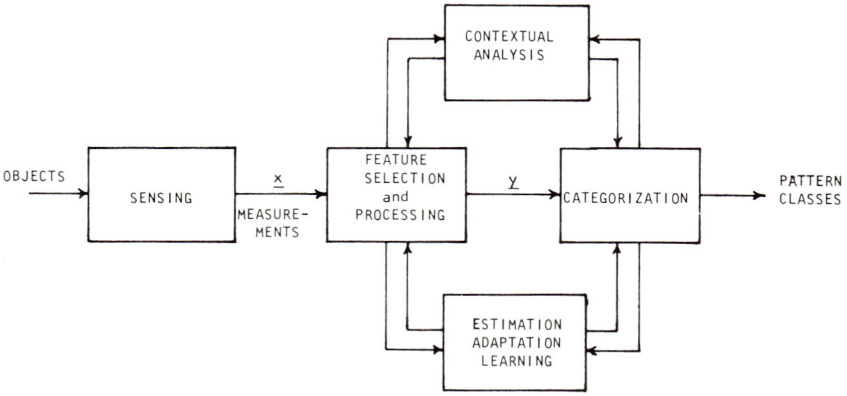

Figure 1: Functional Block Diagram of an Adaptive Pattern Recognition System

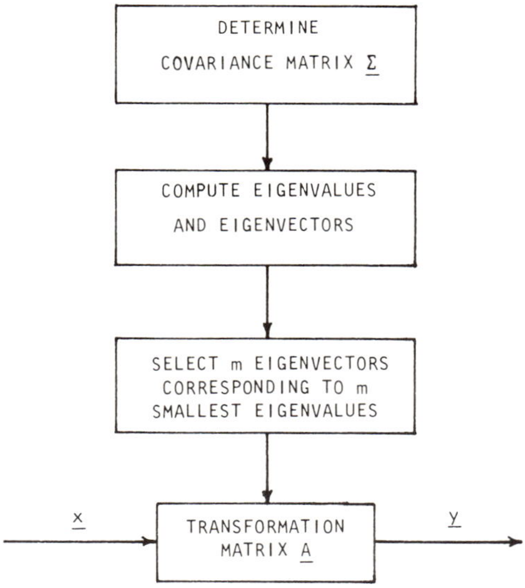

Figure 2: A Feature Selection Flow Chart

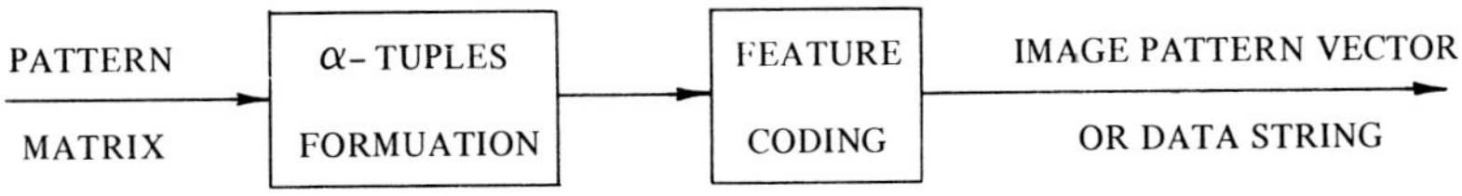

Figure 3: α-Tuple Processing

Figure 4: Illustration of the Selection of α-Tuples

A CONTRIBUTION TO THE INFORMATIONAL ANALYSIS OF PATTERN

Igor Vajda

CZECHOSLOVAK ACADEMY OF SCIENCES
PRAGUE, CZECHOSLOVAKIA

1. The basic problem of pattern recognition theory consists in that one has to separate a relevant information from patterns. Using the information, one classifies the patterns into classes. The process of pattern classification is usually interpreted as a pattern recognition and the classification criteria as an algorithm of the recognition. The quality of the algorithms is usually judged by attributing a numerically expressed loss to every algorithm. The relevancy or irrelevancy of information is to be judged from the viewpoint of losses as well.

Hence, defining a non-empty set J of patterns and a class of rules determining losses, we specify a general pattern recognition problem. Separating the relevant information, we form an algorithm of recognition minimizing losses and representing a solution of the problem under consideration. Therefore, it is important to ask how much information is contained in a pattern and how can one separate the relevant information from a pattern. The solution of this two problems has played an important role in the past development of the pattern recognition theory and, undoubtedly, it will play such a role in the future as well.

In this lecture let me discuss some new aspects of both of these problems in the frame of the classical statistical approach to the pattern recognition problem. As to the amount of information contained in a pattern, it seems that the pattern recognition theory is too inspired by the success of information theory in the field of information transfer. This success was achieved by introducing the Shannon's numerical measure of the amount of information. It seems that the basic problems of pattern recognition theory essentially differ from the asymptotic coding and information transfer problems where the Shannon's information plays the well-known role and hence, in the pattern recognition theory it would be very natural and desirable to ask for other measures of information having more appropriate properties from the viewpoint of its own problems. Some recent studies (see, for example [1,5]) make it possible to understand the relation between the Shannon's information and some more general decision models than the model of information transfer and to discover that the convexity of the function q log q is the cause of some basic properties of the information mentioned above and that the use of a more general approach to the definition of information leads us to an improvement of the characterization of decision models. I should like to touch here some possibilities of improvement of some previous results in the pattern recognition theory by attributing another numerical measure to amount of information. As to the selection of the relevant information from a pattern, I should like to discuss here a new asymptotic approach to the solution of this problem which in some cases leads us to relatively simple methods of the most informative parameters selection as well as to a possibility to introduce analytical methods in the data compression theory.

2. In the frame of the statistical approach to the pattern recognition the loss $L(d)$ attributed to an arbitrary algorithm of pattern recognition d which, in accordance with the considerations above, can be identified with a disjoint decomposition $\{J_\lambda\}$ $\lambda \epsilon \Lambda$, of J, is usually expressed by

$$L(d) = \int_\Lambda \int_J \ell(\lambda, d(y))\, dQ_\lambda(y)\, dQ(\lambda) \tag{1}$$

In this formula Q_λ, $\lambda \epsilon \Lambda$ or Q denote probability measures on a σ-algebra B of subsets of J or on a σ-algebra L of subsets of Λ respectively and ℓ is $L \otimes L$-measurable transformation of the Cartesian product $\Lambda \otimes \Lambda$ into the real line. From the definition of integral, it results a restrictive condition concerning d, namely, J_λ must belong to B for every $\lambda \epsilon \Lambda$. In the frame of pattern recognition it is usual to restrict ourselves to the case when Λ is a finite or countable set. Without loss of generality we may suppose that $\Lambda = \{1, 2, \ldots\}$ and that $\{\lambda\} \epsilon L$ for every $\lambda \epsilon \Lambda$. The measure Q is in this case determined by a system $\{q_\lambda\}$, $\lambda \epsilon \Lambda$, of non-negative numbers defined by $q_\lambda = Q(\{\lambda\}) \geqq 0$ for which $q_1 + q_2 + \ldots = 1$ and the function ℓ is determined by a matrix $\|\ell_{\lambda\lambda'}\|$, $\lambda, \lambda' \epsilon \Lambda$, where $\ell_{\lambda\lambda'} = \ell(\lambda, \lambda')$. Intuitive meaning of the items we have introduced is as follows: Λ is a class of standards. We suppose that every standard yields a pattern $y \epsilon J$ (so-called standard transform); J in accordance with what stated above is a class of all patterns under consideration (in general, all the standards can be contained in J) which are classified by means of the criterion d into the classes J_λ, $\lambda \epsilon \Lambda$. The probability measure Q_λ describes the relation between the standard λ and patterns from J and the number $\ell_{\lambda\lambda'}$ the loss attributed to the case when y is the standard transform of λ and $d(y) = \lambda'$. The numbers $q_1, q_2, \ldots$ define the probabilities of the events $\lambda = 1, \lambda = 2, \ldots$

The abstract space of patterns is in all non-trivial cases of too complicated structure for mathematical investigation or for a technical processing (for example, for evaluation of the probability measures Q_λ). In order to avoid this, the patterns are to be described by means of a more simple variable. Denote by X the domain of x. Then the description of patterns can be presented by a measurable transformation T of (J, B) into (X, A) where A is a σ-algebra of subsets of X probability measures Q_λ, $\lambda \epsilon \Lambda$, induce on the σ-algebra A probability measures P_λ, $\lambda \epsilon \Lambda$ by $P_\lambda = Q_\lambda T^{-1}$

(in all the cases when circumstances admits no restrictions on the patterns we can suppose that $X = J$ and that T is the identical transformation on J, i.e., $P_\lambda \equiv Q_\lambda$, $\lambda \in \Lambda$).

Now we can summarize the considerations of the preceding paragraphs in the following manner. Statistical model of the pattern recognition theory is described by $\{ (X, A, P_\lambda), \{q_\lambda\}, \|\ell_{\lambda\lambda'}\|\}$, $\lambda, \lambda' \in \Lambda$. The problem is to find such algorithms, i.e., such measurable transformations d of X into Λ, for which the losses given by

$$L(d, \|\ell_{\lambda\lambda'}\|) = \sum_{\lambda\lambda'} q_\lambda \ell_{\lambda\lambda'} P_\lambda(d^{-1}\lambda') \qquad (2)$$

(cf. (1)) are as small as possible. Denote $L^*(\|\ell_{\lambda\lambda'}\|) = \inf L(d, \|\ell_{\lambda\lambda'}\|)$, where infimum is taken over the set of all d and denote by d^* (if it exists) the algorithms satisfying the equality $L(d^*, \|\ell_{\lambda\lambda'}\|) = L^*(\|\ell_{\lambda\lambda'}\|)$. It is easy to prove [4] that, if $\|\ell_{\lambda\lambda'}\|$ is an "anti-unique" matrix, i.e., if $\|\ell_{\lambda\lambda'}\| = e = \|e_{\lambda\lambda'}\|$, where $e_{\lambda\lambda'} = 0$ or 1 depending on whether $\lambda = \lambda'$ or not, then d^* exists and is defined in accordance with the well-known Bayes' principle of maximum posterior probability. $L^*(e)$ can be interpreted as a minimum average probability of error.

As an example, let us consider the following problem. Let every $\lambda \in \Lambda$ be of the form $\lambda = t_1, t_2, \ldots, t_m$, $m = 1, 2, \ldots$, where $t_i \in \{+, \cdot\}$, $i = 1, 2, \ldots, m$, i.e., let every $\lambda \in \Lambda$ be a finite sequence of arithmetic operations of addition and multiplication. Define for every integer z and every $\lambda = t_1, t_2, \ldots, t_m$ a number λz by $\lambda z = (\ldots((zt_1z)t_2z)\ldots t_{m-1}z)t_nz$ (in the usual arithmetic sense). It is clear that λz is also an integer. Let the set X of all standard transforms (or their parameter representations) be the class of all two-column and n-row tables, i.e., let $x = \|x_{ij}\|$, $i = 1, 2, \ldots, n$, $j = 1, 2$, where x_{ij}'s are integers. The relation between the standards $\lambda \in \Lambda$ and $x \in X$ can be described arbitrarily, for example, we can put $x_{i1} = \xi_i$, $x_{i2} = \lambda\xi_i$, $i = 1, 2, \ldots, n$ where ξ_i's are independently distributed random variables taking values from the set $\{1, 2, \ldots, n\}$. Here we shall restrict ourselves to the following case: $x_{i1} = i$, $x_{i2} = \lambda.i$, $i = 1, 2, \ldots, n$. It is clear that this relation between λ and x can be interpreted as a statistical one with $P_\lambda(x) = 1$ or 0 depending on whether $x_{i1} = i$, $x_{i2} = \lambda.i$, $i = 1, 2, \ldots, n$ or not. From the definition of transformation $z \rightarrow \lambda z$ it follows immediately that λz as a function of z is a polynomial and that $\lambda \neq \lambda'$ if and only if there is z such that $\lambda z \neq \lambda' z$. Hence every standard $\lambda \in \Lambda$ can be identified with the polynomial λz, i.e.,

$$\lambda \equiv a_n z^n + a_{n-1} z^{n-1} + \ldots + a_1 z ,$$

where all a_i's are non-negative integers. Hence Λ can be identified with the set $\lim_k \Delta_k$, where Δ_k is the set of all sequences of the form $a_1, a_2, \ldots, a_k, 0, 0, \ldots$, where a_i's are non-negative integers with $a_1 + a_2 + \ldots + a_k \geqq 1$. Let $X' \subset X$ be the set of all x, for which there exists $\lambda \in \Delta_n$ such that $P_\lambda(x) = 1$. If $x \in X'$, then there exists exactly one $1 \leqq k \leqq n$ such that the condition $P_\lambda(x) = 1$ is satisfied for exactly one $\lambda' = a'_1, a'_2, \ldots,$

$a'_k, 0, 0, \ldots \epsilon \Delta_k - \Delta_{k-1}$. The corresponding polynomial $\lambda' z$ is defined as interpolational Lagrange's polynomial by

$$\lambda' z = \sum_{i=1}^{n} x_{i2z} \psi_i(z) ,$$

where

$$\psi_i(z) = \frac{\prod_{j \neq i} (z-j)}{\prod_{j \neq i} (i-j)} ; j = 1, 2, \ldots, n , i = 1, 2, \ldots, n .$$

Let us define the algorithm d of recognition by $d(x) = \lambda'$ if $x \epsilon X'$ and $d(x) = 1, 0, 0, \ldots, \epsilon \Lambda$ if $x \notin X'$. If λ can be interpreted as a random variable with probability distribution Q on Λ, then the considerations above we can conclude by the inequality

$$L^*(e) \leqq 1 - Q(\Delta_n) \quad n = 1, 2, \ldots \tag{3}$$

3. Now placing us in the frame of statistical model where λ and x are described by probability distributions, we shall discuss the question of how much information concerning λ is contained in x.

In some cases this question admits a meaningful answer also when λ and x cannot be interpreted as random variables. Let, for example, Λ and X be finite, i.e., $|\Lambda| < \infty$ $|X| < \infty$*) and let every pattern $x \epsilon X$ can or cannot be the standard image of any standard $\lambda \epsilon \Lambda_x \neq \emptyset, \Lambda_x \subset \Lambda$ or $\lambda \notin \Lambda_x$ respectively. Then the difference

$$f(|\Lambda|) - \frac{1}{|X|} \sum_x f(|\Lambda_x|) , \tag{4}$$

where f(q) for $q > 0$ is, for example, continuous and increasing function, can be interpreted as a measure of information $I(\lambda, x)$ contained in the pattern x concerning the standard λ. To illustrate this definition let Λ be the set of all $\lambda = a_1, a_2, 0, 0, \ldots, \epsilon \Delta_2$ (cf. the notation above) for which $a_1 + a_2 \leqq 2$. We shall suppose that the pattern x_1 or x_2 is represented by the value of the polynomial λz at $z = 1$ or $z = 2$ respectively. It is easy to see that in this case $|\Lambda| = 5$ and

λz	x_1	x_2
z^2+z	2	5
$2z^2$	2	8
z^2	1	4
$2z$	2	4
z	1	2

* $|A|$ denotes here and in the sequel the cardinal of A for every set A.

The pair (x_1, x_2) obviously suffices to recognize the polynomial without any error. According to (4) we have

$$I(\lambda, (x_1, x_2)) = f(5)$$

$$I(\lambda, x_1) = f(5) - \frac{f(2) + f(3)}{2}$$

$$I(\lambda, x_2) = f(5) - \frac{3f(1) + f(2)}{4}$$

If we put $f(q) = \log q$*, then $I(\lambda, x_2) - I(\lambda, x_1) = 1/4 + \log\sqrt{3}$. Hence the parameter x_2 is more informative than x_1 (cf. [6]).

If λ and x are described statistically as a pair of random variables, then in accordance with a well-known Shannon's idea, the amount of information $I(\lambda, x)$ contained in x concerning λ can be defined as the average decrease of uncertainty (or entropy) concerning λ which results if x is observed, i.e.,

$$I(\lambda, x) = \int_X [H(\{q_\lambda\}) - H(\{\tilde{q}_\lambda(x)\})]d\bar{P}, \tag{5}$$

where $\{q_\lambda\}$, $\lambda \in \Lambda$, is the prior and $\{\tilde{q}_\lambda(x)\}$, $\lambda \in \Lambda$, the posterior probability distribution of the standard λ, i.e., $q_\lambda(x)$ is the value of the A-measurable Radon-Nikodym derivative of the measure $q_\lambda P_\lambda$ with respect to the probability measure $\bar{P} = \Sigma_\lambda q_\lambda P_\lambda$ at the point $x \in X$. If we accept the Shannon's viewpoint and measure the uncertainty (or entropy) $H(\{q_\lambda\})$ of the distribution $\{q_\lambda\}$, $\lambda \in \Lambda$, numerically by

$$H(\{q_\lambda\}) = - \Sigma_\lambda q_\lambda \log q_\lambda , \tag{6}$$

then from (5) we obtain the following formula

$$I(\lambda,x) = \Sigma_\lambda q_\lambda \int_X f\left(\frac{\tilde{q}_\lambda}{q_\lambda}\right) d\bar{P} , \tag{7}$$

where

$$f(q) = q \log q . \tag{8}$$

It results from [3] that most of important properties of information, such as $I(\lambda,x) \geqq 0$ or $I(\lambda,x) \geqq I(\lambda,Tx)$, where equality occurs if and only if λ and x are independent or T is sufficient respectively, or the following convergence property: $I(\lambda, (x_1, x_2, \ldots)) = \lim_n I(\lambda, (x_1, x_2, \ldots, x_n))$, are based only on the convexity of f in (7) (cf. (8)). Since the information-theoretical analysis of pattern recognition problems is essentially based on

---

* All logarithms in this paper are taken to the base 2.

these properties of the information, it seems to be fruitful to apply a more general approach to the definition of information represented by the formula (7) with an arbitrary convex function f(q) continuous for $q > 0$.

In order to illustrate by an example that this approach is really fruitful, let us consider the problem of data compression as studied by A. Perez [5]. Let P be a probability measure on the Cartesian product $\Lambda \otimes A$ generated by the collection $\{q_\lambda, P_\lambda\}$, $\lambda \in \Lambda$, and let $A' \subset A$ be a sub-σ-algebra of the σ-algebra A representing a compression of patterns from X. Let P′ be the reduction of P on $\Lambda \otimes A'$. Then it can be shown that the probability of error $L^*(e)$ corresponding to the initial σ-algebra A is always less than or equal to the minimum probability of error $L'^*(e)$ corresponding to the reduced σ-algebra A' and that the following estimation is true (see Corollary 3.1 of [5]):

$$L'^*(e) - L^*(e) \leqq \sqrt{2L'^*(e)(1 - L'^*(e))\,[I(\lambda, x) - I'(\lambda, x)]}\ ,$$

where $I(\lambda, x)$ or $I'(\lambda, x)$ is the Shannon's information contained in x concerning λ corresponding to A or A' respectively. The last difference between informations can be, in case $P << P'$ (absolute continuity), written also in the form of relative Shannon's entropy

$$H(P, P') = \int_{\Lambda \otimes X} f\left(\frac{dP}{dP'}\right) dP' \tag{9}$$

for f defined by (8). If, instead of (8), we have considered another convex function, for example $f_a(q) = \text{sign}\,(a-1)q^a$, $a > 0$, $a \neq 1$, then we obtain another version of the estimate considered above, for example (see Theorem 4.2 in [5])

$$\text{sign}(a-1)\left[L'^*(e)\left(\frac{L^*(e)}{L'^*(e)}\right)^a + (1 - L'^*(e))\left(\frac{1 - L'^*(e)}{1 - L^*(e)}\right)^a\right] \leqq H_a(P, P')\ ,$$

where $H_a(P, P')$ is the so-called relative a-entropy of Renyi [2], defined by (9) for $f = f_a$. It was already proved that this estimate of minimum probability of error change is in some cases better than the analogous estimate using Shannon's relative entropy.

I should like to finish the discussion of the problem of information measure by another example convincingly showing us that, as to some problems of pattern recognition, it is suggesting to accept a new approach to the definition of the entropy and information.

Intuitively, it is clear that the average conditional entropy $H(\lambda | x)$ of the standard λ defined by

$$H(\lambda | x) = \int_X H(\{\tilde{q}_\lambda(x)\})\,d\bar{P} \tag{10}$$

(cf. (5)) characterizes the pattern recognition problem in the sense that, roughly speaking, if $H(\lambda|x)$ decreases then also, for a sufficiently wide class of loss matrixes, $L^*(\|\ell_{\lambda\lambda'}\|)$ decreases and conversely. (A. Renyi has proposed to call $H(\lambda|x)$ a "missing information." If $H(\lambda|x) = 0$, then $L^*(\|\ell_{\lambda\lambda'}\|) = 0$ for every sufficiently "reasonable" loss matrix.) Particularly, the relation between $H(\lambda|x)$ and the minimum probability of error $L^*(e)$ is interesting because in solving many problems the need for a judging of the achievable quality of recognition (without any necessity to solve the corresponding optimalization problem including founding of the optimum recognition algorithm d^*) is growing. On exact precision of this relation, methods for such a judging can be based.

If $H(\cdot)$ in (10)is defined by (6), then the well-known theorem of Fano asserts that

$$h(L^*(e)) + L^*(e) \log (|\Lambda|-1) \geqq H(\lambda|x) , \tag{11}$$

where $h(q) = -q \log q - (1-q) \log(1-q)$, and that this lower estimate of $L^*(e)$ is achievable. A. Perez in [5] has obtained an upper estimate of $L^*(e)$, namely, the inequality

$$L^*(e) \leqq 1-2^{-H(\lambda|x)}$$

which is unfortunately not achievable. An achievable upper estimate was found by V. Kovalevskij [7] who has proved that if

$$\frac{m-1}{m} \leqq L^*(e) < \frac{m}{m+1}$$

then

$$\log m + m(m+1) \log \frac{m+1}{m} (L^*(e) - \frac{m-1}{m}) \leqq H(\lambda|x) \tag{12}$$

Therefore, the inequalities (11) and (12) represents the best possible both-sides estimates of the minimum probability of error in terms of average Shannon's conditional entropy. The lack of these estimates is easily remarkable: the lower estimate is too inaccurate when $|\Lambda|$ is large or $|\Lambda| = \infty$.

Let us write in (10)

$$H(\{q_\lambda\}) = \Sigma_\lambda q_\lambda(1-q_\lambda) \tag{13}$$

instead of (6), i.e., let us change the Shannon's approach to the definition of entropy by a "quadratic" one represented by (13). Then it can be proved (see [4]) that

$$H(\lambda|x) \ (1 + \sqrt{1 - H(\lambda|x)}\ )^{-1} \leqq L^*(e) \leqq H(\lambda|x) \tag{14}$$

and, if $|\Lambda| < \infty$, that

$$H(\lambda|x)\left(1+\sqrt{1-\frac{|\Lambda|}{|\Lambda|-1}H(\lambda|x)}\right)^{-1} \leqq L^*(e) \leqq H(\lambda|x)\,. \tag{15}$$

These estimations are achievable, i.e., the best possible ones. In view that the average conditional "quadratic" entropy is always less than or equal to the Shannon's average conditional entropy, in the case of large $|\Lambda|$ or $|\Lambda| = \infty$, the last estimates of minimum probability of error are undoubtedly better than (11) or (12).

The entropy (13) possesses properties similar to properties of the Shannon's entropy (6). For example, if the last of the well-known Fadeev's postulates of the Shannon's entropy is changed by the following requirement

$$H(tq_1, (1-t)q_1, q_2, \ldots, q_n) = H(q_1, q_2, \ldots, q_n) + q_1^2\, H(t, 1-t)$$

for every $0 \leqq t \leqq 1$, then the new system of postulates uniquely defines the "quadratic" entropy. The difference in postulates consists in that we write q_1^2 instead of Fadeev's original q_1 in the second term on the right side.

It seems that the essence of this analogies due to the fact that both (13) and (6) are of the form

$$H(\{q_\lambda\}) = \Sigma_\lambda q_\lambda\, I(q_\lambda)\,,$$

where the "information" $I(q_\lambda)$ contained in the event λ is, in both the cases we have considered, a continuous decreasing function on the interval (0,1) with $I(1) = 0$. It would be interesting to investigate the class of all entropies defined by this relation for sufficiently smooth functions I decreasing on the interval (0,1) with $I(1) = 0$ and to search in the class of conditional entropies obtained by this manner for a more satisfying estimations of the minimum probability of error than (14) or (15). If, for example, we denote by $H_a(\{q_\lambda\})$ the entropy corresponding to $I(q) = c_a(1-q^{a-1})$ for $a > 0$, $a \neq 1$, where $c_a > 0$ is an appropriate norming constant, then replacing in the modified Fadeev's postulates mentioned above q_1^2 by q_1^a, we obtain $H_a(\{q_\lambda\})$ [8]. Which of the average conditional entropies $H_a(\lambda|x)$ gives the closest estimation of $L^*(e)$?

4. The problem of selection of the most informative parameters and the problem of optimal reduction of patterns $x \in X$ are the most actual ones in recent pattern recognition theory, the solutions of which are often obstructed by computing difficulties. I should like to call our attention to a possibility of an asymptotic approach to the solution of this problem which, unfortunately, is not universal but on the other hand is effective. This method is applicable when

$$(X, A, P_\lambda) = \bigotimes_{i=1}^{n} (X_i, A_i, P_{\lambda i}),$$

where $(X_i, A_i, P_{\lambda i}) = (\widetilde{X}, \widetilde{A}, \widetilde{P}_\lambda)$, $i = 1, 2, \ldots, n$, $\lambda \in \Lambda$, and n is large. In the rest of this paper we shall suppose that these conditions are satisfied. An easy example of such a structure of the probability spaces under consideration is the case when $x = (x_1, x_2, \ldots, x_n)$ is a vector with real independently distributed components. This structure corresponds also to the case when, in order to accumulate the information, for every standard λ we observe independent realizations $x_1, x_2, \ldots, x_n$ of the standard transform.

It is possible to prove (see [9]) that in case $|\Lambda| < \infty$ the Shannon's average entropy $H(\lambda|x)$ is asymptotically (for sufficiently large n) equal to 2^{-nD}, i.e., according to (5), $I(\lambda, x) \approx H(\{q_\lambda\}) - 2^{-nD}$, where

$$D = \min_{\lambda \neq \lambda'} D(\widetilde{P}_\lambda, \widetilde{P}_{\lambda'}),$$

and

$$D(\widetilde{P}_\lambda, \widetilde{P}_{\lambda'}) = -\log \int_{C_{\lambda\lambda'}} \left(\frac{d\widetilde{P}_{\lambda'}}{d\widetilde{P}_\lambda} \right)^a d\widetilde{P}_\lambda$$

for some $0 < a < 1$ and where $C_{\lambda\lambda'}$ is the set of equivalence of the measures $\widetilde{P}_\lambda$, $\widetilde{P}_{\lambda'}$. It is very important that the parameter of exponential convergence of $H(\lambda|x)$ to zero depends only on "one-dimensional" measures $\{\widetilde{P}_\lambda\}$, $\lambda \in \Lambda$, which may be relatively simple and that D is, from an extremalization point of view, much more suitable than $L^*(e)$, $H(\lambda|x)$ or $I(\lambda, x)$. If, for example, $\Lambda = \{\lambda_1, \lambda_2\}$ and $P_{\lambda_1}, P_{\lambda_2}$ are Poisson or binomial distributions with parameters λ_1, λ_2 then

$$D = \lambda_1 + a \log \frac{a}{2\lambda_1}$$

or

$$D = a \log \frac{\lambda_1}{a} + (1-a) \log \frac{1-\lambda_1}{1-a},$$

where

$$a = \frac{\lambda_1 - \lambda_2}{\log \frac{\lambda_1}{\lambda_2}}$$

or

$$a = \frac{\log \dfrac{1-\lambda_1}{1-\lambda_2}}{\log \dfrac{\lambda_2(1-\lambda_1)}{\lambda_1(1-\lambda_2)}}$$

respectively. One can hope that a development of general methods for maximalization of D under different conditions of restriction and an evaluation of concrete results in case that $\tilde{P}_\lambda$ corresponds to standard random variables and processes will not present any difficulties.

REFERENCES

[1] A. Perez: Contributions de la théorie l'information à la cybernetique, 4 Congrès international de cybernetique, Namur, 1964.

[2] A. Renyi: On measures of entropy and information, Proceedings of the 4th Berkeley Symposium on Probability and Statistics, Vol. I, Berkeley, 1960.

[3] I. Csiszár: Eine informations theoretische ungleichung und ihre advendung auf den bewels der ergodizitat von Markoffschen ketten, Publ. Math. Inst. Hung. Acad. Sci., 8 (1963), Ser. A, No. 1.

[4] I. Vajda: Estimations of the minimum probability of error under testing of countable many hypotheses, Information transmission problems 4 (1968), No. 1.

[5] A. Perez: Information-theoretical risk estimates in statistical decision, Kybernetika 3 (1967), No. 1.

[6] A.N. Kolmogorov: Three approaches to the definition of information, Information transmission problems 1 (1965), No. 1.

[7] V.A. Kovalevskij: The problem of pattern recognition from the viewpoint of mathematical statistics (in Russian), Reading automata, Kiev, 1965.

[8] I. Vajda: Axioms of a-entropy of a generalized probability scheme (in Czech), Kybernetika 4 (1968), No. 2.

[9] I. Vajda: On the amount of information contained in a sequence of observations, Colloquium on information theory, Debrecen, 1967.

PATTERN RECOGNITION AS AN INDUCTIVE PROCESS

Satosi Watanabe

UNIVERSITY OF HAWAII
HONOLULU, HAWAII

1. Inductive Ambiguity

It is generally accepted that pattern recognition is a special kind of induction, but no serious efforts have so far been made to examine how the various aspects of pattern recognition fit in the general framework of inductive inference. The purpose of this paper is to try to do just that, basing ourselves on the mathematical model of induction proposed previously by the author[1,2,3]. It is hoped that such an attempt will benefit both the abstract study of inductive inference in general and the practical exploration of methods of pattern recognition. It is well-known since the time of David Hume[4] that inductive inference is not a purely logical process, hence pattern recognition cannot be free from logically arbitrary elements inherent in any inductive inference. It is then very important in the methodological study of pattern recognition to clarify how the inductive arbitrariness creeps into the method, and what kind of guiding principle of non-logical nature is actually practiced to make the method work as a technique.

The most harmful bias which is widespread among philosophers and mathematicians hindering a correct appreciation of the depth and breadth of inductive ambiguity stems from the so-called "necessary view" of probability which is usually associated with such eminent names as Keynes[5] and Carnap[6]. According to this view, between any two propositions, taken as the analogues of the logical notions of premise and consequence, there holds in analogies to logical implications, one and only one relation of a certain kind called probability relation, which corresponds to a numerical value which depends only on the two propositions, and not on human opinions or any other element outside these two propositions. Thus, Carnap* introduces the probability c(h,e) of a hypothesis h which is a function only of the hypothesis h and the relevant evidence e. That this view is entirely untenable in the case of induction was demonstrated previously by the present author[1,2]. He enumerated in his papers[2,3] various "extra-evidential"

* It is understood that Carnap has shifted his view in recent years, but the name Carnap is used here as the author of his famous book mentioned as Reference 6 in the bibliography.

factors other than e which affect the probability (credibility) of a hypothesis h. Some of them are worth mentioning here briefly, because an analogous situation exists also in pattern recognition. The inductive arbitrariness, which cannot find its place in the necessary view of probability, finds one of its expressions in these extra-evidential factors.

(1) Effect of other competing hypotheses. If a more credible hypothesis is competing with a given hypothesis, the credibility of the latter will become less than in the absence of the former.

(2) In a scientific theory, hypotheses of different areas and different levels have to be structured into a harmonious and consistent system. Two hypotheses which are equally well confirmed by the evidence may have different credibilities depending on how well they harmonize with other hypotheses in a theory.

(3) Scientists often believe in one hypothesis more than in another because it is simpler or more elegant, or simply more to his taste. Such an esthetic evaluation is not only inevitable but also quite helpful in efficient induction.

(4) A hypothesis h is often a (probabilistically) deductive consequence of another hypothesis of higher level. If this latter hypothesis becomes more credible through a direct confirmation or through an indirect confirmation via other hypotheses of lower levels, then the hypothesis h becomes more credible in spite of the fact that its deductive consequences are not tested by any evidence.

These factors which are extraneous to the "necessary relation" between the hypothesis and the evidence are certainly the most common source of inductive ambiguities, but there is another kind of inductive ambiguity which may be considered separately. The above introduced factors affect the evaluation of the hypotheses, but in order to evaluate them, we shall first have to produce them, because evidently the hypotheses are inscribed nowhere in nature so that we can read them off. The act of generating hypotheses, which may be called abduction to borrow Charles Peirce's terminology, is usually excluded from the theorization of inductive process. Some people believe that it is an unpredictable act of genius outside the realm of rational formulation. Some other people claim that it is a mechanical process, which grinds out all possible hypotheses one by one. Neither of these two extreme views seem to correspond to the actual process of hypotheses generation or abduction. Poincaré's view about the invention in mathematics suggests the existence of an esthetic referee guarding the threshold between the conscious and the unconscious admitting into the conscious only those hypotheses ground out by the unconscious which have esthetic appeal. Undeniably, there is a certain element of truth in this conjecture in the sense that abduction is not a purely logical or necessary process. The abduction is a decisive source of inductive arbitrariness, because we cannot generate or handle all possible hypotheses, and the choice of those which are actually placed for evaluation is made in a highly contingent fashion. We shall discuss more about this in Section 3.

We shall now introduce a mathematical model of induction and try to interpret the process of pattern recognition according to this model, exposing the junctures where the inductive ambiguities are lurking.

2. Mathematical Model of Induction and Pattern Recognition

Needless to say that inductive inference is, in a certain sense, the inverse process of deductive inference. It may then be natural to start our discussion with a brief sketch of deductive inference. Deductive inference involves three components: 1. Hypothesis or Law H_j, 2. Auxiliary Condition A_k, and 3. Experimental Data D_i. In one example, H_j could be a dynamical law of some kind, and A_k could be the initial and boundary conditions, and D_i may be the final condition to be predicted on the ground of H_j and A_k. In another example, hypothesis H_j may say that an animal of a certain given species has probability 1/2 of having red eyes (D_1) and probability 1/2 of having blue eyes (D_2). A_k may state that this particular object O at hand is an animal of this particular species. The deductive consequence is that object O has an equal probability of being red-eyed and blue-eyed. In a still simpler example, H_j may state that all men are mortal, A_k may state that Socrates is a man, and these two premises give probability one to the particular D_i which says that Socrates is mortal. The basic task of deduction is then the calculation of probability $p(D_i | H_j \cap A_k)$ or the determination of the D_i which makes this probability one. In the general case, this conditional probability must be averaged with the help of the probability $p(H_j \cap A_k)$. But in many practical cases, this last probability can be replaced by $p(H_j) \cdot p(A_k)$ where $p(H_j)$ is assumed to be unity for a particular H_j because it is taken for a law, and $p(A_k)$ is assumed to be unity because it is an observed fact. In any event, we see that the general theory must be based on the probability measure $p(H_j \cap A_k \cap D_i)$ defined on the product space $\{H_j\} \otimes \{A_k\} \otimes \{D_i\}$, where $\{H_j\}$ is the set of hypotheses at hand, $\{A_k\}$ is the set of possible auxiliary conditions, and $\{D_i\}$ is the set of possible outcomes.

In the usual inductive inference, we are first given D_i and A_k, and we are interested in guessing the right H_j, i.e., we are interested in evaluating the inverse conditional probability $p(H_j | D_i \cap A_k)$. In a second type of inductive inference, we are given D_i and H_j and we are interested in deriving $p(A_k | D_i \cap H_j)$. In the third type of inductive inference, we are given only D_i and we are interested in deriving $p(A_k \cap H_j | D_i)$.

In the first type of induction, we can assume one particular A_k to be the case, hence we can write $p_k(H_j | D_i) = p(H_j | D_i \cap A_k)$, which assigns an a posteriori probability (in the sense of "after the experience of D_i") to hypothesis H_j. This is an act of hypothesis evaluation. This inductive conditional probability or credibility, as this author usually calls it, is connected with the corresponding deductive probability $p_k(D_i | H_j) = p(D_i | H_j \cap A_k)$ by the well-known Bayes formula.

$$p_k(H_j | D_i) = \frac{p_k(D_i | H_j)\, p_k(H_j)}{\sum_{\ell} p_k(D_i | H_\ell)\, p_k(H_\ell)} \tag{2.1}$$

The most important fact about this Bayes formula is that the deductive conditional probability $p_k(D_i | H_j)$ satisfies the Keynesian postulate because it is determined solely by the definition of H_j and D_i , while the inductive conditional probability $p_k(H_j | D_i)$ does not satisfy the postulate because it depends on the prior probability $p_k(H_j)$ and the denominator $p_k(D_i)$. It is rather surprising that this mathematical formula agrees with our general remarks about the extra evidential factors, because it provides a place, namely, the prior probability, where we can include these factors in the evaluation of a given hypothesis. Moreover, the effect of other competing hypotheses can reflect itself through the denominator. See Reference 3 for more details. Other than these extra evidential factors, the two conditional probabilities are proportional to each other giving a certain justification to the so-called likelihood approach. A special case of this last remark is the fact that the formula incorporates the condition of logical refutation. If the hypothesis H_j gives probability zero to D_i and if this D_i nevertheless happens, the credibility of H_j becomes zero. It can be easily shown that we can use (2.1) successively in a sequential experimentation by substituting the a posteriori probability of a stage for the a priori probability of the next stage, thus "improving" the evaluation of the hypothesis. As the number of stages increases, the influence of the prior probability of H_j on the a posteriori probability of H_j decreases, yet insofar as the experience is finite, the prior probability can always offset the evidential factor[2].

The task of pattern recognition is obviously closely related to the above-sketched inductive inference, but it has its own peculiarity. Suppose that H_j states that each member of class I has probability $f^j_I(D_i)$ of giving experimental result (a representation vector) D_i and each member of class II has probability $f^j_{II}(D_i)$ of giving experimental result D_i. The content of H_j expressed by $f^j_k(D_i)$ may be called a statistical definition of class k. Let A_I state that an object O at hand belongs to class I and A_{II} state that 0 belongs to class II. The deductive probability of object O having the experimental value D_i is then given by $p(D_i) = \sum_j \sum_k p(D_i | A_k \cap H_j)\, p(A_k \cap H_j) = \sum_j [\, f^j_I(D_i)\, p(A_I) + f^j_{II}(D_i)\, p(A_{II})]\ p(H_j)$. When A_k is given, we may write $p_k(D_i) = \sum_j p_k(D_i | H_j)\, p(H_j)$ where $p_k(D_i | H_j)$ is either $f^j_I(D_i)$ of $f^j_{II}(D_i)$ depending on $k = I$ or $k = II$.

During the so-called training period, the classifier, human or machine, is shown a D_i with its class affiliation, i.e., A_k. The effect of the training lies in the evaluation of hypotheses H_j by the Bayesian rule (2.1) in which the probabilities have now to be interpreted respectively as the prior probabilities of hypothesis $p(H_j)$, and the deductive distribution functions, $f^j_k(D_i)$. The formula expresses the "improvement" of the quality of the credibility through the accumulation of experimental facts, $(D_i \cap A_k)$.

When we come to the application period of the pattern recognition process, the classifier is given D_i and is asked the probability of its class-affiliation A_k, i.e., it is required to evaluate $p(A_k | D_i)$ which should be given by

$$p(A_k \mid D_i) = \frac{\sum_j p(D_i \mid A_k \cap H_j)\, p(H_j)\, p(A_k)}{\sum_j \sum_k p(D_i \mid A_k \cap H_j)\, p(H_j)\, p(A_k)} \tag{2.2}$$

This is a case of the second type of inductive inference mentioned above. In a usual pattern recognition algorithm only one H_j is taken as true at one time; as a result, we do not question the probability $p(H_j)$ and use $p(A_k \mid D_i) = p_j(D_i \mid A_k)\, p(A_k) / \sum_k p_j(D_i \mid A_k)\, p(A_k)$ instead of (2.2). We may rationalize this procedure by saying that the hypothesis which receives the highest a posteriori credibility during the training period by (2.1) is assumed to be the law in the application period. But, this is not justifiable from a more fundamental point of view, and the $p(H_j)$ of (2.2) should be equated to the last stage a posteriori probability $p_K(H_j \mid D_i)$ of the training period. The evaluation of credibility of H_j, even after accumulation of experimental facts, ultimately depends on the original extra-evidential evaluation of H_j, hence it is not determined by the experimental data only. Usually the prior probability of class $p(A_k)$ is taken from the actual relative frequency of members of class I and members of class II. But, this also is not always justifiable. In fact, the known class-samples and the unknown samples may be taken from two different populations. In general, being a prior probability, $p(A_k)$ can reflect also all other considerations that the classifier may have and has no necessarily determined value.

This analysis shows that the pattern recognition actually involves two stages of inductive inference of different kinds, and inevitably extra evidential, non-necessary factors are involved in each stage. The usual method of pattern recognition is so formulated that these inductive ambiguities are entirely invisible.

3. Abduction and Clustering

By clustering we mean the task of grouping a given set of objects into a certain number of subsets, whereby nothing more than the properties of each object is known. The subsets here are required to be created in such a way that members of the same subset are tied together more intensely by some kind of bond than members of different subsets. In the case of pattern recognition, on the other hand, the number of classes and a certain number of paradigms, i.e., class samples, are first given (in the training stage), and other objects are later given (in the application stage) without class-assignments. The classifier is then required to place these late-comers into the classes which have been exemplified by the paradigms. In reference to the mathematical model, the pattern recognition assumes that the classifier knows at least the number of classes with certainty, and he knows also more or less distinctly the set $\{H_j\}$ of competitive hypotheses, i.e., possible statistical definitions of classes. In clustering problem, we have to create both of these, hence its task is abductive, according to Section 1. For this reason, clustering involves further inductive ambiguities over and above those involved in pattern recognition. Since the nature of "hypotheses" in the classification problem with which we are dealing here is different from the hypotheses as candidate natural laws in science, the ambiguity which arises in clustering has its own peculiarities.

The bond by which members of a class are supposed to cohere together may be of different nature, similarity, contrast, triangular relation, etc. But, since the majority of problems of clustering is based on the bilateral relation of similarity, we shall limit the following discussion here to the case of similarity, although we can extend a similar discussion easily to more complicated kinds of multilateral relations[7]. If now the definition of similarity can be made on a purely logical basis, then we shall have to acknowledge that there is a certain logical, hence necessary, ground for the abductive phase of clustering. But, as we are now going to show, there is no logical basis in the idea of similarity.

Suppose each object is represented by the yes-or-no answer to n predicates. If each object is represented by a vector whose components are the measured values of some quantities, we can quantize the range of each variable and transform the given vector to a binary vector with a higher number of components. Thus, the assumption that the representative vector is an n-component binary vector (referring to n predicates) is no essential restriction. Now, starting from these n predicates, we can build, in principle, $N = 2^{2^n}$ different logical functions, which are all applicable predicates. Each time there is one logical constraint among the original n predicates, this number N has to be divided by 2, but this will not affect the essence of the following argument which assumes the absence of such logical constraint. The question we pose ourselves is the following: How many among these N predicates are answered yes by an object? The answer is obviously N/2 no matter which object we take, because if N contains a predicate, it contains also its negation. Next, how many among these N predicates are answered yes simultaneously by two given objects, assuming that there is at least one predicate among N which is answered by the two objects differently? The answer is N/4 no matter which pair of 2 objects we take. (See Reference 3 or 7 for the proof).

From this ensues the Theorem of the Ugly Duckling: "Any pair of two objects are as similar to each other as are any other pair of two objects, insofar as the degree of similarity is measured by the number of shared predicates." The condition for validity of this theorem is that we consider only a finite set of predicates which are all applicable to all the objects under consideration, and that each pair of two objects considered must not consist of two identical objects (with reference to the set of predicates). The consequence is that from the logical point of view, there is no such thing as a class of similar objects in the world.

However, we know that our picture of the empirical world consists of classes of similar objects, without which any pre-scientific or scientific system of knowledge would be utterly impossible. The apparent conflict between the aforementioned logical conclusion and this fact of our empirical world can be eliminated if we agree that some predicates are more "important" than some others so that sharing of more important predicates contribute more to the degree of similarity than sharing of less important ones. This shows clearly that the essence of classification lies in weighting and selection of predicates.

Now the central question becomes: Where does the degree of importance originate? In the last analysis, the source of importance must be the purpose for which the classification is to be used. Lettvin's "bug-detector" of the frog's eye[8] places a special and exclusive importance on the predicate: bug-like-ness, because this predicate leads to a classification useful for survival. For a systematic zoology, it may be more satisfactory to place a whale and a monkey in the same class, while for a fishing industry, it may be more convenient to place a whale and a tuna in the same class. There should not be any quarrel between different classifications. It is often vaguely hinted at the goal-orientedness of pattern recognition and clustering, but the above discussion provides a clear explication of the relation between goal and classification.

The foregoing paragraphs showed that similarity or "nearness" derives from the weights or importance of predicates. This relation between nearness and weights is a two-way road. We can in some cases derive weights from the concept of distance, too. Suppose we are given a collection of representative vectors, and assume that the Euclidean distance in this vector space faithfully expresses the desirable concept of distance. Then, we can "evaluate" different coordinate axes according to the degree to which it participates (statistically in the collection) in the distance-measurement. After choosing only the coordinate axes which have turned out to be more important in this evaluation, we can reduce the number of dimensions of the vector space. This is the basis of the methods of SELFIC and CLAFIC to which we shall briefly return in the next section.

In this section, we have slightly over-simplified the problem, giving the impression that clustering is purely an abduction and pattern recognition is purely a double induction. In actual problems, these two aspects are usually intermingled. For instance, the training period of the parametric approach to pattern recognition may be described as evaluation of the members of a well-defined set $\{H_j\}$ of hypotheses, but the non-parametric approach does not always assume a well-defined set $\{H_j\}$, and includes often an abductive aspect in itself.

4. Ambiguity in Decision Making

As we have seen in Section 2, the training period can be described as a stage where the inductive probability of the first kind $p(H_j | D_i \cap A_k)$ is determined. If each object is represented by an n-component vector x, then D_i is a point in the corresponding n-dimensional space. A_k designates the class to which this point belongs. In some cases, A_k can be considered as the (n+1)st component of the vector. In many practical problems, we do not need to know the exact value of the probability $p(H_j | D_i \cap A_k)$, but only to obtain the particular H_j which maximizes this probability. The estimation of the values of parameters in the parametric approach can be considered as doing just that. In this case, the set $\{H_j\}$ is well-defined in such a way that for each k, $p(D_i | H_j \cap A_k) = p(x | H_j \cap A_k)dx$ is a function of a given type containing yet-to-be-determined parameters which depend on H_j. The most plausible values of parameters may be interpreted as those which maximize $p(H_j | x \cap A_k)$. This process actually involves a basic indeterminacy, because the value of the prior credibility $p(H_j)$ cannot be determined on a necessary basis. We usually camouflage this indeterminacy by giving an equal (or almost equal) value to all $p(H_j)$.

In the application stage, we are concerned with the inductive probability of the second kind $\sum_j p(A_k | H_j \cap D_i)\, p(H_j)$ or simply $p_j(A_k | D_i) = p(A_k | H_j \cap D_i)$ with the H_j which has the highest credibility at the moment. In this expression, the D_i is the vector of the new object whose class-belonging is yet to be determined. If there are only two classes I and II, the probability of the object belonging to class I is larger than the probability of its belonging to class II if and only if

$$f(x) \equiv \frac{p(I | H_j \cap x)}{p(II | H_j \cap x)} > 1 . \tag{4.1}$$

If the loss due to "misclassifying" an object of class I into class II is larger than the loss due to "misclassifying" an object of class II into class I, then one would classify the object to class I if and only if

$$f(x) > \theta \tag{4.2}$$

with θ less than unity. In the opposite case, θ must be larger than unity. If the loss function is known, then θ can be determined. The border surface, or "decision function"

$$f(x) - \theta = 0 \tag{4.3}$$

depends on the loss. The loss means the negative of utility and is dependent on the usage for which the classification is made. Here is another place where the logical indeterminacy is lurking.

After we have decided on a value of θ, we can replace $f(x) - \theta$ by the simplest possible function $g(x)$ such that the three conditions $g(x) \gtreqless 0$ coincide with the three conditions $f(x) - \theta \gtreqless 0$. For instance, if $p(I | H_j \cap x)$ and $p(II | H_j \cap x)$ are linear in x (within a certain domain of x), then f(x) is not linear; but we can readily find a linear function g(x). If we assume that g(x) is linear, quadratic, etc., in x, it results in restricting the class of possible H_j's. The limitation of H_j to a certain class represents an extra-evidential arbitrary choice which is another aspect of inductive indeterminacy.

An important fact to note here is that everytime $p(A_k | H_k \cap x)$ is given, we can define a black-and-white decision function f(x) or g(x). There is a great difference in quality of the decision depending on whether f(x) remain close to unity (or θ) for a large domain of x or it becomes close to 0 and ∞ for most of the domain of x. This ambiguity hiding behind the ostensibly clearcut decision can be measured by the inductive entropy

$$U = - \sum_k \int [p(A_k | H_j \cap x) \log p(A_k | H_j \cap x)]\; p(x)dx \tag{4.4}$$

The concept of inductive entropy was previously introduced by the author[1] in a different context but used later in connection with pattern recognition by Kamentsky[9]. It is not difficult to demonstrate that this expression is invariant for a measure preserving transformation[3]. This entails a consequence that the stretching and deformation of the representative space really does not help much the task of pattern recognition as some of the authors had hoped.

If $p(A_k | H_j \cap x)$ is zero or one, this entropy U becomes zero, and there is no ambiguity (of the kind we are presently discussing) behind the decision. Many researchers considered this situation ($U = 0$) is to be upheld at all costs. The usual version of linear decision function method assumes both linearity of $g(x)$ and $U = 0$ for a given set of paradigms. But this so-called linear separability is not always to be hoped for.* In fact, we can always choose H_j in such a way that the condition $U = 0$ is upheld for a given set of paradigms provided there are no two paradigms of different classes which have exactly the same representative vector. But to do this, we may have to choose an extremely complicated function for the domain determined by $p(A_k | H_j \cap x) = 1$. An excessive gerrymandering, however, is against our good intuition. Here we are faced with a conflict between the ideal of a small inductive entropy and the ideal of a smooth function for $p(A_k | H_j \cap x)$. In view of the fact that noise (distortion) is unavoidable and that the variables we have at our disposal may not be sufficient to discriminate all the small differences among objects, we have to be satisfied with a value of U different from zero. Yet if it is too large, the decision may involve too many misclassification.

The method of obtaining a smooth function for $p_j(x | A_k)\, p(A_k) = p_j(A_k | x)\, p(x)$ (which characterizes H_j) from a given set of paradigm points used by Aizerman[10] is an arbitrary choice from among infinitely many other possibilities to choose H_j. Yet, such a method is so to speak a direct generalization of the common practice of connecting the data points by a "smooth" curve, and for this reason it may be given a high intuitive prior credibility, although there is no necessary ground for it[3].

5. Selection of Variables

If the final goal of pattern recognition is to obtain a decision function $g(x)$, then we can say that the whole effort of pattern recognition resides in extracting one variable which is a function of the n given variables, n being the number of components of the data-vector x. In other words, we may consider a general coordinate transformation $x'_i = f_i(x_1, x_2, \ldots, x_n)$, $i = 1, 2, \ldots, n$ such that $f_1 = g$. Then all the remaining coordinate variables x'_i, with $i \neq 1$, are entirely "irrelevant," provided that the decision function $g(x)$ is the "correct" one. Of course, we can never hope for such a one-stroke

*If the number of dimensions is very large for a given number of paradigms, the linear separability is automatically guaranteed. The linearly non-separable case can be transformed to a linearly separable case by a previous transformation of variables.

elimination of the irrelevant factors. The various methods of pattern recognition may be regarded as different ways of gradually eliminating those variables which are deemed to be irrelevant or little relevant.

Very often this gradual elimination of less relevant variables, or equivalently the gradual selection of more relevant variables, is divided into three stages. The first is the selection of variables to be measured which provides the raw data. The second is what is usually called pre-processing (not to be confused with "pre-selection"), whose purpose is to eliminate the variables which are obviously irrelevant, so that the input to the next stage becomes of a manipulable size. The third stage is the main portion of pattern recognition process, which uses a more or less sophisticated guiding principle of selection, leading up to a final decision rule. This division into three stages is obviously little more than a matter of convention or convenience. It is more often motivated by hardware consideration than by methodological significance. Furthermore, the feedback from a higher stage to a lower stage of selection can exist, making all the stages a single inseparable unit.

It should first be recalled that the decision function, in principle, should be derived from the inductive probability of class-affiliation $p(A_k|x)$ which depends on the inductive probability of hypotheses which in turn depend on their prior extra-evidential values. This inductive ambiguity is inherent in the entire method. Second, we should mention that even if we have a clearly defined criterion of relevance, it is seldom possible to find a variable which is found to be absolutely irrelevant. We have often to eliminate those variables which are not irrelevant but only less relevant. This increases the ambiguity in the final decision. An aspect of this situation can be described more interestingly as a conflict between two goals of pattern recognition: (1) A small value of the inductive entropy (4.1), and (2) A small number of variables. Usually, by eliminating less important variables in the pursuit of the second goal, we obtain more and more overlapping of domains interfering with the first goal.

An algorithm used in elimination of the less important (or selection of the more important) variables can be characterized from different points of view. One of the distinctions we can meaningfully make depends on whether the criterion of selection is of an "internal" or "external" origin. In some cases, we have a collection of objects with known properties to be classified, and we can evaluate each variable according to the extent to which it serves either the purpose of distinguishing individual objects from one another in the collection or the purpose of describing the main feature of this collection of objects. In such cases, the criterion of importance derives from the collection itself, hence it is internal. But, in the other cases where the criteria of selection do not derive from the collection of objects under examination itself, they are external.

In clustering problems, none of the objects are given with its class-affiliation, but in pattern recognition problems some of the objects are given with their class-affiliations. They are paradigms. The elimination of the irrelevant which does not depend on paradigms is called "pre-selection" while that which does depend on paradigms is called "post-selection." When a variable is selected, as mentioned above, on the ground that it will effectively serve the purpose of discriminating individual objects, the variable may be called "discriminating feature." On the other hand, a variable is selected as a prominent common property of the members of a given class (as illustrated by the paradigms), it may be called "class feature." A discriminating feature may be a class feature (when the collection consists of members of different classes), but not necessarily. Finally, some methods of elimination may be applied to any problem so long as each object is described by an n-component vector, but some methods are specifically designed to be applied to a particular type of classification problems. The former is a general method and the latter is a specialized method.

For instance, the SELFIC[11,12,13] method, which the author introduced some years ago, is an internal, pre-selective, general method of extracting "discriminating features." The CLAFIC[12], on the other hand, is an internal, post-selective, general method of extracting "class features." The method of Crossing Number Compression[12] used also by the author is an external, pre-selective, specialized method of extracting discriminating features. It is specifically designed for the purpose of character recognition but is not so specific as to be solely useful for a particular alphabet.

In connection with the extraction of feature-variables, a few words have to be spent with regard to the extraction of representative objects and the extraction of components. Most of the clustering algorithms become extremely time-consuming if the number of objects to be classified becomes large. This difficulty can be avoided if we have some method of extracting a smaller number of "representative objects" to which we can first apply the clustering algorithm. The non-representative objects can then be placed, by the pattern recognition technique, into the classes generated by the representative objects with the help of the clustering algorithm. One method of representative-extraction proposed by the author consists of choosing those objects which have large vector-components in the subspace subtended by variables representing discriminating features[14,15]. The results obtained by this method are quite satisfactory.

The component extraction consists of regarding each pattern as consisting of a certain number of definite component parts which are found in many patterns and characterizing each pattern by the relations (relative positions, etc.) existing among the component parts in the pattern. The discovery of components is abductive in nature and requires a very special algorithm to overcome the abundance of ambiguities which exist in the process. Once, however, the components are defined, the relations among components can be treated in more or less the same ways as other properties of the objects.

6. Object-Predicate Reciprocity

The idea, latent in traditional philosophy, of treating symmetrically the extension and intension of a concept, evidenced by such a statement as "the extension and intension are inversely proportional to each other," may be the first indication of the awareness in man's mind about what we call "object-predicate reciprocity" in this section. The last-named idea lies in the fact that the role of objects and the role of predicates qualifying them can be interchanged, mutadis mutandis, to bring about further light in the explication of the notions of concept and class. It is well-known that in counting the number of possible combinations in quantum statistics it is sometimes more convenient to interchange the role of particle (object) and the role of state (predicate). This is an interesting example of the object-predicate reciprocity. The proposal to exploit consciously the object-predicate reciprocity in the pattern recognition problem was made for the first time by the author in a paper mentioned as Reference 16. Details of some results obtained by this method will be reported in Reference 17. Some psychologists in their works with factor analysis are known to have employed sometimes for convenience's sake what corresponds to an interchange of predicates and objects, but there was no systematic, methodological implications in it.

If $x^{(a)}_i$, $i = 1, 2, \ldots, n$, $a = 1, 2, \ldots, \nu$ represents the value of the i-th variable measured on the a-th object, the usual standpoint is to consider an n-component vector $\{x^{(a)}_1, x^{(a)}_2, \ldots, x^{(a)}_n\}$ as representing object a. In the reciprocated viewpoint we consider a ν-component vector $\{x^{(1)}_i, x^{(2)}_i, \ldots, x^{(\nu)}_i\}$ as representing predicate i. The two viewpoints are formally on an equal footing, but the resulting classification, though they must be in accord in general lines, cannot be exactly identical. Hence, this possibility of object-predicate reciprocation adds, so to speak, another degree of freedom to the "arbitrariness" in the problem of classification.

It is interesting to consider how the different tasks of classification transform by the process of reciprocation. The roles of feature-extraction and representative-extraction are interchanged. In the usual viewpoint, representative-extraction is a secondary process, but in the reciprocated viewpoint, it comes first. Clustering, which consists in grouping of (similar) objects, is transformed into grouping of predicates. Pattern recognition, whose task lies in determination of the intension of a concept by a partial extension, becomes a task of determining the extension of a concept by a partial intention.

7. Conclusion

We have shown in this paper that the tasks of classification, namely, clustering and pattern recognition, involve an immense number of non-necessary factors, i.e., those factors which are not determined by logic and the given data. To carry out the task of classification, however, we have to, and we do, make an "arbitrary choice" in the presence of this infinity of alternatives. An arbitrary choice does not mean that it is just as good or just as bad, as any other choice. It means only that its merits cannot be judged from the "necessary" point of view. In fact, the choice used in practice is usually a good one, in the sense that it produces a result which is useful for our purpose. The point is that the choice has to depend strongly on human intuition, and when it is made it is usually transferred to the computing machine sub rosa. Once in the computer, the remaining process is logical and necessary. A suggestion that can be made here is that a serious study of these non-necessary elements in pattern recognition as such will greatly contribute to the advancement of this technique.

Another source of "ambiguity" which has not been discussed in this paper is the possible breakdown of what the author called the postulate of fixed truth set. Such a breakdown can happen in the observed data in different branches of science, such as psychology and sociology other than quantum mechanics where it has already been established. The absence of this postulate will result in the absence of distributive law of logic, and the problem of classification will be faced with an entirely new kind of serious difficulties. The reader is referred to References 18 and 19 for more details.*

Acknowledgment

The work presented in this paper has been partially supported by Air Force Grant No. AF–AFOSR–68–1466.

---

* It may be mentioned that the motivation of Zadeh's idea of fuzzy set[20] is somewhat related to this problem, although he would not go as drastically as the author to the very basis of logic.

REFERENCES

1. S. Watanabe, IBM Journal of Research and Development, Vol. 4, 1960, p. 208.
2. S. Watanabe, Colloquium on the Foundations of Mathematics, Mathematical Machines and Their Applications, Tihany, September 11-15, 1962, Akadémiai Kiadó, Budapest, 1965, p. 67–107.
3. S. Watanabe, *Knowing and Guessing*, John Wiley and Sons, New York Press, (to be published).
4. D. Hume, *A Treatise on Human Nature, Being an Attempt to Introduce the Experimental Method of Reasoning into Moral Subjects,* London, 1739.
5. M. Keynes, *A Treatise on Probability,* London and New York, 1921.
6. R. Carnap, *Logical Foundations of Probability,* Chicago, 1950.
7. S. Watanabe, *Information and Prediction in Science,* (eds. Dockx and Bernays), Academic Press, New York, 1965, p. 39–76.
8. J.Y. Lettvin, *et alia,* Proceedings of I.R.E., Vol. 47, 1959, p. 1940.
9. L.A. Kamentsky and C.N. Liu, IBM Journal of Research and Development, Vol. 7, 1963.
10. M. Aizerman, *et alia, The Probabilistic Problem Concerning the Instruction of Automata to Recognize Classes and the Method of Potential Functions,* Moscow, 1964; *Theoretical Foundations of the Method of Potential Functions in the Problem of Instructing Automata to Partition Input Situations into Classes,* Moscow, 1963.
11. S. Watanabe, *Proceedings of the Fourth Prague Conference on Information Theory, etc., 1965,* Czechoslovakia Academy of Science.
12. S. Watanabe, *Proceedings of Computer and Information Sciences–II* (ed. J. Tou), Academic Press, New York, 1967.
13. S. Watanabe, *Proceedings of BIONICS Conference,* 1966 (in press).
14. S. Watanabe, T. Kaminuma, T. Takekawa, Paper presented at Information Science Conference, September 1967, San Remo, Italy (in preparation).
15. S. Watanabe, T. Kaminuma, T. Takekawa, Paper presented at the Hawaii International Conference on System Sciences, January 29–31, 1968, Honolulu, Hawaii.
16. S. Watanabe, Information and Control, Vol. 4, 1961, p. 2911.
17. S. Watanabe, "Object-Predicate Reciprocity and Its Application to Pattern Recognition", to be presented at IFIP Congress 68, August 5–10, 1968, Edinburgh, Scotland.
18. S. Watanabe, Progress of Theoretical Physics, Supplements 37 and 38, 1966, p. 1966.
19. S. Watanabe, "Modified Concepts of Logic, Probability and Information, etc.", to appear in the Information and Control, 1969.
20. L.A. Zadeh, Information and Control, Vol. 8, No. 3, 1965, p. 338.

INVARIANT RECOGNITION OF GEOMETRIC SHAPES *

Eugene Wong and J. Alan Steppe

DEPT. OF ELECTRICAL ENGINEERING AND COMPUTER SCIENCES
AND ELECTRONICS RESEARCH LABORATORY
UNIVERSITY OF CALIFORNIA
BERKELEY, CALIFORNIA

1. Introduction

In using geometrical figures to convey information, we make little use of the position or orientation of the figures. Rather, the information is contained in their "shapes," which might be defined as those properties of a figure which are invariant under rigid-body motions. An occasional counterexample, such as the numerals 6 and 9 in certain type fonts, only serves to remind us how rare these counterexamples are. It is not surprising, therefore, that most pattern classification problems for geometrical figures involve classes each of which is closed under rigid-body motions. Seldom, if ever, are we required to distinguish a figure from a congruent copy of itself. This paper is concerned with the problem of classifying geometric figures without regard to their positions and orientations. We want to establish procedures which recognize squares of a fixed size in any position and orientation as belonging to the same class.

In formulating pattern recognition problems it is often convenient to distinguish two separate operations in the recognition procedure, namely, *measurement* and *decision*. The problem of *measurement* is to obtain from the sample to be classified a finite set of numbers which are indicative of the class to which the sample belongs. This operation has the dual function of data conversion and data reduction. The operation of *decision* consists of assigning the sample to one of the prescribed classes on the basis of the measured values. The bulk of the pattern recognition literature is devoted to the problem of designing effective *decision* procedures. We shall have something to say about both of these operations. It is intuitively clear that for recognition of geometric shapes, we should begin with measurements

* The research reported herein was supported by the U. S. Army Research Office – Durham under Grant DA–ARO–D–31–124–G776 and Contract DAHCO4–67–C–0046.

which are invariant under rigid-body motions. There are at least two reasons for this. First, such measurements coupled with any decision procedure automatically give rise to invariant recognition. Congruent figures will automatically be assigned to the same class. A second advantage of starting with invariant measurements is efficiency. Positional and orientational information is not relevant to the classification problem and should not be measured.

As was pointed out by Pitts and McCulloch[1], one way of obtaining invariant measurements is to average over all rigid-body motions. This idea of averaging is also basic to the suggestion of Novikoff[2] that the techniques of integral geometry be used in pattern recognition. The basic principle underlying Novikoff's suggestion can be illustrated by a simple example. Suppose that the geometric figures to be recognized are simple closed curves. Suppose we throw straight lives "randomly" at the figures and measure the lengths of their intersections. If "random" is taken to mean that no position or orientation is given a preference, then the average of these intersections will converge to a number which is independent of the position and orientation of the unknown figure. Hence, the average constitutes an invariant measurement. This example also serves to illustrate some of the difficulties associated with the averaging approach. First, to obtain a good approximation to the limiting average may require a large number of lines to be thrown, which is clearly undesirable. Secondly, and more importantly, the average, while invariant with respect to rigid-body motions, may not depend much on shape either. For example, the average of the lengths of intersection between a simple closed curve and random lines is proportional to the area enclosed by the curve. Clearly, this measurement is useful only in discriminating among figures with different areas. Furthermore, since only approximations involving a finite number of lines can be obtained in practice, the figures to be distinguished should have very different enclosed areas, in order for the average length of intersection to be a useful measurement. Invariance is a necessary property for measurements, but not a sufficient property. The most important attribute of a measurement is, after all, its power in discriminating between classes.

While the approach suggested by Novikoff has been developed in somewhat greater detail by Ball[3] and Tenery[4], there appears to have been no study specifically addressed to the two difficulties mentioned earlier; namely, how to keep the number of trial measurements small and how to choose measurements which are not only invariant with respect to motions but also discriminating with respect to shape. This paper summarizes some preliminary results of a study to re-examine the appropriateness of integro-geometric techniques in the recognition of geometric shapes, with special attention being given to the difficulties mentioned earlier. There are two distinct features in our approach which should be pointed out at the very outset. First, we have essentially abandoned the idea of averaging, in favor of treating the observations as "random variables." Secondly, sequential analysis is used and plays an important role in keeping the number of observations small. The preliminary results from a computer study are very encouraging indeed. In assessing these results, however, we must keep in mind certain assumptions. First, these results pertain to noise-free recognition problems. Each class contains only figures congruent to each other, and not deformed figures. In practice, of course, deformations are unavoidable, and they will change the results somewhat. Secondly, these results pertain only to two-category classification problems. The basic procedure extends readily to the multi-category situation, but the more optimistic conclusions may not. Finally, as will be seen, the invariance that we actually achieve is with respect to only those motions which keep the figure within a prescribed retina. The larger the retina, the larger will be the needed number of observations for a given level of performance.

2. Integral Geometry in the Plane

Let R^2 denote the Euclidean plane, on which we can choose an origin and Cartesian coordinates (x,y). Euclidean distance between two points (x,y) and (x_o,y_o) is given by

$$d[(x,y), (x_o,y_o)] = [(x-x_o)^2 + (y-y_o)^2]^{1/2} \tag{1}$$

By a rigid-body motion g we mean a mapping of R^2 onto R^2 which is one of the following types:

(a) g is a translation $t_{(\xi,\eta)}$, $(\xi,\eta) \in R^2$,

$$t_{(\xi,\eta)}(x,y) = (x + \xi,\ y + \eta) \tag{2}$$

(b) g is a proper rotation τ_θ , $0 \leqslant \theta < 2\pi$,

$$\tau_\theta(x,y) = (x \cos\theta - y \sin\theta,\ y \cos\theta + x \sin\theta) \tag{3}$$

(c) g is a succession of translations and rotations.

The collection G of all rigid-body motions is a group. Every rigid-body motion is equivalent to a translation followed by a rotation. This correspondence $g = \tau_\theta\, t_{(\xi,\eta)}$ provides a natural coordinate system $\{(\xi,\eta,\theta); (\xi,\eta) \in R^2, \theta \in [0,2\pi)\}$ for G. Hence, a subset A of G corresponds to a subset $\bar{A}$ of R^2 x $[0,2\pi)$. Consider those subsets A for which the integral

$$\mu(A) = \int_{\bar{A}} d\xi\, d\eta\, d\theta \tag{4}$$

is well-defined. The function $\mu(A)$ has the important invariance property

$$\mu(g_0 A) = \mu(A) \text{ for every } g_0 \text{ in } G \tag{5}$$

where $g_0 A = \{g_0 g;\, g \in A\}$. Furthermore, subject to some mild additional conditions, every function F(A) with this invariance property is a constant multiple of $\mu(A)$. The function $\mu(A)$ is known as an invariant measure (or Haar measure) for the group of rigid-body motions.

As illustrated by the example in the introduction, the measurements that we shall consider are all generated by throwing lines, points, arcs and other geometric objects randomly against the unknown figure which is to be classified. The notion of "randomness" is to be defined in such a way as to be consistent with invariance with respect to rigid-body motions. The way to do this is through the use of the invariant measure. Let ω_0 denote a fixed set of points in R^2. For example, ω_0 may be the horizontal axis $\{(x,0), -\infty < x < \infty\}$, or the origin (0,0). Let M be the collection of all possible copies of ω_0 under rigid-body motions, i.e. $M = \{g\omega_0, g\epsilon G\}$. It turns out that the invariant measure μ of G induces automatically an invariant measure μ_M on M. That is, $\mu_M(\cdot)$ is a non-negative σ-additive set function defined for a class of subsets of M such that

$$\mu_M(g_0 B) = \mu_M(B) \quad \text{for } g_0 \in G$$

By choosing a coordinate system for M, μ_M can be expressed similarly to (4). For example, let M be the set of all infinite straight lines. Every such line can be obtained from the horizontal axis $\omega_0 = \{(x,0), -\infty < x < \infty\}$ by a vertical displacement $t_{(o,y)}$, $-\infty < y < \infty$, followed by a rotation τ_θ, $0 \leqslant \theta < \pi$. Thus, $(y,\theta) \in (-\infty,\infty) \times [0,\pi)$ provides a coordinate system for M. A subset B of M corresponds to a subset $\overline{B}$ of $(-\infty,\infty) \times [0,\pi)$, and up to a positive multiplicative constant $\mu_M(\cdot)$ is given uniquely by

$$\mu_M(B) = \int_{\overline{B}} dy\, d\theta \tag{6}$$

Roughly speaking, integral geometry deals with integration with respect to the invariant measure μ_M for various choices of M.

Let C denote a fixed geometric figure in the plane. Let $f(\omega,C)$ be a real-valued function which depends on C and on elements ω of a given M in such a way that f is invariant when ω and C are simultaneously acted upon by a rigid-body motion. Then, the integral

$$I(C) = \int_M f(\omega,C)\, \mu_M(d\omega) \tag{7}$$

is invariant when C is acted upon by rigid-body motions. This is the average of f. If M is the set of all straight lines, C is a simple closed curve, and $f(\omega,C)$ is the length of intersection between C and ω, then I(C) is proportional to the area enclosed by C. References 2 and 3 contain a number of examples where the integral I(C) can be explicitly computed. More examples can be found in the book by Santalo[5]. In practice, unless I(C) corresponds to a simple quantity such as area or perimeter, I(C) can only be *measured* by generating elements of M according to the invariant measure and average the results. Strictly speaking, only a modification of this can be implemented. Instead of all straight lines, we consider only those that intersect a prescribed retina, and modify the invariant measure accordingly. This will be explained in more detail subsequently. In most cases the number of elements of M that have to be generated may be quite large for a satisfactory approximation to I(C).

The process of estimating I(C) by observing f for a sequence of randomly generated elements from M is analogous to the process of estimating the mean of a distribution by the sample mean of a sequence of sample random variables. The correspondence becomes exact, if we convert the unnormed measure μ_M into a probability measure by the introduction of a retina. Let R, called the retina, be a closed and bounded region in the plane which contains the figure C. Let M_o be the subset of those elements of M that intersect R. For a subset A of M, we define

$$\mathcal{P}(A) = \frac{\mu_M(A \cap M_o)}{\mu_M(M_o)} \tag{8}$$

The function $\mathcal{P}(A)$ is defined whenever $\mu_M(A)$ is defined and is a probability measure. If we are choosing elements from M according to the $\mathcal{P}$ measure, then elements that do not intersect the retina do not get chosen. Of course, $\mathcal{P}$ is no longer a true invariant measure. For a given A in M_o, $\mathcal{P}(A)$ is invariant only for those motions which do not take A out of M_o. The process of estimating I(C) can now be stated precisely as follows: For the function $f(\omega,C)$, let

$$P(x) = \mathcal{P}(\{\omega;\ f(\omega,C) \leqslant x\}) \tag{9}$$

be its probability distribution function. The mean of the distribution is equal to

$$m = \int_{-\infty}^{\infty} x\ d\ P(x) = \frac{1}{\mu_M(M_o)} \int_{M_o} f(\omega,C)\ \mu_M(d\omega) \tag{10}$$

which is not quite I(C) but closely related to it. If, for example, $f(\omega,C) = 0$ whenever ω does not intersect the retina R, then

$$m = \frac{1}{\mu_M(M_o)} I(C) .$$

Now, the sequence of observations on f generated by choosing elements out of M corresponds to a sequence of identically distributed random variables: $f_1(\omega,C)$, $f_2(\omega,C)$, ... , each being distributed with distribution function P(x). The random variables should preferably be chosen to be independent as well. The problem is reduced to one of determining whether the sample mean

$$m_N(\omega) = \frac{1}{N} \sum_{k=1}^{N} f_k(\omega,C)$$

converges to m.

3. Sequential Analysis

From the point of view of pattern recognition there is no reason why we should restrict our attention to sample average. Instead, we should seek the best procedure for deciding the class to which C belongs, using as data a sequence of identically distributed samples. The situation is this: The random variable $f(\omega,C)$ has a distribution function P(x,i) which depends on i, the class to which C belongs. Let $f_1, f_2, \ldots, f_N$ be a sequence of random variables independently and identically distributed according to the distribution function of f. Upon observing a realization of the sequence $f_1, \ldots, f_N$, we want to determine the class number i. Thus posed, the problem becomes a standard problem in statistical classification. In fact, we have here a much nicer statistical problem than is usually encountered in pattern recognition. Normally, the measurements in a pattern recognition problem are neither independent nor identically distributed. It is also difficult to think of another pattern recognition situation where it is natural not to fix the number of measurements, namely, N, a priori. The setting here is perfect for the application of sequential analysis[6].

The basic idea of sequential analysis can be outlined as follows. Our observation is represented by a sequence of independent and identically distributed random variables $f_1, f_2, \ldots$. Given a set of observed values, we are to decide something about the common distribution of $f_1, f_2, \ldots$ The number of observations in a sequential test is not a priori limited. After n observations we can either go on observing or terminate the observations and make the necessary decision concerning the distribution of $\{f_i\}$. Unlike the fixed-sample case, we now have an additional degree of freedom, namely, the flexibility of determining when to stop observing. In sequential analysis one usually tries to minimize the average number of observations consistent with a given level of performance. To be specific, suppose $f_1, f_2, \ldots$

can be distributed according to one of two distribution functions, with density functions $p_1(x)$ and $p_2(x)$ respectively. Now, there are two types of error that can be made; deciding that the density function is $p_1(x)$ when it is in fact $p_2(x)$, and conversely. Suppose we require that the probability of error for these two types of error not to exceed α and β respectively, and design a decision procedure which minimizes the average number of observations that are required to achieve this level of performance. The resulting decision procedure is the celebrated sequential ratio test of Wald[6]. First, two positive numbers A and B, with $B > A$, are computed for the given values of α and β. Suppose $f_1, f_2, \ldots$ are the observed values, then for each $n \geqslant 1$ we compute the likelihood ratio

$$L_n(f_1, \ldots, f_n) = \prod_{k=1}^{n} \frac{p_1(f_k)}{p_2(f_k)} \tag{11}$$

and compare L_n against A and B. As long as L_n lies between A and B, sampling continues. As soon as L_n exceeds B or falls below A, the sampling stops, and we decide in favor of $p_1(x)$ if $L_n > B$, and conversely if $L_n < A$. Clearly, the number of observations depends on the actual values observed, and is thus a random variable.

The sequential procedure can be easily adapted for the pattern recognition problem that we have been discussing. In order to obtain a better assessment for the entire approach to invariant recognition, some numerical computations have been conducted, and more experiments are underway. Preliminary results are summarized in the next section.

4. Experimental Results

All the experiments reported in this section have the following features in common:

(a) M is the set of all infinite straight lines.

(b) The geometric figures to be recognized are all simple closed figures.

(c) $f(\omega,C)$ is the length of intersection between the straight line ω and the figure C.

(d) In each experiment only two classes are involved, and a version of the sequential ratio test is used.

In each experiment two simple closed line figures representing the two classes are chosen. Roughly speaking, the sizes of figures are chosen so as to render the underlying classification problem as difficult as possible. For a fixed retina R, the probability distribution functions $P_1(x), P_2(x)$ corresponding to the two figures are then computed for $f(\omega,C)$ using (8) and (9). We next compute the average number of samples needed for a given pair α and β, probabilities of the two types of error. The main variables of each experiment are α, β and the size of the retina R.

The role of the retina is an important one, because it pertains to the question of invariance. The recognition procedure is invariant only with respect to those motions which keep C within the retina. Naturally, we can expect that the larger the retina, the larger the required sample size. This comes about because for a large retina there is a large probability that the observed intersection is zero, which is not an informative piece of data. Provided that the retina is convex, the average sample size depends only on the perimeter of the retina and not its shape. However, the specific motions that we can tolerate obviously depends on the shape of the retina.

The distribution functions P(x) that we encounter in these experiments can always be written as

$$P(x) = P_o + (1-P_o)\int_0^x p(x')dx' \qquad x \geqslant 0 \tag{12}$$

$$= 0 \qquad x < 0$$

where $P_o \geqslant 0$ is the probability of the length of intersection being zero, and p(x) is a probability density function. As was alluded to earlier, the principal effect of increasing the size of the retina, is to increase P_o. Let $P_i(x)$, i = 1, 2 be the distribution functions corresponding to the two classes, and let P_o^i , $p_i(x)$, i = 1 2 be defined in terms of $P_i(x)$ as in (12). Define for $x \geqslant 0$ the function L(x) by

$$L(x) = \frac{P_o^1}{P_o^2}, \qquad x = 0 \tag{13}$$

$$= \frac{p_1(x)}{p_2(x)}, \qquad x > 0$$

For a sequence of observation $x_1, x_2, \ldots$, let

$$L_n(x_1, \ldots, x_n) = \prod_{i=1}^{n} L(x_i) \tag{14}$$

The sequential test consists of computing L_n and comparing it against A and B as was explained earlier. If the retina is large, then P_o^1/P_o^2 is approximately 1, and both P_o^1 and P_o^2 are nearly 1. This means that there is a large probability that L_{n+1} and L_n are approximately equal. Obviously, this situation would require a large number of samples to reach a decision.

In our computer study, a set of 15 simple basic figures were chosen. This generates 105 pairwise recognition problems. Of these, 5 pairs are presented in the accompanying figures. They are arranged in an increasing order of difficulty, ranging from the trivial problem of separating a circle from a block U, to the rather difficult problem of separating two nearly identical pentagons. In each of these cases, the probabilities of error of the two types have been set to be equal, and two values of this probability for each retina ratio are presented. Retina ratio refers to ratio of perimeters, and retina ratio = 1 is for any retina which encloses either shape in its standard position, and has the same perimeter as the smallest circle which has this property. The average sample size depends on the true class of the figure being tested, and both cases are presented.

We feel that these results are very encouraging. For an example of medium difficulty, consider Case 3: circle vs. square. For a retina ratio of 1 and an error probability of .2 percent, no more than 5 samples are required. For a retina ratio of 2 and the same error probability, the average sample size is 8 or 15 depending on the true class of the observed figure. These results indicate that the procedure proposed in this paper is well within the realm of practicability. Case 5 involves a problem of discriminating two nearly identical pentagons. This is by far the most difficult case among the 105 that were studied. We feel that the difficulty for this case is only in part due to the close similarity of the two shapes, but perhaps more importantly, it is due to the fact that line intersections are ill-suited for discriminating between these two shapes. For a given set of shapes the problem of determining the best manifold M of random objects and the best invariant function $f(\omega,C)$ to be used is undoubtedly the most important open problem in the application of integral geometry to pattern recognition. We feel that the techniques outlined in this paper provide an adequate vehicle for the comparison of two integro-geometric measurements. However, the problem of determining the "best" measurement is not only unsolved, but is yet to be properly posed. We are continuing our study in this direction.

REFERENCES

1. W. Pitts and W.S. McCulloch, "How We Perceive Universals: The Perception of Auditory and Visual Forms," *Bull. Math. Biophysics,* Vol. 9, pp. 127–147, 1947.
2. A.B.J. Novikoff, "Integral Geometry as a Tool in Pattern Perception," *Principles of Self-Organization,* Von Foerster and Zopf,ed., Pergamon Press, pp. 347-368,1962.
3. G.H. Ball, "An Application of Integral Geometry to Pattern Recognition,"Stanford Research Inst., Report for Office of Naval Res., Contract No. 3438/00, 1962.
4. G. Tenery, "Pattern Recognition Function of Integral Geometry," *IEEE Trans. on Military Electronics,* Vol. MIL-7, pp. 196–199, 1963.
5. L.A. Santalo, *Introduction to Integral Geometry*, Hermann and Co., Paris, 1953.
6. A. Wald, *Sequential Analysis,* John Wiley and Sons, Inc., New York, 1947.

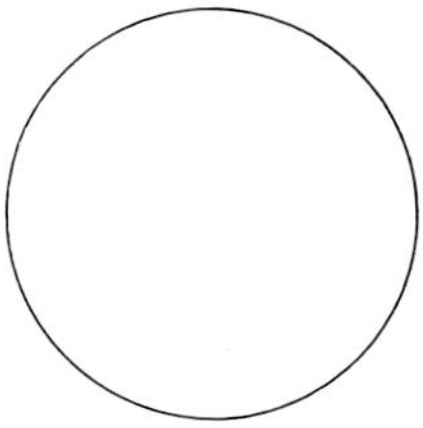

CLASS 1 CIRCLE

CLASS 2 BLOCK U

RETINA RATIO	ERROR RATES	AVERAGE SAMPLE NUMBER OBSERVING 1	OBSERVING 2
1	0.01	0.616	1.00
	0.002	0.646	1.37
2	0.01	1.25	2.30
	0.002	1.31	3.17
3	0.01	6.24	11.5
	0.002	6.53	15.8

Figure 1

CLASS 1 SQUARE

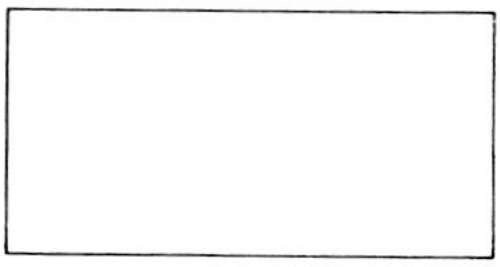

CLASS 2 2:1 RECTANGLE

RETINA RATIO	ERROR RATES	AVERAGE SAMPLE NUMBER OBSERVING 1	OBSERVING 2
1	0.01	5.79	7.97
	0.002	7.96	11.0
2	0.01	11.7	16.2
	0.002	16.1	22.3
10	0.01	58.6	81.3
	0.002	80.6	112.

Figure 2

CLASS 1 CIRCLE

CLASS 2 SQUARE

RETINA RATIO	ERROR RATES	AVERAGE SAMPLE NUMBER OBSERVING 1	OBSERVING 2
1	0.01	2.72	3.19
	0.002	3.73	4.39
2	0.01	5.76	10.9
	0.002	7.92	14.9
10	0.01	28.9	54.7
	0.002	39.7	75.1

Figure 3

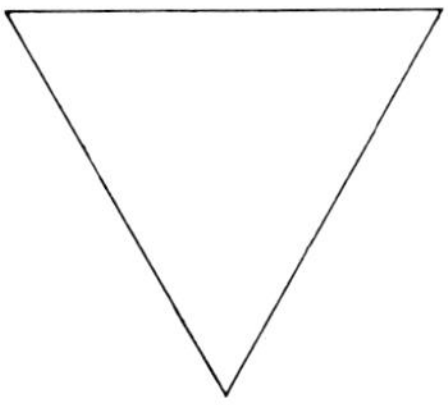

CLASS 1 TRIANGLE

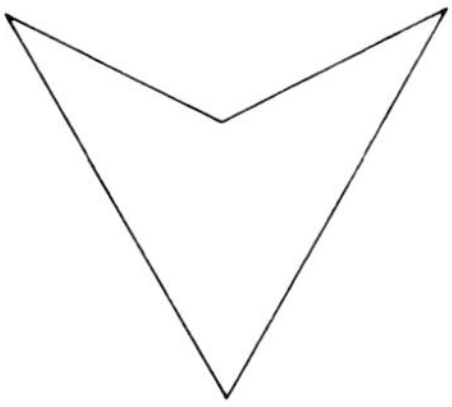

CLASS 2 V

RETINA RATIO	ERROR RATES	AVERAGE SAMPLE NUMBER OBSERVING 1	OBSERVING 2
1	0.01	24.6	29.8
	0.002	33.8	40.9
2	0.01	49.2	59.5
	0.002	67.6	81.8
10	0.01	246.	298.
	0.002	338.	409.

Figure 4

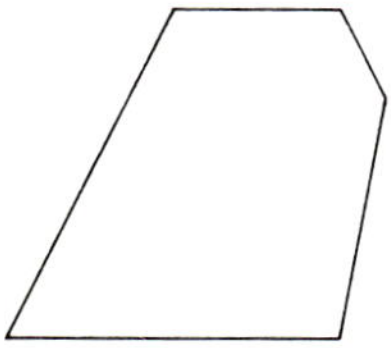

CLASS 1 PENTAGON 1

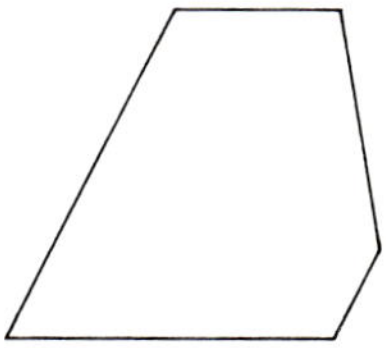

CLASS 2 PENTAGON 2

RETINA RATIO	ERROR RATES	AVERAGE SAMPLE NUMBER OBSERVING 1	OBSERVING 2
1	0.01	261.	271.
	0.002	359.	373.
2	0.01	522.	543.
	0.002	717.	746.
10	0.01	2610.	2710.
	0.002	3590.	3730.

Figure 5

C O M M E N T S

Geoffrey H. Ball – During this five minutes I would like to re-emphasize the role of the *process* by which we do research on pattern recognition. I think we need to explicitly examine our research strategies to see the way we work and the methodology that we use. I feel that this might pay dividends. Consider Fig. 1. Here we show the conventional model of a pattern recognition system. Much of the work has been done within this structure (or paradigm, as it has been called by Kuhn in his book, *The Structure of Scientific Revolutions.*) It occurs to me that a more powerful model that might be worth exploiting is the one shown in Fig. 2. This is a model that one might think of in the context of automatic control theory, but is not one I have seen used in pattern recognition. The basis of the block diagram is that, in some instances, regions within the pattern data space can be defined such that within a given region a certain parameterization of a pattern recognition device is appropriate. Within another region, a different parameterization may be desirable. The kind of situation where this might arise is given in Fig. 3. In each of the three regions two modes, one from Class 1 and one from Class 2, exist. However, the orientation of the modes differs in each region. By first deciding which region we are in and secondly adjusting the adaptive pattern recognizer to be appropriate to that region, we can design a relatively economical pattern recognition device that takes into account these differences in orientation.

The point of offering this model is twofold:

First, that it might be of some intrinsic value in developing new techniques in pattern recognition if it were developed further.

Second, that it offers an example of how stepping back from a given way of viewing the problem can sometimes offer alternatives that may in certain circumstances be more powerful.

Another way of viewing the process of pattern recognition is to use the analogy of the cavalry and a fort. While I intend the example to be primarily humorous, I think it has a certain validity as well.

The cavalry can be characterized as a unit that can stay together and move very fast so that it is difficult to tell where it is going to be at next instant. It has the possibility of splitting up and making many small attacks on a main force so that the main force will feel "there must be an army out there." The cavalry has certain disadvantages in that it is in a sense unstable in that it never quite knows where it is at and can carry no heavy armament. It has no workshop in which to develop new weapons. Existence itself for cavalry is hard enough so that there is little extra time to reflect on the nature of the ground that it is covering. The cavalry has the prime virtue that it is extremely flexible and can shift its available fire power quickly. It also can explore a large region of territory with relatively little expenditure of resources and can follow any leads that may occur.

The fort, on the other hand, has the virtue when adequately manned that it has a high rate of fire and thick walls. The territory around the wall is well known and provides considerable stability. Heavy armament can be supported and developed within the fort itself. However, if there is little activity in the territory where the fort is, then people will take the available time to create problems for themselves to solve. In these instances there is a tendency to develop heavily ornamented weapons. The fort has the further disadvantage that it is extremely rigid and if the climate changes it requires a considerable investment to move the fort.

I would suggest that at the stage of development where we find pattern recognition that we need a mixed strategy with both cavalry and fort being available. Perhaps a suitable analogy is that of the frontier fort supplied by the wagon trains from the east. It is clear that we need the cavalry to do the exploring of the territory around the fort, and it is equally clear that the cavalry needs the fort to come back to replenish its supplies and to have time to reflect on the territory that it has explored.

In presenting this analogy my purpose is not to condemn this or that school of thought within pattern recognition. It is primarily to suggest that each of us from time to time step back and examine the work he has done in the larger context, and at the same time examine the process and the methodology that he is using. If he can see the methodology is inappropriate, then it seems to me the worker ought to attempt to shift his emphasis to development of new methodology rather than attempting to use the old methodology less and less productively.

I would suggest that one area in which methodology needs to be developed, in addition to application of interactive graphic computer systems, is in the area of understanding how we use the "representations" we have available to us for representing the complex real world in which the pattern recognizer is being asked to apply his techniques.

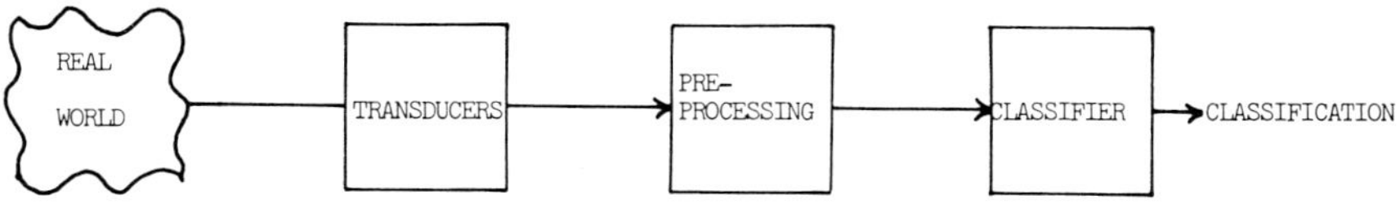

Figure 1: Conventional Pattern Recognition Block Diagram

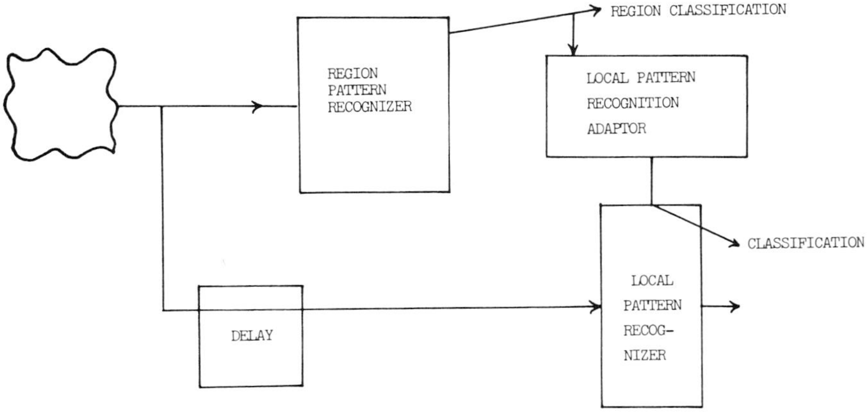

Figure 2: Proposed Block Diagram

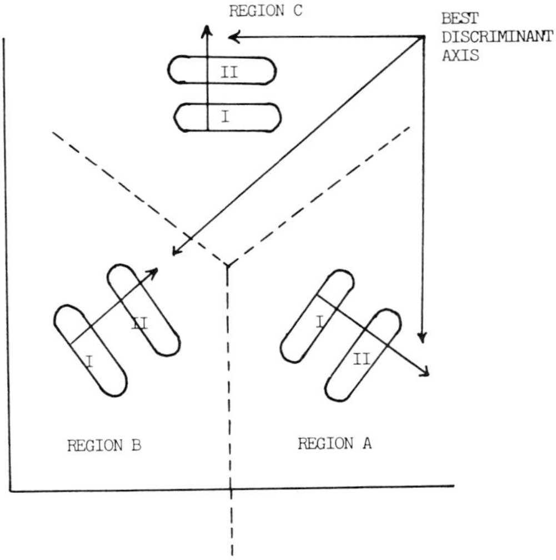

Figure 3: An Example of Data Space with Three Regions

R. B. Banerji, *Simplicity of Description and Significance Tests* – For the purposes of the first part of the present discussion it will be assumed that a "pattern" is a point in an n-dimensional euclidean space (a set of "measurements") and a "class" is a set of patterns whose coordinates satisfy

$$f(\bar{x}) > 0$$

where $f(\bar{x})$ is a polynomial in the components of the n-tuple $\bar{x}$. The polynomial $f(\bar{x})$ will be said to "describe" the pattern and "simplicity of description" will stand for the degree of $f(\bar{x})$.

Any learning algorithm in this environment generates, on the basis of two sets of example vectors, $\{\bar{x}_1, \bar{x}_2, \ldots, \bar{x}_r\}$ and $\{\bar{y}_1, \bar{y}_2, \ldots, \bar{y}_s\}$, a polynomial $g(\bar{x})$ such that

$$g(\bar{x}_i) > 0 \quad (1 \leqslant i \leqslant r)$$

and

$$g(\bar{y}_i) \leqslant 0 \quad (1 \leqslant i \leqslant s)$$

It is predicted, after g is found, that

$$g(\bar{x}) > 0 \text{ if and only if } f(\bar{x}) > 0$$

for all $\bar{x}$.

If a sufficiently realistic hypothesis is available regarding the distribution of $\bar{x}$ in space (not the probability of $\bar{x}$ being in a class but the probability of $\bar{x}$ being available for observation), one can estimate the distribution of the coefficients in g in terms of

i) the coefficients of f
ii) the method used for obtaining g
iii) r and s.

On the basis of these, one can estimate the degree of confidence one has on the aforesaid prediction. No matter what method is used for obtaining g from the samples $\{\bar{x}_i\}$ and $\{\bar{y}_i\}$, it can be asserted that for fixed values of r and s, the confidence will be small if the number of coefficients to be estimated in large.

As an obvious deduction from these arguments, one can state as follows: "In a practical case of pattern learning, involving in the excess of 100 variables, predictions based on any pattern learning scheme is bound to be of low quality unless the description of the class is simple". One can perhaps surmise that the statement remains valid under more general interpretations of the terms used here. There is evidence that the same difficulty occurs if other interpretations be used.

It is to be noted that the simplicity of description is determined by the nature of the class and the manner in which the measurements abstracted from a real-life pattern, and irrespective of any learning algorithm. The crucial question that faces the field of pattern recognition, then, is "How to decide on a set of measurements in terms of which the description of a given class will be simple?" Unfortunately, most of the work in the field is concentrated on learning algorithms and not on this crucial issue.

Obviously, the question raised above cannot be answered without some prior knowledge of the class being learned. This has led some to suggest that every practical pattern recognition problem be solved individually, using human intuition and prior knowledge about the classes to deduce useful measurements or "features". Perhaps this will remain the most practicable approach for some time to come. Meanwhile there might still be some workers in the field who are mainly interested in developing uniform algorithms for pattern learning. For these the question raised above remains crucial. If the question as posed here seems unanswerable, one can perhaps restrict its demands (without unduly decreasing its realism) by raising the following sub-questions:

1. If one's prior knowledge of the class is restricted to the knowledge that it comes from a pre-determined family of classes, what kind of structure has to be assumed for this family to render the question answerable?

2. Are there statistical techniques available for answering the main question if a satisfactory answer is available to sub-question 1 above?

3. If the main question has to be answered by an uniform algorithm, then the universe of discourse available to the algorithm should include the processes which convert the real-life patterns to measurements. This will necessitate that the representation of patterns be something other than points in euclidean space. What representations are appropriate?

It appears that in the past Science has done quite well in answering question 1 above as follows, "The family is restricted to having those classes as members all which can be simply described in terms of a few (currently unknown) measurements."

While answering question 3, it should be borne in mind that the recognition algorithms should take cognizance, not only of the values of the measurements but the nature of the measurements themselves and the relationships that exist between them. The discerning reader can see this for himself. Any clarification of this point would have to be done by means of an inordinately long series of examples for which the present medium is inappropriate.

I am incapable of making any comment on question 2 above. This, therefore, appears to be a good place to bring this article to an end. It may be worthwhile not to mislead the reader by referring to my own obviously incomplete answers to the questions above. I shall be happy to respond to the queries raised by any reader who may be interested.

Paul W. Cooper – Perhaps the most fundamental step in a pattern recognition problem is the very first one, the selection of a classification *criterion*. As philosophers have long pointed out, the questions asked frame and constrain the types of answers that can be expected. A *criterion* plays that role. The criterion is the (subjectively) chosen goal or standard, for which a classification procedure (decision rule) is sought satisfying that criterion. (Although, to some extent the choice of criterion can itself be constrained by the types of models on which one is allowed to build). Probably the best general criterion is *minimum-error-probability*. This is one of those used most widely, often implicitly, but in many cases it isn't formally satisfied. Some criteria selected by experimenters appear to be so arbitrary that one wonders whether they have useful meaning.

I should like to suggest, therefore, that the pattern recognition field could derive benefit from further thought and ideas on the *nature of criteria*. (1) On the one hand, some fundamental criteria could be selected, as, e.g., minimum-error-probability, and experimenters would try to satisfy these, within the constraints of their model. (There is then some basis with which to compare models and techniques.) (2) Secondly, it might be rewarding to give thought to defining *new* criteria. (A really fundamental criterion could be applicable to many models, although it is possible to have ones that are of value even though defined for specific models.)

Michael J.B. Duff – Drew comparison between high energy particle physics and the field of pattern recognition.

Pattern recognition is, at least in part, a practical subject, yet for someone entering this field it is sometimes difficult to find what can be done, e.g.,

(a) Few machines can be bought;
(b) Little common hardware;
(c) Little common software;
(d) Few good practical reviews.

Plea for "rounding off" projects so as to allow better exchanges.

Thomas G. Evans – I propose to take advantage of the diagram left on the board from Professor MacKay's talk this morning to restate very briefly the main theme of my talk on Wednesday.

(It looked something like this:)

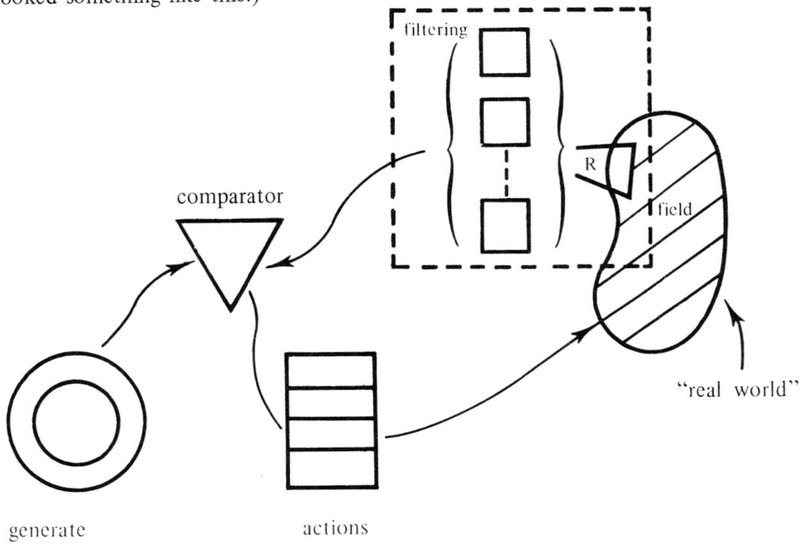

Consider the problem facing the designer of a system organized along the lines shown, intended to be capable of dealing effectively with some corner of the real world. My contention is that when the designer looks in that comprehensive handbook advocated by Don Brick in search of techniques for building the portion of the system that I have surrounded by the dotted line, he will find very little by way of approaches capable of handling complex environments. I argued that one reason for this has been a preoccupation with classification processes, rather than with processes concerned with the making and manipulating of descriptions, that is, constructs reflecting those aspects of the structure of the input pattern that are judged relevant by the designer to the subsequent generation-comparison and action-selecting stages shown in the diagram.

Joseph K. Hawkins – I would like to make three points, two of which are serious and one frivolous.

First, there has been a good deal of discussion at this conference on the notions of fuzzy sets and fuzzy algorithms introduced by Prof. Zadeh. I have been struggling to fit these ideas into my own understanding of pattern recognition network behavior. My tentative conclusion is that these notions will be useful viewpoints from which to look at network behavior because they seem to bring theory a step closer to the real world. For example, it appears to me that the concept of fuzzy behavior is closely related to what we usually think of as reliability. We usually wish to avoid circuit failures in networks, but we are compelled to live with them. Perhaps thinking about fuzzy circuit behavior is a way of doing this. I would like to point out that even at the basic component level in well-behaved digital systems we have fuzzy behavior. When we tell a component to assume the state 1 (or 0), it does so only approximately. The nominal binary level (e.g., 3 volts) is only approximated by the circuit, the actual value being determined by a host of supposedly irrelevant factors such as temperature, output loading and input signal configuration. The component does, however, assume a value which can be unambiguously interpreted (recognized) by subsequent circuits, despite this variation. Perhaps we should develop a theory of "fuzzy numbers" to account for the fact that only in mathematics–and not in the real world–are quantities ever precisely represented.

A second comment I would like to make is in regard to the considerable discussion of "clustering" methods we have had in this conference. It seems to me we want to be very careful of this concept. Some years ago it was generally realized that calculable decision-theory techniques applied directly to sensory patterns were not adequate for accurate classification. There followed a great search for "features" which would reduce the problem to amenable proportions. It seems to have been overlooked that the best feature for recognizing the letter, A, for example, is an A-ness feature extractor. In other words, it seems to me that talking about finding features is just a substitute for talking about the pattern recognition problem. I think that much of the discussion of clustering falls in this category, namely, if clustering can be achieved, then by definition the problem is solved. But note that clusters are likely to be just as non-linear as the original pattern sets. In original pattern space, a pattern and its complement (reversing 0's and 1's) are usually placed in the same class. But in that space these configurations are as far apart as they can get, while intermediate patterns, nearer to one or the other, must be in different classes. I see no reason why this wouldn't also occur in feature space. The presence or absence of a single feature out of hundreds may be the key to changing a classification, while reversing all or most of the features might leave the classification undisturbed. My uneasiness along these lines is reflected in the comments of some participants who have noted that when first-order clustering techniques are applied, it often happens that the residues are the most interesting and informative. Conceptually, I believe that this is also behind some of Prof. Watanabe's comments on the inductive process, which I take to be highly non-linear. I cannot imagine, for example, that Newton would have come up with the concept of gravity had he been given 100 samples each of apples falling from trees and apples not falling from trees, together with our present bag of clustering tricks.

Finally, I note that several participants, particularly Dr. Masson speaking for Prof. Benzecri, have suggested that we turn the techniques of pattern recognition loose upon ourselves, with respect to classification of utterances and perhaps even concepts. This is an undertaking obviously fraught with great peril as well as potential benefit. While it would obviously be an enormous relief if white noise could be filtered from the publication and conference spectrum, we run the risk of creating a closed circular system containing only those concepts which we can recognize which we can recognize which we can recognize . . . .

H.L. Oestreicher – The description of classes and selection of class features is still one of the more difficult procedures in pattern recognition problems which is most frequently approached intuitively. I would like to mention one systematic method in this respect which is quite powerful but not very often used. It can be called "Feature Selection by Source Analysis" and is based upon utilization of any knowledge we may have about the signal source and about the mechanisms by which the signals are generated. This method is best explained by the example of speech sound and word recognition; speech and word recognition is, of course, a pattern recognition problem: the human speech recognition system categorizes acoustic signals into classes which are recognized as words or speech sounds of the English (or some other) language. Although this is strictly an acoustical problem, it is the analysis of the speech generating mechanisms which makes it possible to determine useful characteristic parameters for the word or speech sound. The vowels, as the simplest example of speech sounds, are generated by passing the airstream, which is modulated by the glottis, through the resonant oral cavity. Changing the resonant frequencies by deforming this cavity produces the various vowels. The set of natural frequencies of the oral cavity (called the formants) determines the vowel sound completely and can therefore be used as a set of features for all sounds which are recognized as one specific vowel. As it turns out that the two lowest formants are sufficient to determine the vowel sounds, a set of two features has been found to describe each vowel. Other parameters useful for the description of non-vowel speech sounds are position of the tongue, the lips, etc., providing "features through source analysis" which would be difficult to obtain if the signals were analyzed without knowledge of the generating mechanism.

While this method is well known and widely used for the recognition of speech sounds, it seems that it should also be useful in other completely different pattern recognition problems.

Toshiyuki Sakai – I would like to suggest that various kinds of studies are now combining in the research work of speech recognition:

(a) Speech analysis, quantization and coding
(b) Perception test of synthesized speech expressed in regular expression
(c) Complex pattern matching in transition diagram
(d) Measurement of a large number of natural speech sounds in the regular expression form
(e) Statistics of transition probability of the quantum
(f) Syntactic rules of accent in conversational sentences
(g) Modification technique shared by a computer program and a hardware (speech synthesizer)
(h) On-line, real time audio response from a middle size computer.

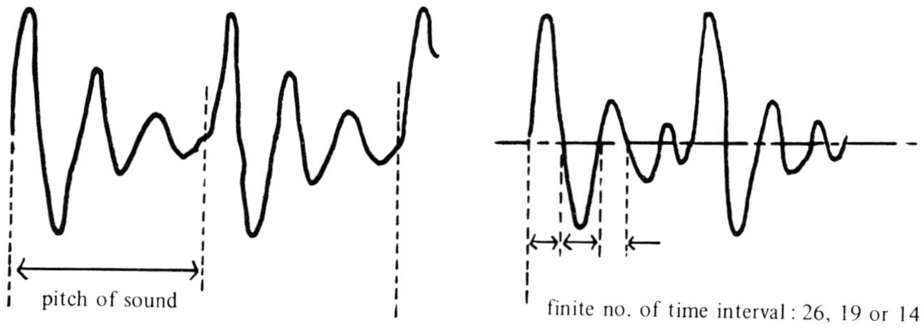

Vowel A: 8–9 8–8 9–3 1–12 9–8 . . . . . .

Phoneme |A| : $7(A)^{10}$

Context:
VcV

V : Vowel
c : consonants

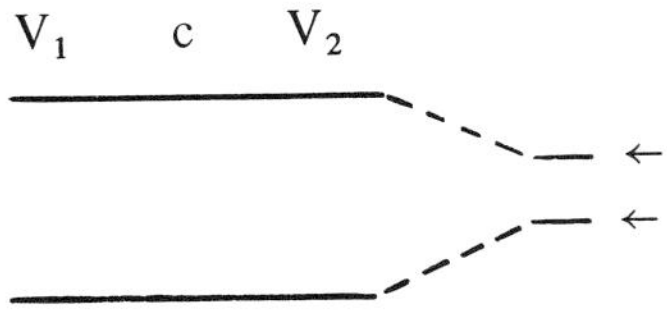

c: calculated 50,100 c/s spectrum spacing

Modification: *Accent (pitch), duration, wave form, phonetic rule of language.*

Math: *Regular expression (Kleene)*

Machine: *70k bits memory for synthesis–real time; state diagram for recognizer; statistics of transition probability; same technique in analysis and synthesis.*

Stephen D. Shapiro – I would like to mention several interrelated problems which deal with changes in the decision boundaries used in a pattern recognizer. Changes in these boundaries may be necessitated for various reasons such as the introduction of new identified samples, the removal of incorrectly identified members of the training set or old samples–when the statistics of the pattern vector are changing. To deal with this at present, for the case of complex decision surfaces, it is usually necessary to form a completely new solution with respect to the effected classes. In principle this should not be required, since it should be possible to utilize the relevant information contained in the surfaces about the retained samples in an efficient way. This remark also applies to the introduction of new classes.

Concerning the recognition of classes with nonstationary inputs, it may be possible to define a "time constant" which is that number of samples required to update the classifier in the presence of change. In the model presented, the quantity d is a measure of this time constant for each elementary volume V_k.

NAME INDEX

C

D

E

F

G

H

I

J

K

L

O

P

R

Y

Z

SUBJECT INDEX

P

R

S